Managing Public Relations and Brand Image through Social Media

Anurag Singh
Banaras Hindu University, India

Punita Duhan
Meera Bai Institute of Technology, India

A volume in the Advances in Marketing, Customer Relationship Management, and E-Services (AMCRMES) Book Series

BUSINESS SCIENCE Reference
An Imprint of IGI Global

Published in the United States of America by
Business Science Reference (an imprint of IGI Global)
701 E. Chocolate Avenue
Hershey PA, USA 17033
Tel: 717-533-8845
Fax: 717-533-8661
E-mail: cust@igi-global.com
Web site: http://www.igi-global.com

Library of Congress Cataloging-in-Publication Data

Library of Congress Cataloging-in-Publication Data

Names: Singh, Anurag, 1974- editor. | Duhan, Punita, 1973- editor.
Title: Managing public relations and brand image through social media / Anurag Singh and Punita Duhan, editor.
Description: Hershey : Business Science Reference, 2016. | Includes bibliographical references and index.
Identifiers: LCCN 2016006121| ISBN 9781522503323 (hardcover : alk. paper) | ISBN 9781522503330 (ebook)
Subjects: LCSH: Public relations. | Branding (Marketing) | Social media.
Classification: LCC HD59 .M246 2016 | DDC 659.20285/4678--dc23 LC record available at https://lccn.loc.gov/2016006121

This book is published in the IGI Global book series Advances in Marketing, Customer Relationship Management, and E-Services (AMCRMES) (ISSN: 2327-5502; eISSN: 2327-5529)

British Cataloguing in Publication Data
A Cataloguing in Publication record for this book is available from the British Library.

Advances in Marketing, Customer Relationship Management, and E-Services (AMCRMES) Book Series

Eldon Y. Li
National Chengchi University, Taiwan & California Polytechnic State University, USA

ISSN: 2327-5502
EISSN: 2327-5529

Mission

Business processes, services, and communications are important factors in the management of good customer relationship, which is the foundation of any well organized business. Technology continues to play a vital role in the organization and automation of business processes for marketing, sales, and customer service. These features aid in the attraction of new clients and maintaining existing relationships.

The Advances in Marketing, Customer Relationship Management, and E-Services (AMCRMES) Book Series addresses success factors for customer relationship management, marketing, and electronic services and its performance outcomes. This collection of reference source covers aspects of consumer behavior and marketing business strategies aiming towards researchers, scholars, and practitioners in the fields of marketing management.

Coverage

- Relationship marketing
- CRM and customer trust
- Legal Considerations in E-Marketing
- Electronic Services
- Database marketing
- Mobile CRM
- Cases on Electronic Services
- CRM in financial services
- Customer Retention
- B2B marketing

IGI Global is currently accepting manuscripts for publication within this series. To submit a proposal for a volume in this series, please contact our Acquisition Editors at Acquisitions@igi-global.com or visit: http://www.igi-global.com/publish/.

The Advances in Marketing, Customer Relationship Management, and E-Services (AMCRMES) Book Series (ISSN 2327-5502) is published by IGI Global, 701 E. Chocolate Avenue, Hershey, PA 17033-1240, USA, www.igi-global.com. This series is composed of titles available for purchase individually; each title is edited to be contextually exclusive from any other title within the series. For pricing and ordering information please visit http://www.igi-global.com/book-series/advances-marketing-customer-relationship-management/37150. Postmaster: Send all address changes to above address.

Titles in this Series

For a list of additional titles in this series, please visit: www.igi-global.com

Handbook of Research on Promotional Strategies and Consumer Influence in the Service Sector
Upendra Singh Panwar (Shri Govindram Seksaria Institute of Technology and Science, India) Raj Kumar (Banaras Hindu University, India) and Nilanjan Ray (Netaji Mahavidyalaya, India)
Business Science Reference • copyright 2016 • 492pp • H/C (ISBN: 9781522501435) • US $335.00 (our price)

Global Marketing Strategies for the Promotion of Luxury Goods
Fabrizio Mosca (University of Turin, Italy) and Rosalia Gallo (Universitat Autònoma de Barcelona, Spain)
Business Science Reference • copyright 2016 • 329pp • H/C (ISBN: 9781466699588) • US $200.00 (our price)

Global Perspectives on Contemporary Marketing Education
Brent Smith (Saint Joseph's University, USA) and Amiram Porath (AmiPorCon Ltd, Israel)
Business Science Reference • copyright 2016 • 293pp • H/C (ISBN: 9781466697843) • US $190.00 (our price)

Competitive Social Media Marketing Strategies
Wilson Ozuem (University of Gloucestershire, UK) and Gordon Bowen (Regent's University London, UK)
Business Science Reference • copyright 2016 • 317pp • H/C (ISBN: 9781466697768) • US $195.00 (our price)

Product Innovation through Knowledge Management and Social Media Strategies
Alok Kumar Goel (CSIR Human Resource Development Centre, India) and Puja Singhal (Amity University, India)
Business Science Reference • copyright 2016 • 421pp • H/C (ISBN: 9781466696075) • US $205.00 (our price)

Fuzzy Optimization and Multi-Criteria Decision Making in Digital Marketing
Anil Kumar (ABV-Indian Institute of Information Technology & Management, India) and Manoj Kumar Dash (ABV-Indian Institute of Information Technology & Management, India)
Business Science Reference • copyright 2016 • 368pp • H/C (ISBN: 9781466688087) • US $200.00 (our price)

Trends and Innovations in Marketing Information Systems
Theodosios Tsiakis (Alexander Technological Educational Institute of Thessaloniki, Greece)
Business Science Reference • copyright 2015 • 454pp • H/C (ISBN: 9781466684591) • US $225.00 (our price)

Capturing, Analyzing, and Managing Word-of-Mouth in the Digital Marketplace
Sumangla Rathore (Sir Padampat Singhania University, India) and Avinash Panwar (Sir Padampat Singhania University, India)
Business Science Reference • copyright 2016 • 339pp • H/C (ISBN: 9781466694491) • US $200.00 (our price)

IGI GLOBAL
DISSEMINATOR OF KNOWLEDGE
www.igi-global.com

701 E. Chocolate Ave., Hershey, PA 17033
Order online at www.igi-global.com or call 717-533-8845 x100
To place a standing order for titles released in this series, contact: cust@igi-global.com
Mon-Fri 8:00 am - 5:00 pm (est) or fax 24 hours a day 717-533-8661

Editorial Advisory Board

List of Reviewers

Table of Contents

Detailed Table of Contents

Prior studies on the use of social media by public relations professionals are often descriptive and did not apply communication theories to fully evaluate the richness of this emerging communication platform. These studies did not explain the technology adoption process of public relations professionals. On the basis of Media Richness Theory, the authors assessed the perceptions of 162 public relations professionals from a national sample in the United States to identify emerging media richness dimensions of social media. This study found that these dimensions are not the same as those in other mass and traditional media platforms. This chapter suggests that social media should not simply be compared to traditional media, because they have demonstrated unique medium characteristics. Both theoretical and managerial implications are discussed.

The Chapter talks about the importance of social media from the view of publicity for an organization. It talks about a few real life situations where organizations have suffered as a result of negative publicity on the social media. That negative publicity can be a disaster for the organization is emphasized. The chapter lists out the causes of negative publicity for an organization in the social media and how it can be tackled as is found in existing literature on negative publicity in the social media. The chapter ends with a series of guidelines to get back on track in the face of negative publicity in the social media.

The primary objective of this chapter is to highlight how social media can be used to strengthen stakeholders' relationships and build social capital for the organization, thereby enabling the organization to build, manage and sustain CR. The chapter begins with a brief overview of existing thought, approaches and terminology related to CR and proceeds to identify the interactions of each stakeholder with the organization through social media. The tenability of various forms of social media as viral videos, blogs, forums and micro blogging websites in furthering CR and the extent of their effectiveness are examined using cases derived from secondary data. Further, the chapter discusses methods of measuring the success of an organization's social media initiatives using different techniques and strategies for restoring reputation post a crisis by using social media. Finally, the chapter demonstrates a systematic process of strategizing and planning CR using social media and creating organizational infrastructure to achieve this end.

Gone are the days when Consumers had fewer product choices and companies had fewer sources of finding the right candidates for their work. Thanks to technology and globalization, things have changed. In this age of technology and speed, it becomes tough to overcome competition and make a successful career or business. One thing that may certainly help in achieving the above is a good reputation. Building a good reputation may take a long time but for maintaining it intact or destroying it entirely just takes few minutes. Online reputation is a newer term which basically deals with the rapport of a person or brand that has been build online. There are several online reputation management firms which earns millions of dollars every year from individuals and organizations just to maintain their good reputation on online platforms. This chapter discusses these concepts and techniques of online reputation management.

This chapter aims to promote brand management through social media in global marketing, thus explaining the theoretical and practical overview of social media, evolving dynamics of brand management, shifts in global marketing dynamics, and brand promotion through social media in global marketing. Social media is a great way to reach a new group of targeted consumers. Social media is utilized as a marketing tool by marketers in creating brand relationship. The integration of social media and brand management is necessary for modern organizations that seek to serve suppliers and customers, increase business performance, strengthen competitiveness, and achieve continuous success in global marketing. The chapter argues that promoting brand management through social media in global marketing has the potential to enhance organizational performance and reach strategic goals in the social media age.

opinion influences the decision making of others and the company. And companies, therefore, need to understand how to structure content and branding strategies where clients not only communicate with the company, but each other, in real time: the social media. Social networks, as currently represent the opportunity to get the engagement of customers and prospects in a way that can not be achieved by other means, become a single source of information that must be integrated into the software of the company, allowing the conversion of conversation into a transaction. So having a database of clients with personal information is no longer enough, and is required to obtain qualitative features that enable the company to know more about consumers and provide, as a result, a greater brand value. The Social CRM is a tool that incorporates the information obtained from the social networks to the traditional CRM, to ensure that the company is better informed about its customers and gets a much more solid basis for decision making, customizing the offer and adding value to the customer.

Chapter 9
Company-Customer Interaction via Social Media: Contributions to the Marketing Mix 160
Manel Hamouda, ISGG, Tunisia

In recent years, social media has become an integral part of internet users' everyday life. Customers are increasingly seen to be more like "content creators" or even company employees rather than mere customers as they were in the past. In this chapter, we try to understand how customers use the various social media platforms to interact and how this interaction influences the company's marketing policy. An overview of the customers' different uses and practices enabled authors to identify several forms of interactions and to detect their effects on pricing, product, place and promotion, the four main components of the marketing mix.

Section 4
Assortment of Impacts of Social Media Adoption

Chapter 10
Virtual Atmosphere, Emotions, Attitudes and Real Use: When "Love is in the Air" in a Virtual Community 172
António C. Moreira, University of Aveiro, Portugal
Mariana Mira Ferreira, University of Aveiro, Portugal
Pedro Macedo, University of Aveiro, Portugal

This study involves several theories, namely: the theory of reasoned action, the technology acceptance model, the theory of planned behavior and the internet banking acceptance model. It aims to understand the relationships between the virtual atmosphere and emotional states, how the individual characteristics (social identity, altruism and telepresence) and emotional states influence attitudes, and how attitudes, past experience and trust influence actual use of a site. To this end, the authors developed three conceptual models explaining the relationships among the above-mentioned variables. Methodologically, descriptive statistics, exploratory factor analysis and the generalized maximum entropy estimator are used to test the three models in a wedding site. Of the eight hypotheses proposed, one can only partially validate hypotheses h1, h2, h3 and h6, while hypothesis h7 is accepted and the remaining are rejected.

This paper examines factors, which affect web 2.0 knowledge sharing and its effect on organizational innovation in small and medium-sized enterprises (SMEs). The study also investigates whether web 2.0 knowledge sharing mediates the relationship between HR (Human Resource) practices and innovation. The proposed research model and its associated hypotheses were tested by using structural equation modelling on a dataset of 552 SMEs. Results suggest that technological and organizational factors are positively associated with web 2.0 knowledge sharing in Ss, while the contrary is found with regard to vertical competition. In addition, results show that web 2.0 knowledge sharing positively influence innovation and that web 2.0 knowledge sharing mediates the relationship between Human Resource (HR) practices and innovation in SMEs.

This chapter examines how Lawson, a convenience store chain in Japan has taken a different approach in utilizing Twitter. This chapter begins with the background of the retail sector in Japan, specifically the convenience store industry as well as a brief description of cute culture. The key elements of Lawson's Twitter account are explored accordingly. Using elements from Esch, Langner, Schimitt & Geus' general model of branding components and relationship to micro blogging, a study was conducted to examine the current and future purchase intentions. While social media proved to help differentiate Lawson from its competitors, it was not the main factor in generating brand loyalty. The findings show that not all followers displayed purchase intentions. The results also identified a gap between the perceptions of Lawson's Twitter account versus the overall corporate brand. This provides the foundation for further research activities in developing more effective methods of maximizing Twitter in enhancing customer experience and subsequently increasing brand equity and loyalty.

The influence of social media on the various facets of society has attracted a lot of attention of the researchers in the last few years who are probing its multifaceted impact. One important aspect of social media is its role in promoting instant gratification. It has far reaching consequences for evolution of self, which in turn has important implications for society and businesses. Drawing from the conceptual foundations of the theories of identity and social comparison, the researchers tried to develop a model as to how the dual role of social media acts to alter the identity and hence behavior. In this context, the significance of the study lies in exposing the intricate interplay between the attributes of social media and the dynamic self. The study goes a long way in providing a deeper understanding of self-concept in connection to social media, which has immense importance for consumer behavior and can help businesses to fine-tune their strategies with the changing consumer psychology.

Foreword

Proliferation of social media is metamorphosing various aspects of public and private interactions. Public spheres, public relations, publicity and image of the brands and organizations appear to be the most affected arenas due to the simple fact that social media is by the masses, for the masses and influences the masses to a greater extent. In organizations, social media has not only altered but has also augmented the media interactions, opinion leadership, publicity management, reputation management, crisis management, brand management, brand image and customer relationship management to name a few. Be it through Facebook, Twitter, Instagram, YouTube, Pinterest, WhatsApp or other similar platforms, social media is proving to be instrumental in breaking news, making it viral and keeping it relevant. Online and offline literature is abound of such examples wherein social media has tremendously affected or has shown the potential to affect the reputation of the organizations, in a positive or negative way, such as American Apparel's Challenger disaster, MasterCard's hashtag hijack, LG's mockery of iPhones, Apple's Bendgate, Dell Hell, Jasmine Revolution, etc. Transformed media landscape, composed of internet citizen journalist, generating content and news and ease of access of internet along with smartphones, necessitates a re-examination of Publicity, PR and Reputation management in this changed scenario.

This comprehensive text was conceptualized with the aim of providing a relevant theoretical framework, the latest empirical researches, problems and future research prospects in the dynamic and fast-evolving area of reputation management and brand management through social media with a specific focus on developing nations. The text was proposed with an aim to bridge the gap in research in the above-referred area. It is a significant contribution to the body of knowledge in the field on social media marketing.

The present treatise divided into five sections contains 15 chapters. The issues covered are customer relationship management and social media, PR, Publicity and reputation management through social media, role of social media in brand management, assessment of impacts of social media adoption and emerging trends in digital marketing. The contents are quite rich and they cover wider issues with respect to social and digital media. Contributions from all over the globe were compiled. Useful contributions were received from distinguished critics of US, Spain and Portugal.

In this highly competitive digital age of global interconnectivity and interdependence, task of brand management has become tough for the professional working in the organizations. The challenges in altered media scenario are both difficult and interesting and people are working on them with enthusiasm and tenacity to provide for solutions to keep up with the ever-changing threats. Practitioners not only need to understand business strategy and to work in tandem with their counterparts in areas such as customer service and advertising, but also to comprehend the public sentiment expressed on social media platforms, in order to help various stake holders achieve their goals. This book is a good step in this direction.

The publication has been targeted at policy makers, technology developers, academicians, researchers, practitioners and students of public relations, brand management and social media to help them in improving their understanding of the subject so that improved marketing strategies can be put in practice. This book provides relevant theoretical frameworks and the latest empirical research findings in the area to contribute substantially to the body of knowledge on managing public relations and brand image through social media.

The editors Dr. Anurag Singh and Punita Duhan have made a sincere attempt to cover various facets of social media as envisioned by practitioners. Valuable insights can be found by reading the whole book. I compliment both the editors for this academic venture, so that academicians, researchers and policy makers may be benefitting by this presentation.

Nageshwar Rao
Indira Gandhi National Open University, India

Nageshwar Rao *is working as in-charge Vice- Chancellor, Indira Gandhi National Open University, New Delhi since November 28, 2014. After completing his term as Vice-Chancellor of Uttar Pradesh Rajarshi Tondon Open University, Allahabad between August 2008 to August 2011, he has joined as Pro Vice Chancellor, Indira Gandhi National Open University New Delhi in December 2013. During the period between August 2011 and December 2013 he was Professor in Pandit Jawaharlal Nehru Institute of Business Management (PJLNIBM) Vikram University, Ujjain where he also served as the Director of the institute for more than 13 years. He was appointed as Dean, Faculty of Management Studies for five terms; Dean, Faculty of Information Technology for one term and Chairman, Board of Studies in Management for four terms at Vikram university Ujjain. He is University Professor in Management for more than 23 years. He was also Reader in Faculty of Management Studies at Banaras Hindu University, Varanasi between 1985 and 1990 and Lecturer in Department of Commerce & Business Administration of University of Allahabad, Allahabad between 1978 to 1985. He has led a cherished First Class career and received his D.Phil from the University of Allahabad and ICWA from institute of Cost and Management Accountants of India, Kolkata. He has been a recipient of Gold Medals and various coveted scholarships of merit. He has contributed to the academics by writing eight books. His popular books are 'Administration on Public Enterprises in India' and 'Communication Skills'. 37 students have been awarded Ph.D. in management under his supervision. To his credit, more than 160 research papers and articles have been published. He has been invited as a Resource person to approximately 25 EDPs (Executive Development Programmes) for Railways, NTPC, National Fertilizers etc. He has attended more than 90 National and International Seminars in management and allied disciplines.He has been a Member of Governing Council, for the Association of Indian Universities in 2010; a Member of Executive Council of Council of Science and Technology, U.P (2008-11); a Member, Academic Council of Banaras Hindu University, Varanasi; a Member of the Academic Council of Mahatma Gandhi Kashi Vidyapeeth, Varanasi; Uttaranchal Open University, Nainital; Vardhman Mahaveer Kota Open University, Banasthali Vidyapeeth, Jaipur, etc. He was the Chairman-Sports Board, Chief Warden- Hostels, Dean Students Welfare, Patron-Students Union and In-charge Professor, Ambedkar Peeth at Vikram University. He was also Hon. Secretary, Institute of Gandhian Thought and Peace Studies, University of Allahabad. He was nominated by Govt. of Madhya Pradesh to be the Director of the Board of Professional Examination Board, Bhopal for a period of four years. He was also the President of Indian Accounting Association. Saraswati Samman was conferred upon him by the Department of Higher Education U.P. Govt (India) on 5th Sep, 2010 and a Prof. B.B.L. Saxena Smriti Hindi Sewa Samman was conferred by Etawah Hindi Sewa Nidhi on 26 December, 2010. He was conferred with a Fellow Membership of the Institute of Cost and Management Accountants of India, Kolkata and also honoured as Fellow Member by the Indian Commerce Association. He was also made honoured by Gramin Patrakar Association Uttar Pradesh for contributions to Journalism in 2011, World Welfare and Astrology Research Institute, Allahabad in 2010 and Bioved Honorary Fellowship Award of Bioved Research Institute of Agriculture and Technology, Allahabad in 2010.*

Preface

Advent of information technology tools, their proliferation and acceptance amongst masses worldwide is one of the most significant developments of mankind. Collaboration, transparency, connectivity accorded by these tools accompanied by continual and continuous improvements mandates the study of impact of these on consumers and marketers alike. Availability of large amounts of publically available personal data at web opens the new vistas for marketers to engage the customers with their brands in ways that are more meaningful. However, in order to tap these vast amounts of data effectively, we need to employ an all encompassing, multidimensional, integrated and action oriented approach towards the customer footprints available at different techno-social mediums. Pervasiveness and influence of these media has led to emergence of the new fields such as social media, digital marketing, e-marketing and online consumer behavior as separate branches/ disciplines in the overriding marketing field.

Whether an organization likes it or not, its brands are being talked about on social media platforms. The organizations have lost the control over the manner in which their brands are being talked about i.e. whether the brands are being discussed in a positive light or in a negative way. This uncontrolled, uninitiated and viral discussion of brands, positive or negative, has become and should be a cause of concern for the marketers, as a single negative remark going viral has the potential of decimating the carefully nurtured and hard-earned reputation of the brands and organizations over the years. Hence, this opens a new arena for marketers to work, in order to manage the public relations and brand image through social media, as social media marketing is different from traditional marketing as it enables an organization to analyze the effectiveness of its marketing campaigns in real time. Emergence of new social platforms, mobile devices and new apps require altered strategies to reach new and existing customers turning social media marketing into a continuously evolving and dynamic field.

This comprehensive text was conceptualized with the aims to provide relevant theoretical framework, latest empirical researches, problems and future research prospects in the dynamic and fast evolving area of reputation management and brand management through social media with specific focus on developing nations. The text was proposed with an aim to bridge the gap in research in the above-referred area so that it is a significant contribution to the body of knowledge in the field on social media marketing. Accordingly, contributors were invited to submit chapters related to managing public relations and brand image through social media in developing countries. Major topics covered in the text include Managing Negative publicity on Social Media, PR and reputation management through social media, Social CRM, Mobile marketing, Impact of Social Media on PR, Role of social media in Personal branding, Brand image management through social media, Online reputation management, e-WOM and Future of Social Media Marketing to name a few.

The publication has been targeted at policy makers, technology developers, academicians, researchers, practitioners and students of public relations, brand management and social media to help them in improving their understanding of the subject so that improved marketing strategies can be put in practice. This book provides relevant theoretical frameworks and the latest empirical research findings in the area so as to contribute substantially to the body of knowledge on managing public relations and brand image through social media.

The book is organized in the following five sections:

Section 1: PR, Publicity and Reputation Management through Social Media
Section 2: Role of Social Media in Brand Management
Section 3: Customer Relationship Management and Social Media
Section 4: Assortment of Impacts of Social media Adoption and
Section 5: Emerging Trends in Digital Marketing

Each section caters to a distinct role played by social media for effective business management. A total of 15 chapters are interspersed in the five sections, a brief description of each of the chapters follows:

First chapter focuses on the role of social media as a tool of PR Practitioners. Study, which was conducted in USA, uses Media Richness Theory to evaluate the richness of this emerging communication medium, as the prior studies were often descriptive in nature. Authors assessed the media richness dimensions of social media based on the perceptions of 162 public relations professionals and concluded that though social media is an emerging as well as powerful tool for PR efforts, it should not be compared to traditional media as both possess some unique medium characteristics.

Second chapter discusses how social media impacts the publicity component of the promotion mix, more specifically the emphasis of the author is on ramifications of the negative publicity, in social media, for the organizations. Author has listed out the reasons and remedies relating to negative publicity on social media by citing real life examples. Author proposes a series of guidelines to get back on track in the face of negative publicity in the social media.

In third chapter, focus is on how social media can be used for building, managing and sustaining Corporate Reputation. Authors begin with an overview of the existing literature related to corporate reputation and then using real life cases exhibit the plausibility of various social media platforms to strengthen stakeholders' relationships and building social capital for the organisation. The methods to measure the success of social media initiatives in organisations, strategies to deal with online reputational crisis and process of creating organizational infrastructure for managing corporate reputation using social media is discussed.

Online Reputation management, an important dimension to be catered to by the organizations in this dynamic and competitive era, is the subject matter of fourth chapter. Emphasizing the importance of building managing and maintaining the reputation, more specifically online reputation, authors talk about the concept of Online Reputation Management (ORM) and various online platforms (such as Weblogs, Microblogs, Folksonomies, Wikis, Social Networks etc.) at the disposal of the organizations to manage the reputation online. Authors have also enumerated the features and advantages of these platforms. Impact of Digital Footprints, Digital Shadow or Passive Digital Footprints on online reputation as well as importance of managing SERP (Search Engine Results Page) has been discussed so that the negative SERPs are pushed down and the positive SERPs are pushed up in the research results. Authors while discussing techniques for sustaining online reputation stressed the need for a global body to monitor and regulate the online reputation management practices to ensure ethical implementation of the same.

Chapter 5 discusses how organizations can use various social media platforms for effective brand management in global marketing. Author gives a thorough literature consolidation of social media and brand management and advocates the brand management through social media as a mean to achieve strategic goals of the organizations. Chapter gives the theoretical and practical overview of social media, evolving dynamics of brand management, shifts in global marketing dynamics, and brand promotion through social media in global marketing.

Chapter 6 analyzes the Spanish Government's use of social media to create, manage and consolidate the Spain Brand image to exhibit the image of Spain as an economic and political power among the first countries in the world. Chapter builds upon the brand basics *viz.* concept of brand, brand image, country brand equity, keys of country brand, management of brand image, effect of the origin on the behavior of the individual and then progresses to emphasize the importance of brand building with specific reference to country brand management. Country brand acting as a differentiator has become a strategic asset and a tool to promote their products, attract investments and promote activities like tourism for the nations has been elaborated upon. How rapid evolution of the internet and social media has brought in new dimensions in the construction of communication strategies for country brand management has been detailed.

Chapter 7 studies the role consumer engagement and swarm intelligence play in managing a brand at social media. Social media facilitates the human swarm and this ability to think collectively influences the online buyers at social media. Organizations need to explore this collective phenomenon as individuals behave in a very different way as a single identity from how they behave collectively in a group. Another crucial aspect, which organizations need to be wary of, is to get involved in dialogue with customers with respect to their brands in order to engage the customers as customer engagement creates the value for the company and adds to its bottom line. Social media and internet have changed the way customer engagement and swarm intelligence affect the consumer behavior and authors have studied the phenomenon empirically using netnography.

Chapter 8 is about Social Customer Relationship Management (SCRM), the paradigm shift in customer relationship management, which is taking place due to the advent, proliferation and embracing of social media. Social media has altered the very character of the customers' interactions with the organizations making this real time, interactive and influential. Authors highlight the need for integration of web 2.0 technologies with the existing business strategy of the so as to utilize the qualitative aspects of digital footprints for converting conversation into a transaction, for better value addition and win-win situations for the different stake holders. Authors have discussed the SCRM philosophy from two perspectives *viz.* strategic and operational by exhibiting two successful case studies for real life.

Chapter 9 asserts that social media, which has become a part and parcel of the internet users' life, has the potential to influence the marketing policy of a firm. Author gives a theoretical review of how the possible customer-company interactions taking place via various platforms of social media can shape and affect the 4P's of marketing mix. Chapter makes an interesting reading because of various examples quoted by the author to substantiate his views.

Chapter 10 caters to an under researched area i.e. consumer behavior associated to wedding in context of virtual environment, which in this case is a website catering to wedding *viz.*www.onossocasamento.pt. Chapter appears to be a unique contribution to the literature, both in terms of analytical tool used and the research gap identified, as it uses GME estimator, robust for small samples sizes (micronumerosity) to analyze virtual atmosphere, emotions, attitudes and real use in a virtual community having wedding, an intangible concept, as its main theme instead of some product transaction. Study assimilated concepts borrowed from Theory of Reasoned Action, Technology Acceptance Model, Theory of Planned Behavior and Internet Banking Acceptance Model. Three models were developed to understand the relationships between the virtual atmosphere and emotional states, how the individual characteristics (social identity, altruism and telepresence) and emotional states influence attitudes, and how attitudes, past experience and trust influence the actual usage of the site. Researchers concluded that out of the four components of the virtual atmosphere only graphics has a positive effect on emotions, whereas Emotions and social identity have a positive effect on attitudes. Individual characteristics of altruism and telepresence as well as trust do not exert any influence on attitudes and real use of the website respectively. In turn, attitudes only partially influence the actual use of site, where as past experiences are strong predictors of real use.

Chapter 11 examines the technological, environmental and organisational factors that may facilitate, motivate or constraint Web 2.0 knowledge sharing in SMEs and the effect of knowledge sharing on organisational innovation. Chapter also investigates whether web 2.0 knowledge sharing mediates the relationship between HR (Human Resource) practices and innovation. Results of the proposed model and hypotheses, tested using Structural Equation Modelling, hinted that technological and organizational factors are positively associated with web 2.0 knowledge sharing in SMEs, with organizational factors–commitment-based HR practices- being the main drivers of Web 2.0 knowledge sharing, and that it mediates the relationship between HR practices and innovation in SMEs. Findings are pertinent in view of the fact that SMEs are using Web 2.0 technologies such as social networking, wikis, and internal blogging to improve collaboration and Web 2.0 knowledge sharing.

Chapter 12 brings to the fore the changes and challenges effected in Japanese retail sector, specifically the convenience store industry, due to the technological innovations induced by social media. Specific focus of the chapter is on the micro bogging strategy adopted by Lawson, one of the top three convenience stores in Japan, to combat the saturation and 'noise' induced by bombarding of messages via social media and to stay relevant and differentiate itself, by taking refuge in Japanese cute culture concept, from the others. The pilot study conducted to explore the perceptions of the customers revealed that though the strategy adopted by store was successful in differentiating it from competitors, yet the positive customer perceptions about social media account did not result in customer actions. This chapter provides readers with insights as to how a Japanese convenience retailer has been able to create a comprehensive shopping experience by incorporating cultural marketing in Social Networking Sites.

Chapter 13 exposes the intricate interplay between the attributes of social media and dynamic self, which is immensely important to understand altered consumer psychology and behavior and in turn to form appropriate business strategies. Researcher has attempted to wade through the so far unchartered vistas in the arena of social media as it discovers the role of social media in instant gratification and the impact of the same on formation and evolution of self. A conceptual model for understanding the mental states and the concept of self in relation to want satisfaction through social media has been propounded, which depicts social media as a satisfier to a need as well as modifier and generator of a need. Model may be useful to unravel the present day state of instant gratification and its ramifications for the business and society more than what the conceptual and analytical studies about social media have exhibited so far.

Chapter 14 explores and assesses the influence of electronic word of mouth (eWOM) on customers' purchasing decisions in hospitality sector in Indian context using secondary sources of data. Experiential and intangible aspects of hospitality business have rather made it binding on the customers to resort to word of mouth to assess the quality of the products and services offered. Era of internet and web 2.0, has led to emergence of (Internet) iWOM or (electronic) eWOM, which is virtual, written, permanent, more trust worthy and san any temporal and geo-political boundaries. Chapter also talks about various types of social media along with their contribution in marketing of hospitality sector. While discussing the impact of reviews on hotel performance, chapter suggests potential strategies for using online guest reviews when marketing.

Chapter 15 explores the interplay of attitude, satisfaction and purchase intentions in context of online shopping in Indian youth. Influence and role of attitudes and satisfaction from past purchases in offline shopping is a well-established fact. However, the changed retail landscape due to induction of internet technologies and more aware customers, researchers attempted to understand the same in context on online shopping, which is fast becoming a preferred mode of shopping amongst youth in India. Researchers found that attitude towards online shopping are a significant factor affecting purchase intentions in online shopping as well. Satisfaction was also found to be mediating the relationship between attitude towards online shopping and purchase intentions to online shopping among Indian youth.

In nutshell, book is an attempt to cover the various facets of social media as envisioned by researchers and practitioners to give valuable insights to the marketing practitioners, policy makers, academicians, researchers and students of Public relations, brand management and Social media by exposing them to various latest research endeavours being undertaken in these fields in a comprehensive manner.

Anurag Singh
Banaras Hindu University, India

Punita Duhan
Meera Bai Institute of Technology, India

Acknowledgment

The editors would like to acknowledge the help of all the people involved in this project and specifically authors, reviewers and editorial advisory board. Without their support, this book would not have become a reality.

First, the editors would like to thank each one of the authors for their contributions. Our sincere gratitude goes to the chapters' authors who contributed their precious time and immense expertise to this book. Erudite contribution of authors is the most important building block of the book.

Second, the editors wish to acknowledge the valuable contributions of the learned reviewers, regarding the improvement of quality, coherence, and content presentation of chapters. Most of the authors also served as referees; we highly appreciate their double task.

Next, the editors are thankful to the editorial advisory board for their timely and valuable guidance and scholarly insights to give final shape to this book.

Also, editors are grateful to Prof. Nageshwar Rao, in-charge Vice- Chancellor, Indira Gandhi National Open University, New Delhi for his prefatory note.

Last, but not the least, editors are grateful to their families for their constant support to help them complete the project in time.

Anurag Singh
Banaras Hindu University, India

Punita Duhan
Meera Bai Institute of Technology, India

Section 1

PR, Publicity and Reputation Management through Social Media

Chapter 1
How Public Relations Practitioners Perceive Social Media Platforms?
A Media Richness Perspective

Ana Isabel Gonzalez Michel
Albertus Magnus College, USA

Thomas E. Ruggiero
The University of Texas at El Paso, USA

Kenneth C. C. Yang
The University of Texas at El Paso, USA

ABSTRACT

Prior studies on the use of social media by public relations professionals are often descriptive and did not apply communication theories to fully evaluate the richness of this emerging communication platform. These studies did not explain the technology adoption process of public relations professionals. On the basis of Media Richness Theory, the authors assessed the perceptions of 162 public relations professionals from a national sample in the United States to identify emerging media richness dimensions of social media. This study found that these dimensions are not the same as those in other mass and traditional media platforms. This chapter suggests that social media should not simply be compared to traditional media, because they have demonstrated unique medium characteristics. Both theoretical and managerial implications are discussed.

INTRODUCTION

Improvements in computers, mobile technologies and integrated technologies have played an essential role in adding ease to the way people communicate with each other (Lica & Tuta, 2011; Margalit, 2014). While the changes generated by "new" technology have presented various opportunities in the field of communication, these fast-paced transformations demand prompt and intelligent adaptation in order to continue the efficient flow of information to its publics (Elliott, 2011; Macario, Ednacot, Ullberg &

DOI: 10.4018/978-1-5225-0332-3.ch001

Reichel, 2011). Among the various communication professions that are faced with the challenges and opportunities of change due to technological advancements is public relations (henceforth, PR) (Berkowitz, 2007; Elliott, 2011; Taylor & Kent, 2010; Supa, 2014). The potential impacts of social media on PR practices have led the Public Relations Society of America, the industry's largest organization, to consider the redefinition of "public relations" (Elliott, 2011). Supa (2014) claims that social media have changed "the purposes of public relations, or its strategic value to organizations" (para 6). Since its inception, PR has relied on traditional media to communicate with the public and its target audience. However, social media have allowed PR professionals direct access to their audiences through interactive and two-way conversation (Elliott, 2011). As such, there is now a transformation of the delivery of the press release directly to the audience (Elliott, 2011; Vorvoreanu, 2008). While PR continues to rely on traditional media platforms, such as newspapers, television and radio to communicate with its target audience, the 21st century has brought an array of challenges and changes that have the potential to impact the future of the profession (Darnowski & Wright, 2010; Elliott, 2011; Supa, 2014; Taylor & Kent, 2010).

These technological advancements such as social media have provided a two-way interactive communication, allowing PR specialists to create dialogue between the organization and its public, instead of the one-way communication model based on interaction between journalist and editors (Berkowitz, 2007; Elliott, 2011). As such, social media have the potential for PR specialists to access new communication tools to reach their audience directly while shifting the purpose and usage of traditional media (Vorvoreanu, 2008). Thus, the innovation of communication technologies has made it non-productive for PR specialists to simply rely on traditional methods to communicate with their audiences (Macario et al., 2011). More importantly, supported by emerging social media platforms, PR professionals have the potential to wield a powerful mechanism in reach and message delivery to target audiences (Macario et al., 2011; Wang & Hung, 2011).

While this potential creates the impetus for PR professionals to embrace social media as a beneficial tool, PR scholars have also cast doubt on their effectiveness in the educational context (Taylor & Kent, 2010) and their limited use in the media relations (Supa, 2014). A fundamental question that is lacking in the current literature is what explains the characteristics of social media as viable and effective PR communication tools. The current sub-set of the literature also did not provide a theoretical framework to support and justify these proposed recommendations to integrate social media into PR campaigns (Iodhia, 2012). In an effort to bolster that theoretical vacuum, this book chapter proposes Media Richness Theory (henceforth, MRT) as a prospective model to assess social media by focusing on their media characteristics as predictive variables to account for PR professionals' decisions to use these emerging platforms. With the support of the MRT theoretical framework, this research aims to gauge the perceptions of PR professionals' use of social media as a medium to communicate to audiences effectively, and to what degree the characteristics of social media facilitate the overall professional tasks necessary for PR professionals. Furthermore, the study also examines the media richness dimensions as perceived by PR professionals, to compare with existing dimensions derived from more traditional media.

BACKGROUND

The Role of Social Media in Public Relations

Although various PR organizations argue that the new frontier in PR practices is social media (Elliott, 2011; Wright & Hinson, 2014), Kent (2010) argued that social media is a concept that has existed for decades. Social media were first introduced toward the end of the 1970's, as *CompuServe* offered a novel avenue for users to communicate through online discussions. In 1990, *America Online* opened the availability for their clients to e-mail as well as chat; and in 1997 *sixdegrees.com* introduced profiles, the ability to search for friends and organize contacts into groups (Brass, 2011).

In the case of PR, the role of social media is essential to help deliver messages and establish and maintain effective campaigns (Kent, 2010). In 2011, the BRASS Programing Planning Committee (2011) suggested that social media permit users to create a public profile, and establish a contact list of for the purpose of sharing the connection and the connections of other users. Kent (2010) also argued that any interactive communication media that allows for two-way interaction and feedback is a form of social media, but he differentiates from modern social networks or social media, which is based on real-time interaction. Wright and Hinson (2010) added that social media provide a platform for anyone to publish digital creative content; give and access real-time feedback via online discussions and allows for the editing of the original message. Later, in their longitudinal study, Wright and Hinson (2014) also observed the interaction between emerging social and traditional media in enhancing public relations practices.

In the current state of two-way interactive communication, the target audience for PR can fulfill multiple roles such as becoming a spokesperson for the company, and influencing his/her network to favor the client (Michaelson & Stacks, 2011). PR professionals seek to inspire the behavior of the recipient based on the reaction to the message, and have the ability to employ the target audience as an extension of their communication efforts (Michaelson & Stacks, 2011). A survey conducted in 2008 to 283 PR professionals from different parts of the United States found that PR specialists were committed to using social media as a PR tool. The survey listed e-mail, blogs and intranet as items of social media (Eyrich, Padman & Sweetser, 2008). Out of the individuals polled, the premier tools for social media used in PR were e-mail (96.1%), intranet (68.2%) and video conferencing (39.1%). By 2010, social media included interactive social networking sites like *MySpace*, *Facebook*, and *LinkedIn*, as well as blogs, podcasts, message boards, online videos, picture albums, and mobile telephone alerts. According to a later poll of 1,060 PRSA members and PRSA prospects, social media engagement among PR specialist should be viewed for its potential and as an important tool with the promise to grow the proficiency of PR in the next five years (Darnowski & Wright, 2010). In comparison to traditional media, social media has the potential to provide an opportunity to offer a two-way messaging platform yielding a clear and open communication with the audience and the message sender (Elliott, 2011; Wright & Hinson, 2009). However, Wright and Hinson's longitudinal study (2014) also reported a discrepancy between PR professionals' recommendations and actual integration of emerging social media into PR practices. In their study of communication strategies, 77% of the PR professionals reported different messages should be used for various social media, while only 57% of their organizations implemented the dissemination of different messages for various social media platforms.

Rapid advancements of technology have led to an increased scrutiny among PR specialists and scholars to evaluate these new outlets, and fostered reluctance to fully embrace social networking, blogging and other forms of social media (Eyrich et al., 2008). Pundits on how to effectively use social media in PR campaigns can be easily found online. For example, Wynne (2014) proposed four rules to create so-called "winning social media for public relations campaigns," by recommending being brief, newsworthy, and helpful and avoiding Facebook. Though PR associations increasingly express a need to adapt social media as a potential tool for outreach based on the large amount of users (Wright & Hinson, 2009, 2014), questions arise as to what social media outlets are most preferred by PR professionals. Thus, the authors posed the following research question:

RQ 1: What is the preferred social media outlet among PR professionals?

MAIN FOCUS OF THE CHAPTER

Issues, Controversies, Problems

Fast-paced innovations in communication technologies and the demands of the 21st century have modified the nature of human communication between individuals (Kupritz & Cowell, 2011). The evolution created by new technologies during the past decade has permitted new forms of interactions between an organization and the people who are interested in it or dependent on it (Turner, Grube, Tinsley, Lee & O'Pell, 2006). With the demand to use time efficiently and to communicate in a clear manner, communicators have analyzed the best way to deliver a message in order to motivate an action based on the message sent (Kupritz & Cowell, 2011). One of the leading theories used in the study of and analysis of media selection is Media Richness Theory (henceforth, MTR) (Daft & Lengel, 1986; Sheer & Chen, 2004). MTR scholars argue that organizations are social systems that must process information, but face obstacles created by uncertainty and equivocality (Daft & Lengel, 1986). As such, MRT analyses the richness of media with the goal of reducing these obstacles in the communication process (Daft & Lengel, 1986). Using rich media is believed to reduce uncertainty and equivocality in the communication process (Daft & Lengel, 1986).

Based on MRT, the richness of a medium is grounded on the availability of the following media characteristics/dimensions: (1) instant feedback, (2) use of multiple cues such as body language and tone of voice, (3) use of natural language, and (4) personal focus on the medium (Trevino, Lengel, Bodensteiner, Gerloff, & Muir, 1990). First, instant feedback is defined as the immediacy as to how the feedback is received from the individual target audience. The faster the feedback, the faster the information will be verified (Daft & Lengel, 1986). As such the immediacy of feedback plays an important role in maintaining clarity and comprehensiveness. MRT also states that, the faster the feedback, the richer the medium (Daft & Lengel, 1986). Thus the variable of instant feedback will measure the immediacy of communication among the PR professionals and their target audience.

Rich media are characterized as personal because they provide immediate feedback from both the speakers, allowing the instant verification of the information shared. According to Daft and Lengel (1984) the richness of the information disseminated has the ability to change understanding of the messages on a given period of time. Aasheim and Stensønes (2011) studied Facebook in an organizational setting and found that personal communication characteristics make it suitable for distribution of information, teamwork, education and moral support during disaster (Ahmed, 2012).

Secondly, in terms of using multiple cues, rich media also provide a large variety of communication cues such as body language, vocal tone and message delivery defined as "natural language" (Daft & Lengel, 1986). Rich media have the capacity for interaction and personal communication that hold the potential to develop a personal focus, and a closer relationship between the message sender and recipient (Sheer & Chen, 2004). According to Daft and Lengel (1986), multiple cues, such as tone of voice and body language allow different items of reference and assist in the defining the message content with less uncertainty. MRT states that the fewer cues will restrict the immediacy of feedback, which can lead to mistakes or confusion (Daft & Lengel, 1986). The use of multiple cues is essential in determining the message, and facilitates the understanding of the message. Shahkat (2011) described Facebook as a medium with a rich and interactive interface.

Third, as to the use of natural language, MRT highlights natural language, inspired by the spontaneous use of gestures and expressions leading to the understanding of the message. Natural language is simple and straightforward, allowing for a common interpretation between message sender and recipient. Information exchanged through natural language allows for immediate understanding without the need for additional interpretations that can lead to confusion. In their study, Koo, Wati, and Jung (2011) noted that social media has the potential to help create ideas, ease message delivery, and promote task understanding. Social media allows its users to utilize a variety of innovative cues, such as capitalized letters, and emoticons used spontaneously depending on the conversation (Lica & Tuta, 2011).

Lastly, personal communication plays an important role in the richness of the media. Since the message requires negotiation and feedback as members work together to create symbols that convey relevant information, it is important to maintain a good relationship with audiences (Trevino et al., 1990). The personal attribute of the communication encourages an emotional attachment to the message, leading to responsibility and involvement to the task communicated (Sheer & Chen, 2004). This variable will aid in understanding the relationship between the PR professional and her or his target audience, which can aid in developing better understanding of the audience, culminating in the audience serving as an extension of the PR efforts in the message delivery.

The continuous development of communication technologies has expanded media richness potential, wherein a web-hosted communication process stimulates easy and immediate access to information on a real-time basis (Iodhia, 2012). Thus, Kupritz and Cowell (2011) argued there is an increasing necessity to re-evaluate communication channels in order to study the value that they add to message delivery. Recent studies have suggested that contrary to earlier predictions, computer-mediated communication is a rich medium (Anandarajan, Zaman, Dai, & Arinze, 2010; Johnson & Keil, 2002; Sheer & Chen, 2004; Turner et al., 2006).

Based on the literature above, the authors proposed the following research question:

RQ2: How do public relations professionals perceive various media richness dimensions in social media?

Solutions and Recommendations

The goal of this research is to establish an academic investigation of the richness of social media as a tool for the practice of PR. In order to accomplish this goal, the study is derived from these core variables of MRT, used to reduce uncertainty and equivocality: (1) instant feedback, (2) use of multiple cues such as body language and tone of voice, (3) use of natural language and (4) personal focus on the medium (Daft & Lengel, 1986). The authors also borrowed from Koo et al. (2011) in developing a survey to determine if social media is a communication tool rich enough to benefit PR practitioners.

Data Collection Method

Qualitative inquiry of how social media affects public relations practices has generated optimistic assessment of these emerging media platforms (Supa, 2014). While qualitative research provides profound insight into the topic being investigated, it is based on small samples that cannot be extrapolated to the perceptions of a larger group (Wrench, Thomas-Maddox, Richmond & McCroskey, 2008). This quantitative study was designed to obtain statistical information regarding a large group of PR professionals. Furthermore, answers to research questions posed by this study required the input of a large pool of national PR professionals from diverse professional backgrounds. In order to reach various PR professionals at different geographic locations within the continental United States, the researcher used an online questionnaire to survey a national sample of PR professionals in the United States. The data gathered is intended to provide information about the PR practitioners, their relationship, perceptions, attitudes, and behaviors in using social media as means of communication.

Participant Recruitment Procedures

The respondents for this investigation were PR specialists gathered through the search engine *Google* to obtain contact information. The contact names and e-mail addresses for survey respondents were gathered by searching under the categories PR specialists, PR director, Public Information Officer and Public Affairs Officer. The survey respondents were obtained, through search engine by looking under, "contact: PR specialist," "contact: public information officer," and "contact: public affairs officer." During the survey collection process, the investigators encountered companies that had more extensive PR departments than others. Some companies had two, three or even up to 30 PR professionals performing different tasks for the organization. In the case of those websites that had more than one PR professional listed, the investigators chose the second person listed. As such, only one contact was selected per organization web-page found with the help of the search engine. With the use of *Google*, the researchers had nationwide access to PR professionals and obtained their contact information in order to send a personalized invitation to participate in the online survey. PR professionals were also invited to participate in the research through *LinkedIn* professional groups.

Instrumentation

On the basis of Koo et al.'s study (2011), seven rich media dimensions in social media were examined. The scales focused on the measurements of *task analyzability*, *task urgency*, *task complexity, social influence, social affinity, the usage of media* and *task performance*. Additionally, the survey was designed with six sections aimed to obtain the perception of PR specialists regarding the richness of social media as perceived by different types of PR industries. Three of these sections focused on the variables of MRT (i.e., feedback, language, personal communication and message delivery). The other two sections were used to obtain demographic information and the social media usage by PR professionals for their professional efforts. The first part of the survey, the demographic information, queried respondents about their gender, ethnic background, the type of industry and years of experience in the field of PR. The survey respondents were also asked their preference and usage of social media outlets and approximately how much time they use social media for their professional purposes.

The Cronbach's alpha coefficients for each dimension range from *Task Analyzability* (.82) to *Task Performance Marketing Related* (.65). The coefficients support the reliability of the scales (Table 1).

Table 1. A Comparison of Koo et al. (2011) and Daft and Lengel (1986) media richness dimensions

Koo et al. (2011) Variables	Definition	Analysis of MRT Core Variables (Daft & Lengel, 1986)
Task Analyzability	The measurement of how clear and understandable the communication guidelines are studied	Instant Feedback, Use of Various Cues, Use of Natural Language, Personal Emphasis
Task Urgency	The measurement of how well a medium can provide rapid response and reaction in the communication process	Instant Feedback
Task Complexity	The use of multiple cues that are needed to help send a clear message with the least amount of confusion	Use of Various Cues, Use of Natural Language
Social Influence	The attitude and influence provided in the message dissemination by people of influence	Personal Emphasis
Social Affinity	Moderates the relationship between the task characteristics	Personal Emphasis
Task Performance	The relation between which communication channel usage matches task characteristics	Instant Feedback, Use of Various Cues, Use of Natural Language, Personal Emphasis

Results

Demographic Data of the Sample

In early 2012, the researchers surveyed 241 respondents. Among them, 162 fully completed the questionnaire and their responses were used for later analyses. Out of the respondents, 44 (27.3%) were male, 117 (72.7%) were female. The ethnicity of the national respondents was comprised of: 115 (71.0%) white, followed by 28 (17.3%) Latino/Hispanic/Chicano, seven (4.3%) African American, six (4.3%) Asian and six (3.7%) preferred to be acknowledged as other. The industries represented by the population included 47 (29%) in agency, 29 (17.9%) non-profit, 29 (17.9%) education, 18 (11.1%) corporate, 18 (11.1%) freelance/independent, 12 (7.4%) government and nine (5.6%) small to mid-size business.

Among the respondents the largest percentage in age distribution was between the ages of 22 to 34. Of the respondents 59 (36.4%) were between the ages of 22 to 34, 45 (27.8%) participants were between the ages of 35 to 44, 42 (25.9%) were between the ages of 45 to 54, 15 (9.3%) were between the ages of 55 to 64 and only one participant (0 .6%) identified in the age range of 65 and over.

The average work experience of the respondents was 14 years, indicating many were very experienced PR professionals. The majority of respondents, 38 of the participants (30.3%) had one to five years in the professional field, 35 (28.5%) shared six to ten years of experience, 23 (14.2%) had 11 to 15 years of PR experience, 20 (12.5%) had 16 to 20 years of PR knowledge, 19 (11.8%) had practiced PR between 21 to 25 years, 15 (9.3%) had 26 to 30 years professional PR involvement, six (3.6%) individuals contributed with 31 to 35 years of experience and two (1.2%) respondents had 40 years of proficiency in PR (Refer to Table 2).

Exploratory Factor Analysis of Media Richness Dimensions

Past research on MRT has shown the multi-dimensionality of media richness. To better identify factors in media richness, the authors ran factor analysis with Principal Component Analysis with Varimax Rotation. The factor analysis has extracted six common factors with their eigenvalue larger than one. These factors accounted for 64.52% of the variance of the data (Table 3). The rotated factor matrix shows overall high

Table 2. Demographic data of the sample

Demographic Characteristics	N	%	Frequency
Gender	162		
Male		27.2	44
Female		72.2	117
Other		.6	1
Age	162		
21 & Under		0	0
22 to 34		36.4	59
35 to 44		27.8	45
45 to 54		25.9	42
55 to 64		9.3	15
65 & Over		.6	1
Ethnicity	162		
African American		4.3	7
Asian		3.7	6
Latino/Hispanic/Chicano		17.3	28
White		71.0	115
Other		3.7	6
Industry	162		
Agency		29.0	47
Corporation		11.1	18
Education		17.9	29
Freelance/Independent		11.1	18
Government		7.4	12
Non-Profit		17.9	29
Small to Mid-Size Business		5.6	9
Work Experience	158		
1-5		30.3	38
6-10		28.5	35
11-15		14.2	23
16-20		12.5	20
21-25		11.8	19
26-30		9.3	15
31-35		3.6	6
36-40		1.2	2

construct validity, except for *Task Urgency*, *Task Performance*, and *Task Complexity* constructs (Table 4). The factor analysis has created six factors that can be labeled as *Task Analyzability* (α=.82), *Task Urgency* (α=.74), *Social Influence* (α=.67), *Social Affinity* (α=.78), *Multiple Cues* (α=.66), and *Task Performance-Marketing Related* (α=.65) (Refer to Table 3 and Table 4).

Task Analyzability is composed of four variables, including "Sending the message through social media is done simply," "Social media allows me to send the message in a clear manner," "Social media allows me to communicate with my audience by using established procedures," and "Social media allows me to disseminate my message with ease of use." *Task Urgency* factor is composed of the following five variables: "Social media is changing how I respond to information from my audience," "The feedback received from my audience enhances the way I practice PR," "Social media allows me to provide my audience fast feedback," "Message delivery on social media can be carried out on a real-time basis," and "My audience expects to receive honest and truthful information through social media." The least preferred factor (*Task Performance-Marketing Related*) was composed of 2 variables: "Social media

Table 3. Cronbach's alpha reliability test of the MRT variables

Construct	Cronbach's Alpfa	Number of Items
Task Analyzability	.82	4
Task Urgency	.74	5
Multiple Cues	.66	2
Social Influence	.67	4
Social Affinity	.78	3
Task Performance Marketing Related	.65	2

Table 4. Factor analysis (Principal Component Analysis with Varimax Rotation)

Construct	Total Variance Accounted	Cumulative %
Task Analyzability	13.27	13.27
Task Urgency	12.81	26.08
Social Influence	11.84	37.92
Social Affinity	10.62	48.54
Multiple Cues	8.95	57.48
Task Performance and Marketing Related	7.04	64.52

delivers the message to my target audience more effectively than traditional media," and "A message sent via social media more likely to influence the behavior and attitude of my audience" (Refer to Table 5).

Social Media Usage among PR Professionals

The authors arranged the discussions in response to two research questions proposed above. The first research question asks PR professionals' preference of a social media outlet. As to the types of social media that PR professionals often use, out of the participating pool of PR professionals 137 provided their percentage of social media use during their eight hour work day. Responses varied from 1% to 100%, but the average professional used social media 15% (M = 15.41, SD = 21.38) of the work day. The large majority of respondents, 94 (58.8%), preferred to use Facebook as the leading social media communication outlet for PR. Twitter was indicated as the second preferred social media outlet among 39 (24.4%) of PR professionals followed by LinkedIn, which is used by 18 (11.3%) of PR specialists. The least used social media outlets among PR professionals included Google + (2.5%), and YouTube (1.3%). Out of the respondents who share their preference for social media outlet, three (1.9%) indicated other and listed blogs and e-mail as their preference to communicate with their target audience.

Results of the survey indicated that the respondents' use of social media was mainly for the dissemination of information through news releases. News releases were selected as the first preference by 65 (47.8%) participating PR professionals. The second most popular function by PR professionals was customer feedback (N=38, 28.8%) (Refer to Table 6).

Media Richness Dimensions as Perceived by PR Professionals

The second research question asks PR professionals about their media richness perceptions of social media. PR professionals in this survey have viewed social media to be strong in task performance- marketing related factor (M=3.40, SD=1.02). However, other rich media dimensions were not perceived favorably among PR professionals: *Task Analyzability* (M=2.30, SD=.89), *Task Urgency* (M=2.04, SD=.62), *Social Influence* (Mean=2.08, SD=.77), *Social Affinity* (M=2.05, SD=.71), and *Multiple Cues* (M=2.39, SD=.90). In addition to the descriptive statistics such as *mean* and *standard deviation*, One-Way Analysis of Variance (ANOVA) procedure was used to compare means of three or more samples through F-distribution (Howell, 2012) as clustered by different PR organizations and industries. One-Way ANOVA allows the researchers to better understand if PR professionals' organizations affect their

Table 5. Extracted factors after rotation

	Extracted Factors					
	1	2	3	4	5	6
Sending the message through social media is done simply	**.84**	-.01	.09	.02	.12	.06
Social media allows me to send the message in a clear manner	**.80**	.26	.07	.19	.08	.15
Social media allows me to communicate with my audience by using established procedures	**.73**	.12	.19	.17	.13	.00
Social media allows me to disseminate my message with ease of use	**.54**	.31	.31	.15	.04	.27
Social media is changing how Ahmed respond to information from my audience	.08	**.76**	.12	-.07	.11	.11
The feedback received from my audience enhances the way I practice PR	.06	**.71**	.09	.19	.11	.23
Social media allows me to provide my audience fast feedback	.33	**.62**	.19	.10	.26	.03
Message delivery on social media can be carried out on a real-time basis	.31	**.53**	.26	-.03	.35	-.23
My audience expects to receive honest and truthful information through social media	.17	**.52**	.13	.19	-.33	.30
Social media helps to pressure organizations to respond quickly to customer's comments and criticism	.03	**.51**	.19	.11	.08	-.44
My peers use social media as a tool to communicate	.31	.08	**.72**	.01	-.16	.05
I am actively engaged in social media	.00	.20	**.70**	.28	.22	-.00
My audience is actively engaged in social media	.00	.18	**.68**	.19	-.03	.37
Social media is a useful tool to communicate	.34	.22	**.67**	.16	.21	.03
I can communicate with my audience comfortably	.21	.09	.20	**.83**	.09	-.02
I identify with my audience	.07	.08	.19	**.81**	.06	.13
I can communicate with my audience regarding issues affecting my client	.09	.04	.04	**.76**	.14	-.06
An effective message delivery through social media requires the use of various electronic cues like sounds, written symbols, videos, and images	.07	.04	-.00	.21	**.75**	.11
Delivery of multiple messages on social media can be carried out concurrently	.40	.20	.00	-.00	**.65**	.05
Social media allows me to use various forms of cues like written visual images, audio and symbols to deliver a clearer and more understandable message	.06	.35	.31	.21	**.60**	.17
Social media delivers the message to my target audience more effectively than traditional media	.15	.26	.13	-.04	.13	**.70**
A message sent via social media more likely to influence the behavior and attitude of my audience	.21	.05	.41	.12	.28	**.59**

Extraction Method: Principal Component Analysis.
Rotation Method: Varimax with Kaiser Normalization.

perceptions of these rich media dimensions on the basis of their perceptions of rich media dimensions. As to the *task analyzability* dimensions, industry types do not affect the perception ($F = 1.86, p > .05$). As to the *task urgency* dimension, no significant statistical difference was found ($F = 1.26, p > .05$). However, statistical significant relationships were found in *social influence* ($F = 2.27, p < .05$) and *social affinity* ($F = 3.07, p < .01$) dimensions. Other two rich media dimensions pertinent to social media were

Table 6. PR functions used in social media

Characteristics	N	%	Frequency
News Release	162		
First Preference		27.2	44
Second Preference		72.2	117
Third Preference		.6	1
Fourth Preference			
Fifth Preference			
Customer Feedback	132		
First Preference		23.5	38
Second Preference		25.9	42
Third Preference		19.8	32
Fourth Preference		10.5	17
Fifth Preference		1.9	3
Finding New Trends	130		
First Preference		19.1	31
Second Preference		25.9	42
Third Preference		25.3	41
Fourth Preference		7.4	12
Fifth Preference		2.5	4
Arrange Promotion	97		
First Preference		10.5	17
Second Preference		18.6	18
Third Preference		16.5	16
Fourth Preference		39.2	38
Fifth Preference		8.2	8
Product Recall	85		
First Preference		10.5	17
Second Preference		11.1	18
Third Preference		9.9	16
Fourth Preference		23.5	38
Fifth Preference		4.9	8

not found statistically significant: *multiple cues* ($F = 2.04$, $p > .05$) and *task performance- marketing related* ($F = 1.16$, $p > .05$) (Refer to Table 7 and Table 8).

Increasingly, social media have been used by corporations and other organizations since 2009 (Eyrich et al., 2008; Wright & Hinson, 2011). Government agencies and non-profit organizations have also adopted social media in their communication campaigns. For example, Ruh and Magallon (2009) found the U.S. military studied the potential of using social media for its internal communication campaigns (cited in Wright & Hinson, 2011). While most PR practitioners are enthusiastic about the impacts of

Table 7. One-Way ANOVA

Media Richness Dimensions	df	F	p-value
Task Analyzability	6/155	1.86	.09
Task Urgency	6/155	1.26	.28
Social Influence	6/155	2.27	.04*
Social Affinity	6/155	3.07	.01**
Multiple Cues	6/155	2.04	.06
Task Performance and Marketing Related	6/155	1.16	.33

social media, journalists and other corporate communication professionals appear to take a more cautious stance (Supa, 2014; Wynne, 2014). Despite this, Wright and Hinton's (2011) three-year longitudinal study concluded that the impacts of social media and other emerging media platforms have increased in the past years. Age was found to be an important predictor of how PR professionals will use these emerging media as younger PR professionals tend to adopt them first. Similar to Wright and Hinson's (2011) finding, Facebook was found to be the most popular social media platform for PR messages in 2010 and 2011, replacing search engines in 2009. The popularity of Facebook is consistent across different PR industry sectors (Refer to Figure 1). However, Wright and Hinson's latest data (2014) have reported that Twitter is now replacing Facebook as the most frequently used medium for public relations activities.

Importantly for this study, Wright and Hinson (2011, 2014) did not preface their study with a robust theoretical context by examining what prompted PR professionals to use these emerging media. This book chapter thus proposed that an examination of the rich media dimensions of these emerging media platforms would help communication scholars understand the adoption process better.

How do PR Professionals Perceive Social Media in Terms of Media Richness Dimensions?

PR professionals among different industry sectors did not perceive the media richness dimensions of social media differently on the following three dimensions: *Task Analyzability*, *Task Urgency*, and *Multiple Cues*. Means in these three dimensions are similar to each other, regardless of what PR sectors these professionals belong to. Two distinct rich media dimensions were found to be significantly different as to how PR professionals perceive the social dimensions of social media. These two rich media dimensions are *Social Influence* and *Social Affinity* dimensions. *Social influence* is defined as the attitude and influence provided in the message dissemination by opinion leaders, in this case spokespersons such as PR professionals. By providing this feedback, this chapter discovered that PR professionals agree that social media carries social influence in the delivery of the message. Participants indicated that they agreed to being actively engaged in social media, and somewhat agreed that their target audience was actively engaged in social media. PR professionals agreed that their peers used social media as a tool for communication and also agreed that social media was a useful tool to communicate. These results show that the majority of participants' perceived social media met their requirements of social influences while communicating with their audience.

On the other hand, *social affinity* is described as a variable that moderates the relationship between the tasks. The social affinity measure is closely related to "likes" feature in many social media platforms (like

Table 8. Descriptive statistics

Rich Media Dimensions	Mean	SD
Task Analyzability		
Agency	2.51	.89
Corporation	2.53	.96
Education	2.27	.81
Freelance/Independent	2.15	.87
Government	2.15	1.24
Non-Profit	1.92	.73
Small to Mid-Size Business	2.61	.74
Task Urgency		
Agency	2.13	.64
Corporation	2.14	.58
Education	2.03	.59
Freelance/Independent	2.00	.68
Government	1.89	.65
Non-Profit	1.83	.54
Small to Mid-Size Business	2.33	.79
Social Influence		
Agency	2.07	.72
Corporation	2.44	1.04
Education	1.97	.72
Freelance/Independent	1.93	66
Government	2.52	.65
Non-Profit	1.81	.70
Small to Mid-Size Business	2.22	.76
Multiple Cues		
Agency	2.34	.81
Corporation	2.54	1.05
Education	2.43	.80
Freelance/Independent	2.20	1.23
Government	2.53	1.17
Non-Profit	2.13	.91
Small to Mid-Size Business	3.30	.84

Facebook). Past research found the importance of this variable in explaining users' behaviors (Panigrahy, Najork, & Xie, 2012). Overall, survey participants agreed that social media meets the requirements of *social affinity* in the communication process. Participants agreed that they identify with their audience, allowing them to communicate comfortably with their target audience, and also communicate with audience issues that affect the client. In this study, *social affinity* measures demonstrated the communicative

Figure 1. Usage of Media: Preferred Social Media Outlet by Industry

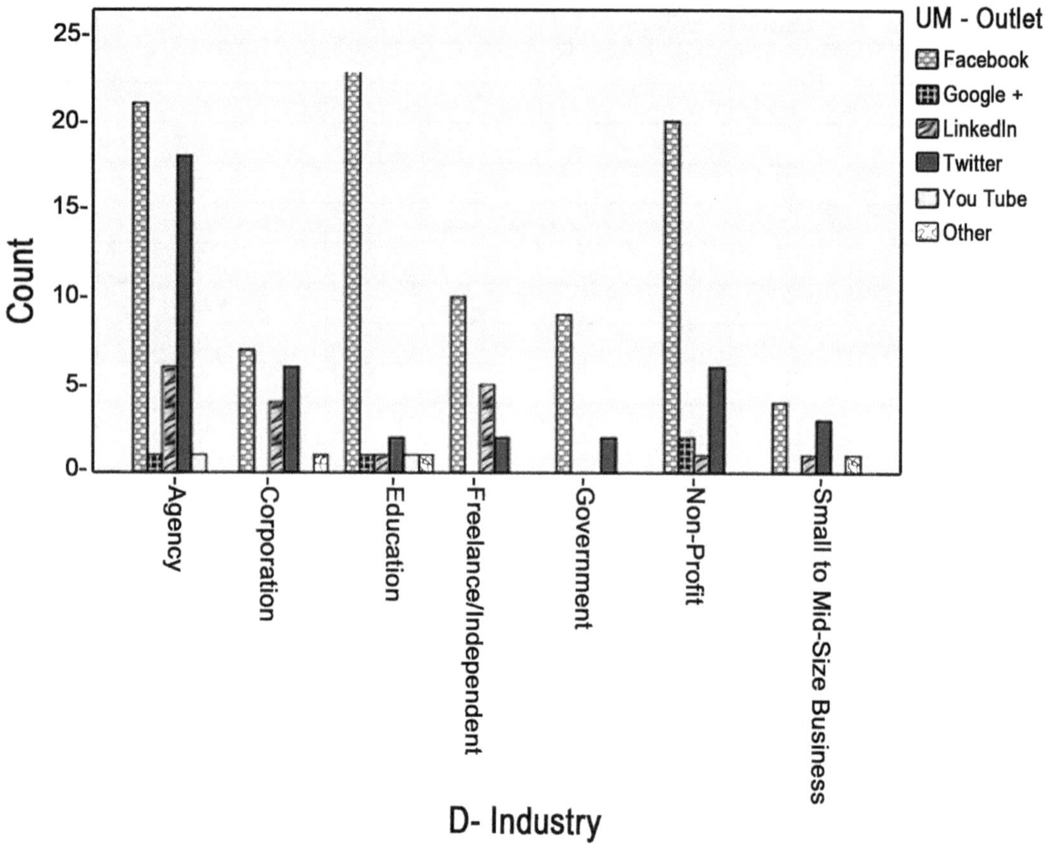

characteristics of social media to allow PR professionals to enhance social relationships with their clients and target audiences for a variety of PR functions.

These social media richness dimensions as perceived by PR professionals in the sample demonstrate the intrinsic and objective characteristics that differentiate social from traditional media. In line with what MRT researchers would argue (Ngwenyama & Lee, 1997), these media characteristics allow researchers to understand what affects PR professionals decision-making process. As anticipated, *social affinity* and *social influence*, two important dimensions that makes social media different from other traditional media, points out the social networking and relationship-building characteristics of social media. On the other hand, media dimensions that are not related to social networking and relationship, such as *Task Analyzability*, *Task Urgency*, and *Multiple Cues*, were not perceived to be different among PR professionals.

FUTURE RESEARCH DIRECTIONS

The study provides a valuable perspective to understanding and clarification of the role of social media as a tool for PR. Prior studies primarily evaluated the superficial perception of PR professionals and social media. This study utilized the media richness theory to provide a vigorous theoretical framework to better evaluate the richness of these emerging social media platforms. The investigation results indicate that social media is a rich communication outlet, and if included in the PR professional tool box, has the potential to increase and aid PR efforts substantially.

There are several limitations worth addressing for future investigations. This survey was originally designed to reveal perceptions of PR professionals regarding the media richness of social media, focusing primarily on social networking sites and avoided the use of blogs, e-mail, web pages, instant messaging and applications available to smart phones and tables. Thus, the sampling procedures in this study might tilt toward media relations, a sub-group of PR professionals. Earlier outreach to more diverse groups such as local, regional and state PR groups at an earlier stage might have produced a larger sample size and a diverse group of PR professionals with various job functions and clients. While it was important to focus on the perceptions of PR professionals through the industry angle, future investigations should also highlight the role and perceptions of ethnicity, gender and age in moderating these relationships.

Technology is constantly changing and new innovations are surfacing constantly. New communication technologies have the potential to facilitate the role of PR professionals, but it is important to evaluate the richness of the communication outlet prior to using it. Among current advancements are the mobile and portable technologies that expose new opportunities for further investigation. Mobile social media provide users with ubiquitous access to their social media accounts at any location. It might be rewarding to research the use of applications of mobile apps for PR purposes, or the PR efforts in reaching their mobile and partible audience. Furthermore, as marketing and PR professionals increasingly emphasize the importance of consumer engagement (Brodie, Illic, Juric, & Hollebeek, 2011), Another recommendation based on the comments expressed by participants are the reasons why companies are hesitant to embrace new technology communications, as well as the challenges and opportunities that these might present to the field of PR.

CONCLUSION

This study confirmed the media richness dimensions as reported in Koo et al. (2011). Traditional MRT employs the following four dimensions to characterize rich media: (1) instant feedback, (2) use of multiple cues such as body language and tone of voice, (3) use of natural language and (4) personal focus on the medium (Trevino et al., 1990). This study identified more media richness dimensions, adding to current MRT categorization. These newly found media richness dimensions are more relevant to the emerging social media dimensions by focusing on their social networking and relationship-building characteristics. With the development of mobile social media applications, other new media richness dimensions (such as ubiquity or pervasiveness) could be found in the future. Despite new media richness dimensions may emerge to better characterize emerging media platforms, some dimensions show their resilience and consistency across multiple platforms and media. For example, multiple cues and instant feedback continue to be distinctive rich media dimensions. Additionally, task analyzability, social influence, social affinity, and task performance are also found to relate social media to PR professionals' use in various contexts.

Furthermore, Sheer and Chen (2004) argued that, on the basis of MRT, media are chosen to fulfill an organization's needs to reduce message equivocality by making the most of media richness dimensions. The study of PR professionals' perceptions of social media suggests that these are likely to influence their choice of social media in conducting various PR functions.

REFERENCES

Aasheim, H., & Stensønes, I. (2011). *Financial institutions in social media; Deliver traditional services in new channels*. Unpublished Master's thesis. Copenhagen Business School. CBS. Retrieved April 1, 2014 from http://hdl.handle.net/10417/2961 25

Ahmed, A. (2012). *Hypothesizing the aptness of social media and the information richness requirements of disaster management*. Proceedings of ECIS 2012. Retrieved from http://aisel.aisnet.org/ecis2012/157

Anandarajan, M., Zaman, M., Dai, Q., & Arinze, B. (2010). Generation Y adoption of instant messaging: An examination of the impact of social usefulness and media richness of use richness. *IEEE Transactions on Professional Communication*, *53*(2), 132–143. doi:10.1109/TPC.2010.2046082

Berkowitz, E. N. (2007). The evolution of public relations and the use of the internet: The implications for health care organizations. *Health Marketing Quarterly*, *24*(3-4), 117–130. doi:10.1080/07359680802125154 PMID:19042531

BRASS Programing Planning Committee. (2011). The business of social media: How to plunder the treasure trove. *Reference and User Services Quarterly*, *51*(2), 127–132. doi:10.5860/rusq.51n2.127

Brodie, R. J., Juric, B., Ilic, A., & Hollebeek, L. D. (2011, January). Consumer engagement in a virtual brand community: An exploratory analysis. *Journal of Business Research*, *66*(1), 105–114. doi:10.1016/j.jbusres.2011.07.029

Daft, R. L., & Lengel, R. H. (1984). Information richness: A new approach to manager information processing and organization design. In B. Staw & L. L. Cummings (Eds.), *Research in Organizational Behavior. Greenwhich, C.T.* JAJ Press.

Daft, R. L., & Lengel, R. H. (1986). Organizational information requirements, media richness and structural design. *Management Science*, *32*(5), 554–571. doi:10.1287/mnsc.32.5.554

Darnowski, C., & Wright, D. (2010). Tomorrow's professional: employer demand for public relations knowledge, skills and abilities. *Presented at Public Relations Society of America Leadership Assembly*. Retrieved from http://www.prsa.org/AboutPRSA/Documents/2010prsaemployerstudy.pdf

Elliott, S. (2011, November 20). Redefining public relations in the age of social media. *New York Times,* Retrieved from http://www.nytimes.com/2011/2011/2021/business/media/redefining-public-relations-in-the-age-of-social-media.html

Eyrich, N., Padman, M., & Sweetser, K. (2008). PR practitioner's use of social media tools and communication technology. *Public Relations Review*, *34*(4), 412–414. doi:10.1016/j.pubrev.2008.09.010

Howell, D. C. (2012). *Statistical methods for psychology* (8th ed.). Independence, KY: Cengage Learning, Inc.

Iodhia, S. (2012). Web based social and environmental communication in the Australian minerals industry: An application of media richness framework. *Journal of Cleaner Production*, *25*, 73–85. doi:10.1016/j.jclepro.2011.11.040

Johnson, R. D., & Keil, M. (2002). Media richness theory: Testing e-mail vs. v-mail for conveying student feedback. *Journal of Informatics Education*, *4*(2), 15–24.

Kent, M. L. (2010). Directions in social media for professionals and scholars. In R. Heath (Ed.), *Handbook of Public Relations* (2nd ed.). Thousand Oaks, CA: Sage.

Koo, C., Wati, Y., & Jung, J. J. (2011). Examination of how social aspect moderates the relationship between task characteristics and usage of social communication technologies in organizations. *International Journal of Information Management*, *31*(5), 445–459. doi:10.1016/j.ijinfomgt.2011.01.003

Kupritz, V. W., & Cowel, E. (2011). Productive management communication: Online and face-to-face. *Journal of Business Communication*, *48*(1), 54–82. doi:10.1177/0021943610385656

Lica, L., & Tuta, M. (2011). Predicting product performance with social media. *Informatica Economica*, *15*(2), 46–56.

Macario, E., Ednacot, E., Ullberg, L., & Reichel, J. (2011). The changing face and rapid pace of public health communication. *Journal of Community Health*, *4*(2), 145–150. doi:10.1179/17538061 1X13022552566254

Margalit, L. (2014, August 29). The psychology behind social media interactions. *Psychology Today*. Retrieved from https://www.psychologytoday.com/blog/behind-online-behavior/201408/the-psychology-behind-social-media-interactions

Michaelson, D., & Stacks, D. W. (2011, Spring). Standardization in public relations measurement and evaluation. *The Public Relations Journal*, *5*(2), 1–22.

Ngwenyama, O. K., & Lee, A. S. (1997, June). Communication richness in electronic mail: Critical social theory and the contextuality of meaning. *Management Information Systems Quarterly*, *21*(2), 145–167. doi:10.2307/249417

Panigrahy, R., Najork, M., & Xie, Y.-L. (2012, February 8-12). How user behavior is related to social affinity. *Proceedings of the Fifth ACM International Conference on Web Search and Data Mining WSDM '12,* Seattle, Washington (pp. 713-722).

Parcell, L. M., Lame, M. O., & Cooley, S. C. (2011). Learning from the trades: Public relations, journalism and news release writing, 1945-2000. *American Journalism*, *28*(2), 81–111.

PRSA.org. (2012). What is Public Relations? PRSA's widely accepted definition. Retrieved from http://www.prsa.org/AboutPRSA/PublicRelationsDefined/#.U8wtf-NdXvE

Shahkat, M. S. A. (2011). The use of Facebook to increase climate change awareness among employees. Proceedings of the International Conference on Social Science and Humanity (Vol. 5, pp. 266–270). Retrieved from http://www.ipedr.com/vol5/no2/59-H10164.pdf

Sheer, V. C., & Chen, L. (2004). Improving media richness theory: A study of interaction goals, message valence and task complexity in manager-subordinate communication. *Management Communication Quarterly*, *18*(1), 76–93. doi:10.1177/0893318904265803

Supa, D. W. (2014). A qualitative examination of the impact of social media on media relations practice. *The Public Relations Journal*, *8*(2). Retrieved from http://www.prsa.org/Intelligence/PRJournal/Vol8/No2/

Taylor, M., & Kent, M. L. (2010). Anticipatory socialization in the use of social media in public relations: A content analysis of PRSA's public relations tactics. *Public Relations Review*, *36*(3), 207–214. doi:10.1016/j.pubrev.2010.04.012

Trevino, L., Lengel, R., Bodensteiner, W., Gerloff, E., & Muir, N. K. (1990). The richness imperative and cognitive style: The role of individual differences in media choice behavior. *Management Communication Quarterly*, *4*(2), 176–197. doi:10.1177/0893318990004002003

Turner, J. W., Grube, J. A., Tinsley, C. H., Lee, C., & O'Pell, C. (2006). Exploring the dominant media: How does media use reflect organizational norms and affect performance? *Journal of Business Communication*, *43*(3), 220–250. doi:10.1177/0021943606288772

Vorvoreanu, M. (2008). Society for new communication research study: ROI of online press releases. *Journal of New Communication Research*, *3*(1), 92–98.

Wang, S., & Hung, J. H. (2011). Voice of America in the post-Cold War era: Opportunities and challenges to external media services via new information and communication technology. *International Communication Gazette*, *73*(4), 343–358. doi:10.1177/1748048511398599

Wrench, J., Thomas-Madox, C., Peck Richmond, V., & McCroskey, J. (2008). *Quantitative research methods for communication: A hands on approach*. New York, NY: Oxford University Press.

Wright, D., & Hinson, M. D. (2009). An updated look at the impact of social media on public relations practice. *The Public Relations Journal*, *3*(2), 2–23.

Wright, D. K., & Hinson, M. D. (2010, Summer). How new communication media are being used in public relations: A longitudinal analysis. *The Public Relations Journal*, *4*(3). Retrieved from http://www.prsa.org/Intelligence/PRJournal/Documents/2010tWrightHinson.pdf

Wright, D. K., & Hinson, M. D. (2014). An updated examination of social and emerging media use in public relations practice: A longitudinal analysis between 2006 and 2014. *The Public Relations Journal*, *8*(2), 1–35.

Wynne, R. (2014, April 28). Winning social media stratégies for public relations. *Forbes*. Retrieved from http://www.forbes.com/sites/robertwynne/2014/04/28/winning-social-media-strategies-for-public-relations/

KEY TERMS AND DEFINITIONS

Equivocality: According to MRT, equivocality refers to confusion, wrongful interpretation, and lack of understanding (Daft & Macintosh, 1981).

Media Richness Theory: Media Richness Theory (MRT) assumes that organizations are social systems that must process information, but have obstacles in uncertainty and equivocality (Daft & Lengel, 1986). Both equivocality and uncertainty are viewed as the reasons behind the lack of effectiveness in an organization caused by faulty communication. Based on MRT, the richness of a medium is grounded on the availability for: (1) instant feedback, (2) use of multiple cues such as body language and tone of voice, (3) use of natural language and (4) personal focus on the medium. Looking for instant feedback, use of multiple cues, natural language and personal focus allows for a medium's ability to transmit a rich message (Trevino, et al., 1990).

Public Relations: According to the Public Relations Society of America (PRSA), public relations refers to the strategic communication functions to "help an organization and its public adapt mutually to each other" (PRSA.org, 2011).

Social Media: According to Andreas Kaplan and Michael Haenlein (2010), social media are defined as "a group of Internet-based applications that build on the ideological and technological foundations of Web 2.0, and that allow the creation and exchange of user-generated content." Social media include collaborative projects (such as Wikipedia), microblogs and blogs, contents (such as YouTube), social networking services (such as Facebook), virtual games, and virtual social life (such as Second Life).

Rich Media: Rich media are personal and can provide immediate feedback from both the speakers, allowing the instant verification of the information shared. Rich media are viewed to have a greater language variety and can convey natural language rather than just numerical information.

Social Influence: The concept is defined as the attitude and influence provided in the message dissemination by opinion leaders, in this case spokes people such as PR professionals.

Social Affinity: The concept moderates the relationship between the task characteristics.

Task Analyzability: The concept refers to the measurement of how clear and understandable the communication guidelines are studied.

Task Complexity: The concept means the use of multiple cues to help send a clear message with the least amount of confusion.

Task Urgency: The concept is defined as the measurement of how well a medium can provide rapid response and reaction in the communication process.

Task Performance: The term refers to the relation between which communication channel usage matches task characteristics.

Uncertainty: According to MRT, uncertainty is defined as the lack of information within an organization.

Chapter 2
Managing Negative Publicity on Social Media:
Getting Back on Track

Himadri Barman
Dibrugarh University, India

ABSTRACT

The Chapter talks about the importance of social media from the view of publicity for an organization. It talks about a few real life situations where organizations have suffered as a result of negative publicity on the social media. That negative publicity can be a disaster for the organization is emphasized. The chapter lists out the causes of negative publicity for an organization in the social media and how it can be tackled as is found in existing literature on negative publicity in the social media. The chapter ends with a series of guidelines to get back on track in the face of negative publicity in the social media.

On January 25, 2013, a pastor who had eaten at an Applebee's restaurant crossed out the automatic 18% tip charged for parties of more than eight and wrote "I give God 10% why do you get 18" above her signature. A waitress at the restaurant took a photo of this and posted it on Reddit. She was subsequently fired for "violating customer privacy" which would have been understandable if Applebee's had not posted a similar receipt that was complimenting them just 2 weeks prior. As news of this incident spread like wildfire and infuriated people across all social media platforms, Applebee's responded with a short post defending their actions on their Facebook page. This quickly drew over 10,000 mostly negative comments, to which Applebee's started responding by posting the same comment over and over again. They were also accused of deleting negative comments and blocking users. The downward spiral continued as Applebee's persisted to defend their actions and argue with users that criticized them. By the following day, after the original post had generated over 19,000 comments, Applebee's decided to hide the post which only created more anger (Thompson, 2015).

In January 2012, McDonald's tried to promote its brand and engage with customers through two promoted trends: #meetthefarmers and #mcdstories. Unfortunately for McDonald's, many Twitter users decided to post their horror stories at the fast food chain using the second one of those hashtags. In short,

DOI: 10.4018/978-1-5225-0332-3.ch002

McDonald's paid to promote a trend that showered the company with negative publicity. McDonald's later admitted that "#mcdstories did not go as planned (Fiegerman, 2012).

When Gap (the garment company) unveiled a new logo in October 2010, the reaction was swift, intense and very, very negative. In fact, somebody set up a Twitter account (@GapLogo) that purported to speak in the unpopular design's voice, and someone else built a site called CrapLogo.me that made it easy to convert any short text into an imitation of the brand's new style. The company tried to pivot off the negative buzz by asking the online hate mob for advice, in a sort of "crowd sourcing" gimmick, but that didn't go over well, either. In just four days, the company capitulated and announced that it would not change its logo after all (Carla, 2011).

UNDERSTANDING NEGATIVE PUBLICITY ON THE SOCIAL MEDIA

The above three are typical instances of negative press on the social media because of a public relations disaster, social media publicity going horribly wrong or negative publicity on social media out of nowhere. ESOMAR (2010) defines Social Media as "Internet based platforms and technologies that permit users' interaction and/or facilitate the creation and exchange of user generated content. Whilst the scope is evolving, currently the most frequently used examples include: Online forums/discussions, communities, blogs, social networks (e.g. Facebook), Video/photo sharing (e.g. YouTube), Multi-person/group communication and/or collaboration platforms (e.g. Twitter), etc." Thus social media includes social networking sites, blogs, micro-blogs, consumer review sites, content community sites, wikis, internet forums, podcasts, etc. A more concise definition is given by *Wikipedia* which defines Social Media as "computer-mediated tools that allow people to create, share or exchange information, ideas, and pictures/videos in virtual communities and networks."

Social media is the new battleground for marketers. Every brand or business house worth its name is present in multiple social media platforms trying to engage the existing and would be customers in a meaningfully way. A study on Fortune 500 companies, conducted by university of Massachusetts Dartmouth Center for Marketing Research, reveals that in 2014, 413 companies (83%) of the Fortune 500 have corporate Twitter accounts with a tweet in the past thirty days while 401 companies (80%) of the Fortune 500 were on Facebook. As per Facebook's 2014 Quarter 4 results, it had 890 million Daily Active Users (DAUs) and 1393 million Monthly Active Users (MAUs). These are phenomenal numbers. Social media is an excellent way to build relationships with customers and build word-of-mouth publicity. This is because social media provides the platform to engage in free or very cost effective public relations and promotional exercises. Social media tools allow publicists to interlock all the activities into a cohesive campaign (Burke, 2010). It is an amazing tool of free publicity that allows direct communication with the target audience without anything in between. From the customer's perspective, social media is playing an increasingly important role as an information source. The role of social media in decision-making is an important one with the consumer sharing thoughts, concerns, and problems on a public forum for all to see, and feeling rewarded for it (Pollitt, 2014). The social media networks on their part also offer numerous benefits to the marketers to tap into their user base. Organizations have also gradually increased awareness regarding the importance of monitoring what their target audience says about them in the online environment (Mindruta, 2013).

To use social media for publicity, organizations need to ("IEEE – Using", 2011):

- Identify the right social-media platform for our audience.
- Plan their content and frequency of updates.
- Build the page, create messages, or develop a following.
- Monitor the site for new followers and comments.

Considerable effort is made and resources are used to develop a publicity plan for the social media. Earning and maintaining a good reputation is challenging for new as well as established businesses. Though the advantages are many as far as using social media for publicity is concerned, there are pitfalls too. According to Nielsen's Global Trust in Advertising report published online in October 2012, there has been increasing confidence in online reviews and on an average, 70% of customers' view online reviews as a trusted source of brand information. Another study by Michael Luca of Harvard Business School in 2014 also points out that a one-star difference in Yelp rating (yelp.com is used by people to search for everything from the city's tastiest burger to the most renowned cardiologist) can affect an organization's revenue by 5 – 9%. While good publicity through likes and positive comments need not convert into more sells or better brand acceptance; negative publicity is more likely to do the reverse. It is also to be accepted that in spite of careful handling of the social media for public relations exercises, negative publicity is bound to happen. Negative publicity is a reality that many businesses face, and one that can have devastating consequences if not handled correctly.

Negative publicity is the adverse publicity that an organization may incur due to a particular reason, which may lead to potentially disastrous consequences. It has to be noted that not all-negative publicity need be counter-productive. In some cases, negative publicity can increase sales when a product or company is relatively unknown, simply because it stimulates product awareness. Whereas a negative review in the New York Times hurt sales of books by well-known authors, for example, it increased sales of books that had lower prior awareness (Berger, Sorensen & Scott, 2010). This chapter of course avoids the potential benefits of negative publicity.

THREADS OF NEGATIVE PUBLICITY ON THE SOCIAL MEDIA

When negative publicity emerges on the social media, businesses could be portrayed as irresponsible, dishonest or appear to be only looking out for their best interests. Although it is possible to make a good name for the business on a local or national scale or for that matter a global scale through social media, doing so can be an uphill task, especially in the face of negative publicity. In social media, negative messages have the ability to spread like wildfire. Negative publicity on the social media can lead to sudden loss of reputation for the organization and trust in it, affect sales of the organization and damage brand equity as well as brand association (Beauchamp, n.d.). Regaining trust is very difficult and time consuming. The veil of anonymity social media can provide also means that so-called 'keyboard warriors' – unknown people posting negative views about a corporation online – can attack firms with the freedom of a person who is unlikely to suffer any consequences from their public acrimony. In the backdrop of this, negative publicity is unwarranted or is to be avoided. Social media expands the spectrum of reputation risks and boosts risk dynamics, and it can have notable effects on corporate-level strategic endeavors, which must be considered in order to be successful in the modern business environment (Aula, 2010).

Public relations practitioners need to be attentive to the following threads of negative publicity. The first four have been obtained from ("Negative Publicity," 2007) while the rest have been formulated from the literature review.

- Disillusioned (ex) employee(s) spreading negative vibes about the organization.
- Angry customer(s) dissatisfied with products/services of the organization.
- Misleading interpretations of blogs/forum posts/interview excerpts about the organization.
- Mischief mongers spreading unsubstantiated rumours about the organization.
- Faulty public relations.
- Unethical activities of the organization.
- Wrong policies of the organization
- Crisis within the organization
- Simply because the organization is relatively unknown.

Public relations practitioners need to be suitably equipped to handle negative publicity on the social media. The sources of negative publicity are the starting point in tackling it. This means that each source must be properly screened and understood. The understanding will be better if the screening is done as completely and carefully as possible.

TACKLING NEGATIVE PUBLICITY ON THE SOCIAL MEDIA

Organizations are typically in a catch-22 situation when tackling negative publicity on the social media. Most organizations never set out with malicious intent, but even the smallest of mistakes can be pounced on by the public or a competitor and spread like wildfire. Whether it is an unsafe product or an environmental calamity, the speed and authority with which organizations tackle such public relations mishaps can determine the future of the organization. As Warren Buffet (2013) famously puts it, "It takes 20 years to build a reputation and five minutes to ruin it. If you think about that, you'll do things differently."

("7-Step Action", 2012) talks about 7 A's to deal with negative publicity by customers on the social media. These are:

- **Assess:** The first step in dealing with negative publicity is to monitor and find out what is being said in the first place.
- **Accept:** Before responding to the negative publicity in any way, the organization should accept the complaint as it is and acknowledge the customer. The organization does not have to accept that it was their mistake. Just the act of acknowledging the customer will calm the customer down to some extent.
- **Ask:** It is also important to get all the facts about the situation before taking any action. The more information the organization has, the better prepared they will be to respond. This also assures other customers that their feedback is taken seriously and the organization is willing to do whatever it takes to satisfy them.
- **Apologize:** "I am sorry" – these are powerful words that can pacify any angry customer. As mentioned earlier, the organization is not acknowledging that it was their mistake with these words. They are merely sympathizing with the customer's situation. If it is truly their mistake, the organization should accept the responsibility and promise to make it better.
- **Act:** After having the facts about the situation and having apologized to the customer, the organization should take appropriate action depending on the situation. It could be in the form of product return, a refund or a coupon for the next purchase. Before doing anything, however, it is again

important to ask the customer what would make him happy and do it. This is not the time to be penny wise and pound-foolish.

- **Affirm:** Sometimes it may be necessary to bring customer's attention to the organization's business policies. The customer may not be aware of them and may have expected something different from what the organization offers. But affirming to the customer will let everyone know that it was not the organization's mistake.
- **Abandon:** After these six steps most customers will be pacified, even thanking the organization for taking care of the situation so promptly and graciously. Some customers, however, will simply not go away. Obviously, they have different intentions. In those cases, it is better to just let go of him and move on. This one fight is not worth fighting.

Thomas, Peters, Howell, and Robbins (2012) have talked about strategies for handling unexpected comments (negative publicity) in the social media. The strategies have been broadly categorized as offensive or defensive initiatives. Offensive strategies, such as partnering (and to a limited extent responding and ignoring/delaying), are more pro-active attempts to constructively engage the consumer in the marketing communication process. Partnering epitomizes an offensive strategy as it engages the consumer in the process and turns over control of the brand to the consumer. In contrast, there are defensive strategies like legal action and censorship in which the marketer is attempting to take control over the message and defend the brand. Defensive strategies may appear as more antagonistic towards consumers. Ignoring or responding strategies have the potential to be perceived as either offensive or defensive in nature, depending on how the message is crafted by the company as well as how the message is received by communities of consumers in the marketplace. The strategies adopted for handling unexpected comments and dealing with negative social media need to incorporate a mixture of both offensive and defensive strategies looking at the situation and context.

CRISIS COMMUNICATION, SCCT AND MANAGING NEGATIVE PUBLICITY ON THE SOCIAL MEDIA

This chapter has looked at the impact of negative publicity in social media on an organization. It has been clearly established that negative publicity of an organization in the social media can have long-term ramifications. Thus, it is imperative to have clear policies and guidelines to manage negative publicity on social media. It is akin to having a disaster mitigation plan because negative publicity on social media may be nothing short of a disaster. Information on the social media travels very fast. Negative publicity will travel faster because of the very nature of the negative content and as such damage control exercises have to be put into place on a war-footing. As social media plays a major role in the diffusion of bad news and crisis communication, companies have started to leverage social media in responding to corporate crises (Park, Cha, Kim, & Jeong, 2012). Otherwise, the organization at the receiving end of negative publicity may be down and out finding it hard to stand again. Organizations need crisis managers to deal with negative publicity and they benefit from understanding how crisis communication can be used to protect reputational assets during a crisis. Public relations play a critical role in crisis management. It provides information, defines an event, places crisis in a context and conveys an organization's position to various publics (Cooley & Cooley, 2011). Much of the crisis communication literature is based on the recommendations of those who have had many years of experience as journalists or public relations professionals. The "evidence" used to prove their points are typically drawn from anecdotes and case studies carefully culled and interpreted to shore up their assumptions (Robertson, 2012). In the real world, crises may happen simultaneously to multiple competing organizations. In such cases, public relations practitioners should watch for other organizations' crisis stances and strategies because others' responses significantly contribute to building public perception of crisis responsibility (Ham, Hong, & Cameron, 2012).

Situational Crisis Communication Theory (SCCT) can be used to create a mechanism for anticipating how stakeholders will react to a crisis in terms of the reputational threat posed by a crisis. SCCT argues that information about past crises is a significant factor that can affect perceptions of a more recent crisis. The theory suggests that to protect an organization's reputation adequately, management must adjust their communication to account for possible past crises about which relevant publics are aware. SCCT focuses on the use of communication to preserve and protect an organization's valuable reputation (Coombs, 2004). SCCT talks about 10 categories of basic organizational crisis communication strategies. Further, these strategies are grouped into four postures (Cheng, 2011):

- **Denial Posture:** Including attack the accuser (confronting person claiming a crisis occurred), denial (asserting no crisis), and scapegoat (shifting the blame to others outside the organization), with an attempt to eliminate the crisis by denying its existence or the organization's responsibility for the crisis;
- **Diminishment Posture:** Which takes the forms of excuse (denying intend to do harm or claiming inability to control) and justification (minimizing severity of damage) with the purpose of weakening the link between the crisis and the organization by claiming the crisis is not the organization's fault;
- **Rebuilding Posture:** Of compensation (providing money or other gifts to the victims) and apology (taking full responsibility), which strives to restore legitimacy by seeking public approval and forgiveness; and
- **Bolstering Posture:** Which includes reminder (telling stakeholders about its past good works), ingratiation (praising stakeholders and/or reminds them of past good works) and victimage (reminding stakeholders that the organization is a victim of the crisis, too).

SCCT with its focus on situations is well geared up to face ticklish situations which negative publicity on the situation can bring about with balanced responses looking at the gravity of a situation.

CONCLUSION

The objective of this chapter was to manage negative publicity on the social media so as quickly get back on track of running the business. With that objective, four guidelines have been formulated for an organization to get back on track in the event of negative publicity on the social media. These guidelines have been formulated based on the contents of ("5 steps", 2012), (Berman, 2015), and (Christopher, n.d.) in addition to the content on dealing with negative publicity on the social media mentioned till now in this chapter.

Guideline 1: Organizations should not quickly react to negative publicity. There is no point trying to out-insult or arguing with the other party in a knee-jerk reaction. It is better to take some time to gather the facts. If the fault lies with the organization, it is important to be honest and accept the fault. It does no harm to the organization's reputation that way. Some clarifications need to be given to let the public know as to why the fault happened and what is being done to prevent such things in the future. On the other hand, if the negative publicity was a handiwork of some rivals as a business ploy or some rumormongers, it has to be countered with all facts put in the public domain and legal measures initiated against the business rivals/rumormongers. Social media channels are great platforms on which to present the organization's side of the story with facts and figures. It should be used to dispel misconceptions. Due to the large audiences they attract, official statements may be posted on them and feedback solicited from the public. Effective communication and engagement is the key. The engagement has to be strategic. Whatever action is taken, it should put the organization in a better position for success and recovery.

Guideline 2: Organizations need to have standard operating procedures (SOPs) for handling negative publicity, considering everything from an exposé on the national news to a nasty online review. Food and Agriculture Organization (FAO) of the United Nations states that, "A Standard Operating Procedure is a document whose purpose is to carry out the operations correctly and always in the same manner. A SOP should be available at the place where the work is done". Responsibilities should be fixed, for example, it is necessary that the organization make someone responsible to liaison with the social media and pubic, if required, and how that person will get the guidance on what to say on social media. When an organization finds itself needing to respond, everyone should know his or her roles beforehand. A negative publicity can spread through social circles quickly. But, what about the one that becomes positive? That travels well too. To translate a negative publicity into positive needs some serious planned work.

Guideline 3: Organizations need to cultivate a positive image in the social media through the organization's customers, employees and other stakeholders. Being known for the right reasons is the key so that negative publicity in the social media will not easily effect the organization.

Guideline 4: Guideline 1 said that organizations should not be reactive when it comes to dealing with negative publicity. But they should be proactive. There have been numerous instances where organizations have neglected the negative publicity they were receiving via social media sites and, consequently, individual posts got astounding numbers of shares, creating negative buzz and harming the company's reputation further. It is a given fact that organizations cannot control what is being said about them in the online environment and it is simply impossible to please everybody. But, by being proactive, the damage can be kept at the bare minimum and even be converted into something positive.

These guidelines serve as a course of action for organizations – big or small in dealing with negative publicity on the social media. It is to be remembered that social media is a necessary evil. Organizations have to live with it. The better it is managed; the better will be the returns. The cost of ignoring negative publicity on the social media may be huge. Negative publicity on the social media must be given the importance it deserves.

REFERENCES

Aula, P. (2010). Social media, reputation risk and ambient publicity management. *Strategy and Leadership*, *38*(6), 43–49. doi:10.1108/10878571011088069

Beauchamp, M. (n. d.). *The Disadvantages of Bad Publicity*. Retrieved from http://yourbusiness.azcentral.com/disadvantages-bad-publicity-3495.html

Berger, J., Sorensen, A. T., & Scott, J. R. (2010). Positive Effects of Negative Publicity: When Negative Reviews Increase Sales. *Marketing Science*, *29*(5), 815–827. doi:10.1287/mksc.1090.0557

Berman, C. (2015). *How Should Firms Respond to Negative Publicity?* Retrieved from http://smallbusiness.chron.com/should-firms-respond-negative-publicity-69199.html

Warren Buffett: his best quotes. (2013). *The Telegraph*. Retrieved from http://www.telegraph.co.uk/finance/newsbysector/banksandfinance/8381363/Warren-Buffett-his-best-quotes.html

Burke, F. (2010). Publicity and Social Media: A Match Made in Heaven. *Huffington Post*. Retrieved from http://www.huffingtonpost.com/fauzia-burke/publicity-and-social-medi_b_547672.html?ir=India

Carla, B. (2011). *Does Negative Publicity Help or Hurt your Business?* Retrieved from https://eotm.wordpress.com/category/publicity/

Cheng, S. S. (2011). A Corporate Hero with Scandal: Lessons Learned from Martha Stewart's Insider Trading Crisis. *International Journal of Humanities and Social Science*, *1*(15), 12–24.

Christopher, J. (n. d.). The 9 Golden Rules for Dealing With Bad Publicity. *Technori.com*. Retrieved from http://technori.com/2013/07/4516-the-9-golden-rules-for-dealing-with-bad-publicity/

Cooley, S. C., & Cooley, A. B. (2011). An examination of the situational crisis communication theory through the general motors bankruptcy. *Journal of Media and Communication Studies*, *3*(6), 203–211.

Coombs, W. T. (2004). Impact of Past Crises on Current Crisis Communication: Insights from Situational Crisis Communication Theory. *Journal of Business Communication*, *41*(3), 265–289. doi:10.1177/0021943604265607

Fiegerman, S. (2012). 11 Biggest Social Media *Disasters*. Mashable.com. Retrieved from http://mashable.com/2012/11/25/social-media-business-disasters-2012/

Ham, C. D., Hong, H., & Cameron, G. T. (2012). Same Crisis, Different Responses: Case Studies of How Multiple Competing Corporations Responded to the Same Explosion-Related Crises. *International Journal of Business and Social Science*, *3*(20), 19–31.

Mindruta, R. (2013). 5 Reasons Why Monitoring is Essential for PR. *BrandWatch*. Retrieved from http://www.brandwatch.com/2013/07/5-reasons-why-social-media-monitoring-is-essential-from-a-pr-perspective/

Negative Publicity Management. (2007). Vinove. Retrieved from http://www.vinove.com/mindscape/internet-marketing/negative-publicity-management/

Park, J., Cha, M., Kim, H., & Jeong, J. (2012). Managing Bad News in Social Media: A Case Study on Domino's Pizza Crisis. In J. G. Breslin, N. B. Ellison, J. G. Shanahan, & Z. Tufekci (Eds.), *ICWSM: The AAAI Press.*

Pollitt, C. (2014). The Role of Social Media in Consumer Decision Making. *LinkedIn.* Retrieved from https://www.linkedin.com/pulse/20140331210413-36910198-the-role-of-social-media-in-consumer-decision-making

Robertson, J. (2012). Tell It All?: Challenging Crisis Communications' Rules. *The Public Relations Journal*, *6*(1), 1–19.

7 . Step Action Plan to Deal with Negative Publicity on Social Media. (2012). *SmallBizViewpoints.* Retrieved from http://www.smallbizviewpoints.com/2012/03/06/7-step-action-plan-to-deal-with-negative-publicity-on-social-media/

5 . steps to handling bad publicity. (2012). *TEC.com.* Retrieved from https://www.tec.com.au/resources/article-library/strategy/5-steps-to-handling-bad-publicity/

Thomas, J. B., Peters, C. O., Howell, E. G., & Robbins, K. (2012). Social Media and Negative Word of Mouth: Strategies for Handing Unexpecting Comments. *Atlantic Marketing Journal*, *1*(2), 87–108.

Thompson, H. (2015). 6 Examples of Social Media Crises: What can we learn? *OurSocialTimes.com.* Retrieved from http://oursocialtimes.com/6-examples-of-social-media-crises-what-can-we-learn/

Using Publicity and Social Media. (2011). IEEE. Retrieved from http://www.ieee.org/conferences_events/conferences/organizers/conference_publicity_social_media.html

World Association of Opinion and Marketing Research Professionals. (2011). *ESOMAR Guideline on Social Media Research.* Amsterdam, Netherlands: ESOMAR.

KEY TERMS AND DEFINITIONS

Applebee's: The Applebee's International, Inc., is an American company which develops, franchises, and operates the Applebee's Neighborhood Grill and Bar restaurant chain.

Crisis Communication: Crisis communication is a part of public relations exercise that is carried out to protect and/or defend an individual, company, or organization facing a public challenge to its reputation.

Defensive Strategies: Attempts by a marketer to take control over a crisis and defend the brand.

Gap: The Gap, Inc., commonly known as Gap Inc. or Gap, is an American multinational clothing and accessories retailer. It was founded in 1969 by Donald Fisher and Doris F. Fisher and is headquartered in San Francisco, California.

McDonalds: The McDonald's Corporation is the world's largest chain of hamburger fast food restaurants.

Offensive Strategies: Pro-active attempts to constructively engage the consumer in the marketing communication process so as to negate a potential crisis.

Public Relations: It is concerned with managing the information flow between an individual or an organization and the public.

Reddit: It is an entertainment, social networking, and news website where registered community members can submit content, such as text posts or direct links, making it essentially an online bulletin board system.

Situational Crisis Communication Theory (SCCT): A theory in the field of crisis communication, which suggests that crisis managers should match strategic crisis responses to the level of crisis responsibility and reputational threat posed by a crisis.

Standard Operating Procedure (SOP): A document whose purpose is to carry out the operations correctly and always in the same manner.

Chapter 3
Managing Corporate Reputation through Social Media

Asha Kaul
Indian Institute of Management, India

Avani Desai
GLS University, India

ABSTRACT

The primary objective of this chapter is to highlight how social media can be used to strengthen stakeholders' relationships and build social capital for the organization, thereby enabling the organization to build, manage and sustain CR. The chapter begins with a brief overview of existing thought, approaches and terminology related to CR and proceeds to identify the interactions of each stakeholder with the organization through social media. The tenability of various forms of social media as viral videos, blogs, forums and micro blogging websites in furthering CR and the extent of their effectiveness are examined using cases derived from secondary data. Further, the chapter discusses methods of measuring the success of an organization's social media initiatives using different techniques and strategies for restoring reputation post a crisis by using social media. Finally, the chapter demonstrates a systematic process of strategizing and planning CR using social media and creating organizational infrastructure to achieve this end.

INTRODUCTION

The emergence of social media has changed the manner of information exchange. Data reveals that the number of Facebook users is more than 1 billion (Facebook Statistics Directory, 2015) and active Twitter users comprise over 115 billion (Statistic Brain, 2013) suggesting a significant drop in traditional newspaper readership with readers switching allegiance to a new and emerging form of technology. Some of the reasons for this shift can be attributed to environmental changes, globalization, speed at which messages need to be transmitted across the globe, the emerging tech-savvy Gen Y and Z, and evolution of communication technologies.

DOI: 10.4018/978-1-5225-0332-3.ch003

Overall, favorable disposition towards social media has also changed the interaction pattern between companies and consumers. One-way communication has given way to dialogue where consumers are at liberty to express their concerns or grievances through multiple platforms as YouTube, Twitter, Facebook, Pinterest, Instagram, blogs etc. Further, increase in reach and decrease in time for messages to traverse has alerted companies to the need for using a social media platform mix to manage stakeholder concerns and their own reputation. Undoubtedly, companies are finding it difficult, though not impossible, to monitor and control online conversations as stakeholders are being influenced more by cyber groups and fan following through this medium than advertising and marketing campaigns. Arguably then, if companies wish to connect with stakeholders, a paradigm shift is required. They need to adopt newer technologies that will shape offline and online public perception and opinion and build corporate reputation (CR).

CR, defined as "a perceptual representation of a firm's past actions and future prospects that describes the firm's overall appeal to all of its key constituents when compared with other leading rivals" (Fombrun, 1996, p. 72),has over the last four decades attracted the attention of academia and practitioners, alike. Researchers have posited that a reputation is "arguably the single most valued formal asset" (Gibson, Gonzales, & Castanon, 2006, p. 15), leading to a sustained competitive advantage (Fombrun, 1996). A favorable reputation "may [thus] enable firms to charge premium prices, attract better applicants, enhance their access to capital markets and attract investors" (Fombrun & Shanley, 1990, p. 223) and impact firm sustainability and performance.

With the advent of social media, building CR has undergone a change because "online reputation is your [organizational] reputation" (Fertik &Thompson, 2010, p. 16). It has thus, become essential to manage CR through social media across all stakeholders, be they shareholders, consumers, employees, business partners, governments, media, or local communities. The criticality of social media management can be comprehended when we consider CR as the net assessment of the company's reputation (Fombrun, 1996), the "overall, affective impression" (Hutton, Goodman, Alexander & Genest, 2001, p. 257) and a sum of sub-reputations for different aspects of its activities (e.g., profitability, or quality of products or services). The challenge for companies is to manage these sub-reputations and generate loyalty by securing eyeballs, building awareness, developing consideration and preference, and stimulating action (Li & Bernoff, 2009).

Empirical studies have attempted to investigate the effect of social media on CR (Seebach, Beck & Denisova, 2013). It is considered a potentially effective and efficient tool for building and maintaining relationships between a company and its publics (Kelleher & Miller, 2006) and can be used to influence the assessments made by stakeholders about a company's products and services, corporate responsibility, success, ability to change and develop, and public image (Aula, 2011). Simultaneously, the reduced corporate control over the communication and messages has also generated much concern and skepticism (Cox, Martinez & Quinlan, 2008) over the use and abuse of social media in CR.

The objective of this chapter is to present learnings from situations of building, maintaining and safeguarding CR, discuss facets of reputation building, develop a social media strategy, and present a functional framework of social media. Finally, it includes some of the best and worst company practices in addressing stakeholder concerns.

Using secondary sources of data, incidences of threats to CR have been analyzed to study company responses to such crises through social media. Practices of companies that have successfully developed strategies for building reputation through social media have been examined using anecdotal evidence. The findings have then been condensed into a set of strategies to enable companies to come up with a policy framework to build, maintain and safeguard CR through judicious use of social media.

UNDERSTANDING CR

As early as 1956, academics developed interest in the term 'reputation', though there was little clarity on what constitutes CR. There were attempts to define the term from multiple perspectives and different disciplines. Much of the understanding emphasized the strong link between 'reputation' and 'image'. A move towards acquiring a clear comprehension of the term 'reputation' gained momentum in the early 2000s with corporate scams, globalization and competition, high stakes and narrowed survival domains. While practitioners and academics struggled to define the term, they agreed on the need to create perceptual images that built stakeholder trust and confidence and helped in the survival and success of a company.

However, to date there is no consensus on the differences and similarities between CR and company image. Some researchers argue that the two terms are identical (Dowling, 1993), some posit that the term reputation has been used loosely to define image (Bernstein, 1984), while others base their interpretation on perceptions of internal and external stakeholders (Dutton et al., 1994). Varying interpretations of CR across disciplines have been posited ranging from social phenomenon (Fombrun & Van Reil, 1997) to game theory (Ferris et al., 2003), to signaling theory (Davies et al., 2003) to marketing (Lin, Li & Huang, 2003; Weiss et al., 1999) to business strategy (Fombrun, 1996; Ferris et al., 2003). The most comprehensive interpretation has been provided by scholars of business strategy who lay emphasis on the essentials of resource-based view and the competitiveness paradigm and stress the need for stakeholder analysis.

Fombrun's (1996) definition of CR as "a snapshot that reconciles the multiple images of a company held by all its constituencies" (p. 72) is probably the most comprehensive which builds on existing scholarship and interpretations across disciplines. A good reputation thus, is an asset, albeit intangible, that can help an organization secure tangible and intangible benefits that are inimical to unforeseen, unprecedented situations and help the organization stay afloat and survive in adverse climate. As the "most valued organizational asset" (Gibson et al., 2006, p. 15), a good CR enables an organization to secure a sustainable competitive edge in the marketplace (Dowling, 2001; Davies et al., 2003), addresses multi-stakeholder perspectives (Bontis et al., 2007) and impacts the financial performance of a company (Fombrun & Shanley, 1990). The benefits of a good reputation are multiple as low organizational costs (Fombrun, 1996), ability to charge premium rates for products (Fombrun & Shanley, 1990), attract a potential pool of candidates (Fombrun, 1996), and secure buy-in of customers (Fombrun, 1996) and investors (Srivastava et al., 1997) etc.

What are the parameters based on which company reputation is measured? There are nine attributes of a good reputation: product and services, innovation, people management, use of corporate assets, social responsibility, quality of management, financial soundness, long-term investment value, global competitiveness. For companies attempting to manage reputation through social media all nine parameters are to be considered and managed. Let us consider the example of Apple. In an assessment conducted in the year 2014 it was found that Apple for eight years in a row has held the number one position. In all the parameters of reputation, it has protected its numero uno status. In February 2014, it was the first company to hit more than $700 billion in market value (Mark, 2015).

The benefits of building and managing CR and associated challenges are huge. The primary reason for this is that reputation is fragile and vulnerable to perceptual biases that are based on "representation of a company's past actions and future prospects that describe a firm's overall appeal to all of its constituents when compared to other leading rivals" (Fombrun, 1996 cited in Smaiziene & Jucevicius, 2009, p. 96). CR is a composite of multiple images collated, filtered over time, or altered with changes in stakeholder perceptions. It can be positive or negative and one over which a company has little or no control. For instance, a company may be perceived to be environmentally responsible or irresponsible by a group of stakeholders because of its core business or its CSR activities. In the current age of social media, companies need to be cognizant and wary of positive and negative perceptual biases that can make or mar their CR.

CHAMPIONING THE CAUSE OF SOCIAL MEDIA

Marketo (2010) defined social media in *The Definitive Guide to B2B Social Media* as "the production, consumption and exchange of information through online social interactions and platforms" (p.5) creating platforms for companies to narrate their stories and tales (Ploof, 2009) and build reputation through narratives (Deetz, 1986) that are communicated through a "collection of stories about an organization" (Smythe, Dorward, & Reback, 1992, p. 19). This implies that stakeholders are the custodians of company reputation and its overall market perception for they possess the capability to co-create, build, control and distribute stories. Constant engagement and collaboration with consumers helps companies to co-create value and build reputation. The point gains further credence when we view the increase in number of social media users over the last five years (Figure 1).

According to a Pew Internet study (2014) on use of online medium for communication, 72 per cent men and 74 per cent women were internet users. A comparative study of the number (Figure 1) and percentage (Figure 2) of online adults using social media websites over a four-year timeframe (2010-14), indicates a significant increase in internet usage mandating a paradigmatic shift in techniques of communication and influence.

The statistics show that though Facebook has been in the lead for the last three years, its growth has stagnated over the last two years. As on date, Facebook is the most preferred medium, and can be used by companies and influencers for reputation management. The example of Pampers Dry Max clearly validates the point.

On 6 May 2010, P&G faced consumer wrath over Pampers Dry Max diapers. The diapers were giving rashes to babies and before P&G realized it, mothers got together on Facebook to discuss issue of rashes and criticize the company. The impact on P&G CR was huge. In one day, on May 6 there was a recorded plunge of 39% in the company's stock price. Within 28 hours, P&G executives implemented a communication strategy to appease the customers. They began by listening to complaints with approximately four employees stationed at the brand's listening post, monitoring and categorizing the posts for

Figure 1. Number of social network users worldwide from 2010 to 2014 (in billions)
http://www.statista.com/statistics/278414/number-of-worldwide-social-network-users/

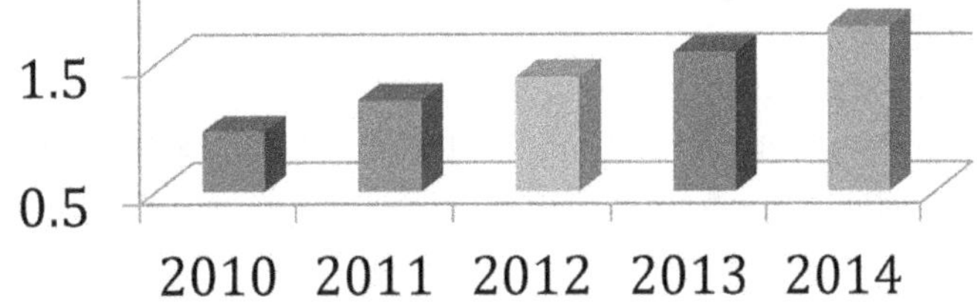

Figure 2. Social Media Sites, 2012-2014
% of online adults who use social media websites (2012-14) http://www.pewinternet.org/2015/01/09/social-media-update-2014/

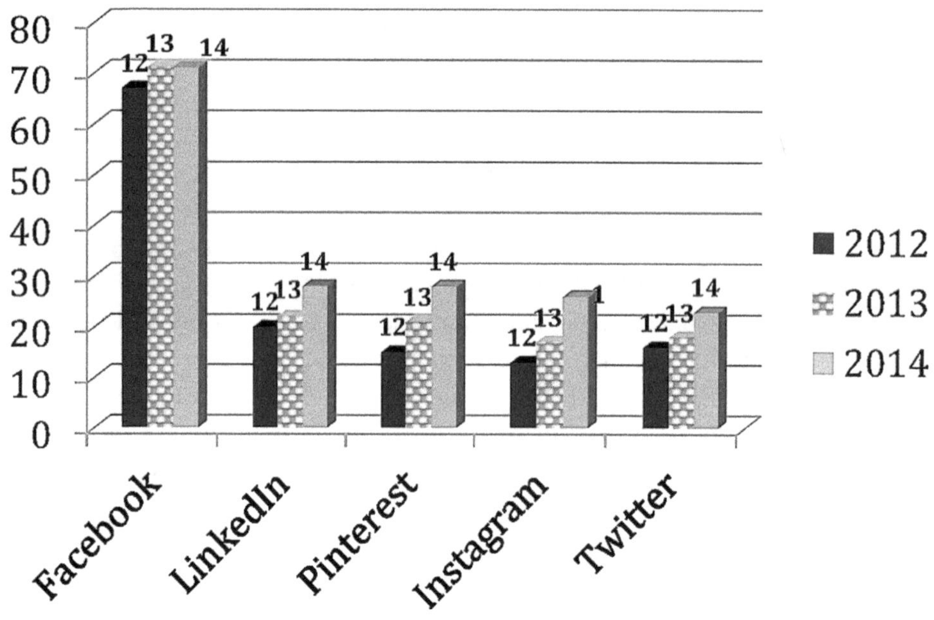

speedy responses. While P&G was patient with the customers, it also decided to take a slightly harsh stand by stressing that the complaints were only from a small group of parents, false rumors etc. Instead of shying away from media, they selected spokespersons from the company and pediatricians to talk to the public. The company addressed calls from customers almost immediately and even invited them to talks with pediatricians at company cost. In this example, the situation snowballed into a crisis because of the interactivity of users on the Facebook page. We can hypothesize that the young mothers who used the diapers were in the age bracket of 25-35. This corroborates with the statistics provided in Figure 3 of maximum usage of social media by Gen Y and Z.

Further, a study conducted by Jeff Bullas (2014) on social media usage by age, recorded a substantial increase in number of internet users (Figure 3). The maximum increase in users was in the age bracket of 18-29, followed by 30-49, 50-64, and 65+. The intensity of usage in the age bracket of 18-29 and 30-49 indicates that social media is their preferred form of communication. Companies can target this segment for they possess the potential of influencing and being influenced.

An analysis of Figures 1, 2 and 3 shows that:

- Social media use/consumption is on the increase
- Facebook is the most frequently used form of online communication
- Facebook has remained the most preferred choice for adult users of online communication in the timeframe from 2012-14.
- Social media is the most preferred medium for Gen Y and Z.
- Gen Y and Z are most susceptible to influence through social media and also play the role of influencers in the same space.

Figure 3. User Timeline: Social Media Usage by Age.
http://www.jeffbullas.com/2014/01/17/20-social-media-facts-and-statistics-you-should-know-in-2014/

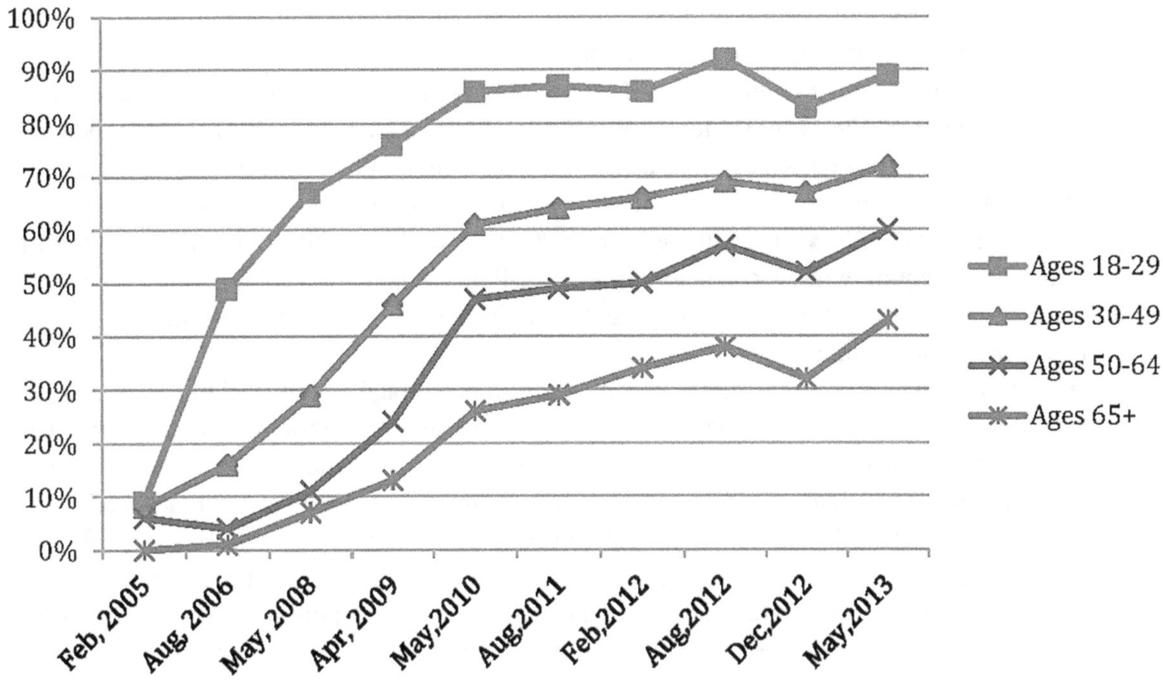

The points stated above indicate the rising popularity of social media. Small wonder then, that companies are using this medium to manage their reputation across age groups. Consider the example of Lenovo which targeted the 18-25 age bracket. To woo customers in this target segment the company launched a 'Please Daddy, Please campaign' on YouTube.

Developing a Strategy

There is overall agreement on the decision that social media should be the company's choice for building reputation. However, the question on choice of strategy for exercising influence remains to be answered. These strategies vary with the targeted company objective. To understand the nature of strategies better, Wilson et al. (2011) conducted a survey on 1,100 companies and found four predominant strategies: predictive practitioner, creative experimenter, social media champion and social media transformer. The defining parameter was the nature of task to be accomplished through social media. For instance, predictive practitioners build their reputation by focusing on any one area, for example, product. This technique was found to be useful for companies and businesses that wished to avoid uncertainty, achieve results and measure the success through established tools. Creative experimenters were a little more adventurous who experimented with small scale tests. For instance, a company may wish to experiment and find out more about the use of social media by its employees. Small questionnaires were distributed which helped the company assess existing practices and implement changes, if required. To be a social media champion, the company required involvement in massive initiatives planned and executed for predictable results. It also involved collaboration across multiple functions within and outside the organization. Finally, a social media transformer strategy was the requirement for large-scale initiatives that extended to external stakeholders, allowing companies to apply customer responses for operationalizing critical business decisions and issues.

What are the decision parameters for application of a strategy? When to take on the role of a social media champion or transformer or predictive practitioner or creative experimenter? Laying down clear-cut guidelines concerning the use of strategies is difficult but critical factors in the decision process are the business needs and required stakeholder influence. Companies and businesses may also choose to alter or build on the existing strategies, techniques and medium of influence for building reputation. For instance, the growth of Facebook (Figure 2) from 2012-14, may be sufficient reason for a company to invest in experimenting with or championing this medium. Strategy is defined with the 'what' of information, the summary of company achievements, ratings or some crucial information that positions the company in a positive light.

Developing a strategy for social media can be understood through the diffusion theory (Rogers, 1962) that is critical from the perspective of developing an online media strategy that helps a company build and manage its reputation. The theory enumerates that innovation and innovative strategy can be communicated through multiple channels over a period of time among members from a social system (Rogers, 1962). Alternately, the theory explains how and why publics change their perspective with reference to ongoing issues and events and adapt to change. For instance, in the case of social media, growth in technology, globalization and other environmental changes reframed public perspective in favor of technologically driven modes of communication. According to Rogers (1962), the process involved four components: innovation, communication channels, time and social system. The most important were identified to be the take-off time for an innovation and its final adoption, which emphasized the role of media and people in gaining knowledge, forming an opinion, adopting or rejecting the same, implementing the new idea and validating the decision point. In the initial phase, the adoption of a new idea was dependent on media and in the second, personal communication. Also referred to as 'inter-media agenda-setting' (McCombs & Shaw, 1993), this new information was introduced by the media into the contemporary social network.

The central issue in strategy formulation and implementation is that there be cohesion and coordination within the different nodes of the company responsible for online conversations with stakeholders. Ad hoc attempts by small groups can often warp the impact and have an adverse effect on company reputation measured in terms of leadership, corporate stewardship, products and services, corporate culture etc. that collectively build social capital. These measures also facilitate stakeholder trust for different structural factors as mentioned above. The greater the company's ability in securing stakeholder commitment and faith through narratives and stories being co-created, the higher is the influence (Aula & Mantere, 2008). The responsibility of garnering support of stakeholders rests with the marketing and sales divisions who are also custodians of social media policies and processes. Their understanding of customer needs, brand building, advertising, relationship management, pricing and the target segment facilitates initiation of favorable conversations. None of these functions is mutually exclusive and all impact engagement with the customer.

Occasionally, there is a consumer/customer call on the social web asking for information, expressing grievance or any other sentiment. The nature and timing of company response is important. Addressing these aberrant calls in a specific manner may or may not have been part of the strategy implementation process but requires immediate attention. An interesting case in point is that of KLM. In April 2010, all flights were stalled for a period of six days following an Icelandic volcanic eruption that produced an ash cloud. Due to a huge number of customer service requests, all call centers were jammed. In this crisis, CEO, KLM, Peter Hartman announced that the airline would invest heavily in an ongoing social media strategy that would be customer-focused. True to its word, KLM proceeded with speed and alacrity, training employees to respond with grace and caution, listening and responding, organizing creative campaigns, and procuring information about customers. All these efforts yielded positive results and KLM gained a reputation of being a global leader in championing social media (Socialbakers, n. d.). Reasons for the success of KLM are not far to seek - quick response mechanism, recognition of customer voice, development of capabilities for monitoring and influencing conversations.

Contrast this with the classic example of the infamous guitar tossing in March 2008 that churned up a social media incident for United Airlines. Dave Carroll, owner of the guitar, after being denied a hearing by the company, created a trilogy of songs and video with the aim of getting a million hits in a year. Though United Airlines was warned of the consequences of ignoring, not listening to customer appeal, the incident cascaded down to consumers and competitors. Their strategies of denying, obfuscating or stalling, which may have been right in bygone years, tarnished their reputation in the age of social media. Things started getting out of control and the statement, "there is no such thing as bad PR" was tossed in social media and multiple interpretations derived (Hendershot-Hurd, 2009). As Jeff Bezos, Founder of Amazon, aptly stated, "If you make customers unhappy in the physical world, they might each tell 6 friends. If you make customers unhappy on the Internet, they can each tell 6000 friends." (Banks, n. d.). A more cooperative stand by United Airlines would have salvaged their reputation. Some corporate strategies to avoid similar results in the future are education of employees to convert them into experts and advocates, with an ability to manage preventable crises and get prepared for the accidental one.

Rushing to the situation and providing an immediate or quick-fix solution that does not match with the overall company objective is not the best approach. The situation requires careful analysis. Speed undoubtedly is important, but equally important is the 'what' and the 'how' of the message. Without first taking cognizance of online dialogue, rushing to take either a defensive or an offensive position can be counter-productive. Processes and procedures should be streamlined for providing a fair response that appeases the customer and yet does not negatively impact company reputation. The existing bond between the company and the consumers should be reiterated, positive experiences recounted and subtle hints or direct messages posted that reinforce the trust and reaffirm the commitment to quality. While responding to customers, apologies or some form of token gifts in the form of discounts, free services etc. can also be given. Ultimately, perception of a good reputation has multiple benefits.

Consider the case of KLM which post the 2010 crisis, ran a campaign through which it studied the social media profile of customers and at destination points gave them surprise gifts as a token of appreciation for flying with KLM (Socialbakers, n. d.).

The success of a social media strategy hinges on providing information to stakeholders, engaging and collaborating with them. As part of the corporate culture and social media policy, companies monitor, assess and analyze, strategize and structure, test, embed and review online conversations. For managing reputation, information on company perception collated from the web is displayed in the form of reviews, star ratings, number of transactions completed, numerical scores etc. The advantage of presenting these scores is that stakeholders can independently interpret, draw conclusions and commence conversations about the company and the brand. These online conversations with the use of automated keywords can be listened to, traced and tracked. In social media analytics, listening is the most important as it enables companies to capture online data. This may comprise all online conversations related to the company or its products and services and competing brands. However, not all of this data may be meaningful. Only relevant bits of information are assembled to create meaning and then archived. The understanding of this data -who is talking, what is being talked about, who shows most sentiment, who builds narratives, etc. provides a clue about online participants high on "sentiment" or "authority". What do customers feel about a product or company? How closely are the views echoed by other stakeholders in the online space? Who commands authority and who is high on sentiment? What is their following? What is the control they exercise over online groups? Various metrics are used to capture user background, interests, concerns, networks of which they are members, and their purchasing behavior. Once the data has been collated, it becomes simple for the company to critically analyze and assess the results and create a road map with a platform mix - blogs, apps, social networks etc. The strategy is then tested on a small scale and ROI calculated before being implemented with appropriate campaigns, allocation of responsibilities, employee incentives and targets. Periodical reviews of success measures, implementation of changes, if required, completes the task of the practitioner, though, it does not warrant online media security from reputational damage. However, to succeed, not one strategy is sufficient. Changes may be initiated, measured and finally adopted during strategy implementation.

Framework for Social Media Functions

The strategy for social media is developed in tandem with the identified functions for implementation. Kietzmann et al. (2011) posited seven elements in the framework for social media functions and presented them in the form of a honeycomb model. Does the user wish to reveal his/her identity? An image can be created of the character and preferences through conversations posted on the social media website. This may be the true or fake identity created by the user. Conversations in social media can take on different forms as tweeting, blogging, discussions etc. Initiating and monitoring these conversations is crucial as a wrong message can lead to hostility among stakeholders and damage reputation. Under the dimension of sharing, users can share and disseminate information. At the same time, companies need to cognize that the platform and the material being shared are trustworthy. Inappropriate content has to be immediately removed and steps taken to rectify or stall inadvertent situations. However, by sharing, companies get to know what is being talked about in cyber space. The interactivity between the company and the users creating possibilities of dialogue is referred to as presence. The higher the presence, greater is the conversational influence (Kaplan & Haenlin, 2010). Another important dimension in the social media context is structure of relationships between influencers and users. Influencers have authority and exercise considerable sway over group members through rational and emotional connect. Listening with a close ear to conversations also helps companies know more about influencers with authority and competing products in the market. These stakeholders influence purchase decisions and enjoy an advisory role in the social media space. They may provide either a positive or a negative impression to the users (Gorry & Westbrook, 2009), creating what is referred to as a reputational threat. What is the interaction between users within groups and communities? The 'group' dimension enables companies to learn more about group attitudes and behaviors. All dimensions discussed above, namely, identity, sharing, conversations, presence, relationships, reputation and groups relate directly to the company and user reputation. Let us consider the example of HMV (2013) and study the framework for social media function.

The HMV example clearly reiterates the functions of social media, and creation of perceptual biases of stakeholders through social media interactivity.

Table 1. Analysis contributed by PGPII students (batch of 2015) for the MCCourse

THE CASE A disgruntled 21-year-old HMV social media executive went rogue (2013) and tweeted live about the mass lay-off of 190 employees from the HMV group, using the company's Twitter account. IDENTITY The HMV Twitter identity was stolen. The account was typically used for promoting new music, games and movies sold by the company, but due to poor security reasons, the executive was able to use the proprietary company account to publish these tweets in the company's name to its followers. CONVERSATIONS & GROUPS The executive was able to reach almost 70,000 people instantly sharing first-hand information on how HMV laid off significant number of employees. SHARING After a while, HMV was able to delete the tweets. However, it was too late. The original tweets garnered rapid and widespread attention and were retweeted over 1300 times within 30 minutes of the original postings. This accelerated the spread of tweets exponentially and made the story reach British, European and American outlets in good time before the next day's morning paper went to press. PRESENCE In HMV's case, the situation was possible because of lack of presence. If other people together with the executive in question had been monitoring the Twitter account, they would have been able to delete the tweets and shut down the disgruntled employee's access to the account. This was however not the case, giving other Twitter users plenty of time to retweet and to share before anyone at HMV knew what was going on. RELATIONSHIPS At the time of this case, HMV had almost 70,000 followers, probably people with an interest in music, video games and movies who would like to receive updates from their provider for these media potential customers. By hijacking the account and posting a series of tweets, the errant employee could have well damaged customer relationships with HMV. REPUTATION The tweets not only allowed bad company news, presented mockingly to spread uncontrolled over the Internet, but also embarrassingly displayed HMVs poorly executed social media strategy. As the reputation of a company in social media is largely associated with professionalism and how well they adopt the social media platform, it was sad to see how the reputation of HMV took a crippling blow because of unmonitored tweets.

IDENTIFYING AND ADDRESSING THREATS

Kietzmann et al.'s (2011) seven dimensions of functionality reiterate that perceptions of stakeholders are more important than reality. The argument gains importance when reputational threat is understood in terms of what the stakeholders attribute to the company. This 'attribution theory' (Weiner, 1986) stresses that blame is attributed for a negative word-of-mouth publicity and perception of responsibility, the process of which is accelerated by the social media (Gonzales-Herrero & Smith, 2008). Such situations of reputational threat are far too frequent in the social media space where all stakeholders, be they investors, consumers, or employees, mould their decisions based on a systematic analysis of conversations and social media reports.

The speed at which messages, positive and negative, are transferred is difficult to control and can, at the speed of lightning tarnish the image of a company (Dellarocas, 2003). Content can be generated, edited and shared with a large number of people in a short span of time. This is compounded by the fact that negative content far outweighs positive information in the minds of the public. The threat is also faced from other social media users who may spearhead rumors about a company, leaving little or no time for the company to respond. In such situations, the worst mistake that a company can make is to ignore these conversations or project lack of awareness. Slighting the consumers by feigning ignorance can have dire consequences for the company as consumers may decide to migrate to competition where they feel their voice will be heard.

The threat from customers who are empowered to comment on the social, ethical and business responsibilities is greater than that from internal stakeholders. Consumers may post content on the product that is negative or may openly criticize services provided by the company. Escalated interactivity with negative content openly visible to individuals and all groups can be a major threat. Often cross-cultural differences stemming from different expectations may also create negative impressions in consumer minds. Products designed for a specific usage in a typical environment with anticipated results may not have a similar impact in other environments or yield expected value. Negative reviews, controversial issues related to ethics, social or business, anti-branding sites, incidents dealing with emotional and irrational criticism can all be used to negatively impact business and reputation. Are the messages truthful and objective or fabricated by sponsored third parties? Companies can address many of the aforementioned issues by hiring experts or consultants who can constantly monitor the ongoing dialogue, listening to conversations, talking to complainants, sorting misunderstandings through humor and wit, apologizing if the need arises, and integrating 'figures of authority' in the social space. One of the interesting examples is of McDonald's, targeted by the anti-branding sites, which harped on the processes of the food giant that impacted the environment. In the wake of these accusations, McDonald was forced to focus on corporate stewardship and created a webpage, which invited feedback from the consumers (Kucuk, 2008).

Not only external but also internal stakeholders can prove to be a threat to the company by acting in unpredictable ways or through acts of commission as posting material on their private blogs or social networking sites. A video was created and uploaded by employees of Dominos Pizza (2009) showing them violating health standards while in the process of preparing pizza. The video went viral with more than a million hits. Discussions abounded on Twitter, which damaged the reputation of the company. Dominos began by firing the employees, and then issuing an apology video (Clifford, 2009). Though the employees claimed that it was just a fun video with no intentions of harming the company's reputation, the damage was huge.

Other related issues as work culture, leadership etc. can be brought to the fore. Their voices can influence external stakeholders. In case of dissent, voices can be intentionally aired through unsanctioned channels. These unfiltered messages influence opinions of hundreds and thousands of people in a short span of time drawing attention to lapses or shortcomings in company policies or behavior. Employees can also make unintentional politically incorrect statements when designated to work for the social media space. All these points clearly indicate that one small voice in the social media space can snowball and have a crippling effect on company reputation. Awareness on the part of companies on what is happening, what changes can be implemented can definitely impact overall impression. Finally, reacting to customer complaints/ grievances or ignoring them is not the best possible strategy. To avoid instances of the type cited above, companies have begun to make their social presence felt and to apply social media tools strategically.

It is important that the timing of what is being said is appropriate and the person/employee using social media is well informed of the external environment. In May 2015, a massive earthquake measuring 7.5 on the Richter scale hit Nepal. While the tremors were felt in India, no damage to people and property was recorded. When both countries were reeling under the impact of the environmental crisis, Lenskart came up with the following advertisement (see Figure 4).

This advertisement created so much anger and fury among the customers that Lenskart had to come out in the open and apologize (Singh, 2015) (see Table 2).

While there are many examples in which employee folly has cost the company much in terms of reputation, it is difficult to predict each and every situation. Maintaining a social presence and being on the vigil are just beginning points in the entire process of exercising control over employee social media presence and conversation.

Figure 4. Lenskart advertisement

Table 2. The apology mail

Dear All,
Today is a sad day for us. We witnessed an earthquake that hit Nepal and North India, which has caused extensive loss of life and property. Our hearts reach out to the many who have been affected by the earthquake.
Today we also sent out an SMS offer which referred to the earthquake in poor taste. This is completely unacceptable to us and is against the standard that we have set for ourselves as a responsible member of society. We are really sorry that this has happened. We have already taken steps to put safeguards in place to ensure that this is never ever repeated.
We would like to tender an unconditional apology to the society at large and especially to the affected families and to everyone whom we have offended. We sincerely hope that you will be able to forgive our lapse.
At Lenskart we pride on being a young and responsible organisation. This incident has strengthened our resolve to work harder and add greater value to our customers and our society.
Sorry we messed up,
Peyush Bansal & Amit Chaudhary
Co-Founders, Lenskart
http://blog.lenskart.com/we-are-sorry/

These reputational threats or rumors, which meet the expectations or perceptions of internal and external customers, reflect lack of company control and responsibility. In social media, both reach and time (Gaines-Ross, 2010) are critical. Within seconds and minutes, messages can traverse to large groups and can escalate a situation, mostly crisis, if not handled in a timely and appropriate manner. The stages of overcoming such crises, unscathed, are listening, monitoring, analyzing conversations, managing stakeholders with flexibility, acting with speed in case of damaging or threatening interactions, extending reach and influencing groundswell. Stakeholders in all probability like to assign blame to the company for unfavorable outcomes. Their views are framed on the perceived responsibility assigned to the company – high or low. Company stratagem is based on an analysis of the stakeholder response and perceptions. "Firms should know when to chime in" (Kietzmann et al., 2011, p. 245) and if a decision is taken to react, should the response be offensive or defensive (Thomas, Peters, Howell & Robbins, 2012)? Should the company join the fray and if yes, what should be the time and manner of approach? An incorrect decision can have an irreversible impact on reputation. The decision in most cases is based on the history of the company, how its past actions will impact the current threat and the stakeholder perceptions (Coombs, 2004) which may view the company as a "victim", or may perceive the crisis or threat as "preventable" or "accidental". Based on these categorizations, stakeholders award a clean chit to the company or lash it for unintended, yet preventable crisis.

As social media can aggravate the situation by spreading news like wildfire, companies need to be constantly on the vigil for establishing control and identifying the three parameters of influence: influential actor, interaction and network (Vollen Broek et al., 2014). Social media actors and influencers who are more experienced and knowledgeable than the average public can be identified by scanning social media platforms. The interaction can be measured in terms of number of mentions, positive and negative, within a specified timeframe by specific users and finally comparing the total number with the reach of a company. This facilitates identification of sentiment of the public by aggregating the positive against the negative mentions. Measurement of sentiment by recognizing conversational trends (McCarthy et al., 2010) helps assess if the issue under consideration is being perceived positively or negatively. For instance, sudden increased reference to a company or issue indicates heightened interest level as well as demonstrates reach. In case a company wishes to initiate dialogue, it can use a forum or a blog. This may help in resolving issues, if any, on products and services and networking.

The challenge before a company in combating crises is design of strategic tools. However, before it approaches the website drawing board, it should ensure that there is a good match with the business objectives. Additionally, to keep reputation intact organizations should build on the notion of customer trust and goodwill. Quality consideration is the second most important criterion for maintaining reputation. Once conversations have been initiated, loyalty paradigms are established. Consumers who have once shown allegiance to a company for its products or services are unlikely to veer in the direction of competing products. Use of a variety of social media activities can create a comprehensive network through which different customers can be speedily approached. The actions taken by a company and the manner of response can, to a great extent, diminish the negative impact. Depending on the gravity of the situation different response strategies as forced compliance, voluntary compliance or denial can be adopted. The company strategy to abet the intensity of the crisis should be perceived as honest. Interactivity with the stakeholders increases the possibility of being heard and perceived as open-minded and customer-focused.

Brands and companies may take years to develop, but can be ruined by one callous comment or one wrong move in social media. Consistent approach in wooing customers is the first step in managing reputation. If there is inconsistency in presence or approach, customers may turn to other competing brands and products where they feel their voice is being heard. Consistency does not imply that companies begin to spam the mail boxes of customers. In 2012, Toyota committed the mistake of creating nine Twitter accounts in the process of marketing the new Toyota Camry. The wrath of the customers forced them to take down many of the pages and apologize to the customers.

Occasionally, distasteful content may be put on social media. While it is a good opportunity to connect with fans and followers, content should be carefully monitored before being uploaded. Negative feedback on the social media space (example of McDonald's) or incorrect timing (example of Lenskart) can be disastrous for a company. Accounts can be hacked (example of HMV) and messages posted creating discontent, sarcasm and skepticism in the social media.

CONCLUSION

Social media technologies as blogs, microblogs etc. have changed the business horizon with both the users and consumers in a win-win situation. Companies are able to advertise their products, create awareness, build consideration and get consumer buy-in at almost one-tenth the cost of normal advertising. Consumers are able to voice their appreciation and grievances, express their personal opinions and thoughts and influence purchase decisions in short spells. In this scenario, both opportunities and risks are huge. Companies can leverage social media to mobilize large groups, which can later be converted to loyal customers. However, on the flip side, even one disgruntled stakeholder or a wrong statement can boomerang, create negativity and nullify all positive attempts of the company to amass reputational capital.

By being constantly on the vigil, companies may avert reputational damage, which may negatively impact the business (Rindova et al., 2005). As social media is not bound by time, space and boundaries, companies can maintain a 24x7 social media management team to monitor interactivity as content that once appears on the web is difficult to delete. To cleanse the social media environment and maintain a good reputational score, companies should constantly monitor, analyze and aggregate stakeholder perceptions.

REFERENCES

Aula, P. (2011). Meshworked reputation: Publicists' views on the reputational impacts of online communication. *Public Relations Review*, *37*(1), 28–36. doi:10.1016/j.pubrev.2010.09.008

Aula, P., & Mantere, S. (2008). *Strategic Reputation Management*. New York: Routledge.

Banks. (n. d.) Jeff Bezos on customer service. Retrieved from http://blog.paylane.com/jeff-bezos-on-customer-service/

Bernstein, D. (1984). *Company Image and Reality: A Critique of Corporate Communications. Holt, Rinehart and Winston*. Eastbourne: The Advertising Association.

Bontis, N., Booker, L., & Serenko, A. (2007). The mediating effect of organizational reputation on customer loyalty and service recommendation in the banking industry. *Management Decision*, *45*(9), 1426–1445. doi:10.1108/00251740710828681

Clifford, S. (2009). Video Prank at Domino's Taints Brand. Retrieved from http://www.nytimes.com/2009/04/16/business/media/16dominos.html?_r=0

Coombs, W. T. (2004). Impact of past crises on current crisis communications: Insights from situational crisis communication theory. *Journal of Business Communication*, *41*(3), 265–289. doi:10.1177/0021943604265607

Cox, J. L., Martinez, E. R., & Quinlan, K. B. (2008). Blogs and the corporation: Managing the risk, reaping the benefits. *The Journal of Business Strategy*, *29*(3), 4–12. doi:10.1108/02756660810873164

Davies, G., Chun, R., Da Silva, R. V., & Roper, S. (2003). *Corporate Reputation and Competitiveness*. UK: Routledge.

Deetz, S. (1986). Metaphors and the discursive production and reproduction of organization. In L. Thayer (Ed.), *Organization-Communication: Emerging Perspectives I* (pp. 168–182). Norwood, NJ: Ablex Publishing Co.

Dellarocas, C. (2003). The Digitization of word-of-mouth: Promise and challenges of online reputation systems. *Management Science*, *49*(10), 1407–1424. doi:10.1287/mnsc.49.10.1407.17308

Dowling, G. (2001). *Creating Corporate Reputations: Identity, Image and Performance*. UK: Oxford University Press.

Dowling, G. R. (1993). Developing your corporate image into a corporate asset. *Long Range Planning*, *26*(2), 101–109. doi:10.1016/0024-6301(93)90141-2

Dutton, J. E., Dukerich, J. M., & Harquail, C. V. (1994). Organisation images and member identification. *Administrative Science Quarterly*, *39*(2), 239–263. doi:10.2307/2393235

Ferris, G. R., Blass, R., Douglas, C., Kolodinsky, R. W., & Treadway, D. C. (2003). Personal reputation in organizations. In J. Greenberg (Ed.), *Organizational Behaviour: The State of the Science* (pp. 211–246). New Jersey: Lawrence Erlbaum Associates.

Fertik, M., & Thomson, D. (2010). *Wild West 2.0: How to Protect and Restore Your Online Reputation on the Untamed Social Frontier*. New York: AMA.

Fombrun, C. J. (1996). *Reputation: Realizing Value from the Corporate Image*. Boston: Harvard Business School.

Fombrun, C. J., & Shanley, M. (1990). What's in a name? Reputation building and corporate strategy. *Academy of Management Journal*, *33*(2), 233–258. doi:10.2307/256324

Fombrun, C. J., & Van Riel, C. (1997). The reputational landscape. *Corporate Reputation Review*, *1*(1 & 2), 5–13. doi:10.1057/palgrave.crr.1540024

Gaines-Ross, L. (2008). *Corporate Reputation: 12 Steps to Safeguarding and Recovering Reputation*. Hoboken, NJ: John Wiley & Sons.

Gibson, D., Gonzales, J. L., & Castanon, J. (2006). The importance of reputation and the role of public relations. *Public Relations Quarterly*, *51*(3), 15–18.

González-Herrero, A., & Smith, S. (2008). Crisis communications management on the Web: How internet-based technologies are changing the way public relations professionals handle business crises. *Journal of Contingencies and Crisis Management*, *16*(3), 143–153. doi:10.1111/j.1468-5973.2008.00543.x

Gorry, G. A., & Westbrook, R. A. (2009). Winning the internet confidence game. *Corporate Reputation Review*, *12*(3), 195–203. doi:10.1057/crr.2009.16

Hendershot-Hurd, K. (2009). What to do when Social Media creates a Shit Storm. Retrieved from http://virtualimpax.com/2009/07/13/soial-media-shit-storm/

Hutton, J. G., Goodman, M. B., Alexander, J. B., & Genest, C. M. (2001). Reputation management: The new face of corporate public relations? *Public Relations Review*, *27*(3), 247–261. doi:10.1016/S0363-8111(01)00085-6

Kaplan, A., & Haenlein, M. (2010). Users of the world, unite! The challenges and opportunities of social media. *Business Horizons*, *53*(1), 59–68. doi:10.1016/j.bushor.2009.09.003

Kelleher, T., & Miller, B. (2006). Organizational blogs and the human voice: Relational strategies and relational outcomes. *Journal of Computer-Mediated Communication*, *11*(2), 395–414. Retrieved from http://jcmc.indiana.edu/vol11/issue2/kelleher.html doi:10.1111/j.1083-6101.2006.00019.x

Kietzmann, J. H., Hermkens, K., McCarthy, I. P., & Silvestre, B. S. (2011). Social media? Get serious! Understanding the functional building blocks of social media. *Business Horizons*, *54*(3), 241–251. doi:10.1016/j.bushor.2011.01.005

Kucuk, S. U. (2008). Negative Double Jeopardy: The role of anti-brand sites on the internet. *Journal of Brand Management*, *15*(3), 209–222. doi:10.1057/palgrave.bm.2550100

Lin, Z., Li, D., & Huang, W. (2003). Reputation, Reputation system and reputation distribution – An explanatory study in online consumer-to-consumer auctions. In R. Azari (Ed.), *Current security management & ethical issues of information technology* (pp. 249–266). USA: Idea Group Inc.

Mark, D. (2015). Apple is once again #1 most admired company in the world. *Loopinsight.com*. Retrieved from http://www.loopinsight.com/2015/02/20/apple-is-once-again-1-most-admired-company-in-the-world/

Marketo (2010). *The Definitive Guide to B2B Social Media: A Marketo Workbook*. San Mateo, CA Retrieved from http://docs.cdn.marketo.com/Guide-B2B-Social-Media-Part2.pdf

McCarthy, I. P., Lawrence, T. B., Wixted, B., & Gordon, B. R. (2010). A multidimensional conceptualization of environmental velocity. *Academy of Management Review*, *35*(4), 604–626. doi:10.5465/AMR.2010.53503029

McCombs, M. E., & Shaw, D. L. (1993). The evolution of agenda-setting research: Twenty-five years in the marketplace of ideas. *Journal of Communication*, *43*(2), 58–67. doi:10.1111/j.1460-2466.1993.tb01262.x

Neff, J. (2010). How Pampers Battled Diaper Debacle. *Adage.com*. Retrieved from http://adage.com/article/news/pampers-battled-diaper-debacle/143777/

Pew Research Centre social networking fact sheet. (n. d.). Pew Internet. Retrieved from http://www.pewinternet.org/fact-sheets/social-networking-fact-sheet/

Ploof, R. (2009). Johnson & Johnson does new media. Retrieved from http://ronamok.com/ebooks/jnj_case_study.pdf

Rindova, V. P., Williamson, I. O., Petkova, A. P., & Sever, J. M. (2005). Being good or being known. *Academy of Management Journal*, *48*(6), 1033–1049. doi:10.5465/AMJ.2005.19573108

Rogers, E. M. (1962). *Diffusion of Innovations*. New York: Free Press.

Seebach, C., Beck, R., & Denisova, O. (2013). Analyzing social media for CR management: How firms can improve business agility. *International Journal of Business Intelligence Research*, *4*(3), 50–66. doi:10.4018/ijbir.2013070104

Singh, R. (2015). 'Shake it off like the earthquake', says Lenskart ad after Nepal tragedy. *Zeenews*. Retrieved from zeenews.india.com/news/sci-tech/shake-it-off-like-the-earthquake-says-lenskart-ad-after-nepal-tragedy_1585108.html

Smaiziene, I., & Jucevicius, R. (2009). Corporate Reputation: Multidisciplinary richness and search for a relevant definition. *Inzinerine Ekonomika-Engineering Economics*, *2*(62), 91–101.

Smythe, J., Dorward, C., & Reback, J. (1992). *Corporate Reputation: Managing the New Strategic Asset*. London: Century Business.

Social Bakers. (n. d.) KLM: A Truly Socially devoted company. Retrieved from https://cdn.socialbakers.com/www/archive/storage/www/klm-sociallydevoted.pdf

Srivastava, R. K., Crosby, J. R., McInish, T. H., Wood, R. A., & Capraro, A. J. (1997). Part IV: How do reputations affect corporate performance: The value of corporate reputation: Evidence from the equity markets. *Corporate Reputation Review*, *1*(1), 62–68. doi:10.1057/palgrave.crr.1540018

Statistic Brain. (2013). Twitter statistics. Retrieved on May 6, 2015 from http://www.statsticsbrain.com/twitterstatistics

Statistics Directory. (n. d.). Facebook. Retrieved from http://www.socialbakers.com/statistics/facebook/

Thomas, J. B., Peters, C. O., Howell, E. G., & Robbins, K. (2012). Social media and negative wordof mouth: Strategies for handing unexpecting comments. *Atlantic Marketing Journal*, *1*(2), 7.

Vollenbroek, W., Vries, S., Constantinides, E., & Kommers, P. (2014). Identification of influence in social media communities. *International journal of web based communities*, 10(3), 280-297.

Weiner, B. (1986). *An Attributional Theory of Motivation and Emotion*. New York: Springer-Verlag. doi:10.1007/978-1-4612-4948-1

Weiss, A. M., Anderson, E., & MacInniss, D. J. (1999). Reputation management as a motivation for sales structure decisions. *Journal of Marketing*, *63*(4), 74–89. doi:10.2307/1251975

Wilson, H. J., Gulnan, P. J., & Parise, S. (2011). What's your social media strategy? *Harvard Business Review*, (July - August), 23–25.

Chapter 4
Concept and Importance of Online Reputation Management

Vinod Kumar Singh
GurukulKangri University, India

Naman Sharma
Amity University, India

ABSTRACT

Gone are the days when Consumers had fewer product choices and companies had fewer sources of finding the right candidates for their work. Thanks to technology and globalization, things have changed. In this age of technology and speed, it becomes tough to overcome competition and make a successful career or business. One thing that may certainly help in achieving the above is a good reputation. Building a good reputation may take a long time but for maintaining it intact or destroying it entirely just takes few minutes. Online reputation is a newer term which basically deals with the rapport of a person or brand that has been build online. There are several online reputation management firms which earns millions of dollars every year from individuals and organizations just to maintain their good reputation on on-line platforms. This chapter discusses these concepts and techniques of online reputation management.

INTRODUCTION

In this age of paramount competition and dynamic business environment, it becomes necessary for organizations to maintain a healthy Public Relations (PR). PR is defined as that management function that identifies, establishes and maintains mutually beneficial relationships between an organization and various publics on whom its success or failure depends (Cutlip, Center & Broom, 2000). Brand, Image and Reputation are the three terms that are often used interchangeably (Riel & Berens, 2001). Chartered Institute of Public Relations (CIPR), UK relates public relations with reputation of a person/organization:

Public relations are about reputation. It is the result of what you do, what you say and what others say about you. Public relations practice is the discipline, which looks after reputation with the aim of earning understanding, support and influencing opinion and behavior. (www.cipr.co.uk)

DOI: 10.4018/978-1-5225-0332-3.ch004

There are few empirical proof in support of above definition stating how public relations can help in building reputation (Plowman, Briggs &Huang, 2001; Walker, 2010) and changing opinion and behaviors of people (Cutlip, Center & Broom, 2000). Researchers concerning corporate reputation took its inspiration from the concept of corporate image. Corporate image is generally considered as the company's brand equity (Caruana & Chircop, 2000). Corporate image is considered to be made up of two components: tangible characteristics that can be measured and evaluated easily and emotional characteristics such as feelings, attitudes and beliefs of the people towards organizations (Kandampully & Hu, 2007).

Losing reputation is a far greater sin for an organization than losing money. (Warren Buffet)

Every individual, product or organization is considered only as good as its general perception amongst the masses. This general perception is formally known by the term 'Reputation'. People strive for good reputation and avoid receiving any negative reputation. A good reputation in general signifies the approval or acceptance of an individual or organization by their potential customers or stakeholders. In times of difficulty, a good reputation may also help a particular organization or individual to stand on his feet again while a bad reputation will only lead to its final collapse. Hence, organizations and individuals generally take the matter of reputation very seriously. Talking more in Indian terms, people in India are always known for their trait of treasuring their reputation more than other materialistic things in life. It is due to this very reason, Indian organizations have absorbed the same quality and hence there is always a fight of reputation going on between them. Talking more about reputation a more refined and accepted dictionary definition of 'Reputation' is

Overall quality or character as seen or judged by people in general; a place in public esteems or regard: good name. (Merriam – Webster dictionary)

How crucial is this 'Reputation' can be understood by some examples such as Xiaomi who is known for its technologically advanced and popular cellphone handsets like RedMi witnessed a sharp decline in its sales when Indian Air Force raised some security concerns over its data storage policies. Similar incident can be cited for Blackberry which again is very big name in Cellphone industry. Another example that can be taken is of Cadbury and Nestle; they have to change their entire packaging for chocolates in India few years back when they were alleged for distributing contaminated chocolates in the market. Quite clearly, reputation of an organization or individual can be considered as make or destroy factor in its endeavors. There are a number of reasons why reputation shall be considered crucial for an individual or a business. Some of these are:

- Starting a new venture.
- Applying for a loan.
- Asking for promotion at workplace.
- Attracting new customers.
- Searching for a new job.
- Leading a new team.
- Launching new product/services.

With the corporate names getting only bigger by each day and competition turning out to be fierce than ever, the need for professional aid in maintaining a healthy reputation is felt now more than ever before.

BACKGROUND

Reputation is considered as an outcome of all organizational actions and conducts, being hard to segregate a unique variable and to recognize it as the one that most influences the opinion of stakeholders (Schultz, Moritsen & Gabrielsen, 2006). Reputation Management is now established as a separate line of business whose market is now worth billions of dollars. Organizations in order to achieve their goals and remain competitive in the market rely more and more to improve their corporate reputation (Argenti & Druckenmiller, 2004). The importance of corporate reputation can be understood by the following statement:

It's the role of public relations to make sure that the organization is getting credit for the good it does. Great reputations are built on doing this consistently over a period of time in which a track record of delivering on promises and engendering trust is evident to everyone. All members of an organization have a contribution to make to building and sustaining reputation. (Murray and White, 2004)

Not only the big corporate honchos but also celebrities, politicians and other personalities from time to time take help of professional reputation management consultancies to make or remake their reputation within their targeted social circles. A good example of this can be taken from political campaigning, months before the elections, a series of positive ad campaigns are run for political parties at all possible platforms such as social sites (Online), Television and Newspapers (Media), Public meetings (Social gatherings) etc. to attract new voters or sometimes to erase the wrong image in minds of existing voters. In India alone, these political campaigns account for billions of rupees and often are under the radar of Election commission for over budgeting. Formally speaking, Reputation Management can be defined as the holistic exercise concerning the careful monitoring of an Individual's or Corporate's (and its brands) reputation, addressing issues and incidents which are negatively influencing it, generating routine mass feedback on their client's reputation and prompting early warning signals to any potential reputation related problems. It is also worth noticing that generally speaking reputation is considered as a positive side of any entity but Gardberg and Fombrun (2002) in their research put forward both the positive and negative reputation of organizations. Hence Reputation Management is more than just building a positive outlook for someone or something, it is also to deviate the general mindset from the negative perceptions. If we speak in a rather layman language Reputation Management is an art of building good reputation and avoiding bad reputation for any individual or brand. With recent technology, Reputation Management is no longer limited to the traditional print media and television advertising, it has evolved to faster, more efficient online platforms such as Facebook and other social networking sites, where the reputation can be created or destroyed in the matter of minutes. The chapter will discuss in detail the concept of online reputation management along with the current platforms and techniques of sustaining reputation management. The chapter will also brush up certain ethical concerns regarding the online reputation management.

ONLINE REPUTATION MANAGEMENT (ORM)

Gone are the days when reputation of an individual or a brand was made in years through never ending hard work and performance. Now all you need to do is give some money to brand management firm and within days rather hours the whole nation will know about you and your products. Nowadays, from a needle to space ship, everything you want to know is available just a click away from you and not only the products and places but one can gather a lot of details about celebrities, leaders or any normal person just like that in a fraction of second. Just type your name in any search engine online such as Google or Bing and countless links will be available at your disposal. Not all the results obtained have any linkage with you, your identity or your personal and professional life. It may be also possible that your real profile doesn't appear at all on the first or second page of search. Reputation of person depends upon how much other people know about that person, his/her job and lifestyle and nowadays all these details are easily accessible through World Wide Web. Just assume a situation in which you are appearing for a job interview, during the final round job interviewer asks you about your achievements and you tell him about how you won a College Science Olympiad contest in your final year. Now as everybody owns a smartphone now days, it will only take less than a minute for the interviewer to type your name along with the contest name and Google it. First few links will be establishing good remarks in your name that how you won the contest and all the important people praising your performance. There will be few pictures of you holding the first prize standing along with some famous personalities and guest of honor. Suddenly, there will be a positive environment created in the interview room in your favor. Google has got some recommendation in your favor which might ultimately help you in grabbing that job. Assume a whole different outcome now, suppose the person bluffs about his/her achievements. In similar situations, when the interviewer googles the candidate's name for the same, obviously the search results speak a different story all together. All of a sudden, his reputation is put on a stake, all his qualifications and skills are seemed to be questionable and of course there will be no job.

Organizations spend millions of dollars every year just to make sure that their current online reputation is kept intact and not to fall into the obsolete zone. It has become next to impossible in this era to work out a successful business of any kind without publicizing it on some online platform. Weblogs, Micro blogs, Folksonomies, Wikis and Social networks are just a few, but very powerful media for creating and sustaining online reputation and are backed by very well-articulated and organized management known as the Online Reputation Management (ORM).

DIGITAL FOOTPRINTS AND SERP

With the emergence and growth of internet and World Wide Web in recent decades, everyone is present everywhere and can be accessed by anyone at any time. We are surrounded by so much of technology at so many levels that it is almost impossible for any civilized human for not to have a presence on internet. Just assume a baby who is born just two days back, his parents/relatives may tweet about their excitement or may have posted a photo on Facebook/Instagram. Some may have also uploaded a video of him/her laughing on YouTube. Even if none of the above has happened, at least the District Registrar of Birth/Death record must have updated their database of newly born and the child's name along with his/her date of birth and time of birth is available on internet. All these records/photos/tweets etc. concerning a particular person/product are known as 'Digital footprints' of the concerned person/product. All these digital footprints are there for the child even when he is merely few days old; imagine the case for him when he will be like 21 years of age. Driving License, Voter Id, Class X mark sheet, Blogs, Facebook account, Gmail, Twitter and so on, there will be thousand may be millions of footprints all over the internet and it is next to impossible to erase all these footprints. These footprints are what constitute the reputation for particular person. This can also be interpreted in the terms that individuals must be very cautious while creating any online content, posting anything personal on internet and definitely must be very proactive while handling any data online as all these things are forming digital reputations for them. It is also interesting to note that most of the data that is there online about a person or an organization is not really posted by themselves but through other sources. This particular phenomenon is known by terms like 'Digital Shadow' (Gantz & Reinsel, 2009) and 'Passive Digital Footprints' (Madden, Fox, Smith, & Vitak, 2007).

For companies, these footprints become all the more important as one negative footprint and it will be there against them forever. Imagine an American cosmetic manufacturer planning to launch a new product in India. A social activist search for the product and found that there are some cases pending in American court against the products of that company. Just imagine the impact of those pending cases in overall marketing of concerned product in India. All that activist has to do is to write a negative review about the product on his blog and his millions of followers will share it on social networking sites, making pledges not to buy and use that product and write an online appeal letter to the government to not to allow the said company to distribute the said product in India. All this negative reputation without even using the actual product and just imagine that company winning the case in the court few months later, it is like they have lost a big market just because of a negative footprint on internet.

Google is not a search engine. It's a reputation management system. (Wired magazine)

Now consider this, suppose you are planning to buy a new cellphone. If you do not already have a brand in your mind, then most probably you will do what a majority of urban consumers do nowadays i.e. pre purchase search on internet. The moment you search for keyword "Cellphones" on a search engine such as Google or Bing, a number of links appear on screen which when clicked route you to the desired webpage containing information about a specific handset etc. The links that appear on the webpage are known as SERP (Search Engine Results Page). You replace your search with "Budget Smartphones" and again a number of different SERP appear concerning the various handsets. At times there are few SERP highlighted on the top and goes with the caption 'Sponsored'. The search engines make a lot of money from these Sponsored SERPs. It is a well-known fact that person rarely go beyond the first two-three pages of search engines and general perception is like that first four of five SERP contains the best products. In general, the first few SERPs belong to industry leaders who have maximum sales and positive reviews and all this led the person searching for it to make up his mind in favor of any one of them. However, there is another side to this very convenient process. What about the phones which are not appearing on the first page? What if they are as good as the big names? May be they did not care enough to maintain their social presence as prominent as their rivals and due to this they have missed a client or let's say millions of client as per the booming e-retailing sector. This is due to this specific reason companies today have separate budget for maintaining their good ranking within SERP listing of various leading search engines. Some companies also pay exclusively for a particular position in SERP list to increase the probability of the person searching for the desired product to have a look on their website for at least once. Another perspective importance for SERP is that when a company or individual has got some negative reputation in the past then the concerned company/individual will try its level best to push these negative search results to page 4 or more so that the likelihood of any one finding out about these negative reviews decreases. Hence, many of times it has been found that a lot of activities or news is created in favor of particular person or brand so that whenever someone search for it these news/activities comes at the top and engage the person. Once again SERP turn out to be an important tool for managing the online reputation.

ONLINE PLATFORMS FOR REPUTATION MANAGEMENT

Besides search engines, there are various other online platforms available for maintaining and improvising the reputation of an organization or individual. These platforms are in forms of Weblogs, Microblogs, Folksonomies, Wikis, Social Networks such as Facebook, Google+ etc. Stakeholders and personnel of reputation management firms often make use of these platforms to address a particular issue at times or to neutralize any bad publicity that is being circulated online. We will discuss these platforms along with their features and advantages in this section.

Weblogs or simply blogs are online platforms through which a person can share a personal message or opinions with people. In online reputation management these Weblogs act as excellent platform for building a good rapport for brands and individuals. Author of the blog details the several positive features of product or individual and answers the concerns of public in detailed manner. Organizations even reach out to their potential customers with the help of their corporate blogs and sometimes even make use of media to reach out to their customers (Peters, 2011). These blogs act as an excellent source to disseminate the additional information related to a product or individual that has not yet been covered by any other media source such as television, newspaper etc. Sometimes these blogs are also discussed in traditional media (television, newspaper, radio) which further enhance its reach and overall capability to affect the reputation of an organization/individual (Portmann, 2008). www.blogger.com is one of the popular Weblogs today. Blogger.com allows its users to create their own personalized blogs for free. The stake holders of any organization can make use of this facility in order to create their own blogs and spreading positive reviews and clarifications regarding their company's brands.

Unlike Weblogs, which are directed to all of internet, *Microblogs* are confined only to few members of a personal social network like followers and friends. This platform is exclusively used as a passive source of information. This source can be personal/public in nature maintained by the individuals or it can be maintained at times by the organizations for their products and services (Portmann & Hutter, 2011). These Microblogs are also used by media for spreading awareness and reporting purposes and it is considered that information spread through this medium travels faster and expands exponentially (Peters, 2011). However, Peters (2011) also believed that due to its limitation on number of words (generally up to 140 words), this medium has a very limited effect on the overall reputation of any individual or brand as it lacks much details and generally limited to spreading the news. Nevertheless, the importance of Microblogs cannot be overruled in online reputation management. Twitter is considered as one of the most popular Microblog and consists millions of celebrities and companies, which in turn have millions of followers. These companies/individuals used this twitter so as to update their fans/customers about their upcoming projects or to neutralize any controversy floating against them.

Folksonomies, sometimes also known by the name social tagging, are the bookmarks of an organization/individual's particular act or service. In simpler terms, this is platform where several users tag their experience/opinions regarding a particular product or person at one place. These experience/opinions then act as reference for organizations/concerned individuals to gather the details on their current market reputation and then they can act accordingly. Folksonomies are important to reputation management as they act as a more specific source of information than any other traditional search engines (Peters, 2011). Sometimes Media also uses these Folksonomies as a source for their information and thereby spread the news in market/general public regarding the particular person or organization and hence affects the reputation of the same (Portmann & Hutter, 2011).

Wikis are yet another medium to slowly enhance the online reputation for any particular brand or person. Wikis especially Wikipedia is an excellent source of information for anything or anyone. The best feature of Wikis is that it is easily editable and hence the individual or organizational members can themselves edit and enhance the content of related Wiki to bring forth the concerned best feature or positive attributes. Wikis are also known for the fact that besides containing some well-known information on the subject it also contains critical information on the same (Peters, 2011). Wikipedia also allows the rating of page which also indirectly influences the reputation of a firm as if any wrong information is flourished on that page then it will receive relatively low ratings. Although, it can be said that the reliability of Wikis is low but the truth is that most of the articles are written by a small group of authors and small closed group of administrators control the Wikipedia and hence its credibility is good (Stegbauer, 2009).

Social Networking Sites (SNS) also sometimes known by the popular term social media has changed the way one used to communicate and interact a decade or two ago. What makes social networking sites unique is not that they allow individuals to meet strangers, but rather they enable users to articulate and make their social networks visible. This can result in connections between individuals that would not otherwise be made (Haythornthwaite, 2005) and these connections help in dissemination of information to endless people in relatively short span of time. Kim et al, (2009) summarize the usage of social media into three types: individuals, government, and business. For individual users, first of all, social media creates a new way of communication beyond the traditional way of email, phone call, and text messaging. SNS provides a new source of collective knowledge, and user can seek answers to specific questions through one-to-one basis or one-to-many dialogs within his network. Users are also allowed to join several online communities and groups based on any interest or hobby to interact with others, keep up with the world, and seek advice from each other. Furthermore, it shows that a large number of users have a strong desire for self-expression and self-satisfaction. These users when apply for a job or loan, recruiters can check the credentials of the applicants by visiting these social networking sites and look upon the profiles of the candidate before making their final decision. In addition, with the huge database since each site has gathered millions of members' information, it can be used as online world wide directories of people. For government, they could easily reach a large number of people to disseminate information and receive feedback for governance purpose.

For business purpose, social media provides rich features for online networking which is essential for a company's intranet. They could conduct everyday operations on the site. Meanwhile, business can also benefit from external networks their employees maintain on the open social webs. For example, they can use the external social web for recruitment and information gathering, and the most significant utilization is in marketing. Businesses now increasingly post their product release announcement and photos to such social media sites like YouTube, Facebook, and Flickr for product promotion. They also monitor the comments replied by potential customers about their products, and about using social media as a marketing tool. Social networks at times are also used to severe the reputation of anyone or any brand as competitors sometimes float negative reviews on social networks and due to the fact that information travels faster on these social networks, a large number of people witness the change in their perception regarding that product/person and its reputation is tarnished. The individual/brand then has to clarify and counteract on those rumors and it takes some time to contain the damage that has already been done to them. It is also noticed that sometimes jokes and funny pictures floated on the Social Networking Sites (SNS) dent the reputation of any particular person or organization. This is especially seen in the case of political campaigns. The supporters of a particular party deliberately post and promote cartoon strips and jokes against opposition parties on Facebook and Twitter and due to their humorous contents; it spreads on the online channels very quickly. What happens next is that despite knowing the fact that all these content is probably fake and intended only to make people laugh, still many supporters of concerned party feel humiliated and at times due to influence of these disturbing posts lose their faith in the party. In past many such incidents has been noticed and Government as well as Courts have taken action against the accused, but still a lot has to be done in this area through making cyber laws strict and quickly enforceable.

Hence, due to all these above reasons it is now evident that social networking sites are an important medium to moderate the reputation for any individual and business. Some of the famous and most popular social networks today are Facebook, Google+, LinkedIn, Research Gate, MySpace, and YouTube etc. These SNSs have got millions of active users who possess power to make or break reputation of individuals/brands in matter of minutes.

TECHNIQUES FOR SUSTAINING ONLINE REPUTATION

At times, it is said that creating a reputation of you is tough but what is even tougher is to maintain that reputation in future. One of the major tasks of reputation management is to bridge the gap between how an individual/ company perceive itself and how others view it. According to a research conducted by BrandYourself and Harris Interactive, as much as 86% of online US adults use search engines such as Google and Bing to find out information regarding some other persons. Further, this research also strengthened the fact that from time to time the employers (especially in US) use online search to find out more about the applicants before hiring them. Clearly, the reputation management today has got many individual and organizational uses that are beyond ignoring. But the big question is how to sustain this online reputation especially when someone has got so many competitors who may engage in unethical practices just to ruin your reputation at the first chance they got. One way of doing this is by taking professional help from experts. Many big organizations and professionals make use of specialized service providers such as BrandYourself, HootSuite, KnowEm and Harris Interactive for their effective reputation management. These reputation management service providers assist one to get his desired results such as acquiring good search results on his name, managing social media, getting relevant analytics or acquiring influential domain names etc. However, for the people who cannot afford to utilize the services of these reputation management experts, there are some simple steps as suggested by www.reputationmanagement.com to create their positive online reputation:

- **Lay a Strong Foundation First:** It is advised that instead of waiting for any negative review to appear first and then using the resources to rectify, it is better to setup a strong positive environment beforehand as it also helps in neutralizing the false reviews before they turn into anything damaging.

- **Claim All Online Properties:** It is then advised by the website that it is always wise for someone to claim all his online properties even if it is currently of no use to them. This act prevents fraudulent and mischievous entities from misusing these accounts for creating negative reviews.
- **Register Domains:** The first and most important step for anyone who is worried about his or his brand is to register all relevant domains on his name; as if someone else got it done then it is very costly at times to buy it back.
- **Make use of your Accounts:** Having an official account gives a responsibility of handling that account on regular basis. It is important to connect with the followers/consumers so as to satisfy their queries and concerns. This also strengthens the protective shield against any future negative reviews and negative publicity.
- **Link Positive Online Results:** One may also link any positive news/article that has been published in his favor with his online accounts. This not only helps in improving the overall image but it also indirectly directs the search engines to improve the ranking of their search results.
- **Press Release and Conversations:** It is also advised through the websites to hold regular conversations with the followers or people in general to help improve the relationship and also to use press releases on regular basis to push some positive reviews in the market.

Besides the above steps to create positive online reputation, certain other measures can be taken such as sharing photos and discussing initiatives and future plans. All these little things somehow help one to connect with people. It is also advised to link all these platforms if possible so as to provide simultaneous updates and greater reach with the audience.

There are also some ways available through which one can repair his/brand's dented online reputation:

- **Removing Online Content:** If an online content is posing any trouble, it is only wise to take it off. It is easy however when it is self-posted but in case it has been posted by someone else, one may always request the concerned person personally to take the content off the website/online platform. Even if the persuasion does not work, there are ways to push down the content lower in the search results by posting rather positive reviews on the matter from multiple platforms.
- **Picking up a Unique Name:** Sometimes bad reputation is earned simply because of a common name that can be misunderstood for a criminal or devious person. It is hence advisable to always choose a unique name for online presence. This name should be such that clearly denotes that it is an official handle for you.

For maintaining a good positive reputation online, there are some simple rules that may be followed such as never post something private online, don't pass any angry comments to someone online, use strong and difficult passwords especially if you are using public systems for your online activities and simply think twice before posting online etc. Though these rules seem simple and basic these are essential, when it comes to maintaining a healthy positive online reputation and hence must be followed at any cost.

ETHICAL CONCERNS

Sometimes it has been found that in pursuit of leaving a positive footprint on the mind of readers/viewers an individual/ organization may float certain falsified information on the web, which may help with building up of his/its reputation but certainly fell down on the ethical grounds. There have also been incidents when organizations hire some bloggers to write positive reviews for their brands. But what is most disturbing is organizations/individuals to ask/bribe/threat bloggers/individuals to take down negative contents from their online platforms (Krazit, 2011). However, this act sometimes proves costly to these firms/individuals especially if their intention to hide negative reviews is exposed to public. Also it has been found that in order to create a positive vibe for a particular person or brand sometimes the owner itself make dozens of fake profiles and start spamming supportive contents on different blogs and social networks. This helps them to push down the negative SERP a little down while claiming untested positive contents (Copland, 2007). Now the important thing here is how often these spams are identified? For a normal reader like me and you, this seems like a true content and we believe what we read or see online. These things certainly alter our perception towards certain celebrities, products and persons. On ethical grounds however, we are definitely got cheated by them. MacDonald (2013) in his online article on ethics and business practices revealed that a common perception within business community is that acting ethically is only limited to the extent that it no longer affects their profitability. This clearly shows the low level of commitment of business entities towards ethical online practices. A part of this can be blamed to stiff competition and fake negative reviews thrown to them but mostly it is the weak will power of these organizations to practice fair. Although many organizations try to avoid or discard any negative situation that has been put forward to them, there have been instances in history where practicing ethics have helped an organization to not only protect their reputation rather to further cement it strongly. One such example is of Maple Leaf Foods. In year 2008, Maple Leaf Foods of Canada was alleged for a food contamination case in which 20 people lost their life and several people found to be seriously ill. The company also suffered huge financial loses. Normally, companies deny their involvement in any such mishaps but instead Maple Leaf Foods decided to take full responsibility for the same. The company apologized to the patients, their families and other citizens of Canada. Surprisingly, instead of venting their anger on company, the customers and citizens of Canada were moved by this act and in no time, they forgave the company and embraced their products again. This strategic move actually helped the Maple Leaf Foods to sustain and regain their lost reputation (Greenberg & Elliot, 2009).

In summary, the online reputation management at present doesn't have any clear boundaries so as to ensure the ethical climate in the practice. There have been reported incidents of posting fake negative reviews to boost self-reputation and hampering others, making of fake blogs in order to push down unwanted SERPs, paying others (third party) to post positive reviews on brands and individuals and adding malicious contents on other product/people post. It would be wrong to say that there have been no attempts all together to bring in any sense of moral responsibility in this industry.

In order to bring in the ethical climate in this area the Online Reputation Management Association has been running a certification program but it is still not very popular (Tozzi, 2008). To help out individuals and organizations to sustain their good name in online galleries, Google in year 2011 also took an initiative by introducing a toolset that helps with the monitoring of their concerned online contents and help them with the removal of unwanted content. There is a strong need for a global body that can monitor and regulate the online reputation management practices and ensure that no one is unnecessary benefited or harmed from the same.

CONCLUSION

Ever since the organizations have transcended the geographical boundaries, the competition within as well outside the industries has increased many folds. It becomes inevitable for firms to engage in some sort of deliberate efforts to leave a positive imprint on the mind of its potential or existing consumers failing which they may lose their market share. This deliberate effort is linked to the cementation of their Reputation. Reputation is generally measured in the terms of good or bad reputation. In recent times not only the big organizations but also individuals and job seekers are becoming increasingly concerned about their reputation. Reputation of an organization plays an important role in its success or downfall and hence major companies throughout the world employ professionals to manage their reputation in the market. Reputation Management can be defined as the holistic exercise concerning the careful monitoring of an Individual or Corporate's (and its brands) reputation, addressing issues and incidents which are negatively influencing it, generating routine mass feedback on their client's reputation and prompting early warning signals to any potential reputation related problems.

With the advent of internet and World Wide Web, the war for building and destroying reputation has reached a whole new level. Concept of digital footprints has revolutionized the world. There is so much of data available on the net concerning a person or brand that it is literally impossible for someone to completely erase their footprints from the web. This online presence is known by the term digital foot print. There have been instances when a third person creates these footprints and in that case, it is known as passive digital footprints. So even if someone restricts or withholds any information about him from the world, there will always be someone to put it online, which makes it impossible for one to hide anything from digital world. When we search for any brand or person on Google or any other search engine, various links are displayed. These links are known as Search Engine Results Page (SERP). For sustaining a good online reputation management, the companies and individuals focus on pushing down negative SERPs to subsequent pages and keeping the positive SERP on first couple of pages. This is due to this specific reason companies today have separate budget for maintaining their good ranking within SERP listing of various leading search engines. Some companies also pay exclusively for a particular position in SERP list so as to increase the probability of the person searching for the desired product to have a look on their website for at least once.

Besides the search engines such as Google and Bing, there are various other online platforms available for maintaining and improvising the reputation of an organization or individual such as Weblogs, Microblogs, Folksonomies, Wikis and Social Networking Sites (SNS) such as Facebook, Google+ etc. Weblogs are online platforms through which a person can share a personal message or opinions with people. In online reputation management these Weblogs act as excellent platform for building a good rapport for brands and individuals. Author can furnish the several positive features of product or individual and answers the concerns of general public in detailed manner. Organizations even reach out their potential customers with the help of their corporate blogs and sometimes even make use of media to reach out their customers (Peters, 2011). Microblogs are confined to few members of a personal social network like followers and friends. This platform is exclusively used as a passive source of information on individuals or organizations. This passive information can be added on microblogs by the individuals and at times also by the organizations regarding their products and services. Folksonomies is a platform where several users tag their experience/opinions regarding a particular product or person at one place. These experience/opinions then act as reference for organizations/concerned individuals to gather the details on their current market reputation and then they can act accordingly. Folksonomies are important to reputation management as they act as a more specific source of information than any other traditional search engines. Wikis such as Wikipedia is considered as an excellent source of information for anything or anyone. One of the best features of Wikis is that it is easily editable and hence the individual or organizational members can themselves edit and enhance the content of related Wiki to bring forth the concerned best feature or positive attributes. The numbers of users on Social Networking Sites (SNS) are increasing exponentially day by day. What took Radio 38 years to reach 50 million people only took a little more than month for Facebook to reach (McKinsey & Company, 2012). Users of social networking sites interact with each other despite the language and geographical barriers that exist between them and news travel faster between them than ever before. Contents on social networking sites are an important medium to moderate the reputation for any individual and business. Some of the famous and most popular social networks today are Facebook, Google+, LinkedIn, Research Gate, MySpace, and YouTube etc. These SNSs have got millions of active users who possess power to make or break reputation of individuals/brands in matter of minutes.

Experts suggest certain rules to maintain and sustain a good online reputation for a brand or individual. These rules can be summarized in certain points such as never post something private online, don't pass any angry comments to someone online, use strong and difficult passwords especially if you are using public systems for your online activities and simply think twice before posting online etc. These rules ensure maintenance of a healthy and positive online reputation of a person or an organization. To repair a dented online reputation, one can remove the malicious content by requesting the platform administrator or push down the negative SERPs from the search engines. One may also try using some unique names for posting online contents as sometimes the common usernames create confusion in the mind of the readers and they misjudge and assume negative reputation for certain people and products.

The online reputation management at present doesn't have any clear boundaries so as to ensure the ethical climate in the practice. There have been reported incidents of posting fake negative reviews to boost self-reputation and hampering others, making of fake blogs in order to push down unwanted SERPs, paying others (third party) to post positive reviews on brands and individuals and adding malicious contents on other product/people post. There is strong need for a global body that can monitor and regulate the online reputation management practices and ensure that no one is unnecessary benefited or harmed from the same.

REFERENCES

Argenti, P. A., & Druckenmiller, B. (2004). Reputation and the corporate brand. *Corporate Reputation Review*, *6*(4), 368–374. doi:10.1057/palgrave.crr.1540005

Caruana, A., & Chircop, S. (2000). Measuring corporate reputation: A case example. *Corporate Reputation Review*, *3*(1), 43–57. doi:10.1057/palgrave.crr.1540098

Copeland, J. (2007). The ethics of reputation management (or, "getting stuff deleted from Google"). *Moz.com.* Retrieved from http://moz.com/blog/reputation-management

Cutlip, S., Center, A., & Broom, G. (2000). *Effective Public Relations*. New Jersey: Prentice Hall.

Firestein, P. J. (2006). Building and protecting corporate reputation. *Strategy and Leadership*, *34*(4), 25–31. doi:10.1108/10878570610676864

Gantz, J., & Reinsel, D. (2009). As the Economy Contracts, the Digital Universe Expands, IDC. Retrieved from http://idcdocserv.com/EMC_MMWP_Digital_Universe

Gardberg, N. A., & Fombrun, C. J. (2002). For better or worse – the most visible American corporate reputations. *Corporate Reputation Review*, *4*(4), 385–391. doi:10.1057/palgrave.crr.1540159

Greenberg, J., & Elliott, C. (2009). A cold cut crisis: Listeriosis, Maple Leaf Foods and the politics of apology. *Canadian Journal of Communication*, *34*(1), 189–204.

Haythornthwaite, C. (2005). Social networks and Internet connectivity effects. *Information, Communication, & Society*. *PubMed*, *8*(2), 125–147.

Kandampully, J., & Hu, H. H. (2007). Do hoteliers need to manage image to retain loyal customers? *International Journal of Contemporary Hospitality Management*, *19*(6), 435–443. doi:10.1108/09596110710775101

Kim, S., Haley, E., & Koo, G. Y. (2009). Comparison of the paths from consumer involvement types to ad responses between corporate advertising and product advertising. *Journal of Advertising*, *38*(3), 67–80. doi:10.2753/JOA0091-3367380305

Krazit, T. (2011). A primer on online reputation management. *Cnet.com*. Retrieved from http://news.cnet.com/8301-30684_3-20028997-265.html

MacDonald, C. (2013) Ethics and online reputation management. *CSR news.net*. Retrieved from http://csr-news.net/main/2013/08/29/ethics-and-online-reputation-management/

Madden, M., Fox, S., Smith, A., & Vitak, J. (2007). Digital Footprints. *Pew Internet & American Life Project*. Retrieved from http://www.pewinternet.org/Reports/2007/Digital-Footprints/1-Summary-of-Findings.aspx?r=1

Turning buzz into gold: How pioneers create value from social media. (2012). McKinsey & Company. Retrieved from https://www.mckinsey.com/~/media/.../Turning_buzz_into_gold.ashx

Melewar, T. C. (2008). *Facets of corporate identity, communication and reputation*. New York: Routledge. doi:10.4324/9780203931943

Merrit, J. (2015). The ultimate guide to ORM. *ReputationManagement.com*. Retrieved from https://www.reputationmanagement.com/

Murray, K., & White, J. (2004). *CEO Views on reputation management*. London: Chimes Communications.

Peters, P. (2011). *Reputations Management in Social Web*. Norderstedt: Social Media Verlag.

Plowman, K. D., Briggs, W. G., & Huang, Y. H. (2001). In R. L. Heath (Ed.), *Handbook of Public Relations* (pp. 301–310). California: Sage Publications. doi:10.4135/9781452220727.n23

Portmann, E., & Hutter, R. (2011). Blogosphäre –soziale Netzwerkeals Trendsetter. *HMD Praxis Der Wirtschaftsinformatik*, *48*(4), 37–48. doi:10.1007/BF03340604

Schultz, M., Moritsen, J., & Gabrielsen, G. (2006). Sticky reputation: Analyzing a ranking system. *Corporate Reputation Review*, *4*(1), 24–41. doi:10.1057/palgrave.crr.1540130

Stegbauer, C. (2009). *Wikipedia: Das Ratsel der Kooperation*. Wiesbaden: VS. doi:10.1007/978-3-531-91691-0

Tozzi, J. (2008). Do reputation management services work? *Businessweek.com*. Retrieved from http://www.businessweek.com/stories/2008-04-30/do-reputation-management-services-work-businessweek-business-news-stock-market-and-financial-advice

Van Riel, C. B. M., & Berens, G. (2001). Balancing corporate branding policies in multi business companies. In P. J. Kitchen & D. E. Schultz (Eds.), *Raising the corporate umbrella: corporate communications in the 21st century*. Basingstoke: Palgrave.

Walker, K. (2010). A systematic review of the corporate reputation literature: Definition, measurement, and theory. *Corporate Reputation Review*, *12*(4), 357–387. doi:10.1057/crr.2009.26

KEY TERMS AND DEFINITIONS

Digital Footprint: It refers to the data that is left behind by users on online platforms.

ORM: It is the practice of relationship management on various online platforms.

Public Relations: It is the practice of managing information spread between an individual or an organization.

Reputation: It is a widespread belief that someone or something possesses a particular characteristic.

Reputation Management: It is a process of influencing and/or controlling an individual's or business's reputation.

SERP: Search Engine Research Page are links that are provided on a search engine during a query.

Social Network: It is a social structure that is made up of a set of social actors (individuals/organizations) and a set of the dyadic ties between these actors.

Section 2

Role of Social Media in Brand Management

Chapter 5
Role of Social Media in Brand Promotion:
An International Marketing Perspective

Kijpokin Kasemsap
Suan Sunandha Rajabhat University, Thailand

ABSTRACT

This chapter aims to promote brand management through social media in global marketing, thus explaining the theoretical and practical overview of social media, evolving dynamics of brand management, shifts in global marketing dynamics, and brand promotion through social media in global marketing. Social media is a great way to reach a new group of targeted consumers. Social media is utilized as a marketing tool by marketers in creating brand relationship. The integration of social media and brand management is necessary for modern organizations that seek to serve suppliers and customers, increase business performance, strengthen competitiveness, and achieve continuous success in global marketing. The chapter argues that promoting brand management through social media in global marketing has the potential to enhance organizational performance and reach strategic goals in the social media age.

INTRODUCTION

The emergence of social media has facilitated the consumer's communication in global marketing (Abzari, Ghassemi, & Vosta, 2014). Social media activities generated by consumers in brand communities are claimed to have a potential impact on interaction among brand entities and brand building (Luo, Zhang, & Liu, 2015). Online platforms and social networks directly influence the consumer-brand relationship (Enginkaya & Yılmaz, 2014). Companies create the official fan pages on social networking sites such as Facebook, Twitter, and LinkedIn to provide customers with information about their brands, products, and promotions (Zadeh & Sharda, 2014). The purpose of a brand website is to create a positive brand experience for customers (Culache & Obadă, 2014).

Understanding how brands operate on social media is very important for contemporary marketing, researchers, and brand managers (Habibi, Laroche, & Richard, 2014). Gensler et al. (2013) stated that

DOI: 10.4018/978-1-5225-0332-3.ch005

the dynamic, ubiquitous, and real-time interaction enabled by social media significantly changes the landscape for brand management. Eisingerich et al. (2015) stated that Facebook is a global phenomenon. Social networking sites have become some of the primary sources of communication for people to find people in their network and brands (Bright, Kleiser, & Grau, 2015). Building and leveraging the brand community on social networking sites is one of the popular social media strategies that companies employ to build a consumer-brand relationship (Park & Kim, 2014).

The strength of this chapter is on the thorough literature consolidation of social media and brand management. The extant literature of social media and brand management provides a contribution to practitioners and researchers by describing the multifaceted applications of social media and brand management to appeal to the different segments of social media and brand management in order to maximize the business impact of social media and brand management in global marketing.

BACKGROUND

Advances in information and communications technology (ICT) has brought new challenges and opportunities to the relationship marketing, in which brand communities has received the attention from researchers and businesses (Hudson, Roth, Madden, & Hudson, 2015). Social media based on information technology (IT) enables the combination of competences, capabilities, and knowledge that underpin value co-creation in dynamic relationships with their partners (Srivastava & Gnyawali, 2011). It is essential to understand the ways in which brands can preserve the one-to-one characteristics and intimate relationship qualities offered by social media is essential (Labrecque, 2014).

Marketing the brands through social media becomes the precise, personal, interesting, interactive, and social perspectives (Jothi, Neelamalar, & Prasad, 2011). Sukoco and Wu (2010) indicated two main motivations for customers to join a brand community (i.e., self-related motivation and social-related motivation). Self-related motivation refers to members' interest to experience enjoyment, gain knowledge regarding a brand, and maintain their self-esteem. Social-related motivation refers to members' interest to join brand communities to have some affiliation with other members and acquire social status to maintain their collective self-esteem. Through social networks, consumers are entrenched in the dissemination of information. Consumers are brands' storytellers and the new brand ambassadors (Booth & Matic, 2011).

The rise of social media in organizational settings has initiated the new horizons for strategic communication (Zerfass & Schramm, 2014). Social media is defined as a method of technological innovations in terms of both hardware and software that facilitate the inexpensive content creation, interaction, and interoperability by online users (Berthon, Pitt, Plangger, & Shapiro, 2012). Social media is considered as consumer-generated media that covers a variety of new sources of online information used by consumers, who are intent on sharing information with others (Blackshaw & Nazzaro, 2004). Malthouse et al. (2013) stated that the rise of social media is challenging the traditional notion of customer relationship management.

Due to its popularity and widespread use, social media is recognized as a new platform, which can be used as a competitive marketing tool by business firms (Hassan, Nadzim, & Shiratuddin, 2015). The development of social media shapes people's connections with others via the different social media platforms (Colliander & Dahlén, 2011). Social media involves the social communication and builds reputations (Tang, Gu, & Whinston, 2012). Social media enables the broad communication and the collaboration (Li & Bernoff, 2009). Social media can facilitate organizations to tap into the collective intelligence, creativity, and the passion of employees and customers for business decision (Bradley & McDonald, 2011).

ROLE OF SOCIAL MEDIA IN BRAND PROMOTION: AN INTERNATIONAL MARKETING PERSPECTIVE

This section explains the theoretical and practical overview of social media, evolving dynamics of brand management, shifts in global marketing dynamics, and brand promotion through social media in global marketing.

Social Media: A Value Proposition in Brand Management

Social media has attracted much attention in the industry and education sectors (Ngai, Tao, & Moon, 2015). Weinberg et al. (2013) indicated that social media applications transform the ways that companies execute many processes such as product development, marketing, sales, customer service, staffing, and change management. Social media can be utilized for a variety of relevant purposes such as creating conversations and access to information and knowledge (e.g. online communities and blogs), managing content that reflects the organizational beliefs and values (e.g. wikis), and sharing market information (e.g. social media command centers) (Weinberg et al., 2013). Social media can itemize hierarchies and create business opportunities for people to contribute (Qureshi & Zigurs, 2001).

Social media is viewed as a group of Internet-based applications that build on the ideological and technological foundations of the Web 2.0 technological essence, and allow the exchange of user generated content (Kaplan & Haenlein, 2010). Social media is the product of Internet-based applications that build on the technological foundations of the Web 2.0 (Parveen, Jaafar, & Ainin, 2015). The Web 2.0 is a platform in which software and content are developed by different participants in a collaborative manner (Laroche, Habibi, Richard, & Sankaranarayanan, 2012). Berthon et al. (2012) stated that the Web 2.0 technologies have three effects (i.e. a shift in the locus of activity from the desktop to the website, a shift in the locus of value production from the firm to the consumer, and a shift in the locus of power away from the firm to the consumer).

Social media is a platform that facilitates information sharing and participation from users of the media in order to create and distribute the content (Steenkamp & Hyde-Clarke, 2014). Social media platforms have shifted the emphasis of the Internet services from being consumption-based toward becoming more interactive and collaborative, thus creating new online opportunities for interaction between organizations and the public (Henderson & Bowley, 2010). Distinct from the traditional forms of media, social media involves both web-based and mobile technologies (Mou, Atkin, Fu, Lin, & Lau, 2013). Organizations should consider using social media because of the changing trends among consumers (Parveen et al., 2015). It allows individuals to be visible to others toward establishing connections with others (Kasemsap, 2014a). Social media enables the development of knowledge value chain to customize the useful information for a technological business growth (Kasemsap, 2014b).

Social media takes a variety of forms, including weblogs, social blogs, microblogging, wikis, podcasts, pictures, video, rating, and social bookmarking (Kim & Ko, 2012). It includes the new sources of online information (e.g., social networking sites, blogs, chat rooms, rating websites, photo sharing websites, and podcasts), which are used for educating customers about issues related to products and brands (Mangold & Faulds, 2009). Mangold and Faulds (2009) stated that marketing managers should recognize the power and critical nature of the discussions executed by consumers using social media. Professional public relations often organize events as part of their media relations strategy aimed at attracting media attention and gaining publicity to communicate the organization's message to its public groups (Toledano & Riches, 2014).

Social media refers to technology-facilitated dialog conducted through platforms such as Facebook, Twitter, LinkedIn etc. involving blogs, wikis, content sharing, social networking, and social bookmarking (Reilly & Hynan, 2014). Social media is important for business-to-business (B2B) companies (Shih, 2009). B2B companies can use social media and social networking sites to communicate with their customers and suppliers, build relationships and trust, as well as to identify prospective partners in terms of B2B selling (Shih, 2009). Social media becomes more important as an internet marketing tool given adoption by general public (Michaelidou, Siamagka, & Christodoulides, 2011). Social networking sites are valuable due to the potential to increase demand for products (Moran & Gossieaux, 2010).

The advent of Web 2.0 has created new ways to communicate, collaborate and share content (Enders, Hungenberg, Denker, & Mauch, 2008). The increase in the Web 2.0 has enabled consumers to actively act and react on what companies are doing, without being dependent on the third parties for media access (Cormode & Krishnamurthy, 2008; O'Reilly, 2007). Building on the foundation of the Web 2.0, social media applications have facilitated the remarkable growth in human interaction in modern times (Balakrishnan, Dahnil, & Yi, 2014). There has been an exponential increase in the volume of user generated content available in the social media platforms of the Web 2.0 genre (Callarisa, García, Cardiff, & Roshchina, 2012). The Web 2.0 technological core refers to the mixed technological and media core that allows the instantaneous communication at relatively low cost and utilizes various formats (e.g., text, video, audio, and photos), global reach, and different delivery platforms (Kaplan & Haenlein, 2010; Mangold & Faulds, 2009).

User generated content contains a certain level of creativity (Vickery & Wunsch-Vincent, 2007). User generated content has enabled new opportunities for developing and exchanging knowledge and culture through groups and communities. In brand-related user generated content, consumers pose questions to marketers and respond to companies' questions (Smith, Fischer, & Yongjian, 2012). Social media platform allows the development of new activities and provides the powerful capabilities in a virtual environment (Erdem & Cobanoglu, 2010; Kim & Hardin, 2010; O'Connor, 2010). Social media is a platform that enables the like-minded people to gather in groups, discuss, share information, photos, and videos (Fournier & Avery, 2011; Mangold & Faulds, 2009).

Social media has changed the way people interact with each other and with companies (Hanna, Rohm, & Crittenden, 2011; Kietzmann, Hermkens, McCarthy, & Silvestre, 2011). Social media makes significant contributions to companies in pursuit of consumer engagement, brand awareness, and connectivity (Enginkaya & Yılmaz, 2014). Social media leads consumers to company-generated advertisements in social media (Akar & Topçu, 2011) whereas the real experience of experienced consumer is easily attainable. Social media has altered the ways that people communicate, collaborate, and connect with others. Social media gives marketers a method for direct interaction which constitutes an ideal environment for creating brand community (Scarpi, 2010), establishing relationships, and gaining a better understanding of consumers (Kozinets, 2002).

Social media becomes the center of attention in many industries concerning the advantages of social media in connecting businesses to end-consumers in a timely manner and at a low cost (Kaplan & Haenlein, 2010), by facilitating the various areas of marketing such as promotions, marketing intelligence, sentiment research, public relations, marketing communications, product, and customer management (Akar & Topçu, 2011). People join social networks to fill the needs such as self-presentation, self-expression, and self-esteem (Wilcox & Stephen, 2013; Yeo, 2012). Facebook has over one billion active users (Habibi et al., 2014). The unique aspects of social media and its immense popularity have revolutionized the marketing practices (Hanna et al., 2011) and consumer behavior from information acquisition to the post-purchase behavior (Mangold & Faulds, 2009; Powers, Advincula, Austin, & Graiko, 2012).

Companies have embraced social media because of its potential for engagement and collaboration with consumers (Hudson et al., 2015). Managers can leverage social media by shaping consumer discussions (Kaplan & Haenlein, 2010; Mangold & Faulds, 2009), and others have offered strategies for measuring the success of social media marketing campaigns (Hoffman & Fodor, 2010). Through social media platforms, consumers' activities regarding innovation and interactions within a community become more effective (Lee, Kim, & Kim, 2012; Lee, Xiong, & Hu, 2012).

Evolving Dynamics of Brand Management

Consumers form relationships with brands is documented in the marketing literature (Aggarwal & Zhang, 2006; Foo, Douglas, & Jack, 2008; Johnson & Grimm, 2010). With any brand, the goal of brand management is to attract customers to ensure brand and product success (Zavattaro, Daspit, & Adams, 2015). Managing brands is about keeping the brand performance alive (Singh & Sonnenburg, 2012). A determinant of brand success is brand equity evaluated from a consumer perspective toward evaluating an individual's willingness to pay a premium price for a branded product over a non-branded alternative (Gartner & Ruzzier, 2011). Product design is an integral component of a brand and an important driver of brand equity (Kumar, Townsend, & Vorhies, 2015).

Consumer-based brand equity is evaluated in four dimensions (e.g., brand awareness, brand associations, perceived brand quality, and brand loyalty) (Buil, Martinez, & de Chernatony, 2013). Brands can be differentiated according to their physical attributes (Kohli, Suri, & Kapoor, 2015). Brands get reinforced through creating participation and allowing external audiences to identify with them (Yan, 2011). Brand appears in marketing literature as a powerful tool of differentiation for products and companies (Clifton, 2003). Brand consumption is implemented in a collective context in which consumption value is a social process of stakeholder interactions (Merz, He, & Vargo, 2009). Brand consumption becomes the social co-production of shared meanings (de Chernatony & Segal-Horn, 2001; Tuominen, 2007).

Establishing a good brand relationship is vital for brand management in emerging markets (Kasemsap, 2014c). Customer value and customer satisfaction can facilitate a higher degree of brand loyalty in modern organizations (Kasemsap, 2014d). Social media has the opportunity to capitalize on brand image transferability, which enables marketers to build the brand with larger audiences than ever before (Kasemsap, 2015a). To be the successful global retailers, the ability to adjust the retail marketing mix elements and retail brand strategy regarding specific target-market conditions, is practically crucial in retail settings (Kasemsap, 2015b).

From a cultural perspective, brand orientation is defined as a certain type of corporate culture (Schmidt & Baumgarth, 2015). Examples of brand-oriented behaviors are corporate identity and corporate design (van Riel & Balmer, 1997), integrated marketing communication (Ewing & Napoli, 2005), the measurement of brand equity (Keller, 2008), the impact of brand orientation on managerial practice (Hankinson, 2002), and employer branding (Barrow & Mosley, 2005). A brand community is a non-geographically bound community based on a structured set of social relationships among brand admirers (Muniz & O'Guinn, 2001) providing an effective process for establishing the long-term bonds between consumers and brands (Thompson & Sinha, 2008). The consumer-centric, relational, and co-creative practices are increasingly described as the foundation of good ties between consumers and communities (McAlexander, Schouten, & Koenig, 2002).

Marketing scholars invest the considerable effort to understand the various practices' roles in the process of harmonious relationships within brand community (Nuttavuthisit, 2010; Schouten, McAlexander, & Koenig, 2007). Brand communities and events can set the stage for members and other brand-related elements to involve a high context communication through which consumption experiences, brand stories, their symbolic interpretations, and other valuable resources are shared among members (Habibi et al., 2014). This perspective leads to strengthen the bonds among members, co-create value, provide higher participation, and enhance brand loyalty (Schau, Muñiz, & Arnould, 2009; Zhou, Zhang, Su, & Zhou, 2012).

According to social capital theory (Coleman, 1988), brand community is a potential form of social network through which consumers realize social capital. Sharing information and resources is the essence of brand communities (Muniz & O'Guinn, 2001) and consumers derive the hedonic and utilitarian values through participating in brand community events (McAlexander et al., 2002). Brand community provides many benefits for the brand and marketers such as sharing information and keeping in touch with the highly devoted consumers (Andersen, 2005), integrating consumers into the brand identity (Andersen, 2005; McAlexander et al., 2002), obtaining the valuable market research from consumers for innovation (von Hippel, 2005), and co-creating the value with consumers (Schau et al., 2009). Regarding brand management, co-creating with consumers can be a strategic method to positively influence the product perceptions and the behavioral intentions (van Dijk, Antonides, & Schillewaert, 2014).

Muniz and O'Guinn (2001) stated that brand communities encompass three perspectives of traditional community (i.e., shared consciousness, shared rituals and traditions, and shared obligations to society). Shared consciousness refers to the intrinsic feelings of connectedness among group members and manifests itself through processes as oppositional brand loyalty (Kuo & Feng, 2013; Muniz & O'Guinn, 2001), and in-group/out-group differentiation (Algesheimer, Dholakia, & Herrmann, 2005). Shared rituals and traditions are the symbolic ways of communication that perpetuate the cultural norms of the community and transfer them to members and those outside of the community. Shared rituals and traditions help build and preserve community identity (Muniz & O'Guinn, 2001) and manifest themselves in a celebration of brand history toward sharing the brand-related stories and using a specific jargon within the community (Casaló, Flavian, & Guinaliu, 2010). Shared obligations to society are a felt sense of duty and obligations to the community and its members (Muniz & O'Guinn, 2001).

Brand community is a group of consumers with a shared enthusiasm for a social identity with members who jointly engage in the group action to achieve the collective goals and express the mutual commitment (Bagozzi & Dholakia, 2006). Due to the characteristics of brand community based on social media (e.g., no time constraint, non-geographically bound, high information transparency, and multi-party communication), it is an important platform for placing a variety of value co-creation practices, where consumers can easily share the consumption experiences and interact with each other (Muniz & Schau, 2005).

In brand communities, consumers are self-motivated and enthusiastic in exchanging, sharing and debating ideas, and contribute to the improvement of products and services, which play an important role in developing the consumer-brand loyalty via the relational marketing (Anderson & Weitz, 1992). The social relationships built within a brand community can create the consumer exit barriers and maintain the longevity of consumer loyalty (Algesheimer et al., 2005; McAlexander et al., 2002). Value co-creation practices strengthen the interaction among the members of a brand community which helps bring members closer and increase the member's affective connection to the brand (Carlson, Suter, & Brown, 2008; Zaglia, 2013).

A brand community is defined in terms of the relationships in which the consumers situated, including relationships between the consumer and the brand, and among fellow consumers (Muniz & O'Guinn, 2001). Building and enhancing brand communities and consumer experiences within the context of brand community play a significant role in making consumers loyal to the brand (Brodie, Ilic, Juric, & Hollebeek, 2013; Jang, Olfman, Ko, Koh, & Kim, 2008). Consumers establish enduring relationships with the elements of brand community and draw values from the long-term interactions through value co-creation practices, which make them to trust and love the brand (Stokburger-Sauer, 2010; Zhou et al., 2012).

B2B branding increases the buyers' satisfaction with their purchase decision (Low & Blois, 2002; Michell, King, & Reast, 2001) and reduces their level of perceived risk and uncertainty (Bengtsson & Servais, 2005; Mudambi, 2002; Ohnemus, 2009). A strong B2B brand results in the enhanced quality perceptions in the market (Cretu & Brodie, 2007) and allows organizations to transfer brand equity in other categories through extensions (Hutton, 1997). A strong B2B brand raises the barriers to entry for competitive brands, leads to higher demand, and allows companies to command a premium price. In the distribution channel, a strong B2B brand increases the company's negotiating power, and promotes opportunities for licensing (Low & Blois, 2002; Ohnemus, 2009).

Building and maintaining brand loyalty are one of the central themes of research for marketers for a very long time (Bennett & Rundle-Thiele, 2002; Chaudhuri & Halbrook, 2001). Brand loyalty can be conceptualized as the final dimension of consumer brand resonance symbolizing the consumer's ultimate relationship and the level of identification with a brand (Keller, 2008). Brand loyalty brings sales revenues, market share, profitability to the firms, and help them grow or at least maintain themselves in the marketplace (Aaker, 1991, Kapferer, 1997; Keller, 2008). Marketers have utilized the various methods to maintain the brand loyalty of their customers, including brand elements, classical marketing mix variables, and the new methods of marketing (e.g., events, sponsorships, one-to-one marketing activities, Internet marketing, and social media marketing) (Keller, 2008; Kotler & Keller, 2007).

Shifts in Global Marketing Dynamics

In this highly competitive century, social media offers both opportunities and challenges (Shih, Lin, & Luarn, 2014). With social networking sites, business organizations are able to showcase their brands to consumers and also to communicate with them (Reyneke, Pitt, & Berthon, 2011). Consumers can help firms generate new business and promote brand through tweeting and blogging (Hassan et al., 2015). Brands conducting social media interactions with consumers are essential in global marketing (Dholakia & Durham, 2010). The likelihood for individuals to buy products normally increases after they follow a brand via social media (Cruz & Mendelsohn, 2010). A positive experience from direct brand interaction through social media will lead to repeat purchases and recommendations (Cruz & Mendelsohn, 2010).

Consumers are motivated to generate and broadcast online content primarily for intrinsic reasons such as the enjoyment that the act of creating something provides, promoting themselves to attract attention and initiate conversation, or to influence others (Berthon, Pitt, & Campbell, 2008). In social media settings, a brand can encourage the consumers' participation by initiating conversation through seeding (Schau et al., 2009), provoking (Deighton & Kornfeld, 2009), engaging, and providing a platform for conversations, which is exemplified by Dove's Real Beauty campaign. Dove evolved from a product-focused brand to a brand that told a story to a brand that co-created a story with consumers.

The initiation of Dove's co-created performance in social media was Dove's posting "The Evolution Spot" in October 2006 on YouTube (seeding). The spot showed a normal looking woman being transformed into the stereotype of a beautiful woman, driving home the point that the idea of beauty created by the beauty industry was not real (provoking). Within three months, this spot had been viewed three million times (Deighton, 2008) which encouraged Dove to take the campaign to its own Internet website, inviting women to discuss beauty and share their views with women around the world (engaging and providing a platform). The initiative received an overwhelming response from women.

Social media provided Dove with multiple touch points (e.g., YouTube, company websites, blogs, and Facebook), allowing the brand owner to give the different forms of extrinsic motives for the consumer to participate in conversations (Singh & Sonnenburg, 2012). Conversations in social media were generated where none would have taken place naturally otherwise (Godes & Mayzlin, 2009). Because people think in terms of events or series of events (narratively) rather than in terms of the validity of an idea (argumentatively), they express themselves with stories (Weick, 1995). The consumers' stories, combined with the brand owner's story, co-created the Dove brand performance (Singh & Sonnenburg, 2012).

Starbucks is an international coffee house chain founded in Seattle, Washington, in 1971. Starbucks, as one of the top ten most followed brands on Twitter, uses tweets to share knowledge with customers and promote their latest products, campaigns, and events (Chua & Banerjee, 2013). With an average of ten tweets per day on Twitter, Starbucks extracts relevant knowledge from a network of current and prospective customers who express their expectations about the brand (Chua & Banerjee, 2013).

The development of social media challenges the ways that marketing academicians and practitioners conceptualize and manage brands. Social media has a major impact on business (Corstjens & Umblijs, 2012; Sands, Harper, & Ferraro, 2011), thus transforming consumer behavior, relationships, and traditional brand practice (Kaplan & Haenlein, 2010). Consumers possess the extensive opportunities to engage with brands (Christodoulides, Jevons, & Bonhomme, 2012; Helm & Jones, 2010). The results of the increased brand access practically mandate the changes in branding strategies in the social media platforms (Naylor, Lamberton, & West, 2012).

With the advent of social media, consumers are more exposed to the brand's pages, comments, and marketers, which facilities communication, information dissemination, and the capability of members to be in touch with each other in brand community (Hudson et al., 2015). The platform of social network provides the favorable condition to execute value co-creation practices (e.g., social networking, community engagement, impression management, and brand use) and bring members and other elements of a brand community to a high-context interaction, which strengthens the triangular relationships of consumer-brand-other consumers within brand community (Muniz & O'Guinn, 2001).

The most prevalent motives for companies to use social media are to enhance trustworthiness, brand attitude, and customer commitment (van Noort & Willemsen, 2011; Weinberg & Pehlivan, 2011). As social media is acquiring greater importance for global marketing and advertising via internet and social networking sites, understanding the dynamics of users' relationship formation with the social media-related brands becomes imperative for managers and scholars (Pentina, Zhang, & Basmanova, 2013). Social networking sites containing the user generated comments can affect the creation of brand, providing companies with the greater effectiveness in the communication process for their products and services, as well as with the greater awareness in brand loyalty, perceived quality, and brand associations (Wang, Hsu, Hsu, & Hsieh, 2011; Xiang & Gretzel, 2010).

Social media serves as a marketing communications tool that facilitates organizational activities among peers, customers, business partners, and organizations in terms of collaborative product development (Mangold & Faulds, 2009; Porter & Donthu, 2008), the creation of knowledge-sharing communities (Fernando, 2010; Kasavana, Nusair, & Teodosic, 2010; Yates & Paquette, 2011), the implementation of corporate dialog at the financial institutions (Bonsón & Flores, 2011), marketing strategies for brand management (Jin, 2012; Laroche, Habibi, & Richard, 2013), and collaborative learning (Peppler & Solomou, 2011). In a quest for connecting with customers, brands promote developing communities to interact with consumers (Baldus, Voorhees, & Calantone, 2015). Social media has intensified the personal interaction between the brand and its community (Nambisan & Watt, 2011).

Social media introduces the direct-to-consumer processes and creates the new distribution channels, which affect the brand promotion and bridge the gap between organizations and consumers and among consumers (Hyde, 2008; Pan & Li, 2011). Using social media as the marketing communications tool can be effective if the organization behind the social media page (e.g., the organization's Facebook page and Twitter account) is comfortable with social media and understands it (Eagleman, 2013). The networked nature of social media allows the like-minded people to gather in groups and subgroups with a common interest (Mangold & Faulds, 2009). There are many groups in social media that are centered on a certain brand (Habibi et al., 2014). The rise of social media challenges the way that firms manage their brands (Gensler et al., 2013).

Consumers have shifted their information seeking behavior with regard to products and services from offline sources to electronic word of mouth (eWOM) sources such as social networking sites (Gruen, Osmonbekov, & Czaplewski, 2006). Social networking sites provide a substantive part of the available eWOM (Dijkmans, Kerkhof, & Beukeboom, 2015). The eWOM facilitates information sharing without face-to-face interaction (Sun, Youn, Wu, & Kuntaraporn, 2006). Marketing communications have a positive influence on brand equity, brand loyalty, brand awareness, and brand value (Yoo, Donthu, & Lee, 2000).

Brand Promotion through Social Media in Global Marketing

Businesses can promote products and services, provide instant support, and create an online community of brand enthusiasts through all forms of social media such as social networking sites, content communities, virtual worlds, blogs, microblogging sites, online gaming sites, social bookmarking, news sites, and forums (Weinberg, 2009; Zarella, 2010). Social media enables consumers to share information with their peers about the product and service brands (Mangold & Faulds, 2009). Social media helps firms build brand loyalty through social networking sites, conversation, and community building (McKee, 2010). Consumers utilize social networking sites to keep up with the brand's products and the promotional campaigns (Mangold & Faulds, 2009).

Social media brand characteristics appear more important in their impact on a customer's trust in a brand (Christou, 2015). Consumers learn about brands by using blogs and social networks and by letting others know their opinions (Yan, 2011). There is the amplification of reputation with the support of social media over traditional mediums (Barwise & Meehan, 2010). Social media is a space in which customers can find out what people or brands of interest are doing in global marketing (Dong-Hun, 2010). Social media users become the producers of brand content, while companies strengthen their relationships with customers (Crittenden, Hanna, & Rohm, 2011). Because customer satisfaction results from the fulfillment of created expectations, brands on Facebook must take care to quickly answer the fans' questions (Gamboa & Goncalves, 2014).

As major brands have established their communities and fan pages within online social networks and started offering commerce opportunities delivered through social media platforms, crowdsourcing applications have become some of the most engaging tools in digital marketing realm, enabling brands to realize the potential for their fans' input into the product development and the market development processes (Huberman, 2008). Internal crowdsourcing can effectively control the shared collaboration and promote a type of trust associated with an ethic of contribution (Simula & Vuori, 2012). Browsing online social networks promotes the individual's self-esteem (Wilcox & Stephen, 2013). Online platforms empower stakeholders to play an active role in brand meaning co-creation (Vallaster & von Wallpach, 2013). Understanding the fans' behaviors on the online social networks is important to the content providers to enable the enhanced organization of brand-post information and the improved design of effective online communities toward implementing the effective marketing campaigns (Zadeh & Sharda, 2014).

Twitter has received increasing attention as a unique communication tool that facilitates eWOM (Kim, Sung, & Kang, 2014). Twitter is used as a social channel to promote communication and to help companies develop the relationships with consumers (Jansen, Zhang, Sobel, & Chowdury, 2009). Companies frequently utilize interpersonal messages in their Twitter posts in order to develop the relationships with their consumers (Kwon & Sung, 2011; Lin & Pena, 2011). Twitter users follow the exchange relationship norms and evaluate a brand with the exchange relationship-oriented messages more favorably than communal relationship-oriented messages (Li & Li, 2014). Consumers generate the brand-related tweets on Twitter to express their sentiments, complaints, and opinions concerning brands (Jansen et al., 2009). The communicational challenge for marketers is the identification of eWOM as the online influencer (Kunz, Hackworth, Osborne, & High, 2011). The eWOM is a powerful method to select a brand (Casaló et al., 2010). Consumers receive and share information about products and services through digital platforms with other consumers via social networking sites and online comments (Clemons, 2009).

Microblogging platforms have grown to be a highly social technology (Zhang, Benyoucef, & Zhao, 2015). Microblogging platforms can be adopted as a new marketing tool (Culnan, McHugh, & Zubillaga, 2010; Li & Shiu, 2012). Companies can create microblog accounts, also known as brand microblogs, to attract the consumers' attention (Zhang et al., 2015). Examining participation on brand microblogs can help companies recognize how to attract the consumers' attention and to reinforce their influence in social media (Jansen et al., 2009; Zhang, Zhao, Zhang, & Lee, 2014).

Participation in online communities is an increasing concern in the existing literature (Bagozzi & Dholakia, 2006; Fang & Neufeld, 2009; Zhang, Hahn, & De, 2013). Bateman et al. (2010) stated that participation in the online communities involves three aspects of activities (i.e., reading messages, posting replies, and moderating discussions) among community members. The easiness of participating in the online social communities removes both the physical and temporal barriers, thus increasing the likelihood of participation from consumers who may not have been able or inclined to do so previously. The access of social media has moved beyond the fixed physical space of the computer screen to the ubiquitous mobile channel of the smartphone. Instant consumption is activated by brand and conversation-related content from other connected channels of communication (e.g., radio and television) (Davis & Sajtos, 2008).

The combination of both brand community and social media promotes the brand community based on social media, whose distinctive platform for consumers who share the common interests about brands is the main differentiator compared with the traditional brand community (Hudson et al., 2015). Kietzmann et al. (2011) stated that the rapidly growing popularity of social networking sites has provided brand community with a new platform to retain the existing customers and attract the new customers. With the support of social media, brand communities provide the effective venues where marketers can obtain the insight into the consumers' needs, and where the relationship between brand and consumers is established (Kim et al., 2014; McWilliam, 2012).

Social media integrates consumers with their own voice, not as passive respondents in their relationships with brands as in the past (Miller & Lammas, 2010). Consumers' voices are strong to the extent that marketing experts warn brands to focus on brand protection rather than brand building (Fournier & Avery, 2011). Brands, offering identity extensions and seeking visibility over social networks, try to create the interaction and engagement with consumers via their online presence (Enginkaya & Yılmaz, 2014). Brand-post popularity can be defined as a mixture of factors such as vividness, interactivity, the content of the brand post, and the number of times that the brand post is mentioned by fans (de Vries, Gensler, & Leeflang, 2012). Brand-post popularity reflects the number of brand fans toward providing an indication of the brand's recognition on social media (de Vries et al., 2012).

FUTURE RESEARCH DIRECTIONS

The strength of this chapter is on the thorough literature consolidation of social media and brand management. The extant literature of social media and brand management provides a contribution to practitioners and researchers by describing the multifaceted application of social media and brand management to appeal to the different segments of social media and brand management in order to maximize the business impact of social media and brand management in global marketing. The classification of the extant literature in the domains of social media and brand management will provide the potential opportunities for future research. Future research direction should broaden the perspectives in the implementation of social media and brand management to be utilized in the knowledge-based organizations.

Practitioners and researchers should recognize the applicability of a more multidisciplinary approach toward research activities in implementing social media and brand management in terms of knowledge management-related variables (e.g., knowledge-sharing behavior, knowledge creation, organizational learning, learning orientation, and motivation to learn). It will be useful to bring additional disciplines together (e.g., strategic management, marketing, finance, and human resources) to support a more holistic examination of social media and brand management in order to combine or transfer existing theories and approaches to inquiry in this area.

CONCLUSION

This chapter aimed to promote brand management through social media in global marketing, thus explaining the theoretical and practical overview of social media, evolving dynamics of brand management, shifts in global marketing dynamics, and brand promotion through social media in global marketing. Companies and content marketers need to start taking social media seriously, and become active in the various social networks related to the audience in their industry. Social media presents potential opportunities for the new forms of communication and commerce between marketers and consumers. Social media is a great way to reach a new group of targeted consumers. Social media is a source of communication, information, and entertainment, but increasingly, it also acts as a vehicle for brand promotion.

Social media represents a fundamental shift in how buyers and sellers interact, as they face each other through an electronic connection, and its interactivity provides the opportunity for brands to establish a dialog with customers in modern business. Brands that can build a following by being genuinely interesting and posting engaging, entertaining, and relevant contents create far more opportunities for themselves to sell to consumers. The biggest value that social media offers over traditional media channels is the ability to perform specific audience targeting. The unique value of social media is that it is one of the rare channels that can be viewed as paid, earned, shared, and owned media at the same time for a brand. In order to get the most out of a channel, brands should have a coordinated strategy for all marketing channels, with extensive knowledge of how to target audiences, run advertising, and create optimized content for that specific channel.

Social media is practically utilized as a marketing communications tool by practitioners and marketers in creating brand relationship in global marketing. The integration of social media and brand management is necessary for modern organizations that seek to serve suppliers and customers, increase business performance, strengthen competitiveness, and achieve continuous success in global marketing. Therefore, it is essential for modern organizations to promote their social media and brand management applications, develop a strategic plan to regularly check their practical advancements, and immediately respond to social media and brand management needs of customers in modern organizations. Promoting brand management through social media in global marketing has the potential to enhance organizational performance and reach strategic goals in the social media age.

REFERENCES

Aaker, D. A. (1991). *Managing brand equity*. New York, NY: Free Press.

Aggarwal, P., & Zhang, M. (2006). The moderating effect of relationship norm salience on consumers' loss aversion. *The Journal of Consumer Research*, *33*(3), 413–419. doi:10.1086/508524

Akar, E., & Topçu, B. (2011). An examination of the factors influencing consumers' attitudes toward social media marketing. *Journal of Internet Commerce*, *10*(1), 35–67. doi:10.1080/15332861.2011.558456

Algesheimer, R., Dholakia, U. M., & Herrmann, A. (2005). The social influence of brand community: Evidence from European car clubs. *Journal of Marketing*, *69*(3), 19–34. doi:10.1509/jmkg.69.3.19.66363

Andersen, P. H. (2005). Relationship marketing and brand involvement of professionals through web-enhanced brand communities: The case of Coloplast. *Industrial Marketing Management*, *34*(1), 39–51. doi:10.1016/j.indmarman.2004.07.002

Anderson, E., & Weitz, B. (1992). The use of pledges to build and sustain commitment in distribution channels. *JMR, Journal of Marketing Research*, *29*(1), 18–34. doi:10.2307/3172490

Bagozzi, R. P., & Dholakia, U. M. (2006). Open source software user communities: A study of participation in Linux user groups. *Management Science*, *52*(7), 1099–1115. doi:10.1287/mnsc.1060.0545

Balakrishnan, B. K. P. D., Dahnil, M. I., & Yi, W. J. (2014). The impact of social media marketing medium toward purchase intention and brand loyalty among generation Y. *Procedia: Social and Behavioral Sciences, 148*, 177–185. doi:10.1016/j.sbspro.2014.07.032

Baldus, B. J., Voorhees, C., & Calantone, R. (2015). Online brand community engagement: Scale development and validation. *Journal of Business Research, 68*(5), 978–985. doi:10.1016/j.jbusres.2014.09.035

Barrow, S., & Mosley, R. (2005). *The employer brand: Bringing the best of brand management to people at work*. Chichester, UK: John Wiley & Sons.

Barwise, P., & Meehan, S. (2010). The one thing you must get right when building a brand. *Harvard Business Review, 88*(12), 80–84.

Bateman, P. J., Gray, P. H., & Butler, B. (2010). The impact of community commitment on participation in online communities. *Information Systems Research, 22*(4), 841–854. doi:10.1287/isre.1090.0265

Bengtsson, A., & Servais, P. (2005). Co-branding on industrial markets. *Industrial Marketing Management, 34*(7), 706–713. doi:10.1016/j.indmarman.2005.06.004

Bennett, R., & Rundle-Thiele, S. (2002). A comparison of attitudinal loyalty measurement approaches. *Journal of Brand Management, 9*(3), 193–209. doi:10.1057/palgrave.bm.2540069

Berthon, P. R., Pitt, L. F., & Campbell, C. (2008). Ad lib: When consumers create the ad. *California Management Review, 50*(4), 6–30. doi:10.2307/41166454

Berthon, P. R., Pitt, L. F., Plangger, K., & Shapiro, D. (2012). Marketing meets Web 2.0, social media, and creative consumers: Implications for international marketing strategy. *Business Horizons, 55*(3), 261–271. doi:10.1016/j.bushor.2012.01.007

Blackshaw, P., & Nazzaro, M. (2004). *Consumer-generated media (CGM) 101: Word of mouth in the age of the web-fortified consumer*. Cincinnati, OH: Intelliseek.

Bonsón, E., & Flores, F. (2011). Social media and corporate dialogue: The response of global financial institutions. *Online Information Review, 35*(1), 34–49. doi:10.1108/14684521111113579

Booth, N., & Matic, J. A. (2011). Mapping and leveraging influencers in social media to shape corporate brand perceptions. *Corporate Communications: An International Journal, 16*(3), 184–191. doi:10.1108/13563281111156853

Bradley, A. J., & McDonald, M. P. (2011). *The social organization: How to use social media to tap the collective genius of your customers and employees*. Boston, MA: Harvard Business Review Press.

Bright, L. F., Kleiser, S. B., & Grau, S. L. (2015). Too much Facebook? An exploratory examination of social media fatigue. *Computers in Human Behavior, 44*, 148–155. doi:10.1016/j.chb.2014.11.048

Brodie, R. J., Ilic, A., Juric, B., & Hollebeek, L. (2013). Consumer engagement in a virtual brand community: An exploratory analysis. *Journal of Business Research, 66*(1), 105–114. doi:10.1016/j.jbusres.2011.07.029

Buil, I., Martinez, E., & de Chernatony, L. (2013). The influence of brand equity on consumer responses. *Journal of Consumer Marketing, 30*(1), 62–74. doi:10.1108/07363761311290849

Callarisa, L., García, J. S., Cardiff, J., & Roshchina, A. (2012). Harnessing social media platforms to measure customer-based hotel brand equity. *Tourism Management Perspectives*, *4*, 73–79. doi:10.1016/j.tmp.2012.04.005

Carlson, B. D., Suter, T. A., & Brown, T. J. (2008). Social versus psychological brand community: The role of psychological sense of brand community. *Journal of Business Research*, *61*(4), 284–291. doi:10.1016/j.jbusres.2007.06.022

Casaló, L. V., Flavián, C., & Guinalíu, M. (2010). Relationship quality, community promotion and brand loyalty in virtual communities: Evidence from free software communities. *International Journal of Information Management*, *30*(4), 357–367. doi:10.1016/j.ijinfomgt.2010.01.004

Chaudhuri, A., & Holbrook, M. B. (2001). The chain of effects from brand trust and brand affect to brand performance: The role of brand loyalty. *Journal of Marketing*, *65*(2), 81–93. doi:10.1509/jmkg.65.2.81.18255

Christodoulides, G., Jevons, C., & Bonhomme, J. (2012). Memo to marketers: Quantitative evidence for change. How user-generated content really affects brands. *Journal of Advertising Research*, *52*(1), 53–64. doi:10.2501/JAR-52-1-053-064

Christou, E. (2015). Branding social media in the travel industry. *Procedia: Social and Behavioral Sciences*, *175*, 607–614. doi:10.1016/j.sbspro.2015.01.1244

Chua, A. Y. K., & Banerjee, S. (2013). Customer knowledge management via social media: The case of Starbucks. *Journal of Knowledge Management*, *17*(2), 237–249. doi:10.1108/13673271311315196

Clemons, E. K. (2009). The complex problem of monetizing virtual electronic social networks. *Decision Support Systems*, *48*(1), 46–56. doi:10.1016/j.dss.2009.05.003

Clifton, R. (2003). The future of brands. In R. Clifton (Ed.), *Brands and branding* (pp. 227–241). New York, NY: Bloomberg Press.

Coleman, J. S. (1988). Social capital in the creation of human capital. *American Journal of Sociology*, *94*, 95–120. doi:10.1086/228943

Colliander, J., & Dahlén, M. (2011). Following the fashionable friend: The power of social media. *Journal of Advertising Research*, *51*(1), 313–320. doi:10.2501/JAR-51-1-313-320

Cormode, G., & Krishnamurthy, B. (2008). Key differences between Web 1.0 and Web 2.0. *First Monday*, *13*(6), 2. doi:10.5210/fm.v13i6.2125

Corstjens, M., & Umblijs, A. (2012). The power of evil: The damage of negative social media strongly outweigh positive contributions. *Journal of Advertising Research*, *52*(4), 433–449. doi:10.2501/JAR-52-4-433-449

Cretu, A. E., & Brodie, R. J. (2007). The influence of brand image and company reputation where manufacturers market to small firms: A customer value perspective. *Industrial Marketing Management*, *36*(2), 230–240. doi:10.1016/j.indmarman.2005.08.013

Crittenden, V. L., Hanna, R., & Rohm, A. (2011). We're all connected: The power of the social media ecosystem. *Business Horizons*, *54*(3), 265–273. doi:10.1016/j.bushor.2011.01.007

Culache, O., & Obadă, D. R. (2014). Multimodality as a premise for inducing online flow on a brand website: A social semiotic approach. *Procedia: Social and Behavioral Sciences*, *149*, 261–268. doi:10.1016/j.sbspro.2014.08.227

Culnan, M. J., McHugh, P. J., & Zubillaga, J. I. (2010). How large U.S. companies can use Twitter and other social media to gain business value. *MIS Quarterly Executive*, *9*(4), 243–260.

Davis, R. A., & Sajtos, L. (2008). Measuring consumer interactivity in response to campaigns coupling mobile and television media. *Journal of Advertising Research*, *48*(3), 375–391. doi:10.2501/S0021849908080409

de Chernatony, L., & Segal-Horn, S. (2001). Building on services' characteristics to develop successful service brand. *Journal of Marketing Management*, *17*(7–8), 645–669. doi:10.1362/026725701323366773

de Vries, L., Gensler, S., & Leeflang, P. S. H. (2012). Popularity of brand posts on brand fan pages: An investigation of the effects of social media marketing. *Journal of Interactive Marketing*, *26*(2), 83–91. doi:10.1016/j.intmar.2012.01.003

Deighton, J. (2008). Dove: Evolution of a brand. Harvard Business School (Case No. 9-508-047). Boston, MA: Harvard Business School Press.

Deighton, J., & Kornfeld, L. (2009). Interactivity's unanticipated consequences for marketers and marketing. *Journal of Interactive Marketing*, *23*(1), 2–12. doi:10.1016/j.intmar.2008.10.001

Dholakia, U. M., & Durham, E. (2010). One café chain's Facebook experiment. *Harvard Business Review*, *88*(3), 26.

Dijkmans, C., Kerkhof, P., & Beukeboom, C. J. (2015). A stage to engage: Social media use and corporate reputation. *Tourism Management*, *47*, 58–67. doi:10.1016/j.tourman.2014.09.005

Dong-Hun, L. (2010). Growing popularity of social media and business strategy. *SERI Quarterly*, *3*(4), 112–118.

Eagleman, A. N. (2013). Acceptance, motivations, and usage of social media as a marketing communications tool amongst employees of sport national governing bodies. *Sport Management Review*, *16*(4), 488–497. doi:10.1016/j.smr.2013.03.004

Eisingerich, A. B., Chun, H. H., Liu, Y., Jia, H., & Bell, S. J. (2015). Why recommend a brand face-to-face but not on Facebook? How word-of-mouth on online social sites differs from traditional word-of-mouth. *Journal of Consumer Psychology*, *25*(1), 120–128. doi:10.1016/j.jcps.2014.05.004

Enders, A., Hungenberg, H., Denker, H. P., & Mauch, S. (2008). The long tail of social networking: Revenue models of social networking sites. *European Management Journal*, *26*(3), 199–211. doi:10.1016/j.emj.2008.02.002

Enginkaya, E., & Yılmaz, H. (2014). What drives consumers to interact with brands through social media? A motivation scale development study. *Procedia: Social and Behavioral Sciences*, *148*, 219–226. doi:10.1016/j.sbspro.2014.07.037

Erdem, M., & Cobanoglu, C. (2010). The impact of consumer-generated media and social networking in hospitality: The implications for consumers and hospitality managers. *Journal of Hospitality Marketing & Management*, *19*(7), 697–699. doi:10.1080/19368623.2010.507990

Ewing, M. T., & Napoli, J. (2005). Developing and validating a multidimensional nonprofit brand orientation scale. *Journal of Business Research*, *58*(6), 841–853. doi:10.1016/j.jbusres.2003.09.012

Fang, Y., & Neufeld, D. (2009). Understanding sustained participation in open source software projects. *Journal of Management Information Systems*, *25*(4), 9–50. doi:10.2753/MIS0742-1222250401

Fernando, I. (2010). Community creation by means of a social media paradigm. *The Learning Organization*, *17*(6), 500–514. doi:10.1108/09696471011082367

Foo, M., Douglas, G., & Jack, M. A. (2008). Incentive schemes in the financial services sector: Moderating effects of relationship norms on customer-brand relationship. *International Journal of Bank Marketing*, *26*(2), 99–118. doi:10.1108/02652320810852772

Fournier, S., & Avery, J. (2011). The uninvited brand. *Business Horizons*, *54*(3), 193–207. doi:10.1016/j.bushor.2011.01.001

Gamboa, A. M., & Goncalves, H. M. (2014). Customer loyalty through social networks: Lessons from Zara on Facebook. *Business Horizons*, *57*(6), 709–717. doi:10.1016/j.bushor.2014.07.003

Gartner, W. C., & Ruzzier, M. K. (2011). Tourism destination brand equity dimensions: Renewal versus repeat market. *Journal of Travel Research*, *50*(5), 471–481. doi:10.1177/0047287510379157

Gensler, S., Völckner, F., Liu-Thompkins, Y., & Wiertz, C. (2013). Managing brands in the social media environment. *Journal of Interactive Marketing*, *27*(4), 242–256. doi:10.1016/j.intmar.2013.09.004

Godes, D., & Mayzlin, D. (2009). Firm-created word-of-mouth communication: Evidence from a field test. *Marketing Science*, *28*(4), 721–739. doi:10.1287/mksc.1080.0444

Gruen, T. W., Osmonbekov, T., & Czaplewski, A. J. (2006). eWOM: The impact of customer-to-customer online know-how exchange on customer value and loyalty. *Journal of Business Research*, *59*(4), 449–456. doi:10.1016/j.jbusres.2005.10.004

Habibi, M. R., Laroche, M., & Richard, M. O. (2014). Brand communities based in social media: How unique are they? Evidence from two exemplary brand communities. *International Journal of Information Management*, *34*(2), 123–132. doi:10.1016/j.ijinfomgt.2013.11.010

Hankinson, P. (2002). The impact of brand orientation on managerial practice. *International Journal of Nonprofit and Voluntary Sector Marketing*, *7*(1), 30–44. doi:10.1002/nvsm.165

Hanna, R., Rohm, A., & Crittenden, V. L. (2011). We're all connected: The power of the social media ecosystem. *Business Horizons*, *54*(3), 265–273. doi:10.1016/j.bushor.2011.01.007

Hassan, S., Nadzim, S. Z. A., & Shiratuddin, N. (2015). Strategic use of social media for small business based on the AIDA model. *Procedia: Social and Behavioral Sciences*, *172*, 262–269. doi:10.1016/j.sbspro.2015.01.363

Helm, C., & Jones, R. (2010). Brand governance: The new agenda in brand management. *Journal of Brand Management*, *17*(8), 545–547. doi:10.1057/bm.2010.20

Henderson, A., & Bowley, T. (2010). Authentic dialogue? The role of "friendship" in a social media recruitment campaign. *Journal of Communication Management*, *14*(3), 237–257. doi:10.1108/13632541011064517

Hoffman, D. L., & Fodor, M. (2010). Can you measure the ROI of your social media marketing? *MIT Sloan Management Review*, *52*(1), 41–49.

Huberman, B. A. (2008). Crowdsourcing and attention. *Computer*, *41*(11), 103–105. doi:10.1109/MC.2008.450

Hudson, S., Roth, M. S., Madden, T. J., & Hudson, R. (2015). The effects of social media on emotions, brand relationship quality, and word of mouth: An empirical study of music festival attendees. *Tourism Management*, *47*, 68–76. doi:10.1016/j.tourman.2014.09.001

Hutton, J. G. (1997). A study of brand equity in an organizational-buying context. *Journal of Product and Brand Management*, *6*(6), 428–439. doi:10.1108/10610429710190478

Hyde, K. F. (2008). Information processing and touring planning theory. *Annals of Tourism Research*, *35*(3), 712–731. doi:10.1016/j.annals.2008.05.001

Jang, H., Olfman, L., Ko, I., Koh, J., & Kim, K. (2008). The influence of on-line brand community characteristics on community commitment and brand loyalty. *International Journal of Electronic Commerce*, *12*(3), 57–80. doi:10.2753/JEC1086-4415120304

Jansen, B. J., Zhang, M., Sobel, K., & Chowdury, A. (2009). Twitter power: Tweets as electronic word of mouth. *Journal of the American Society for Information Science and Technology*, *60*(11), 2169–2188. doi:10.1002/asi.21149

Jin, S. A. A. (2012). The potential of social media for luxury brand management. *Marketing Intelligence & Planning*, *30*(7), 687–699. doi:10.1108/02634501211273805

Johnson, J. W., & Grimm, P. E. (2010). Communal and exchange relationship perceptions as separate constructs and their role in motivations to donate. *Journal of Consumer Psychology*, *20*(3), 282–294. doi:10.1016/j.jcps.2010.06.018

Jothi, P. S. J., Neelamalar, M., & Prasad, R. S. (2011). Analysis of social networking sites: A study on effective communication strategy in developing brand communication. *Journal of Media and Communication Studies*, *3*(7), 234–242.

Kapferer, J. N. (1997). *Strategic brand management: Creating and sustaining brand equity long term*. London, UK: Kogan Page.

Kaplan, A. M., & Haenlein, M. (2010). Users of the world, unite! The challenges and opportunities of social media. *Business Horizons*, *53*(1), 59–68. doi:10.1016/j.bushor.2009.09.003

Kasavana, M. L., Nusair, K., & Teodosic, K. (2010). Online social networking: Redefining the human web. *Journal of Hospitality and Tourism Technology*, *1*(1), 68–82. doi:10.1108/17579881011023025

Kasemsap, K. (2014a). The role of social networking in global business environments. In P. Smith & T. Cockburn (Eds.), *Impact of emerging digital technologies on leadership in global business* (pp. 183–201). Hershey, PA: IGI Global. doi:10.4018/978-1-4666-6134-9.ch010

Kasemsap, K. (2014b). The role of social media in the knowledge-based organizations. In I. Lee (Ed.), *Integrating social media into business practice, applications, management, and models* (pp. 254–275). Hershey, PA: IGI Global. doi:10.4018/978-1-4666-6182-0.ch013

Kasemsap, K. (2014c). The role of brand management in emerging markets. In I. Samanta (Ed.), *Strategic marketing in fragile economic conditions* (pp. 167–184). Hershey, PA: IGI Global. doi:10.4018/978-1-4666-6232-2.ch009

Kasemsap, K. (2014d). The role of brand loyalty on CRM performance: An innovative framework for smart manufacturing. In Z. Luo (Ed.), *Smart manufacturing innovation and transformation: Interconnection and intelligence* (pp. 252–284). Hershey, PA: IGI Global. doi:10.4018/978-1-4666-5836-3.ch010

Kasemsap, K. (2015a). The role of social media in international advertising. In N. Taşkıran & R. Yılmaz (Eds.), Handbook of research on effective advertising strategies in the social media age (pp. 171–196). Hershey, PA: IGI Global. doi:10.4018/978-1-4666-8125-5.ch010

Kasemsap, K. (2015b). The roles of corporate marketing strategies and brand management in the global retail industry. In E. Pantano (Ed.), *Successful technological integration for competitive advantage in retail settings* (pp. 310–339). Hershey, PA: IGI Global. doi:10.4018/978-1-4666-8297-9.ch014

Keller, K. L. (2008). *Strategic brand management: Building, measuring and managing brand equity*. Upper Saddle River, NJ: Prentice Hall.

Kietzmann, J. H., Hermkens, K., McCarthy, I. P., & Silvestre, B. S. (2011). Social media? Get serious! Understanding the functional building blocks of social media. *Business Horizons*, *54*(3), 241–251. doi:10.1016/j.bushor.2011.01.005

Kim, A. J., & Ko, E. (2012). Do social media marketing activities enhance customer equity? An empirical study of luxury fashion brand. *Journal of Business Research*, *65*(10), 1480–1486. doi:10.1016/j.jbusres.2011.10.014

Kim, E., Sung, Y., & Kang, H. (2014). Brand followers' retweeting behavior on Twitter: How brand relationships influence brand electronic word-of-mouth. *Computers in Human Behavior*, *37*, 18–25. doi:10.1016/j.chb.2014.04.020

Kim, J., & Hardin, A. (2010). The impact of virtual worlds on word-of-mouth: Improving social networking and servicescape in the hospitality industry. *Journal of Hospitality Marketing & Management*, *19*(7), 735–753. doi:10.1080/19368623.2010.508005

Kohli, C., Suri, R., & Kapoor, A. (2015). Will social media kill branding? *Business Horizons*, *58*(1), 35–44. doi:10.1016/j.bushor.2014.08.004

Kotler, P., & Keller, K. L. (2007). *A framework for marketing management*. Upper Saddle River, NJ: Prentice Hall.

Kozinets, R. V. (2002). The field behind the screen: Using netnography for marketing research in online communities. *JMR, Journal of Marketing Research*, *39*(1), 61–72. doi:10.1509/jmkr.39.1.61.18935

Kumar, M., Townsend, J. D., & Vorhies, D. W. (2015). Enhancing consumers' affection for a brand using product design. *Journal of Product Innovation Management*, *32*(5), 716–730. doi:10.1111/jpim.12245

Kunz, M. B., Hackworth, B., Osborne, P., & High, J. D. (2011). Fans, friends, and followers: Social media in the retailers' marketing mix. *Journal of Applied Business and Economics*, *12*(3), 61–68.

Kwon, E. S., & Sung, Y. (2011). Follow me! Global marketers' Twitter use. *Journal of Interactive Advertising*, *12*(1), 4–16. doi:10.1080/15252019.2011.10722187

Labrecque, L. I. (2014). Fostering consumer–brand relationships in social media environments: The role of parasocial interaction. *Journal of Interactive Marketing*, *28*(2), 134–148. doi:10.1016/j.intmar.2013.12.003

Laroche, M., Habibi, M. R., & Richard, M. O. (2013). To be or not to be in social media: How brand loyalty is affected by social media? *International Journal of Information Management*, *33*(1), 76–82. doi:10.1016/j.ijinfomgt.2012.07.003

Laroche, M., Habibi, M. R., Richard, M. O., & Sankaranarayanan, R. (2012). The effects of social media based brand communities on brand community markers, value creation practices, brand trust and brand loyalty. *Computers in Human Behavior*, *28*(5), 1755–1767. doi:10.1016/j.chb.2012.04.016

Lee, D., Kim, H. S., & Kim, J. K. (2012). The role of self-construal in consumers' electronic word of mouth (eWOM) in social networking sites: A social cognitive approach. *Computers in Human Behavior*, *28*(3), 1054–1062. doi:10.1016/j.chb.2012.01.009

Lee, W., Xiong, L., & Hu, C. (2012). The effect of Facebook users' arousal and valence on intention to go to the festival: Applying an extension of the technology acceptance model. *International Journal of Hospitality Management*, *31*(3), 819–827. doi:10.1016/j.ijhm.2011.09.018

Li, C., & Bernoff, J. (2009). *Marketing in the groundswell*. Cambridge, MA: Harvard Business School Press.

Li, Y. M., & Shiu, Y. L. (2012). A diffusion mechanism for social advertising over microblogs. *Decision Support Systems*, *54*(1), 9–22. doi:10.1016/j.dss.2012.02.012

Li, Z., & Li, C. (2014). Twitter as a social actor: How consumers evaluate brands differently on Twitter based on relationship norms. *Computers in Human Behavior*, *39*, 187–196. doi:10.1016/j.chb.2014.07.016

Lin, J. S., & Pena, J. (2011). Are you following me? A content analysis of TV networks' brand communication on Twitter. *Journal of Interactive Advertising*, *12*(1), 17–29. doi:10.1080/15252019.2011.10722188

Low, J., & Blois, K. (2002). The evolution of generic brands in industrial markets: The challenges to owners of brand equity. *Industrial Marketing Management*, *31*(5), 385–392. doi:10.1016/S0019-8501(00)00131-0

Luo, N., Zhang, M., & Liu, W. (2015). The effects of value co-creation practices on building harmonious brand community and achieving brand loyalty on social media in China. *Computers in Human Behavior*, *48*, 492–499. doi:10.1016/j.chb.2015.02.020

Malthouse, E. C., Haenlein, M., Skiera, B., Wege, E., & Zhang, M. (2013). Managing customer relationships in the social media era: Introducing the social CRM house. *Journal of Interactive Marketing*, *27*(4), 270–280. doi:10.1016/j.intmar.2013.09.008

Mangold, W. G., & Faulds, D. J. (2009). Social media: The new hybrid element of the promotion mix. *Business Horizons*, *52*(4), 357–365. doi:10.1016/j.bushor.2009.03.002

McAlexander, J. H., Schouten, J. W., & Koenig, H. F. (2002). Building brand community. *Journal of Marketing*, *66*(1), 38–54. doi:10.1509/jmkg.66.1.38.18451

McKee, S. (2010). *Creative B2B branding (no, really): Building a creative brand in a business world.* Oxford, UK: Goodfellow Publishers.

McWilliam, G. (2012). Building stronger brands through online communities. *MIT Sloan Management Review*, *41*(3), 43–54.

Merz, M. A., He, Y., & Vargo, S. L. (2009). The evolving brand logic: A service-dominant logic perspective. *Journal of the Academy of Marketing Science*, *37*(3), 328–344. doi:10.1007/s11747-009-0143-3

Michaelidou, N., Siamagka, N. T., & Christodoulides, G. (2011). Usage, barriers and measurement of social media marketing: An exploratory investigation of small and medium B2B brands. *Industrial Marketing Management*, *40*(7), 1153–1159. doi:10.1016/j.indmarman.2011.09.009

Michell, P., King, J., & Reast, J. (2001). Brand values related to industrial products. *Industrial Marketing Management*, *30*(5), 415–425. doi:10.1016/S0019-8501(99)00097-8

Miller, R., & Lammas, N. (2010). Social media and its implications for viral marketing. *Asia Pacific Public Relations Journal*, *11*(1), 1–9.

Moran, E., & Gossieaux, F. (2010). Marketing in a hyper-social world: The tribalization of business study and characteristics of successful online communities. *Journal of Advertising Research*, *50*(3), 232–239. doi:10.2501/S0021849910091397

Mou, Y., Atkin, D., Fu, H., Lin, C. A., & Lau, T. Y. (2013). The influence of online forum and SNS use on online political discussion in China: Assessing "Spirals of Trust.". *Telematics and Informatics*, *30*(4), 359–369. doi:10.1016/j.tele.2013.04.002

Mudambi, S. (2002). Branding importance in business-to-business markets three buyer clusters. *Industrial Marketing Management*, *31*(6), 525–533. doi:10.1016/S0019-8501(02)00184-0

Muniz, A. M. Jr, & O'guinn, T. C. (2001). Brand community. *The Journal of Consumer Research*, *27*(4), 412–432. doi:10.1086/319618

Muniz, A. M. Jr, & Schau, H. J. (2005). Religiosity in the abandoned Apple Newton brand community. *The Journal of Consumer Research*, *31*(4), 737–747. doi:10.1086/426607

Nambisan, P., & Watt, J. H. (2011). Managing customer experiences in online product communities. *Journal of Business Research*, *64*(8), 889–895. doi:10.1016/j.jbusres.2010.09.006

Naylor, R. W., Lamberton, C. P., & West, P. M. (2012). Beyond the like button: The impact of mere virtual presence on brand evaluations and purchase intentions in social media settings. *Journal of Marketing*, *76*(6), 105–120. doi:10.1509/jm.11.0105

Ngai, E. W. T., Tao, S. S. C., & Moon, K. K. L. (2015). Social media research: Theories, constructs, and conceptual frameworks. *International Journal of Information Management*, *35*(1), 33–44. doi:10.1016/j.ijinfomgt.2014.09.004

Nuttavuthisit, K. (2010). If you can't beat them, let them join: The development of strategies to foster consumers' co-creative practices. *Business Horizons*, *53*(3), 315–324. doi:10.1016/j.bushor.2010.01.005

O'Connor, P. (2010). Managing a hotel's image on TripAdvisor. *Journal of Hospitality Marketing & Management*, *19*(7), 754–772. doi:10.1080/19368623.2010.508007

Ohnemus, L. (2009). B2B branding: A financial burden for shareholders? *Business Horizons*, *52*(2), 159–166.

O' Reilly, T. (2007). What is Web 2.0: Design patterns and business models for the next generation of software. *Communications & Stratégies*, *65*, 17–37.

Pan, B., & Li, X. R. (2011). The long tail of destination image and online marketing. *Annals of Tourism Research*, *38*(1), 132–152. doi:10.1016/j.annals.2010.06.004

Park, H., & Kim, Y. K. (2014). The role of social network websites in the consumer–brand relationship. *Journal of Retailing and Consumer Services*, *21*(4), 460–467. doi:10.1016/j.jretconser.2014.03.011

Parveen, F., Jaafar, N. I., & Ainin, S. (2015). Social media usage and organizational performance: Reflections of Malaysian social media managers. *Telematics and Informatics*, *32*(1), 67–78. doi:10.1016/j.tele.2014.03.001

Pentina, I., Zhang, L., & Basmanova, O. (2013). Antecedents and consequences of trust in a social media brand: A cross-cultural study of Twitter. *Computers in Human Behavior*, *29*(4), 1546–1555. doi:10.1016/j.chb.2013.01.045

Peppler, K. A., & Solomou, M. (2011). Building creativity: Collaborative learning and creativity in social media environments. *On the Horizon*, *19*(1), 13–23. doi:10.1108/10748121111107672

Porter, C. E., & Donthu, N. (2008). Cultivating trust and harvesting value in virtual communities. *Management Science*, *54*(1), 113–128. doi:10.1287/mnsc.1070.0765

Powers, T., Advincula, D., Austin, M. S., Graiko, S., & Snyder, J. (2012). Digital and social media in the purchase-decision process: A special report from the advertising research foundation. *Journal of Advertising Research*, *52*(4), 479–489. doi:10.2501/JAR-52-4-479-489

Qureshi, S., & Zigurs, I. (2001). Paradoxes and prerogatives in global virtual collaboration. *Communications of the ACM*, *44*(12), 85–88. doi:10.1145/501317.501354

Reilly, A. H., & Hynan, K. A. (2014). Corporate communication, sustainability, and social media: It's not easy (really) being green. *Business Horizons*, *57*(6), 747–758. doi:10.1016/j.bushor.2014.07.008

Reyneke, M., Pitt, L., & Berthon, P. R. (2011). Luxury wine brand visibility in social media: An exploratory study. *International Journal of Wine Business Research*, *23*(1), 21–35. doi:10.1108/17511061111121380

Sands, S., Harper, E., & Ferraro, C. (2011). Customer-to-noncustomer interactions: Extending the "social" dimension of the store environment. *Journal of Retailing and Consumer Services*, *18*(5), 438–447. doi:10.1016/j.jretconser.2011.06.007

Scarpi, D. (2010). Does size matter? An examination of small and large web-based brand communities. *Journal of Interactive Marketing*, *24*(1), 14–21. doi:10.1016/j.intmar.2009.10.002

Schau, H. J., Muñiz, A. M. Jr, & Arnould, E. J. (2009). How brand community practices create value. *Journal of Marketing*, *73*(5), 30–51. doi:10.1509/jmkg.73.5.30

Schmidt, H. J., & Baumgarth, C. (2015). Brand orientation: A case study approach within the context of social entrepreneurial businesses. *Procedia: Social and Behavioral Sciences*, *175*, 24–31. doi:10.1016/j.sbspro.2015.01.1170

Schouten, J. W., McAlexander, J. H., & Koenig, H. F. (2007). Transcendent customer experience and brand community. *Journal of the Academy of Marketing Science*, *35*(3), 357–368. doi:10.1007/s11747-007-0034-4

Shih, C. C. (2009). *The Facebook era: Tapping online social networks to build better products, reach new audiences, and sell more stuff.* Boston, MA: Prentice Hall.

Shih, C. C., Lin, T. M. Y., & Luarn, P. (2014). Fan-centric social media: The Xiaomi phenomenon in China. *Business Horizons*, *57*(3), 349–358. doi:10.1016/j.bushor.2013.12.006

Simula, H., & Vuori, M. (2012). Benefits and barriers of crowdsourcing in B2B firms: Generating ideas with internal and external crowds. *International Journal of Innovation Management*, *16*(6), 1–19. doi:10.1142/S1363919612400117

Singh, S., & Sonnenburg, S. (2012). Brand performances in social media. *Journal of Interactive Marketing*, *26*(4), 189–197. doi:10.1016/j.intmar.2012.04.001

Smith, A. N., Fischer, E., & Yongjian, C. (2012). How does brand-related user-generated content differ across YouTube, Facebook, and Twitter? *Journal of Interactive Marketing*, *26*(2), 102–113. doi:10.1016/j.intmar.2012.01.002

Srivastava, M. K., & Gnyawali, D. R. (2011). When do relational resources matter? Leveraging portfolio technological resources for breakthrough innovation. *Academy of Management Journal*, *54*(4), 797–810. doi:10.5465/AMJ.2011.64870140

Steenkamp, M., & Hyde-Clarke, N. (2014). The use of Facebook for political commentary in South Africa. *Telematics and Informatics*, *31*(1), 91–97. doi:10.1016/j.tele.2012.10.002

Stokburger-Sauer, N. (2010). Brand community: Drivers and outcomes. *Psychology and Marketing, 27*(4), 347–368. doi:10.1002/mar.20335

Sukoco, B. M., & Wu, W. Y. (2010). The personal and social motivation of customers' participation in brand community. *African Journal of Business Management, 4*(5), 614–622.

Sun, T., Youn, S., Wu, G., & Kuntaraporn, M. (2006). Online word-of-mouth (or mouse): An exploration of its antecedents and consequences. *Journal of Computer-Mediated Communication, 11*(4), 1104–1127. doi:10.1111/j.1083-6101.2006.00310.x

Tang, Q., Gu, B., & Whinston, A. B. (2012). Content contribution for revenue sharing and reputation in social media: A dynamic structural model. *Journal of Management Information Systems, 29*(2), 41–76. doi:10.2753/MIS0742-1222290203

Thompson, S. A., & Sinha, R. K. (2008). Brand communities and new product adoption: The influence and limits of oppositional loyalty. *Journal of Marketing, 72*(6), 65–80. doi:10.1509/jmkg.72.6.65

Toledano, M., & Riches, M. (2014). Brand alliance and event management for social causes: Evidence from New Zealand. *Public Relations Review, 40*(5), 807–814. doi:10.1016/j.pubrev.2014.09.001

Tuominen, P. (2007). Emerging metaphors in brand in brand management: Towards a relational approach. *Journal of Communication Management, 11*(2), 182–191. doi:10.1108/13632540710747398

Vallaster, C., & von Wallpach, S. (2013). An online discursive inquiry into the social dynamics of multi-stakeholder brand meaning co-creation. *Journal of Business Research, 66*(9), 1505–1515. doi:10.1016/j.jbusres.2012.09.012

van Dijk, J., Antonides, G., & Schillewaert, N. (2014). Effects of co-creation claim on consumer brand perceptions and behavioural intentions. *International Journal of Consumer Studies, 38*(1), 110–118. doi:10.1111/ijcs.12071

van Noort, G., & Willemsen, L. M. (2011). Online damage control: The effects of proactive versus reactive webcare interventions in consumer-generated and brand-generated platforms. *Journal of Interactive Marketing, 26*(3), 131–140. doi:10.1016/j.intmar.2011.07.001

van Riel, C. B. M., & Balmer, J. M. T. (1997). Corporate identity: The concept, its measurement and management. *European Journal of Marketing, 31*(5/6), 340–355. doi:10.1108/03090569710167574

Vickery, G., & Wunsch-Vincent, S. (2007). *Participative web and user-created content: Web 2.0 wikis and social networking*. Paris, France: Organization for Economic Cooperation and Development.

von Hippel, E. (2005). *Democratizing innovation*. Cambridge, MA: MIT Press.

Wang, Y., Hsu, K., Hsu, S., & Hsieh, P. (2011). Constructing an index for brand equity: A hospital example. *Service Industries Journal, 31*(2), 311–322. doi:10.1080/02642060902759145

Weick, K. E. (1995). *Sensemaking in organizations*. Thousand Oaks, CA: Sage Publications.

Weinberg, B. D., de Ruyter, K., Dellarocas, C., Buck, M., & Keeling, D. I. (2013). Destination social business: Exploring an organization's journey with social media, collaborative community and expressive individuality. *Journal of Interactive Marketing, 27*(4), 299–310. doi:10.1016/j.intmar.2013.09.006

Weinberg, B. D., & Pehlivan, E. (2011). Social spending: Managing the social media mix. *Business Horizons*, *54*(3), 275–282. doi:10.1016/j.bushor.2011.01.008

Weinberg, T. (2009). *The new community rules: Marketing on the social web*. Sebastopol, CA: O'Reilly Media.

Wilcox, K., & Stephen, A. (2013). Are close friends the enemy? Online social networks, self-esteem, and self-control. *The Journal of Consumer Research*, *40*(1), 90–103. doi:10.1086/668794

Xiang, Z., & Gretzel, U. (2010). Role of social media in online travel information search. *Tourism Management*, *31*(2), 179–188. doi:10.1016/j.tourman.2009.02.016

Yan, J. (2011). Social media in branding: Fulfilling a need. *Journal of Brand Management*, *18*(9), 688–696. doi:10.1057/bm.2011.19

Yates, D., & Paquette, S. (2011). Emergency knowledge management and social media technologies: A case study of the 2010 Haitian earthquake. *International Journal of Information Management*, *31*(1), 6–13. doi:10.1016/j.ijinfomgt.2010.10.001

Yeo, T.E.D. (2012). Social-media early adopters don't count: How to seed participation in interactive campaigns by psychological profiling of digital consumers. *Journal of Advertising Research*, *52*(3), 297–308. doi:10.2501/JAR-52-3-297-308

Yoo, B., Donthu, N., & Lee, S. (2000). An examination of selected marketing mix elements and brand equity. *Journal of the Academy of Marketing Science*, *28*(2), 195–211. doi:10.1177/0092070300282002

Zadeh, A. H., & Sharda, R. (2014). Modeling brand post popularity dynamics in online social networks. *Decision Support Systems*, *65*, 59–68. doi:10.1016/j.dss.2014.05.003

Zaglia, M. E. (2013). Brand communities embedded in social networks. *Journal of Business Research*, *66*(2), 216–223. doi:10.1016/j.jbusres.2012.07.015

Zarella, D. (2010). *The social media marketing book*. Sebastopol, CA: O'Reilly Media.

Zavattaro, S. M., Daspit, J. J., & Adams, F. G. (2015). Assessing managerial methods for evaluating place brand equity: A qualitative investigation. *Tourism Management*, *47*(1), 11–21. doi:10.1016/j.tourman.2014.08.018

Zerfass, A., & Schramm, D. M. (2014). Social media newsrooms in public relations: A conceptual framework and corporate practices in three countries. *Public Relations Review*, *40*(1), 79–91. doi:10.1016/j.pubrev.2013.12.003

Zhang, C., Hahn, J., & De, P. (2013). Continued participation in online innovation communities: Does community response matter equally for everyone? *Information Systems Research*, *24*(4), 1112–1130. doi:10.1287/isre.2013.0485

Zhang, K. Z. K., Benyoucef, M., & Zhao, S. J. (2015). Consumer participation and gender differences on companies' microblogs: A brand attachment process perspective. *Computers in Human Behavior*, *44*, 357–368. doi:10.1016/j.chb.2014.11.068

Zhang, K. Z. K., Zhao, S. J., Zhang, H., & Lee, M. K. O. (2014). An empirical research of the factors affecting users to follow companies' microblogs. *International Journal of Networking and Virtual Organisations*, *14*(1/2), 129–145. doi:10.1504/IJNVO.2014.065081

Zhou, Z., Zhang, Q., Su, C., & Zhou, N. (2012). How do brand communities generate brand relationships? Intermediate mechanisms. *Journal of Business Research*, *65*(7), 890–895. doi:10.1016/j.jbusres.2011.06.034

ADDITIONAL READING

Antorini, Y. M., Muniz, A. M., & Askildsen, T. (2012). Collaborating with customer communities: Lessons from the Lego group. *MIT Sloan Management Review*, *53*(3), 73–79.

Healy, J. C., & McDonagh, P. (2013). Consumer roles in brand culture and value co-creation in virtual communities. *Journal of Business Research*, *66*(9), 1528–1540. doi:10.1016/j.jbusres.2012.09.014

Hollebeek, L. D., Glynn, M. S., & Brodie, R. J. (2014). Consumer brand engagement in social media: Conceptualization, scale development and validation. *Journal of Interactive Marketing*, *28*(2), 149–165. doi:10.1016/j.intmar.2013.12.002

Hughes, D. J., Rowe, M., Batey, M., & Lee, A. (2012). A tale of two sites: Twitter vs. Facebook and the personality predictors of social media usage. *Computers in Human Behavior*, *28*(2), 561–569. doi:10.1016/j.chb.2011.11.001

Kalafatis, S. P., Remizova, N., Riley, D., & Singh, J. (2012). The differential impact of brand equity on B2B co-branding. *Journal of Business and Industrial Marketing*, *27*(8), 623–634. doi:10.1108/08858621211273574

Kuksov, D., Shachar, R., & Kangkang, W. (2013). Advertising and consumers' communications. *Marketing Science*, *32*(2), 294–309. doi:10.1287/mksc.1120.0753

Kuo, Y. F., & Feng, L. U. (2013). Relationships among community interaction characteristics, perceived benefits, community commitment, and oppositional brand loyalty in online brand communities. *International Journal of Information Management*, *33*(6), 948–962. doi:10.1016/j.ijinfomgt.2013.08.005

Lipsman, A., Mudd, G., Rich, M., & Bruich, S. (2012). The power of "like": How brands reach (and influence) fans through social-media marketing. *Journal of Advertising Research*, *52*(1), 40–52. doi:10.2501/JAR-52-1-040-052

Liu, F., Li, J., Mizerski, D., & Soh, H. (2012). Self–congruity, brand attitude, and brand loyalty: A study on luxury brands. *European Journal of Marketing*, *46*(7/8), 922–937. doi:10.1108/03090561211230098

Luu, T. T. (2012). Behind brand performance. *Asia-Pacific Journal of Business Administration*, *4*(1), 42–57. doi:10.1108/17574321211207962

Malhotra, A., Malhotra, C. K., & See, A. (2012). How to get your messages retweeted. *MIT Sloan Management Review*, *53*(2), 60–66.

Mann, B. J. S., & Kaur, M. (2013). Exploring branding strategies of FMCG, services and durables brands: Evidence from India. *Journal of Product and Brand Management*, *22*(1), 6–17. doi:10.1108/10610421311298650

Marzocchi, M., Morandin, G., & Bergami, M. (2013). Brand communities: Loyal to the community or the brand? *European Journal of Marketing*, *47*(1/2), 93–114. doi:10.1108/03090561311285475

Mayzlin, D., & Yoganarasinhan, H. (2012). Link to success: How blogs build an audience by promoting rivals. *Management Science*, *58*(9), 1651–1668. doi:10.1287/mnsc.1110.1510

Moe, W. M., & Schweidel, D. A. (2012). Online product opinions: Incidence, evaluation, and evolution. *Marketing Science*, *31*(3), 372–386. doi:10.1287/mksc.1110.0662

Noble, C. H., Bing, M. N., & Bogoviyeva, E. (2013). The effects of brand metaphors as design innovation: A test of congruency hypotheses. *Journal of Product Innovation Management*, *30*, 126–141. doi:10.1111/jpim.12067

Olsen, L. E., & Lanseng, E. J. (2012). Brand alliances: The role of brand concept consistency. *European Journal of Marketing*, *46*(9), 1108–1126. doi:10.1108/03090561211247874

Onishi, H., & Manchanda, P. (2012). Marketing activity, blogging and sales. *International Journal of Research in Marketing*, *29*(3), 221–234. doi:10.1016/j.ijresmar.2011.11.003

Pham, M. T., Geuens, M., & De Pelsmacker, P. (2013). The influence of ad-evoked feelings on brand evaluations: Empirical generalizations from consumer responses to more than 1000 TV commercials. *International Journal of Research in Marketing*, *30*(4), 383–394. doi:10.1016/j.ijresmar.2013.04.004

Quintal, V., & Phau, I. (2013). Brand leaders and me-too alternatives: How do consumers choose? *Marketing Intelligence & Planning*, *31*(4), 367–387. doi:10.1108/02634501311324852

Romaniuk, J., & Nenycz-Thiel, M. (2011). Behavioral brand loyalty and consumer brand associations. *Journal of Business Research*, *66*(1), 67–72. doi:10.1016/j.jbusres.2011.07.024

Sashi, C. M. (2012). Customer engagement, buyer-seller relationships, and social media. *Management Decision*, *50*(2), 253–272. doi:10.1108/00251741211203551

Schnittka, O., Sattler, H., & Zenker, S. (2012). Advanced brand concept maps: A new approach for evaluating the favorability of brand association networks. *International Journal of Research in Marketing*, *29*(3), 265–274. doi:10.1016/j.ijresmar.2012.04.002

Sharifi, S. S. (2014). Impacts of the trilogy of emotion on future purchase intentions in products of high involvement under the mediating role of brand awareness. *European Business Review*, *26*(1), 43–63. doi:10.1108/EBR-12-2012-0072

Smock, A. D., Ellison, N. B., Lampe, C., & Wohn, D. Y. (2011). Facebook as a toolkit: A uses and gratification approach to unbundling feature use. *Computers in Human Behavior*, *27*(6), 2322–2329. doi:10.1016/j.chb.2011.07.011

Stahl, F., Heitmann, M., Lehmann, D. R., & Neslin, S. A. (2012). The impact of brand equity on customer acquisition, retention, and profit margin. *Journal of Marketing*, *76*(4), 44–63. doi:10.1509/jm.10.0522

Wang, X., Yu, C., & Wei, Y. (2012). Social media peer communication and impacts on purchase intentions: A consumer socialization framework. *Journal of Interactive Marketing*, *26*(4), 198–208. doi:10.1016/j.intmar.2011.11.004

KEY TERMS AND DEFINITIONS

Brand: A trademark or distinctive name identifying a product, service, or organization.

Brand Loyalty: The tendency of customers to keep buying the same brand of a particular product instead of trying other brands.

Brand Management: A function of marketing that uses techniques to increase the perceived value of a product line or brand over time.

Brand Strategy: A plan for the systematic development of a brand to enable it to meet its agreed objectives.

Facebook: The name of a social networking service and website, launched in 2004.

Marketing: The ways in which a company encourages people to buy its products by deciding on price, type of customer, and advertising policy.

Social Media: The computer application that people use in order to create and share information through social networking sites.

Social Networking Sites: Websites that are designed to help people communicate and share information with a group.

Twitter: A social networking website, which allows users to publish short messages that are visible to other social media users.

Chapter 6

Country Brand Management:
Assessing the Role of Social Media in Creating the Image of Marca España (Spain Brand)

Neus Soler-Labajos
Open University of Catalonia, Spain

Ana Isabel Jiménez-Zarco
Open University of Catalonia, Spain

ABSTRACT

In the recent years the country brand has become a strategic asset for the nations. Rather than showing the culture and traditions of a place, the name of a country acts as a differentiator from everything that comes with the territory, increasing the value perceived by the customer in any product or service by having a specific origin. Because the fact that a product is "typical" of a place allows the name of the place to become a geographical indicator of quality. So Nations use the brand country as a tool to promote their products, attract investments and promote activities like tourism. For this reason, they are developing public policies aimed at the construction, promotion and consolidation of the brand image of the country. This book chapter analyzes how the Spanish Government has used the social media to create and consolidate the Spain Brand image with the aim to establish an image of Spain as an economic and political power among the first countries in the world.

INTRODUCTION

Traditionally, from the marketing point of view brands have been defined as a strategic intangible asset. As a source of competitive advantage, brands have been managed in order to create and consolidate organizational brand equity. In this sense, Kotler and Armstrong (1996) show that the combination of brand name and brand significance has become a core competitive asset in an ever-growing number of contexts.

DOI: 10.4018/978-1-5225-0332-3.ch006

Nowadays, the brand concept has been expanded, exceeding the organizational and business context. Thus, in the current economic climate, there is a lot of talk about country brands; not only how these influence the national and supranational economic decisions,[1] but also the way how they are perceived influences on consumer behavior toward the country and the products that originate from it.

According to Keller et al., (2011), both corporate and product or service brands, have a social and emotional value to the user as country brands. So they have personality and speak for the user, and enhance the perceived utility and desirability of the product, organization or country. But besides, brands have value to investors and organizations, thus consumer preferences and loyalty translate into organizations' financial gains, market position, brand reputation and equity.

In the special case of country brands, these effects are seen in improving credibility and brand reputation of both the country and its products. Thus, country reputation is likely to influence people's decisions related to purchasing, investing, changing residence and travelling (Laroche et al., 2005). The reputation depends on the Country image. Image is defined as the sum of beliefs and impressions people hold about places. The images represent a simplification of a large number of associations and pieces of information connected to a place, while reputation refers to how a particular brand (whether for an individual or a company) is viewed by others. A favorable brand reputation means consumers trust your company, and feel good about purchasing your goods or services. An unfavorable brand reputation, however, will cause consumers to distrust your company and be hesitant about purchasing your products or services.

There is a product of mind trying to process and pick out essential information from huge amounts of data about a place (Martin & Eroglu, 1993).

The ability of country brands to create value has led governments to design policies aimed to the creation and consolidation of a strong and positive country brand image. Traditionally, the management of the country brand is based on a careful communication strategy, with a double objective: (1) link the country brand to positive associations with different origins and natures, (2) create a positive opinion in consumers and an attitude towards the country brand.

During the past decade, the rapid evolution of the internet, and especially in the social media, has offered new opportunities and challenges to the country brand management. They provide the opportunity to connect with consumers using richer media with greater reach (Thackeray et al., 2008). The interactive nature of these digital media not only allows brand managers to share and exchange information with their consumers, but also allows consumers to share and exchange information with each other. Besides, managers have the opportunity to shift relations with consumers from dialogue to trialogue, in which consumer engage in meaningful relationships with one another and with the country brand (Tsimonis & Dimitriadis, 2014). But among the challenges came the opportunity for consumers to use the social media besides the obvious use of searching information and communicating with boundaries, it is nowadays possible to use social media to express feelings and thoughts.

Considering the last ideas, this book chapter proposes to analyze how the Spanish Government has used the Internet and social media to create and consolidate the Spain Brand image. For that, the chapter is divided into two different sections. The first one reviews the theoretical framework about the country brand image concept, and how social media networks are used in the construction of communication strategies. The second section presents the case of the Spain Brand, identifying the different associations that make up its image, and analyzing the communication strategies used in the network as well as the results it has obtained in recent years.

BRAND BASICS

Today no one casts doubt on the strategic nature of the brand, as well as the fact that the consumer is the agent on which depends its success or failure in the markets. Since the beginning of the 1990s, abundant works analyze the concepts of brand, image and capital, noting its importance in strategic terms, and showing how all this is a direct result of the degree of knowledge that the consumer has about the brand, and the influence this knowledge has on the affective and behavioral dimensions of the subject against the brand (Keller et al., 2011; Kim & Kim, 2005; Stahl et al., 2012).

Considering the above, several issues arise in relation to the companies' brand situation: Do the companies and organizations have the ability to affect the position and capital of its brands in the markets? While at the macro level, the fundamental question is to know if it is possible to apply the logic of the brand in the country context.

Regardless of the field, organizations and administrations expend high efforts and resources to the brand management. The objective consists of the design, establishment and management of a strong and positive brand image. To do this, it is not only needed to control the reality of the brand and make a proper projection of it through the different channels of communication. Moreover, it is required to understand the mechanisms through which the consumer sets the image, and the way in which this influences the different dimensions of its performance.

WHAT IS A BRAND?

Technically, and as Kotler and Armstrong,(1996) show, a brand is defined as "a name, term, sign, symbol, or design, or combination of them which is intended to identify the goods and services of one seller or group of sellers and to differentiate them from those of competitors". Brands are born to be used in business, marketing, and advertising. Initially, livestock branding was adopted to differentiate one person's cattle from another's by means of a distinctive symbol burned into the animal's skin with a hot branding iron.

In accounting, a brand defined as an intangible asset, is often the most valuable asset, on a corporation's balance sheet. Brand owners manage their brands carefully to create shareholder value, and brand valuation is an important management technique that ascribes a money value to a brand, and allows marketing investment to be managed (e.g. prioritized across a portfolio of brands) to maximize shareholder value. Although only acquired brands appear on a company's balance sheet, the notion of putting a value on a brand forces marketing leaders to be focused on long term stewardship of the brand and managing for value.

But the brand is, after all, the sum total and ultimate expression of all the collected activities undertaken by the brand owner (or on the owner's behalf) and the experiences of the brand user. These activities and experiences do not always match, work in accord or act synergistically in an integrative way to achieve the best out of the brand's potential.

THE BRAND IMAGE

Branding is a complex concept, and to some extent controversial in the field of marketing management. Many works have tried to offer a definition of this concept (Table 1).Table 1. Definitions of the concept of brand

- **Plummer (1985):** A complex concept that refers to the personality of the brand and the attributes and benefits or consequences associated with its use.
- **Aaker (1994) :** Set of associations usually organized by way of meaning.
- **Kapferer (1992):** It is the way in which the audience plays a set of signals from the products, services and communications issued by the brand.
- **Biel (1992):** Set of attributes and associations which the consumer connects to the brand.
- **Keller (1993;1998):** Set of associations linked to the brand that consumer keeps in memory.
- **Aaker (1996):** It is how the brand is perceived by consumers.
- **Kotler and Amstrong (1996) :** A set of beliefs that the consumer keeps about the brand.
- **Schmitt and Simonson (1998) :** Mental reflection of the identity and the set of associations that build it.
- **Nandan (2005):** External perception of consumers about a brand.
- **Faircloth (2005):** Overall mental image that consumers have of a brand, which is uniqueness in comparison to the other brands.
- **Royand Banerjee (2007) :** Consumer's thoughts and feelings towards a brand.
- **Iversen and Hem (2008):** Personal symbolism that consumers associate with the brand, which comprises of all the descriptive and evaluative brand-related information.
- **Kapferer (2012):** From the point of view of the receiver, the image of brand focuses on how certain groups perceive a product, a brand, a politician, a company or a country; and he decodes all the signs of them or the communication covered by the brand. (Source: Own elaboration)

Dobni and Zinkhan (1990) point out that it is difficult to find a high degree of agreement among the different definitions offered, both in relation to the concept of image, and that concerning the role that it plays for the subject. However, it is possible to highlight a series of traits and characteristics common to all of them. The brand image is characterized by being a concept generated by the receiver, and has a complex and multidimensional nature.It is the result of a mental process of the consumer - or potential consumer - that receives information about the brand. In this process the individual collects, evaluates and associate information that relates to the brand, and that comes from different sources (Janiszewski & Van Osselaer, 2000).

Boush et al. (1987) point out that the image includes cognitive and affective aspects of the subject in relation to the brand. Along this line, Roy and Banerjee (2007) describe the brand image as a set of thoughts and feelings that an individual has towards a brand. Faircloth (2005) and Iversen and Hem (2008) go beyond, designating the brand image as the mental representation that consumers have globally about a brand.

This mental representation is determined by the degree of knowledge that the individual has about the brand, and includes personal and intrinsic elements of the individual, such as his beliefs or thoughts towards the brand. All this makes the image, that the individual has about the brand, unique and different, so it is considered that the image makes it possible to differentiate the brand from the rest. According to

Batra et al., (1993) the content of the image has been operationalized along the marketing literature in terms of: (1) general characteristics, feelings and impressions; (2) perceptions of the product; (3) beliefs and attitudes; (4) the brand personality; (5) relationship between characteristics of the brand and the feelings and emotions aroused in the consumer.

Hsieh and Li (2008) point out that when consumers have a favorable image, the brand message has a strong influence in comparison with messages from a competing brand. Their paper shows what previously noted in other works of research in the field of marketing: that the brand image is an important determinant of consumer behavior. On this particular, Burman et al., (2009), among others, indicate how this influence occurs in three dimensions that make up the behavior of the individual: cognitive, affective and behavioral. Thus, the double cognitive-affective component identified in the associations that make up the image, influences the level of knowledge or attitude that the individual develops toward the brand. In addition, the degree of knowledge and/or the displayed attitude influence, or at least guide, the behavioral dimension of human behavior. For example, a favorable brand image exerts a positive effect on the behavior of purchases in terms of increasing in loyalty (Zeithaml, 1988; Zins, 2001), acceptance of higher price levels in the brand, or generation of an intensive positive word of mouth communication (Martenson, 2007).

The knowledge and attitude towards the brand have the ability to determine or at least guide the behavioral dimension of human behavior (Burmann et al., 2008). This would explain, for example, why consumers having a favorable image, value most favorably messages issued by the brand -compared to the competition-. (Hsieh & Li, 2008); develop high rates of loyalty towards the same (Zeithaml, 1988; Zins, 2001), purchase intent (Fakharmanesh & Miyandehi. 2013) or generate a strong and positive word of mouth communication (Martenson, 2007). More recently, Ismail and Spinelli (2012) provide that brand image influences love towards the brand and that love is what generates the word of mouth communication.

Finally, as a mental representation, the image is characterized by some stability necessary for its survival and concretion. But in spite of this, it is also true that the image is not something static, but has a dynamic structure, sensitive, to the changes experienced by the agents and the own social environment in which brand is inserted, in the same way that as it happens to the subject both internally and externally (Folgado et al., 2011).

COUNTRY BRAND EQUITY

It is widely recognized that the name of a country can often act in a similar way as the name of a brand (Anholt, 2006) and, hence, has the ability to add to or subtract from the perceived value of a product (Aaker, 1991; Keller 1993). For example, products bearing a "made in Germany", "made in U.S.A." or "made in Japan" label are generally evaluated much more favorably by consumers than products with, for example, a 'made in Hungary' or "made in Bangladesh" label, due to the reputation of the former countries as top world manufacturers and exporters (Kaynak et al., 2000). Consequently, it seems that countries whose name evoke positive (or negative) associations with consumers also contain a positive (or negative) country equity (Iversen and Hem, 2008). In line with these findings, Shocker, Srivastava, and Ruekert (1994, p. 150) suggest that "country-of-origin effects may be part of the brand equity of certain names", while Shimp et al (1993) introduce a new construct called country equity "to disentangle the equity contained in a brand (the conventional notion of brand equity) from that contained in the country with which the brand is associated".

A comparison of the different definitions and conceptualizations of country equity reveals that some researchers (Iversen & Hem, 2001) refer to country equity at the individual consumer level, meaning that they are mainly interested in the differential effect of the country origin as a non-physical product attribute on consumers' perceptions and response (e.g., in terms of customer perceived value, product perceptions, and preferences). An example for such a conceptualization is provided by Iversen and Hem (2001) who describe country equity as "that portion of consumer affect toward a brand or a product that is derived purely from the product's associations with a particular country". Other researchers (e.g., Kotler et al., 2010) refer to country equity at the aggregate country level and conceptualize it in terms of general assets and liabilities of a country (which is of course not limited to consumers' perceived value of products originating from a particular country as indicated by the first research stream).

THE KEYS OF THE COUNTRY BRAND: THE TYPICALITY AND THE COUNTRY BRAND AS GEOGRAPHICAL INDICATOR OF QUALITY

The true capacity of the *country brand* resides in its ability to increase the value perceived by the customer in any product or service by having a specific origin. Because the fact that a product is "typical" of a place allows the name of the place to become a geographical indicator of quality.

Increasingly, public administrations and business organizations have noted the enormous power of the country brands. In markets as diverse as the agri-food, technology, or fashion and accessories, the origin of a product determine its degree of differentiation. The origin is synonymous with expertise, tradition and know-how, as well as at the same time it becomes a guarantee of quality, exclusivity and excellence.The concept of typicality is not defined in marketing literature in a clear way, although there is an intuitive approach to it based on geographical origin, age, methods of preparation, customs, etc. (Albert & Muñoz, 1999). There are three dimensions on which the typicality articulates: quality, differentiation and territory. From a marketing perspective, quality is a customer perception of the overall quality or superiority of a product against others with regard to its purpose or intention (Aaker, 1996; Zeithalm, 1988).Such perceived superiority depends on the subject, the moment in which the assessment is made and the type of product being assessed and the need that is intended to satisfy. In this way, it is observed as the quality is a relative, subjective and dynamic concept that can be assessed in multiple ways by consumers (Janiszewski & Van Osselaer, 2000).A different dimension,although deeply associated with perceived quality, is the differentiation, whether from the production and presentation (internal qualitative component) or from the recognition of the difference by the consumer, or perceived image of the product (external qualitative component). To the consumer differentiation produces a higher degree of satisfaction because of the tailored products to different market segments; to the producer, the differentiation is a source of competitive advantages. Against standardization, differentiation is based from an economic point of view in the models of monopolistic competition, where each company tries to isolate itself from the competition in prices and achieve a certain degree of market power, making that its products are perceived and valued as unique by consumers who make up a target market or a particular segment (Agarwal et al., 2009).

From a strategic perspective, the differentiation of a product has at least two meanings: the first one says that a company follows a strategy of differentiation when it offers a product differentiated from the rest of the competitors for a given target audience; in the second, company differentiates its products to adapt or better meet the needs of different targets (Yagüe, 1996). In this second meaning, the differentiation is an inseparable strategy from the segmentation, because it is necessary that the markets are segmented so that companies can address products specifically adapted to the needs of all or some of the segments. Since in this approach the perceived quality is one of the main axes on which companies design and execute their strategies of differentiation (Albert & Muñoz, 1999).

On the other hand, both from production and from an appreciation of consumers, the typicality of a product is largely associated with the origin of the product, i.e. the territory. The territory, in its triple geographical, historical and cultural dimension, determines the typicality of a product (Letablier & Nicolas, 1994). Geographically the territory conditions the production by its natural pedoclimatic characteristics. Culturally, the territory provides typicality to associate the production and consumption of a product to the customs or collective representations around the same (Steenkamp & Dekimpe, 1997). Historically, the typicality is represented by the anchor or settlement at the time of the practices, methods or knowledge about the product (previously, continuity and permanence).With all this, to consider a product typical, this one should be associated spatially to a territory and culturally with customs or modes, with a minimum of permanence in time or age, and owning individual qualitative characteristics that differ it from other products (Albert & Muñoz, 1999). Naturally, the consumer who observes all of these features in a product has bases to establish a judgment on the degree of quality of the product and the degree of adaptation to his needs. However, on multiple occasions the so-called typical products make use of an external sign or official recognition which guarantees its quality. Sometimes this endorsement is the only possible way to publicly demonstrate the quality of the product.

THE MANAGEMENT OF BRAND IMAGE

Ind and Riondino (2001), and Stuart and Jones (2004), among others, point out how the internet has brought a revolution to corporate brands. In spite of this, however, there are few papers that analyze the effects that this generates in the processes of formation and management of the brand image.Christodoulides (2011) points out that the development of the internet has altered the way in which companies manage the image of their brands. But there are still many questions as, for example, there is still a lack of solid evidence about how brand values can be transferred via the network (Frías et al., 2008). The understanding of how this phenomenon occurs is essential for those responsible for marketing, given the need to develop an integrated management of the brand image.

In a dynamic and interactive environment like the present, companies have changed the mode of communicating with its customers. Companies choose other models based on the continued dialogue with the customer, where internet plays a key role as a channel of communication, in front of a hierarchical model where communication, descending and unidirectional, is based on the use of mass media (Christodoulides, 2011).

And with the increased use of technologies based on the internet,the importance of meaning in the relationship between companies and customers has increased, at the same time it has significantly changed the role played by customers. Thus, the interactivity offered by new technologies - bidirectionality, saving time, control and responsiveness - (Bolton & Saxena-Iyer, 2009), have enhanced the involvement of customers in product development and in the creation of content in relation to the brand (Edvardsson et al., 2011). With all this, now consumers have the ability to speak directly with the brands, and about the brands, with other consumers.

One of the main issues contained in the literature is the role of the brand image as a strategic tool for the development of loyalty. In the field of e-business the meaning of brand building has increased with the explosion of the number of competitive options that have appeared in a short period of time. The Internet offers unique tools of interaction with the brand building that were not previously available through the traditional mass media aimed at brand building strategies (Beerli & Martin, 2004).

A study of trends in building brand on the internet (Nemes, 2000) has shown the importance of the domain names as an extension of the brand name. Consumers not only prefer well-known and easy-to-remember names, but rather the content of the web also plays a significant role in improving the overall image of the brand. Elements such as the language, the use of certain colors, or certain audiovisual resources can influence the users of a same web differently. Thus, the fact that the internet is a global site makes necessary for enterprises and organizations to consider the existing multicultural reality when designing their webs (Alcántara et al., 2013). However, an excessive control of branding on the internet can return to the company violently. This practice is known as the Streisand effect, which is concerned with trying to control the content of the publications on the Internet, eliminating what has been published can cause the opposite effect, further disseminating the information relating to a trade mark or a person (Liarte, 2013).

Indeed, the users of the network are a potential source of information, which can be used by other individuals in the creation of the brand image (Varadarajan et al., 2010).On the internet not only companies or intermediaries publish on brands, also users can make comments, express opinions and create content on brands. The user generated content (UGC) is a new term appeared in the literature which defines as consumers' created contents that are accessible via the Internet; it reflects a degree of creative effort and is generated for free outside the routines and professional practices. However, in practice UGC is not a so recent concept. In fact, already in 1996, the work of Hoffman and Novack shows that the eruption of the internet promotes a model of communication based on interactivity, where multiple actors can become senders and receivers of messages through multiple media.The specific literature on the creation of the UGC is limited and is in the early stages of research on this phenomenon, in such a way that the few published works are focused on the study of the motivations of the UGC (Berthon et al., 2008). Focusing on the creation of ads by users, Berthon et al. (2008) identify in the individual three main motivations for creating these ads: (1) intrinsic enjoyment for the expression, (2) own promoting, and (3) change of perceptions which aims to show the brand differently to other consumers.

Christodoulides et al., (2012) identify four antecedents of the creation of UGC related to the brand: (1) co-creation, by which the value of a brand is perceived to be produced jointly between the company and consumers, (2) empowerment, to the extent that the brand is perceived to empower consumers, (3) concept of oneself, to the extent that the brand is perceived to match the concept of oneself that consumershave, that means the creation of the UGC is used as a communication vehicle of the identity of oneself, and (4) community, to the extent that a brand is perceived to promote a community of consumers; in this case the creation of the UGC is on the interaction between the community and the development of a sense of belonging. These authors show that engage with the UGC affects consumer brand perceptions. In 2011, the increase in the UGC through electronic media represents one of the latest market dynamics (Christodoulides et al., 2011).

The digital WOM (word of mouth), also known as eWOM, is one of the means through which individuals create content on the network. This is defined as the development of a "word of mouth" communication via internet, i.e. communication that keep consumers on the purchase experience and consumption of a product through digital media (Hennig-Thurau et al., 2004). Consumers can express informally their opinions and experiences through the network, and these can be viewed by people from all over the world. Works like Chu and Kim's (2011) analyze the motivations of individuals to engage in eWOM. Most of them indicate the intention to build relational capital, in such a way that through this type of communication, the need for social interaction is satisfied and opinions about products and brands are shared through internet (Hennig-Thurau et al., 2004). In addition, recipients can respond to issuers, thus developing relationships and increasing their social interactions (Chu & Kim, 2011). Other authors, on the other hand, point to a motivation of pride or strengthening of self-confidence as a reason to develop eWOM. This motivation arises from the desire to be socially recognized by others. In this way, recommendations to third parties allows the issuer gain attention and respect and provide to be considered an important source of reliable information (Hennig-Thurau et al., 2004).The e-WOM can help other consumers make a right choice. In this sense Berger and Schwartz (2011) point to how the eWOM can affect the three dimensions that shape the behavior of individuals against the brand. In particular, it promotes the degree of knowledge about the product and brand, influences the development of the attitude, and finally, has an impact on the intent and purchase behavior developed later.However, the effect of the eWOM on individuals can be asymmetric. In this way, it is observed that a positive view has a greater influence than a negative opinion. In particular, Romaniuk (2011) suggests that this effect may be up to four times higher in the event that initiated communication is positive in nature; in comparison, the effects of the negative WOM, are smaller and insignificant. On the other hand, Dean and Lang (2008) have shown that when a negative eWOM becomes a viral message, the harmful effect caused is observed not only about the brand but also competitor brands in the same category of products. The relationship between customers and brands has reached such importance that companies consider these relations as a significant component of the own capital of the brand (Blackston, 1992). However, the ability of companies to control the image of their brands is currently very low, especially when there are ways and communication channels such as those previously listed. That is why many managers believe that the only role that can be played in relation to the brand is that of a guardian, protecting, and not controlling the meaning and the public image of the brands (Blackston, 1995).The web has changed the way in which consumers are involved in the communication process. So that individuals become more demanding, and not only want to be consumers of the product, but also participate in the development of its marketing mix. This new conception of the individual as a producer-consumer, known as prosumer, supposes a whole change in the way in which companies have to create and market their products and brands. Focusing strictly on the field of brand communications, the prosumer is characterized by playing an active role in them, given that he is able to create, enrich and even control the process of communication. The UGC allows consumers to transform and play creatively with brands. The development of the internet, Web 2.0 applications and peer-to-peer communications, offer consumers unprecedented opportunities to become creative (Christodoulides et al., 2011).As a consequence of the creativity of consumers, marketers have discovered that in addition to the organizations, the consumers are also able to create value, not only to trademarks but also to other consumers. To capture that value, the minds of management and business models must change (Berthon et al., 2007), and to consider from this moment that consumers are at the same time co-creators (Christodoulides et al., 2011).

The change of the model of communication "from one to many" to the communication "from many to many" exemplified by the internet and the interactive technologies shows that the flow of communication is no longer unidirectional (from transmitter to the receiver). In addition, several interactions can take place not only between consumers and marketers, but also within the communities of consumers (Zhou et al., 2012). Consumers also have access to tools that allow them to create their own content and spread it easily and fast. The bandwidth and peer-to-peer technology enables consumers to create and share their views and experiences with regard to brands with other consumers through entries in blogs, videos, sounds, product references. And it could be said that the UGC related to the brand is an activity related to the consumption (Christodoulides et al., 2011).

Now consumers are demanding to participate actively in decision-making concerning their favorite brands. Faced with this situation, companies have to find a new way of approaching the marketing to make its brands attractive and easy to connect with consumers both individually and collectively. The brand has to be proactive, trying not only to understand the motivations that lead consumers to pour views on them, but also to give a quick and appropriate response to the same. The UGC is an important mechanism of feedback which allows to enter in the particular perception of consumers about a brand. For this reason it has to be analyzed closely. Companies will receive attention from creative consumers if they reach a community around its brand, create a brand identity that identifies with the desires of consumers and develop brands that are customized with the direct input of consumers (Christodoulides et al., 2011).

New rules for engaging on the social web are explored in relation to their contribution to impair or improve corporate reputation and brand image. The web allows to increase the flow of free information, unfiltered, by an audience with rights as the professional writers (Shirky, 2008).

It is necessary to have transparency and responsibility to operate effectively in an environment where people are engaged in an active way in conversations online. These fast changes affect directly the marketing communication, and it is necessary to review the rules of reputation and brand management. For the reputation and brand management is not enough anymore to know how an organization is perceived and the image that its audience has, whose formation is based on its communication efforts; in addition, it is necessary to inquire into the conversations that take place online between users and consumers (Jolly, 2001).Organizations are increasing the need to implement the reputation management and take the risk to which are subjected in the commitment to the vast community through the social web. A clear understanding of how the reputation in this environment can be handled is vital to the business. Agents are gradually using talks to share industry information, taking an active role as consumers detective, investigative journalists and influencers of opinion. The Web 2.0 is a tool to empower consumers and citizens. In this new environment the effective management of brand and reputation requires brands to collaborate with different agents. The social web makes participants to navigate through a shared and negotiated construction of the understanding of meaning. The social web baptizes a new type of professional consumers or prosumers (Davis & Moy, 2007).

The way a company behaves online and is perceived by its wide audience is far more important than philanthropy, donations to charity, ostentatious websites or even corporate social responsibility annual reports printed on recycled paper; in short, online reputation is very important. In the era of the social web a chat in an informal meeting room can be online in seconds while the information slipped through the bulk mail can be published and commented on blogs in a matter of minutes. These activities can potentially damage the image of a company and create the perception of corporate irresponsibility (Jones et al., 2009).

The power of the networks of the web sites has contributed extraordinary to increase the speed, reach and interactivity of social communication. As the number of people grows in networks, connectivity also increases. If these people link to other content, then the value increases exponentially (Hendler & Golbeck, 2008).

A correct planning of the online conversations can help companies to build and maintain a presence, reputation and brand image (Christodoulides et al., 2011). Fill (2005) talks about how the reputation of the global brands can be questioned or even tarnished through spoof websites where doubts can damage their integrity, hence the need for greater transparency, participation and collaboration. Ind (2003) suggests that a wide social perspective of the brand management is fundamental for a company to keep its relevance in the marketplace. In a social setting, a brand is drawn by the corporation and also by the community that it adheres. In an environment of corporate social behavior, messages should be clear and convincing, since customers are more likely to attribute greater perceived value and greater satisfaction to the products or services produced by socially responsible companies (Luo and Bhattacharya, 2006). On the social web, there is little room for the monologue (Lewis, 2001).

Reputation in the social Web is mainly built with the participation in the community, collaboration and content creation punctuated by reputation aggregators known as search engines, the door that people use to find content online (Weber, 2007). Unsolicited emails, advertising and the intrusion into the social web may damage the image and reputation of the business. The hyperlinks and the rankings of web pages used by the search engines, increase the chances of the image recognition and contribute to the building of the online reputation of the organization (Weber, 2007). On the social web emission (broadcasting) has been replaced by participation, collaboration and exchange, which can be baptized as social emission (social casting) (Greaves & Mika, 2008). Under these circumstances, organizations have to adapt and rethink their online corporate reputation and their brand communication strategies between their management practices (Christodoulides et al., 2011). The social web, allows the agents of the organization and the public to co-create the brand image and reputation. The property of this process is shared and inevitably brings risk factors (Fill, 2005).

THE EFFECT OF THE ORIGIN ON THE BEHAVIOR OF THE INDIVIDUAL

The presence of an indicator of origin-quality of a recognized and prestige brand makes the consumer to enlarge the image that exists of the brand. The strengthening of existing partnerships and the incorporation of new ones allow the subject to recognize new benefits of the product on a cognitive level and extend and reinforce his recognition of the former, to develop new attitudes and feelings towards the product on an affective level, and even to show a greater intent to purchase, or even to reach the very act of purchase, on a behavioral level (Steenkamp, 1997).

The importance attached to the origin as a source of information and meaning has rekindled its interest in marketing research (Lampert & Jaffe, 1998). The place of origin of products can be considered a major source of advantages for enterprises, able to alter the assessment that the consumers of the products or brands make (Agrawal & Kamakura, 1999). The image of a product, service or brand plays an important role in consumer purchasing decisions, but this image is formed by various variables, so that the place of manufacture or origin of the product becomes an element capable of defining, or at least alter the image of the same (Bigné et al., 1993).The role of the geographical indicators of quality in the creation of attitudes and as a determinant of consumer behavior can be analyzed considering the classical approach formulated by the attitude as a conjunction of three elements: the cognitive component, the affective and the behavioral. Despite this distinction, based on a more current conception, attitude is usually considered more specifically, as the affective or the evaluative dimension understood as the overall evaluation toward an object (Fuchs & Reichel, 2006). In this way, the cognitive dimension reflects the structure and contents of beliefs and knowledge about attributes that characterize the products and brands. These beliefs serve as a knowledge base to form assessments that define the attitude. The behavioral dimension is also the result of the attitude embodied in the provision for action in terms of intended acquisition, provision and use of products and services (Keller, 1998).The influence of the quality indicators and the determination of attitudes is given this way first by beliefs and associations that this feature generates in consumers. Considered as an attribute that is external to the physical characteristics of the product, it is assumed that the origin is used by the consumer as a basis to infer associations relating to the quality, results or other specific characteristics about the product, especially when the product or brand is unknown, or when it is possible to evaluate it without having previously existed an act of consumption (Steenkamp, 1997). Through the personal experience, the information gained through other sources, and even stereotypes or existing topics on the areas (Roth & Romeo, 1992), the consumer develops a series of associations related to the place of origin of the product that later will form the image of the brand to which it is bound.

The type of relevant associations for the evaluation that can be generated by consumers from the information on the place of origin is very varied. These partnerships can range from beliefs about certain specific and intrinsic characteristics of the product - for example color or flavor of a wine - to more general beliefs that refer to global product aspects such as quality, attributes related to dimensions of personality, values or symbolic representations of the kind of cultural identity or tradition. The association of quality therefore plays a crucial role in the evaluation component derived from the geographical indicators of quality. The organization and rules surrounding geographical indicators make sure procedures of manufacture and quality of the raw materials are controlled and certified. This fact added to the idea of a greater specialization and know-how of the companies generate higher quality perceptions that positively affect the attitudes. This perception of superior quality determines an effect more direct and palpable on the value perceived by the consumer and, thus, in his confidence (Agrawal & Kamakura, 1999).In addition to these associations, there are others of second order, related to the economic, social and cultural characteristics of the geographic area that may also have effects on the evaluative dimensions of individuals. In this case, if consumers keep a positive (or negative) image over the area, it tends to generalize a positive or negative attitude toward all trademarks and/or products associated with the site (Roth & Romeo, 1992). These associations, together with the rest of associations more generic related aspects of personality, styles of life or culture and traditions, have a more limited effect on evaluations and behaviors of individuals, because its impact on the added value are minor.All these factors determine that, ultimately, the positive evaluation of the product or the brand will increase consumer confidence, and therefore will increase the perceived value or reduce the risk associated with the purchase (Bigné et al., 1993).In the literature, it has been suggested that the image created in the minds of consumers about the origin can be considered as the fifth element of the marketing mix, along with the product, price, communication and distribution (Baker & Currie, 1993). Laroche et al., (2005) goes beyond and describes the image of the area of origin as the image of the products. For this author, the image of a geographic area allows the classification of its products, fortification and development of favorable attitudes and beliefs. Even, sometimes the influence of the image of the area is so strong in subjects, that they develop perceptions about the products that may not be correlated with their actual attributes (Baker & Michie, 1995). This fact would explain phenomena such as ethnocentrism in consumers, where the attitude and preference for domestic products tend to be higher (Steenkamp, 1997).

However, although in a way more or less general, most of papers agree in pointing out the existence of these effects, as well as highlighting the importance of the 'origin' in relation to the decision-making process of consumers. It is necessary to clarify to what extent it can be a really relevant attribute. This fact has led some authors to point out that in practice actual consumers are influenced by origin, but to a lesser extent than research indicate (Agrawal & Kamakura, 1999; Bigné et al., 1993). An important conclusion from the previous studies is that the effect shown by origin is lower in those situations where the consumer uses more information criteria to assess the product. Referred works highlight that the effect of origin on consumers is only detected in certain products, and with uneven intensity, and accordingly is not justified to grant the origin as a generalized effect of any product or country. In any way in a real situation of consumption, as Agrawal and Kamakura (1999) point out, the consumer tends to use additional sources of information, the effect of the origin of the country significantly decreased. Despite all this, one thing is clear, all developed research points to that place of origin presents an important effect in the consumer behavior, whether in its dimension of cognitive, affective or behavioral. Obviously, the results of the studies are determined by: the type of design proposed for the research, the type of product, and considered consumers.

In our opinion the importance attached to the place of origin by consumers has to be taken into account by the managers as an element of marketing to use. Just pointing out the origin of the product on the label, sometimes will facilitate both the identification of the product and the improvement of evaluation. The support of an identifier of the origin of the products that certifies officially the origin of the products, will reinforce the advantage granted by origin to the companies, and its effect on their products or brand.

BRAND SPAIN CASE STUDY

States are increasingly aware of the importance of their image, reputation, i.e. of their brand. What has triggered the rise of these initiatives of image is the globalization, that spans all areas (economical, political and cultural) and, from this point of view, it seems logical that among theGovernments there is an increased awareness that the image of the country is a fundamental asset to defend the interests of the States in the new international economic and political relations.

In a global market of goods, services and persons, the States must sell its best image to attract most beneficial flows that may come from other countries (Moisescu, 2009). Along with the need to attract financing, the brand image of the country serves as an indicator or element that guarantees the quality of the products coming from it.

In this way, the country brand facilitates the access of its products in foreign markets. Finally, the territory itself becomes a liquefiable marketing element. As a tourism product, the existence of a brand that brings to spin a set of favorable associations that are related to the territory, promotes its positioning in the national tourist context.In this situation, there are developing public policies aimed at the construction, promotion and consolidation of a brand image country. Such is the case of the Spain Brand, i.e. a state policy whose effects are to be seen in the long term. It is aimed at strengthening the country's image, both among Spanish citizens and beyond Spanish borders. By Royal Decree 998/2012, June 28, the position was established as the High Commissioner for "*Marca España*" (BrandSpain) from the Spanish Government in the planning, promotion and coordinated management of the activities by public and private agencies aimed at building a stronger image about Spain.The Spain Brand is an inclusive and integrator project with the vocation of permanence in the long term.The project aims to establish an image of Spain as an economic and political power among the first countries in the world; a view of a traditional and modern country at the same time; solid and supportive; different; flexible and open to change. It is to highlight the many strengths of Spain in the areas of culture, heritage, language, science, technology, tourism, fashion, gastronomy and solidarity.

To do this, the Spain Brand has the invaluable help of the Crown, of the whole of the administrations, embassies, consulates and sectorial offices abroad, companies, the media, citizens abroad, civil society and all those, including foreigners, who share the values that inspire the project. In particular, the Spain Brand Board gathers the heads of the leading actors in the project to analyze their main courses of action. It is an informal body, presided over by the High Commissioner for "*MarcaEspaña*" from the Spanish Government and made up by the presidents or directors of the following organizations:

- Office of the Secretary of State for Communications of the Presidency of the Government
- High Sports Board
- Office of the Secretary-General for Food and Agriculture (MAGRAMA)
- Office of the Secretary-General for Defense Policy (MINISDEF)
- Spanish Olympic Committee
- Instituto Cervantes
- Real Instituto (R. I.) Elcano
- ICEX
- TURESPAÑA
- Carolina Foundation
- Directorate-General for International Economic Relations (MAEC)
- Directorate-General for Media and Public Diplomacy (MAEC)
- Directorate-General for Trade and Investment
- Directorate-General for Economic Policy (Ministry of Economy and Competitiveness)
- RTVE
- EFE news agency
- Spanish Ambassador for Cultural Diplomacy
- Ministry of Education, Culture and Sport

The *MarcaEspaña* Board performs its action through working groups:

- Public diplomacy
- Economic diplomacy
- Sport diplomacy
- Cultural and social policy
- Communication, media
- Civil society
- Institutional actors
- Self-governing regions and local governments

The First Steps For The Spain Brand History

The history of the Spain Brand is a success story of how can be created a brand country linked to modernity, innovation and the Mediterranean lifestyle. Because from 1939 to 1975 Spain was isolated Internationally. A non-democratic government system, and an economic policy that isolated the country from the European environment, managed to project a negative image of Spain. But despite its negative history, Spain has been able to achieve a positive and believed image. Experts on location branding, note that Spain is among the best examples of modern successful national branding because it is built on what truly exist.

The political transition to a democratic system, next to exit the economic crisis at the end of the decade of 1980 made possible that Spain offered an image of modern and stable country. But definitely, it is the celebration of sports and cultural events of first level, as the Barcelona Olympics in 1992 or the Universal Exposition of Seville, which attach permanently the position of Spain on the international scene.

But the real starting point for the birth of the Project Spain Brand is situated in the year 2001. The achievements in relation to the external image, make that from the public sphere is token the awareness of the need to manage comprehensively the brand country. At the end of 2001, the Elcano Royal Institute, the Association of Leading Brands of Spain, the ICEX (Ministry of Economy), the Ministry of Foreign Affairs and DIRCOM (the Association of Directors of Communication), constituted the work platform for the Project Spain Brand(PME) to "move forward in a coordinated way in the construction of an image of Spain to respond to the new economic, social and cultural reality of the country".The PME consisted of several phases:

1. A collection of information on the foreign image of Spain, based on polls of general population opinion or opinion leaders.

The study's conclusions leave no doubt. Spain, above all by the effect of the transition to democracy, has a very good political image as a Latin country, and improving, with high and increasing levels of confidence towards the country and its people, which generate more sympathy than antipathy (although not everywhere). In addition, it also has an excellent, cultural and artistic image.

However, and as halo effect, there is a strong stereotype that influences negatively the foreign image of Spain. On the one hand, the economic picture is good and certainly improves, but Spain continues being perceived as a country with an economic capacity below the real. On the other hand, the "Spain is different", based on an excellent image as a tourist destination, already solidly seated, generates tensions among its high evaluation as a place to rest, and its mediocre assessment as a suitable place to work. Fr this reason the "made in Spain" is regularly assessed as a result of a very little knowledge of the Spanish brands and products and of a certain traditional image of no advanced country.

2. The second phase of the PME is about listening.

Through round tables, the actors and most relevant institutions gave their opinion about the reality and the problems of the foreign image of Spain: experts in history, sociology and marketing; the Public Administration, central, regional and municipal; the business world; journalism, advertising and communication professionals; Spain brand ambassadors (Spanish personalities from various fields who have achieved some popularity abroad); and, finally, policymakers of image in other countries.

The necessary conclusions to draft a guideline of the Spain brand communication were token from the first and the second phase. In the third and last phase, work was conducted by a team of experts and managers of communication which, after the track of the previous phases, formulated proposals of positioning and communication discussed and approved by the organizers of the PME.

One of the first elements in the creation of the Spain Brand was the one concerning the graphic identity. Its first branding efforts incorporate absorb, and embrace a wide variety of activities under one graphic identity to form and project a multi-faceted yet coherent interlocking and mutually supportive whole. For this, its national promotional program uses Joan Miró's sun to symbolize the step change in the modernization of Spain. With it, it is unified graphical a myriad of activities, publicity events and ads, even though the different programs are driven by both public and private sectors (see Figure 1).

The New Efforts: Towards Strengthening The Spain Brand

The efforts made over the past decades have allowed to consolidate an image of Spain as a modern and growing country. Problems related to ignorance or mistrust generated by Spain -and everything related to it- over the last two decades have been overcome. And the current international context, along with the country's external position, requires rethinking the Spain brand.

One of the key points in the current management of the Spain brand has consisted in the harness -and above all the profitable- any activity, news or event that allows to project a positive image of the country abroad. Under this premise, from Spain Brand have been launched several initiatives that are intended to highlight the contribution of Spanish organizations and individuals abroad. For example, cases of professional and human effort that have contributed to the development of their host countries, the strengthening of bilateral relations with Spain and the knowledge, through their works and behavior, of the traits that define the contemporary Spanish society: diversity, creativity, solidarity, innovation and generosity.

Figure 1. The use of JoanMiró's sun as the image of the Spain Brand

This has been supported by advertising on a national and regional level, and strengthened by the privatization and rapid global expansion of the Spanish multinationals such as Telefonica and Bank of Santander into Latin American, the impact of hosting the Barcelona Olympics, the rebuilding of great cities like Bilbao, with the Guggenheim Museum, the films of Almodóvar and even the prominence of actresses such as Penélope Cruz. It was, partially, a careful planning and coordination, and part, individual inspired and corporate action. Spanish designers as AdolfoDomínguez or ManoloBlahnik, the film maker PedroAlmodóvar and the architect Santiago Calatraba, pooled their artistic talents and worked together as a team to assist the Spanish government in expressing a Spain that was fresh, free and more competitive.

The net result is that Spain's branding effort is both efficient and impactful: one symbol leverages everything together in the eyes of Spain and the world.

The Spain Brand Focus: The Tourism Sector

One of the principal focus of *MarcaEspaña* is to consolidate Spain as a power in the tourism sector. It, thus, boosts the competitiveness of companies and Spanish tourist destinations and renews the world leadership of Spain for the next decades, contributing to the generation of wealth, employment and social welfare.

Through the impetus of the Strategic Marketing Plan, several goals are set out, seeking to increase the profitability of the sector. Among the designated objectives to be achieved in the medium and long term are:

1. To increase the volume of tourism revenue.
2. Diversifying the origin, temporality, destination and motivation of travelers.
3. To increase the power of the tourism brand of Spain.

In particular, and in regard to the biennium 2014-2015, the above objectives are realized in different sub-goals. In relation to the increase in the volume of tourism revenue, it is intended to increase the number of overnight stays and average expenditure of the travelers. With regard to travelers, the objectives are realized in broadening the market of issuance of travelers, as well as increase the reasons why visiting Spain.In relation to the origin of the travelers, the interest focuses on two sources: the first to consolidate the strength in markets traditionally issuers of travelers (EU scope, Russia). The second objective is to attract new travelers from distant markets, which so far have been insensitive to Spain as a tourist destination. In this sense, the major areas of interest are located in countries such as China, India or South Korea, the Persian Gulf (Saudi Arabia, Arab Emirates and Qatar), or countries in the Southeast Asia (Malaysia, Indonesia, Thailand). And another focus of interest is set in travelers from Japan, New Zealand, Austria and Canada, together with the Latin-Americans (Mexico, Colombia, Brazil) who, traditionally, have shown a certain sensitivity to the Spanish culture as a motivation to visit the country. Tourists from these markets show a great capacity for spending, making it one of the main markets in terms of average expenditure and sales free of taxes.

In regard to the motivations for travel, the main objective is to lure travelers attracted by the culture, food and traditions, nature, shopping or sports. In this way, against the traditional *sun and beach* that has usually been the motivation to visit Spain, it is trying to reinforce an *experiential tourism*, which strengthens the position of inside geographical destinations –not coastal zones- and, simultaneously, deseasonalizes the tourism activity -traditionally located in summer-.

Aiming to get the above objectives, the marketing activities have revolved around increasing the power of the Spain Brand. In particular, the work has been on the line of:

1. Improving the positioning of the image of the brand in the consolidated markets.
2. Increasing the visibility in emerging markets.

Traditionally the brand image has been developed according to the known cycle AIDA (knowledge, interest, desire and action). Depending on the phase of the cycle in which the brand is located, it is necessary to implement a set of actions intended to strengthen its power, increase its notoriety or increase its differentiation. That is to say, to tend to position or reposition the brand.

The 2014-15 plan wants the brand positioning -or repositioning- is established in terms of *global brand source* or *warranty*; that is, as a brand that not only is linked to tourism, but as an image of brand country, able to protect and distinguish the different types of product.

In general terms the Spain brand enjoys prestige. However, it should be noted that during the period 2008-2013 the image has undergone some erosion. The economic crisis has seriously damaged the image of Spain as an economic power, both at European level and globally. During the year 2014, the data confirm an improvement of the image of Spain abroad (marcaespaña.es, 2015), both in the economic field as business, cultural, tourist, gastronomic and sports. Meanwhile, in the strictly tourist spot, Spain is suffering competition from new destinations. It is for this reason that in the most of the source markets of tourists, Spain has lost share as a holiday destination, and only the Russian market has maintained a strengthened growth since 2011.

Communication as the Key to the Repositioning of the Brand: Internet, Social Networks, and the Power of the UGC

The need to reach a global audience, with the aim of creating awareness and differentiation, leads to an important part of the marketing action carried out in relation to the Spain brand to focus on the development of communications actions on the internet and social networks.Especially in the year 2015, the Spain Brand works intensely on its presence in the Network. Under the slogan "Everything you expect and much more than you imagine", the Spain Brand tries to create and convey a sense of ownership and pride. The renewal of the web, increasing the presence in social networks and the launch of a promotional video are the few first steps.

The internet is a fundamental element in the communication policy of the Spain Brand. With the creation of the web *marcaespaña.es*, the High Commissioner of the Spain Brand has an excellent showcase to be known in the world (see Figure 2).

The web spreads information about activities and events that have to do with the image of Spain abroad. But in addition, the web has put emphasis on the flexibility and participation. Flexibility is possible because it is accessible from the different mobile devices. With respect to participation, it should be noted that the web has a section where it is called the direct involvement of the people, with the aim of collecting ideas and advertise the Spain Brand internationally (see Figure 3).

Figure 2. Web of the Spain Brand

Figure 3. The participation section of the web of the Spain Brand

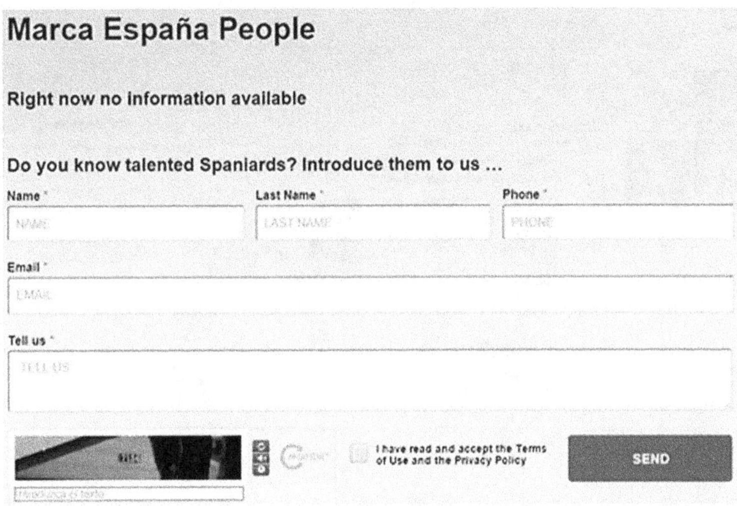

The Spain Brand has used social networks as a means of communication. Its presence on networks such as Facebook and Twitter is active. One of the main objectives of the presence in social networks is that users tell stories about Spain and the Spanish (see Figure 4).

The presence of famous people helps the broadcast of the Spain Brand on social networks. Such is the case of athletes of elite, or chefs, and designers of renowned prestige, that voluntary and free of charge work with the Spain Brand in the international dissemination of the brand (see Figure 5).

Figure 4. The Spain Brand on Facebook

Figure 5. The Brand Spain in Twitter

An element to highlight is the importance of social networks as a means of expression of individuals. Users of social media can express opinions, explain experiences and create content on the Web, which are capable of influencing opinion and behavior that others have about a brand or a territory (Llodrà, 2013).

Today the UGC (User Generated Content) is such that even in the traditional AIDA model, used to work the brand image, recommendation phase has been added and the action has been divided into acquisition and repetition. Because with the emergence of social networks the behavior dimension of the individual behavioral segment presents different conducts such as buying, buybacks and recommendation (see Figure 6).

Figure 6. The AIDA model

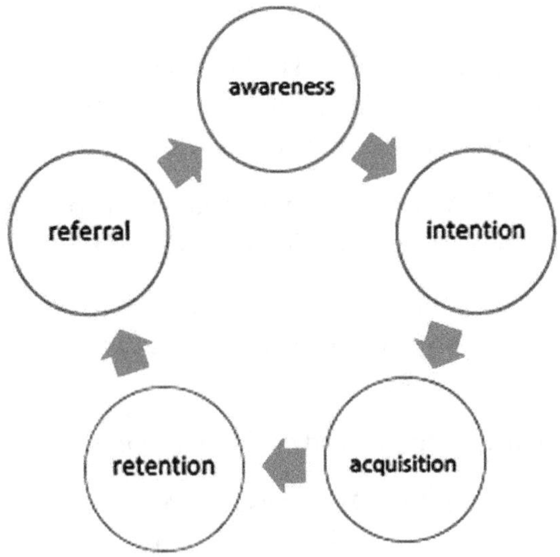

In this way, with the presence on the network, the Spain Brand not only allows to present the main features of the culture, economy and society of the country, but it also makes possible the experiences of people, both famous and anonymous, are known and can be used by potential users of products of Spain in their decision making process.

REFERENCES

Aaker, D. A. (1991). *Managing brand equity*. New York, NY: Free Press.

Aaker, D. A. (1996). *Building strong brands*. New York, NY: The Free Press.

Agarwal, R., Ganco, M., & Ziedonis, R. H. (2009). Reputations for toughness in patent enforcement: Implications for knowledge spillovers via inventor mobility. *Strategic Management Journal*, *30*(13), 1349–1374. doi:10.1002/smj.792

Agrawal, J., & Kamakura, W. A. (1999). Country of origin: A competitive advantage? *International Journal of Research in Marketing*, *16*(4), 255–267. doi:10.1016/S0167-8116(99)00017-8

Albert, P.C. & Muñoz, A.C. (1999). Signos distintivos en productos agroalimentarios. *Distribución y consumo*, *9*(45), 71-83.

Alcantara-Pilar, J. M., Del Barrio-García, S., & Porcu, L. (2013). A cross-cultural analysis of the effect of language on perceived risk online. *Computers in Human Behavior*, *29*(3), 596–603. doi:10.1016/j.chb.2012.10.021

Anholt, S. (2006). *Competitive identity: The new brand management for nations, cities and regions*. Palgrave Macmillan. doi:10.1057/9780230627727

Baker, M. J., & Currie, C. A. (1993). Country of origin: the fifth element of the marketing mix? *Proceedings of theMarketing Education Group Conference* (pp. 149-167).

Batra, R., Lehmann, D. R., & Singh, D. (1993). The brand personality component of brand goodwill: some antecedents and consequences. In D. A. Aaker & A. L. Biel (Eds.), *Brand equity and advertising* (pp. 83–96). Hillsdale, NY: Lawrence Erlbaum Associates Inc.

Berger, J., & Schwartz, E. M. (2011). What drives immediate and ongoing Word of mouth? *JMR, Journal of Marketing Research, 48*(5), 869–880. doi:10.1509/jmkr.48.5.869

Berthon, P. R., Pitt, L. F., McCarthy, I., & Kates, S. M. (2007). When customers get clever: Managerial approaches to dealing with creative consumers. *Business Horizons, 50*(1), 39–47. doi:10.1016/j.bushor.2006.05.005

Biel, A. L. (1992). How brand image drives brand equity. *Journal of Advertising Research, 32*(6), 6–12.

Bigne, J. E., Sanchez, M. I., & Sanchez, J. (2001). Tourism image, evaluation variables and after purchase behavior: Interrelationship. *Tourism Management, 22*(6), 607–616. doi:10.1016/S0261-5177(01)00035-8

Blackston, M. (1992). Observations: Building brand equity by managing the brand's relationships. *Journal of Advertising Research, 32*(3), 79–83.

Blackston, M. (1995). The qualitative dimension of brand equity. *Journal of Advertising Research, 35*(4), 2–7.

Bolton, R., & Saxena-Iyer, S. (2009). Interactive service: A framework, synthesis and research directions. *Journal of Interactive Marketing, 23*(1), 91–104. doi:10.1016/j.intmar.2008.11.002

Boush, D. M., Shipp, S., Loken, B., Gencturk, E., Crokett, S., Kennedy, E., & Strobel, J. et al. (1987). Affect generalization to similar and dissimilar brand extensions. *Psychology and Marketing, 4*(3), 225–237. doi:10.1002/mar.4220040306

Burmann, C., Zeplin, S., & Riley, N. (2009). Key determinants of internal brand management success: An exploratory empirical analysis. *Journal of Brand Management, 16*(4), 264–284. doi:10.1057/bm.2008.6

Christodoulides, G., Jevons, C., & Blackshaw, P. (2011). The voice of the consumer speaks forcefully in brand identity: User-generated content forces smart marketers to listen. *Journal of Advertising Research, 51*(1), 101–111. doi:10.2501/JAR-51-1-101-111

Chu, S., & Kim, Y. (2011). Determinants of consumer engagement in electronic word-of-mouth (eWOM) in social networking sites. *International Journal of Advertising, 30*(1), 47–75. doi:10.2501/IJA-30-1-047-075

Davis, C. & Moy, C. (2007, October). Coming to Terms With Business Transparency. *Admap Magazine*, Issue 487, Oxon: WARC, pp. 19-22.

Dean, D. H., & Lang, J. M. (2008). Comparing three signals of service quality. *Journal of Services Marketing, 22*(1), 48–58. doi:10.1108/08876040810851950

Dobni, D., & Zinkhan, G. M. (1990). In Search of Brand Image: A Fundation Analysis. *Advances in Consumer Research. Association for Consumer Research (U. S.), 17*(1), 110–119.

Edvardsson, B., Tronvoll, B., & Grubet, T. (2011). Expanding understanding of service exchange and value co-creation: A social construct approach. *Journal of the Academy of Marketing Science*, *39*(2), 327–339. doi:10.1007/s11747-010-0200-y

Faircloth, J. B. (2005). Factors influencing nonprofit resource provider support decisions: Applying the brand equity concept to nonprofits. *Journal of Marketing Theory and Practice*, *13*(3), 1–15. doi:10.1080/10696679.2005.11658546

Fakharmanesh, S., & Miyandehi, R. (2013). The Purchase of Foreign Products: The Role of Brand Image, Ethnocentrism and Animosity: Iran Market Evidence. *Iranian Journal of Management Studies*, *6*(1), 147–162.

Fill, C. (2005). *Marketing communications: engagements, strategies and practice*. Prentice Hall.

Folgado, J. A., Oliveira, P. A., & Hernádez, J. M. (2011). Imagen del destino y marca turística: sinergias e implicaciones. *Proceedings of the International Conference on Tourism and management studies* (Book 1), Algarve Portugal (pp. 904-914).

Frías, D. M., Rodriguez, M. A., & Castañeda, J. A. (2008). Internet vs. travel agencies on pre-visit destination image formation: An information processing view. *Tourism Management*, *29*(1), 163–179. doi:10.1016/j.tourman.2007.02.020

Fuchs, G., & Reichel, A. (2006). Tourist destination risk perception: The case of Israel. *Journal of Hospitality & Leisure Marketing*, *14*(2), 83–108. doi:10.1300/J150v14n02_06

Greaves, M., & Mika, P. (2008). Semantic Web and Web 2.0. *Journal of Web Semantics*, *6*(Jan), 1–3. doi:10.1016/j.websem.2007.12.002

Hendler, J., & Golbeck, J. (2008). Metcalfe's law, Web 2.0, and the Semantic Web. *Web Semantics: Science, Services, and Agents on the World Wide Web*, *6*(1), 14–20. doi:10.1016/j.websem.2007.11.008

Hennig-Thurau, T., Gwinner, K., Walsh, G., & Gremler, D. (2004). Electronic word-of-mouth via consumer-opinion platforms: What motivates consumers to articulate themselves on the Internet? *Journal of Interactive Marketing*, *18*(1), 38–52. doi:10.1002/dir.10073

Hsieh, A. T., & Li, C. K. (2008). The moderating effect of brand image on public relations' perception and customer loyalty. *Marketing Intelligence & Planning*, *26*(1), 26–42. doi:10.1108/02634500810847138

Ibrahim, E., & Gill, J. (2005). A positioning strategy for a tourist destination, based on analysis of customers perceptions and satisfactions. *Marketing Intelligence & Planning*, *23*(2), 172–188. doi:10.1108/02634500510589921

Ind, N. (2003). *Beyond Branding: How the new values of transparency and integrity are changing the world of brands*. London: Kogan Page.

Ind, N., & Riondino, M. C. (2001). Branding on the Web: A real revolution? *The Journal of Brand Management*, *9*(1), 8–19. doi:10.1057/palgrave.bm.2540048

Iversen, N. M., & Hem, L. E. (2008). Provenance associations as core values of place umbrella brands: A framework of characteristics. *European Journal of Marketing*, *42*(5/6), 603–626. doi:10.1108/03090560810862534

Janiszewski, C., & Van Osselaer, S. M. (2000). A connectionist model of brand-quality associations. *JMR, Journal of Marketing Research*, *37*(3), 331–350. doi:10.1509/jmkr.37.3.331.18780

Jolly, A. (2001). *Managing Corporate Reputations*. London: PRCA.

Jones, B., Bowd, R., & Tench, R. (2009). Corporate irresponsibility and corporate social responsibility: Competing realities. *Social Responsibility Journal*, *5*(3), 300–310. doi:10.1108/17471110910977249

Kapferer, J. N. (1992). *Strategic Brand Management*. London: Kogan Page.

Kapferer, J. N. (2012). *The new strategic brand management: Advanced insights and strategic thinking*. Kogan Page.

Kaynak, E., Kucukemiroglu, O., & Hyder, A. S. (2000). Consumers' country-of-origin (COO) perceptions of imported products in a homogenous less-developed country. *European Journal of Marketing*, *34*(9/10), 1221–1241. doi:10.1108/03090560010342610

Keller, K. L. (1993). Conceptualizing, measuring, and managing customer-based brand equity. *Journal of Marketing*, *57*(1), 1–22. doi:10.2307/1252054

Keller, K. L. (1998). *Strategic brand management: Building, measuring, and managing brand equity*. Upper Saddle River, NJ: Prentice Hall.

Keller, K. L., Parameswaran, M. G., & Jacob, I. (2011). *Strategic brand management: Building, measuring, and managing brand equity*. Pearson Education India.

Kim, H. B., & Kim, W. G. (2005). The relationship between brand equity and firms' performance in luxury hotels and chain restaurants. *Tourism Management*, *26*(4), 549–560. doi:10.1016/j.tourman.2004.03.010

Kotler, P., & Armstrong, G. (1996). *Principles of Marketing* (7th ed.). Englewood Cliffs, NJ: Prentice Hall, Inc.

Kotler, P., Kartajaya, H., & Setiawan, I. (2010). *Marketing 3.0: From products to customers to the human spirit*. New York: John Wiley & Sons Inc. doi:10.1002/9781118257883

Kotler, P. H. (1991). *Marketing Management: Analysis, Planning, and Control* (8th ed.). Englewood Cliffs, NJ: Prentice-Hall, Inc.

Lampert, S. I., & Jaffe, E. D. (1998). A dynamic approach to country-of-origin effect. *European Journal of Marketing*, *32*(1/2), 61–78. doi:10.1108/03090569810197471

Laroche, M., Papadopoulos, N., Heslop, L., & Mourali, M. (2005). The influence of country image structure on consumer evaluations of foreign products. *International Marketing Review*, *22*(1), 96–115. doi:10.1108/02651330510581190

Letablier, M. T., & Nicolas, F. (1994). Genèse de la typicité. *Sciences des Aliments*, *14*(5), 541–556.

Lewis, S. (2001). Measuring corporate reputation. *Corporate Communications: An International Journal*, *6*(1), 31–35. doi:10.1108/13563280110381198

Liarte, S. (2013). Image de Marque et Internet. Comprendre, éviter et gérer l'effet «Streisand». Décisions marketing, (69, Janvier-Mars), pp.103-110

Luo, X., & Bhattacharya, C. B. (2006). Corporate social responsibility, customer satisfaction, and market value. *Journal of Marketing*, *70*(4), 1–18. doi:10.1509/jmkg.70.4.1

Martenson, R. (2007). Corporate brand image, satisfaction and store loyalty: A study of the store as a brand, store brands and manufacturer brands. *International Journal of Retail & Distribution Management*, *35*(7), 544–555. doi:10.1108/09590550710755921

Moisescu, O. I. (2009). *Country branding: Conceptualization and review.* International Conference Marketing from Information to decision 2nd edition.

Nandan, S. (2005). An exploration of the brand identity-brand image linkage: A communications perspective. *The Journal of Brand Management*, *12*(4), 264–278. doi:10.1057/palgrave.bm.2540222

Nemes, J. (2000) Domain names have brand impact. *B to B Chicago*, 85(12), 20.

Plummer, J. (1985). Brand personality: a strategic concept for multinational advertising. *Proceedings of theMarketing Educators Conference*. New York, NY: Young & Rubicam.

Romaniuk, J. (2011). Advertising is More Influential than Word-of-mouth? That would be Something to Talk About! *Proceedings of ANZMAC*. Retrieved from http://anzmac.info/conference/2011-proceedings

Roth, M. S., & Romeo, J. B. (1992). Matching Product Category and Country Image Perceptions: A Framework for Managing Country-Of-Origin Effects[corrected title: Matching Product Category and Country Image Perceptions: A Framework for Managing Country-Of-Origin Effects]. *Journal of International Business Studies*, *23*(3), 477–497. doi:10.1057/palgrave.jibs.8490276

Roy, D., & Banerjee, S. (2007). CARE-ing strategy for integration of brand identity with brand image. *International Journal of Commerce and Management*, *17*(1/2), 140–148. doi:10.1108/10569210710776512

Shimp, T. A., Samiee, S., & Madden, T. J. (1993). Countries and their products: A cognitive structure perspective. *Journal of the Academy of Marketing Science*, *21*(4), 323–330. doi:10.1007/BF02894524

Shirky, C. (2008). *Here comes everybody: The power of organizing without organizations*. Penguin books.

Stahl, F., Heitmann, M., Lehmann, D. R., & Neslin, S. A. (2012). The impact of brand equity on customer acquisition, retention, and profit margin. *Journal of Marketing*, *76*(4), 44–63. doi:10.1509/jm.10.0522

Steenkamp, J. B. E. (1997). Dynamics in consumer behavior with respect to agricultural and food products. In Agricultural marketing and consumer behavior in a changing world (pp. 143-188). Springer US. doi:doi:10.1007/978-1-4615-6273-3_8 doi:10.1007/978-1-4615-6273-3_8

Steenkamp, J. B. E., & Dekimpe, M. G. (1997). The increasing power of store brands: Building loyalty and market share. *Long Range Planning*, *30*(6), 917–930. doi:10.1016/S0024-6301(97)00077-0

Stuart, H., & Jones, C. (2004). Corporate branding in marketspace. *Corporate Reputation Review*, *7*(1), 84–93. doi:10.1057/palgrave.crr.1540213

Thackeray, R., Neiger, B. I., Hanson, C. L., & McKenzie, J. F. (2008). Enhancing promotional strategies within social marketing programs: Use of Web 2.0 social media. *Health Promotion Practice*, *9*(4), 338–343. doi:10.1177/1524839908325335 PMID:18936268

Tsimonis, G., & Dimitriadis, S. (2014). Brand strategies in social media. *Marketing Intelligence & Planning*, *32*(3), 328–344. doi:10.1108/MIP-04-2013-0056

Varadarajan, R., Srinivasan, R., Vadakkepatt, G. G., Yadav, M. S., Pavlou, P. A., Krishnamurthy, S., & Krause, T. (2010). Interactive technologies and retailing strategy: A review, conceptual framework and future research directions. *Journal of Interactive Marketing*, *24*(2), 96–110. doi:10.1016/j.intmar.2010.02.004

Weber, L. (2007). *Marketing on the Social Web: how digital customer communities build your business*. New Jersey: John Wiley and Sons.

Zeithaml, V. A. (1988). Consumer perceptions of price, quality, and value: A means-end model and synthesis of evidence. *Journal of Marketing*, *52*(3), 2–22. doi:10.2307/1251446

Zhou, Z., Zhang, Q., Su, C., & Zhou, N. (2012). How do brand communities generate brand relationship? Intermediate mechanisms. *Journal of Business Research*, *65*(7), 890–895. doi:10.1016/j.jbusres.2011.06.034

Zins, A. (2001). Relative attitudes and commitment in customer loyalty models. International. *Journal of Service Industries management*, 12(3), 269-294.

KEY TERMS AND DEFINITIONS

Brand: It is technically defined as the name, term, sign, symbol, or design, or combination of them which is intended to identify the goods and services of one seller or group of sellers and to differentiate them from those of competitors. But after all, it is the sum total and ultimate expression of all the collected activities undertaken by the brand owner and the experiences of the brand user.

Brand Equity: A set of attributes linked to the brand, as the name recognition, the perceived quality, the loyalty of consumers and other associations that have to do with it, that set a value added or subtracted from the product or service offered.

Brand Image: It is the mental representation that consumers have about a brand globally as to how the brand is perceived by them.

Country Brand: It is the name of a country acting in a similar way as the name of a brand, which has the ability to increase the value perceived by the customer in any product or service by having a specific origin.

Country Brand Equity: Defined as the tangible and intangible, internal (iconography, landscape, culture) and external (country image perceptions, external portrayal in popular culture, brand ambassadors) assets or liabilities of the nation.

Country of Origin Effect: It represents the perception about a certain country that is extended to the products made in that country. It is, practically, the consumer's perception of a product, which is influenced by the brand's nationality.

Perceived Quality: A consumer's opinion aboutthe ability of a product or a brand to fulfill his/her expectations based, nor that on the excellence of the product, on the brand's public image, the consumer experience with the other products of the company, and the influence of the opinion leaders, consumer peer group and others.

ENDNOTES

1 For instance at the European Union, country brands influence decisions in Brussels, those of the Central Bank or the members of the EU, and how they can influence the rankings of default, credit, etc.

Chapter 7
Role of Consumer Engagement and Swarm Intelligence in Management of a Brand at Social Media

Rajshree Singh
Amity University, India

ABSTRACT

The traditional media has its own place and will always be there but the revolution in marketing era will change the thinking of the society as a whole and the various communication channels will always be in flux. The ability to think collectively seeks cognitive architectures of collective intelligence which today from consumer's perspective is to become a human swarm with the use of social media. With the growth of social media, marketing companies need something more innovative to engage and interact with their customers. As the marketplace becomes noisier, with more products being introduced, fight is not just mindshare but share of attention. Various organizations have started exploring the power of such a large user membership to influence the online buyers at social media and are attempting to engage consumers with their brands, which will finally influence their brand image. The chapter explores the extent of consumer experience and engagement, how online consumers are engaged towards a specific brand. The methodology for study is empirical evidence through netnography, and result of this study is through correlation and regression model. Findings confirm the factors contributing to consumer engagement and swarm intelligence in management of a brand at social media.

1. INTRODUCTION

Through social networking websites, people cross boundaries, language barriers, and share information with others. The information available on these websites easily becomes the voice of many. Every day we see different types of individuals and they behave in a very different way as a single identity from how they behave collectively in a group. Human swarm mindset is an array of project and it is very

DOI: 10.4018/978-1-5225-0332-3.ch007

important to maximize the number of happy customers. These days, individuals are having access to lot of information because of social networking websites. Organizations are working on social networks for marketing, but they lack in understanding the behavior of individuals who are present on the social network. An individual, who is there on the social network, is independent and will find the solution himself or herself by sharing knowledge, information, and intelligence with others. So, it is very important to understand that an independent individual, who is present on a social network, can act as reader and writer by sharing his own set of thoughts with others and also passing the intelligence over the passage of time. Companies need to understand the power of online communities and also start providing the social networking apps that can give best results from the social networks.

Companies should use their own system by using their own game rules. Organizations need to define new protocols of communication and find various modes or channels to reduce the language barriers worldwide. They need to provide the appropriate interface to fulfill the requirement of communication through social networks and the applications should have the database and knowledge management system for all the users. This knowledge management system will maintain the data of various users and the information regarding the experiences, reviews, and feedback. This type of application will work as a source of information for users in future related to marketing activities. There is a need for hosting the appropriate content on a firm initiative, which by matching consumer requirements helps develop a relationship between firm and consumer (Ahuja & Medury, 2010), thus helping them in their decision-making and facilitating purchase intentions.

2. BACKGROUND

2.1. What Is "Swarm Intelligence"?

The emergent collective intelligence of groups of natural or artificial agents. (Bonabeau et al., 1999)

Swarm intelligence in simple terms, can be described as the "Collective wisdom". Animals show swarm behavior and animals make group, move together without even told what to do. Due to technology advancement, human behavior has become more relevant to this swarm behavior. Through social networking websites, people cross boundaries, language barriers, and share information with others. The information available on these websites easily becomes the voice of many. Every day we see different type of individuals and they behave in a very different way as a single identity than to collectively in a group. Human swarm mindset is an array of project and it is very important to maximize the number of happy customers.

As per mosquito interactive, swarm marketing is a method of interactive marketing that creates and manages a literal swarm of thousand. Swarm marketing is not SEO (search engine optimization) and PPC (page per click). Swarm marketing includes both SEO and PPC and it is a simple concept that develops one unique page for every useful search term for which an organization has an offerings. These days, individuals are having access to lot of information because of social networking websites. Swarm intelligence works as a collective intelligence tool and the companies needs to understand the hidden benefits of swarm intelligence.

Companies need to understand the power of human swarm and should start providing the social networking apps that can give best results from the social networks. Companies should use their own system by using their own game rules. They can use various practices to help human swarm and take the benefits. Organizations need to define new protocols of communication and find various modes or channels to reduce the language barriers worldwide. They need to provide the appropriate interface to fulfill the requirement of communication through social network and the applications should have the database and knowledge management system for all the users. This knowledge management system will maintain the data of various users and the information regarding the experiences, reviews and feedback. This type of application will work as source of information for users in future related to marketing activities.

Therefore, it is very important to understand the human swarm thinking and their information-sharing pattern on social network. Companies need to understand the pattern of sharing information and find out various activities by which they can attract these types of human swarm. Human swarm will help an organization to build a string brand, which will help an organization to fulfill their long term objectives. Human swarm do various type of activities on social network like updating their status, liking various posts, writing comments, sharing posts and commenting on other posts. Marketers need to find out human swarm of different traits and personalities like bloggers, scientists, students, writers, journalists, musicians etc. by the help of these human swarms. It will be easy for marketers to integrate all the possible options to find the solution for the problem. The way of information flowing and the source of information have changed because instead of using the expert source of information, individuals are relying on their own source of information like friends, family, peers, reference groups, fellow online members on social networks. To control this voice about the brand is not an easy task. If a brand will be able to connect with human swarm then it can outperform. So the marketing has moved from traditional way to new way of brighter world where people create brands, products and services and then talk about it with other people.

2.2. Harnessing the Swarm: What It Meant for Innovation

Researchers studying socialization in online learning note that definitions are quite broad, suggesting that, *Socialization* is about people being able to mingle and establish network. People share views and information and build connections, it is a tool for interpersonal and interactional skills. While these definitions cover a broad range of concepts, online consumers need a variety of experiences and exposure to differing views and perspectives to develop the skills to think for themselves and effectively get engaged and develop their opinion.

Swarm intelligence accelerates creativity across a large group of network of consumers and develops a strong consumer engagement. Rather than pay agencies to create video, content, image, and brand, a company can go to analyze online swarm behavior and innovate their product.

When organizations develop social network they need to develop a system where individuals can share their opinions to give direction for future users to follow the same ideal route for communicating value to the market place, this will help marketers promote their brands since the internet allows for interactions across geographical boundaries that transcend the possibilities within physical medium. In many ways online interactions offer socialization opportunities that go beyond what most traditional ways can provide, whether it is taking part in a discussion with people from another country, online interaction foster collaboration among a diverse and geographically dispersed group of consumers.

Irwin (2006) and Berge (2006), suggest “Socialization is about people being able to mingle and establish connections on one or more levels. They speak with one another; share ideas and information and confirm the connections made through an agreed upon means.”

More broadly, Giddens (1999), define socialization as "the process by which, through contact with other human beings, one becomes a self-aware, knowledgeable human being, skilled in the ways of a given culture and environment."

Today, consumers are becoming a human swarm with the use of digital media. The traditional media has its own place and will always be there. But the revolution in marketing era will change the thinking of the society as a whole and the various communication channels will always be in flux. So swarm marketing is based on swarm intelligence, which is described as "collective wisdom". The swarm theory shows how marketing can harness the crowd of modern communities and build influential brands.

Socialization in online social networking sites can be categorized into one or more of several categories that are discussed below:

- Interaction with friends within the online social communities
- Communication with other peers within the online social networking communities
- Online communication and activities facilitated by Social networking websites such as Facebook, Twitter, Myspace, and YouTube
- Activities that involve bringing people within social networking sites closer

2.2.1. Consumer Engagement and Branding in Social Media via Swarm Intelligence

There is existing research on online social communities, however, these research rarely show how user preferences can be accommodated with online interaction process. Most previous research in online communities highlights preferences focusing on a specific content. Thus, there is little emphasis on a coherent structure – no integrative framework to interpret collaborative interaction with other friends. Active participation on online activities of similar interest group promotes a group dynamics and team building exercise online, especially in context to active forum. This creates an active knowledge-sharing platform with peers within online social networking communities such as Facebook, Twitter, Myspace, and YouTube. In the online community, the terms 'relationship marketing' and CRM are often used interchangeably (Parvatiyar & Sheth, 2002). The heart of marketing is maintaining long-term relationships, which is the goal of marketing practice (Berry et al., 2006). Five macro-environmental factors responsible for the growth of relationship orientation in marketing (Sheth & Parvatiyar, 2000) include the following:

- Rapid technological advancements, especially in the field of information technology
- The adoption of total quality programs by companies
- The growth of the service economy
- Organizational development processes leading to the empowerment of individuals and teams

Swarm Intelligence has its role in Consumer Engagement through activities that involve bringing people within social networking sites closer. Shevlin (2006) emphasized on the process of buying, using and consuming the product, there is an emotional, psychological and physical investment by the consumer onto the brand. The challenge for the organizations is to convince consumers that their efforts, money and commitment is of worth to a brand, henceforth marketers emphasize in process of building, nurturing and preserving relationships and enhance the customer lifetime values (CLV) and improve the customer equity (CE) over the lifetime of a brand.

The challenge for marketers in digital world is to hold on to the visitors on to their websites, and engage them towards an experience for a relationship. Peoplemetrics (2010) conducted a survey in 2008 across 10,000 customers which revealed highly engaged customers led their companies to grow 13% above the industry average and low engagements of customers (digitally) to companies declining by 36% as against the industry average which in turn affected their Return on Investment. Customer engagement relates to product involvement and frequency of his repeat purchase which depicts how emotionally he is attached to it. Neuro marketing studies have helped find out some relationships between the emotional attachment of consumers with brands and their brain activity levels. Familiar brands produced higher levels of brain activity in areas associated with positive emotions.

Sprott and Czellar (2009) iterated the concept of brand engagement in self-concept which represents consumer tendency of how they view or associate themselves with a brand. The self-concept emphasizes on how consumers become less time and price sensitive with their favorite brands and display a high propensity of brand engagement compared to their sensitivity to other products. Muniz and O'Guinn (2001), suggested how people vary in brand engagement in identity building and expression through brand communities. The self–brand connection scale (Escalas, 2004) measures the strength of the link between a certain brand and of self.

Thus organizations should just do not concentrate on promotion or advertisement for market engagement but should emphasize to get involved in dialogue with customers to respect their brand thus raising the expectation the consumer creates value to the firm.

To assess the current scenario of swarm intelligence in marketing, no literature is available yet some relevant examples are:

Frito Lay's and Maggie – Frito Lay's have used swarm intelligence as a tool. Especially for world cup 2011, Lay's have asked consumers to choose flavors according to their choice and taste in the advertisement. Through swarm intelligence, company will get various inputs, then will screen the ideas and finally will develop new product. By doing this, company has a competitive edge above their competitors. Nestle has done an advertisement for Maggie in which company had asked for new recipes from consumers. Company had tried to increase the sale by creating an emotional bond with crowd. Company wanted to associate with childhood of many adults and advertisement increased the sale for company among adults. Nestle had got various responses from people and finally company had launched a campaign (Me and Meri Maggie) on Television.

Procter & Gamble – According to a research done by Contagiuos Magazine et al. (2009), P&G use vocalpoint.com nationwide as a website. It has around 2,40,000 female users as a virtual swarm in the US to promote their brands. Vocalpoint crowd has the access to all the information about the new product, which will come in the market after some time. They try their products before the masses – and if they like then they tell others, If they do not like then they tell P&G. It is a very cost effective and marketing effective mechanism. P&G always promote their Always and Tampax brands through Beinggirl.com website. P&G has found BeingGirl to be four times effective as compared to price television advertising. Through InnoCentive.com, P&G capture a group of 140,000+ freelance scientists to R&D section. P&G has a programmer called "Connect & Develop" which source out product and service innovations from outside.

India Currency Design –India came up with an open competition for currency symbol design. From a swarm intelligence perspective, the step of swarm for redesigning the symbol was a hit. Around 8,000 initial entries came for first screening and finally 3,000 entries shortlisted and finally five finalists were selected. The judging panel consisted of various design experts and representatives from government body. The five finalists have got 5,000 rupees and winner Udaya got 2,50,000 rupees as prize amount.

Amazon – Amazon was one of the first companies who have started swarm intelligence with the launch of Mechanical Turk in 2005. It works as a platform for workers to complete "Human Intelligence Tasks" – mainly projects, which cannot be done by one person or machine, such as extracting information from web pages. Texteagle, the company allows mobile and desktop users to participate in their projects. Users perform various tasks like describing the content of an image, rating the quality of web search results, or transcribing and translating text from other language. This unique platform works in a unique way; the tasks, which are very difficult for in-house trained artificial intelligence workers but are relatively easy for an untrained worker, get finished outside. Due to swarm intelligence, company achieves economies of scale by distributing the work to nations where small payments are a significant source of income. There are various success factors like data transferability, the increased ease of breaking work into separate tasks, the development of tools to track, aggregate and assess the quality of work performed remotely have made swarm intelligence happen in real world. This trend will increase in future also because there will be seamless requirement of technology related work.

Sunsilk Gang of Girls: Hindustan Unilever Ltd. initiative from an effort by Sunsilk to develop a greater understanding and connect between the consumer and the brand by building another interface with them. The brand stands for togetherness, fun and expertise which the online site Sunsilkgangofgirls.com propagated which it claimed was India's first "online all-girl community". The site was a branded space promoting Sunsilk while at the same time providing a social networking space for girls. Through this initiative, HUL was able to study changing Indian consumer preference, which helped them re-launch improved variants of Sunsilk.

To elaborate further Co-creation and Online Community is a step towards consumer engagement, Prahalad (2005) describes Co-creation as the service experience of a consumer to allow him co-construct his personal experience, hence allowing him cocreate a value with the organization where firm and consumer converge creating demand and supply which is contextual hence value is co-created at point of interaction unlike in target market where value creation became restricted towards value chain, and market acts like a forum.

Organizations should not alone rely on financial metrics to measure their brand equity they should also pay attention towards various variables associated to measure customer attention towards online social network media. Investments in social media networks lead to reciprocal, empathetic, long lasting and authentic customer engagement especially when it comes to online social communities specially brand communities.

Organizations can create market by understanding the economic value especially through non-monetary route of social media as customer opinions represent customer experience.

Online brand communities' loyalty is mapped through actual customer experience, which seeks variations as per what customer desires. It should be the organization adaptation of new techniques and processes thus focusing on Customer experience for delivering loyalty-building experience.

A customer's perception of organizations is built as a result of the interactions and organizations can push up their bottom-line when they gather positive customer feedback (Pan and Lee, 2003). Organizations should emphasize on evaluating consumer online interactive behavior and their perception about their brand. In order to optimize customer experience, organizations put efforts on their internal stakeholders to tap customer experience management and this should be enabled with online systems and tools for better customer experience management.

An effort in this respect for online community trust is well reflected on websites of e-commerce especially Amazon.

2.2.2. Online Community

An online community is a group of people with some shared interests, who connect and interact with each other over time. Relationship of some sort is implied (Preece & Krichmar, 2003). The dawn of the information age found groups communicating electronically rather than face to face. A computer-mediated community uses social software to regulate the activities of the participants. These are places where people gather to share knowledge, build recognition, and tap opportunities. Initially sensed to be resource pools for value addition, where people ventured to fulfil their need for self-actualization, participation in online communities and forums started as a medium for exchange of ideas and information, and now organisations have started using these communities for marketing through consumer evangelism and support. A web-based communication model utilizes the features of the network for B2C as well as peer-to-peer communication. On the internet, electronic tribes structured around consumer interests have been growing rapidly. To be effective in this new environment, managers must consider the strategic implications of the existence of different types of both virtual community and community participation (Kozinets, 1999). Consumers join these forums because of the multifaceted opportunities they provide to members. Not only do they provide information on products and services and latest promotional schemes, they are also triggers for innovation. As like-minded people converge together, these are new cliques where organisations can use opinion leaders for evangelism, while harnessing consumer-generated content for product improvement and co-creation. Corporates like Dell have introduced ‘Ideastorm’ as a virtual interaction centre for consumers who participate in the development and enhancement of Dell’s products and services by sharing their ideas online. Enabling interactive electronic dialogue with user communities is one way of getting closer to the customers.

The demographic composition of the user population has also changed to include people of all ages, different cultures, educational backgrounds, as well as experience and technical skills. This has led to a change in the range of people participating in various kinds of online communities. In today’s era, although some communities require members to have particular skills or qualifications, there are millions of ‘open’ communities in which anyone with internet and web access can participate. As a result, the majority of users in these open communities and many others are not technical people. Today’s online community participants come from all walks of life. Hence, online communities appear to have significant potential for organisations trying to interact and build relationships with their consumers. Here, customer orientation is given a new meaning and the contents and processes of exchange between companies and customers are reconsidered if firms want to retain their customers and cooperate with them (Hemetsberger, 2002). What deserve significant mention is that online communities represent a set of core values such as consumer culture, consumer perceived value, conviviality and strong democracy, thereby building consumer equity and consumer retention. By leveraging the content created by the consumers in the online forums, organizations can form strategies for targeting consumers appropriately, make alterations to products, improve services and improve consumer retention.

2.2.2.3. Online Business Communities

In the present scenario, many business companies view building online 'brand' communities as a marketing strategy. These companies seek to build a new kind of relationship with their customers through these communities. Many companies are currently hosting interactive B2C online community sites organised around their brand, products, and services to create reinforcing, competitively distinct and long-lasting relationships with customers (McWilliam, 2000). They aim to expand their markets and accumulate detailed customer profiles for target-marketing new and existing products and services. Companies are often using these business communities to test new product ideas, involve customers in product development, monitor customer purchase patterns, and gauge early demand for products.

The Kodak company's website has an embedded discussion board that serves as a gathering place for the discussion of photography. The various service providers such as Yahoo and Microsoft host a large number of online communities to encourage traffic to their sites where they carry advertisements.

In an online community, the members share the same physical space – that is, co-presence – and have access to shared resources. Co-presence breeds kinship among consumers. Consumers make purchases on the basis of opinions of their peers; belonging to the same community enhances trust in the opinion of others. These members have a shared goal, interest, need, or activity that provides the primary reason for belonging to the community. If organizations seed these communities with their evangelists (brand propagators) and they are able to become opinion leaders, they can influence the opinion and decision of entire consumer communities. Members are engaged in repeated, active participation and there are often immense interactions, strong emotional ties, and shared activities occurring between participants. Reciprocity of information, support, and services between members is thus obvious. The online communities can be used for customer engagement, which ultimately leads to consumer empowerment. These communities act as catalysts for strengthening the bond between company and consumer, building long-lasting relationships with the consumer, creating, maintaining, and tightening the feedback loop, identification, and resolution of customer issues, and creating customer loyalty through personal investment in order to maintain competitive business edge. These communities allow for greater interactivity among members, boosting self-disclosure reciprocity. These communities are also a useful complement to CRM solutions. They help in more accurate profiling of customers based on interests and behaviors, and thus they can be used to reinforce or manipulate brand image through better penetration of markets. They have enormous potential to be used as a 'test group' to gauge new products or advertising campaigns. Last but not least, these communities help companies to design a path for growth and change.

2.2.3. Customer Relationship Management

CRM is an enterprise-wide initiative that belongs to all areas of an organisation (Singh & Agrawal, 2003). It reflects the comprehensive strategy and process of acquiring, retaining, and partnering with selective customers to create superior value for the company and the customer.

The goals of CRM are:

- Build long-term and profitable relationships with chosen customers
- Getting closer to those customers with every point of contact with them (Shainesh & Sheth, 2006).

CRM is an enterprise-wide approach to understanding and influencing customer behavior through meaningful communication to improve customer acquisition, customer retention, customer loyalty, and customer profitability. CRM can be viewed as an application of one-to-one marketing and relationship marketing, responding to an individual customer on the basis of what the customer says and what else is known about that customer (Peppers et al., 1999). It is a management approach that enables organizations to identify, attract, and increase retention of profitable customers by managing relationships with them (Hobby, 1999) and further identifying strategically significant customers (Buttle, 2001). In the academic community, the terms 'relationship marketing' and CRM are often used interchangeably (Parvatiyar & Sheth, 2002). The heart of marketing is relationships, and nurturing long-term relationships should be the goal of marketing practice (Berry et al., 2006). Five macro-environmental factors responsible for the growth of relationship orientation in marketing (Sheth & Parvatiyar, 2000) include the following:

- Rapid technological advancements, especially in the field of information technology.
- The adoption of total quality programs by companies.
- The growth of the service economy.
- Organizational development processes leading to the empowerment of individuals and teams.
- An increase in competitive intensity leading to concern for customer retention.

Increased competition reduces brand loyalty, making the job of the marketers more complex. Further, customers also become indifferent to the myriad marketing messages being thrust upon them. As a result, marketing needs to be more well directed and specific, because customers, whether consumers or businesses, do not want more choices. They want exactly what they want, when, where, and how they want it, and technology now makes it possible for companies to give it to them (Joseph et al., 1995). Customers have hidden or overt preferences that marketers can reveal by building a learning relationship. Earlier, marketers were attempting to interpret consumer needs on the basis of their buying behaviors. Now with the arrival of consumer-generated media, which has been discussed in the next section, marketers have another avenue to learn about the consumer. The objective is to keep the consumers satisfied and keep them loyal towards the company or brand. CRM, which has also been described as 'information-enabled relationship marketing', (Ryals & Payne, 2001) comprises processes used by organizations to manage consumer relationships, which also include collecting, storing, and analysing data, and is often termed as data-driven marketing. CRM attempts to provide a strategic bridge between information technology and marketing strategies aimed at building long-term relationships and profitability. This requires 'information intensive strategies' (Glazer, 2002).

For decades, businesses tried to determine what their customers wanted using focus groups that offered feedback about how well customers liked certain products. As the business world got more complex and markets became more competitive, the kind of information that could be gleaned from focus groups became inadequate for most businesses. They did not provide enough information, nor was the information valuable after a product was already released. Realizing the limitations of focus groups and similar marketing practices, companies decided that they needed to know more about who their customers were, how they interacted with the company, and how the company could reach out to customers in a meaningful way. This idea of getting a '360° view' of customers was a nice concept, but it was never really achievable within the limited spectrum of marketing and communication tools that were available (Wright, 2006). This is where interactive marketing had a vital role to play. Marketing has moved from a transaction-based effort to a conversation. Interactive marketing can be defined as the ability to address the customer, remember what the customer says, and address the customer again in a way that illustrates that we remember what the customer has told us (Blattberg & Deighton, 1996). The collaborative web is evolving as a significant interactive marketing tool, and the ability to remember what the customer has said is made easier when we can collect customer information online and communicate with the customer easily using the connectivity provided by the internet. The posts and reviews help in increasing the organizational brand equity, as the consumer perception for a product varies and depends a lot on the discussion on these communities. The online communities have more discussions about the competitor's products too and about new features, which increase the perceived value by stakeholders, which can be utilized for the growth of the company.

2.2.3.1. Reciprocity, and Online Trust are Important Dimensions of CRM

Reciprocity

It represents a pattern of behaviour in which people respond to friendly or hostile actions with similar actions even if no material gains are expected. Furthermore, when people discover that they have similar problems, requirements, opinions, or experiences, they may feel closer, more trusting, and be prepared to reveal even more. This has a 'snowball effect' in that the more people discover that they are similar to each other, the more they tend to like each other and the more they tend to disclose about themselves. This is known as 'self-disclosure reciprocity' and it is powerful online. The reciprocity can be in the form of exchanges of the same kind of aid or helping a mutual friend in the network. Even if reciprocity does not happen immediately, it can happen months or years later, possibly with another person in the community. In healthy communities, reciprocity is a general and accepted norm among members.

Online Trust

Online trust is positively associated with returns on CRM initiatives because CRM is focused on targeted customer segments, and effective communication and interaction with these segments and customers is directly related to online trust. Thus, we can conclude by saying that higher the degree of online trust, greater the degree of involvement of the customers, which eventually leads to effective CRM. As per Mooradian et al (2006) the degree of trust dependence in CRM may be driven by customer power and the influence of competitive intermediaries among other factors. Trust can be defined as "the willingness of a party to be vulnerable to the actions of another party based on the expectation that the other will perform a particular action online trust is important in both business-to-business and business-to-consumer e-business. Consumers and businesses, feeling the pressure of economic downturn and terrorism, increasingly look to buy from and do business with organizations with the most trusted websites and electronic networks. Companies' perception of online trust has steadily evolved from being a construct involving security and privacy issues on the internet to a multidimensional, complex construct that includes reliability/credibility, emotional comfort, and quality for multiple stakeholders such as employees, suppliers, distributors, and regulators, in addition to customers. Further, trust online spans the end -to- end aspects of e-business rather than being just based on the electronic storefront.

3. RESEARCH METHOD

The study is both qualitative and quantitative in nature and since a selected online community conversation is observed hence by passively monitoring the approach of research adopted was Netnography Ahuja, Medley (2010). Objective is to identify the possible extent for online consumer engagement exercise for Smartbit campaign initiative by Samsung via socio media site Facebook and launched an attractive online facebook campaign called "smart-Bid", where the participants had the opportunity to win a brand new Samsung Galaxy smart-phone.

Quantitative variables under study include:

For research, author selected Samsung, which had recently launched an attractive online facebook campaign called "smart-Bid". The typology of the content in Samsung Discussions is organized are:

1. The status of a participant of the community which is depicted by its *Number of points*, and these points are reflection of the active response of the participant to another member, this is measured by reciprocity and accuracy of responses by the members of community.
2. The Number of days a participant spends in the online community, which indicates their presence with respect to their time spent, this depicts longevity of the member from their date of registration.
3. The Number of Views other participants of the community go through and it is a measure of their active engagement.
4. The active participation of the community members is measured by their volumes of messages through number of their posts.
    a. **Target Sample:** Online brand community users of Samsung on Facebook page for Smartbid.
    b. **Sampling Technique:** Judgmental Sampling
    c. **Community Observation and Data Collection:** The selected online communication in Facebook page of users who have liked the 'Smartbid' page is observed.

4. ANALYSIS AND FINDINGS

USING CORRELATION ANALYSIS: An attempt was made to fit correlation model to the data collected from the Online group of Samsung Community and a relationship is observed between points (reciprocity) and views (engagements) as in appendix 1 across a set of 50 customers.

A High correlation is found between no. of views and no. of points compared to other variables. The Pearson correlation coefficient (r) calculated among the number of points and views is (r=0/524, p<0/01). The substantial value of correlation coefficient indicated that there is a significant relationship between the number of points and views is 52 percent, hence suggesting members in the Facebook forum are active participants and their replies in the forum which is a measure of their active consumer participation towards this campaign

USING REGRESSION ANALYSIS FOR PREDICTION: Since a high correlation is found between No. of points and no. of views, hence an attempt was made to fit a regression model to the data collected from the Online group of Smartbid and a significant linear relationship was observed between points(reciprocity) and views(engagement). Approximately R^2 value suggests that 96 per cent of variation in the no. of views was explained by the no. of points (Netnography), calculations done across a set of

50 consumers, in SPSS 20, for Samsung Galaxy-Y. The expected no. of views (*Y*) can be predicted by including the value of no. of points (*X*)in the given equation (refer also Appendix 2)

$Y = 2198.881 + 0.462\, X$

The effect of *No of views* (b=.462, p=.000) is significant and its coefficient is positively indicating a reasonably strong correlation was observed between the no. of points and no. of views. Views further demonstrated an incremental growth trend of 0.462 per unit increase in points to the no. of times a participant post is viewed by other members. This is indicative of *engagement* of the participant that is 46% of the participants in the online forum are actively engaged in conversation and product information sharing.

The t-test coefficient for no of views is 17.924 is significantly different from 0 because its p-value is 0.000, which is smaller than 0.05.

The Durbin-Watson statistic for this problem is 1.10, which falls within the acceptable range from 1.50 to 2.50. The analysis satisfies the assumption of independence of error associated with one observation are not correlated with the errors of any other observation

Hence there is a significant relationship of Reciprocity and engagement of customers contributing towards a ripple effect in social media which can lead towards strong brand equity.

5. CONCLUSION

Shevlin (2006) emphasized on the process of buying, using and consuming the product, there is an emotional, psychological and physical investment by the consumer onto the brand. The challenge for the organizations is to convince consumers that their efforts, money and commitment is of worth to a brand, henceforth marketers emphasize in process of building, nurturing and preserving relationships and enhance the customer lifetime values (CLV) and improve the customer equity (CE) over the lifetime of a brand.

The challenge for marketers in digital world is to hold on to the visitors on to their websites, and engage them towards an experience for a relationship. Customer engagement relates to product involvement and frequency of his repeat purchase which depicts how emotionally he is attached to it, also of later switching cost for a customer is progressively declining (Sedley,2006). Neuromarketing studies have helped find out some relationships between the emotional attachment of consumers with brands and their brain activity levels. Familiar brands produced higher levels of brain activity in areas associated with positive emotions.

Sprott (2009), iterated the concept of Brand engagement in self-concept which represents consumer tendency of how they view or associate themselves with a brand. The self-concept emphasizes on how consumers become less time and price sensitive with their favorite brands and display a high propensity of brand engagement compared to their sensitivity to other products. Muniz and O'Guinn (2001) suggested how people vary in brand engagement in identity building and expression through brand communities. The self–brand connection scale (Escalas, 2004) measures the strength of the link between a certain brand and of self.

Thus organizations should just do not concentrate on promotion or advertisement for market engagement but should emphasize to get involved in dialogue with customers to respect their brand thus raising the expectation of the savvy consumer to create the value that engagement delivered to the bottom line.

REFERENCES

Ahuja, V., & Medury, Y. (2010). Corporate blogs as e-CRM tools: Building consumer engagement through content management. *Journal of Database Marketing & Customer Strategy Management*, *17*(2), 91–105. doi:10.1057/dbm.2010.8

Amit, R., & Zott, C. (2001). Value creation in e-business. *Strategic Management Journal*, *22*(6-7), 49–520. doi:10.1002/smj.187

Berry, L. L., Wall, E., & Carbone, L. (2006). Service clues and customer assessment of the service experience: Lessons from marketing. *The Academy of Management Perspectives*, *20*(2), 43–57. doi:10.5465/AMP.2006.20591004

Buttle, F. (2001). The CRM value chain. *Marketing Business*, February, 52–55. Retrieved from http://www.wtcbrescia.it/upload/0-FButtle_CRMvalchain.pdf

Blattberg, R. C., & Deighton, J. (1996). Manage marketing by the customer equity test. *Harvard Business Review*, *74*(4), 136–144. PMID:10158473

Bonabeau, E.M.D. (1999). Swarm Intelligence: From Natural to Artificial System. New York: Oxford University Press.

Escalas, J. E. (2004). Narrative Processing: Building Consumer Connections to Brands. *Journal of Consumer Psychology*, *14*(1–2), 168–180. doi:10.1207/s15327663jcp1401&2_19

Giddens, A. D. M. (1999). *Introduction to Sociology, 5/e*. W. W. Norton & Company Inc.

Glazer, R. (2002). Measuring the value of information: The information-intensive organization. *IBM Systems Journal*, *32*(1), 99–110. doi:10.1147/sj.321.0099

Grewal, D., & Gopalkrishnan, R. (2003). The Internet and The Price-Value-Loyalty Chain. *Journal of Business Research*, *56*(5), 391–398. doi:10.1016/S0148-2963(01)00227-2

van der Heijden, H., Verhagen, T., & Creemers, M. (2003). Understanding online purchase intentions: Contributions from technology and trust perspectives. *European Journal of Information Systems*, *12*(1), 41–48. doi:10.1057/palgrave.ejis.3000445

Hemetsberger, A. (2002). Fostering cooperation on the internet: Social exchange processes in innovative virtual consumer communities. *Advances in Consumer Research. Association for Consumer Research (U. S.)*, *29*(1), 354–356.

Hobby, J. (1999). Looking after the one who matters. *Accountancy Age*, 28, 1741-2439.

Alavi, S., Ahuja, V., & Medury, Y. (2011). Journal of Database Marketing & Customer Strategy Management. *Database Marketing & Customer Strategy Management*, *18*(2), 83–96.

Humphreys, P., Samson, A., Roser, T., & Cruz Valdivieso, E. (2009). *Co creation: New pathways to value*. London: LSE Enterprise.

Irwin, C., & Berge, Z. (2006). Socialization in the Online Classroom. E-Journal of Instructional Science and Technology, 9(1).

Joseph, P. B., Peppers, D., & Rogers, M. (1995). Do you want to keep your customers forever. *Harvard Business Review*, *73*(2), 103–104.

Kim, H., Damhorst, M., & Lee, K. (2002). Apparel involvement and advertisement Processing. *Journal of Fashion Marketing and Management*, *6*(3), 277–302. doi:10.1108/13612020210441364

Kozinets, R. (1999). E-tribalized marketing: The strategic implications of virtual communities of consumption. *European Management Journal*, *17*(3), 252–264. doi:10.1016/S0263-2373(99)00004-3

Lindquist, J. D., & Sirgy, J. M. (2009). *Shopper, Buyer and Consumer Behaviour theory, Marketing applications and Public Policy implications* (4th ed.). Ohio: Cengage Learning.

McWilliam, G. (2000). Building stronger brands through online communities. *Sloan Management Review*, *41*(3), 43–54.

Mooradian, T., Renzl, B., & Matzler, K. (2006). Who trusts? Personality, trust and knowledge sharing. *Sage Journals Online Management Learning*, *37*(4), 523–540.

Muniz, A. M. Jr, & O'Guinn, T. C. (2001). Brand Community. *The Journal of Consumer Research*, *27*(4), 412–432. doi:10.1086/319618

Pan & Lee. (2003). *Using E-CRM for a Unified View of the Customer*. New York, NY: ACM Press.

Parvatiyar, A., & Sheth, J. (Eds.). (2002). *Handbook of Relationship Marketing*. Thousand Oaks, CA: Sage.

The Importance of Customer Satisfaction and Customer Engagement in Business Outcomes. (2010). *Peoplemetrics*, Retrieved from http://www.peoplemetrics.com/

Peppers, D., Rogers, M., & Dorf, B. (1999). 'Is your company ready for one-to-one marketing? *Harvard Business Review*, *77*(1), 151–160. PMID:10345390

Preece, J., & Krichmar, D. M. (2003). Online communities: focusing on sociability and usability. In J. Jacko & A. Sears (Eds.), *Handbook of Human-Computer Interaction* (pp. 596–620). Mahwah, NJ: Lawrence Erlbaum Associates.

Prahalad, C. K., & Ramaswamy, V. (2004). Building New Strategic Capital for Co-Creation. Strategy. *Journal of Interactive Marketing*, *18*.

Ryals, L., & Payne, A. F. T. (2001). Customer relationship management in financial services: Towards information-enabled relationship marketing. *Journal of Strategic Marketing*, *9*(1), 3–25. doi:10.1080/713775725

Sedley, R. (2006). cScape Customer Engagement Director. Retrieved from http://www.e-consultancy.com/publications/customer-engagement-report

Shainesh, G., & Sheth, J. (2006). *Conceptual Foundations of CRM, Customer Relationship Management, A Strategic Initiative*. Chennai, India: Macmillan.

Sheth, J. N., & Parvatiyar, A. (2000). *'The evolution of relationship marketing', Handbook of Relationship Marketing* (pp. 119–148). India: Sage Publications Ltd. doi:10.4135/9781452231310.n5

Singh, D., & Agrawal, D. P. (2003). CRM practices in Indian industries. *International Journal of Customer Relationship Management*, *5*(3), 241–257.

Sprott, D., Czellar, S., & Spangenberg, E. (2009). Brand Engagement self concept. *JMR, Journal of Marketing Research*, Feb., 2009.

Shevlin, R. (2006). Marketing Whims? Retrieved from http://marketingwhims.blogspot.com/2006/04/disengaging-from-arfs-definitionof05.html

Shim, S., & Bickle, M. C. (1994). Benefit segments of the female apparel market: Psychographics, shopping orientations, and demographics. *Clothing & Textiles Research Journal*, *12*(2), 1–12. doi:10.1177/0887302X9401200201

Shim, S., & Chen, Y. Q.Yen Qiong Chen. (1996). Acculturation characteristics and apparel shopping orientations; Chinese students and spouses from the People's Republic of China residing in the Southwest. *Clothing & Textiles Research Journal*, *14*(3), 204–215. doi:10.1177/0887302X9601400306

Suresh, Shivaram, & Mohan (2004), Does Online Customer Experience Affect the Performance of E-commerce Firms. Journal of Business, 77(2 Part 2).

Visser, E. M., & Du Preez, R. (2001). Apparel shopping orientation: two decades of research. *Journal of Family Ecology and Consumer Sciences*, 29, 71-81. Retrieved from www.up.ac.za/academic/acadorgs/saafecs/vol29/visser.html

Wright, J. (2006). The power of blogs for business. *Blog Marketing*. Retrieved from http://www.blog-marketingbook.com/

KEY TERMS AND DEFINITIONS

Branding: The process involved in creating a unique name and image for a product in the consumers' mind, mainly through advertising campaigns with a consistent theme. Branding aims to establish a significant and differentiated presence in the market that attracts and retains loyal customers. (American Marketing Association Dictionary. Retrieved 2015-06-14. The Marketing Accountability Standards Board (MASB) endorses this definition as part of its ongoing Common Language in Marketing Project.

Consumer Engagement: Customer engagement marketing places conversions into a longer term, more strategic context, and is premised on the understanding that a simple focus on maximising conversions and aims at encouraging customer loyalty and advocacy through word-of-mouth. (Eisingerich, Andreas B.; Kretschmer, Tobias (March 2008). "In E-Commerce, More is More". Harvard Business Review 86: Pages 20–21).

Consumer Experience: It is the product of an interaction between an organization and a customer over the duration of their relationship. This interaction includes a customer's attraction, awareness, discovery, cultivation, advocacy and purchase and use of a service. (Richardson, A. (2010). 'Understanding the customer experience'. Retrieved 2015-06-14 from Harvard Business Review Blog Network: http://blogs.hbr.org/cs/2010/10/understanding_customer_experie.html).

Customer Relationship Management: It is an enterprise-wide initiative that belongs to all areas of an organisation and reflects the comprehensive strategy and process of acquiring, retaining, and partnering with selective customers to create superior value for the company and the customer. (Singh,

D. and Agrawal, D.P. (2003) 'CRM practices in Indian industries', International Journal of Customer Relationship Management, Vol. 5, No. 3, pp.241–257).

Online Business Community: An online community is a virtual community whose members interact with each other primarily via the Internet. (Plant, Robert. (Jan. 2004). Online Communities. Technology in Society 26 (Issue 1). Retrieved 2015-06-14 http://0www.sciencedirect.com.sculib.scu.edu/science/article/pii/S0160791X030009 9X).

Social Media: Social media are computer-mediated tools that allow people to create, share or exchange information, ideas, and pictures/videos in virtual communities and networks. Social media is defined as "a group of Internet-based applications that build on the ideological and technological foundations of Web 2.0, and that allow the creation and exchange of user-generated content. (Kaplan Andreas M., Haenlein Michael (2010). "Users of the world, unite! The challenges and opportunities of social media". Business Horizons 53 (1). p. 61).

Swarm Intelligence: Swarm intelligence (SI) is the collective behavior of decentralized, self-organized systems, natural or artificial. The concept is employed in work on artificial intelligence. (E. Bonabeau, M. Dorigo, & G. Theraulaz. Swarm Intelligence: From Natural to Artificial System. Oxford University Press, New York, 1999).

APPENDIX 1

Table 1. Cronbach's alpha is 0.647, which indicates a internal consistency for our scale with this specific sample. Reliability Statistics

Cron bach's Alpha	Cronbach's Alpha Based on Standardized Items	N of Items
.647	.648	4

Table 2. Correlations

		Reciprocity	Longetivity	Participation	Engagement
Reciprocity	Pearson Correlation	1	.381	.137	.524
	Sig. (2-tailed)		:001	.000	.000
	N	50	50	50	50
Longevity	Pearson Correlation	.381	1	.185	.394
	Sig. (2-tailed)	.001		.232	.000
	N	50	50	50	50
Participation	Pearson Correlation				
	Sig. (2-tailed)	.137 .000	.185 .232	1	.255 .000
	N	50	50	50	50
Engagement	Pearson Correlation	.524	.349	.255	1
	Sig. (2-tailed)	.000	.000	.000	
	N	50	50	50	50

Strong positive correlation was found between Reciprocity and Engagement (r=0/524,p<0/01)

APPENDIX 2

Table 3. Model Summary[b]

Model	R	R Square	Adjusted R Square	Std. Error of the Estimate	Durbin-Watson
1	.983[a]	.966	.961	.1686.5	1.109

Table 4. Coefficients[a]

Model		Unstandardized Coefficients		Standardized Coefficients	t	Sig.
		B	Std. Error	Beta		
1	(Constant)	2198.881	782.346		2.522	.239
	No of points	.462	.033	.825	17.924	.000

Section 3

Customer Relationship Management and Social Media

Chapter 8
Social CRM:
The Role of Social Media in Managing Customer Relations

Neus Soler-Labajos
Open University of Catalonia, Spain

Ana Isabel Jiménez-Zarco
Open University of Catalonia, Spain

ABSTRACT

The advent of the web 2.0 in general and the social networks in particular has altered the consumer behavior with brands, consumer becoming the protagonist of his relationship with the companies. The consumer is no longer passive, but someone who belongs to an interactive user community, whose opinion influences the decision making of others and the company. And companies, therefore, need to understand how to structure content and branding strategies where clients not only communicate with the company, but each other, in real time: the social media. Social networks, as currently represent the opportunity to get the engagement of customers and prospects in a way that can not be achieved by other means, become a single source of information that must be integrated into the software of the company, allowing the conversion of conversation into a transaction. So having a database of clients with personal information is no longer enough, and is required to obtain qualitative features that enable the company to know more about consumers and provide, as a result, a greater brand value. The Social CRM is a tool that incorporates the information obtained from the social networks to the traditional CRM, to ensure that the company is better informed about its customers and gets a much more solid basis for decision making, customizing the offer and adding value to the customer.

INTRODUCTION

The management of relationships that organizations have with their environment is one of the main focuses of interest to companies. Currently, the creation of a stable and strong relationships with those closest agents and in particular with customers, is the main objective of the marketing programs of companies.

In particular, it is essential the management of the relationships that companies establish in the network, especially those settled with customers through social networks. Social networks have become

DOI: 10.4018/978-1-5225-0332-3.ch008

a channel through which individuals - potential consumers - not only to create and issue opinions, but also exchange information and relate. The emergence of phenomena such as the communities of brand or the sale through social networks, has been possible thanks to the diffusion that the applications 2.0 have reached between individuals.

In this context, the Social CRM (in later SCRM) is an essential element. The SCRM is a philosophy, a business strategy designed to engage the customer in a mutually beneficial relationship (win win) that relies on technology, social tools, business rules, workflow and processes, in order to enrich the current knowledge about customers, incorporating social information about them and to provide them with more value. The technological tools that bring together ranges from platforms to post centrally in social networks, monitoring software, up to the community management, etc. The SCRM does not imply having to make a profound change in the company's business, but a change of strategy towards an evolution of how the brand has to communicate with its customers and potential customers. Currently consumers and users have increasingly more channels of communication to express their opinions, feelings, etc., such as the digital channels Facebook, Twitter, LinkedIn, Pinterest, among others.Whereas the previous ideas, the present chapter aims to study the benefits that the use of the SCRM can bring to the company and its results, and how organizations manage relationships with customers from two perspectives: strategic and operational.

To do this, and after understanding the connection of this type of management with the so-called relationship marketing, we will detail the benefits that implementing a CRM system brings to the company, analyzing the performance and its various modalities. We will also study the conversion experienced by the traditional CRM to become social, in response to the advent of social media that occurs at the Network, where conversations are generated with full of information for the company, detailing the distinguishing features of this new system of customer relationship management that incorporates the social factor.

Then we will establish its functions and detail the actions to be developed to implement a successful strategy, summarizing the criteria that will determine the choice of the optimal SCRM tool. Finally, we will illustrate the chapter with the exhibition of two case studies, both successful, the first related to the implementation of the SCRM in marketing campaigns, the second exemplifying the benefits of the SCRM when adopted as a philosophy.

1. CUSTOMER RELATIONSHIP MANAGEMENT: FROM THE TRADITIONAL SYSTEM TO THE SOCIAL

In this section we will analyze the CRM concept both from a strategic and operational perspective. We will finish it analyzing Internet in the logic of the CRM, attended to its role as a source of dissemination, communication and relationship between the company and its prospects.

1.1. The History of Marketing: From the Transactional Marketing to the Relationship Marketing

The marketing concept is dynamic, and this is seen by the different definitions that have been offered on it over the time, including the different approaches that were responding to the problems presented by the discipline in its respective eras.

In 1935 the American Marketing Association (AMA) laid the groundwork for what would be the paradigm which then dominate in marketing, the transactional marketing, understood as a function applicable to organizations that should encourage the exchange of value between the parties. Based on this, in 2004, the same AMA defines marketing as the process of planning and executing the conception, pricing, promotion and distribution of ideas, goods and services to create exchanges that satisfy the objectives of the individual and the organization.

That is, from this perspective the marketing was geared towards an appropriate mix of four variables (marketing mix) that would successfully influence the consumer to buy a particular product. It was considered, in this way, that the patient, anonymous and passive, was only the "other" involved agent in the process, who was given a treatment. Because satisfying the customer through the exchange of values was one of the central ideas of the approach, but still, who assumed the active role of the terms of trade was the company. And in this sense, then, the marketing mix actually had an orientation focused more on the product than the consumer.

In the nineties of the last century, when the transactional marketing approach does not solve the problems arising from the intensity of competition between companies, the changes in the consumer and the concern for quality and interest of organizations to develop customer loyalty strategies, the *relationship marketing* appears as the way to create, maintain and deepen customer relationships (Berry, 1983, 1995).

In this sense the relationship marketing is deployed to a new concept based on the incorporation of a long-term vision marketing that takes into account the needs of consumers really and that values the developing of stable relationships in the markets.

The concept of value is at the center of the corporate competitive strategy (Morgan and Hunt, 1994). Offering customers a greater value than the competition becomes the only way to lure and keep their loyalty, so it is considered essential to deal with them and deeply meet them. But this is possible only if the organization management aims towards the market and customer satisfaction. And for the company, these actions have serious implications which modify the process of marketing management.

The new marketing management involves understanding it as a comprehensive and interactive process that extends to all departments and functions developed within and outside the organization (Berry, 1995). As such, the marketing has to get the correct management of all relationships, within the network of market relations, as a way to improve the relationship between business and consumers. Also the use, under the direction of marketing, of the new technologies applied to production and information processes, allows not only the adjustment of supply to consumer requirements, but the generation of communication between agents, improving their relationship and allowing the customer integration into the company.

Thus, relationship marketing emphasizes not only the loyalty of customers, but cultivating long-term relationships with the set of agents with which the company relates, becoming the strategic vision that can foster exchanges in terms of collaboration and added value. According to McKenna (1991) "Marketing evolves as technology evolves (...). In a world of mass production, which corresponded was a mass marketing. In a flexible manufacturing world, which corresponds is a flexible marketing. Technology comes first, followed by the ability to sell. Technology includes adaptability, programmability and customer adequacy; now comes the marketing that offers these qualities to the market".

In the same line, Alfaro (2004), relationship marketing is the integrated effort to identify and maintain a network of customers, with the goal of continually reinforce it to the benefit of both parties, through individual contacts and interactions that create value over the time.

Although ultimately, relationship marketing is just one marketing concerned with creating, developing and maintaining relationships with customers and other exchange partners, so everyone involved in it gets benefits.

The table 1 summarizes the main differences between transactional and relationship marketing (Sanchez et al., 2010, p7).

1.2. What is the Consumer Relationship Management (CRM)

The same that the concept of relationship marketing is obtained from the evolution of other principles, such as one to one marketing (Rogers and Peppers, 1993), which is based on the premise of treating differently to different clients (since each customer is different, deserves a different treat), the natural evolution of relationship marketing, driven by the technological revolution, also derives a new concept: Customer Relationship Management (CRM).

Its theories are aimed at a comprehensive understanding of customers and their needs, to properly segment the audience and provide it what it needs, when it needs it and how it needs it. And what makes this evolution is the sophistication of technology dedicated to the storage and analysis of customer data, driven, undoubtedly, by new technologies (Pratt, 2007).

But while technology is an important part of CRM, they do not have to be confused. Because CRM is, mainly, a marketing strategy designed to proactively build consumer preference for a particular company, causing his loyalty and, therefore, a greater economic benefit to this.

In this sense, therefore, the concept takes on a double meaning: first refers to the business strategy, focused on building and managing long-term relationships with top customers to optimize their value long term (customer lifetime value), reducing costs and ensuring and increasing his loyalty; and secondly, to software applications required to process the information of those customers and develop the relationship.

So, CRM is not just a computer application, but a strategic orientation of the company to the customer whose success does not depend on the amount of inverted technology, but the ability of the company to lead a process of deep transformation of what initially seems.

Although supported by technology, CRM is a strategy to achieve and increase retention rates of customers of the company, obtaining a better economic performance.

Table 1. Transactional marketing versus relationship marketing

Transactional Marketing	Relationship Marketing
Focused on individual sales	Focused on retaining customers
Oriented to product features	Oriented to product benefits
Providing a short-term view	Providing a long-term vision
Little emphasis on customer service	Greater emphasis on customer service
Low level of customer engagement	High level of customer engagement
Moderate level of customer contact	High level of customer contact
Quality focused essentially on the product	Quality as a concern of everybody

Source: Sánchez et al., (2000)

1.3. Internet as a Relational Element

In the logic of the relationship marketing, - understood both as a philosophy of business and a information management system - Internet occupies an essential place. And it is that the advent of the Web 2.0 revolutionized the Internet and the way of understanding social relations, fostering a culture of participation and interaction. Unlike static websites, where users are limited to the passive viewing of content that have been created for them, the social web is primarily characterized by user participation as an active content creator, shared with the rest of the users.

The term was coined in 2004 by Tim O'Reilly, acknowledged leader of the movement of free software and open source, to refer to a second generation in the history of the Internet services, with the emergence of new services such as social networking, blogs, wikis, etc., which promote collaboration and content sharing among users.

The great value of the Web 2.0 is to reduce the distance between the website visitors and those who publish information in it, because today any user can access a content manager (blog, platforms for publishing images and videos, etc..) and publish information on the Web.

Therefore, the Web 2.0 offers new features that allow to talk about the Internet not only as a great resource, but as a platform for working with resources.

On the other hand, technologies 2.0, which are constantly developing and promoting a more interactive and collaborative web, are included in the so-called social software (social web applications).

And among today's main social software tools include social networks or communication platforms on the Internet, where users share content and interact with those who have their own tastes and interests. As forms of social interaction, they bring together users with the same needs, which are organized to leverage their resources.

From the business perspective, social networks are erected, then, as a powerful tool that brings significant advantages, for being a source of opportunity to disseminate its news on products, provide personalized customer service, interact with the public and get it loyal and achieve greater brand visibility.

That is, that thanks to the Web 2.0 and the software that configures it, social relationships between users with common interests are favored and new and different ways of communicating are fostered, as well as the sharing of knowledge, content publishing, and development of virtual communities in networks that tighten the link between user and brand and other users.

And it is this dynamic change in the nature of relations which has led to the passage of transactional marketing, product-oriented and based on the four Ps (product, price, place, promotion) to relationship marketing, which focuses on the consumer and settles on the four Cs (customer, cost, convenience, conversation).

Thus, the integration of the Internet into the communication channels of business and in managing the relationships with clients enables to:

- Meet customer, his needs, tastes, preferences and expectations, and assess the degree of interest that the client represents for the company.
- Strengthen the link with the customer, through dialogue and exchange of information and content that is relevant to him/her.
- Create and develop a user community that fosters participation, collaboration and involvement of these with the company or brand.

- Customize the treatment and the relationship with clients to direct them only the information that is of interest to them, and relieve them of noise or saturation of information that normally suffer.
- Foster lasting relationships between users and the brand, which benefit each other and boost customer loyalty.

The internet has enhanced the excellence of the one to one marketing, and companies check they can know their customers and treat them individually, after applying segmentation and community building techniques.

The main contributions of the Internet to the relationship marketing are the following:

- Bidirectional communication.
- Reduced interaction costs.
- Increased effectiveness and efficiency of communication actions.
- Public segmentation.
- Marketing customization.
- Improved business processes.
- Better customer service.

2. INFORMATION SYSTEMS IN ENTERPRISES: THE ROLE OF CRM

The information system of an enterprise is the set of resources available to it to capture, process and communicate information in an effective way (providing the necessary information) and efficient (performing it with the least possible resources).

Information systems must be adapted to the specific needs of the company and its organizational structure. And in the process of implementing it must be considered the information that already holds the company, integrating it into the system.

According to the schema presented by Hall (2012) in Figure 1, an enterprise information system performs three activities:

- Receives data from internal and external sources.
- Acts on the data for processing them.

Figure 1. Activities of the enterprise information system

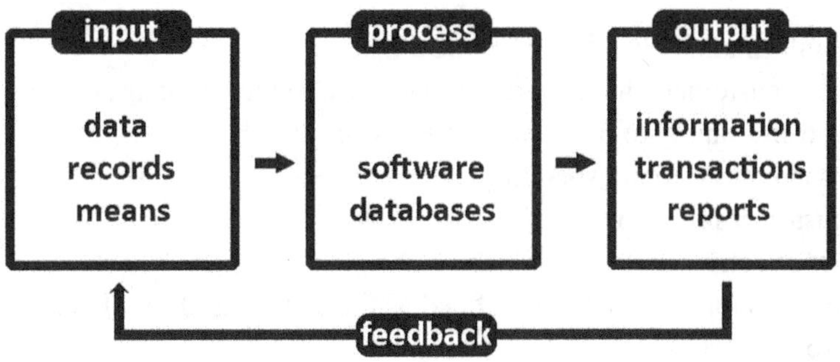

- Distribute the processed information to the user and to get feedback.

The activities described are developed according to the following elements:

- Input or phase whereby the information system takes data to be processed.
- Storing the data in information structures called files.
- Processing the stored data, according to a predetermined sequence of operations or calculations.
- Output or capacity of the system to return the processed information, which will be distributed to the user and / or reused by the system.
- Computer resources, consisting of the hardware and software electronic elements on which the information system is supported.
- Human resources or set of people who design, use and interact with the information system.

The Customer Relationship Management (CRM) represents the technological solution to the growing need for companies to strengthen customer relationships by developing relationship marketing.

CRM is the specific software that allows the company to control and measure contact with its customers. It stores customer data and automates connection therewith, according to the information held. This value is added to the offer made by the company, differentiating the brand from its competitors and improving the quality of attention that is provided to the customer.

The CRM projects take their name from the computer technology industry, since their methods and programs are related to the computer technology and the Internet.

Therefore, CRM is the joint application of the theories of relationship marketing and computer tools that facilitate its implementation and development.

Gillin and Schwartzman (2010,p.117) show that the axes on which CRM systems gravitate are closely related to concepts encompassing the relationship marketing:

- Economy focused on the customer, not the product.
- Customer knowledge derived from the information obtained about him/her, to develop products and services at the level of his expectations.
- Bidirectional communication with the customer based on dialogue and interaction.
- Customizing communication with customers, after their segmentation.
- Creation of stable and lasting relationships with customers, for their loyalty.

Consequently, the objectives that are intended to achieve using CRM solutions are as follows (Hall, 2012, p.516):

- Maximize the information obtained from the client.
- Identify potential customers that generate more profit to the company.
- Improve service and supply to be made to the customer.
- Increase thee share of customer spending.
- Increase the customer retention rate.
- Achieve a more effective marketing.
- Create opportunities for cross-selling, defined as the tactics used to sell accessory or complementary products to the customer.

- Streamline processes and reduce costs.
- Facilitate the introduction of new products quickly.
- Identify new business opportunities.

In any case, although the CRM projects settle in technology, for their development is essential to take into account the factors that are considered traditionally as pillars of any business management program (Smith, 2009):

- **Strategy:** The CRM project must meet the needs of the company in terms of customer relationships and align with corporate strategy and its tactical and operational requirements.
- **People:** The project results will reflect the use performed by persons of the technology itself. Culture, training and internal company communication are key to its success. To ensure that members of the company focus on the customer, requires a cultural change in the company and to promote the empowerment, by which it is conferred on individuals the feeling of being masters of their work, in order to promote their sense of commitment and
- **Processes:** The implementation of technology results in business processes, optimizing their efficiency and effectiveness. The CRM facilitates the development of customer-focused strategies and, therefore, their retention, maximizing their profitability.
- **Technology:** The CRM manages a data warehouse with the information on the management of sales and customers of the company, automating processes. The CRM solution adopted should be established based on the needs and resources of the company.

The Figure 2 illustrates the composition of CRM for its optimal performance.

2.1. Benefits of Implementing a CRM

The purpose of CRM is to improve direct communication between the company and its customers, and that is why is defined as the art or skill favoring customer relations by establishing contact with consumers.

Figure 2. CRM composition

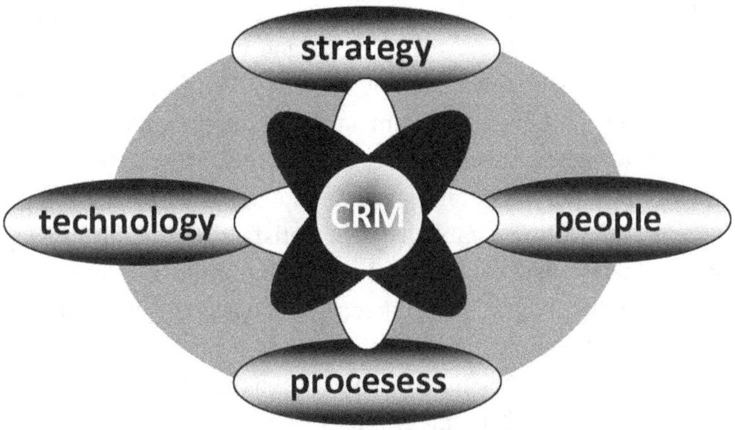

The CRM requires, therefore, a business philosophy that focuses on the customer and a company culture that strongly support the processes of marketing, sales and service, because applications will only allow to implement the customer relationship management when the company holds successful strategy and culture for it.

According to Kim et al., (2003) the benefits to the company of using the CRM system are:

- **Information:** Information is a value in itself. From the analysis and use of information, future customer behavior is predicted, which allows the company to anticipate its range of products and services in accordance with the requirements thereof. This results in customer satisfaction and provides a competitive advantage to the company. In addition, the possession of information allows customer segmentation, in order to distinguish those who are more profitable for business.
- **Corporate Coherence:** The customer orientation makes the organization a flexible entity with a sense of team, whose decisions are linked to customer satisfaction. By centralizing all customer information, CRM avoids to possess inconsistent or outdated data.
- **Integration of the Customer Interaction Channels:** The sales force, channel distribution, telephone service, Internet, in short, the channels that allow the communication of the customer with the company, which until the arrival of CRM worked individually, with the use of this system are integrated, centralizing the collected information in different channels, making them easier to manage and maximizing their performance.
- **Ease and Convenience:** The CRM allows to have the information in a flexible and timely way. And since the level of customer satisfaction is not static (it may vary during the relationship with the company), it allows to develop a dynamic profile of customers, in order to track them and know the reasons for their dissatisfaction, if it occurs, for acting immediately, trying to prevent loss.
- **Marketing Benefit:** The CRM reduces marketing costs, to facilitate the launch of campaigns that are more effective because they target a known audience, and more efficient, for the possibility to customize the message or offer, generating a higher percentage of response. Meeting customers involves knowing the ratio of lost customers, the causes for leaving the company, their satisfaction and loyalty level, the products most consumed, etc. With this information the planning of marketing campaigns adjusts better to the reality, the target is more defined and therefore greater chances of success are obtained.
- **Sales Benefit:** Using CRM improves and increases sales effectiveness, by the identification produced of the best customers and the development of cross selling (selling second and third products to the customer, complementary to the first) and up selling (selling products with higher value added; more advanced, sophisticated or updated). With the cross-selling the sales volume increases, because of the number of complementary products that are sold; the up selling, in turn, increases the amount of sale, by raising the level of the customer spending. In addition, customer loyalty causes more often purchase, and since he is also liable to pay a higher price (price premium) than the one competition establishes, the satisfaction the customer gets through proper management of information and the personalized attention he receives, opens the possibility to raise prices and get a higher margin sales, increasing the average customer profitability.
- **Customer Benefit:** To get complete information on the product, increases the satisfaction of the customer and creates a multichannel interaction between the customer and the company, that properly managed, promotes loyalty. The integration of systems and processes that are continuously

fed back ensures that the customer perceives that the company anticipates his/her needs, meets his/her expectations, dispenses him/her a personalized treatment and offers him/her security service.

Table 2 summarizes the advantages obtained by the company in its different areas with the implementation of a CRM.

2.2. Types of CRM

The origin of CRM solutions goes back to the automation systems of the sales force (SFA or Sales Force Automation) that in its path of growth were adding new tools and methodologies to approach a customer care environment that different sectors of an organization could access.

With the advent of the Internet as a medium and the technology they are integrated with electronic commerce (e-commerce), coupling the concept to the Internet reality. Thus, the interaction of the Network with traditional CRM systems leads to new alternatives, known as e-CRM (Electronic Customer Relationship Management) or e-BRM (Electronic Business Relationship Management).

Thus, according to Kiss and Bichier (2005), the traditional classification describes the CRM types as follows, although other more recent studies add more:

- **Analytical CRM:** It Captures, stores, extracts, processes, interprets and reports customer data. It is responsible for analyzing data from various sources to segment customers and identify potential relationships. It intensively uses storage technologies and information processing, such as databases, data warehouse and data mining, providing business intelligence.
- **Operational CRM:** It manages the different functions of sales automation, marketing and customer service, benefiting vision or complete customer knowledge and collaboration between dif-

Table 2. Benefits that use of CRM is given to the organization areas

Area	Benefit
Marketing	Attracting new customers
	Increasing market share
	Using different channels of distribution
	Boosting business with existing customers
	Customer value
	Fast and permanent access to updated information
Sales	Increased volume and margin sales
	Identification of greater potential customers
	Improving the efficiency of the sales process
Customer service	Improving the quality service
	Reducing the cost of service
	Increased service revenue
	Increasing the customer satisfaction and loyalty

ferent departments of the company, which translates into a more personalized customer service. It focuses on direct customer interactions.

- **Collaborative CRM:** It facilitates interaction with customers through the different channels they use to communicate with the company (mail, phone, fax, web, email, etc.), providing a value added service. It coordinates the various areas of the company, when accessing communication channels, making customer information properly flow through all its departments.

To the exposed classification some authors add a fourth type of CRM, the *strategic*, arguing that the high impact that the system generates into the culture and processes of the company should be considered in terms of corporate strategic planning.

Finally, as we previously said, now, from the use of Internet technologies, on the one hand, and the tendency to achieve improved relations between employees, on the other, two new forms of CRM are defined:

- **E-CRM:** The Electronic Customer Relationship Management is defined as an integrated process that uses the Internet, to develop a series of activities aimed at customer retention, by increasing his satisfaction with the products and services the company offers. It allows to get an interactive, personalized and relevant customer communication through both traditional channels (outlets, call centers, etc.) and electronic (online stores, e-mail, etc.), using a mixture of technology and people that achieve effective communication.
- **ERM:** The Employee Relationship Management seeks to provide technological solutions to promote and improve relations with and between employees of the company, with the aim that they form a team and perfect the development of tasks.

2.3. CRM Functionality: The Virtuous Circle

There are different ways of conceiving the CRM, depending on market orientation (which develops a customer service of added value), the orientation of processes (focused on optimizing customer information and reducing service costs), or its focusing on defensive actions (which seeks to neutralize the advantages of competition).

Anyway, the main function of CRM, as illustrated in the Figure 3, is summarized in the so-called virtuous circle, which aims to achieve to target the right customer, at the right time, with the right offer and by the most optimal channel.

The virtuous circle of CRM summarizes the functions of the system through a scheme that begins with the creation of a relationship with the customer to obtain information about him/her, providing knowledge about his/her habits and preferences. This allows customer segmentation, according to the different profiles, to personalize communications and fit the offering products and services to his needs. Which leads to greater customer satisfaction, which drives loyalty and retention, resulting in increased sales, which also are made with lower service costs, as well as in obtaining more information yet, beginning the cycle again.

The Figure 4 illustrates the operation of the circle.

Figure 3. Virtuous circle of CRM

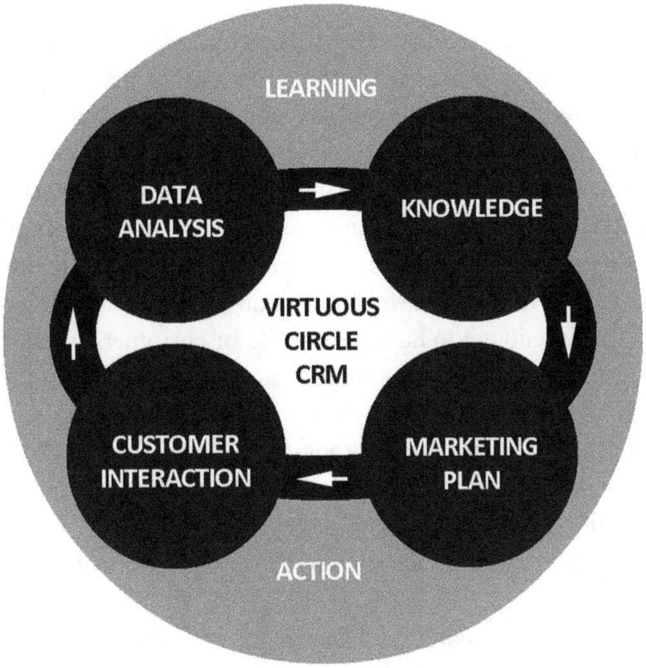

Figure 4. Operation of the virtuous circle of CRM

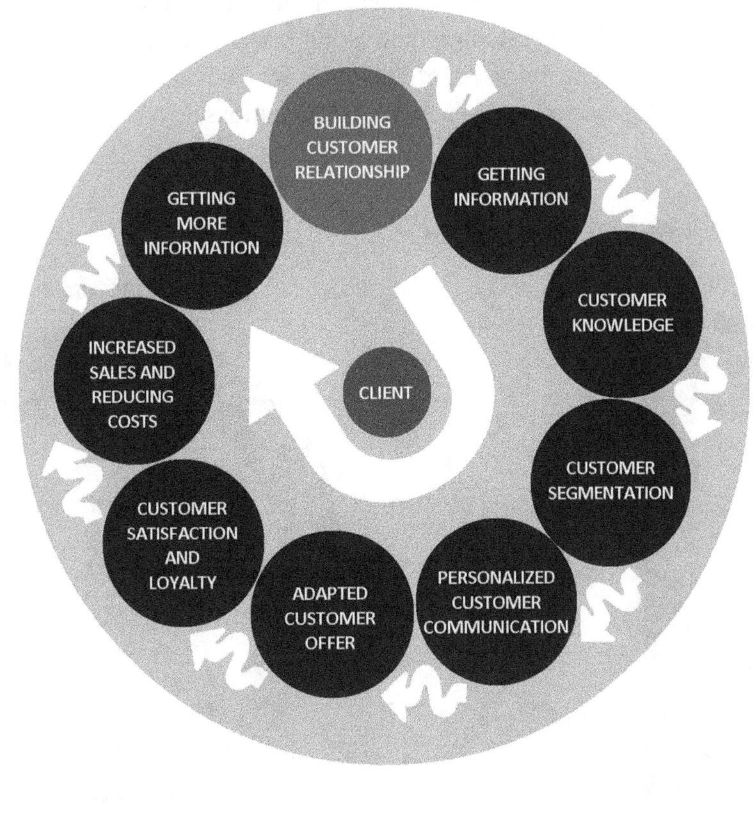

3. THE SOCIAL CRM

The advent of Web 2.0 in general and social media in particular has altered the behavior of the consumer against brands, making him/her the protagonist of the relationship that keeps with the companies. Because the consumer is no longer passive, but someone who belongs to an interactive community whose opinion influences decisions of others and the organization itself.

Companies, therefore, need to manage the information coming from conversations and relationships. Social networks provide the opportunity to get engagement from customers and prospects in a way that can not be achieved by other means and, therefore, become a single source of information to be integrated into the software of the company, to enable the conversion of conversation into a transaction.

In short, that it is no longer enough to have a database of customers with personal information, but it is required to get qualitative characteristics that reveal more about consumers, in order to provide, consequently, a greater brand value.

The Social CRM (SCRM) is a tool that incorporates the traditional CRM information from social networks, so that the company is better informed about its customers, getting a more solid basis for decision making, customizing the offering and to inject customer value.

The Social CRM increases knowledge acquired by the company about costumers by the interactions they make on social media.

So while traditional CRM revolves around data and information that companies can get from their clients through the various functions based on marketing, sales and customer service, data that initiate the CRM system and allow segmentation of these customers, the SCMR incorporates the role of public relations, managing the social presence of brands and customer engagement.

Unlike traditional CRM, where the client is not part of the system, the SCRM locates her/him at the center. The company works with the customer, motivating her/him to build a relationship and to shape its own experiences, in order to generate a beneficial value for both parties.

The Figure 5 illustrates the operation of the two CRM solutions.

Figure 5. Operation of traditional and social CRM systems

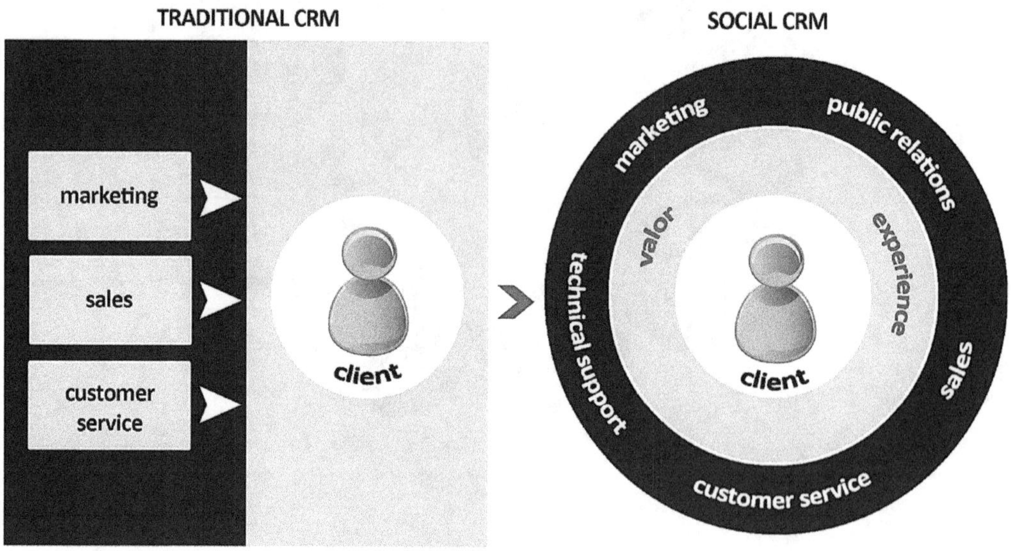

Thus, while the traditional CRM is reduced to a client list that details who these people are, at what level the company meets them and what interaction history have with the entity, the SCRM incorporates talks to the data, acquiring a social form. Conversations and relationships that, besides, are not generated from the company to the customer, but between the company and the customer, under the control of the client, and between the same customers.

And so, if the main goal of traditional CRM is to obtain the optimum value of the client during the course of the relationship the company has with her/him, in the current environment, where the communication control is in the hands of the customer, the SCRM strategy emerges as the dialogue management, not the client. It is based on the ability of the company to fit the client's interests with business objectives, relying on the engagement.

Greenberg (2009) defines the Social CRM as "a philosophy and business strategy, which relies on a technology platform, business parameters, working dynamics, processes, and social characteristics, designed to link the client in a collaborative conversation that seeks mutual benefit in a transparent and trusted environment. It is the answer given by the company to the conversation that controls the client".

In short, it is based on establishing and cultivating collaborative relationships with customers to deliver value and personalized experience.

Greenberg himself details the distinguishing features of this new system of customer relationship management that incorporates the social aspect:

- The SCRM is a CRM extension, not a substitute. It represents a change that adds new features and functions, but is still based on the idea of profitable relationships with customers of the company, rather than reaching new customers. The system goes to the transactional relationship with customers to the direct interaction with them, but without deleting the transaction or data associated with it.
- Given the high expectations of today's consumer and the power of his demands, companies need to build its SCRM strategy in collaboration with the clients themselves.
- Companies must synchronize their own business goals with the client's objectives, in order to that the relationship benefits both parties. Because the intersection of the interests of both parties allows the creation of a collaborative value chain that generates both an individual and joint benefit. The core of the SCRM is the co-creation, the ability of the parties to create value for both.
- The SCRM varies the perspective of the type of client that is optimal for the company. Now, more than the life cycle that the client has, what most reflects the direct economic value of a customer during the course of his relationship with the company is his influence on others when talking about it.

The Figure 6 the evolution experienced by the traditional CRM to become social.

According to Malthouse et al., (2013) and as noted in the above Figure 6, the Social CRM defines:

- **A People Relationship Management (PRM):** In Internet is not always possible to know whether the user is a customer, so that the relations of the company acquire a new dimension, based on interaction with people, not only with customers.
- **The Network Relationship:** Since customers relate, the multichannel relation of traditional CRM takes the form of network relation, where the company is not the central point of interaction of the relationship, but another node in the network.

Figure 6. Social CRM operation compared to traditional

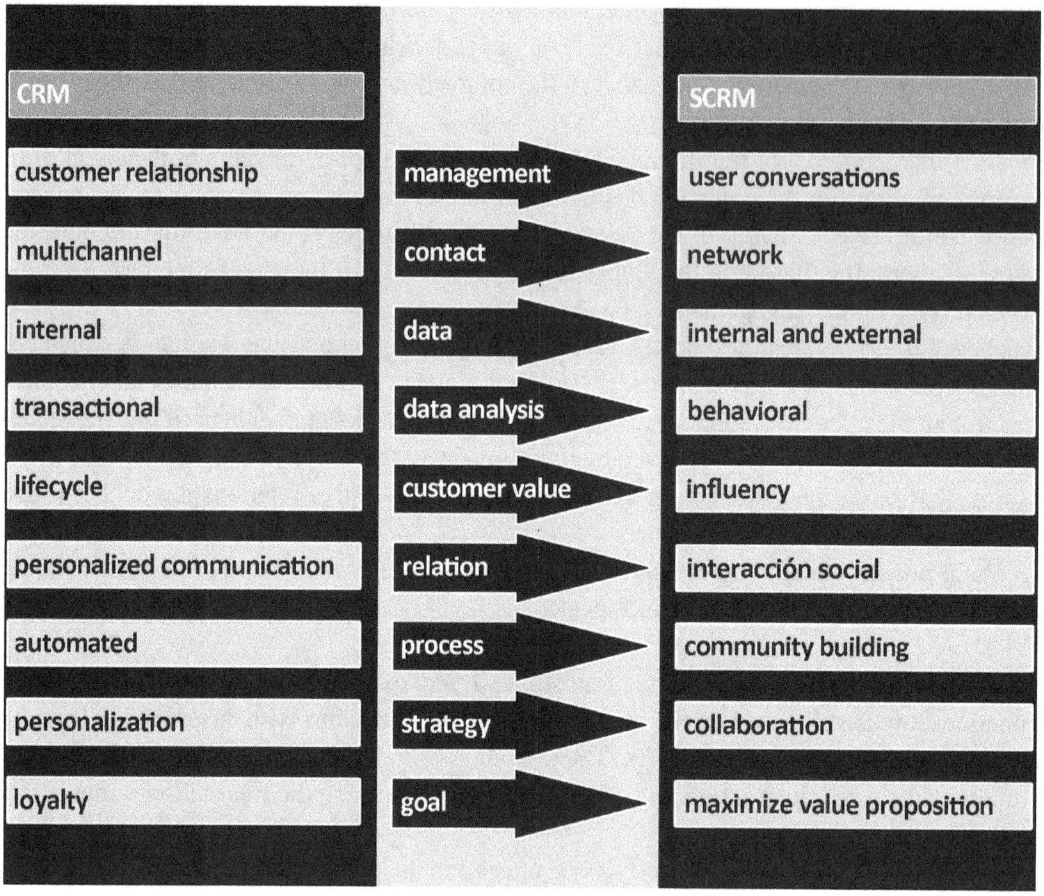

- **Personalized Interaction:** Although traditional CRM tries to establish a more personal communication with customers, the Social CRM requires much more customized and scalable interactions.
- **A Combination of Internal and External Data:** The Social CRM offers the possibility of combining the customer transactional data (internal) with which the company gets on the Internet (external) to achieve a better understanding.
- **Qualitative Data Analysis:** The SCRM adapts the data analysis process from a transactional or quantitative environment to another one more behavioral or qualitative.

3.1. Advantages and Results of the Social CRM

The CRM is a multichannel discipline that connects with customers through the pathways they use or prefer. Social media, meanwhile, represent the most fruitful current source of intelligence in real time, in relation to the customer awareness and sentiment, which feeds the marketing and sales developed in the core of CRM.

The successful development of a Social CRM that improves the customer experience and maximizes the value proposition that the company offers the customer will generate the following results:

- Knowledge of current and potential customers:

Not only for the analysis of data generated internally by the company, but with the same information that the customer gives related to behavioral, sometimes voluntarily and consciously.

- Knowledge of business:

The extraction of feedback left by customers on social channels can generate business knowledge in order to use it to improve the products, how to present them, how to make them reach customers, etc. Comments and opinions from users about the brand and products facilitate the decision-making and allow adaptation of products and services to the wishes and needs of the consumer. Which in turn promotes innovative processes and products.

- Creating social intelligence:

Social intelligence refers to the ability of companies to collect, analyze and process information available in order to increase their competitiveness and quality of customer service. It is based on the ability of firms to learn from the client, to leverage content generated on social networks to create useful information for helping to guide the decisions of the company and reducing risk.

- Ease of segmentation:

The user's presence on social networks provides two types of value for the company: the individual, based on purchases made and its recurrence, and the one generated by his participation in the Network, defined by the ability to influence he has with respect to the decision to buy from other users.

Therefore, the users segmentation based on the value provided allows to launch different marketing strategies, according to the value it is desired to boost: the individual or the network value.

- Increased customer loyalty and engagement:

By providing information and customizing the actions of communication with customers, their retention rate increases and long-term relationships based on trust and win-win strategies (characterized because they benefit all the members) are created.

- Increased turnover:

The increased level of customer satisfaction translates into higher sales and lower price elasticity (sales don't suffer much if prices rise).

- Profitability of resources and cost reduction:

By personalizing the customer service it can be transferred to social channels, increasing efficiency (the response to inquiries and complaints is much faster and agile) and reducing costs.

- Improvement or reinforcement of brand image:

The presence in social networks increases the relationship and interaction with customers, which positively affects the brand recognition and awareness and establishes a level of trust that drives sales figures upward.

In parallel, the benefits obtained to integrate and automate the SCRM with a multichannel strategy are:

- **Scalability and Scope:** The automation allows to develop active listening (learning process made by the company or brand to understand the message from the perspective of the person who emits it; to understand what the consumer transmits) and work engagement creation through a large volume and variety of content generated by the brand, influencers (opinion leaders) and the same users. The content comes from both history and customer intelligence in real time, as the platforms of social media, the CRM and other transactional systems, web analytics, the ratios of satisfaction and market research services.
- **Speed and Performance:** The automation enables rapid detection of cases, the answer, routing, resolution and agent productivity. It also allows downsizing staff in interactions requiring assistance.
- **Customization:** The automation allows to customize optimally events, promotions, campaigns, etc. made by the company or brand, and in particular the actions of listening and creating engagement, allowing to manage conversations with greater depth.
- **Integration of Channels:** The automation supports a comprehensive integration of channels, including telephone, e-mail, chat, SMS, mail, social media, web, e-commerce, etc.
- **Regulatory Compliance:** The automation generates consistency and transparency in the rules established for the creation of engaging, workflows, policies and audits, during the CRM process.
- **Analytics:** The automation enables stakeholders to make more comprehensive and profound analysis, including dashboards, reports, KPI (key performance indicators; outcome measurement parameters), alerts, trends, predictive models, analysis of social network and incurring users, segmentation, sales and up and cross selling analysis, etc.

In short, crossing traditional CRM data with those obtained in social networks not will only allow to offer a better customer service, but will enable extracting more value for the same data.

3.2. Features of Social CRM

The Social CRM needs traditional CRM to make sense. Without client and customer data there is no chance to improve the knowledge. Social listening is the basis of the strategy, but Social CRM is based on the traditional one, trying to supplement the data this one collects, by incorporating new behaviors.

While the interactions that are of interest to the company are produced in the social media (evaluations of the brand and its products, recommendations or criticisms, statements of tastes and preferences, etc.), the so-called social thermometer of CRM allows to know the opinion of customers who are already part of the database of the company (i.e., of the traditional CRM program) about the company, at an aggregated level. Conversations and interactions that customers make are detected, analyzing those related to the company and competition, to measure the social climate of the clients.

Thus, broadly speaking, and according to Schoenbachler et al., (1997) there are four types of customers in the database of the company:

- **In Flight Risk:** Customers who relate to competition or criticize our brand.
- **Discontents:** Customers with a bad experience with the brand or product, but that do not disqualify it.
- **Pleased:** Customers who refer to the brand in neutral or positive terms.
- **Evangelists:** Organic prescribers, customers that recommend the brand selflessly.

Knowing the social status of the database the CRM is socialized, incorporating new knowledge about customers, in order to bring more value in interactions with them and get higher returns. The socialization of CRM will allow a better segmentation, based on the attitudes and feelings that show people, to create more comprehensive value proposals for them.

Personal data, social networking profile, online influence level, intensity of the relationship with the brand, customer seniority, products he purchases, how often, seasonal consumption, shopping channel, consumption figure, etc.; collectively, and in order to segment customers: spaces of interaction, talking subjects, social and cultural motivations, used language code, hierarchy of the community, etc. In general it is to qualify the database, to amplify the potential of CRM with information voluntarily bring people, to achieve a deeper understanding of the customer that the purely demographic and economic, which will allow to optimize efforts and resources to plan strategies.

According to Heller et al., (2011) the SCRM includes activities divided into four areas:

- **Customer:** It collects efforts to integrate the contacts made with customers in social media with CRM systems and corporate customer care. Workflows are defined, channels are integrated and incidents are managed and resolved. The integration of social networks in CRM systems and customer service of the company improves the performance of pre and post service.
- **Loyalty:** The SCRM is to build customer relationships and try to customize them the maximum. Social networks, in turn, allow to create a community of users to maintain constant communication, building strong and lasting relationships.
- **Sales:** The links are built through the content that is shared, so that followers or fans of the brand have already a previous affinity with it and represent potential customers for the company. There are developed social features aimed at generating traffic to online stores, to increase social shopping (e-commerce in social networks, a method of sale that encourages communication and interaction with the company) and to further the recommendations that users make about the brand and its products.
- **Innovation:** Constant feedback received from customers can develop relevant and sustainable competitive improvements in the product or service and encourage innovation. Monitoring social media is developed (to detect and follow conversations in which is talked about the brand and its products) orienting it to innovation and fostering open innovation (internal and external talent collaborating, to create and improve products and services) .

4. DEFINITION AND IMPLEMENTATION OF STRATEGIES OF SCRM

New concepts of social customer, collaborative partner, vendor informed ... push organizations to better understand what social enterprise means.

Social enterprise is one that understands the ecosystem in which is immersed, leverages relationships with people and provides much as it gets. And the organization that understands this new normality can provide better products and build lasting and closer relationships with the members of the ecosystem.

But focusing to achieve this goal requires aligning the internal and external perspectives of the organization. The company 2.0 focuses on promoting collaborative strategies with employees, partners and suppliers. The SCRM, however, is directed outward, through people, processes and technology, to respond to the social customer. The two perspectives are mixed, so that the feedback the company receives from the customer is integrated with other data, analyzed, and incorporated into business processes, which extend to the outside. The process repeats and generates a constant relationship between the customer and the company.

The Social CRM is a customer loyalty strategy that supports the defined objectives to optimize the customer experience. For the strategy to be successful the power of social networks and the impact generated in the business must be considered.

However, a social media strategy is not a Social CRM strategy. The marketing department of the company may have established the brand presence in social networks, for example, by promoting the interaction of customers, and the customer service area perhaps solves the customer doubts intervening in social forums, initiatives that use social media to communicate with customers, but do not make up a strategy of SCRM because they do not include a strategic approach of customer loyalty (representing what customers represent in the value chain) or consider a governance plan, guidelines and shared visions that optimize business benefits.

When a SCRM strategy is established organizations can better determine the influence of their social activities within the entire lifecycle of the customer, both through traditional channels and nontraditional.

In our opinion, the best practices to implement a successful strategy of Social CRM, based on proven strategies, are the following:

- Treating the SCRM as part of the complete CRM strategy:

Internal consensus and understanding of the organization with respect to the objectives to achieve with the project is needed. Any plan recognizes the new reality of social customer and prosecutes value for the customer and the company, but each strategy will be different because it will be based on the specific goals of each organization, the customer base available and its business processes.

The best Social CRM projects are what develop as a natural extension of the existing CRM strategies in the company. Because social media channels differ from traditional, but only represent new ways of customer interaction. Therefore, the management of customer relations should be conducted in a holistic, integrated way, without distinguishing between social and traditional.

- Choosing the tools properly:

The easiest way to address this dilemma is to determine which tools use current and potential customers. Knowing in what social networks are, what means use, the company may choose the tools to be used in the strategy, according to its own criteria established for their adaptation and to identify opportunities to create value.

- Integrate the SCRM and workflows of the users:

A key objective of Social CRM is to create a fluent, integrated and consistent experience across departments and functions that are geared to the customer. Therefore, data obtained from the social sources have to be included in the existing CRM system without keeping them apart. In this way, employees can access and act on the social information in the same way as performed with any other information.

The implementation of the SCRM should enrich and expand existing processes, without separating them, integrating the CRM tools with the existing workflows.

- Focus on value:

The best SCRM strategies combine value for the customer and the company. The exchange of feedback is a benefit for both, so when defining the strategy should be considered the value the social component will bring. Also, before starting the project, it will be essential to determine how the outcome will be measured, setting benchmarks for measuring progress (KPI).

- Perspective:

While it is not possible to anticipate the future, you must provide the appearance of new tools and social channels that will transform the current scenario, ensuring the implementation of an open and flexible CRM that can tailor updates, additions and changes.

4.1. Tools and Applications

With the arrival of the requirements imposed by the SCRM new solutions to monitor, capture and cross data with the company systems are needed, setting a new scenario of analysis of the environment and customers.

The best solutions are those that not only integrate social networks, but also the information that resides in the CRM systems of the company, such as contact information, communications history and workflows.

The latest updates from CRM services introduce already new roles that enhance the user experience, guiding the user through the process of pre-defined and opportunity management. They add new definitions of business processes to manage simple contacts and accounts and track, getting businesses understand better their customers and can maintain optimal communication and collaboration with them.

The systems integrate with networks that simplify the work of sharing customer information between the different areas of the company and enable companies to open new communication channels and connect with other users, both inside and outside the organization.

The CRM software applications that connect traditional business with social media deliver to the companies the tools to:

- Leverage efficiently the information customers generate, share and disseminate in the network, with the aim of improving the development and supply of its products and services.
- Establish a link with customers and maintain a closer and fluid relationship with them, in order to know their opinion and detect problems or opportunities.
- Manage communication campaigns in social channels.

Also the SaaS platforms (Software as a Service) are based on the functionality of social networks planning and management, integrating monitoring conversations, launching campaigns and real-time interaction with customers or community of fans of the brand. Monitoring the activity allows to measure the degree of user participation and identify influencers and brand ambassadors, and segment customers in the networks. And the system encourages collaboration between the departments of the company, promoting a business environment 2.0.

Monitoring and data analysis help to establish marketing strategies in social networks, optimizing the creation of campaigns by segmenting audiences. The campaign management allows to plan and publish content directed to the right persons at the right time. The activity in real time allows viewing from one environment different conversations that occur in different social networks, optimizing processes management to meet the objectives set (loyalty, sales, etc.). The engagement helps brand to identify the most effective strategy for involving the fan, follower or user and interact with him/her.

Thus, social collaboration links social networks with the sales processes of the brand, facilitates the information sharing between teams dedicated to manage the social media and allows all departments involve in the making decisions of the company.

The criteria for choosing a good CRM tool applied to the social field can be many and varied, they depend on the site (web or platform) it is wanted to monitor and the objectives pursued. There are hundreds of solutions and applications on the market, some free, some for sale, and choosing the one that best suits the needs of the business is not easy. However, the most complete and efficient application, in our view, should include the following:

- **Integration with Social Networks:** Both to receive information and to participate in social networks and other websites in daily use by prospective and current clients of the company.
- **Content Filtering:** Since it is not possible to monitor and control the activity of a large number of users on various social networks, it is required to filter content according to the needs: by region, age, keywords, etc.
- **Customizable Database:** It is required to incorporate data and custom fields, to differentiate users.
- **Reports:** The preparation of reports allows to follow the activity developed to modify the strategy in social media, if appropriate, and monitoring the impact of campaigns.
- **Compatibility:** Because in the current market, there is not a product that integrates the processes of social network analysis, campaign management and real-time SCRM, applications that are chosen should complement and enable compatibility of data.
- **Friendly Interface:** The tool must be attractive and intuitive, easy to use, especially when it comes to control conversations and figures.
- **In the Cloud:** Most CRM applications allow to place the activity on the Internet, in order to access data from any location.

4.2. Examples of Use of SCRM

The SCRM can seem a significant investment in time, technology and money, but it is flexible enough to benefit all types of businesses. Following are two real examples of how companies from different sectors have used it successfully: the first related to the implementation of the system in marketing campaigns, the second exemplifying the benefits to adopt it as a company philosophy.

1. **L'Oréal:** Applying SCMR in the marketing campaigns:

For more than a century, L'Oréal has been involved in the adventure of beauty. The small company founded by Eugène Schueller in 1909 has become the number one cosmetic group in the world. Nowadays, L'Oréal, is the leading brand of feminine beauty products, with a presence in 130 countries. The company is the owner of 28 beauty lines including Garnier, Maybelline and Lancôme, knows consumers are increasingly multibrand shoppers. For years, it has segmented customers simply as L'Oréal Paris shoppers or Maybelline brand loyalists. But new commerce channels create an abundance of choice, which makes consumers inherently less loyal.

"For the past 20 years, each brand did what they wanted to do," Christophe Eymery, head of digital for L'Oréal Australia, said in an interview at Salesforce's Connections event. "At this stage, the problem is avoiding marketing to become more streamlined. The direction and change is coming from the top.".

One of the most important challenges the company faces was the need of increasing the top of mind and the sales of products through the beauty salons in the United States.

To achieve this it facilitated access to 5,000 salons to a maximization program in Facebook, under a technology-based CRM and social marketing, which complemented the individual page for each salon, allowing appointments with customers and provide information on trends in court hair and products.

The result led to an increase in sales of US $ 4,000 per salon, with a total increase of $ 20,000,000, detailed information on results and return on investment (ROI) per salon. The program won the Forrester Groundswell Award and earned 21,000,000 impressions and 2,200,000 interactions.

2. **Disney:** Applying SCMR as business philosophy:

The Walt Disney Company has always been a pioneer in applying techniques of community building, both online and offline, and its constant aim is to improve the customer experience.

Through its website, and through the Social CRM, adds behavior and sentiment data coming from the activity of the online community, bringing them together with demographic data to better understand the needs and the type of interaction its customers and prospects want.

The latest novelty of the company is its new initiative to try to improve the live visitor experience, using data obtained from customers to present offers and resources in real time.

So with the use of Radio Frequency Identification (RFID) sensors, experiences could be adapted according to individual preferences of visitors, because they could meet transactional customer data (length of visit, shopping, etc.), demographic data (size of the group, age, etc.), and behavioral (where they went, what they did, etc.) and use predictive models to increase customer satisfaction and revenue of the company.

Thus, for example, it could be detected that a family has not made a dinner reservation and contact the family to suggest nearby restaurants (i.e., that depending on the habits, preferences and level of customer spending, it can be offered what people need) or, knowing that a significant percentage of child crosses the street to buy an ice cream after riding an attraction, installing an ice cream pushcart next to the attraction, increasing the income.

So, on the web, the social CRM adds behavioral and sentimental data from the online community activity to traditional transactional and demographic data, to enable the company to better understand the needs, lifecycle stage and desired interactions of the prospects and customers. And, while this strategy is not possible for companies that don't have an entire ecosystem like Disney does at its resort, they can do this online, using private social communities.

Because the online customer communities provide valuable information, discussions and connections to customers and prospects, while giving the company rich insight into what it would take to strengthen customer relationship and improve the customer experience.

Thus, as more customers and prospects use the web to research solution, find support and build connections, companies have the opportunity to significantly increase sales and customer retention by using the online communities in conjunction with their CRM system to get actionable data about their target audiences.

FUTURE RESEARCH DIRECTIONS

In anticipation of the very near future, although the focus of the strategy concerns the relationship with the customer, it is already predicted the need to focus on the customer experience through mobile, as it is the device that currently generates higher expectations. Companies should focus on providing a user experience through mobile applications, providing a unique customer value. So they will have to convert soon the Customer Relationship Management into Customer Experience Management (CEM), in order to enhance brand visibility and increase conversion rates and revenue.

CONCLUSION

The CRM system is a business strategy supported by a technological tool (software) for competitively managing the relationships the organization has with its stakeholders, in order to meet market requirements and add value to its products and services.

At present, when it is considered fundamental the orientation towards the client, the relationship (which can be created through CRM) and interaction (obtained by SCRM) with the public, provides valuable information to businesses. One interesting point is to know the difference between CRM and SCRM. In this sense, Social CRM is about companies attempting to get back into the conversations being controlled by the customer - listening and engaging to build trust and value. It also gives companies the opportunity to stimulate conversations with and between customers, and use these to build relationships sooner than would traditionally have taken place, managing a pipeline of opportunities more effectively and producing a higher return. Social CRM is an integral component of an overall CRM strategy. However, social CRM is also different in the sense that traditional CRM has been about structuring and controlling data to manage relationships more effectively; by its very nature, social CRM is unstructured and much more difficult to categorize.

Social CRM offers information to business, which, converted into knowledge allows planning strategies to generate value that increases customer satisfaction, increasing his loyalty. And customer loyalty towards the brand, therefore, raises the level of sales of the company, so that ultimate benefit is generated for both. Thus, SCRM enables the brand to extend its personality to engage with consumers on consumer terms, at the time they want, where they play, where they work, when they are travelling and through channels that they chose. Consumers can engage at a level to suit themselves; on a peripheral level or at a level that involves more interaction with the brand. Content, designed to entertain, inform, educate or provide insight, can be designed to connect with consumers, communicate relevantly with those that show interest and convert them to win sales and even advocacy. Consumer marketing experts are working with partners to develop data – light, ultra low cost CRM approaches (especially when compared with CRM databases in the past), which may be able to first identify and then target high value to consumers.

Therefore, what really matters is getting the proper management of the relationship with the customer, because of the beneficial results derived from it. The CRM, in short, is only the system or solution that facilitates this task to businesses.

REFERENCES

Alfaro, M. (2004). *EDITAREDITARTemas clave de marketing relacional.*Madrid: McGraw-Hill.

Berry, L. L. (1983). *Relationship marketing*. American Marketing Association.

Berry, L. L. (1995). Relationship marketing of services—growing interest, emerging perspectives. *Journal of the Academy of Marketing Science*, *23*(4), 236–245. doi:10.1177/009207039502300402

Gillin, P., & Schwartzman, E. (2010). *Social marketing to the business customer: Listen to your B2B Market, generate major account leads, and build client relationships.* New York, NY: John Wiley & Sons, Inc.

Greenberg, P. (2009). CRM at the Speed of Light (4th ed.). New York, NY: McGraw-Hill.

Hall, J. (2012). *Accounting information systems*. Andover, Hampshire: Cengage Learning.

Heller Baird, C., & Parasnis, G. (2011). From social media to social customer relationship management. *Strategy and Leadership*, *39*(5), 30–37. doi:10.1108/10878571111161507

Kim, J., Suh, E., & Hwang, H. (2003). A model for evaluating the effectiveness of CRM using the balanced scorecard. *Journal of Interactive Marketing*, *17*(2), 5–19. doi:10.1002/dir.10051

Kiss, C., & Bichler, M. (2005, October). Leveraging network effects for predictive modelling in customer relationship management. *Proceedings of the15th Annual Workshop on Information Technologies & Systems (WITS)*. doi:doi:10.2139/ssrn.883588 doi:10.2139/ssrn.883588

Malthouse, E. C., Haenlein, M., Skiera, B., Wege, E., & Zhang, M. (2013). Managing Customer Relationships in the Social Media Era: Introducing the Social CRM House. *Journal of Interactive Marketing*, *27*(4), 270–280. doi:10.1016/j.intmar.2013.09.008

McKenna, R. (1991). Marketing is everything. *Harvard Business Review*, 69(1), 65-79.

McKenna, R. (1991). *Relationship Marketing: Successful Strategies for the Age of the Customer*. Perseus Book Group.

Morgan, R. M., & Hunt, S. D. (1994). The commitment-trust theory of relationship marketing. *Journal of Marketing*, *58*(3), 20–38. doi:10.2307/1252308

Pratt, J. (2007). What is CRM. *Construction Business Development*, 71.

Rogers, M., & Peppers, D. (1993). *The One to One Future*. New York, NY: Doubleday.

Sánchez, M., Gil, I., & Mollá, A. (2000). Estatus del Marketing de Relaciones. *Revista Europea de Dirección y Economía de la Empresa*, *9*(3), 47–64.

Schoenbachler, D. D., Gordon, G. L., Foley, D., & Spellman, L. (1997). Understanding consumer database marketing. *Journal of Consumer Marketing*, *14*(1), 5–19. doi:10.1108/07363769710155820

Smith, A. D. (2009). The impact of e-procurement systems on customer relationship management: A multiple case study. *International Journal of Procurement Management*, *2*(3), 314–338. doi:10.1504/IJPM.2009.024814

ADDITIONAL READING

Baran, R. J. (2013). *CRM: The Foundation of Contemporary Marketing Strategy*. Mason, OH: Thomson Higher Education.

Baran, R. J., Zerres, C., & Zerres, M. (2008). *Customer Relationship Management (CRM)*. From http://bookboon.com/es/customer-relationship-management-ebook

Bergeron, B. (2002). *Essentials of CRM: A Guide to Customer Relationship Management*. New York, NY: John Wiley & Sons, Inc.

Cook, N. (2008). *Enterprise 2.0: How Social Software Will Change the Future of Work*. Hampshire, England: Gower Publishing.

Dyche, J., & Levy, A. (2006). *Customer Data Integration: Reaching a Single Version of the Truth (SAS Institute Inc.)*. Hoboken, New Jersey: John Wiley & Sons, Inc.

Freeland, J. (2002). *The Ultimate CRM Handbook: Strategies and Concepts for Building Enduring Customer Loyalty and Profitability*. New York, NY: McGraw-Hill.

Gartner Research Inc. (2003). *Building Business Benefits From CMR. Executive Report*. Stamford, CT: Gartner, Inc.

Goldenberg, B. J. (2015). *The Definitive Guide to Social CRM: Maximizing Customer Relationships with Social Media to Gain Market Insights, Customers, and Profits*. New Jersey, NJ: Pearson Education.

Goodman, J. A. (2014). *Customer Experience 3.0: High-Profit Strategies in the Age of Techno Service*. New York, NY: American Management Association.

Heller, C., & Parasnis, G. (2011). From social media to Social CRM. *IBM Institute for Business Value*. Retrieved from http://www-935.ibm.com/services/us/gbs/thoughtleadership/ibv-social-crm-whitepaper.html

Metz, A. (2011). *The Social Customer: How Brands Can Use Social CRM to Acquire, Monetize, and Retain Fans, Friends, and Followers*. New York, NY: McGraw-Hill.

Pearson, A. W. (2014). *Going Mobile: Going Social*. China: Intelligentsia Media.

Tsiptsis, K., & Chorianopoulos, A. (2010). *Data Mining Techniques in CRM: Inside Customer Segmentation*. New York, NY: John Wiley & Sons, Inc. doi:10.1002/9780470685815

Williams, D. S. (2014). *Connected CRM: Implementing a Data-Driven, Customer-Centric Business Strategy*. Hoboken, New Jersey: John Wiley & Sons, Inc.

KEY TERMS AND DEFINITIONS

Business Information System: The set of resources available to a company to capture, process and communicate information in an effective and efficient way.

Business Intelligence: Processes, tools and technologies to turn data into information and information into knowledge that helps to make decisions, in order to effectively lead the business activity.

CRM: The Customer Relationship Management is a business strategy focused on the customer and supported by the combination of people, processes and technology, in which the goal is to gather as much information as possible about customers to build long-term relationships and increase their satisfaction.

Relationship Marketing: The method to establish, maintain and strengthen relationships with customers, by identifying the most profitable customers and establishing a close relationship with them to know their needs and maintain a product development according to them throughout time.

SCRM: The Social Customer Relationship Management is a business strategy that relies on the basis of traditional CRM, adding a social component for establishing a collaborative conversation with the customer, in order to achieve mutual benefit.

Social Media: Applications, platforms and online communication tools that facilitate the relationship, interaction, collaboration and content generation and distribution between users.

Social Networks: Communications platforms on the Internet where users share content and interact with those who have their own tastes and interests. They represent a powerful tool 2.0 that provides very significant advantages to the company, for being a source of great opportunity that allows it to get a wider dissemination of its news and updates on products, customer interaction and loyalty, providing personalized attention and obtaining greater brand visibility.

Chapter 9
Company-Customer Interaction via Social Media:
Contributions to the Marketing Mix

Manel Hamouda
ISGG, Tunisia

ABSTRACT

In recent years, social media has become an integral part of internet users' everyday life. Customers are increasingly seen to be more like "content creators" or even company employees rather than mere customers as they were in the past. In this chapter, we try to understand how customers use the various social media platforms to interact and how this interaction influences the company's marketing policy. An overview of the customers' different uses and practices enabled authors to identify several forms of interactions and to detect their effects on pricing, product, place and promotion, the four main components of the marketing mix.

INTRODUCTION

The use of social media is continuously being considered as a basic element of companies' marketing strategies that aim at reaching their customers. In fact, Web 2.0 has already attracted the attention of marketers who seem interested to invest in social media applications. Each social media platform like blogs, forums and online communities affects marketing performance (e.g., sales). Therefore, it is essential to understand their relative importance and their interrelatedness (Stephen & Galak, 2009). Customer behavior is also disturbed by the rapid growth of social media (Goh Heng & Lin, 2013; Birke, 2013). Customers now dispose of a new role with the dominance of media in their everyday life. Sawhney, Verona and Prandelli (2005) as well as Vargo and Lusch (2004) agree that customers today are increasingly seen as proactive participants in the interactive process of value co-creation and not just passive receivers of marketing initiatives (Hollebeek, 2013), like they used to be in the past. According to the traditional view of the value creation process, customers have long been considered outside of the company's sphere (Prahalad & Ramaswamy, 2004), which is centered instead on a company-oriented

DOI: 10.4018/978-1-5225-0332-3.ch009

vision. However, nowadays, this vision should be revised. Customers are increasingly becoming active participants in interactive processes that have multiple feedback loops (Brodie, Ilic, Juric & Hollebeek, 2013) as well as instantaneous communication (even in real time) (Hoffman & Novak, 1996). These interactions between customer and company are made easy by the development of User-Generated Content (UGC). UGC represents a new type of virtual environment where users contribute, collect, and explore content generated by other users or by an organization (Di Gangi & Wasko, 2009). The company is now seeking to co-create value with customers by preferring to opt for customized interactions between the customer and the company via several social media formats such as online forums, bulletin boards, list servers, chat rooms, email, personal web pages, social networks and blogs (De Valck, Van Bruggen & Wierenga, 2009). These customer-company interactions through social media (Nambisan & Baron, 2007) bear on the components of the marketing mix (Mangold & Faulds, 2009). The marketing mix is a term that refers to the way a company makes choices and allocates its resources across the four axes of this mix, commonly known as the four Ps (McCarthy, 1960): Product, Price, Place and Promotion. Therefore, we will try in this theoretical review to determine the possible customer-company interactions at the level of each component of the marketing mix. This synthesis would enable us to identify potential uses of social media during customer-company interaction. Then, through concrete real examples, we try to show the best practices of social media in order to optimize their use for the benefit of the company.

ROLE OF CUSTOMER IN PRODUCT POLICY

To better adapt themselves and succeed in a rapidly changing media environment, marketers need to adjust their choices and practices regarding product policy. Online forums, virtual design tools and prototyping facilities are all social media formats that will allow companies to revisit some product policy practices and especially engage their customers in many initiatives or actions related to their products (Nambisan, 2002). Indeed, in the context of product policy, customer- company interaction via web interfaces may take place at several levels.

First, social media may be put at the service of a key element of product policy, which is the brand. The power of social media in developing the brand has been highlighted by numerous studies conducted mainly by international organizations (Miller, Fabian, & Lin, 2009). Web interfaces are in fact a means for companies to place their product at the heart of an online brand community. "Brand communities" are formed when individuals become interdependent around a group identity and rituals and share moral responsibility with the members of this community (Muniz & O'Guinn, 2001). A brand community is able to generate collective actions over time. Many roles can be assigned to brand communities that would allow for sharing of information, recalling history and culture of the brand, assisting new members and mounting pressure on members to remain faithful to the conventional group and the brand (Thompson & Troester, 2002). However, managing a brand community seems to be a very delicate task. On the one hand, brand owners seek to put pressure to guide the community along the brand, and on the other hand, they delegate some degree of brand control in favor of community members (Muniz & O'Guinn, 2001). Moreover, several examples illustrate the success of brand communities. Starbucks, for example, has a Facebook page counting 1,727,314 fans in 2009 (in 2014 it was 36,931,586 fans). The brand is also present on Twitter, YouTube and has its own community Web pages (MyStarbucksIdeas, Starbucks V2V and StarbucksRed). The success of an online brand community reports to the inclusion of a variety of brand-related interests, likely to generate a sense of belonging (Brown, Broderick & Lee,

2007). "MyStarbucksIdeas", for example, gives users the ability to share, vote, discuss and come up with new ideas for Starbucks.

The presence of a company on social networking sites may also result in a wider range of strategic and operational benefits. By inviting feedback, or just observing the conversations, a company may learn about the needs of its customers and adjust its actions. A company may even involve community members in the co-creation of value by allowing them the generation of ideas to modify an existing brand or creating a new one. In this regard, Sawhney et al., (2005) argue that in general co-creation in virtual environments may promote a key element of the marketing plan, new product development (Bugshan, 2014). In terms of product design, General Electric Plastics, for example, relies heavily on the cooperation of its customers to develop a specific application. This has become a custom for the company. By providing their customers with an access to online tools and a library of components, GE transfers design effort and risk on the side of its customers (Thomke & von Hippel, 2002). When innovating or creating new products, working with customers appears to be necessary. Indeed, even before starting the design of new products, the company could seek the views of its customers in order to know what to produce. The use of social media can greatly facilitate this task. Online surveys, for example, are very useful tools to better understand the implicit and explicit needs of customers (Sawhney et al., 2005). Companies could even create online concept labs to test the reaction of customers to the new products that are under development (e.g. an experiment conducted by the Volvo company) (Sawhney et al., 2005).

The use of social media may also take place at the end of the development phase of a new product. Indeed, as soon as the product is ready, new technologies such as rapid prototyping, simulation and combinatorial methods will allow companies to generate and test different product versions quickly but especially at a lower cost (Thomke, 1998).

ROLE OF CUSTOMER IN PRICING POLICY

The use of social media also seems to influence companies' pricing strategies. Bakos (1997) estimated that the internet would be able to increase customer participation in the market, leading to effective competition between prices and creating improved relationships between buyers and sellers. According to Ratchford (2009), internet may influence prices through two characteristics that may lead to lower search and transaction costs and then to lower prices, thanks to increased competition. The first feature is that internet is a new medium for disseminating information that can significantly reduce search costs, improve information collected from customers, increase competition and thus lower prices. Xie and Shugan (2001) suggest that since as e-tickets, smart cards and other forms of online payment instruments (prepaid vouchers, discounted advance tickets) became common, transactions have become less complex and prepaid sales transaction costs have reduced. Zettelmeyer, Morton, and Silva-Risso (2006) confirm the finding of a reduction in transaction costs. Using on the one hand, a set of data on transaction prices, and on the other hand data from a survey of recent car buyers, Zettelmeyer et al. (2006) conclude that web access to data and references to prices led to a decline in transaction prices (by about 1.5%). The authors also suggest that internet benefits especially those who do not like to negotiate. Moreover, since the need to move in the stores was no longer necessary, it was conceived from the start that internet would be able to reduce search costs to lower levels, making market prices much more competitive (Ratchford, 2009). Hence, the ability to conduct online transactions can eliminate geographic barriers, and help create markets for the less traded products.

The second feature is the emergence of online auctions, which became possible through internet. Online auctions now account for about a third of internet transactions (Bajari & Hortacsu 2004). The popularity of sites such as eBay suggests that auctions are increasingly becoming a basis for pricing goods and services online (Prahalad & Ramaswamy, 2004). In a B to B context, for example, there has been an increase in the number of online auctions for manufactured products (Bolton & Iyer, 2009). The auction is indeed a form of interaction between buyer and seller and became popular for three main reasons: it provides immediate savings, it provides an effective sales process and finally it continuously offers new possibilities through emerging technologies (Jap, 2002).

On the other hand, a new trend offered by interactive virtual formats is to give customers the opportunity to choose between price fixing and price selection (Chernev, 2003). Research has shown that customers often tend to prefer to choose rather than to fix a price. Companies are likely to benefit mostly by offering a range of different prices to each customer segment (Bolton & Iyer, 2009). A predetermined selection of reference prices may simplify customer choices by imposing a structure that fits the nature of the decision-making task (Chernev, 2003). Comparing pricing segmentation tactics used by companies on the internet, Grewal, Hardesty and Iyer (2004) found that customers are likely to show more trust, perceive fairness of price and have more positive purchase intentions towards a company that uses "tactical purchase timing" rather than a "tactical buyer identification" strategy.

Finally, the nature of the online environment itself is changing. Increasing access to internet through wireless channels (phones and PDAs) would enable customers to gather information while they are doing online shopping. For example, they can check online prices of a particular computer model when they are at a retailer, or they can consult relevant information on prices when negotiating with a car salesman (Ratchford, 2009).

ROLE OF CUSTOMER IN PLACE POLICY

Varadarajan et al. (2010) tried to study how interactive technologies (such as social media) are likely to affect retailers' strategies. The authors conclude that because of their potential for gathering information that could be objectively evaluated by the customer, these interactive technologies have generated new business models that affected the selection process in the store. Zafu.com is an example of a very successful website that allows women to identify quickly the clothing brands that offer them their favorite models and therefore reduce the time they spend in the fitting cabins (Berry et al., 2010). "1-800 Flowers.com", was the first retailer to launch its first Facebook page, enabling visitors to purchase items directly from the fan page of the retailer without the need to visit its commercial website (SAS Study, 2011). Since social media is increasingly used by customers as a platform to review products and services, many companies grew aware that social media should be integrated into their marketing plans in general and their retailing policy in particular.

A study conducted by Capgemini (Bansal, 2013) shows that banks, as service providers, grew aware of the importance of social media in their interaction with customers. Furthermore, these social media platforms are becoming an important part of a multi-channel strategy for banks. Analysis of data from their social media platforms has transformed the banks' customer relationship management system into a customer social relationship management. Inputs to customer social relationship management allows banks to develop a deep knowledge of its customers' behavior, including their feelings, wants and needs.

Through social media, banks may benefit from a high level of personal interactions with customers at a relatively low cost compared to that of the branch. Capgemini study (Bansal, 2013) assumes that the potential of social media tools using customer data is "still to be explored," given the potential implications on decisions on credits, loans etc. The challenge for banks would be to integrate and transform social media from a simple social screening process aiming at establishing e-reputation to a "social to lead" vision aiming at business expansion and strengthening of the decision-making process.

However, several studies like that of Kacen, Hess, and Chiang (2013) put an emphasis on the negative effects of this customers' migration-to-internet process on retailers' strategies. These effects relate to reducing switching costs, the possibility to compare prices across retailers, and even reducing contact especially with service providers. However, a study by Lorenzo-Romero et al. (2013) revealed the main advantages received by retailers who integrate social media into their retailing policy. Most retailers agree that the most important advantage of social media consists in improving customer relationship (83.9%). Consistent with the work of Berry et al., (2010), who noted that retailers often give much more importance to their transactional role (the emphasis is on the quality and quantity of supply) than to their post-transactional role (i.e., the creation of strong relationships with customers). For the authors, the use of virtual environments is a powerful medium for managing customer relationships. Moreover, disposing of a direct communication channel with customers (one to one, many to many), improved after-sales and customer support services as well as the ability to obtain information from customers (current or potential) at lower costs are also among the key benefits of social media (Lorenzo-Romero, Constantinides & Alarcon-Del-Amo, 2013).

Otherwise, Brennan and Schafer (2010) identified four major trends in the use of social media by companies. The first trend is social monetization. Thanks to the availability of analysis tools of social media performance (Turner & Qualman, 2013), retailers are able to better assess the ROI (Return On Investment) of these media and then identify their directly related expenses. Social omnipresence is the second trend generated by social media. As mobile telephony has become ubiquitous, the same would be for social media. The line between social and mobile media is already blurred because for the customer one of the first major uses of mobile is the ability to access social media. Retail managers can effectively integrate mobile marketing efforts with social media to create offers customized to fit the preferences of each customer (Bansal, 2013). Another trend offered by social media is Location-Based Applications such as Foursquare, Gowalla, Shopkick or Loopt. To attract new customers, maintain a loyal customer base and establish a strong social network, retailers are increasingly confident that these goals can be achieved through the applications that are available on smartphones. LBAs allow for targeting and proposing specific solutions tailored to local customers. Several retailers, including Best Buy, American Eagle, Macy's, Sports Authority, Crate & Barrel and Simon Malls, use Shopkick to reward customers for a visit to their stores by making them earn points. Shopkick is based on gaming techniques that challenge users to take photos of store products in exchange of shopkick points. The points can be exchanged against gifts and participation in gift cards in the store. Finally, the fourth trend, according to Brennan and Schafer (2010), is "social gaming". "Social gaming" is a new technology that will allow bricks and mortars to reverse online the traditional shopping experience. The specialized clothing and accessories store Wet Seal has recently launched the "Shop with Me" application, a technology platform designed to enable customers to get easily and quickly the opinions of their friends and family on their potential purchases while they do their shopping online.

ROLE OF CUSTOMER IN PROMOTION POLICY

According to Mangold and Faulds (2009), social media is a "hybrid" component of the promotion mix. Not only does it allow companies to communicate with their customers (the traditional sense of communication), but it also provides an opportunity for customers to get directly in touch with other customers (not the traditional sense). The use of social media has allowed many companies to develop "viral" marketing" (Kaplan & Haenlein, 2011), which is to convey a message quickly from one person to a group, and each in turn informs another group of their circle (Ferguson, 2008). With the less and less effective influence of traditional media on customer behavior and the declining levels of audience of conventional media (Palmer & Lewis, 2009), viral marketing has become an indispensable tool for companies' promotion strategies thanks to the proliferation of social media. Several examples illustrate the success of social media in viral communication. In order to promote a new children's book, the publishing house "Newgate" distributed excerpts from the book to opinion leaders found on online forums. The company had in fact used more than 400,000 forums, targeting about 11 million "e-fluentials" (online opinion leader), which in their turn have reached 55 million customers (Cardwell, 2002). Opinion leaders of these forums read first these pre-published chapters to publish thereafter their positive opinions and recommendations. The book ended up being ranked in the New York Times' best-seller list. Another example is the "Ford Fiesta Movement", a campaign by Ford before the launch of its new Ford Fiesta, also using social media. The company engaged with an online community, inviting 100 young people to use the car for six months and then report on their experiences. The report is available on several social media including Twitter, Facebook, Myspace and YouTube. Each of these 100 "agents" conducted each month a mission based on a special theme designed to provide a rewarding experience. Over 4,000 applications were submitted and the videos posted on YouTube by the participants have been viewed over 640 000 times (Dilworth, 2009).

However, in contrast to the traditional paradigm of marketing communication in which contact between the customer and the company is strictly controlled, conversations between customers (content, time, frequency) on the various social media platforms are not at all under managers' direct control (Mangold & Faulds, 2009). Therefore, social networks can thus be both a threat and an opportunity for companies as they can quickly diffuse discontent of unsatisfied customers. For example, HSBC bank announced in 2007 that it intended to terminate interest-free overdrafts for students who graduated. It was forced to give up this decision after a wave of attacks on Facebook (Palmer & Lewis, 2009). Other cases illustrate the misuse of viral marketing, like an Exxon employee who was posting messages on Twitter (Havenstein, 2008) or the two employees of Domino Pizza in North Carolina who posted a video of a disgusting meal preparation on YouTube that harmed the company's reputation (Vogt, 2009). Thus, managers should be able to promote, but mainly to guide in a positive way and in the interests of the missions and goals of the company, posts and conversations between customers on social media. Some practices are already in place like exclusive online offers or the support shown by the company on social media to the most important causes for customers such as ecology, fight against serious diseases etc. (Mangold & Faulds, 2009).

SOCIAL MEDIA -CHANGING CONTOURS OF BUYER-SELLER RELATIONSHIP

Social networks have not only changed the lives of customers, but they have also revolutionized companies' marketing strategies. In the online marketing mix, social media seems to be increasingly taken into account, because it is the source of true interaction between customers themselves or between customers and the company (Prahalad & Ramaswamy, 2003). Indeed, throughout this chapter we tried to identify these interactions at the level of each component of the marketing mix. At the product level, social media is a powerful tool, on the one hand, in gathering communities around the one key element of product policy, that of the brand. On the other hand, regarding value co-creation, social media allows communities to generate ideas, modify an existing product or create a new product. As for price, proliferation of social media is found to influence pricing strategies by reducing search and transaction costs. Social media offers buyer-buyer or buyer -seller new interaction formats such as online auctions. As for retailing policy, being an essential component in a multi channel strategy, social media has contributed to a better management of customer relationship through a more direct and personal contact. Social monetization, social ubiquity, LBAs and social gaming are all tools offered by social media, which also facilitated customer-retailer interactions. As for the promotion mix and with the less and less effective influence of traditional media, social media is favourable to the development of corporate communication. Through interactions between customers themselves, social media has succeeded in developing a "viral" communication, which allowed companies to convey their messages to as many customers as possible in a short period of time. Moreover, with specific analysis tools of social media performance (e.g. 33Across, Brandwatch, Google Analytics etc.) (Turner & Qualman, 2013), companies would be able to collect, store and analyze important data obtained from customers. These data could be used later to quantify influence, to predict future volume of conversations on social media and even to anticipate and predict potential problems around the overall activity of the company. The company would be a proactive rather than a reactive organization.

FUTURE RESEARCH DIRECTIONS

This research therefore can be helpful for both researchers and marketing practitioners. For academics, a better understanding of the roles and uses of social media at the level of each component of the marketing mix could be useful to enrich the existing literature. As for practitioners, they could be inspired by the real examples the chapter proposed on very successful cases of the use of social media by several companies to propose initiatives related to their product, price, place and promotion. Therefore, SMEs and especially micro-enterprises can take advantage of the best uses of social media to develop their marketing strategies. We are aware that other uses of social media for each P were not dealt with due to the purely theoretical stance of our research. Indeed, in this chapter, we focused on examples, which are the most famous in the virtual environment. As technology is constantly evolving with the development of innovative online tools and new standards, including the Web 3.0, the forms and uses of social media can thus be influenced. This research can be extended on various fronts. For example, for the purposes of the company's internal marketing, a study of social media as a tool to increase employees' efficiency and collaboration would be an interesting line of future research.

REFERENCES

Bajari, P., & Hortacsu, A. (2004). Economic Insights from Internet Auctions. *Journal of Economic Literature*, *42*(2), 457–486. doi:10.1257/0022051041409075

Bakos, Y. (1997). Reducing Buyer Search Costs: Implications for Electronic Marketplaces. *Management Science*, *43*(12), 1676–1692. doi:10.1287/mnsc.43.12.1676

Bansal, A. (2013). Trends in Retail Banking Channels: Meeting Changing Client Preferences (Capgemini report). Retrieved from http://www.capgemini.com/resource-file-access/resource/pdf/trends_in_retail_banking_channels_meeting_changing_client_preferences.pdf

Berry, L. L., Bolton, R. N., Bridges, C. H., Meyer, J., Parasuraman, A., & Seiders, K. (2010). Opportunities for Innovation in the Delivery of Interactive Retail Services. *Journal of Interactive Marketing*, *24*(2), 155–167. doi:10.1016/j.intmar.2010.02.001

Birke, D. (2013). *Social Networks and their Economics: Influencing Consumer Choice*. Chichester: Wiley. doi:10.1002/9781118699638

Bolton, R., & Iyer, S.S. (2009). Interactive Services: A Framework, Synthesis and Research Directions. *Journal of Interactive Marketing*, *23*(1), 91–104. doi:10.1016/j.intmar.2008.11.002

Brennan, B., & Schafer, L. (2010). *Branded! How Retailers Engage Consumers with Social Media and Mobility*. New Jersey: Wiley.

Brodie, R. J., Ilic, A., Juric, B., & Hollebeek, L. (2013). Consumer engagement in a virtual brand community: An exploratory analysis. *Journal of Business Research*, *66*(1), 105–114. doi:10.1016/j.jbusres.2011.07.029

Brown, J. B., Broderick, A. J., & Lee, N. (2007). Word of mouth communication within online communities: Conceptualizing the online social network. *Journal of Interactive Marketing*, *21*(3), 2–20. doi:10.1002/dir.20082

Bugshan, H. (2014). Co-innovation: The role of online communities. *Journal of Strategic Marketing*, *23*(2), 175–186. doi:10.1080/0965254X.2014.920905

Cardwell, A. (2002, April 1). Viral marketing, subliminal advertising. *ZD Net Inter@ctive Week*. Retrieved from http://www.ennex.com/~Marshall/viral/ref/20020401-Cardwell.pdf

Cherney, A. (2003). Reverse Pricing and Online Pricing Elicitation Strategies in Consumer Choice. *Journal of Consumer Psychology*, *13*(1), 51–62. doi:10.1207/153276603768344780

De Valck, K., Van Bruggen, G., & Wierenga, B. (2009). Virtual communities: A marketing perspective. *Decision Support Systems*, *47*(3), 185–203. doi:10.1016/j.dss.2009.02.008

Di Gangi, P., & Wasko, M. (2009). Steal My Idea! User Innovation Community Influence on Organizational Adoption of User Innovations: A Case Study of Dell Ideastorm. *Decision Support Systems*, *48*(1), 303–312. doi:10.1016/j.dss.2009.04.004

Dilworth, D. (2009, April 9). Ford debuts social media campaign for new Fiesta. *DM News*. Retrieved from www.dmnews.com/Ford-debuts-social-media-campaign-for-new-Fiesta/article/130445/

Ferguson, R. (2008). Word of mouth and viral marketing: Taking the temperature of the hottest trends in marketing. *Journal of Consumer Marketing*, *25*(3), 179–182. doi:10.1108/07363760810870671

Goh, K. Y., Heng, C. S., & Lin, Z. (2013). Social Media Brand Community and Consumer Behavior: Quantifying the Relative Impact of User- and Marketer-Generated Content. *Information Systems Research*, *24*(1), 88–107. doi:10.1287/isre.1120.0469

Grewal, D., Hardesty, D. M., & Iyer, G. R. (2004). The Effects of Buyer Identification and Purchase Timing on Consumers' Perceptions of Trust, Price Fairness and Repurchase Intentions. *Journal of Interactive Marketing*, *18*(4), 87–100. doi:10.1002/dir.20024

Havenstein, H. (2008, August 4). Exxon Mobil's brand 'hijacked' by impersonator on twitter. *Computer World*. Retrieved from www.computerworld.com/action/article.do?command1/4viewArticle Basic&articleId1/49111524

Hoffman, D. L., & Novak, T. P. (1996). Marketing in hypermedia computer-mediated environments: Conceptual foundations. *Journal of Marketing*, *60*(3), 50–68. doi:10.2307/1251841

Hollebeek, L. (2013). The customer engagement/value interface: An exploratory investigation. *Australasian Marketing Journal*, *21*(1), 17–2. doi:10.1016/j.ausmj.2012.08.006

Jap, S. (2003). An Exploratory Study of the Introduction of Online Reverse Auctions. *Journal of Marketing*, *67*(3), 96–107. doi:10.1509/jmkg.67.3.96.18651

Kacen, J. J., Hess, J. D., & Chiang, W. K. (2013). Bricks or Clicks? Consumer Attitudes Toward Traditional Stores and Online Stores. *Global Economics and Management Review*, *18*(1), 12–21. doi:10.1016/S2340-1540(13)70003-3

Kaplan, A. M., & Haenlein, M. (2011). Two hearts in three-quarter time: How to waltz the social media/viral marketing dance. *Business Horizons*, *54*(3), 253–263. doi:10.1016/j.bushor.2011.01.006

Lorenzo-Romero, C., Constantinides, E., & Alarcon-Del-Amo, M. C. (2013). Social Media as Marketing Strategy: An Explorative Study on Adoption and Use by Retailers. In M.R. Olivas-Luјàn & Bondarouk (Eds.), Social Media in Strategic Management, (pp. 197–215). Bingley: Emerald Group Publishing Ltd.

Mangold, W. G., & Faulds, D. J. (2009). Social media: The new hybrid element of the promotion mix. *Business Horizons*, *52*(4), 357–365. doi:10.1016/j.bushor.2009.03.002

McCarthy, E. J. (1960). *Basic Marketing: A Managerial Approach*. Homewood, IL: Irwin.

Miller, K. D., Fabian, F., & Lin, S. J. (2009). Strategies for online communities. *Strategic Management Journal*, *30*(3), 305–322. doi:10.1002/smj.735

Muniz, A. Jr, & O'guinn, T. (2001). Brand community. *The Journal of Consumer Research*, *27*(4), 412–432. doi:10.1086/319618

Nambisan, S. (2002). Designing Virtual Customer Environments for New Product Development: Toward a Theory. *Academy of Management Review*, *27*(3), 392–413.

Nambisan, S., & Baron, R. A. (2007). Interactions in virtual customer environments: Implications for product support and customer relationship management. *Journal of Interactive Marketing*, *21*(2), 42–62. doi:10.1002/dir.20077

Palmer, A., & Koenig-Lewis, N. (2009). An experiential, social network-based approach to direct marketing. *Direct Marketing: An International Journal*, *3*(3), 162–176. doi:10.1108/17505930910985116

Prahalad, C. K., & Ramaswamy, V. (2003). The New Frontier of Experience Innovation. *Sloan Management Review*, *44*(4), 12–18. Retrieved from http://sloanreview.mit.edu/article/the-new-frontier-of-experience-innovation/

Prahalad, C. K., & Ramaswamy, V. (2004). Co-creation experiences: The next practice in value creation. *Journal of Interactive Marketing*, *18*(3), 5–14. doi:10.1002/dir.20015

Ratchford, B. T. (2009). Online Pricing: Review and Directions for Research. *Journal of Interactive Marketing*, *23*(1), 82–90. doi:10.1016/j.intmar.2008.11.001

SAS. (2011). Improving Revenue and Customer Engagement with Social Media Analytics, *Retail Touchpoints White Paper*. Retrieved from http://www.sas.com/resources/whitepaper/wp_30521.pdf

Sawhney, M., Verona, G., & Prandelli, E. (2005). Collaboration to Create: The Internet as a Platform for Customer Engagement in Product Innovation. *Journal of Interactive Marketing*, *19*(4), 4–17. doi:10.1002/dir.20046

Stephen, A. T., & Galak, J. (2009). The complementary roles of traditional and social media in driving marketing performance. Retrieved from http://www.insead.edu/facultyresearch/research/doc.cfm?did=46238

Thomke, S. (1998). Managing Experimentation in the Design of New Products. *Management Science*, *44*(6), 743–762. doi:10.1287/mnsc.44.6.743

Thomke, S., & Von Hippel, E. (2002). Customers as Innovators: A New Way to Create Value. *Harvard Business Review*, *80*(4), 74–81. PMID:12024760

Thompson, C. J., & Troester, M. (2002). Consumer Value Systems in the Age of Postmodern Fragmentation: The Case of the Natural Health Microculture. *The Journal of Consumer Research*, *28*(4), 550–571. doi:10.1086/338213

Turner, J., & Qualman, E. (2013). The 83 Best Social Media and Mobile Marketing Tools for Small- to Mid-Sized Businesses. Retrieved from http://www.oahefcu.coop/elements/uploadFiles/83%20Best%20Tools.pdf

Varadarajan, R., Srinivasan, R., Vadakkepatt, G.G., Yadav, M., Pavlou, P.A., Krishnamurthy, S., & Krause, T. (2010). Interactive Technologies and Retailing Strategy: A Review, Conceptual Framework and Future Research Directions. *Journal of Interactive Marketing*, *24*(2), 96–110. doi:10.1016/j.intmar.2010.02.004

Vargo, S., & Lusch, R. (2004). Evolving to a new dominant logic for marketing. *Journal of Marketing*, *68*(1), 1–17. doi:10.1509/jmkg.68.1.1.24036

Vogt, P. (2009, April 24). Brands under attack: marketers can learn from domino's video disaster, *Forbes*. Retrieved from www.forbes.com/2009/04/24/dominos-youtube-twitter-leadership-cmonetwork- marketing.html

Xie, J., & Shugan, S. M. (2001). Electronic Tickets, Smart Cards and Online Prepayments: When and How to Advance Sell. *Marketing Science*, *20*(3), 219–243. doi:10.1287/mksc.20.3.219.9765

Zettelmeyer, F., Morton, S., & Silva-Risso, J. (2006). How the Internet Lowers Prices: Evidence from Matched Survey and Automobile Transaction Data. *JMR, Journal of Marketing Research*, *43*(2), 168–181. doi:10.1509/jmkr.43.2.168

KEY TERMS AND DEFINITIONS

Co-Creation: Any act of collective creativity based on collaboration between two or more people. As a business strategy, co-creation allows and encourages a more active involvement from the customer in the design or development of future products, often with the help of tools that are provided by the firm.

Interaction: A process by which two or more people or things communicate with or react to each other.

Marketing-Mix: A set of actions, or tactics, that a company uses to promote its service or product in the market. The 4Ps make up a typical marketing mix: Price, Product, Promotion and Place.

Online Brand Community: A dedicated group of members embedded in online social networks where they communicate and exchange information on specific brand and/or product.

Social Media: A collection of tools and online means of communication that are used by individuals and businesses to share information and to develop social and professional contacts.

UGC: User-Generated Content refers to any digital content that is produced and shared by end users on social media platforms on the internet. Video, blogs, discussion forums, posts, digital images, audio files are some forms of UGC.

Web 2.0: Basically refers to the transition from static HTML Web pages to a more dynamic Web that is more organized and is based on serving Web applications to users. Web 2.0 is a second generation in the development of the World Wide Web that is focused on user collaboration, sharing of user generated content and social networking.

Section 4

Assortment of Impacts of Social Media Adoption

Chapter 10

Virtual Atmosphere, Emotions, Attitudes and Real Use:

When "Love is in the Air" in a Virtual Community

António C. Moreira
University of Aveiro, Portugal

Mariana Mira Ferreira
University of Aveiro, Portugal

Pedro Macedo
University of Aveiro, Portugal

ABSTRACT

This study involves several theories, namely: the theory of reasoned action, the technology acceptance model, the theory of planned behavior and the internet banking acceptance model. It aims to understand the relationships between the virtual atmosphere and emotional states, how the individual characteristics (social identity, altruism and telepresence) and emotional states influence attitudes, and how attitudes, past experience and trust influence actual use of a site. To this end, the authors developed three conceptual models explaining the relationships among the above-mentioned variables. Methodologically, descriptive statistics, exploratory factor analysis and the generalized maximum entropy estimator are used to test the three models in a wedding site. Of the eight hypotheses proposed, one can only partially validate hypotheses h1, h2, h3 and h6, while hypothesis h7 is accepted and the remaining are rejected.

INTRODUCTION

Consumer behavior is influenced by many factors. Individuals need to know in advance how their behavior influences and is influenced by others (Gefen & Straub, 2004; Gefen, 2000). However, as consumer behavior is difficult to control, the use of methods that could help understand consumer behavior has become essential to understand the individual's needs (Gefen, 2000).

DOI: 10.4018/978-1-5225-0332-3.ch010

The influence of the environment on consumer behavior has been studied by psychologists. Even before traders consider this important area of study, landscapers, architects and interior decorators had already recognized consumer behavior as relevant (Donovan & Rossiter, 1982).

The world is constantly and rapidly changing, technology being currently one of its main engines. Digital technologies have contributed to consumer behavior modification constantly presenting new forms of marketing of goods and services (Schiffman & Kanuk, 2006).

Since the mid-1980s, with strong growth in the 1990s, several studies have allowed the construction of models that attempt to predict what behaviors might be associated with the acceptance of the technology. The continuous increase of such studies is justified by the significant growth in the presence of technology in our daily lives. Currently, it is relatively easy for any of us to access a computer, tablet or smartphone with internet access, and is increasingly simple and familiar to use them to make online purchases. However, to know how and why individuals use certain sites, especially those linked with very high involvement as is the case of wedding-related sites, are understudied and there is a lack of general knowledge about how users behave.

This research aggregates concepts associated with consumer behavior and environment, consumer emotions, consumer attitudes and actual use of an online service related to weddings. Moreover, one of the main contributions of this chapter is related to the evaluation of these variables in a virtual community. Another contribution is that this is the first study of its kind analyzing a virtual community using the generalized maximum entropy (GME) estimator, which is robust when using small samples sizes (micronumerosity).

This study has important contributions for several areas, namely for public relations, brand image and social media: firstly, it uses unique characteristics as virtual atmosphere, emotions and attitudes in a high-involvement virtual community; and secondly, it uses a robust estimation method when small samples are at stake, the GME.

For a better understanding of the relationships between consumer behavior and environment, consumer emotions, consumer attitudes and actual use of an online service, this study has the following main objectives:

- To understand what components of the virtual atmosphere have more influence on pleasure/arousal, as emotional states;
- To realize if individual characteristics (social identity, altruism and telepresence) and emotional states influence attitudes;
- To understand whether attitudes, past experience and trust influence the wedding site actual use;

CONSUMER BEHAVIOR

Solomon (2002, p. 24) defines consumer behavior as the study of the processes involved when individuals or groups select, buy, use or have products, services, ideas or experiences to satisfy needs and wants. Consumer behavior is seen as a continuous process of exchange where there is a transaction between two or more people who give and receive something of value (Solomon, 2002). Although the moment of exchange is an important part of consumer behavior, there is an increasingly tendency to include in this process the issues that influence the consumer before, during and after his/her purchase.

Pinheiro et al. (2006) defends interdisciplinarity as essential to the study of consumer behavior. This includes and combines concepts and methodologies of a wide field of knowledge such as psychology, economics, sociology, cultural anthropology, semiotics, demography and history.

Over time and based on the principle of interdisciplinarity, several thinkers and scientists from various fields made their theories about human behavior. As such, this chapter presents a summary of what the different theories defend, with special focus on the consumption. Among the various theories, the following ones are highlighted: the theory of economic rationality, behavioral theory, psychoanalytic theory and cognitive learning theory.

The theory of economic rationality is a theoretical approach centered on psychological utilitarianism, where consumer behavior is based on maximizing the degree of psychological satisfaction and pleasure obtained from the use of purchased products and services. That is, the study focuses on maximizing the benefits (satisfaction and pleasure) at the lowest possible cost (discomfort or suffering).

This theory states that the frequent use of a good (product or service) causes a decrease in the utility perception by consumers, in other words, the more you use that product or service, the degree of satisfaction received from its usage will continuously decrease (Giglio, 2005).

According to Pinheiro, Castro, Silva, and Nunes (2006) and Giglio (2005), the theory of economic rationality has some limitations because it is too focused on the effects that the purchase/use causes the consumer, not studying the psychological processes that give rise to the same purchase and not taking into account individual, social and cultural differences that determine the intention of consumption.

The behavioral theory highlights the importance of systematic study of the stimuli present in the consumer environment, because they produce reactions, positive (approach) or negative (removal) on consumers, compared to products available, consumption being considered as the set of physiological reactions and observable behavioral stimuli generated by those found in the environment (Pinheiro et al., (2006).

Pinheiro et al. (2006) suggest that the behavioral theory should be used as an alternative to the theory of economic rationality when it comes to understanding the cognitive, motivational and emotional processes involved in choosing and buying decision. However, because it only gives importance to extrinsic environmental factors, the need to study the consumer's mind arises, mainly the gap that occurs between stimulus presentation and the implementation or not of the purchase behavior, to better understand the purchasing process.

According to Pinheiro et al. (2006), for psychoanalytic theory, the human mind is divided into two spheres, one conscious, the other unconscious, knowing that the second has a strong determination on the former. Thus, the behavior expressed in consciousness is a distorted expression of repressed desires that reside in the unconscious.

In this theory, the intention to purchase is defined by desires, expectations, anxieties and conflicts that are located in the unconscious plan of the man´s mind. Consumption is then an attempt to satisfy these desires, projecting them in the products available in the market. The choice of products takes place according to the capacity of satisfying, even partially and temporarily unconscious impulses.

Considering the psychoanalytic theory, organizations should seek to create strategies that highlight features that awaken the unconscious desire of consumers (Giglio, 2005).

Today, cognitive learning theory is the most used by behavioral researchers because it integrates the aspects of the product, the consumer and the environment. This theory shows consumer behavior as a decision-making process where the individual solves problems and uses actively the information that surrounds itself in order to master its environment. Learning is determined by the best process that each individual finds to retain new knowledge, new experiences, that is, learning consists of a change of the cognitive structure of the subject and is based on the way he perceives, selects, organizes and attributes meaning to objects and events (Solomon, 2002).

The cognitive theory of learning is emphasized by the importance of cognitive factors such as perception, motivation, learning, memory, attitudes, values and personality, socio-cultural factors such as group influence, family, culture and social class and even situational factors such as the localized influence of the environment at the time of purchase (Pinheiro et al., 2006). The individual learns by doing. The learning process is intentional. The individual seeks to learn due to its internal needs, its curiosity and its expectations (motivation).

According to this theory, the various purchasing decisions can be classified by the type of product, consumer motivation, frequency of purchase, search and information processing, according to the perception of the alternatives for the consumer and situational influences.

Beliefs, Attitudes and Behavior: Cognitivist Theory of Emotions

According to Kotler (1998), the consumer is the target of psychological, personal, social and cultural influences, as shown in Table 1.

Solomon (2002) based himself on these factors to develop its cognitivist theory of emotions, according to which the behavioral attitudes of individuals are sensitive to rational assessment and revision by them during the decision process before consumption.

Perceived attitudes of consumers are based on three components: affect, behavior and cognition, known as ABC. The feeling regards to how a consumer feels about an attitude object. The behavior includes the consumer's intention to do something about an object; however, not all intentions give rise to behaviors. Cognition refers to consumer beliefs about an attitude object.

All components (ABC) are important, but the relative importance varies according to the user's level of motivation in relation to the attitude object, depending on the level of involvement of consumers in the purchase decision.

The impact of these three components is explained by three effect hierarchies developed by researchers in the field: standard learning hierarchy, low engagement hierarchy and experiential hierarchy.

The standard learning hierarchy presupposes a high involvement in the purchase decision-making process. The consumer conducts a deep research about a particular product and develops a set of beliefs concerning the product. After evaluating these beliefs, a certain feeling about around the product is developed. This assessment leads to a certain behavior, or in other words, a positive or negative purchase decision. In this case, the user's action is the result of consumer's cognitive information positioning.

Table 1. Factors that influence the purchase decision process

Buyer			
Cultural Factors	**Social Factors**	**Personal Factors**	**Psychological Factors**
• Culture • Subculture • Social Classes	• Reference Groups • Family • Roles and social positions	• Age and stage of life cycle • Occupation • Economic conditions • Lifestyle • Personality	• Motivation • Perception • Learning • Beliefs and Attitudes

Source: Kotler (1998)

In low-involvement hierarchy the consumer does not have a strong preference for a brand, it acts based on the knowledge it already has about the product and limits itself to evaluating it, after purchasing it. The choice made by the consumer is enhanced by good or bad experiences with the product after purchase. Clearly, the consumer attitude is based on the learning processes that result from consumer behavior.

Experiential hierarchy emphasizes the importance of emotional response as a central-spectrum attitude. Thus, the consumer acts upon the emotional responses and their attitudes can be influenced by intangible product attributes, such as the package design, where the consumer attitude is based on the hedonic consumption.

STORE ATMOSPHERE

For most consumers, a particular store, regardless of the product offering, may be more or less attractive than another if it is able to induce in them welfare sensations rather than convey feelings of irritation or annoyance. Spies, Hesse and Loesch (1997) state that consumers tend to spend more money when they are in a positive frame of mind than when they are more negative. Thus, there is a direct relationship between the store features (atmosphere) and buying behavior of consumers, which should be explored in order to maximize consumption.

Baker (1986) presented a typology of three categories to characterize the elements of the store environment: the social, environmental and design factors. Social factors relate to people that are in the store, whether customers or employees. The design factors relate to visual elements that make up the store environment, such as color, layout, cleanliness and signs. Environmental factors are not visual elements of the environment, such as temperature, light, music and the smell (Baker, Grewal, & Parasuraman, 1994).

Bitner (1992) divided the components of the atmosphere into three groups: environmental conditions, space and functionality, and symbols, signs and artifacts. Environmental conditions include temperature, lighting, noise, music and the smell. The spatial arrangement is related to how the machinery, equipment and furniture are arranged in space, as well as the shape and size of these. Functionality refers to the ability of these elements to facilitate the performance and the achievement of the objectives of consumers. The symbols, signs and artifacts are used to identify a location, indicate a direction or communicate the behavior rules of the place and may be indications of the company name, location of entrances and exits or indication of local permissions and prohibitions (Bitner, 1992).

The physical store has the ability to appeal to all senses of the individual through endless combination of environmental elements, structural, social and aesthetic; however, in the online store, the store environment is limited to a screen, making it impossible to use the same taxonomy of the atmosphere elements (Eroglu, Machleit, & Davis, 2001).

In the virtual environment, Eroglu et al. (2001) consider that the store's atmosphere has two categories of elements: high relevance tasks and low relevance tasks. The highly relevant tasks refer to descriptive of the site, verbal or images that appear on the screen and that facilitate and enable the goal of buying by the consumer. Examples of such stimuli are the description of the goods, the price, terms of sale, delivery and return policies, availability of samples and site maps or search functions. The low relevance tasks refer to the information of the site that is not important for the purchase itself, although they may make the purchase experience more enjoyable, such as colors, background patterns, fonts, animations, music, the blanks, among others (Eroglu et al., 2001).

Hausman and Siekpe (2009) divided the elements of the atmosphere as computational factors and human factors. The computational factors are those whose presence provides functionality, being characterized as highly relevant tasks. These include the technical aspects, the navigation aspects, impartiality and information content. Human factors are elements that contribute to user satisfaction when using the site, being low relevance tasks. These elements can be the specific pleasure, cognitive result, reliability, user training, the visual appearance and organization of the information content.

By studying the effects of the store's atmosphere in consumer purchasing behavior, the SOR (stimuli, organism, and response) model was derived from environmental psychology (Donovan & Rossiter, 1982; Eroglu et al., 2001; Koo & Ju, 2010; Mehrabian & Russell, 1974). Mehrabian and Russell (1974) suggest that the model should have the following components: a taxonomy of stimuli, a set of intermediate variables and a response taxonomy. The stimuli function as a history of emotional states of the consumer (organism), whose response can result in purchasing behavior (response) (Donovan & Rossiter, 1982; Koo & Ju, 2010; Mehrabian & Russell, 1974).

Donovan and Rossiter (1982) applied the model for the first time to the retail context. The components of the shop's atmosphere were considered the stimulus, the emotional states (pleasure, arousal and dominance) the organism and the attitudes and intent of behavior (approach and retraction) the answer.

The stimuli (S) are the physical characteristics used during the creation of the environment, being represented by a set of attributes that affect consumer perceptions (Eroglu et al., 2001; Sherman, Mathur, & Smith, 1997). These attributes enter the consumer's mind consciously or unconsciously waking him or urging him to action (Koo & Ju, 2010). An appropriate taxonomy of stimuli is difficult to achieve because any environmental setting has a large number of stimuli involved. It takes a lot of experience in the store to determine what kind of stimulus evokes that kind of emotional response in order to result in an approach/ retraction behavior (Donovan & Rossiter, 1982).

The organism (O) refers to the internal processes and structures involved between external stimuli to the individual and his reactions, final actions or responses emitted by the consumer (Sherman et al., 1997), which cause changes in the emotional and cognitive state of the consumer (Koo & Ju, 2010). The consumer converts the stimuli into meaningful information and uses it to understand the environment before making any judgment or draw any conclusions. These processes are based on perception, physiological, feeling and thought activities. Perception can be characterized by the judgments that a consumer has when he/she comes into contact with the price of a product. Physiological activities can be produced by agglomeration in the shop, resulting in the consumer's perspiration. Feeling is expressed in terms of agitation, enjoyment and arousal and is derived from the feeling achieved during shopping trip (Koo & Ju, 2010).

Mehrabian and Russell (1974) defend that there are three emotional states that moderate the approach and retraction behavior: pleasure, arousal and dominance, known as PAD. Donovan and Rossiter (1982) and Sherman et al. (1997) stated that any environment can produce an emotional state that can be characterized in any of the PAD dimensions.

Pleasure refers to the degree to which an individual feels good, cheerful, happy or satisfied in a given situation. Pleasure is related to how an individual feels encouraged by the atmosphere, or excited, active or alert in a certain situation. Dominance refers to the control an individual feels over the situation (Donovan & Rossiter, 1982; Koo & Ju, 2010; Wu, Cheng, & Yen, 2008). However, Donovan and Rossiter (1982) decided to exclude dominance of the model, because they consider that this dimension requires a cognitive interpretation by the individual, making it not purely applicable in situations that require emotional responses (Donovan & Rossiter, 1982; Eroglu et al., 2001; Koo & Ju, 2010; Sherman et al, 1997).

The response (R) is the final result, or the final action, of consumers, that include psychological reactions that express their satisfaction or dissatisfaction with the consumption experience (Koo & Ju, 2010; Sherman et al., 1997). Mehrabian and Russell (1974) state that all responses to an environment should be considered as approximation or withdrawal behaviors, considering four antagonistic aspects: approximation behaviors are reflected as positive responses like a "physical" desire to stay in a particular environment; the desire to explore the environment; the desire to communicate with other individuals in the environment; the degree of improvement of "performance and satisfaction" of tasks. Retraction behaviors are negative responses like "physical" desires of leaving a given environment; a tendency to remain inanimate in the environment; avoid interaction with other individuals in the environment; the degree of retreat of the "performance and satisfaction" with tasks (Donovan & Rossiter, 1982).

Eroglu et al. (2001) applied the model to the online retail context. They propose that some of the atmospheres of the virtual store, mediated by the involvement and the atmospheric response, influence the internal affective and cognitive states of consumers that involve themselves in the type of response (clearance or approach) that consumers have given the online shopping experience.

Eroglu, Machleit, and Davis (2003) empirically tested the model presented showing the significant effect of the atmosphere of the site on consumer attitudes, satisfaction and in approach behaviors.

Following the study of Eroglu et al. (2001), Koo and Ju (2010) they developed a research model in order to test the effect of the atmospheric stimuli of online stores in the emotional states of consumers, which, in turn, influence their buying intentions. They state that the stimuli are the atmospheric elements of virtual stores (graphics, colors, links and menus), the organism is the set of emotions (pleasure and arousal) that translate the feeling of users when they search and buy products online. The answer is the set of intentions that the consumer presents (continue or not to use the online store). Here, perceptual curiosity is introduced as a moderating variable between stimuli and the emotions of consumers (Koo & Ju, 2010).

The results are not uniform. While Eroglu at al. (2003) confirm that most of the atmospheric stimuli (graphics, colors, links and menus) have a positive impact on pleasure and arousal, which in turn affect the costumers' intention, Koo and Ju (2010) and Mummalaneni (2005) contend, on the other hand, that menus have a negative impact on the consumer's emotions.

TECHNOLOGY ACCEPTANCE MODEL

Since the early 1980s (Yuanquan, Jiayin, & Huaying, 2008) the need to understand the relationship between technology and the consumer began to emerge, but it was during the 1990s, especially in the second half of the decade, that the research in this area took considerable proportions (Silva & Dias, 2007). Given the principles of consumer behavior and the need to adapt that understanding to the constant technological changes, the researchers sought to build models to better understand the impact of technology on human behavior. Consumers who use the technologies are called users.

Nowadays, it is easy to understand the reason of this sudden need. The truth is that, as Silva and Dias (2007) report, the amount of information flowing through the information systems is so vast that it is impossible to manipulate it without the help of technology. However, according to Davis (1989), the important thing is not the capacity of the technological system, but rather the acceptance of the technology by the user. Davis (1989) considers that the reason why a certain technology is or is not used is of great importance. The truth is that possible failures of technology are directly connected with the non-acceptance by the target audience, as well as the inappropriate use of it. Individuals are no longer the targets of technology, starting to become the responsible ones for it, as active elements.

The theory of reasoned action (TRA) is considered by many researchers as the first concrete model with applicability in measuring the acceptance of technologies by users (Moutinho & Roazzi, 2010).

This theory accepts the principle of man's rationality and defends their ability to assimilate and transform information into effective decisions that directly influence their behavior (Moutinho & Roazzi, 2010). The success of this model is due to its applicability in the analysis of dependent behavior of a direct intention of the individual, that is, the TRA believes that people behave rationally, evaluating the environmental conditions to decide whether to perform or not a particular behavioral intention.

For Fishbein and Ajzen (1975), the main objectives of the TRA model are: (1) understand and predict the behavior of individuals and (2) identify accurately the degree of intent with which the individual has those behaviors. In turn, this behavior intention has two basic determinants (Moutinho & Roazzi, 2010): (1) the behavioral attitude, referring to the personal aspects, and (2) the subjective standard, with reference to social influence.

In the mid-1980s, Fred Davis was invited by the Massachusetts Institute of Technology (MIT) to build a research whose assumption was the assessment of the market potential for new products of the brand IBM Canada and to obtain an explanation of the determining factors in the use of computers (Silva & Dias, 2007). In 1986, Davis, considered by many the "father" of TAM, proposed in his doctoral thesis (Dias, Zwicker, & Vicentin, 2003) a TAM model that was intended to focus on the reasons why users accept or reject the new technology and to provide proposals regarding how to improve the acceptance process, providing a support for prediction and explanation of acceptance levels of a certain technology. Since its introduction, this model has been tested extensively by many researchers and it is assumed that it correctly forecast the use of technology in more than 40% of the situations (Dias et al., 2003).

Davis' model is an adaptation of the TRA, proposed by Fishbein and Ajzen (1975), where it is assumed, as already mentioned, that the beliefs, attitudes and intentions are basic assumptions for the understanding of a particular behavior.

Davis added to this specific model for information technology (Silva & Dias, 2007) two basic constructs to predict behavioral intention of an individual in respect of information systems and technologies: perceived ease of use and perceived usefulness (Dias et al ., 2003).

Perceived ease of use refers to the degree to which a user believes that by using a system he/she will be free for effort, so this system does not raise difficulties or obstacles in its use. While the perceived usefulness refers to the degree that a user associates to the belief that using this system will be able to improve their performance, that is, by streamlining their tasks, they increase their performance level (Dias et al. 2003; Silva & Dias, 2007).

These beliefs are interconnected since both assume that the individual will have a sense of satisfaction with the use of technology, resulting therefore in positive results. Both these constructs are conditioned by external variables (e.g. situational and socio-cultural factors).

Consequently, the perception obtained on the perceived ease of use and perceived usefulness, allow the individual to generate a set of attitudes that may or may not influence the intention of a certain behavior to use the technology in question. The correlation between all these elements is essential for understanding of the results obtained from the analysis of acceptable levels of an information technology system.

According to Silva and Dias (2007, p. 83), "the use of information systems would be mainly determined by the intention of use that the individual shows."

In turn, this behavioral intention to use will be substantiated by the real use of technology and the perceived utility before it. The idea that is obtained is that the more the feelings toward technology are positive, the greater the intended use and there will be a greater propensity to actual use, therefore, higher the acceptance.

TAM, as a behavioral model, can only be considered taking into principal the issues related to the user, their perceptions and motivations related to the use of the system.

The usefulness of this model transcends the ability to forecast the degree of acceptance of the technology by identifying the reason for non-acceptance, if any, allowing for corrections and improvements.

The Theory of Planned Behavior (TPB) appears as an extension of the TRA, about a decade later, being proposed by Icek Ajzen (Silva & Dias, 2007).

Ajzen complements the TRA adding the construct of perceived behavioral control, noting that the intentions and behaviors may also be influenced by other factors, such as the individual´s current habits or past behaviors and their results. Some behaviors are so habitual and routine that individuals are not fully aware of what led them to act, as if they had no voluntary power over this action (Moutinho & Roazzi, 2010). TPB adds to the TRA the existence of beliefs about control that are referred as the perceived behavioral control. These are related to the perception of control that the individual has, or not, on their behavior and the degree of ease and / or difficulty encountered while implementing it (Moutinho & Roazzi, 2010).

TPB seeks to predict and explain human behavior in specific environments and conditions (Silva & Dias, 2007). It is assumed that an individual in full control of a situation may act in accordance with the intention of previous behavior or not: in fact behavioral intentions reflect only the motivation to act, while the execution of an action does not only depend on this, but also on the greater or lesser control over the behavior (Moutinho & Roazzi, 2010).

The internet banking acceptance model (IBAM) derives from the need that Alsajjan and Dennis (2009) found to measure the degree in which online banks were accepted by consumers. The authors observed that the most used models to measure the adoption of e-commerce were the behavioral models such as the TAM and TPB and decided to adopt them to the online banking context. Later, Dennis, Jayawardhena, and Papamatthaiou (2010) considered the model was extendable to online businesses in general.

By investigating about TAM, Alsajjan and Dennis (2009) found that some previous studies on TAM suggested that the perceived usefulness and perceived ease of use were not the only constructs that mediated the impact of external variables on attitudes and intentions and they also added that the perceived ease of use has no direct impact on attitudes.

Alsajjan and Dennis (2009) also analyzed the perceived behavior control of TPB, which they considered is a close measure of the perceived use of the TAM. This behavioral control tries to assess difficult behaviors in the adoption of technology while perceived ease of use relates to the individual's self-efficacy. Thus, they interpreted the perceived ease of use and the perceived behavioral control as a single construct, the perceived viability. They also added the variable trust as they consider it as "the heart of all kinds of relationships" (Alsajjan & Dennis, 2009, p. 958).

Gefen, Karahanna, and Straub (2003) add that any technology acceptance model which presents more social dimensions should include trust, especially when it involves uncertainty and risk, as in the case of online banking or e-commerce itself.

VIRTUAL COMMUNITIES

Humans are social animals; they are all part of groups, where each individual tries to please others, following clues of how to behave by watching others around him/her (Solomon, 2002). The term reference group is defined as an individual or group capable of having significant relevance in the ratings, aspirations and behaviors of an individual (Solomon, 2002), and has been subject to new perspectives as such groups are identified as being loyal to a product or an activity (Solomon, 2002).

Reference group is considered to be any person or group of persons exercising influence, consciously or unconsciously, on the behavior of an individual (Bearden & Etzel, 1982) and may be composed of family, friends or colleagues, whose opinion is considered important / relevant (Valck, Bruggen, & Wierenga, 2009).

A reference group can exert influence on consumer decisions, since the attitude, values and behavior of its members represent standards that the individual uses to make his/her own assessments. However, the degree of this influence depends on the personality of the individual, the nature of the product and social factors (Leal, Hor-Meyll, & Pessôa, 2013). An individual with no experience or information about a product is more easily influenced by the advice or examples of others who he/she considers reliable, as they have similar values to theirs, thus influencing their purchase decision (Shen, Huang, Chu, & Liao, 2010).

In today's world, internet is increasingly used by consumers to communicate, both with companies, in exchange for information or transaction of goods and services, and among each other, sharing views and experiences about a good or service (Thomsen, Straubhaar, & Bolyard, 1998). The communication over internet allows consumers to overcome geographical and temporal barriers that previously existed facilitating the creation of reference groups based on common interests, many of them related to consumption (Leal et al., 2013), called virtual communities.

Virtual communities are social aggregations as chats, fora and social networks through which people with the same interests, experiences, tasks and concerns can interact with each other (McKnight, Choudhury, & Kacmar, 2002) for a period of time and a certain degree of engagement, to create personal relationships (Hagel & Armstrong, 1997; Leal et al, 2013; Valck et al., 2009; Wu, Chen, & Chung, 2010), where members tend to act as if these societies exist physically, governed by common rules, values and codes of conduct (Hagel & Armstrong, 1997; Leal et al., 2013)

An individual, at the time of joining a virtual community, usually is not familiar with the environment, with the community members, or with the codes of conduct as he/she does not have many social ties or commitments to the community; their visits are used to acquire information and gain knowledge (Leal et al., 2013). However, over time, the lack of initial knowledge is overcome and the individual becomes more confident in the exchange of information and increases the regularity of participations (Langerak, Verhorf, Verlegh, &Valck, 2004).

The access to information, the desire to interact socially and the interest in finding specific information related to a purchase decision are amongst the most common reasons to generate a virtual community (Ridings, Gefen, & Arinze, 2006): Social interaction is very strong involving time, effort and empathy in helping each other. This investment is made without interest in retribution; however, the individual expects to be compensated in the form of gratitude or mutual aid (Chan & Li, 2010).

The information exchanged in virtual communities' influences purchasing decisions as they are understood by consumers as coming from consumption partners and, as such, without commercial interest or manipulation intent (Shen et al., 2010).

A virtual community has both social and business functions. From a social perspective, the virtual community promotes interaction between individuals through a communication platform and social network. The objective of its members is to develop friendships, share interests and exchange information (Hagel & Armstrong, 1997; Wu et al., 2010). From a business point of view, the virtual community works as a commerce and marketing platform that allows interaction between vendors, intermediaries and buyers (Schubert & Ginsburg, 2000; Wu et al., 2010) with three main functions (Hagel & Armstrong, 1997; Wu et al., 2010): to allow suppliers to leverage the ideas of consumers in terms of design and customization of new products; to serve as an incentive mechanism to transaction trends and; to reach a large mass of individuals at reduced costs. Virtual communities are still relatively informal and their business value depends on the willingness of consumers to exchange information. For a community to be profitable traffic flow must be constant and loyalty to the site is mandatory (Wu et al., 2010).

The biggest difference between these groups on the Internet groups is that their participation is voluntary, conscious and written, so it is possible to consider carefully about what one would write (Bagozzi & Dholakia, 2002; Leal et al., 2013), while in the traditional reference group participation can be imposed by factors such as the proximity of residence. In virtual communities people are free to participate or not and can always decide on not being a part of the group when it ceases to be of interest to them. This can make the virtual communities most influential than traditional communities where the individual does not always feel deeply connected with it (Valck et al., 2009).

INDIVIDUAL CHARACTERISTICS

Most information systems are task-oriented, i.e., they aim to provide useful information for users to improve their decision making. Thus, many studies have attempted to examine the cause-effect relationships between environmental and human characteristics and the intention to use a system (Kwon & Wen, 2010).

Technology acceptance models set out in this chapter provide some variables to connect the individual characteristics and intention to use. However, when it comes to online communities, where there is a human relationship involved, these variables seem not to be enough. Thus, the social identity, altruism and telepresence dimensions are considered relevant for this study.

Social identity derives from social psychology, but has recently been expanded to the area of organizational research (Ashforth & Mael, 1989), being characterized by the solidarity that an individual has to the social group to which it belongs to according to his/her social norms, which discriminates him/her from other groups (Riedlinger, Gallois, McKay, & Pittam, 2004).

In online communities, social identity is the perception of belonging to a community where individuals are motivated to interact with each other, being able to influence their attitudes (Kwon & Wen, 2010).

Kwon and Wen (2010) classify altruism in two types: genetic altruism and reciprocal altruism. Genetic altruism is when an individual sacrifices him/herself in favor of another, i.e., to help others knowing that this might bring him/her negative consequences, while reciprocal altruism happens when an individual helps another based on the belief that he/she will also be helped by the other in the future (Ashtona, Paunonen, Helmes, & Jackson, 1998), without the intention of having any reward, but a reciprocal help.

Altruism is considered a strong candidate to explain human behavior although it is still difficult to understand due to the economic vision of society that is oriented to the maximization of personal profits (Kwon & Wen, 2010).

Telepresence exists to describe a type of feeling that the user is exposed to when in a virtual environment. The user feels like he is in the environment, as if physically there, although he is only connected virtually (Kwon & Wen, 2010). That is, in the case of virtual communities the user feels like he/she is really directly contacting with other users, even though the contact is only virtual and not physical.

This sense of telepresence allows the user to create human relationships with other users who are remotely located and if the experience is considered as positive, it is expected to develop positive attitudes (Kwon & Wen, 2010; Li et al., 2002). Telepresence also seems to influence the person interactivity and subjective norms (Walther 1996) by converting the cognitively generated experiences produced by machine and person interactivity into the simulated perception of direct experience of a real shopping environment (Suntornpithug & Khamalah, 2010).

TRUST AND PAST EXPERIENCE

Moorman, Deshpande, and Zaltman (1993) defined trust as the willingness to rely on somebody that you believe in. For Morgan and Hunt (1994) trust is the perception to believe in the partner's reliability and integrity. In a more commercial context, Corbitt, Thanasankit, and Yi (2003, 204) consider that trust is "the expectation that the other party will behave in accordance with their commitments, negotiate honestly and not take advantage, even if the opportunity arises."

In the literature, many authors consider that trust is crucial in the relationship between businesses and consumers (Brei, 2001; Corbitt et al. 2003; Moorman et al., 1993; Morgan & Hunt, 1994). More specifically, they consider it a central aspect in the online purchase intentions (Corbitt et al. 2003; Fortin, Dholakia, & Dholakia, 2002; Goode & Harris, 2007; Lee & Turban, 2001).

The lack of trust is considered the most serious problems in online activities knowing that it is not easy to maintain loyalty in the environment. The community needs to develop ways to encourage members to believe in each other and to be loyal. Trust is the way to attract an individual to participate in a virtual community and to remain faithful to it (Wu & Tsang, 2008).

Dennis, Merrilees, Jayawardhena, and Wright (2009) suggested that online consumer trust would have a positive effect on the intentions of that consumer. In the same year, Alsajjan and Dennis (2009), with its IBAM model proved that purpose on the online bank. Subsequently, Dennis et al. (2010) considered that this model could be extended to online businesses in general, and therefore that online consumer trust influences their intentions.

The study by Kim, Ferrin, and Rao (2008) confirms that consumer trust influences directly and indirectly its intention to purchase, having a positive effect on it, especially in electronic context. The authors also state that trust is the strongest predictors of purchase intentions.

With regard to virtual communities, trust is an important catalyst to facilitate social interaction and relationships in the long term (Wu et al., 2010).

Gefen (2000) argues that familiarity is another way for individuals to reduce uncertainty and simplify their relationships with others. This is an understanding of what, why, where and when others do what they do, often based on previous interactions, experiences and learnings.

The model of Klein (1998) suggests that online shopping past experience is a significant antecedent of internet research behavior. Shim, Eastlick, Lotz, and Warrington (2001) stated that previous shopping experiences are positively related to online purchase intentions. Familiarity allows consumers to determine future expectations and create ideas about these future expectations based on previous interactions (Chen & Barnes, 2007).

Shim and Drake (1990) stated that as online consumers become more experienced, their trust increases and tend to buy more and to become less concerned with uncertainty.

That said, trust and familiarity are truly different: familiarity refers to the understanding of current attitudes of others, trust is related to beliefs about future actions that are more dynamic, complex and risky (Gefen, 2000). Familiarity reduces uncertainty by establishing a structure; trust reduces uncertainty letting people hold relatively reliable expectations on favorable actions of others (Gefen, 2000).

In line with Hoffman et al. (1999) and Suntornpithug & Khamalah (2010) study, customer's lack of perceived behavioral control is assumed to reflect past experience as well as anticipated obstacles. As such, past experience and trust are expected to positively influence real use.

WEDDING AND EMOTIONS

Marriage is an ancient institution that is based on two traditional pillars: a psychological (emotional) contract largely unconscious and a transition to a cohabitation that leads to a more intrinsic relationship between both partner's elements (Fonseca & Duarte, 2014).

The prenuptial period is important as it antecedes the constitution of the couple and consists of a period of time where emotions and the excitement of creating a new identity sense are important. It is a period where there is a strong individualization process that allows both spouses analyze their differences and shape to each other, ensuring their individualities.

Love and intimate relationships are part of individuals every day's life (Wright, Simmons, & Campbell, 2007). They are also a basic need to love and be loved (Fletcher, 2002). Although marriage is the most common form of the official intimate relationships, in Portugal there has been a progressive growing of other forms of cohabitation as previous experience to marriage (Leite, 2003).

Although the formal role of marriage as essential unit of economic survival gave way to a symbol of individual freedom enjoyed in Western societies (Leite, 2003), it has always associated a romantic ideal of love (Acevedo & Aron, 2009; Duarte, 2011; Ribeiro, 2002).

Nowadays we are witnessing a change of values and representations about marriage and its purposes, denoting a more secular and devaluating the sacramental and institutional vision aspect (Leite, 2003). To Aboim (2005), Portugal and the western world is witnessing a plural form and definition of marriage involving dating, living together, cohabitation as a variable set of transitory informal marital experiences. In general, the research reflects the continuing desire to celebrate the marriage, regardless of their informal marital experience, being positively perceived by young people, particularly as a commitment (Martin, Specter, Martin, & Martin, 2003).

The expectations from each partner, the expectations for marriage, the expectations of and for both families of origin, the expectations for marriage as an institution and the ideal partner image or concept are well expressed in the epigenetic model of marital expectations proposed by Bhatti (1993).

There are several factors that influence expectations about marriage: social norms and the socio-cultural context (Juvva & Bhatti, 2006), the structure and family experiences since childhood (Flouri & Buchanan, 2001), and the experience gained with the partners and romantic relationships they have established (Hall, 2006).

It is worth mentioning that most studies that analyze online services are based on the transaction of products. This study aims to analyze consumer behavior based on an online community related to marriage, which is an intangible concept.

METHODOLOGY AND DATA

In the former sections a review of the literature covered the main topics of this chapter: consumer behavior and environment, consumer emotions, consumer attitudes and actual use of an online service. As referred above this study has the following main objectives:

- To understand what components of the virtual atmosphere have more influence on pleasure/arousal, as emotional states;
- To realize if individual characteristics (social identity, altruism and telepresence) and emotional states influence attitudes;
- To understand whether attitudes, past experience and trust influence online site actual use;

This research focuses on the study of the behavior of individuals participating in an online community related with wedding: the site www.onossocasamento.pt. As such, from the review of previous literature, the problem was delimited, and we proceeded with the formulation of hypotheses and subsequent data collection.

Models and Hypotheses

In this study the influence of the virtual atmosphere in the real use of a system is going to be analyzed.

To develop this model, we started with the Mehrabian and Russell's (1974) SOR model. The virtual atmosphere constructs, conceptualized by graphical components, colors, links and menus and emotions, conceptualized by pleasure and arousal, were withdrew from Koo and Ju (2010). Situational attitudes, perceived ease of use, perceived usefulness and subjective norm were considered as components of attitude.

Although the connection between emotions and attitudes has not been addressed before, they are often referred to as antecedents of intention to use, particularly in the theory of reasoned action, technology acceptance model and theory of planned behavior. As such, it was decided to test the relationship of emotions as antecedents of attitudes.

Individual characteristics, more specifically the social identity, altruism and telepresence, were proposed by Kwon and Wen (2010) as antecedents of perceived ease of use, perceived usefulness and perceived encouragement.

Trust comes from the online bank acceptance model suggested by Alsajjan and Dennis (2009), which can be extended to online commerce in general. Past experiences have been proposed by Dennis et al. (2009) for a review of the site real use. The evaluation of real use is supported by the theory of rational action, the technology acceptance model and the theory of planned behavior.

In accordance with the research objectives, a questionnaire-based quantitative approach was adopted, which was developed by extensively reviewing the literature on virtual atmosphere, emotions, social identify, altruism, telepresence, attitude, trust, past and real use, to identify reliable measures used in previous studies. Based on the theoretical background, we established and tested three research models, as shown in Figure 1, and the detailed hypotheses were defined.

Based on the literature review performed previously, and based on the presented models, following research hypotheses are put forward:

H1: The virtual atmosphere has a positive effect on emotions;
H2: Emotions have a positive effect on attitudes;
H3: Social identity has a positive effect on attitudes;
H4: Altruism has a positive effect on attitudes;
H5: Telepresence has a positive effect on attitudes;
H6: Attitudes have a positive effect in real use;
H7: Past experiences have a positive effect in real use;
H8: Trust has a positive effect on real use.

In order to assess the validity of the hypotheses, we built a questionnaire for members of online communities related to the event "Marriage". The questionnaire consists of ten sets of questions, one for each main construct being assessed: virtual atmosphere, emotions, attitudes, social identity, altruism, telepresence, trust, past experiences and real use.

Figure 1. Models Proposed

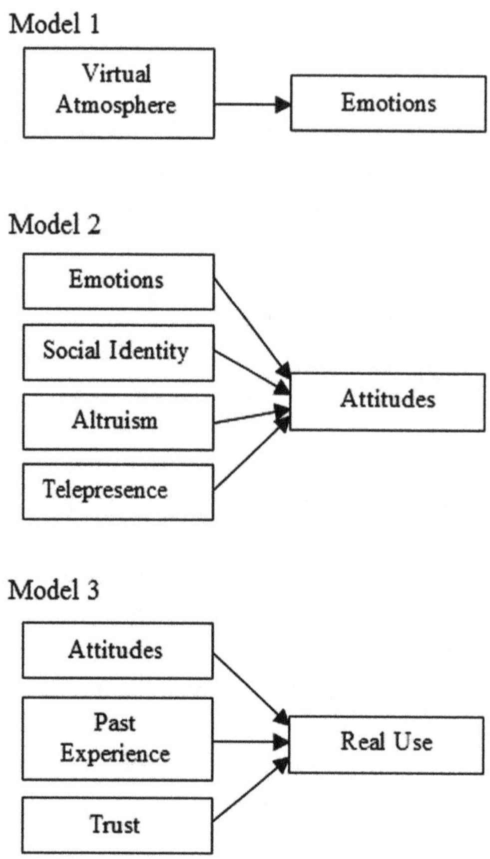

The Virtual atmosphere is composed of four different constructs, as shown in Table 2: Graphics (four items); Colors (three items); Links (four items); and Menus (four items). Social identity and altruism and telepresence were adapted from Kwon and Wen (2010). These are shown in Tables 3, 4, and 5. Emotions are subdivided in two constructs: Pleasure (five items) and arousal (four items). These two scales were adapted from Koo and Ju (2010), as shown in Table 6.

Attitude is a variable composed of four different constructs: Situational attitude, Perceived utility, Perceived ease of use, and Subjective norm. Situational attitude uses five items adapted from Suntornpithug and Khamalah (2010). The four items of perceived utility are adapted from Lee (2008). Perceived ease of use uses four items adapted from Venkatesh and Davis (2000) and Venkatesh and Morris (2000). Finally, Subjective norm uses three items adapted from Suntornpithug and Khamalah (2010). The items and constructs that compose attitude are shown in Table 7. Trust, which is shown in Table 8, was adapted from Suntornpithug and Khamalah (2010). Finally, Actual use, as shown in Table 9, was adapted from Kwon and Wen (2010).

The study was carried out between October 2013 and February 2014 on "Our wedding" website (in Portuguese: "O nosso casamento"; www.onossocasamento.pt). The questionnaire required the knowledge of the users concerning the different services and platforms available on the website. The

Table 2. Items and constructs that compose Virtual Atmosphere

Graphics	Source
It is fun watching the graphics such as picture, animation in the website. The website looks nice because of graphics. The graphics in the website are beautiful. The graphics of the website are visually comforting.	Adapted from Koo & Ju (2010)
Colors	
The website emphasizes newly displayed merchandises with distinctive colors. The colors in the website are visually appealing. Visually appealing colors are used in the website to distinguish important contents and emphasized parts from others.	
Links	
The website presents buttons and/or paths to help customers find products/services. The website shows buttons and shortcut paths to make customers find out products they already know. The website makes it possible to find out what customers want within three clicks from the first page. The website provides convenient links to move into the sub-sites.	
Menu	
The menus of the websites appear clean and neat. The segmentations of the website are quite satisfying. Menus of the website fit with the website design. Menus of the website are consistent with the overall style.	

Table 3. Items of Social Identity

	Source
As a member of the community, my position is very important to me. As a member of the community, I am the type of person who likes to engage in my community. Activities in my community are the important part in my life.	Adapted from Kwon & Wen (2010)

Table 4. Items of Altruism

	Source
I tend to encourage people who are in a real crisis or need. I usually help people when they ask me the solution. I give congratulation when people tell me good news.	Adapted from Kwon & Wen (2010)

Table 5. Items of Telepresence

	Source
When my online visit ends, I felt like I actually met other people. I felt that this site creates a new world. While engaged with this site, I felt I was in a different society. While engaged with this site, the site's world was more real or present to me compared to the "real world".	Adapted from Kwon & Wen (2010)

Table 6. Ite ms and constructs that compose Emotions

Pleasure	Source
Using online shopping site is Contented–depressed Happy–unhappy Satisfied–unsatisfied Pleased–annoyed Free–restricted	Adapted from Koo & Ju (2010)
Arousal	
When I use online shopping stores, I'm Aroused–not aroused Wide awake–sleepy Excited–calm Frenzied–sluggish	

questionnaire was posted online on "Our wedding" website forum and users were kindly asked to answer the questionnaire. With this strategy, there is no interviewer bias since the interviewer played no part in the interview process. Although this cannot be considered a random sampling procedure, the initial idea was to implement a process of systematic random sampling. In future work, a fully random sampling procedure should be accomplished. Traditional approaches to minimize non-responses were also implemented in this study.

The population under study is all the users of "Our wedding" website and the sample is composed of 72 voluntary answers from website users (76.4% female, 23.6% male; 1.4% less than 21 years old, 73.6% between 21 and 30 years old, 22.2% between 31 and 40 years old, 2.8% more than 40 years old).

All constructs were measured using a likert scale with 'strongly disagree' and 'strongly agree' options as the anchors. The initial questionnaire was based on practical experience gained from rigorous analysis provided by academics and online experts to validate its construction, language clarity and to obtain comments and suggestions to improve its readability. The questionnaire was pretested with 20 master students to evaluate its consistency.

Table 7. Items and constructs of Attitudes

Situational Attitude	Source
Shopping with this online store is pleasant. Shopping with this online store has many benefits (e.g., fast, easy, convenient, and etc.). I am content shopping with this online store. Shopping with this online store satisfies my needs. In general, I have good attitudes toward online shopping with this online store.	Adapted from Suntornpithug & Khamalah (2010)
Perceived Usefulness	**Source**
This site enables me acquire more information or perform my searches. Using this site would improve my efficiency when doing my searches. This site is a useful. Generically, this site is of added value.	Adapted from Lee (2008)
Perceived Ease of Use	**Source**
My intention when using this site was clear and comprehensible. Interacting with this site does not demand a lot of mental effort. The process of using this site is clear and understandable. I think the site is easily maneuverable.	Adapted from Venkatesh & Davis (2000) and Venkatesh & Morris (2000)
Subjective Norm	**Source**
I would like very much to make purchases with this online store because others think I should do it. If other buyers think that purchases with this online store are valuable, then I should buy online. Others strongly support my purchasing with this online store.	Adapted from Suntornpithug & Khamalah (2010)

Table 8. Items of Trust

	Source
I feel secure about the electronic payment system of this online store. This online store ensures that transactional information is protected from being accidentally altered or destroyed during transmission on the Internet. I think that the security of my personal information is at stake when shopping with this online store. I think that this online store implements security measures to protect my information from hackers. I think that this online store has the ability to verify my identity for security purpose. It bothers me when this online store asks me for personal information. I think that this online store is collecting too much personal information from me. I think that this online store will use my personal information for other purposes without my authorization. I think my personal information in this online store's database is not accurate. I think that unauthorized people (i.e., hackers) have access to my personal information when shopping at this online store. There might be general misrepresentations or fraud shopping with this online store. I feel shopping with the online store has low potential for non-delivery of ordered products. In general I trust shopping with this online store.	Adapted from Suntornpithug & Khamalah (2010)

Table 9. Items of Actual use

	Source
I spend to use this site frequently I spend a lot of time on this site I exerted myself to use this site	Adapted from Kwon & Wen (2010)

A descriptive statistical analysis was firstly used to describe all the variables through different graphics and statistics, followed by an Exploratory Factor Analysis (EFA) and, finally, a regression analysis using the generalized maximum entropy estimator.

Normality of the items was tested through different procedures such as normality tests, QQ-plots, skewness and kurtosis statistics (Curran, West, & Finch, 1996). Cronbach's alpha was used to estimate the internal consistency of scale's items (Pestana & Gageiro, 2003). EFA was used for data reduction purposes: the idea is to describe the variability among the large sets of correlated variables to acquire a small set of variables, usually known as latent factors. Kaiser-Meyer-Olkin (KMO) measure of sampling adequacy and Bartlett's test of sphericity were used to evaluate the suitability of factor analysis (Pestana & Gageiro, 2003). The descriptive statistics, the EFA, the normality tests and the QQ-plots were implemented using SPSS-20 software.

Finally, to explore the three models discussed previously, a regression analysis procedure was implemented. Since the analysis is based in a small sample (the micronumerosity problem), a maximum entropy approach was chosen instead of other traditional approaches such as the ordinary least squares or maximum likelihood estimator. For instance, it is worth to mention that maximum likelihood estimator is attractive mainly due to its large-sample properties. For reader's convenience, the maximum entropy (ME) principle and the generalized maximum entropy (GME) estimator are briefly discussed next.

The ME principle was first established by Jaynes (1957a, 1957b) based on physics (the Shannon entropy and statistical mechanics) and statistical inference. The ME principle provides a tool to make the best predictions from the (usual limited) available information. However, as noted by Jaynes (2003, p. 369), "[...] the principle of maximum entropy is not an Oracle telling which predictions *must* be right; it is a rule for inductive reasoning that tells us which predictions *are most strongly indicated by our present information*." An interesting feature of ME is that it can be seen as an extension of Bernoulli's principle of insufficient reason (Jaynes, 1957a).

To illustrate the ME principle, the famous die problem discussed by Jaynes (2003) is briefly discussed. Only with the average outcome y from a large number N of independent rolls of a dice, how to estimate the probability vector $p=(p_1,p_2,...p_6)$? Considering that the observed frequency distribution of the sample is unknown, only with this information at hand (the average of the results), the ME principle can be applied to select the probability vector p that maximizes

$$-\sum_{k=1}^{6} p_k \ln p_k,$$

subject to the model constraint

$$\sum_{k=1}^{6} kp_k = y$$

and the additivity constraint

$$\sum_{k=1}^{6} p_k = 1.$$

The formal solution is easily derived for the die problem using the Lagrangian function and the corresponding first-order optimality conditions. In Figure 2, the estimated ME distributions for different values of y are presented. Note that, as expected, when y=3.5, the estimated ME distribution is a uniform distribution.

The ME principle is often used for solving ill-posed problems, for example, in physics, informatics, linguistics, biology, medicine, communication engineering, statistics and economics. Some examples of applications of the ME principle can be found in Dionísio et al. (2008), Golan and Dose (2001), Park and Bera (2009) and Vinod and López-de-Lacalle (2009), among many others.

As noted by Golan et al. (1996), statistical data are frequently limited and affected by collinearity implying that the associated statistical models may be ill-posed, unless simplifying assumptions or procedures are imposed to generate seemingly well-posed statistical models that can be estimated with traditional statistical tools. Giving heed to this problem, Golan et al. (1996) generalized the ME formalism and developed the GME estimator, which is useful in models exhibiting collinearity, in models with small samples sizes (micronumerosity) and non-normal errors, as well as in models where the number of parameters to be estimated exceeds the number of observations available (under-determined models).

The GME estimator contributed to the development of the ME econometrics literature in the recent years. In view of the fact that ill-posed real-world problems seem to be the rule rather than the exception

Figure 2. Estimated ME distributions for the die problem

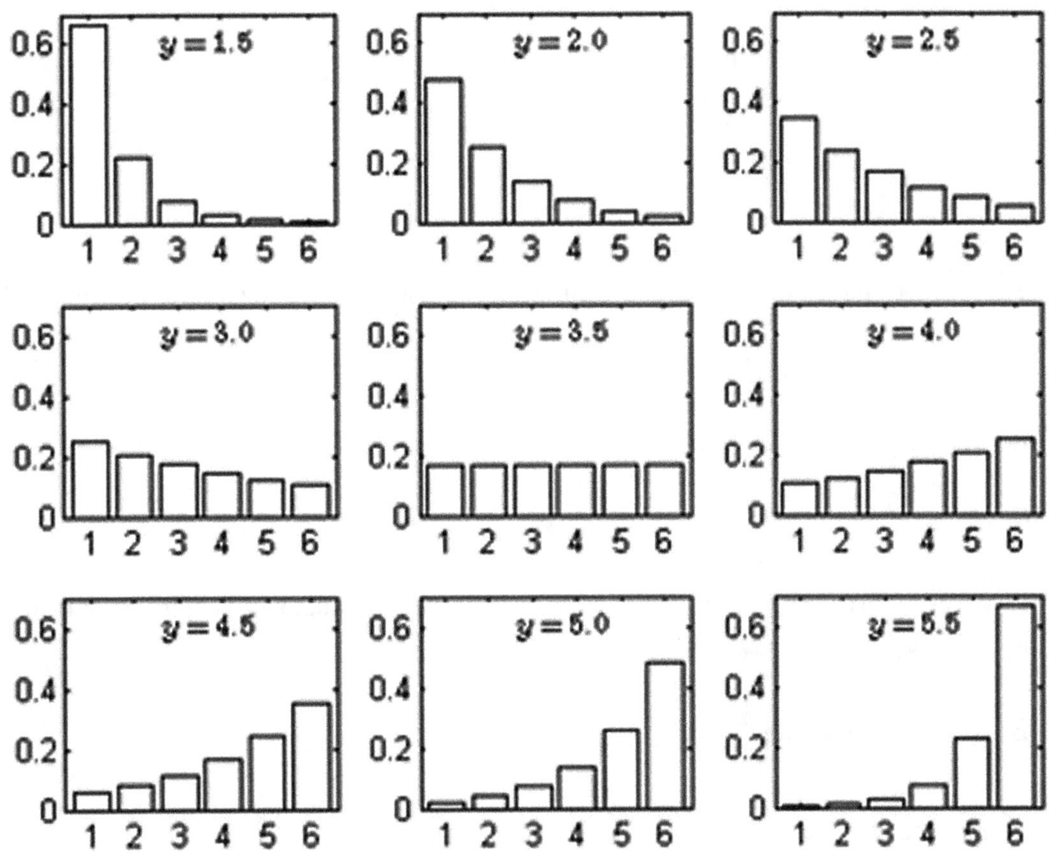

in statistics, the GME estimator has acquired special importance in the toolkit of statistical techniques, by allowing statistical formulations free of restrictive and unnecessary assumptions. For applications of the GME estimator see, among many others, Campbell et al. (2008), Ferreira et al. (2010), Macedo et al. (2014) and Robaina-Alves et al. (2015), and the references therein.

Considering the linear regression model defined in matricial form as

$$y = X\beta + e,$$

where y denotes a $(N \times 1)$ vector of noisy observations, β is a $(K \times 1)$ vector of unknown parameters, X is a known $(N \times K)$ matrix of explanatory variables and e is a $(N \times 1)$ vector of random errors, usually assumed to have a conditional expected value of zero and representing spherical disturbances, Golan et al. (1996) treat each β_k as a discrete random variable with a compact support and $M \geq 2$ possible outcomes, and each e_n as a finite and discrete random variable with $J \geq 2$ possible outcomes. Assuming that both the unknown parameters and the unknown error terms may be bounded *a priori*, the linear model can be presented as

$$y = XZp + Vw,$$

where

$$\beta = Zp = \begin{bmatrix} z'_1 & 0 & \cdots & 0 \\ 0 & z'_2 & \cdots & 0 \\ \vdots & \vdots & \ddots & \vdots \\ 0 & 0 & \cdots & z'_K \end{bmatrix} \begin{bmatrix} p_1 \\ p_2 \\ \vdots \\ p_K \end{bmatrix},$$

with Z a $(K \times KM)$ matrix of support values and $p > 0$ a $(KM \times 1)$ unknown weight vector, and

$$e = Vw = \begin{bmatrix} v'_1 & 0 & \cdots & 0 \\ 0 & v'_2 & \cdots & 0 \\ \vdots & \vdots & \ddots & \vdots \\ 0 & 0 & \cdots & v'_N \end{bmatrix} \begin{bmatrix} w_1 \\ w_2 \\ \vdots \\ w_N \end{bmatrix},$$

with V a $(N \times NJ)$ matrix of support values and $w > 0$ a $(NJ \times 1)$ unknown weight vector. In matricial form, the GME estimator is given by

$$\arg\max_{p,w} \left\{ -p' \ln p - w' \ln w \right\},$$

subject to the model constraint,

$$y = XZp + Vw,$$

and the additivity constraints for p and w, respectively,

$$1_K = \left(I_K \otimes 1'_M\right)p,$$

$$1_N = \left(I_N \otimes 1'_J\right)w,$$

where ⊗ represents the Kronecker product. The GME estimator generates the optimal vectors $\hat{p}$ and $\hat{w}$ that can be used to form point estimates of the unknown parameters and the unknown errors through the reparameterizations defined previously. Additional details can be found in Mittelhammer et al. (2013).

The support matrix Z is defined by the researcher based on prior information. When such information does not exist wide bounds can be used. In this work, the supports in Z are defined through [–10, 10] for all the parameters of the models, considering five points $\left(M = 5\right)$. Different supports with wide bounds were also used to test the stability of the estimator and the results were similar to the ones presented next. The supports in the matrix V are defined symmetrically and centered on zero, considering $J = 5$ and using the three-sigma rule with the empirical standard deviation of the noisy observations.

Since the GME estimator is consistent and asymptotically normally distributed, some asymptotic results can be used to test hypotheses on model parameters (Mittelhammer et al., 2013). However, since this work is based in a small sample, the bootstrap method is used to resampling residuals (1000 trials) and 95% confidence intervals (CI) are obtained by using the percentile method.

The GME estimation procedures are conducted in MATLAB software and all the code was computed by us. However, for those that are not familiar with programming and optimization procedures, the GME estimator with tests and statistics is available, for example, in SAS and LIMDEP software.

RESULTS

Some descriptive statistics are presented in Table 10. Based on the skewness and kurtosis values one can admit there is no reason to reject the normality hypotheses (Curran et al., 1996).

Tables 11, 12 and 13 present some results of the EFA. Virtual atmosphere is composed of four factors/variables, emotions are composed by two factors/variables and attitudes are composed by four factors/variables. The remaining variables (social identity, altruism telepresence, trust and real use) are unifactorial variables. Generally speaking, one can consider that the results are acceptable in terms of cumulative variance, Cronbach's alpha and KMO.

The three research models defined previously are now discussed. For simplicity purposes, the estimated coefficients (EC) and the associated confidence intervals (CI) are presented only for those variables that are considered relevant according to the maximum entropy estimation.

Thus, according to the GME estimator, Virtual atmosphere-graphics is the only independent variable that is considered relevant (EC: 0.594; 95% CI: 0.373 – 0.778) to explain the dependent variable Emotions-pleasure (Model R^2: 38%) in Model 1, as shown in Figure 3. This means that, when the other

Table 10. Some descriptive statistics

Variable/Construct	Mean	Standard Deviation [Min; Max]	Skewness [Min; Max]	Kurtosis [Min; Max]
Virtual Atmosphere	3.75	[0.698; 1.212]	[-1.032; 0.187]	[-0.905; 1.062]
Emotions	3.52	[0.828; 1.179]	[-1.067; 0.151]	[-1.085; 1.337]
Attitudes	3.71	[0.765; 1.250]	[-1.489; 0.889]	[-0.791; -2.373]
Social Identity	2.77	[1.071; 1.237]	[-0.087; 0.125]	[-0.974; -0.705]
Altruism	3.49	[1.061; 1.213]	[-0.953; -0.302]	[-0.589; 0.732]
Telepresence	2.81	[1.119; 1.202]	[-0.146; 0.222]	[-1.032; -0.486]
Trust	2.85	[0.768; 1.267]	[-0.910; 0.525]	[-1.047; 1.399]
Real Use	2.74	[0.927; 1.278]	[-0.441; 0.518]	[-0.971; -0.590]

Table 11. Exploratory factor analysis: virtual atmosphere and emotions

	Virtual Atmosphere				Emotions	
	Graphics	Colors	Links	Menus	Pleasure	Arousal
Eigenvalue	2.819	1.857	2.152	2.816	3.316	2.375
Cumulative variance	70.477	61.899	53.792	70.399	66.327	59.386
Cronbach's α coefficient	0.858	0.683	0.706	0.855	0.850	0.740
KMO	0.783	0.597	0.678	0.793	0.838	0.699

Table 12. Exploratory factor analysis: attitudes

	Situational Attitudes	Perceived Utility	Perceived Ease of Use	Subjective Norm
Eigenvalue	3.674	2.898	2.892	1.986
Cumulative variance	73.489	72.462	72.303	66.195
Cronbach's a coefficient	0.909	0.870	0.872	0.739
KMO	0.851	0.688	0.748	0.625

variables are fixed, the rate of change of the conditional mean of the Emotions-pleasure with respect to the Virtual atmosphere-graphics is estimated to be approximately between 0.373 and 0.778 units.

The coefficients associated to the Colors, Links and Menus are not statistically significant and thus should not be interpreted. In other words, no statistically significant linear dependence is detected between the mean of Emotions-pleasure and these independent variables. Moreover, there is no statistically significant linear dependence between Virtual atmosphere and Emotions-arousal.

Considering Model 2 in Figure 4, there are four significant relations, according to the GME estimator. They are:

Table 13. Exploratory factor analysis: social identity, altruism, telepresence, trust and real use

	Social Identity	Altruism	Telepresence	Trust	Real Use
Eigenvalue	2.383	2.384	2.977	5.128	1.843
Cumulative variance	79.445	79.464	74.416	36.627	61.445
Cronbach's α coefficient	0.866	0.867	0.882	0.742	0.615
KMO	0.703	0.705	0.788	0.802	0.745

Figure 3. Research Model 1

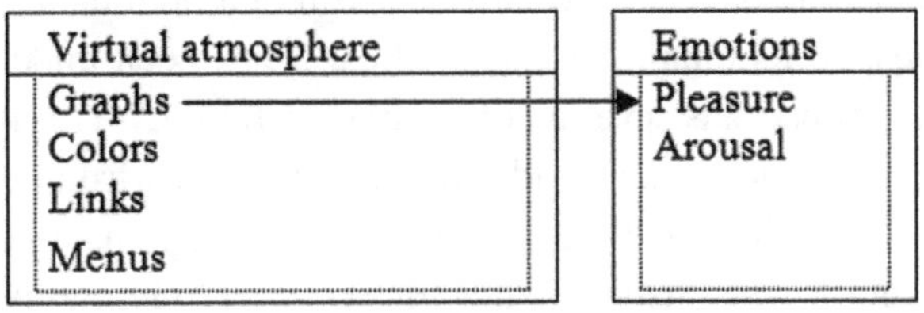

Figure 4. Research Model 2

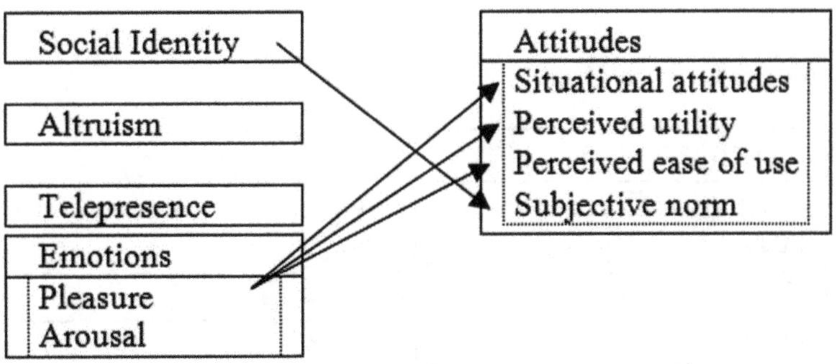

- The Emotions-pleasure is considered significant (EC: 0.769; 95% CI: 0.614 – 0.929) to explain the Attitudes-Situational attitudes (Model R^2: 59%);
- The Emotions-pleasure is considered significant (EC: 0.565; 95% CI: 0.360 – 0.736) to explain the Attitudes-Perceived utility (Model R^2: 46%);
- The Emotions-pleasure is considered significant (EC: 0.574; 95% CI: 0.364 – 0.771) to explain the Attitudes-Perceived ease of use (Model R^2: 34%);
- The Social identity is considered significant (EC: 0.422; 95% CI: 0.141 – 0.677) to explain the Attitudes-Subjective norm (Model R^2: 30%).

The coefficients associated with the remaining variables of Model 2 not mentioned above are not statistically significant.

Finally, according to the GME estimator, there are four significant relations in Model 3, as can be seen in Figure 5. The Attitudes-Situational attitudes (EC: 0.114; 95% CI: 0.013 – 0.223), the Attitudes-Perceived utility (EC: 0.142; 95% CI: 0.009 – 0.218), the Attitudes-Perceived ease of use (EC: 0.131; 95%

CI: 0.005 – 0.211) and Past experience (EC: 0.002; 95% CI: 0.001 – 0.003) are considered relevant to explain the Real use (Model R^2: 42%). The coefficients associated with the variables Attitudes-Subjective norm and Trust are not statistically significant.

Taking into account the abovementioned results one can only partially validate hypotheses H1, H2, H3 and H6, while hypothesis H7 is accepted and the remaining are rejected. The outcomes of the hypotheses are shown in Table 14.

CONCLUSION

Consumer behavior, especially associated to wedding, is full of emotionality and romanticism, as "love is in the air." However, despite its unique characteristics, it has been under researched in the virtual environment. As such, this chapter has several contributions: firstly, it is original in what concerns the analysis of virtual atmosphere, emotions, attitudes and real use in a virtual community involving wedding as its main theme. Secondly, it is the first study of its kind analyzing a virtual community using the GME estimator, which is robust when using small samples sizes (micronumerosity).

A first conclusion is that the relationship between virtual atmosphere and emotions, as well as emotions and attitudes, are poorer than expected. Two reasons can be advanced for this. In fact, the studies analyzed in the literature were obtained for online customers and not for online users, namely when

Figure 5. Research Model 3

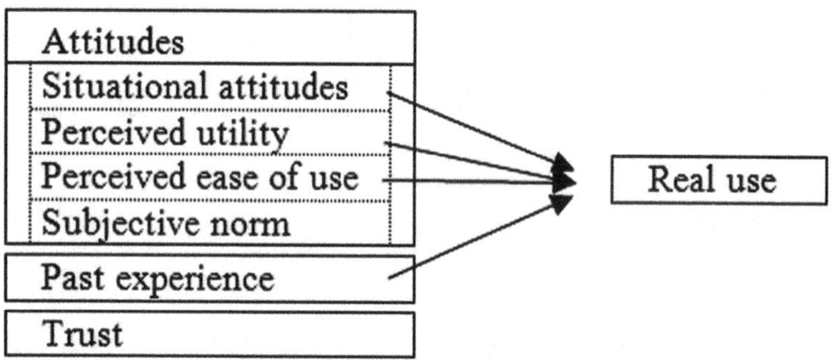

Table 14. Validated hypotheses under investigation

Hypotheses	Results
H1: Virtual atmosphere has a positive effect on emotions.	Partially accepted
H2: Emotions have a positive effect on attitudes.	Partially accepted
H3: Social identity has a positive effect on attitudes.	Partially accepted
H4: Altruism has a positive effect on attitudes.	Rejected
H5: Telepresence has a positive effect on attitudes.	Rejected
H6: Attitudes have a positive effect on real use.	Partially accepted
H7: Past experience has a positive effect on real use.	Accepted
H8: Trust has a positive effect on real use.	Rejected

these users are looking for information for marriage, or as referenced "when love is in the air." The big difference between customers and users of online technology in the research carried out is that the site provides information on weddings and lacks a commercial vocation. As a result, we are facing users, not buyers, which may have biased the results of relations between the two aforementioned variables.

One has also to take into account that this model was tested in relation to the wedding site. Thus, it is relevant to take into consideration some aspects. The site analyzed portrays marriage as more than an engagement contract between two people; wedding is portrayed as the event created around that day/event. The target audience is the groom and bride, that is, those people who decided to marry but have not yet done it.

Being more than a psychological contract, marriage is a particularly emotional event in the life of two people. Utopically, marriage is seen as a unique and singular event, traditionally being associated with something that happens only once in life, which has clear emotional influences over the event experienced.

Because it is a singular, unique event, the site under study is of interest to users during the period of time previous to marriage. After marrying the site loses interest, at least in relative terms.

Culturally, it is also known that women are more emotional than men. Hosftede (1980) used this information to set one of the four cultural dimensions, masculinity vs. femininity. He considered that in more masculine cultures prevail focus on results, success and competition and in more feminine cultures the well-being and the quality of interpersonal relationships especially valued, men being more rational, while women being more emotional. In this study, the majority of respondents (76.4%) are women, so the emotional issue is here more emphasized.

In any case, as presented in the literature review, the social perspective, cohabitation and transient informal conjugality that have been evolving in Western society makes this study the starting point for further studies, as the results (lack of greater validity of the assumptions presented) may indicate that this exploratory study may require a greater depth to the target audience segmentation level associated with marriage, as well as greater conceptual clarity of the depth of emotional involvement associated with marriage.

This work had as its main focus to answer the following three questions:

- To understand what components of the virtual atmosphere have more influence on pleasure/arousal, as emotional states;
- To realize if individual characteristics (social identity, altruism and telepresence) and emotional states influence attitudes;
- To understand whether attitudes, past experience and trust influence online site actual use;

Overall, the results show that the virtual environment partially influences emotions. More specifically, only the graphics have an influence on pleasure, not validating the assumptions that (a) the colors, links and menus have a relationship with emotions and (b) arousal is influenced by any of the virtual atmosphere components. These results are very different from those obtained by Koo and Ju (2010). For them both emotions, pleasure and arousal, are influenced by the graphics, colors and links. Only the menus have no influence on emotions.

Small changes in the sites atmospheric characteristics can sometimes have a big impact on the consumer's emotions. Although this is not an easy task, it is important that managers know well the interests of users to go match their needs and preferences. Thus, according to the results of this study, a possible conclusion is that we need to understand how important are colors, links and menus when emotional users are at stake.

A more likely conclusion is that emotions, as measured by Koo and Ju (2010), are more relevant to online customers but not so relevant for online users of a site with a high emotionally load, which is the case of brides and grooms, given the importance of marriage. In these circumstances the virtual atmosphere loses some of its influence on emotions due to the fact that online users are most influenced by intrinsic motives than by the virtual atmosphere. In any case, it is necessary to consider the various segments associated with the target audience in order to analyze their influence in these relationships.

With regard to the relationship between emotions and attitudes, only pleasure exerts partial influence on attitudes, particularly in situational attitudes, perceived usefulness and perceived ease of use. The subjective norm is not influenced by emotions. Arousal has no influence on any of the attitude factors.

The relationship between emotions and attitudes was proposed in this study in order to adapt the relationship between emotions and the intention to use, proposed by Koo and Ju (2010). On the one hand, it was intended to test how emotions influence attitudes and, on the other hand, how attitudes influence the real use. It is clear that while pleasure is a clear antecedent of attitudes, arousal has no influence.

In the case of users with a high emotional charge one can say that pleasure plays an important role associated with the event, eventually placing on second place any arousal associated with situational attitudes, perceived usefulness and perceived ease of use. As such, the components joy, happiness or satisfaction are more relevant than the components associated with excitation, especially since they are closer to the emotional reality of the site's users associated with marriage.

The other antecedents of attitudes – social identity, altruism and telepresence – do not significantly influence attitudes. Kwon and Wen (2010) concluded that there is a relationship between the social identity and perceived utility, as well as with the perceived ease of use. Regarding altruism and telepresence, they only found influence with the perceived ease of use. They did not study situational attitudes and subjective norm. The results did not match those of Kwon and Wen (2010), which can be explained by the fact that perceived usefulness, perceived ease of use or subjective norm are associated with various non-anticipated website user profiles (dating, living together, cohabitants) seeking information on weddings.

In turn, telepresence and altruism, associated more with individual characteristics than to social ones, portray that the reality of the site is closer to an informational reality than to a participatory one, which eventually limits the participation with other users' networks.

Although Suntornpithug and Khamalah (2010) consider there is a direct influence between trust and intention to use, in this study the relationship between trust and real use did not occur.

Although past experiences have been suggested by Dennis et al. (2009) without any empirical validation, it is possible to affirm that positive past experiences lead to a higher real use, which represents the users' website behavioral perspective, which can be regarded as behavioral trust. Thus, it appears that past experience with the site is a strong antecedent of the actual use of "Our Wedding" site. On the other hand, the lack of relationship between trust and real use might be explained by the construct, as it was built including too many items that do not represent the emotional involvement of the users, which in turn may explain the poor variance of the construct trust.

Considering the goals established in this work, one can state that they were partially accomplished:

- The hypotheses 1, 2 and 3 were partially corroborated. From the four components of the virtual atmosphere, only the graphics have influence on the pleasurable emotions. However, virtual environment has no influence in the arousal. Also the arousal does not have any influence on attitudes. On the other hand, social identity and emotions have influence on attitudes;

- The individual characteristics (altruism and telepresence) do not play any role in attitudes, as well as trust does not have influence on the real use of the website;
- Past experiences are a strong predictor of real use;
- Attitudes partially influence the actual use of the website.

This work has some limitations and thus additional efforts in future research are recommended:

- Will be necessary a fully random sampling procedure and a large sample to provide more reliability of the inference process;
- The questionnaire has 75 questions, which can in certain circumstances limit the website users' involvement in this study. A simplification on the questionnaire should be accomplished;
- The questionnaire was implemented in a very specific website. Marriage being mostly a singular event in the life of an individual, active participation in the website is relatively situational.

FUTURE RESEARCH DIRECTIONS

It is necessary to restructure the model based on the results obtained. It would be advisable to categorize the components of the virtual atmosphere, emotions and attitudes as independent variables, not only to replicate the models of the theory of planned behavior, but also to test the perceived ease of use, intention to use and actual use.

It is necessary to apply the model in a more global and general type of site where relational issues are more relevant than situational ones, or where the engagement / involvement is not as intricate as is the wedding as emotional event. It may also be tested in a more commercial environment where the purchase intent is more pragmatic than the merely use intention.

It is advisable to deepen the study of the differences between genders and ages, as there can be clear perceptual and behavioral differences among them that have not been studied in this sample due to the limitation of the number of respondents.

With respect to attitudes, the model considered situational attitudes, perceived usefulness, perceived ease of use and the subjective norm as components of attitudes. However, the clustering of variables was not proven and they shall be considered as independent variables in future studies.

In future studies, it is necessary to take into consideration target audiences associated with marriage *lato sensu,* as there are behavioral, social and emotional differences that can lead to a deeper and differentiated analysis.

ACKNOWLEDGMENT

This work was partially supported by Portuguese funds through the CIDMA - Center for Research and Development in Mathematics and Applications, and the Portuguese Foundation for Science and Technology ("FCT - Fundação para a Ciência e a Tecnologia"), within project UID/MAT/04106/2013.

REFERENCES

Aboim, S. (2005). A formação do casal: Formas de entrada e percursos conjugais. In K. Wall (Ed.), *Famílias em Portugal – percursos, interacções, relações sociais* (pp. 85–116). Lisbon: Imprensa de Ciências Sociais.

Acevedo, B. P., & Aron, A. (2009). Does a long-term relationship kill romantic love? *Review of General Psychology, 13*(1), 59–65. doi:10.1037/a0014226

Alsajjan, B., & Dennis, C. (2009). Internet banking acceptance model: Cross-market examination. *Journal of Business Research, 63*(9-10), 957–963. doi:10.1016/j.jbusres.2008.12.014

Ashforth, B. E., & Mael, F. A. (1989). Social identity theory and the organization. *Academy of Management Review, 14*(1), 20–35.

Ashtona, M. C., Paunonen, S. V., Helmes, E., & Jackson, D. N. (1998). Kin altruism, reciprocal altruism, and the big five personality factors. *Evolution and Human Behavior, 19*(4), 243–255. doi:10.1016/S1090-5138(98)00009-9

Bagozzi, R. P., & Dholakia, U. M. (2002). Intentional social action in virtual communities. *Journal of Interactive Marketing, 16*(2), 2–21. doi:10.1002/dir.10006

Baker, J. (1986). The role of the environment in marketing services: The consumer perspective. In A. John, J. A. Czepeil, C. A. Congrarn, & J. Shanahan (Eds.), *The service challenge: Integrating for competitive advantage* (pp. 79–84). Chicago, IL: American Marketing Association.

Baker, J., Grewal, D., & Parasuraman, A. (1994). The influence of store environment on quality inferences and store image. *Journal of the Academy of Marketing Science, 22*(4), 328–339. doi:10.1177/0092070394224002

Bearden, W. O., & Etzel, M. J. (1982). Reference group influence on product and brand purchase decisions. *The Journal of Consumer Research, 9*(2), 183–194. doi:10.1086/208911

Bhatti, R. S. (1993). Changes in the institution of marriage and family structures: Problems and solutions. *Paper presented at the International Conference on Respect for Life: The Priority of the Nineties*, St. John's Medical College and Hospital, Bangalore, Karnataka.

Bitner, M. J. (1992). Servicescapes: The impact of physical surroundings on costumers employees. *Journal of Marketing, 56*(2), 57–71. doi:10.2307/1252042

Brei, V. A. (2001). *Antecedentes e consequências da confiança do consumidor final em trocas relacionais com empresas de serviço: Um estudo com o usuário de internet banking no Brasil* [Unpublished master dissertation]. Universidade Federal do Rio Grande do Sul.

Campbell, R., Rogers, K., & Rezek, J. (2008). Efficient frontier estimation: A maximum entropy approach. *Journal of Productivity Analysis, 30*(3), 213–221. doi:10.1007/s11123-008-0103-9

Chan, K. W., & Li, S. Y. (2010). Understanding consumer-to-consumer interactions in virtual communities: The salience of reciprocity. *Journal of Business Research, 63*(9-10), 1033–1040. doi:10.1016/j.jbusres.2008.08.009

Chen, Y.-H., & Barnes, S. (2007). Initial trust and online buyer behaviour. *Industrial Management & Data Systems*, *107*(1), 21–36. doi:10.1108/02635570710719034

Corbitt, B. J., Thanasankit, T., & Yi, H. (2003). Trust and e-commerce: A study of consumer perceptions. *Electronic Commerce Research and Applications*, *2*(3), 203–215. doi:10.1016/S1567-4223(03)00024-3

Curran, P. J., West, S. G., & Finch, J. F. (1996). The robustness of test statistics to nonnormality and specification error in confirmatory factor analysis. *Psychological Methods*, *1*(1), 16–29. doi:10.1037/1082-989X.1.1.16

Davis, F. D. (1989). Perceived usufulness, perceived ease of use, and user acceptance of information technology. *Management Information Systems Quarterly*, *13*(3), 319–339. doi:10.2307/249008

De Valck, K., Van Bruggen, G. H., & Wierenga, B. (2009). Virtual communities: A marketing perspective. *Decision Support Systems*, *47*(3), 185–203. doi:10.1016/j.dss.2009.02.008

Dennis, C., Jayawardhena, C., & Papamatthaiou, E.-K. (2010). Antecedents of internet shopping intentions and the moderating effects of substitutability. *International Review of Retail, Distribution and Consumer Research*, *20*(4), 411–430. doi:10.1080/09593969.2010.504008

Dennis, C., Merrilees, B., Jayawardhena, C., & Wright, L. T. (2009). E-consumer behaviour. *European Journal of Marketing*, *43*(9/10), 1121–1139. doi:10.1108/03090560910976393

Dias, M. C., Zwicker, R., & Vicentin, I. C. (2003). Análise do modelo de aceitação de tecnologia de Davis. *Revista. SPEI*, *4*(2), 15–23.

Dionísio, A., Reis, A. H., & Coelho, L. (2008). Utility function estimation: The entropy approach. *Physica A*, *387*(15), 3862–3867. doi:10.1016/j.physa.2008.02.072

Donovan, R. J., & Rossiter, J. R. (1982). Store atmosphere: An environmental psychology approach. *Journal of Retailing*, *58*(1), 34–57.

Duarte, C. (2011). Conflito e violência nas relações conjugais: Uma perspectiva sistémica. In P. M. Matos, C. Duarte, & M. E. Costa (Eds.), *Famílias: Questões de desenvolvimento e intervenção* (pp. 103–123). Oporto: LivPsic.

Eroglu, S. A., Machleit, K. A., & Davis, L. M. (2001). Atmospheric qualities of online retailing: A conceptual model and implications. *Journal of Business Research*, *54*(2), 177–184. doi:10.1016/S0148-2963(99)00087-9

Eroglu, S. A., Machleit, K. A., & Davis, L. M. (2003). Empirical testing of a model of online store atmospherics and shopper responses. *Psychology and Marketing*, *20*(2), 139–150. doi:10.1002/mar.10064

Ferreira, P., Dionísio, A., & Pires, C. (2010). Adopt the euro? The GME approach. *Journal of Economic Interaction and Coordination*, *5*(2), 231–247. doi:10.1007/s11403-010-0062-x

Fishbein, M., & Ajzen, I. (1975). *Belief, attitude, intention and behavior: An introduction to theory and research.* Reading, Massachusetts: Addison-Wesley.

Fletcher, G. J. (2002). *The new science of intimate relationships.* New York: Blackwell. doi:10.1002/9780470773390

Flouri, E., & Buchanan, A. (2001). What predicts traditional attitudes to marriage? *Children & Society*, *15*(4), 263–271. doi:10.1002/chi.674

Fonseca, S., & Duarte, C. (2014). Do namoro ao casamento: Significados, expectativas, conflito e amor. *Psicologia: Teoria e Pesquisa (Brasília)*, *30*(2), 135–143. doi:10.1590/S0102-37722014000200002

Fortin, D. R., Dholakia, R. R., & Dholakia, N. (2002). Emerging issues in electronic marketing: Thinking outside the square. *Journal of Business Research*, *55*(8), 623–627. doi:10.1016/S0148-2963(00)00202-2

Gefen, D. (2000). E-commerce: The role of familiarity and trust. *Omega*, *28*(6), 725–737. doi:10.1016/S0305-0483(00)00021-9

Gefen, D., Karahanna, E., & Straub, D. W. (2003). Trust and TAM in online shopping: An integrated model. *Management Information Systems Quarterly*, *27*(1), 51–90.

Gefen, D., & Straub, D. W. (2004). Consumer trust in B2C e-commerce and the importance of social presence: Experiments in e-products and e-services. *Omega*, *32*(6), 407–424. doi:10.1016/j.omega.2004.01.006

Giglio, E. M. (2005). *O comportamento do consumidor*. São Paulo: Thomson.

Golan, A., & Dose, V. (2001). A generalized information theoretical approach to tomographic reconstruction. *Journal of Physics. A. Mathematical Nuclear and General*, *34*(7), 1271–1283. doi:10.1088/0305-4470/34/7/304

Golan, A., Judge, G., & Miller, D. (1996). *Maximum Entropy Econometrics: Robust estimation with limited data*. Chichester: John Wiley & Sons.

Goode, M. M., & Harris, L. C. (2007). Online behavioural intentions: An empirical investigation of antecedents and moderators. *European Journal of Marketing*, *41*(5/6), 512–536. doi:10.1108/03090560710737589

Hagel, J. (1999). Net gain: Expanding markets through virtual communities. *Journal of Interactive Marketing*, *13*(1), 55–65. doi:10.1002/(SICI)1520-6653(199924)13:1<55::AID-DIR5>3.0.CO;2-C

Hagel, J. I., & Armstrong, A. G. (1997). *Net gain: Expanding markets through virtual communities*. Boston, MA: Harvard Business School Press.

Hall, S. (2006). *Marital meaning: Exploring young adults' belief systems about handbook of couple therapy*. New York: Guilford Press.

Hausman, A. V., & Siekpe, J. S. (2009). The Effect of web interface features on consumer online purchase intentions. *Journal of Business Research*, *62*(1), 5–13. doi:10.1016/j.jbusres.2008.01.018

Hoffman, D. L., Novak, T. P., & Peralta, M. (1999). Building consumer trust online. *Communications of the ACM*, *42*(4), 80–85. doi:10.1145/299157.299175

Hofstede, G. (1980). *Culture's consequences: international differences in work-related values*. Beverly Hills: Sage.

Jaynes, E. T. (1957a). Information theory and statistical mechanics. *Physical Review*, *106*(4), 620–630. doi:10.1103/PhysRev.106.620

Jaynes, E. T. (1957b). Information theory and statistical mechanics. II. *Physical Review*, *108*(2), 171–190. doi:10.1103/PhysRev.108.171

Jaynes, E. T. (2003). *Probability Theory – The Logic of Science*. Cambridge: Cambridge University Press. doi:10.1017/CBO9780511790423

Juvva, S., & Bhatti, R. S. (2006). Epigenetic model of marital expectations. *Contemporary Family Therapy*, *28*(1), 61–72. doi:10.1007/s10591-006-9695-2

Kim, D. J., Ferrin, D. L., & Rao, H. R. (2008). A trust-based consumer decision-making model in electronic commerce: The role of trust, perceived risk, and their antecedents. *Decision Support Systems*, *44*(2), 544–564. doi:10.1016/j.dss.2007.07.001

Klein, L. R. (1998). Evaluating the potential of interactive versus experience goods. *Journal of Business Research*, *41*(3), 195–203. doi:10.1016/S0148-2963(97)00062-3

Koo, D.-M., & Ju, S.-H. (2010). The interactional effects of atmospherics and perceptual curiosity on emotions and online shopping intention. *Computers in Human Behavior*, *26*(3), 377–388. doi:10.1016/j.chb.2009.11.009

Kotler, P. (1998). *Administração de Marketing*. São Paulo: Atlas.

Kwon, O., & Wen, Y. (2010). An empirical study of the factors affecting social network service use. *Computers in Human Behavior*, *26*(2), 254–263. doi:10.1016/j.chb.2009.04.011

Langerak, F., Verhorf, P. C., Verlegh, P. W., & de Valck, K. (2004). Satisfaction and participation in virtual communities. In B. E. Kahn & M. F. Luce (Eds.), *Advances in consumer research* (Vol. 31, pp. 56–57). Valdosta, GA: Association for Consumer Research.

Leal, G. P., Hor-Meyll, L. F., & Pessôa, L. A. (2013). Influence of virtual communities in purchasing decisions: The participants' perspective. *Journal of Business Research*, *67*(5), 882–890. doi:10.1016/j.jbusres.2013.07.007

Lee, M.-C. (2008). Factors influencing the adoption of internet banking: An integration of TAM and TPB with perceived risk and perceived benefit. *Electronic Commerce Research and Applications*, *8*(3), 130–141. doi:10.1016/j.elerap.2008.11.006

Lee, M. K., & Turban, E. (2001). A trust model for consumer internet shopping. *International Journal of Electronic Commerce*, *6*(1), 75–91.

Leite, S. (2003). A união de facto em Portugal. *Revista de Estudos Demográficos*, *33*, 97–140.

Li, L. H., Daugherty, T., & Biocca, F. (2002). Impact of 3-D advertising on product knowledge, brand attitude, and purchase intention: The mediating role of presence. *Journal of Advertising*, *31*(3), 43–59. doi:10.1080/00913367.2002.10673675

Macedo, P., Silva, E., & Scotto, M. (2014). Technical efficiency with state-contingent production frontiers using maximum entropy estimators. *Journal of Productivity Analysis*, *41*(1), 131–140. doi:10.1007/s11123-012-0314-y

Martin, P. D., Specter, G., Martin, D., & Martin, M. (2003). Expressed attitudes of adolescents toward marriage and family life. *Adolescence*, *38*(150), 359–367. PMID:14560887

Mcknight, D. H., Choudhury, V., & Kacmar, C. (2002). The impact of initial consumer trust on intentions to transact with a web wite: A trust building model. *The Journal of Strategic Information Systems*, *11*(3/4), 297–323. doi:10.1016/S0963-8687(02)00020-3

Mehrabian, A., & Russell, J. A. (1974). *An approach to environmental psychology*. Cambridge, MA: The MIT Press.

Mittelhammer, R., Cardell, N. C., & Marsh, T. L. (2013). The data-constrained generalized maximum entropy estimator of the GLM: Asymptotic theory and inference. *Entropy*, *15*(5), 1756–1775. doi:10.3390/e15051756

Moorman, C., Deshpandé, R., & Zaltman, G. (1993). Factors affecting trust in market research relationships. *Journal of Marketing*, *57*(1), 81–101. doi:10.2307/1252059

Morgan, R. M., & Hunt, S. D. (1994). The commitment-trust theory of relationship marketing. *Journal of Marketing*, *58*(July), 20–38. doi:10.2307/1252308

Moutinho, K., & Roazzi, A. (2010). As teorias da ação planejada: Relações entre intenções e comportamentos. *AvaliaçãoPsicológica*, *9*(2), 279–287.

Mummalaneni, V. (2005). An empirical investigation of website characteristics, consumer emotional states and on-line shopping behaviors. *Journal of Business Research*, *58*(4), 526–532. doi:10.1016/S0148-2963(03)00143-7

Murteira, B. J. F. (1993). *Análise exploratória de dados - Estatística descritiva*. Lisbon: McGraw-Hill.

Park, S. Y., & Bera, A. K. (2009). Maximum entropy autoregressive conditional heteroskedasticity model. *Journal of Econometrics*, *150*(2), 219–230. doi:10.1016/j.jeconom.2008.12.014

Pestana, M. H., & Gageiro, J. N. (2003). *Análise de Dados para Ciências Sociais - A Complementaridade do SPSS*. Lisbon: Sílabo.

Pinheiro, R. M., Castro, G. C., Silva, H. H., & Nunes, J. M. (2006). *Comportamento do consumidor e pesquisa de mercado*. São Paulo: FGV Management.

Ribeiro, T. (2002). Da diversidade do feminino e do masculino à singularidade do casal [Unpublished doctoral dissertation]. University of Lisbon.

Ridings, C., Gefen, D., & Arinze, B. (2006). Psychological barriers: Lurker and Poster motivation and behavior in online communities. *Communications of the Association for Information Systems*, *18*, 329–354.

Riedlinger, M. E., Gallois, C., Mckay, S., & Pittam, J. (2004). Impact of social group processes and functional diversity on communication in networked organizations. *Journal of Applied Communication Research*, *32*(1), 55–79. doi:10.1080/0090988042000178130

Robaina-Alves, M., Moutinho, V., & Macedo, P. (2015). A new frontier approach to model the eco-efficiency in European countries. *Journal of Cleaner Production*, *103*, 562–573. doi:10.1016/j.jclepro.2015.01.038

Schiffman, L. G., & Kanuk, L. L. (2009). *Comportamento do consumidor*. São Paulo: LTC.

Schubert, P., & Ginsburg, M. (2000). Virtual communities of transaction: The role of personalization in electronic commerce. *Electronic Markets*, *10*(1), 45–55. doi:10.1080/10196780050033971

Shen, Y.-C., Huang, C.-Y., Chu, C.-H., & Liao, H.-C. (2010). Virtual community loyalty: An interpersonal-interaction perspective. *International Journal of Electronic Commerce*, *15*(1), 49–74. doi:10.2753/JEC1086-4415150102

Sherman, E., Mathur, A., & Smith, R. B. (1997). Store environment and consumer purchase behavior: Mediating role of consumer emotions. *Psychology and Marketing*, *14*(4), 361–378. doi:10.1002/(SICI)1520-6793(199707)14:4<361::AID-MAR4>3.0.CO;2-7

Shim, S., & Drake, M. F. (1990). Consumer intention to utilize electronic shopping: The Fishbein behavioral intention model. *Journal of Direct Marketing*, *4*(3), 22–33. doi:10.1002/dir.4000040305

Shim, S., Eastlick, M. A., Lotz, S. L., & Warrington, P. (2001). An online prepurchase intentions model: The role of intention to search. *Journal of Retailing*, *77*(3), 397–416. doi:10.1016/S0022-4359(01)00051-3

Silva, P. M., & Dias, G. A. (2007). Teorias sobre aceitação de tecnologia: Por que os usuários aceitam ou rejeitam as tecnologias de informação? *Brazilian Journal of Information Science*, *1*(2), 69–91.

Silvestre, A. L. (2007). *Análise de dados e estatística descritiva*. Lisbon: Escolar Editora.

Solomon, M. R. (2002). *O comportamento do consumidor: Comprando, possuindo e sendo*. São Paulo: Bookman.

Spies, K., Hesse, F., & Loesch, K. (1997). Store atmosphere, mood and purchasing behavior. *International Journal of Research in Marketing*, *14*(1), 1–17. doi:10.1016/S0167-8116(96)00015-8

Suntornpithug, N., & Khamalah, J. (2010). Machine and person interactivity: The driving forces behind influences on consumers' willingness to purchase online. *Journal of Electronic Commerce Research*, *11*(4), 299–325.

Thomsen, S. R., Straubhaar, J. D., & Bolyard, D. M. (1998). *Ethnomethodology and the study of online communities: Exploring the cyberstreets.Proceedings of IRISS Conference*, Bristol.

Venkatesh, V., & Davis, F. D. (2000). A theoretical extension of the technology acceptance model: Four longitudinal field studies. *Management Science*, *46*(2), 186–204. doi:10.1287/mnsc.46.2.186.11926

Venkatesh, V., & Morris, M. G. (2000). Why don't men even stop to ask for directions? Gender, social influence, and their role in technology acceptance and usage behavior. *Management Information Systems Quarterly*, *24*(1), 115–140. doi:10.2307/3250981

Vinod, H. D., & López-de-Lacalle, J. (2009). Maximum entropy bootstrap for time series: The meboot R package. *Journal of Statistical Software*, *29*(5), 1–19. doi:10.18637/jss.v029.i05

Wright, D. W., Simmons, L. A., & Campbell, K. (2007). Does a marriage ideal exist? Using Q-sort methodology to compare young adults and professional educators' views on healthy marriages. *Contemporary Family Therapy*, *29*(4), 223–236. doi:10.1007/s10591-007-9044-0

Wu, C.-S., Cheng, F.-F., & Yen, D. C. (2008). The atmospheric factors of online storefront environment design: An empirical experiment in Taiwan. *Information & Management*, *45*(7), 493–498. doi:10.1016/j.im.2008.07.004

Wu, J.-J., Chen, Y.-H., & Chung, Y.-S. (2010). Trust factors influencing virtual community members: A study of transaction communities. *Journal of Business Research*, *63*(9-10), 1025–1032. doi:10.1016/j.jbusres.2009.03.022

Wu, J.-J., & Tsang, A. S. (2008). Factors affecting members' trust belief and behaviour intention in virtual communities. *Behaviour & Information Technology*, *27*(2), 115–125. doi:10.1080/01449290600961910

Yuanquan, L., Jiayin, Q., & Huaying, S. (2008). Review of relationships among variables in TAM. *Tsinghua Science and Technology*, *13*(3), 273–278. doi:10.1016/S1007-0214(08)70044-0

KEY TERMS AND DEFINITIONS

Altruism: Occurs when an individual sacrifices him/herself in favor of another knowing that this might bring him/her negative consequences, without the intention of having any reward, but a reciprocal help.

Marriage: Is an ancient institution based on two traditional pillars, a psychological (emotional) contract largely unconscious and a transition to a cohabitation that leads to a more intrinsic relationship between two partners.

Social Identity: Is characterized by the identity and solidarity an individual creates with certain individuals or groups. This identity generates behaviors or concepts that discriminate them from other individuals or groups.

Store Atmosphere: Is the set of environmental conditions, space and functionality, and symbols, signs and artifacts that might influence the direct relationship between the store features (atmosphere) and buying behavior of consumers. As such, store atmosphere needs to be explored in order to maximize consumption. In the case of virtual environments, one may refer to virtual atmosphere.

TAM: Technology Acceptance Model or TAM is a model that was developed to understand the reasons why users accept or reject the new technology and to provide proposals regarding how to improve the acceptance process, providing a support for prediction and explanation of acceptance levels of a certain technology.

Telepresence: Is the feeling that a user or a consumer has when exposed to a virtual environment experience. In the case of virtual communities, the user feels like he/she is directly contacting with other users, even though the contact is only virtual and not physical. The sense of telepresence allows a user to create human relationships with other users who are remotely located.

Wedding: Is an event full of emotionality and romanticism associated to a marriage. Normally, wedding is portrayed as the event created around the day/event when marriage occurs.

Chapter 11
Antecedents and Consequences of Adopting Social Networking Technologies for Knowledge Sharing in Small Firms:

Pedro Soto-Acosta
University of Murcia, Spain

Simona Popa
University of Murcia, Spain

ABSTRACT

This paper examines factors, which affect web 2.0 knowledge sharing and its effect on organizational innovation in small and medium-sized enterprises (SMEs). The study also investigates whether web 2.0 knowledge sharing mediates the relationship between HR (Human Resource) practices and innovation. The proposed research model and its associated hypotheses were tested by using structural equation modelling on a dataset of 552 SMEs. Results suggest that technological and organizational factors are positively associated with web 2.0 knowledge sharing in Ss, while the contrary is found with regard to vertical competition. In addition, results show that web 2.0 knowledge sharing positively influence innovation and that web 2.0 knowledge sharing mediates the relationship between Human Resource (HR) practices and innovation in SMEs.

INTRODUCTION

The Web 2.0 (or social web) constitutes an internet-based digital platform that enables the creation of social networks, facilitating information dissemination and knowledge sharing (Joo and Normatov, 2013; Palacios-Marqués et al., 2015a; Pan, 2012; Paroutis and Al Saleh, 2009; Sigala and Chalkiti, 2014). Consequently, firms are deploying Web 2.0 technologies such as social networking, wikis, and internal blogging to improve collaboration and Web 2.0 knowledge sharing within their boundaries (Levy, 2009; Lim et al., 2010; Xin et al., 2014). In addition, although the literature suggests that findings from stud-

DOI: 10.4018/978-1-5225-0332-3.ch011

ies examining KM practices in large companies are unlikely to be generalisable to SMEs, very few and recent studies focus on this specific type of firms (Chan et al., 2012; Huy et al., 2012; Lopez-Nicolas and Soto-Acosta, 2010). Meanwhile, SMEs are of enormous importance for economic growth, employment and wealth creation. For example, in Europe, SMEs represent around 99% of the total number of firms.

Extant research has demonstrated that, although firms have extensively adopted internet technologies, technology use is an important link to business value and that such link is sometimes limited especially in small and medium-sized enterprises (SMEs) (Devaraj & Kohli, 2003; Zhu & Kraemer, 2005). In this sense, studies in SMEs suggest that, although having a proper information technology (IT) infrastructure can facilitate knowledge creation, it does not necessarily mean that knowledge is created (Lopez-Nicolas & Soto-Acosta, 2010).Thus, implementing IT applications, by itself, is not enough to ensure a better outcome in terms of knowledge sharing. Knowledge will not necessarily circulate freely firm wide just because accurate IT to support such circulation is available (Brown & Duguid, 2000).Therefore, it is important to understand the key factors that facilitate and motivate Web 2.0 knowledge sharing in SMEs. Beyond technological and environmental factors, existing investigation has recognized the importance of organizational factors in influencing internet-based technologies adoption and use (Gu et al., 2012). Organizational factors may constrain or facilitate the implementation and usage of Web 2.0 technologies for knowledge sharing. For instance, the literature suggests that organizational human resource (HR) practices that create a commitment-based environment may affect the organizational social climate that motivates employees to work together and share knowledge (Collis and Smith, 2006), since these practices influence the interactions, behaviours and motivation of employees. In contrast, for instance, performance pressure has been found to undermine knowledge sharing (Gardner, 2012).

Furthermore, one of the main characteristics of the Internet-based technology is that it is founded on the democratization of knowledge, so it facilitates the appearance of natural flows of collaboration and knowledge, which, in turn, may favour creativity and innovation (Pérez-López & Alegre, 2012; Popa et al., 2016). In this sense, literature suggests that knowledge is an antecedent of innovation through organizational learning (Lopez-Nicolas & Soto-Acosta, 2010; Nonaka & Takeuchi, 1995; Templeton et al., 2002). Although there is research that has analyzed the relationship between KM and innovation (Darrow, 2005; López-Nicolás & Meroño-Cerdán, 2011), little is known about whether and how different factors promote or hinder Web 2.0 knowledge sharing and the effect of Web 2.0 knowledge sharing on innovation in SMEs. To delve into these questions, this paper develops an integrative conceptual model to assess the effect of different factors on Web 2.0 knowledge sharing and its effect on innovation in SMEs. In addition, this study analyzes whether Web 2.0 knowledge sharing mediates the relationship between commitment-based HR practices and innovation. With this aim in mind, the rest of our study is organized as follows. Next, the literature review and hypotheses are presented. Following that, the research methods drawing from a sample of 552 SMEs are described. Then, data analysis and results are examined and, finally, conclusions, limitations and future research guidelines are presented.

THEORETICAL BACKGROUND AND HYPOTHESES

Factors affecting Web 2.0 Knowledge Sharing

The Technology-Organization-Environment (TOE) theory conceptualizes the context of adoption and implementation of technological innovations as consisting of three aspects: technological context, organizational context and environmental context (Tornatzky & Fleischer, 1990). The technological context refers to the characteristics of the technological innovation, the organizational context describes characteristics of the organizations, and the environmental context implies characteristics of the environment in which the adopting organizations operate (Tornatzky & Fleischer, 1990; Thong, 1999). This framework has been considered in the literature as one of the main theoretical frameworks to analyze factors, which affect the adoption and use of different ITs including: electronic business (e.g. Bordonaba-Juste et al., 2012; Soto-Acosta et al, 2015; Xu et al., 2004), electronic collaboration (Chan et al., 2012), mobile commerce (San Martín et al., 2012), enterprise resource planning (Zhu et al., 2010), electronic data interchange (Kuan and Chau, 2001), and information and open systems (Chau & Tam, 1997; Thong, 1999). Also, very recent studies specific to the adoption and use of internet technologies have employed this theoretical approach (Bordonaba-Juste et al., 2012; Chan et al., 2012; Gu et al., 2012; Palacios-Marqués et al., 2015b; San Martín et al., 2012). Thus, drawing upon literature analyzing internet technologies adoption/use and the TOE theory, this paper proposes several hypotheses to investigate factors that influence Web 2.0 knowledge sharing in SMEs.

Web 2.0 knowledge sharing is expected to be influenced by firms' technology, since IT plays a pivotal role to support KM processes. Technology competence depends on tangible and intangibles resources, though the latter are more likely to generate competitive advantages (Bharadwaj, 2000; O'Sullivan & Dooley, 2010; Soto-Acosta & Meroño-Cerdan, 2008; Soto-Acosta et al., 2010a, 2010b). Tangible IT resources such as Information Systems integration have been found significant in studies using the TOE framework (e.g. Zhu et al., 2006Zhu and Kraemer, 2005). Information Systems integration in the e-business context is conceptualized as front-end integration and back-end integration (Zhu et al., 2004). Similarly, Information Systems integration may influence Web 2.0 knowledge sharing, since it enables efficient communication and collaboration. Regarding IT intangible resources, IT skills have been identified as one of the main factors that influence the level of e-business use (Bordonaba-Juste et al., 2012). Firms that have IT professionals are more likely to adopt IT innovations because they can better adapt IT applications to their organizations and develop their own specific ones (Lin & Lee, 2005). Therefore, information systems integration and IT expertise may be important technological issues to explain Web 2.0 knowledge sharing. The following hypotheses incorporate our expectations:

Hypothesis 1: Information Systems integration is positively associated with Web 2.0 knowledge sharing.
Hypothesis 2: IT expertise is positively associated with Web 2.0 knowledge sharing.

Beyond technological factors, the TOE framework has acknowledged the importance of organizational factors in influencing internet-based technologies adoption and use (Gu et al., 2012). Technology enablers are a necessary, but not a sufficient condition, for employees to collaborate and share knowledge. That is, although it is essential to develop interaction networks that allow individuals not only to access the same information but also to come together and collaborate through the network, knowledge creation and acquisition rarely occurs if individuals do not interact (Alavi & Leidner, 2001). Thus, building a positive social climate may be crucial to motivate employees to work together and share knowledge (Valkokari, 2012). This is even more crucial when sharing tacit knowledge, which requires more interaction between employees (Fox, 2000).The literature distinguishes between transaction-based HR practices, which focus on individual short-term exchange relationships, and commitment-based HR practices, which emphasize mutual long-term exchange relationships, suggesting that the latter may contribute to such a social climate (Tsui et al., 1995). In fact, Collis and Smith (2006) found that commitment-based HR practices influence positively knowledge exchange among workers by creating a positive social climate. Based on this discussion, the following hypothesis is proposed:

Hypothesis 3: Commitment-based HR practices are positively associated with Web 2.0 knowledge sharing.

The TOE framework considers the environmental context that influences the adoption and implementation of technological innovations. According to Thong (1999), competition is the business environment in which the business operates. Early studies on technology diffusion found that competition increases firms' incentives to adopt new technologies so as to remain competitive (Thong, 1999). Competition intensity is an important driver of internet technologies adoption (Chong et al., 2009; Wang et al., 2010; Zhu et al., 2003; Zhu et al., 2006). Studies have found that external pressure from customers and suppliers affect e-business adoption (Del Aguila & Padilla, 2008; Wang & Ahmed, 2009). However, research (e.g. Chan et al., 2012; Zhu et al., 2006) has also shown that competition may deter firms from using internet technologies, challenging the traditional wisdom about competition and innovation diffusion. Zhu et al. (2006) found a positive relationship between competition and e-business adoption, but a negative relationship between competition and the extent of e-business use. Similarly, Chang et al. (2012) found that competition intensity is negatively related to the extent of e-collaboration use in SMEs. Thus, internet technologies use is less tied to competition intensity than initially thought in both large and small businesses. Too much competitive pressure lead firms to change rapidly form one technology to another without sufficient time to infuse the technology into the company (Zhu et al., 2006). Porter's (1985) five forces refers to horizontal competition (threat of substitute products, the threat of existing rivals, and the threat of new entrants), and vertical competition (the bargaining power of suppliers and the bargaining power of customers). Thus, although competition encourage technology adoption, it is not necessarily good for technology use. This discussion leads to the following hypothesis regarding vertical competition and Web 2.0 knowledge sharing:

Hypothesis 4: Vertical competition from customers is negatively related to Web 2.0 knowledge sharing.
Hypothesis 5: Vertical competition from suppliers is negatively related to Web 2.0 knowledge sharing.

Web 2.0 Knowledge Sharing and Innovation: Direct and Mediated Associations

Knowledge has been recognized as the main driver of new products, services and processes (Choy et al., 2006; Lopez-Cabrales et al., 2009). However, the literature suggests that the ability to create new knowledge, which enables firms to innovate especially in dynamic environments, comes mostly from the collective ability of employees to share and combine knowledge (Nahapiet & Goshal, 1998). In this sense, there are a number of studies that suggest that knowledge sharing is an antecedent of innovation. For instance, Capon et al. (1992) found that encouraging scientific discussions enhances the firm ability to innovate. Other studies link knowledge sharing and innovation to inter-functional coordination and the use of networks (Darrow, 2005). Thus, since innovation largely depends on tacit knowledge, knowledge sharing is a major requisite for innovation (Nonaka, 1994).

Collaborative technologies and virtual spaces, where participants can share knowledge and information in real time, have been found to be positively related to innovation in SMEs (Meroño-Cerdán et al., 2008; Popa et al., 2016). Similarly, Web 2.0 technologies can be used to distribute and share individual experience and innovation throughout the organization and offer the chance of applying knowledge for the creation of new products and/or services or processes. These technologies facilitate the execution of the innovation process with users and partners from remote places. Thus, the benefits from Web 2.0 knowledge sharing, which include efficient information and knowledge sharing as well as working with no distance limitations, are expected to be positively related to innovation.

Social exchange theory argues that employees balance their level of commitment with the company's level of commitment to them (Blau, 1964; Wayne et al., 1997). Base on this, Eisenberger (2001) suggested that employees contribute to firm success in response to the rewards or care they receive from the organization. Commitment-based HR practices may be considered as kind of group incentives (Park & Kim, 2013; Peterson & Luthans, 2006). However, recent research found that HR practices are not directly related to innovation unless they take into consideration employees' knowledge (Lopez-Cabrales et al., 2009). Group-incentive improves employees' attitude toward organizational communication (Hanlon & Taylor, 1991). Thus, commitment-based HR practices may affect innovation positively through Web 2.0 knowledge sharing. In other words, commitment-based HR practices are expected to motivate employees to work together and share knowledge through social networks, such strong climate for cooperation and knowledge sharing is expected to contribute to innovation. Thus, the following hypotheses are suggested:

Hypothesis 6: Web 2.0 knowledge sharing is positively associated with organizational innovation.
Hypothesis 7: Web 2.0 knowledge sharing mediates the relationship between Commitment-based HR practices and organizational innovation.

The set of relationships is illustrated in Figure 1.

Figure 1. Knowledge Sharing Relationships

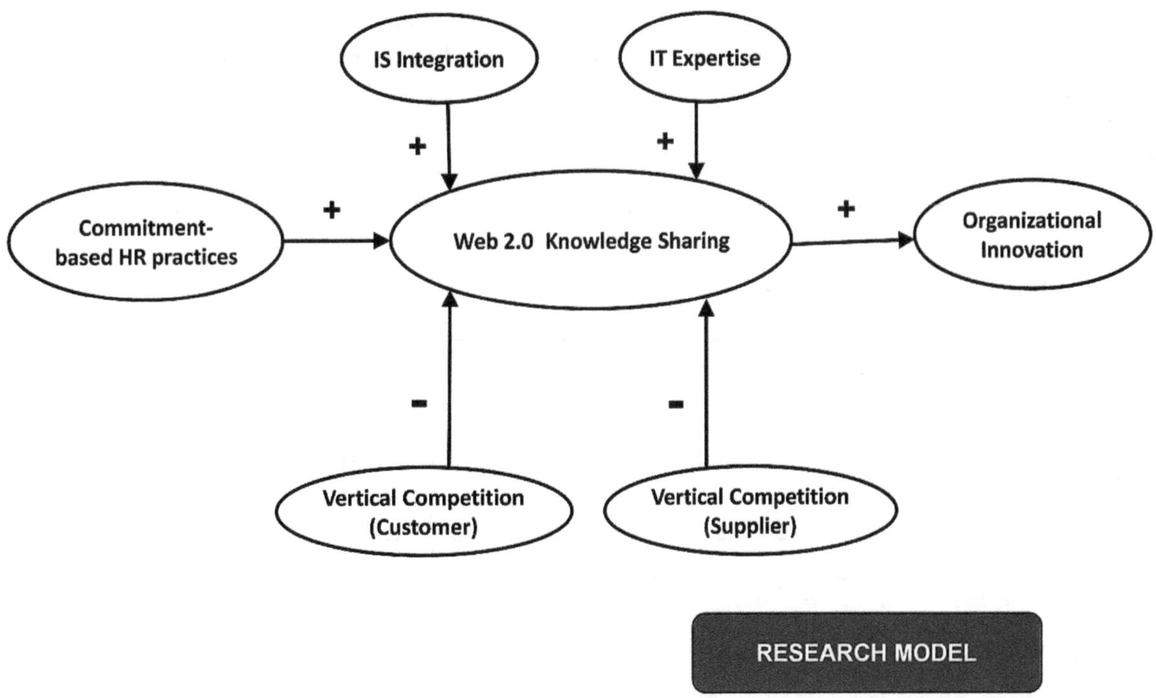

RESEARCH METHODOLOGY

Data Collection and Sample

The target population of our study are SMEs from Spain. Nonetheless, to ensure a minimum firm complexity in which ITs may be relevant, only firms with at least 15 employees were used. Data collection was conducted in two stages: a pilot study and a questionnaire were conducted. Five SMEs were randomly selected from a database to pretest the questionnaires. Based on these responses and subsequent interviews with participants in the pilot study, minor modifications were made to the questionnaire for the next phase of data collection. Responses from these five pilot-study firms were not included in the final sample.

The population considered in this study was the set of all Spanish enterprises, with at least 15 employees, located in the southeast of the country and which have their primary business activity in one of the following business activities: manufacturing, commercial, services and construction. A total of 2246 firms were identified and contacted for participation. The survey was administered to the CEO of the companies via personal interview and the unit of analysis for this study was the company. In total, 552 valid questionnaires were obtained, yielding a response rate of 24.6 percent. The dataset was examined for potential bias in terms of non-response by comparing the characteristics of early and late participants in the sample. These comparisons did not reveal significant differences in terms of general characteristic and model variables, suggesting that non-response did not cause any survey bias.

Common Method Variance

Most researchers agree that common method variance is a potentially serious bias threat in behavioural research, especially with single informant surveys. Several procedures were used to empirically determine whether or not common method bias threatened the interpretation of our results: a) the Harman one-factor test; and b) a confirmatory factor-analytic approach to Harman one-factor test; and c) the common latent factor approach.

The rationale for the first test is that, if common method bias poses a serious threat to the analysis and interpretation of the data, a single latent factor would account for all manifest variables or one general factor would account for the majority of the covariance among the measures. In our case, the one-factor

Table 1. Profile of respondents (N= 552)

Profile of Respondents	Percentage
Industry	
Manufacturing	32.06%
Commercial	25.00%
Services	19.38%
Construction	23.55%
Number of employees	
15-49	71.73%
50-249	28.27%

model obtained using principal components analysis revealed several factors in the unrotated factor solution. However, still other researchers using this technique have used confirmatory factor analysis (CFA) as a more sophisticated test. A worse fit for the one-factor model would suggest that common method variance does not pose a serious threat. The one-factor model yielded a $\chi 2 = 548.63$ with 65 degrees of freedom (compared with the $\chi 2 = 64.40$ with 55 degrees of freedom for the measurement model). However, there are several limitations for these procedures. Therefore, additional statistical remedies are recommended for this purpose. One approach is to use latent variable models (Podsakoff et al., 2003). This method involves adding a first-order factor to all of the measures, as indicators, to the researcher's theoretical model. The common latent factor approach yielded a $\chi 2 = 145.43$ with 55 degrees of freedom (compared to the $\chi 2 = 64.40$ with 55 degrees of freedom for the measurement model). The fit is considerably worse for the the common latent factor approach than for the measurement model, suggesting that common method bias is not a serious threat in our study.

Measures

Measurement items were introduced on the basis of a careful literature review. Confirmatory factor analysis (CFA) was used to test the constructs. Based on the CFA assessment, the measurement models were further refined and then fitted again. Constructs and associated indicators in the measurement model are listed in the Appendix and discussed below. To facilitate cumulative research, operationalizations tested by previous studies were used.Scales were measured on a 5-point Likert scale with anchors from strongly disagree (1) to strongly agree (5).

Several variables were operationalized as multi-item constructs. Information Systems Integration assessed the extent to which internal information systems and databases are connected, and the extent to which company information systems are linked to business partners' databases and systems. Items for technology integration are based on Zhu et al. (2006). *Commitment-based HR practices* were operationalized based on Collins and Smith (2006), Delery and Doty (1996) and Youndt et al. (1996). Overall, 8 items were adapted to measure Commitment-based HR practices: selection policies and training and development policies for long-term growth and team building. *Web 2.0 knowledge sharing* measured the extent of use of Web 2.0 technologies for sharing collective knowledge between employees. Web 2.0 knowledge sharing scale is based on Soto-Acosta and Meroño-Cerdan (2006) and Meroño-Cerdán et al. (2008). *Innovation* was measured following items in previous studies (Lee and Choi, 2003; López-Nicolás and Meroño-Cerdán, 2011; Soto-Acosta et al., 2014; Soto-Acosta et al., 2015) and represents new technological knowledge and ideas into new products and processes.

Other constructs were directly operationalized as observed variables. Based on previous IT literature, *IT expertise* was measured by the number of IT professionals (Bordonaba-Juste et al., 2012; Zhu and Kraemer, 2005; Zhu et al., 2004).*Vertical Competition* was measured following two of Porter's (1985) concepts of five competitive forces. Such operationalization has been previously used as well in the IT literature (Thong, 1999; Zhu et al., 2004).

Instrument Validation

The unidimensionality and reliability of the dataset was assessed by different procedures. First of all, an initial exploration of unidimensionality was done using principal component factor analyses. In each analysis, the eigen-values were greater than 1, lending preliminary support to a claim of unidimensionality in the constructs. Following that, CFA was performed via the EQS 6.2 statistical software to assess the unidimensionality of each construct. In this sense, construct reliability, convergent and discriminant validity were assessed. The measurement model presented a good fit to the data ($\chi 2$ (55)=64.40; CFI = 0.98; IFI = 0.98; GFI = 0.96; RMSEA = 0.033). All traditionally reported fit indexes were within the acceptable range. This study measures commitment-based HR practices as a single construct made up of two dimensions: commitment-based selection policies (CBSP) and commitment-based training and development policies (CBTDP). A second-order factor analysis demonstrated that the two dimensions reflect the higher-order construct ($\chi 2$ (3)= 6.701; CFI = 0.99; IFI = 0.99; GFI = 0.99; RMSEA = 0.04).

Construct reliability assesses the degree to which items are free from random error and, therefore, yield consistent results. This study calculated reliability of measures using Bagozzi and Yi's (1998) composite reliability index and Fornell and Larcker's (1981) average variance extracted index. For all the measures, both indices were higher than the evaluation criteria, namely 0.6 for composite reliability and 0.5 for the average variance extracted. Convergent validity assesses the consistency across multiple constructs. As shown in table 2, after dropping insignificant items, all estimated standard loadings are significant (p<0.01) and of acceptable magnitude, suggesting good convergent validity (Sethi & King, 1994).

To assess the discriminant validity–the extent to which different constructs diverge from one another– Forell and Larcker's (1981) criterion, that the square root of average variance extracted for each construct (diagonal elements of the correlation matrix in table 3) should be greater than the absolute value of inter-construct correlations (off-diagonal elements), was used. All constructs met this criterion,

Table 2. Measurement model: confirmatory analysis and scale reliability

Construct	Indicators	S. Loadings	Reliability
Information Systems integration	TI1	0.819[a]	CR = 0.78 AVE = 0.64
	TI2	0.782***	
IT expertise	ITP	*n/a*	*n/a*
CBSP	HR1	0.835[a]	CR = 0.82 AVE = 0.60
	HR2	0.720***	
CBTDP	HR3	0.789[a]	CR = 0.76 AVE = 0.61
	HR4	0.884***	
	HR5	0.640***	
Vertical Competition (Customer)	VCC	*n/a*	*n/a*
Vertical Competition (Supplier)	VCS	*n/a*	*n/a*
Web 2.0 Knowledge sharing	WKS1	0.852[a]	CR = 0.84 AVE = 0.63
	WKS2	0.775***	
	WKS3	0.753***	
Organizational Innovation	OI1	0.872[a]	CR = 0.84 AVE = 0.64
	OI2	0.815***	
	OI3	0.713***	

Fit statistics for measurement model: $X^2(55) = 64.40$; CFI = 0.98; IFI = 0.98; GFI = 0.96; RMSEA = 0.033.

[a]Fixed items in the scale; *** p<0.01; CR: Composite reliability; AVE: Average variance extracted; n/a. Loadings, CR and AVE are not applicable to single-item constructs.

suggesting that the items share more variance with their respective constructs than with other constructs. Table 3 also provides an overview of the means, standard deviations and correlations of the constructs.

EMPIRICAL RESULTS

This paper performs structural equation modelling (SEM) to test the hypotheses, using maximum likelihood estimation techniques to test the model. The fit of the structural model was satisfactory ($\chi2(89)$= 108.06; RMSEA=0.031; CFI=0.98 IFI=0.98 GFI=0.95), suggesting that the nomological network of relationships fits the data and the validity of the measurement scales (Churchill, 1979).This model is presented in Figure 2.

Figure 2 shows the standardized path coefficients with their respective significant levels. The relationship between information systems integration and Web 2.0 knowledge sharing was not statistically significant, indicating that information systems integration is not related to Web 2.0 knowledge sharing in SMEs. The relationship between IT expertise and Web 2.0 knowledge sharing was positive and statistically significant (0.10, $p<0.05$), this result show that hiring specialized IT personnel in the firm is an important factor for Web 2.0 knowledge sharing. The relationship between commitment-based HR practices and Web 2.0 knowledge sharing was positive and statistically significant (0.81, $p<0.01$), being commitment-based HR practices the strongest path in the proposed model. This indicates that the presence of commitment-based HR practices is a critical factor driving Web 2.0 knowledge sharing in SMEs. Regarding the relationship between vertical competition, only the relationship between vertical competition from customers and Web 2.0 knowledge sharing was found statistically significant (-0.21, $p<0.05$). In addition, results show that Web 2.0 knowledge sharing contributes positively to innovation (0.49, $p<0.01$). Finally, as presented in table 4, the indirect effect of commitment-based HR practices on innovation through Web 2.0 knowledge sharing was positive and significant (0.40, $p<0.01$), supporting the mediating effect of Web 2.0 knowledge sharing in the relationship between commitment-based

Table 3. Descriptive statistics and discriminant validity

Constructs	Av.	SD	Correlation Matrix							
			(1)	(2)	(3)	(4)	(5)	(6)	(7)	(8)
1. IS integration	3.07	1.31	**0.80**							
2. IT expertise	0.73	2.79	0.13*	*n/a*						
3. CBSP	3.38	1.05	0.11*	0.04	**0.78**					
4. CBTDP	3.26	0.91	0.35**	0.06	0.35***	**0.78**				
5. Vertical C. (C)	3.61	1.09	-0.08	-0.07	0.06	-0.03	*Na*			
6. Vertical C. (S)	3.03	1.08	0.10	-0.03	-0.04	0.08	0.24**	*n/a*		
7. Web 2.0 KS	2.94	1.29	0.07	0.12*	0.31**	0.28**	-0.15**	0.08	**0.80**	
8.Org. Innovation	3.20	0.92	0.08	0.18**	0.28**	0.23**	0.05	-0.03	0.31**	**0.80**

Significance levels: p<0.05; p<0.01***; n/a. Variance extracted is not applicable to the single-item constructs.
Diagonal values in bold represent the square root of the AVE

Figure 2. Nomological network of relationships

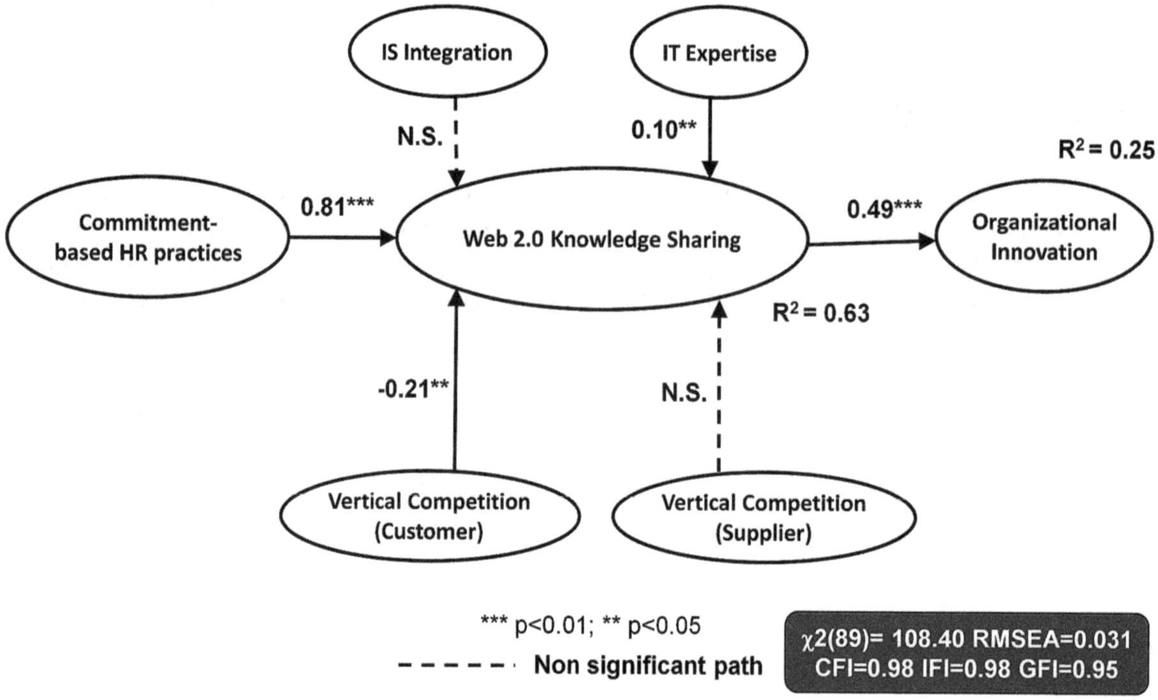

Table 4. Direct and indirect effects

Direct Effect	
C-B HR practices Web 2.0 KS	0.81***
Web 2.0 KS Innovation	0.49**
Indirect Effect	
C-B HR practices Innovation	0.40***

Note: p<0.01***

HR practices and innovation. Implications of these results are discussed in the next section. Through this analysis, this study found support for hypotheses H2, H3, H4, H6 and H7, whereas it did not find support for hypotheses H1 and H5.

DISCUSSION

The empirical results have shown that factors have different effects on Web 2.0 knowledge sharing. Within the technological context, results found that though IT expertise is positively associated with Web 2.0 knowledge sharing, while a non-significant relationship was found for the relationship between technology integration and Web 2.0 knowledge sharing. The first finding confirms recent research (Bordonaba-Juste et al., 2012), which found that IT expertise is one of the main factors that affect the extent of e-business use. However, the second finding counters existing research analyzing internet technologies (e.g. Zhu et al., 2006, Zhu and Kraemer, 2005), which found that technology integration is positively related to the extent of e-business use (Zhu et al., 2006) and positively associated to e-business value (Zhu and Kraemer, 2005). A possible explanation to this can be that previous studies have focused on aggregate measures of the organizational adoption and use of internet technologies and, within that context, tangible IT assets such as technology integration may be more crucial. In contrast, within the specific context of SMEs and Web 2.0 knowledge sharing, intangible IT resources (Bharadwaj, 2000; O'Sullivan and Dooley, 2010; Soto-Acosta et al., 2010a) such as hiring specialized IT personnel seem to be the major technological drivers of knowledge sharing. These results support the idea that IT per se does not create value, because every firm can purchase IT in the marketplace. Rather, IT value creation depends more on intangible IT assets (Soto-Acosta and Meroño-Cerdan, 2008). For instance, Soto-Acosta et al. (2010b) found that intangible IT resources such as IT skills and IT training are critical determinants of how IT is deployed in the organization, which, in turn, affect business value.

Within the organizational context, the effect of commitment-based HR practices on Web 2.0 knowledge sharing is analyzed. Results showed a positive relationship between these two constructs, being commitment-based HR practices the strongest factor in our proposed model. This finding supports previous studies (Collins and Smith, 2006) which, though not focusing on internet technologies, found that commitment-based HR practices were significantly related to knowledge exchange among workers, while, in addition, Gardner (2012) found that performance pressure undermines knowledge sharing. Thus, SMEs should focus on commitment-based HR practices, rather than on transaction-based HR practices, in order to create a social climate, which promotes Web 2.0 knowledge sharing. Results regarding factors from the environmental context suggest a negative relationship between customer power and Web 2.0 knowledge sharing and a non-significant relationship between supplier power and Web 2.0 knowledge sharing. These findings partially support recent research (Chan et al., 2012; Zhu et al., 2006), which found that competition may deter firms from using internet technologies. Thus, although external pressure from customers and suppliers affect e-business adoption (Del Aguila & Padilla, 2008; Wang and Ahmed, 2009), competition is not necessarily good for technology use. Too much competitive pressure lead firms to change rapidly form one technology to another without sufficient time to use the technology (Zhu et al., 2004; Zhu et al., 2006). Our findings also confirm previous research using SMEs. In this sense, Chang et al. (2012) found that competition intensity is negatively related to the extent of e-collaboration use in SMEs. Thus, this finding demonstrates that Web 2.0 knowledge sharing emerges from internal organizational and technological resources rather than from external pressure.

Furthermore, results suggest a positive relationship between Web 2.0 knowledge sharing and innovation. These findings support previous research suggesting that knowledge sharing is an antecedent of innovation (e.g. Capon et al., 1992; Griffin & Hauster, 1996) as well as studies suggesting that internet technologies uses (including knowledge sharing) are related to innovation (Meroño-Cerdán et al., 2008). Therefore, although the literature suggests that innovation cannot be easily split into separate phases or stages and innovation does not neatly proceed in a linear fashion (Anderson et al., 2004), the characteristics of Web 2.0 knowledge sharing make it suitable to enhance efficient information and knowledge sharing, which, in turn, leads to higher innovation outcomes. In addition, results support the mediating effect of Web 2.0 knowledge sharing in the relationship between commitment-based HR practices and innovation. This finding confirms previous research, which found that HR practices are not directly related to innovation unless they take into consideration employees' knowledge (Lopez-Cabrales et al., 2009). Thus, commitment-based HR practices are expected to motivate employees to work together and share knowledge through social networks, such strong climate for cooperation and knowledge sharing is expected to contribute to innovation. Thus, commitment-based HR practices are expected to motivate employees to work together and share knowledge through social networks and such strong climate for cooperation and knowledge sharing is expected to contribute, by extension, to innovation.

CONCLUSION, LIMITATIONS AND FUTURE RESEARCH

The literature considers KM as a set of practices including knowledge acquisition/creation, knowledge dissemination, and knowledge utilization (Darroch, 2003; Jayasingam et al., 2012; Tiwana, 2003). These practices share the use of knowledge as the crucial factor to add and generate value (Alavi & Leidner, 2001; Pérez-López & Alegre, 2012). However, to transfer or create knowledge, interaction of some kind has to take place between the actors. In this sense, knowledge sharing has been considered as essential to achieve the desired outcomes of KM practices (Valkokari, 2012). Thus, it is believed that organizations' survival and success depend on the effort and interactions of employees as they carry the skills and generate knowledge to transform new ideas into innovations. Today, firms are using Web 2.0 technologies in order to enhance knowledge sharing and collaboration (Sigala & Chalkiti, 2014). Thus, it is becoming essential for firms to assimilate Web 2.0 technologies to support information and knowledge sharing within firms. Although previous studies have advanced our understanding of the subject, the literature tend to focus in large businesses, with very few and recent studies analyzing SMEs (Chang et al., 2012). This study shed lights on the factors that affect Web 2.0 knowledge sharing and its effect on innovation in SMEs. The study also investigates whether Web 2.0 knowledge sharing mediates the relationship between HR practices and innovation. Results suggest that organizational factors–commitment-based HR practices- are the main drivers of Web 2.0 knowledge sharing and that it mediates the relationship between HR practices and innovation in SMEs. These findings suggest that firms must pay attention to different factors in order to enhance Web 2.0 knowledge sharing and that commitment-based HR practices create a context that enhances Web 2.0 knowledge sharing which, in turn, leads to new knowledge and innovation.

As any other research, the present study suffers from some limitations, which can be addressed in future research. First, the sample used was from Spain. It may be possible that the findings could be extrapolated to other countries, since economic and technological development in Spain is similar to other OECD Member countries (Meroño & Soto-Acosta, 2005). However, in future research, a sampling frame that combines firms from different countries could be used in order to provide a more international perspective on the subject. Second, developing solid instruments in the IT literature is still an ongoing procedure of development, testing and refinement (Zhu et al., 2004; Zhu et al., 2006). Although reliability and validity were empirically tested in our data set, further confirmatory studies are necessary to determine the external validity of the results. Particularly, as discussed in the hypotheses section, competition constructs in our study capture vertical competition, which needs to be enriched in further research to include horizontal competition. Future research designs could consider other important organizational context factors such as organizational strategy and culture. Third, this research takes a static, cross-sectional picture of contextual factors affecting Web 2.0 knowledge sharing, which makes it difficult to address the issue of how contextual factors and their importance may change over years. A longitudinal study could enrich the findings. These suggestions should be taken into account in future studies to increase the validity of our findings.

REFERENCES

Alavi, M., & Leidner, D. E. (2001). Review: knowledge management and knowledge management systems: conceptual foundations and research issues. *Management Information Systems Quarterly*, *25*(1), 107–136. doi:10.2307/3250961

Anderson, N. R., De Dreu, C., & Nijstad, B. A. (2004). The routinization of innovation research: A constructively critical review of the state-of-the-science. *Journal of Organizational Behavior*, *25*(2), 147–203. doi:10.1002/job.236

Bagozzi, R. P., & Yi, Y. (1998). On evaluation of structural equations models. *Journal of the Academy of Marketing Science*, *16*(1), 74–94. doi:10.1007/BF02723327

Bhagwat, R., & Sharma, M. K. (2007). Information system architecture: A framework for a cluster of small- and medium-sized enterprises (SMEs). *Production Planning and Control*, *18*(4), 283–296. doi:10.1080/09537280701248578

Bharadwaj, A. S. (2000). A resource-based perspective on information technology capability and firm performance: An empirical investigation. *Management Information Systems Quarterly*, *24*(1), 169–196. doi:10.2307/3250983

Bhatt, G. D., & Grover, V. (2005). Types of information technology capabilities and their role in competitive advantage: An empirical study. *Journal of Management Information Systems*, *22*(2), 253–277.

Bordonaba-Juste, V., Lucia-Palacios, L., & Polo-Redondo, Y. (2012). Antecedents and consequences of e-business use for European retailers. *Internet Research*, *22*(5), 532–550. doi:10.1108/10662241211271536

Brown, J. S., & Duguid, P. (2000). Balancing act: How to capture knowledge without killing it. *Harvard Business Review*, *78*(3), 73–80.

Capon, N., Farley, J. U., Hulbert, J., & Lehmann, D. R. (1992). Profiles of product innovators among large US manufacturers. *Management Science*, *38*(2), 157–169. doi:10.1287/mnsc.38.2.157

Chan, F. T. S., & Chong, A. Y.-L. (2012). An empirical investigation of factors affecting e-collaboration diffusion in SMEs. *International Journal of Production Economics*, *138*(2), 329–344. doi:10.1016/j.ijpe.2012.04.004

Chau, P. Y. K., & Tam, K. Y. (1997). Factors affecting the adoption of open systems: An exploratory study. *Management Information Systems Quarterly*, *21*(1), 1–25. doi:10.2307/249740

Chong, A. Y. L., & Chan, F. T. S. (2012). Radio Frequency Identification (RFID) in the healthcare industry: A multi-stage diffusion analysis. *Expert Systems with Applications*, *39*(10), 8645–8654. doi:10.1016/j.eswa.2012.01.201

Choy, C. S., Yew, W. K., & Lin, B. (2006). Criteria for measuring KM performance outcomes in organisations. *Industrial Management & Data Systems*, *106*(7), 917–936. doi:10.1108/02635570610688850

Churchill, G. A. (1979). A paradigm for developing better measures of marketing constructs. *JMR, Journal of Marketing Research*, *16*(1), 64–73. doi:10.2307/3150876

Collins, C. J., & Smith, K. G. (2006). Knowledge exchange and combination: The role of human resource practices in the performance of high-technology firms. *Academy of Management Journal*, *49*(3), 544–560. doi:10.5465/AMJ.2006.21794671

Darroch, J. (2003). Developing a measure of knowledge management behaviors and practices. *Journal of Knowledge Management*, *7*(5), 41–54. doi:10.1108/13673270310505377

Darroch, J. (2005). Knowledge management, innovation and firm performance. *Journal of Knowledge Management*, *9*(3), 101–115. doi:10.1108/13673270510602809

Del Aguila-Obra, A., & Padilla-Melendez, A. (2008). Organizational factors affecting Internet technology adoption. *Internet Research*, *16*(1), 94–110. doi:10.1108/10662240610642569

Delery, J. E., & Doty, D. H. (1996). Modes of theorizing in strategic human resource management: Test of universalistic contingency, and configurational performance predictions. *Academy of Management Journal*, *39*(4), 802–835. doi:10.2307/256713

Devaraj, S., & Kholi, R. (2003). Performance impacts of information technology: Is actual usage the missing link? *Management Science*, *49*(3), 273–289. doi:10.1287/mnsc.49.3.273.12736

Dholokia, R. R., & Kshetri, N. (2004). Factors impacting the adoption of the internet among SMEs. *Small Business Economics*, *23*(4), 311–322. doi:10.1023/B:SBEJ.0000032036.90353.1f

Eisenberger, R., Armeli, S., Rexwinkel, B., Lynch, P. D., & Roades, L. (2001). Reciprocation of perceived organizational support. *The Journal of Applied Psychology*, *86*(1), 42–51. doi:10.1037/0021-9010.86.1.42

Fornell, C., & Larcker, F. D. (1981). Evaluating structural equation models with unobservable variables and measurement error. *JMR, Journal of Marketing Research*, *18*(1), 39–50. doi:10.2307/3151312

Fox, S. (2000). Communities of practice, foucault and actor network theory. *Journal of Management Studies*, *37*(6), 853–867. doi:10.1111/1467-6486.00207

Gardner, H. K. (2012). Performance pressure as a double-edged sword: Enhancing team motivation but undermining the use of team knowledge. *Administrative Science Quarterly*, *57*(1), 1–46. doi:10.1177/0001839212446454

Gibbs, J. L., & Kraemer, K. L. (2004). A cross-country investigation of the determinants of scope of e-commerce use: An institutional approach. *Electronic Markets*, *14*(2), 124–137. doi:10.1080/10196780410001675077

Griffin, A., & Hauser, J. R. (1996). Integrating R&D and marketing: A review and analysis of the literature. *Journal of Product Innovation Management*, *13*(3), 191–215. doi:10.1111/1540-5885.1330191

Gu, V. C., Cao, Q., & Duan, W. (2012). Unified Modeling Language (UML) IT adoption— A holistic model of organizational capabilities perspective. *Decision Support Systems*, *54*(1), 257–269. doi:10.1016/j.dss.2012.05.034

Hanlon, S. C., & Taylor, R. R. (1991). An examination of changes in work group communication behaviors following installation of a gain sharing plan. *Group and Organization Studies*, *16*(3), 238–267. doi:10.1177/105960119101600302

Hong, W., & Zhu, K. (2006). Migrating to Internet-based e-commerce: Factors affecting e-commerce adoption and migration at the firm level. *Information & Management*, *43*(2), 204–221. doi:10.1016/j.im.2005.06.003

Huy, L. V., Rowe, F., Truex, D., & Huynh, M. Q. (2012). An empirical study of determinants of e-commerce adoption in SMEs in Vietnam an economy in transition. *Journal of Global Information Management*, *20*(3), 23–54. doi:10.4018/jgim.2012070102

Jayasingam, S., Ansari, M. A., Ramayah, T., & Jantan, M. (2013). Knowledge management practices and performance: Are they truly linked? *Knowledge Management Research & Practice*, *11*(3), 255–264. doi:10.1057/kmrp.2012.5

Joo, J., & Normatov, I. (2013). Determinants of collective intelligence quality: Comparison between Wiki and Q&A services in English and Korean users. *Service Business*, *7*(4), 687–711. doi:10.1007/s11628-013-0183-0

Kuan, K. Y., & Chau, Y. K. (2001). A perception model for EDI adoption in small businesses using a technology-organization-environment framework. *Information & Management*, *38*(1), 507–521. doi:10.1016/S0378-7206(01)00073-8

Lee, H., & Choi, B. (2003). Knowledge management enablers, processes, and organizational performance: An integrative view and empirical examination. *Journal of Management Information Systems*, *20*(1), 179–228.

Levy, M. (2009). Web 2.0 implications on knowledge management. *Journal of Knowledge Management*, *13*(1), 120–134. doi:10.1108/13673270910931215

Lim, S., Trimi, S., & Lee, H. (2010). Web 2.0 service adoption and entrepreneurial orientation. *Service Business*, *4*(3-4), 197–207. doi:10.1007/s11628-010-0097-z

Lopez-Cabrales, A., Pérez-Luño, A., & Cabrera, R. V. (2009). Knowledge as a mediator between HRM practices and innovative activity. *Human Resource Management*, *48*(4), 485–503. doi:10.1002/hrm.20295

López-Nicolás, C., & Meroño-Cerdán, A. L. (2011). Strategic knowledge management, innovation and performance. *International Journal of Information Management*, *31*(6), 502–509. doi:10.1016/j.ijinfomgt.2011.02.003

Lopez-Nicolas, C., & Soto-Acosta, P. (2010). Analyzing ICT adoption and use effects on knowledge creation: An empirical investigation in SMEs. *International Journal of Information Management*, *30*(6), 521–528. doi:10.1016/j.ijinfomgt.2010.03.004

Meroño-Cerdan, A., & Soto-Acosta, P. (2005). Examining e-Business impact on firm performance through website analysis. *International Journal of Electronic Business*, *3*(6), 583–598. doi:10.1504/IJEB.2005.008537

Meroño-Cerdan, A., Soto-Acosta, P., & Lopez-Nicolas, C. (2008). How do collaborative technologies affect innovation in SMEs? *International Journal of e-Collaboration*, *4*(4), 33–50. doi:10.4018/jec.2008100103

Nahapiet, J., & Ghoshal, S. (1998). Social capital, intellectual capital, and the organizational advantage. *Academy of Management Review*, *23*(2), 242–266.

Nonaka, I. (1994). A dynamic theory of organizational knowledge creation. *Organization Science*, *5*(1), 14–37. doi:10.1287/orsc.5.1.14

Nonaka, I., & Takeuchi, H. (1995). *The knowledge-creating company: how Japanese companies create the dynamics of innovation*. New York: Oxford University Press.

O'Sullivan, D., & Dooley, L. (2010). Collaborative innovation for the management of information technology resources. *International Journal of Human Capital and Information Technology Professionals*, *1*(1), 16–30. doi:10.4018/jhcitp.2010091102

Palacios-Marqués, D., Merigó, J. M., & Soto-Acosta, P. (2015a). Online social networks as an enabler of innovation in organizations. *Management Decision*, *53*(9), 1906–1920. doi:10.1108/MD-06-2014-0406

Palacios-Marqués, D., Soto-Acosta, P., & Merigó, J. M. (2015b). Analyzing the effects of technological, organizational and competition factors on web knowledge exchange in SMEs. *Telematics and Informatics*, *32*(1), 23–32. doi:10.1016/j.tele.2014.08.003

Park, R., & Kim, J. (2013). Individual employees' responses to group incentives: The moderating role of innovation. *Journal of Business and Psychology*, *28*(2), 175–187. doi:10.1007/s10869-012-9270-9

Pérez-López, S., & Alegre, J. (2012). Information technology competency, knowledge processes and firm performance. *Industrial Management & Data Systems*, *112*(4), 644–662. doi:10.1108/02635571211225521

Peterson, S. J., & Luthans, F. (2006). The impact of financial and nonfinancial incentives on business-unit outcomes over time. *The Journal of Applied Psychology*, *91*(1), 156–165. doi:10.1037/0021-9010.91.1.156

Podsakoff, P. M., Mackenzie, S. B., Lee, J., & Podsakoff, N. P. (2003). Common method biases in behavioral research: A critical review of the literature and recommended remedies. *The Journal of Applied Psychology*, *20*(5), 879–903. doi:10.1037/0021-9010.88.5.879

Popa, S., Soto-Acosta, P., & Loukis, E. (2016). Analyzing the complementarity of web infrastructure and eInnovation for business value generation. *Program*, *50*(1), 118–134. doi:10.1108/PROG-09-2015-0065

Porter, M. E. (1985). *Competitive Advantage*. New York: Free Press.

San Martín, S., López-Catalán, B., & Ramón-Jerónimo, M. A. (2012). Factors determining firms' perceived performance of mobile commerce. *Industrial Management & Data Systems*, *112*(6), 946–963. doi:10.1108/02635571211238536

Sethi, V., & King, W. (1994). Development of Measures to Assess the Extent to Which an Information Technology Application provides Competitive Advantage. *Management Science*, *40*(12), 1601–1627. doi:10.1287/mnsc.40.12.1601

Sigala, M., & Chalkiti, K. (2013). Investigating the exploitation of web 2.0 for knowledge management in the Greek tourism industry: An utilisation–importance analysis. *Computers in Human Behavior*, *30*(1), 800–812.

Soto-Acosta, P., Casado-Lumbreras, C., & Cabezas-Isla, F. (2010a). Shaping human capital in software development teams. The case of mentoring enabled by semantics. *IET Software*, *4*(6), 445–452. doi:10.1049/iet-sen.2010.0087

Soto-Acosta, P., Colomo-Palacios, R., & Popa, S. (2014). Web knowledge sharing and its effect on innovation: An empirical investigation in SMEs. *Knowledge Management Research & Practice*, *12*(1), 103–113. doi:10.1057/kmrp.2013.31

Soto-Acosta, P., Martinez-Conesa, I., & Colomo-Palacios, R. (2010b). An empirical analysis of the relationship between IT training sources and IT value. *Information Systems Management*, *27*(3), 274–283. doi:10.1080/10580530.2010.493847

Soto-Acosta, P., & Meroño-Cerdan, A. (2006). An analysis and comparison of web development between local governments and SMEs in Spain. *International Journal of Electronic Business*, *4*(2), 191–203. doi:10.1504/IJEB.2006.009790

Soto-Acosta, P., & Meroño-Cerdan, A. (2008). Analyzing e-Business value creation from a resource-based perspective. *International Journal of Information Management*, *28*(1), 49–60. doi:10.1016/j.ijinfomgt.2007.05.001

Soto-Acosta, P., Popa, S., & Palacios-Marqués, D. (2015). *E-business, organizational innovation and firm performance in manufacturing SMEs: An empirical study in Spain*. Technological and Economic Development of Economy;

Templeton, G. F., Lewis, B. R., & Snyder, C. A. (2002). Development of a measure for the organizational learning construct. *Journal of Management Information Systems*, *19*(2), 175–218.

Thong, J. Y. L. (1999). An integrated model of information systems adoption in small businesses. *Journal of Management Information Systems*, *15*(4), 187–214. doi:10.1080/07421222.1999.11518227

Tiwana, A. (2003). *The knowledge management toolkit: orchestrating it, strategy and knowledge platform*. Upper Saddle River, NJ: Prentice Hall.

Tornatzky, L. G., & Fleischer, M. (1990). *The process of technological innovation. Lexington. MA*. Lexington: Lexington Books.

Tsui, A. S., Pearce, J. L., Porter, L. W., & Tripoli, A. M. (1997). Alternative approaches to the employee-organization relationship: Does investment in employees pay off? *Academy of Management Journal*, *40*(5), 1089–1121. doi:10.2307/256928

Valkokari, K., Paasi, J., & Rantala, T. (2012). Managing Knowledge within networked Innovation. *Knowledge Management Research & Practice*, *10*(1), 27–40. doi:10.1057/kmrp.2011.39

Wang, Y., & Ahmed, P. (2009). The moderating effect of the business strategic orientation on e-commerce adoption: Evidence from UK family run SMEs. *The Journal of Strategic Information Systems*, *18*(1), 16–30. doi:10.1016/j.jsis.2008.11.001

Wang, Y. M., Wang, Y. S., & Yang, Y. F. (2010). Understanding the determinants of RFID adoption in the manufacturing industry. *Technological Forecasting and Social Change*, *77*(5), 803–815. doi:10.1016/j.techfore.2010.03.006

Wayne, S. J., Shore, L. M., & Liden, R. C. (1997). Perceived organizational support and leader-member exchange: A social exchange perspective. *Academy of Management Journal*, *40*(1), 82–111. doi:10.2307/257021

Xin, J. Y., Ramayah, T., Soto-Acosta, P., Popa, S., & Ping, T. A. (2014). Analyzing the use of the Web 2.0 for brand awareness and competitive advantage: An empirical study in the Malaysian hospitability industry. *Information Systems Management*, *31*(2), 96–103. doi:10.1080/10580530.2014.890425

Xu, S., Zhu, K., & Gibbs, J. (2004). Global technology, local adoption: A cross-country investigation of Internet adoption by companies in the United States and China. *Electronic Markets*, *14*(1), 13–24. doi:10.1080/1019678042000175261

Youndt, M. A., Snell, S. A., Dean, J. W. Jr, & Lepak, D. P. (1996). Human resource management, manufacturing strategy and firm performance. *Academy of Management Journal*, *39*(4), 836–866. doi:10.2307/256714

Zhu, K., & Kraemer, K. (2005). Post-adoption variations in usage and value of e-business by organizations: Cross-country evidence from the retail industry. *Information Systems Research*, *16*(1), 61–84. doi:10.1287/isre.1050.0045

Zhu, K., Kraemer, K., & Xu, S. (2003). Electronic business adoption by European firms: A cross-country assessment of the facilitators and inhibitors. *European Journal of Information Systems*, *12*(4), 251–268. doi:10.1057/palgrave.ejis.3000475

Zhu, K., Kraemer, K. L., & Xu, S. (2006). The process of innovation assimilation by firms in different countries: A technology diffusion perspective on e-business. *Management Science*, *52*(10), 1557–1576. doi:10.1287/mnsc.1050.0487

Zhu, K., Kraemer, K. L., Xu, S., & Dedrick, J. (2004). Information technology payoff in e-business environments: An international perspective on value creation of e-business in the financial services industry. *Journal of Management Information Systems*, *21*(1), 17–54.

Zhu, Y., Li, Y., Wang, W., & Chen, J. (2010). What leads to the post-implementation success of erp? An empirical study of the Chinese retail industry. *International Journal of Information Management*, *30*(3), 265–276. doi:10.1016/j.ijinfomgt.2009.09.007

KEY TERMS AND DEFINITIONS

B2B: Business to business. Commercial transactions between businesses conducted over IP (internet protocol).

E-Marketplace: A B2B Internet trading forum in which multiple buyers and sellers exchange goods and services within an industry group or geographic region.

Extranet: A private, secure extension of the intranet running on Internet protocol that allows selected external users to access some parts of an organisation's intranet.

Innovation: New knowledge and ideas transformed into new products and/or services, new technologies, new processes and new organizational forms or structures.

Internet: Relates to Internet Protocol based networks: www, extranet over the internet, EDI over the internet, internet-enabled mobile phones.

Intranet: An internal company network using Internet protocol to enable communications within an organization.

Knowledge Management: A set of practices including knowledge acquisition/creation, knowledge dissemination, and knowledge utilization.

Supply Chain Management: An internet-based software solution that supports the management of logistics and inventory along the entire value chain and connects business partners.

Web 2.0: An Internet-based digital platform that enables the creation of social networks.

APPENDIX

Measures

Information Systems Integration

- Extent to which internal enterprise information systems and databases are integrated (1-5)
- Extent to which enterprise information systems and databases are integrated to that of business partners (clients, suppliers...) (1-5)

IT Expertise

- Number of IT professionals (#)

Commitment-Based HR Practices

- Our selection system focuses on the potential of the candidate to learn and grow (1-5)
- Internal candidates are considered over external candidates for job openings (1-5)
- Selection processes are formalized and rigorous (1-5)
- Our company provides career path opportunities (1-5)
- Our company support employees willing to take further training (1-5)
- Promotion is based on objective criteria (seniority, objectives.) (1-5)
- Performance appraisals are used to plan skill development and training (1-5)
- Job rotation is used to expand the skills of employees and team building

Vertical Competition (Customers and Suppliers)

- Pressure clients exert on purchasing conditions (1-5)
- Pressure suppliers exert on purchasing conditions (1-5)

Web 2.0 Knowledge Sharing

- Extent to which the employees participate in organizational electronic discussion forums (1-5)
- Extent to which Web 2.0 technologies are used for building collective knowledge (1-5)
- Extent to which the employees upload information on organizational social networks or wikis (1-5)

Organizational Innovation

- The number of new or improved products/services launched to the market is above the average of your industry (1-5)

- The number of new or improved processes is above the average of your industry (1-5)
- Changes introduced in products and services during the last five years are very important (1-5)

Note. (1-5): five-point Likert scales; (#): continuous variable.

Chapter 12
We Need to Look Cute! But Is It Really Effective?
The Adoption of Culture in Twitter by a Japanese CVS

Caroline S.L. Tan
University of Tsukuba, Japan

ABSTRACT

This chapter examines how Lawson, a convenience store chain in Japan has taken a different approach in utilizing Twitter. This chapter begins with the background of the retail sector in Japan, specifically the convenience store industry as well as a brief description of cute culture. The key elements of Lawson's Twitter account are explored accordingly. Using elements from Esch, Langner, Schimitt & Geus' (2006) general model of branding components and relationship to micro blogging, a study was conducted to examine the current and future purchase intentions. While social media proved to help differentiate Lawson from its competitors, it was not the main factor in generating brand loyalty. The findings show that not all followers displayed purchase intentions. The results also identified a gap between the perceptions of Lawson's Twitter account versus the overall corporate brand. This provides the foundation for further research activities in developing more effective methods of maximizing Twitter in enhancing customer experience and subsequently increasing brand equity and loyalty.

INTRODUCTION

The ubiquity and influence of social media today has changed the landscape of communication and businesses. The retail sector that had undergone changes from the birth of the internet and e-commerce now embraces further technological innovation with social media where the exchange of information is easily made globally and in real time. Today with just a tweet consumers are able to influence and affect each other's purchase behaviors as well as company's reputation, image and even brand equity. While social media is used by many businesses, the increase in the variety and number of micro blogging sites has led to a saturation, which ultimately becomes 'noise' to the consumers as they are constantly

DOI: 10.4018/978-1-5225-0332-3.ch012

bombarded with messages. This presents the need for businesses to constantly come up with strategies to stay relevant and differentiate themselves, yet at the same time keep things novel and fresh. While at the same time, this increases the need for research focusing on exploring models and core elements that ensures effective utilization of SNS.

This chapter takes a look at the micro blogging strategy that is adopted by one of the top three convenience stores in Japan. While the strategy adopted clearly sets it apart from that of its competitors, the extent of effectiveness of the social media account in shaping purchase behavior provides the backdrop of this chapter. Using Esch, Langner, Schimitt and Geus' (2006) general model of branding components and relationship to micro blogging, a study was conducted to examine the current and future purchase intentions of Twitter users with regards to Lawson.

This chapter also serves to provide a snapshot of how a convenience store chain has taken a different approach in utilizing Twitter in capturing different market segments and at the same time establishing a presence in the social media world. This chapter also looks at showcasing how a Japanese convenience retailer is different in terms of their strategy in managing customer relationship and customer engagement. While most convenience retailers abroad merely focus on push strategy promotions via micro blogs, Japanese convenience retailers look to creating a comprehensive shopping experience incorporating cultural marketing.

First, the chapter starts with an introduction of the convenience store retail industry and background in Japan followed by a brief explanation on cute culture. The approaches undertaken by Lawson as the number two convenience store chain in Japan, in its expansion of value-added services particularly with the utilization of Twitter in brand building and enhancing customer experience are then addressed accordingly. Lawson incorporated popular culture in the management of its social media account in differentiating itself. A brief explanation of the popular culture adopted by Lawson is given, namely cute culture and its place within the Japanese society.

While convenience stores in Japan are turning to Twitter in gaining differentiation, and building their brand image, the perception of the customers is pertinent to determine if such an initiative is indeed bearing fruit. To explore this aspect, a small-scale study was undertaken to explore the customers' purchase drivers, and the extent of influence and role Twitter plays in shaping their decisions. The findings show that while customers to a certain extent find the use of SNS helpful, there was a gap in the perception of the social media accounts especially Twitter versus the overall corporate brand where the social media accounts proved to have established a brand of its own away from the convenience store itself. While social media proved to help differentiate Lawson from its competitors, it was not the main factor in generating brand loyalty. The study basically serves as a preliminary study to uncover the direction of future research.

CONVENIENCE STORE RETAIL INDUSTY BACKGROUND

The retail landscape in Japan has been undergoing major changes such as mergers between major departments stores and continual growth in luxury goods consumption (Japan retail market, 2014; Japanese department store rivals merge, 2007). In terms of retail channels, convenience stores have been enjoying a steady growth in revenue and store expansion since 2003, outperforming department stores and supermarkets while department stores have been experiencing a decline (Savilis World Research, 2014).

The vast arrays of products and services that are offered by convenience stores have propelled steady consumption that continuously boosts strong sales.

Japan is experiencing changes in its demographics, where this island nation is witnessing smaller household sizes and an aging population, convenience stores have focused on product and service diversification that target these market segments, such as community services, utility bill payments and pre-cooked packaged foods in different portion offerings. Focus on women and Generation M has also led to diversification of products such as desserts and even the opening of convenience stores in residential areas that have close proximity to the customers' homes (Japan retail foods, 2013; Japan retail market, 2014). Major convenience stores have also been actively engaged in strategic partnerships in order to strengthen their presence and business, for example 7-Eleven partnered with Japan Rail West to convert subsidiary retail spaces to 7-Eleven outlets (Convenience stores turning to the elderly, 2014; Japan retail market, 2014).

There are more than 50,000 convenience stores all over Japan as of March 2014 with 7-Eleven having the largest number of stores with 16,086 outlets and Lawson coming in second with 11,653 (Japan Franchise Association, 2015; Konbini, 2014). An extensive network in both cities and the rural areas contribute to sales growth and brand recognition and strength.

The convenience store was first introduced in 1927 in the United States and it took nearly four decades to make its way to Japanese soil in 1964 (Chiao, Chou, Lu & Liu, 2011). Initially convenience stores were merely operating from 7am to 11pm, hence the name 7-Eleven however, as the value derived from this retail business model proved to be indispensable to consumers the business hours changed to 24-hours from 1963 (Sparks, 2000). While the concept of convenience has been found to change over time (Shove, 2002), this change is also reflected in the taste, preference and expectations of customers towards convenience stores. Today in Japan, customers do not only expect convenience stores to be a one-stop center for consumer goods but also a place where convenience carries a broader meaning to include services that are supported by technology. Based on a survey conducted by Nifty (2013), more than 10% of the 4,880 respondents go to the convenience store everyday while a 21% of the respondents indicated that they frequent convenience stores around 2-3 times per week. This was followed by 20% that stated that they patronize convenience stores once a week.

The convenience store plays an extremely vital role in Japan's society. It is more than just a place to buy food, medicine, toiletries and stationary. Japanese convenience stores offer a wide range of services such as utility bill payments and tax payments. Tickets to concerts, games and even the museums can easily be purchased at selected convenience stores. The convenience stores also accept pre-payments for online purchases from different merchants such as Amazon. Mobile payment, or m-payments in Japan using cellphones, called *'osaifukeitai'* which literally means wallet cell phone was introduced in 2004 (Vodafone Global Enterprise, 2013). This created a new method of paying for purchases made at the convenience store where customers just scan their cellphones at the cash counter. Apart from these services, the convenience stores are equipped with automated teller machines, or ATMs where customers can perform deposits, withdrawals and money transfers. Harden (2008) states that," At FamilyMart, customers can make appointments for someone to vacuum their home. At 7-Eleven (now run by a Japanese-owned company), there's a drop-off laundry service. . . Nearly any bill in Japan -- utility, phone, cable or tax -- can be paid at a convenience store. About $80 billion worth were paid that way last year." The growing vast array of services that are offered are also a boon to the elderly as they 'assist' the elderly in providing them a one stop center, in the form of the convenience store that caters to all their daily needs be it paying of bills and purchasing of consumables. The breadth of products and services offered coupled by the technology provides a smooth and seamless experience to the customer.

Kumamoto (2012) and Sakaguchi (2008) found that convenience stores also offer the 'convenience of shelter and safety' for those in need of help and 'potential' victims of crimes. Sakaguchi (2008) listed that in 2007, about 6,000 children who were lost took shelter and sought for help from convenience stores while approximately 13,000 women sought refuge at convenience stores from stalkers and other criminals. Clearly, value of the convenience store extends beyond retail.

Japan sits on the Pacific Ring of Fire hence it is a nation that experiences earthquakes and seismic shifts often. The last major earthquake that struck Tohoku region on March 11, 2011 claimed 15,884 lives as of February 10, 2014 (CNN, 2014). Convenience stores have always been helping in times of crisis. Harden (2008) highlighted that convenience stores let government agencies take advantage of their ubiquity for the delivery of water and other supplies in emergencies. Apart from providing their store premises as a base for delivering of emergency supplies, convenience stores also play an active role in contributing to the daily provisions required by victims of such natural disasters and crisis. Seven &i Holdings, the parent company of 7-Eleven Japan delivered 30,000 two-liter bottles of mineral water and 1,000 sweet bread rolls to the disaster headquarters in Miyagi (Public Relations Office Government of Japan, 2011). Many chains such as Family Mart launched mobile convenience shops in the form of trucks that delivered food, beverages, and household commodities to the worst-hit areas, where access to basic and daily necessities were limited (Aviles, 2011).

The changes and expansion in both, the role of and services offered by the convenience store, showcase how Japanese convenience retailers are different in terms of their strategy in managing customer relationship and developing loyalty as well as increasing customer purchase. While most convenience retailers abroad merely focus on push strategy promotions, Japanese convenience retailers look to creating a comprehensive shopping experience bordering on lifestyle marketing.

LAWSON CONVENIENCE STORE

The origin of the company dates back to 1939 in the United States where it was a milk store hence the company logo features milk can against a blue background. While the company did not start as a convenience store, the business model shifted after it became an affiliate of Consolidated Foods Inc. in 1959 where it established its convenience store business. Lawson introduced various products and services such as home deliveries in 1982 followed by copying and printing services a year later, in 1983.Lawson continued to expand its services and in 1998, it introduced 'Loppi' (derived from 'Lawson's Online Shopping'), a multimedia terminal where customers are able to perform various transactions such as shopping and making travel arrangements to payments at their fingertips.

Lawson strengthened its CSR efforts in 2009 when it decided to take the first step in addressing the issue of sustainability by replacing 10% of the company's commercial vehicles with electric cars with Mitsubishi's iMiEV (EV World, 2008; O'Dell, 2009). The decision to make a public statement through corporate vehicle choices enhanced Lawson's image and brand value, while at the same time it demonstrated consistency with the company's mission of creating happiness and harmony in the communities.

In July 2001, Lawson took a creative approach in creating brand extension and changing the landscape of the convenience store industry by opening the first of many Natural Lawson convenience stores. The concept was basically tailored for the female consumer market where the emphasis of the brand was for females who embrace a comfortable life of beauty and health. Subsequently in May 2005, Lawson opened its first 'Lawson Store 100' with the concept of a supermarket, convenience store and 100-yen store merged into one store. In July 2010, Lawson launched another private label line called Lawson Select, targeted at working women and the elderly who do not have the time or energy to patron local supermarkets that is located further away from their homes versus the convenience store.

Japan is faced with an aging population. As of October 2013, people age 65 or older makes up about a quarter of the population (Reynolds, 2014). Based on a report that was compiled with the cooperation of the government, by 2060 approximately 40% of Japan's population would be 65 or older, and the population would shrink about 30% versus that of 2010 (Japan Times, 2014; The Economist, 2014). This has led retailers to look at ways to capture the elderly segment and to meet the demands of these customers. This has contributed to the growth of internet Supermarkets or widely known as online 'Net super' in Japan. Internet supermarkets have been gaining popularity among housewives in the 30s and 40s, as they opt to make purchases online instead of going to the brick and mortar stores (Nakata, 2011). With the growing popularity of internet supermarkets, Lawson launched the 'Radish Lawson Supermarket' service in October 2011, with customers being able to access the online supermarket from November 11, 2011.

In retail, from established department stores such as Macy's to home products such as Ikea, most companies have embraced social media as part of a necessary marketing tool. Convenience stores, for instance 7-eleven, are not left behind and have also jumped on the social media bandwagon. While convenience stores essentially promise convenience, in Japan convenience stores have redefined the meaning of convenience, offering a plethora of products and services ranging from fresh sushi, concert tickets to paying income taxes (Harden, 2008). Lawson, the second largest convenience store chain in Japan with more than 10,000 shops in Japan and more than 400 in China and Indonesia as well as the US (Jitpleecheep, 2012; Kyodo, 2012; Tong, 2012; Uyeno, 2012) has taken a different approach in managing its Twitter account. Unlike their competitors, namely 7-Eleven, FamilyMart and MiniStop, Lawson has integrated cute culture in differentiating its Twitter account and creating a character that has since inception seen an increase in terms of number of characters introduced thus cultivating social groups.

LAWSON AND TWITTER

Social media plays a vital role in the daily lives of many globally including Japan where Twitter and Line seem to enjoy immense popularity (Yarow, 2012; Sakawee, 2014). Convenience stores have embraced social media with each chain having their presence on Twitter and Facebook. In terms of revenue, 7-Eleven claims the top spot followed by Lawson, Family Mart, and Circle K Sunkus respectively (Garbage News, 2014). The social media adoption of the top four players from the respective company website as of October 2014 shows that Facebook and Twitter are the most common services where posts and tweets about the latest products and promotions are being made on a regular basis. While the contents are similar to that of other retail brands such as Starbucks and Seijoishii (a supermarket chain) that feature their new products and promotions as well as seasonal goods via their social media accounts, Lawson took a more creative way of utilizing the different social media services.

Twitter is one of the main micro blogging sites that have taken the world by storm. While Facebook initially struggled to take off in Japan, Twitter proved to be an instant success due to culture and the different needs of the Japanese users (Beck, 2013). Twitter has been acknowledged as an essential business tool in customer engagement as celebrities and businesses alike utilize it to communicate with their customers and also to build their brands. As tweets are real time, this gives a closer sense of connection as followers feel that they have a 'personal' connection with the people, company or brand that they are following. While businesses look to micro blogging to build their brands and market share, one interesting fact is that on a global level not a single retail company is listed in the top 100 most followed Twitter accounts (Twitaholic, 2015). However, in Japan as of August, 2014, the convenience store 7-Eleven Japan ranks 19 and has amassed more than 1.5 million followers while its competitor Lawson sits at number 67 with 826,288 followers (Meyou, 2015).

As companies turn to Twitter in order to expand their market, various strategies are formulated in order to attain differentiation and attract as well as retain followers. The individuals who use twitter to stay in touch and communicate with friends or 'followers' and get real time information and news, are less inclined to follow companies and businesses or even brands, based on the top 200 Twitterholics based on followers. Celebrities, entertainers and sports stars clearly dominate the rankings. While Comcast and BestBuy used a real person rather than a logo to front their Twitter pages, BestBuy did not manage their tweets well as they were too formal unlike Comcast at @comcastcares (Comm& Robbins, 2010). The standard advice given to corporations wanting to successfully manage their Twitter accounts is to be human and this goes beyond having a human face to front the page, corporations need to tweet in a less formal and more 'human' tone in order to establish a relationship with their followers (Comm& Robbins, 2010; Kabani, 2012; Kerpen, 2011; Scott, 2011).

Lawson Japan is no stranger to the social media realm as it has various social media accounts ranging from Mixi to Line.Even though they are the second largest convenience store in Japan, the number of their Twitter account followers surpasses that of their main rivals by nearly five fold (as of August 2015) as illustrated in Table 1.

Lawson approaches its Twitter account from a different perspective as opposed to its rivals. 7-Eleven tweets about new products as well as promotions. This basically involves sending out straightforward tweets informing its followers about new offerings and selections as well as promotion announcements. On the other hand, Lawson takes the approach of creating a character and putting a face to their social media accounts. What Lawson has done is basically it introduced a character and subsequently crafted a story and the background setting. This can be seen as a move to humanize Twitter (as has been done by JetBlue and Dell in the past; however, in both JetBlue and Dell's cases they did not create any characters), while at the same time it is a means to build a specific brand image in reaching out to specific customer segments, as characters are important and the creation is key in the success of most brands in Japan.

Lawson's Characters

Japan is known as the Country of Cute where cute is ubiquitously found in decorations and illustrations (Bremner, 2002; Craft, 2005; Craig, 2000; Schilling, 1997; Yano, 2000). According to a survey done by

Table 1. Top three convenience stores' Twitter information

Ranking	Store	Joined Twitter	No. of Followers (as of July 31, 2014)
1	7-Eleven	11 April 2012	1.52M
2	Lawson	1 April 2010	823,000
3	FamilyMart	1 Dec 2009	409,000

CREA in 1992, *'kawaii'* or cute is the most habitually and widely used in modern day Japan (CREA, November 1992, p. 58, quoted in Kinsella, 1995). There are various elements that embody the definition of cute such as naiveté and neediness (Harris, 2001; Lebra, 1984; Masabuchi, 1994; McVeigh, 2000; Merish, 1996; West, 2008; Yano, 2004). Among the famous Japanese characters that embody the essence of cute ranges from Pikachu to Doraemon, the well-loved robot cat from the future. Popular cute culture icon, Hello Kitty is also another epitome of cuteness and has fans both locally as well as overseas (Belson & Bremmer, 2003). The appeal of cuteness has witnessed the success of characters in terms of sales of goods and brand equity. As of 2008, Hello Kitty alone has contributed to half of Sanrio's $1billion turnover (Walker, 2008) while in 2012 Kumamon, a mascot character created by the local government of Kumamoto prefecture generated a total of US$ 285 million in revenue from the sales of its goods (Otagaki, 2013).

Cute or '*kawaii*' culture has dictated the demand for goods and services; leading to the rise of 'maid cafes' and concepts such as grotesque cute and increasing Japan's soft power (NBC News, 2006; Nye, 2006; Sugawa, 2000). There are unwritten rules of how to dress, carry oneself and behave; body gestures and the like that would qualify and determine if a person is cute. These 'rules' are religiously adhered to by, both women and men in their efforts to be seen as cute. Aside from clothing and displayed behavior, mascots and characters are key in embodying cute culture (Drake, 2001; Kato, 2002; Mead, 2002; Roach, 1999). Characters and mascots have become the face of various companies where they are believed to enhance the sales of products and services, even politicians and local governments are also using mascots (Hughes, 2010; Kyodo News, 2012; Otagaki, 2013; Suzuki, 2012; Torres, 2012).

As characters are dominant in Japanese cute culture, Lawson created the main character named Akiko, fondly referred to as Akiko-chan who works at the convenience store. She is introduced as a college sophomore working part-time at the convenience store. The key reason that Akiko applied for a part-time job at Lawson is said to be due to the fact that she adores the uniform (cerulean blue and white stripped shirt). She is painted as personable, cheerful and chatty. Her tweets are made to sound cute and chirpy. Akiko-chan also provides daily horoscope to those who tweet her as well as advice and information on a range of topics from cooking to music and even hairstyles. Akiko-chan is also the face of the other Lawson social media websites. When Lawson first launched its Twitter account, Akiko-chan was the only person introduced. As followers grew, Lawson introduced Akiko-chan's brother as well as her extended family, for instance cousin, and friends and coworkers. Lawson has also created different groups of friends for Akiko, be it friends from university as well as people whom she befriended while on holiday. Each character's information is also provided, for instance, where Akiko-chan met her friends and their hobbies. Followers are introduced to the other characters and their backgrounds as this adds more depth to the characters where followers can empathize with the characters. Figure 1 and Figure 2 illustrate the growth in network that Akiko-chan currently has from July 2014 to August 2015.

Natural Lawson has also introduced a character named Misato and while she does not have a twitter account at the time of writing, she has a Facebook account and she has also been included in Akiko's network on the upper left as illustrated in Figure 2 further establishing Akiko's position as the central figure and the face of Lawson. Misato has not been heavily featured and she is not prevalent in Natural Lawson stores as well since Natural Lawson is merely a sub-brand of Lawson. The characters and their backgrounds make them human-like, especially since they interact with each other and form relationships. Akiko also tweets other characters from other companies like Sanrio and follows them as well on Twitter. She even has a comic strip that shares Akiko's experiences working at Lawson that is featured on the corporate website under Lawson's Social Media. In past comic strips she was featured praising

Figure 1. Akiko's network as of July 2014 (www.lawson.co.jp, 2014)
Source: www.lawson.co.jp, 2014

her new coworker, a part-timer who happened to be Slime from Dragon Quest (Loo, E., 2012). This brought Akiko attention as fans of Dragon Quest took notice of the 'collaboration' which incidentally caught everyone by surprise to see the character Slime working in Lawson. Akiko's world maybe a virtual one but she has connections to the 'It' people or characters from the manga and gaming world. Such collaborations are undertaken with the aim of garnering followers and hopefully loyal customers from those who are into gaming, anime and manga.

As cute culture is an extremely popular sub-culture in Japan, it alone has led to the birth of various products, concepts and even vocabulary. The number of character goods that are available in shops is astounding especially in the heart of the electric district in Tokyo known as Akihabara. For anime and manga, similarly characters and character goods dominate the scene. Apart from characters, music is also heavily influenced by cute culture. Various pop groups such as AKB48 have dominated the Japanese music scene while in the virtual world some manga and anime characters are also portrayed as singers or members of bands and pop groups with an actual legion of fans and followers. For the past few years, signing characters voiced by a synthesizer has gained immense popularity. This character is known as a Vocaloid. Yamaha developed vocaloid, which is a singing voice synthesizer. The boom in vocaloid has also led Lawson to develop a new character in order to attract more customers. The surge in vocaloid popularity was mainly due to Hatsune Miku, a female character with long light teal hair and

Figure 2. Akiko's network as of August 2015 (www.lawson.co.jp, 2015)
Source: www.lawson.co.jp, 2015

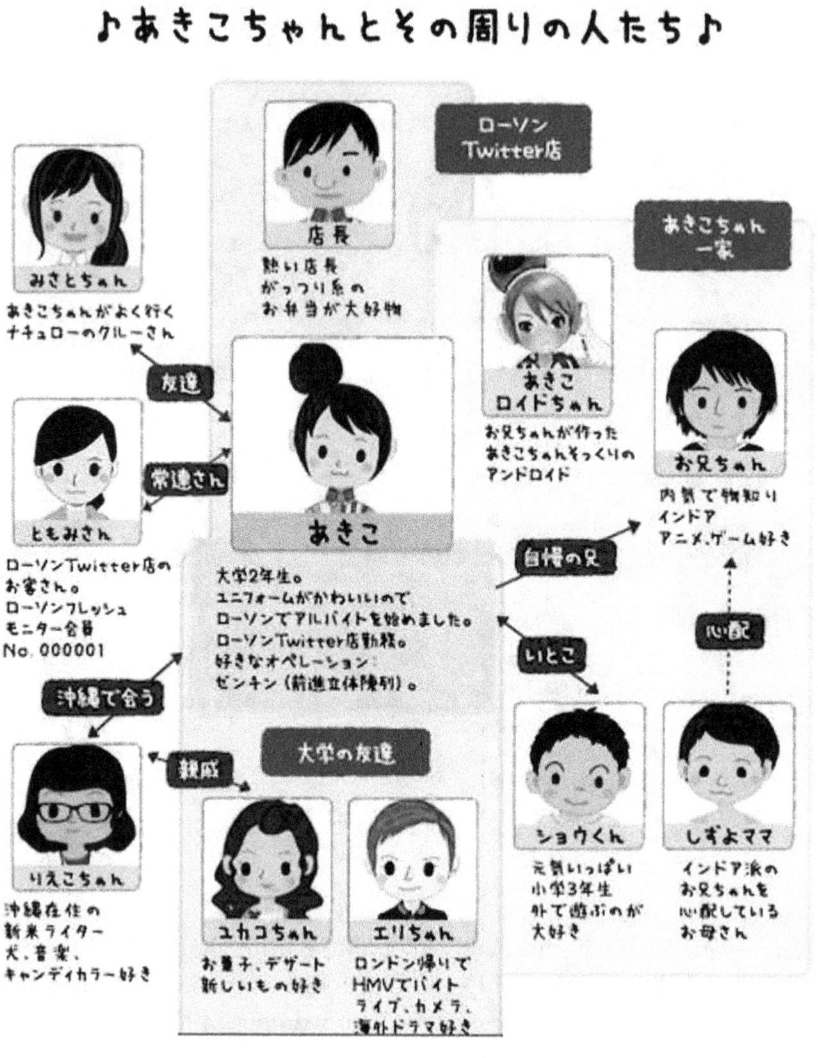

voiced by the synthesizer thus she is known as a 'vocaloid'. Lawson decided to unveil a vocaloid version of Akiko-chan named Akikoroid where a contest was held to find the 'raw voice' of Akikoroid (before programming the raw voice using the vocaloid). Followers are now introduced to this vocaloid named Akikoroid-chan. The surge in vocaloid popularity in Japan is undeniable as Hatsune Miku has staged sold out concerts and has also performed overseas recently. Akikoroid-chan introduces the followers to music and video as well as Lawson channel. She has also recorded and released her own music.

Human Like Traits

Akiko-chan and her extended social circles have been given human-like traits. Their backgrounds, hobbies and in the case of Akikoroid-chan the story of how she was made gives the followers not only a deeper understanding of each character but also help forge bonds with them too. When Akiko's character was formed, Lawson decided to let the public help choose her face as well as her voice, which in turn contributed to her popularity (The Asahi Shimbun, 2011). While the focus of the other convenience stores is providing information about the products, Akiko-chan and her team share other kinds of information such as entertainment and beauty that is indirectly linked to the store's products or services. Auditions were also carried out to find the voice for Akiko-chan where followers were given the chance to give their feedback on the voice and the search process was shared with the followers. The selected voice was generally reviewed as cute by the followers further substantiating the role of cute culture in humanizing the Twitter character.

Another important character in Akiko's world is her brother. While Akiko works part-time and has a growing social circle, her brother has been given a completely opposite character. He is a self-professed geek who likes games and anime. He is supposed to be the brains behind creating Akikoroid. He doesn't like going out and prefers to stay indoors, at home. He is the brainy one and is reputed to know many things but he is shy and finds it difficult to talk to people. Finally, he is known as the Einstein of Otaku (otaku is a Japanese word used to refer to geek or someone who has obsessive interests). As the otaku culture is the main culture in the Akihabara district, Akiko's brother is aimed at gaining the empathy and penetrating this particular target segment.

Tweeting and Blogging Style

In terms of tweeting style, Akiko-chan's tweets as well as the writing style of the blogs are made in an informal tone. Followers are made to feel as if they are reading tweets and the blogs of college students, whom they can relate to or resemble that of their friends. The language used in the tweets and blogs is very casual making it sound as if the characters are 'talking' to their friends and peers. Japanese language has different sets of words and expressions that must be used in formal situations and are completely different from those used when communicating with friends and family. Lawson has opted to use the latter instead of the former and that has appealed more to the customers and followers. While Akiko maintains the twitter account and tweets on a daily basis, her brother is in charge of blogging. He also keeps a very casual, friendly tone when he blogs. Both tweeting and blogging are presented in a convivial tone and create the atmosphere where followers would feel like they are really friends.

Contents

The tweets that Akiko sends out are usually about the promotions that are being and will be held in the Lawson stores. She also attaches pictures of products such as that of the luscious foods and tweets about the information of both product and promotion. On top of that, coupons and discounts are also given on Twitter. Lawson collaborates with various parties such as Final Fantasy and Nintendo as well as celebrities such as Big Bang. The information of the new products or concerts is also tweeted.

While Akiko manages the sharing of information about promotions and products, her brother on the other hand blogs about product rankings and news about products. As he manages the blog, he is able to write longer pieces about promotions and provide more information. He also poses questions and asks followers to provide their feedback about the products offered by Lawson, including the products that are developed by Lawson. Not only does this help with engagement with the customers, Lawson is also able to mine data from the customers and understand customer preferences better in order to make better product development decisions.

Lifestyle

While Akiko-chan and her friends, family and coworkers have shared their background and stories, Lawson goes further in humanizing their social media by incorporating other areas of interests such as music and movies as well as videos. The characters recommend music and videos as well as movies. As entertainment is an important aspect of our daily lives, leveraging on the followers' interests creates more value for Lawson's Twitter as well as other social media accounts. The characters not only talk about upcoming movies and albums but Akikoroid-chan also releases singles and music videos as well as collaborates with singers such as Chatmonchy, a Japanese female rock band. Akiko-chan has also crossed over to the gaming world as she befriended Lightning in 2013 to promote Final Fantasy XIII and Slime from Dragon Quest X (Loo, E., 2012; http://twitter.com/akiko_lawson). The merging of various characters further adds a surreal dimension to the characters.

Study

Businesses today are faced with the challenges of a volatile marketplace and extremely stiff competition. To remain competitive, organizations have to develop new strategies while incorporating new technology and accommodating shifts in consumer behavior. As consumers form relationships with brands, not products and corporations, it is pertinent that brands establish relationships with consumers in order to gain loyalty and brand equity (Decker, 1998; Gobe, 2001; Lindstrom, 2005). Emotional branding brings a new layer of credibility and personality to a brand by connecting powerfully with people on a personal and holistic level (Gobe, 2001). Feelings and emotions evoked are the basis in creating successful, smashing brands.

Conceptualizing a brand through personalization has become a very powerful way to build brand identity (Gobe, 2001; Schmitt, 1999). This has propelled the importance of word of mouth and to a greater degree today, electronic word of mouth or eWOM. Research has proven that word of mouth (WOM) has significant influences on the purchases of products and services by customers, new as well as repeat (Engel, Blackwell & Kegerreis, 1969; Katz & Lazarsfeld, 1955; Richins & Root-Shaffer, 1988). Micro blogging plays an important role in this aspect as it has a direct influence on brand image, perception, brand awareness and satisfaction (Brown, Barry, Dacin & Gunst, 2005; Jansen, Zhang & Sobel, 2009; Reynolds, 2006; Urban, 2005). Esch, Langner, Schmitt & Geus (2006) shows the relationship and effects on branding from eWOM microblogs as illustrated in Figure 3. Esch et al. (2006) found that micro blogging has a significant influence on brand knowledge and is linked to brand relationship.

Figure 3 illustrates how purchase behavior is shaped by the influence of micro blogging in both brand knowledge and brand relationship. Brand knowledge can, either directly influence behavioural outcome or it can affect brand relationship that in turn shapes behavioural outcome. In this study, the first path is examined; namely brand knowledge and the effects on current or future purchases.

Based on the first path, the study was conducted to test the following hypotheses:

H0: Brand image leads to current purchase.
H1: Brand awareness leads to current purchase.

Figure 3. General model of branding components and relationship to micro blogging
Note: From 'Are brands forever? How brand knowledge and relationships affect current and future purchases.' By Esch, Langner, Schmitt & Geus, 2006, Journal of Product & Brand Management, 15(2), p. 101.

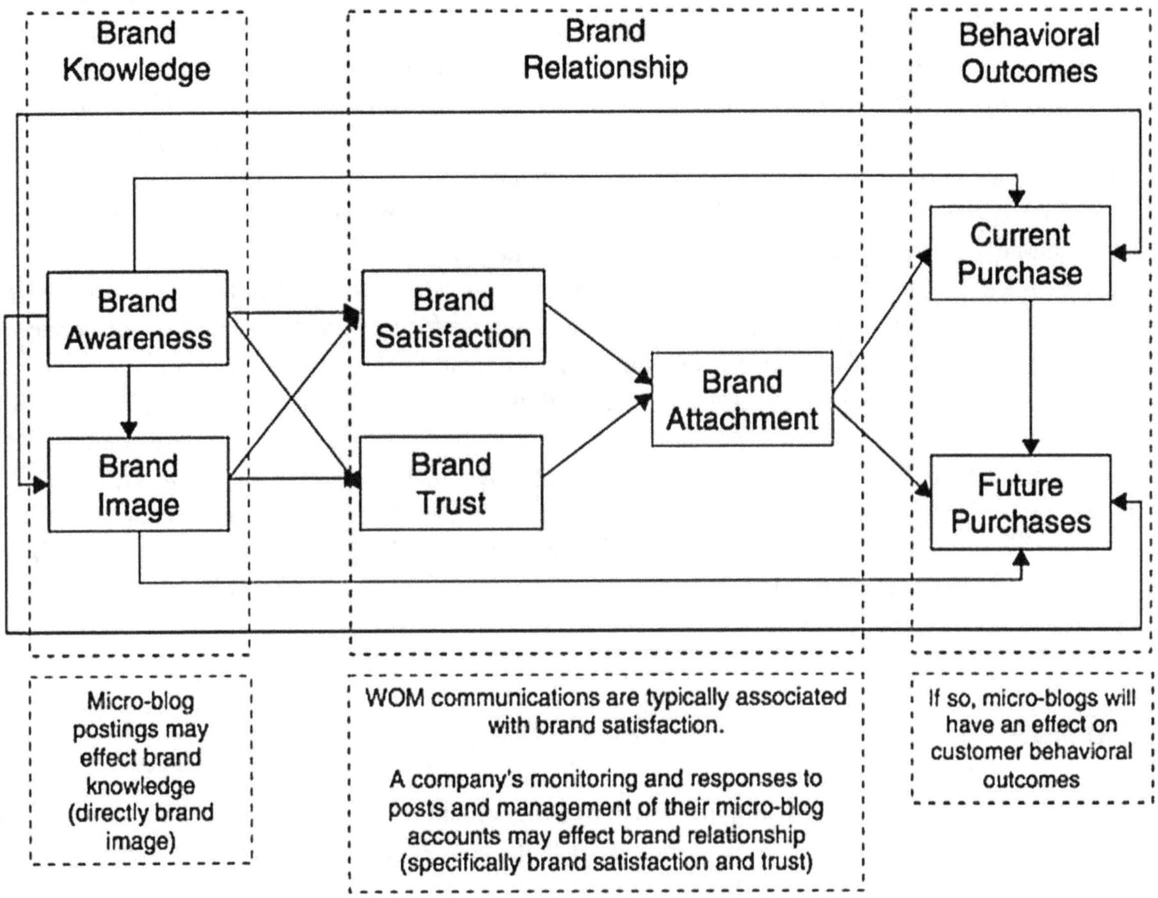

H2: Brand awareness leads to future purchase.
H3: Customers who purchase because of Twitter will continue to make future purchases.
H4: Customers who purchase based on Twitter develop a positive impression.
H5: Brand image and impression will drive future purchase behavior.
H6: Cute culture is successfully incorporated in Lawson's Twitter.

A pilot study was conducted with a total number of 120 self-administered questionnaires being distributed with a response rate of 64.2%. The respondents were asked to provide their opinions using a 5-point Likert scale on their convenience store patronage as well as SNS usage. The first part of the questionnaire basically gathered the demographic information such as gender and age group. The age group segregation was done based more on the purchase power; for instance lower purchase power category that covered college students and those younger such as teenagers and tweens. Various key areas were addressed in the questionnaire with one of the core areas exploring the reasons that drove the choice of convenience store chain selection (including and excluding close proximity as a choice) as well as the extent of information about products and promotions obtained from various channels such as Twitter, flyers and TV commercials.

Respondents were also asked about their purchase choices, covering core areas such as the drivers behind the purchases and response to promotions from various sources. Apart from purchase, the questionnaire also addressed reasons for following the social media accounts of convenience stores. Respondents were asked to provide their thoughts on Lawson's Akiko chan and her network. Understanding the perception and decision-making drivers of customers were paired alongside comprehending the role and influence of social media in shaping customers' preferences and actions. Another area of importance was to uncover the extent of success Lawson has in its approach in managing its social media accounts. The questionnaire also explored the current and future purchase choices.

Open-ended questions using word association, where respondents were asked to indicate two words that come to mind when they see pictures of the different convenience stores, provided the respondents the ability to share their different perception and opinions about the brands respectively.

The data from the questionnaire was then analyzed using descriptive statistics, and Spearman Correlation accordingly. As ordinal data was used in the study, both the median and interquartile range (IQR) values were the main focus for interpretation, with the median reflecting what the average respondents might think or the likeliest response, while the IQR shows the dispersion of the responses. Spearman correlation was used to test the statistically significance relationship between responses to two Likert scale questions. For the open-ended questions descriptive statistics was used to reflect the frequency and percentages.

FINDINGS

Table 2 lists the median and IQR for purchase due to trigger and information from the various sources such as Twitter, and Facebook. Basically, the respondents' answers reflected that when it came to pur-

Table 2. Descriptive Statistics for Purchase

			Statistic	Std. Error
Purchase Due to Twitter Promo	Mean		2.40	.135
	95% Confidence Interval for Mean	Lower Bound	2.13	
		Upper Bound	2.67	
	5% Trimmed Mean		2.34	
	Median		2.00	
	Variance		1.402	
	Std. Deviation		1.184	
	Minimum		1	
	Maximum		5	
	Range		4	
	Interquartile Range		2	
	Skewness		.483	.274
	Kurtosis		-.673	.541

continued on following page

Table 2. Continued

			Statistic	Std. Error
Purchase Due to FB Promo	Mean		1.78	0.79
	95% Confidence Interval for Mean	Lower Bound Upper Bound	1.78	
			2.09	
	5% Trimmed Mean		1.93	
	Median		2.00	
	Variance		.483	
	Std. Deviation		.695	
	Minimum		1	
	Maximum		3	
	Range		2	
	Interquartile Range		1	
	Skewness		.087	2.74
	Kurtosis		-.882	.541
Purchase Due to TV Ad	Mean		2.81	.100
	95% Confidence Interval for Mean	Lower Bound Upper Bound	2.61	
			3.00	
	5% Trimmed Mean		2.82	
	Median		3.00	
	Variance		.764	
	Std. Deviation		.874	
	Minimum		1	
	Maximum		5	
	Range		4	
	Interquartile Range		1	
	Skewness		-.212	2.71
	Kurtosis		-.111	.541
Purchase Due to Flyer	Mean		2.34	.099
	95% Confidence Interval for Mean	Lower Bound Upper Bound	2.14	
			2.53	
	5% Trimmed Mean		2.29	
	Median		2.00	
	Variance		.753	
	Std. Deviation		.868	
	Minimum		1	
	Maximum		5	
	Range		4	
	Interquartile Range		1	
	Skewness		.642	.274
	Kurtosis		.994	.541

chases made at the convenience store, most of them often made purchases triggered by the promotions on Twitter, Facebook and Flyers. This is based on the Likert-scale where 1 indicates Never, 2 reflects Rarely, 3 indicates Sometimes, 4 indicates Often and 5 reflects Always.

Table 3 shows the descriptive statistics for the question that looks at the reasons the respondents follow the social media accounts of convenience stores. The Likert scale was used wherein 1 represents Strongly Agree, 2 indicates Agree, 3 refers to Neither Agree Nor Disagree, 4 reflects Disagree and 5 represents Strongly Disagree. As demonstrated from the median value on an average, respondents tend to follow social media accounts to get product information (shown by the median of 2 which indicates agree). However, obtaining product news does not guarantee purchase as demonstrated by the results reflecting the following of social media is driven by the want to make purchases from the store, with a median of 3 which is neither agree nor disagree. Respondents mainly indicated in the questionnaires that they liked to have information of new merchandise upon which they will then evaluate their need for that specific product. Hence, the want to obtain new product news is not necessarily converted into an act of purchase rejecting H1, as brand awareness did not lead to current purchase behavior.

An interesting finding from this was that while respondents showed a tendency to make purchases upon triggers from social media regarding specific daily specials and promotions, the respondents themselves perceived that they were mainly motivated to follow the SNS accounts to get product information and not to make purchases. The findings showed that respondents were making purchases based on price or promotion triggers and not brand image or brand awareness, rejecting H0.

While H1 was rejected, further analysis was done to understand the relationship between obtaining information from Twitter and making purchases. Spearman's rho was tabulated and only one pair showed significant correlation as reflected in Table 4. The Spearman's rho demonstrated a negative correlation between making purchases based on promotion tweets and obtaining information from Twitter. In terms of obtaining information from Twitter, this aspect covers a different angle on information that is not about the product or service but about latest news and information, both local and international and breaking stories. The results displayed that the more respondents made purchases based on tweets received, the

Table 3. Descriptive statistics for reasons for following SNS

			Statistic	Std. Error
Follow SNS for Merchandise News	Mean		2.48	.126
	95% Confidence Interval for Mean	Lower Bound	2.23	
		Upper Bound	2.73	
	5% Trimmed Mean		2.42	
	Median		2.00	
	Variance		1.227	
	Std. Deviation		1.108	
	Minimum		1	
	Maximum		5	
	Range		4	
	Interquartile Range		1	
	Skewness		.558	.274
	Kurtosis		-.378	.541

continued on following page

Table 3. Continued

			Statistic	Std. Error
Follow SNS for Purchase	Mean		3.29	.108
	95% Confidence Interval for Mean	Lower Bound Upper Bound	3.07	
			3.50	
	5% Trimmed Mean		3.26	
	Median		3.00	
	Variance		.891	
	Std. Deviation		.944	
	Minimum		2	
	Maximum		5	
	Range		3	
	Interquartile Range		1	
	Skewness		.163	.274
	Kurtosis		-.885	.541
Follow SNS due to Brand	Mean		2.99	.100
	95% Confidence Interval for Mean	Lower Bound Upper Bound	2.79	
			3.19	
	5% Trimmed Mean		3.01	
	Median		3.00	
	Variance		.776	
	Std. Deviation		.881	
	Minimum		1	
	Maximum		5	
	Range		4	
	Interquartile Range		2	
	Skewness		-.211	2.74
	Kurtosis		-.608	.541
Follow SNS due to Interesting Messages	Mean		2.51	.109
	95% Confidence Interval for Mean	Lower Bound Upper Bound	2.29	
			2.72	
	5% Trimmed Mean		2.49	
	Median		3.00	
	Variance		.911	
	Std. Deviation		.955	
	Minimum		1	
	Maximum		5	
	Range		4	
	Interquartile Range		1	
	Skewness		.121	.274
	Kurtosis		-.488	.541

Table 4. Spearman's Rho

			Purchase Due to Twitter Promo	Obtain Info from Twitter
Spearman's rho	Purchase Due to Twitter Promo	Correlation Coefficient	1.000	-.364**
		Sig. (2-tailed)	77	.001
		N		77
	Obtain Info From Twitter	Correlation Coefficient	-.364**	1.000
		Sig. (2-tailed)	.001	
		N	77	77

**. Correlation is significant at the 0.01 level (2-tailed).

lesser they are using twitter to obtain information. Hence, a gap exists between the followers where one group focuses on merely obtaining information and not for making purchases while those who tend to purchase based on tweets are not seeking news and information. Hence, the first brand awareness in this instance basically focuses on followers obtaining promotion information, which then drives their purchase intention and behavior. However, there is also a group aware of Lawson and obtains information about it, but this does not lead to purchase.

Respondents selected reasons for choosing Lawson over the other convenience store chains. They were given two different sets of options to choose from; the first includes location as a factor while the second excludes location. The findings are illustrated in Figure 4 accordingly. Respondents were given 'others' as an option however none of the respondents chose this option. Based on the data, it shows that product or merchandise variety and price are fairly stable factors that continue to drive purchase decisions, rejecting H1, and H2 respectively.

Table 5 explores the correlations between the following

1. Purchase made because of Twitter and the impression that followed.
2. Current purchase made because of Twitter will drive future purchase.
3. Brand impression and image will drive future purchase.

Figure 4. Reasons for Selecting Lawson (With and Without Location)

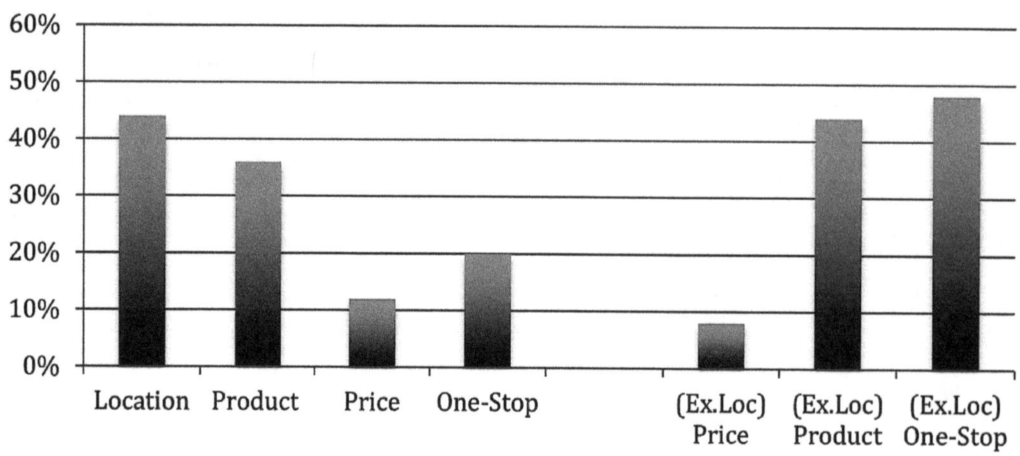

Table 5. Correlations

			CVS	Purchases Because of Twitter	Impression After Twitter	Future Purchases Reasons
Spearman's rho	CVS	Correlation Coefficient	1.000	.025	.136	-.013
		Sig. (2-tailed)		.832	.237	.913
		N	77	77	77	77
	Purchases Because of Twitter	Correlation Coefficient	.025	1.000	.072	-.107
		Sig. (2-tailed)	.832		.531	.356
		N	77	77	77	77
	Impression After Twitter	Correlation Coefficient	.136	.072	1.000	-.091
		Sig. (2-tailed)	.237	.531		.431
		N	77	77	77	77
	Future Purchase Reasons	Correlation Coefficient	-.013	-.107	-.091	1.000
		Sig. (2-tailed)	.913	.356	.431	
		N	77	77	77	77

As illustrated below, all three pairings did not reflect any significant correlation therefore, rejecting H3, H4 and H5 accordingly.

The questionnaire also looked at the number of respondents who had social media presence, mainly Twitter and Facebook. Next tabulation was carried out from the responses that indicated social media presence and whether they followed Lawson on social media or otherwise, as illustrated in Figure 5. Clearly more follow Lawson on Twitter versus Facebook however the figure is lower than those who do not follow Lawson on both social media accounts. A large percentage of 47% indicated that they did not follow, as they did not want to get product or service information cluttering their social media accounts. While the balance was not aware of Lawson's existing social media accounts (31%) and 22% indicated that it did not occur to them to follow the social media accounts.

Figure 5. Percentage of Lawson Customers Who Follow Lawson's Social Media Accounts

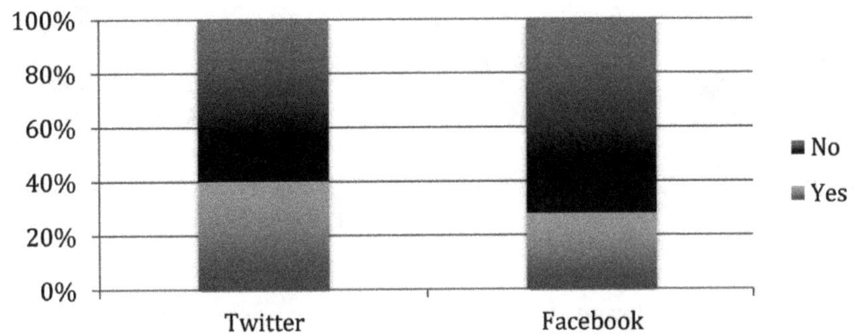

Respondents were also asked to provide their perception regarding the Lawson brand as well as the social media accounts; namely Akiko and 'her network' of family, friends and colleagues, shown in Figure 6.

Evidently, as a brand Lawson lives up to the perception of convenient (43%) followed by innovation (21%) and good variety of product (19%). However, the perception of Lawson's social media presence elicited a different set of responses. While the corporate brand was strongly associated with the aspects of convenience stores, Lawson's social media was linked to distinct aspects that were more 'experiential' from sensorial stimuli such as cute (47%), unique (27%) and fun (21%). The words that the respondents used basically reinforced the success in terms of incorporating cute culture in social media by Lawson, supporting H6. When a comparison was done with the social media perception of the other convenience store brands, Lawson managed to differentiate itself, as respondents basically found the competitors' social media accounts similar to other businesses where the company only provides promotion news and product updates.

DISCUSSION AND RECOMMENDATIONS

The strategy that Lawson took with managing its social media was not only to fuse cute culture but to also develop the characters and create them into your average middle class people who have jobs, school and interests. The blurring of lines between the characters and actual rock singers and gaming characters with the collaboration and crossovers further fuels the humanizing of Akiko-chan and her family, friends and coworkers. As a matter of fact, Lawson is the only convenience store chain that maximizes its presence in the realm of social media. Apart from Twitter and Facebook, Lawson also has accounts in the following social media service

1. Snapeee (a photo sharing social media service that is focused on connecting the world through '*kawaii*')
2. Cameran (a celebrity photo sharing service)
3. Book Reco (a book review site)
4. Google+

Figure 6. Brand and Social Media Perception

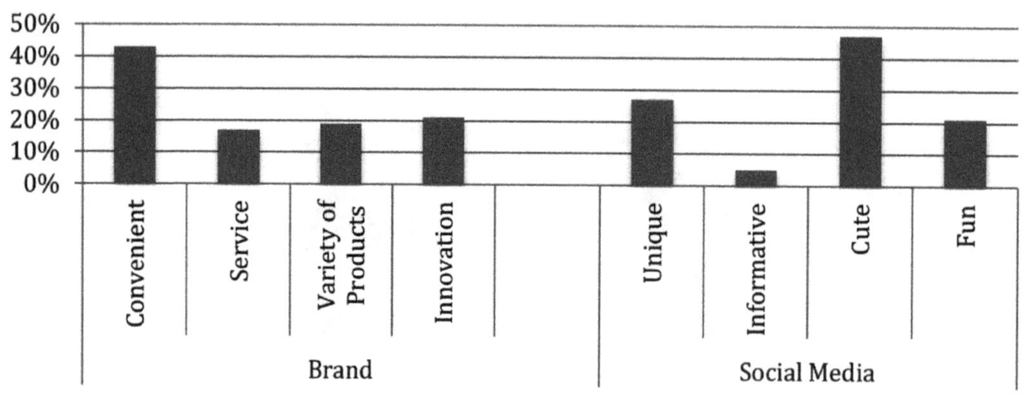

5. Line
6. YouTube
7. Mixi
8. Kakao Talk
9. NicoNicoDoga (the Japanese equivalent to YouTube)
10. Naver
11. Pinterest
12. Tumblr
13. Pixiv
14. Mobage
15. Gree
16. UStream
17. Vine
18. Foursquare
19. Instagram
20. Tokyo Otaku Mode

According to Lawson's Integrated Report 2014 from their corporate website, as of July 31, 2014 Lawson's Akiko-chan has an impressive number of more 13 million 'followers' from all the social media accounts.

The findings from the pilot study brought to light a few core issues. Firstly, Lawson is able to effectively differentiate their social media versus that of their competitors. The respondents were able to identify the cute factor and experience imbued in Lawson's social media. The tie-up strategy with various characters from games such as Dragon Quest has further established Akiko-chan's image and increased awareness amongst specific consumer groups such as those in the gaming community. The development of character background that has human-like traits that followers can identify and bond with further strengthens the relationship between followers and the brand character.

While this is a good first step, there is a gap between perceptions of the brick-and-mortar establishment versus its online presence. While the findings showed that customers found the social media usage cute and attractive, when asked they still thought of Lawson's stores from the perspective of a convenience store. The findings also reveal that customers chose to purchase from Lawson due to elements such as location, product and service (the plethora of services makes it a one-stop center). Hence there was no differentiating element versus their competitors. Therefore, while followers found Lawson's Twitter to be cute, it ended there. Therefore, brand awareness and image from their SNS do not necessarily shape purchase intention and behavior.

Being a convenience store, even without a single social media account customers are already aware of the convenience store brand. The ubiquity of the convenience store in Japan makes it a challenge to shape brand image or even create awareness. The utilization of social media provides more of a platform to proliferate promotions and merchandise news in order to inform and remind customers of the available offerings, and at the same time drive revenue. The preference amongst convenience store chain brands is first and foremost shaped by location/ convenience to the customer followed by product or merchandise choices. In order to build brand loyalty it is important to formulate a strategy that looks at bridging social media and emphasizing the main factors that shape customer selection and preference. This creates a need for Lawson to further develop their own identity while more importantly at the same time, bridge the gap between the customer perception towards their social media presence and the brick-and-mortar stores.

As mentioned earlier in this study, a gap exists, as there is a weak linkage between Akiko-chan's perceived brand image versus the brand image of Lawson convenience store itself. Based on this study, the perception of Lawson's brick-and-mortar establishment is that of any other convenience store while its social media presence is perceived differently; to that of a cute and more fun image. There has to be consistency in the brand image in order to forge relationships between their Twitter followers and the convenience store brand itself. As the direction of the Twitter and other social media accounts taken is to utilize cute culture, the potential customer segment is sizable as the cute sells very well in Japan. Not only that, the collaboration with various anime and game characters has paved the way to penetrate the 'otaku' segment which is known to spend a lot on character goods and memorabilia.

Another issue that was uncovered from the pilot study was the rather low percentage of customers who followed Lawson's social media. On the other hand, those who made purchases based on tweets received were focused on promotions and they were not as engaged with the social media characters. The findings also showed that the respondents tend to follow social media accounts to gain merchandise news. This leads to the issue of getting more customers to follow and engage with the characters and social media accounts as engagement leads to emotional bonds and loyalty. On the other hand, this also creates the opportunity to convert non-followers into followers and then customers. The reach of social media especially Twitter is extensive since Twitter is widely used in Japan. There should be a two-pronged approach in managing the social media accounts. The first is to develop a strategy to acquire followers. Combining product and service offering and communicating in a unique, catchy way instead of the normal product promotional news will attract attention and lead to a viral effect. Right from the start, Lawson has to engage potential followers and provide them an experience of being able to communicate and of being heard.

Apart from customer acquisition, the management of SNS especially Twitter should also look beyond product promotion in strengthening their customer retention activities. The second prong is to create a retention strategy. Many social media followers do not really pay much attention to tweets or news after a while. Therefore, while a certain account may have a high number of followers, it does not translate to active and loyal customers. One of the core factors of retention is location and proximity to the customer. While this does ensure repeated purchase, there is still a need to create and develop other differentiation strategies that will get the customer to make the choice of not opting for proximity when making their purchase. The point card system has long been prevalent in the Japanese retail sector. Almost all convenience store chains have their own point card where customers get points for each purchase that can be exchanged for goods or used as 'electronic' money. While this is a good strategy, the study showed that only a small percentage of respondents viewed this a factor in shaping their convenience store selection choice. The breadth of services that are offered by convenience stores are extensive. However, it did not appear as a core factor in store preference in this study. Creating a continuous follower engagement strategy is key in ensuring retention. Followers ought to be kept active in interacting with either each other, or with Akiko and Lawson. Community forums and events can be held periodically in specific areas such as a pop up event or across the nation in order to continuously forge bonds with their followers.

FUTURE RESEARCH DIRECTIONS

The findings demonstrated that there is still a lot of work to be done in order to achieve effectiveness in the management of social media. As this study also demonstrated that there is a gap between sns and store brand image, future study on bridging the gap would be essential. Future research on determining factors for acquiring and retaining followers in attaining loyalty should also be undertaken. These research areas are pertinent as the findings can be explored further to see if they are applicable to other forms of businesses and industries since majority of businesses and organizations are either actively using social media or has the interest to do so.

CONCLUSION

In today's digital age, companies have been turning to social media to reach out to customers. While most companies have Twitter and Facebook, the most glaring fact is that the top followed Twitter accounts are not that of corporations and businesses. In this rat race of gaining consumer engagement and brand equity, companies have to explore different methods and means in getting customers to not only start following them on Twitter but to continuously actively follow them and make repeated purchases. This demonstrates the prevalent issue faced by businesses as they take to utilizing social media. Many corporations and brands have flocked to creating Twitter accounts yet it serves as a mere promotion announcement tool which, in the end becomes 'noise' and does not successfully engage the followers. Creating engagement has to cover two main areas; namely customer acquisition when the tweets capture customer attention and engages them while building a relationship at the same time. Another area would be customer retention, having to keep things fresh with continual engagement and strengthening of relationship with the follower.

Lawson not only shares promotion information and coupons over social media but also gets their followers involved in the process of product development and product selection. These efforts led to their growing 'friends' or follower base. This chapter provides readers with insight on how a Japanese convenience retailer are able to effectively incorporate culture in SNS with the objective of getting customers to actively follow them and consume their products. The findings paved the way for the foundation for further research activities in developing more effective methods of maximizing Twitter in enhancing customer experience and subsequently increasing brand equity and loyalty.

REFERENCES

Aviles, K. (2011, September). Mobile Convenience Stores Designed to Serve Japan's Earthquake Survivors. *Nasdaq*. Retrieved from http://community.nasdaq.com/News/2011-09/mobile-convenience-stores-designed-to-serve-japans-earthquake-survivors.aspx?storyid=94186

Beck, T. (2013). Why the Japanese Love Twitter But Not Facebook. *Fast C@mpany*. Retrieved from http://www.fastcolabs.com/3016498/why-the-japanese-love-twitter-but-not-facebook

Belson, K., & Bremner, B. (2003). *Hello Kitty: The Remarkable Story of Sanrio and the Billion Dollar Feline Phenomenon*. New York: John Wiley & Sons.

Bremner, B. (2002). In Japan, cute conquers all. *Businessweek*. Retrieved from http://www.businessweek.com/stories/2002-06-24/in-japan-cute-conquers-all

Brown, T. J., Barry, T. E., Dacin, P. A., & Gunst, R. F. (2005). Spreading the word: Investigating antecedents of consumers' positive word-of mouth intentions and behaviors in a retailing context. *Journal of the Academy of Marketing Science*, *33*(2), 123–138. doi:10.1177/0092070304268417

Businessess tap into growing power of social media. (2011, October 31). *The Asahi Shimbun*. Retrieved from http://ajw.asahi.com/article/behind_news/social_affairs/AJ2011103116169

Chiao, Y. L., Lu, C. h., Chou, Y. Y., & Liu, P. l. (2011). Towards a human-centric and smarter convenience store service experience.*Proceedings of the International Conference of Social Science and Humanity* (pp. 84 – 88). Singapore: IACSIT Press.

CNN. (2013, July 17). 2011 Japan Earthquake – Tsunami Fast Facts. *CNN Library*. Retrieved from http://www.cnn.com/2013/07/17/world/asia/japan-earthquake---tsunami-fast-facts/

Comm, J., & Robbins, A. (2010). *Twitter Power 2.0: How to Dominate Your Market One Tweet at a Time*. New York: Wiley.

Convenience stores turning to the elderly. (2014, January 16). *Japan Times*. Retrieved from http://www.japantimes.co.jp/life/2014/01/16/general/convenience-stores-turning-to-the-elderly/#.U9-5QpS1aCU

Craft, L. (2005, August 7). Japan As A World Leader In Pop Culture. *The Washington Times*. Retrieved from http://www.wpherald.com/storyview.php?StoryID=20050807-030608-2858r

Craig, T. (2000). *Japan Pop! Inside the World of Japanese Popular Culture*. New York: M.E. Sharpe, Inc.

Decker, C. (1998). *P&G 99*. London: Harper Collins Business.

Drake, K. (2001, June 25). Kwest for kawaii. Time. Retrieved from http://content.time.com/time/arts/article/0,8599,131022,00.html

Engel, J. E., Blackwell, R. D., & Kegerreis, R. J. (1969). How information is used to adopt an innovation. *Journal of Advertising Research*, *9*(December), 3–8.

Esch, F. R., Langner, T., Schmitt, B. H., & Geus, P. (2006). Are brands forever? How brand knowledge and relationships affect current and future purchases. *Journal of Product and Brand Management*, *15*(2), 98–105. doi:10.1108/10610420610658938

Garbage News. (2014, October 9). Konbinishitennou no uriagedakanadowogurafukashitemiru. Retrieved from http://www.garbagenews.net/archives/1974644.html

Gobe, M. (2001). *Emotional Branding*. New York: Allworth Press.

Harden, B. (2008, November 8). Japanese Stores Take Convenience To a New Level. *Washington Post Foreign Service*. Retrieved from http://www.washingtonpost.com/wp-dyn/content/article/2008/11/07/AR2008110703512.html

Harris, D. (2001). *Cute, Quaint, Hungry And Romantic: The Aesthetics of Consumerism*. New York: Da Capo Press.

Hughes, F. (2010, January 22). Naïve yurukyara win hearts across Japan. *The Japan Times*. Retrieved from http://blog.japantimes.co.jp/japan-pulse/naive-yuru-kyara-win-hearts-across-japan/

Jansen, B. J., Zhang, M., Sobel, K., & Chowdury, A. (2009). Twitter Power: Tweets as electronic word of mouth. *Journal of the American Society for Information Science and Technology*, *60*(11), 2169–2188. doi:10.1002/asi.21149

Japan Franchise Association. (2015, July). Retrieved from http://www.jfa-fc.or.jp/folder/1/img/20150820110725.pdf

Japan retail market. (2014, July). Retrieved from http://pdf.savills.asia/asia-pacific-research/japan-research/japan-retail/retail-spotlight-07-2014.pdf

Japan retails foods. (2013, December). Retrieved from http://gain.fas.usda.gov/Recent%20GAIN%20Publications/Retail%20Foods_Tokyo%20ATO_Japan_12-12-2013.pdf

Japanese culture is becoming a cult of cute. (2006, June 14). *NBC News*. Retrieved from http://www.nbcnews.com/id/13320352/ns/business-world_business/t/japanese-culture-becoming-cult-cute/#.Veg-Fjiyqqko

Japanese department store rivals merge. (2007, March 14). *The New York Times*. Retrieved from http://www.nytimes.com/2007/03/14/business/worldbusiness/14iht-dai.4904532.html

Jitpleecheep, P. (2012, August 24). Saha Group in talks with Japan's Lawson. *The Bangkok Post*. Retrieved from http://www.bangkokpost.com/business/economics/309100/saha-group-in-talks-with-japan-lawson

Kabani, S. (2012). *The Zen of Social Media Marketing: An Easier Way to Build Credibility, Generate Buzz, and Increase Revenue*. Dallas, Texas: Ben Bella Books.

Kato, M. (2002). The Japanese obsession with adorable icons is rooted in cultural tradition. *Eye Magazine*. Retrieved from http://www.eyemagazine.com/feature/article/cute-culture

Katz, E., & Lazarsfeld, P. F. (1955). *Personal influence: The part played by people in the flow of mass communication*. New York: Free Press.

Kerpen, D. (2011). *Likeable Social Media: How to Delight Your Customers, Create an Irresistible Brand, and Be Generally Amazing on Facebook (And Other Social Networks)*. New York: McGraw-Hill.

Kinsella, S. (1995). Cuties in Japan. In L. Skov & B. Moeran (Eds.), *Women, media, and consumption in Japan* (pp. 220–254). Honolulu: University of Hawaii Press.

Kumamoto, Y. (2008, Sept. 26). Stores Defend 24-Hour Operations." The Japan Times Online. *The Japan Times*. Retrieved from http://www.japantimes.co.jp/text/nn20080926f2.html

Kyodo. (2012, July 26). Non-Japanese promoted to top posts to help in long-term bid to move into foreign markets. *The Japan Times*. Retrieved from http://www.japantimes.co.jp/text/nb20120726a7.html

Lawson, A. (2013, October 29). Akiko 4'koma' Lightning returns Final Fantasy XIII (Lawson HMV limited) release memorial collaboration. Plain clothes Light-chan is cute [Tweet]. Retrieved from https://twitter.com/akiko_lawson/status/395424838560403456/photo/1

LeBra, T. (1984). *Patterns of Japanese Behavior*. Honolulu: University of Hawaii Press.

Lindstrom, M. (2005). *Brand Sense*. New York: Free Press.

Loo, E. (2012, July 4). Dragon Quest's Slime is hired by convenience store. *Anime News Network*. Retrieved from http://www.animenewsnetwork.com/interest/2012-07-04/dragon-quest-slime-is-hired-by-convenience-store

Masabuchi, S. (1994). *Kawaiishokogun*. Tokyo: NHK Publishing.

McVeigh, B. (2000). How Hello Kitty commodities the cute, cool and camp: "Consumutopia" versus "control" in Japan. *Journal of Material Culture*, *5*(2), 225–245. doi:10.1177/135918350000500205

Mead, R. (2002, March 18). Shopping Rebellion. What the kids wants. The New Yorker. Retrieved from http://www.newyorker.com/magazine/2002/03/18/shopping-rebellion

Merish, L. (1996). Cuteness and Commodity Aesthetics: Tom Thumb and Shirley Temple. In R.G. Thomson (Ed.), Freakery: Cultural spectacles of the extraordinary body (pp 185-203). New York: New York University Press.

Meyou. (2015, September 3). Twitter nihonforowa ranking. Retrieved from http://meyou.jp/ranking/follower_allcat

Nakata, H. (2011, October 25). Net super trend food for thought. Retrieved from http://www.japantimes.co.jp/news/2011/10/25/reference/net-super-trend-food-for-thought/#.VHxyLleUfpU

Nifty Konbininitsuite no angketto ranking. (2013, May 24). Retrieved from http://chosa.nifty.com/life/chosa_report_A20130524/1/?theme=A20130524&report=1&theme=A20130524&report=1

Nye, J. (2006). Transformational Leadership and US grand strategy. *Foreign Affairs*, *85*(4), 139–148. doi:10.2307/20032047

O'Dell, J. (2009, January 5). Major Japanese retailer says Mitsubishi's I-MiEV battery electric car is way to go. Retrieved from www.edmunds.com/autoobserver-archive/2009/01/major-japanese-retailer-says-mitsubishis-i-miev-battery-electric-car-is-way-to-go.html

Otagaki, Y. (2013, November 13). Soft samurai wins hard battle of mascots. *The Wall Street Journal*. Retrieved from http://blogs.wsj.com/japanrealtime/2013/11/26/soft-samurai-wins-hard-battle-of-mascots/

Public Relations Office Government of Japan. (2011, Oct. 5). Retrieved from http://www.gov-online.go.jp/eng/publicity/book/hlj/html/201105/201105_03.html

Report, L. I. (2014). Retrieved from http://lawson.jp/en/ir/library/annual_report.html

Reynolds, G. (2006). *An army of Davids: How markets and technology empower ordinary people to beat big media, big government, and other Goliaths*. Nashville, TN: Thomas Nelson.

Reynolds, I. (2014, April 16). Japan's Population Shrinks For Third Year As Aging Increases. *Bloomberg News*. Retrieved from http://www.bloomberg.com/news/2014-04-15/japan-s-population-shrinks-for-third-year-as-ranks-of-aged-grow.html

Richins, M. L., & Root-Shaffer, T. (1988). The role of involvement and opinion leadership in consumer word-of-mouth: An implicit model made explicit. *Advances in Consumer Research. Association for Consumer Research (U. S.)*, *15*, 32–36.

Roach, M. (1999, December 7). Cute Inc. *Wired*. Retrieved from http://archive.wired.com/wired/archive/7.12/cute.html

Sakaguchi, M. (2008). *Naruhodo Databook 1: Konbini No Shikake*. Tokyo: Otsuki Shoten.

Sakawee, S. (2014, March 27). Line now has 390 million users with Japan and Thailand as top countries. Retrieved from https://www.techinasia.com/line-390-million-users-japan-thailand-top-countries/

Savilis World Research. (2014, July). Spotlight Japan retail market. Retrieved from http://pdf.savills.asia/asia-pacific-research/japan-research/japan-retail/retail-spotlight-07-2014.pdf

Schilling, M. (1997). *The encyclopedia of Japanese pop culture*. New York: Weatherhill.

Schmitt, B. H. (1999). *Experiential Marketing: How to Get Customers to Sense, Feel, Think, Act, Relate*. New York: Free Press.

Scott, D. M. (2011). *The New Rules of Marketing & PR: How to Use Social Media, Online Video, Mobile Applications, Blogs, News Releases, and Viral Marketing to Reach Buyers Directly*. New York: Wiley.

Seiryokuzu, K. (2014, March). Retrieved from http://todo-ran.com/t/kiji/10327

Shove, E. (2002). Converging Conventions of Comfort, Cleanliness and Convenience. Retrieved from http://www.lancaster.ac.uk/fass/resources/sociology-online-papers/papers/shove-converging-conventions.pdf

Sparks, L. (2000). Seven-Eleven Japan and The Southland Corporation: A marriage of convenience? *International Marketing Review*, *17*(4/5), 401–415. doi:10.1108/02651330010339923

Sugawa, K. (2000, April 25). Change in premiership and Japan's soft power. *The Asahi Shimbun*.

Suzuki, R. (2012, November 17). Nation in the grips of yurukyara fever. Yomiuri Online. Retrieved from http://www.yomiuri.co.jp/dy/photos/newjapan/newjapan121117.htm

The incredible shrinking country. (2014, March 25). *The Economist*. Retrieved from http://www.economist.com/blogs/banyan/2014/03/japans-demography

Tong, C. (2012, July 2). Japan-Based Convenience Store Chain. *Pacific Business News*. Retrieved from http://www.bizjournals.com/pacific/news/2012/07/02/japan-based-convenience-store-chain.html

Top 100 Twitterholics based on followers. (2015). *The Twitaholic.com*. Retrieved from http://twitaholic.com/top100/followers/

Torres, I. (2012, December 26). The battle for cute in Japan rages on in the 'yuru-kyara' mascot competition. Japan Daily Press. Retrieved from http://japandailypress.com/the-battle-for-cute-in-japan-rages-on-in-yuru-kyara-mascot-competition-2620436/

Urban, G. (2005). *Don't just relate-advocate: A blueprint for profit in the era of customer power*. Upper Saddle River, NJ: Wharton School Publishing.

Uyeno, K. (July 2005). Japanese convenience store debuts in Hawaii. Retrieved from http://www.khon2.com/mostpopular/story/Japanese-convenience-store-debuts-in-Hawaii/Dl5b-ZHMIEmDgcj_M-q44A.cspx

Tokyo Drift: how Japan leads the way on m-payment. (2013, May 13). Vodafone Global Enterprise. Retrieved from http://enterprise.vodafone.com/insight_news/2013-08-13-tokyo-drift-how-japan-leads-the-way-on-m-payments.jsp

Walker, E. (2008, May 21). Top car: how 'Hello Kitty' conquered the world. *The Independent*. Retrieved from http://www.independent.co.uk/news/world/asia/top-cat-how-hello-kitty-conquered-the-world-831522.html

West, M. I. (2008). *The Japanification of Children's Popular Culture: From Godzilla to Miyazaki*. Maryland: Scarecrow Press.

Japanese convenient store operator orders 150 Mitsubishi electric cars. (2008, December 31). *EVWorld*. Retrieved from http://evworld.com/news.cfm?newsid=20038

Yano, C.R. (2000). Dream girl: imagining the girl-next-door within the heart/ soul of Japan. *U.S-Japan Women's Journal* (English Supplement), 19, 122-141.

Yano, C. R. (2004). Kitty Litter: Japanese Cute At Home and Abroad. In J. Goldstein, D. Buckingham, & G. Brougere (Eds.), *Toys, Games, and Media* (pp. 57–58). New York: Routledge.

Yarow, J. (2012, January 6). There's one place in the world where Twitter is bigger than Facebook. Retrieved from http://www.businessinsider.com/theres-only-one-place-in-the-world-where-twitter-is-bigger-than-facebook-2012-1#ixzz3KYbyX0W0

KEY TERMS AND DEFINITIONS

Brand Image: The general belief and perception held by both actual and potential customers about the brand.

Brand Awareness: The extent of familiarity and recognition of the brand by potential customers.

Cute Culture: The sub-culture that emphasizes the elements of cute and childlikeness.

Purchase Intention: The plan to purchase certain goods or services in the near future.

Twitter: An online, free, microblogging, social networking service that allows users to send 140-character messages known as 'tweets'.

Vocaloid: Singing voice synthesizer software developed by Yamaha Corporation.

Yurukyara: Mascots that are created to promote a business, product, service, cause, place or region and event.

Chapter 13

Social Media and Business: In Search of Missing Links

Saurabh Gupta
Banaras Hindu University, India

Anurag Singh
Banaras Hindu University, India

Punita Duhan
Meera Bai Institute of Technology, India

ABSTRACT

The influence of social media on the various facets of society has attracted a lot of attention of the researchers in the last few years who are probing its multifaceted impact. One important aspect of social media is its role in promoting instant gratification. It has far reaching consequences for evolution of self, which in turn has important implications for society and businesses. Drawing from the conceptual foundations of the theories of identity and social comparison, the researchers tried to develop a model as to how the dual role of social media acts to alter the identity and hence behavior. In this context, the significance of the study lies in exposing the intricate interplay between the attributes of social media and the dynamic self. The study goes a long way in providing a deeper understanding of self-concept in connection to social media, which has immense importance for consumer behavior and can help businesses to fine-tune their strategies with the changing consumer psychology.

INTRODUCTION

There have been three fundamental inventions and discoveries in the history of mankind- fire, wheel and money, and it shall not be an exaggeration if this list is extended to include internet. It has really revolutionized the world of ours. It has led to massive churning in the cultural, social, political and economic spheres, the ripples of which are being felt across the countries, across the societies, across the cultures and above all, across the individuals. One of the direct offspring of internet is social media, which has emerged as the strongest force shaping our thoughts & actions. Social media can be defined

DOI: 10.4018/978-1-5225-0332-3.ch013

as web based applications that allows individuals to connect with strangers to satisfy their social needs. That is why it is usually referred to as Social Networking Sites. Some examples are Facebook, Twitter, LinkedIn, WhatsApp etc. Man is a social animal, and consequently, the advent of social media was bound to have a massive effect as is becoming evident now. Social Networking Sites (SNSs) like Facebook are blurring the boundaries of time and space and are going to alter the contours of conduct of businesses in the coming years.

The influence of social media on the various facets of society has attracted a lot of attention of the researchers in the last few years who are probing its multifaceted impact. The key assumption underlying this study is that studying the effects and influence of social media necessitates an interdisciplinary approach. The pace at which social media and Information Communication technology (ICT) is changing is so fast that new *Avatars* of SNSs are encountered every now and then. However, amidst all these developments, it may be argued that it is the alteration and transformation in the self-identity resulting from the coalition of social media with the lives of present generation, which can provide with a firm framework to further understand the influence of social media on the society in general and business, in particular. Though empirical and theoretical studies have started flowing in regarding the implications of social media in the field of management, still it remains enigmatic as to how managers can fine tune their strategies in the fields of human resource management, marketing management, production and operation management and so on to effectively deal with the impact of social media on their businesses.

Till now little is known about the effect of social media-individual interaction and its effect on the dynamism of self and consequently on behavior of the individuals. This in turn limits our knowledge of the consumer behavior in terms of choice making and well-being, for instance, to what extent social networking sites fulfill the social needs (other needs?) of individuals? Does this have any influence on the buying behavior of consumers especially those goods and services which have social value like trendy clothes, latest automobiles etc. How does it influence, say, gift-giving behavior? There are several such questions that need attention and whose answers have the capability to transform the way businesses are carried on; be it the way of communicating to the consumers, be it the way consumers evaluate the various choices and be it the customer relationship management (CRM) practices.

The remainder of the paper proceeds as follow. First of all, background and approach of the study has been presented. Next, the salubriousness of social media for the evolution of identity has been analyzed followed by development of a model of social media and need interaction. A separate section has been devoted to the discussion on the implications of this dynamism of self, due to social media for the businesses. Finally, concluding remarks have been made.

BACKGROUND AND APPROACH

Social Media these days have intruded into the life of more than billion people over the globe and for youth it has become a vital tool for connecting and sharing information. People share thoughts, feelings, pictures, accomplishments etc. with their friends and families through social media. By engaging in such behavior, they not only satisfy their social need but also question their identity and self. When reinforced by the growing individualism and instant gratification it has far-reaching consequences. This has not only implications for the development and evolution of self but has certain sociological and psychological notions of the need relevant for the business as well. How this social media shapes the self and what ramifications it is likely to have for the businesses in the coming time remains *terra incognita* among researchers and hence the motivation for this study.

A plethora of research has been undertaken regarding the impact and influence of social media. These studies have focused on such factors as sociability, intimacy, friendship (Lavin & Barrow, 2001; Anderson, 2001; Bargh & Mckenna, 2004; Cummings et. al, 2006). There are studies on individual and group characteristics (Flanagin, 2005; Lenhart et al., 2005; Quan- Haase, 2008; Valkenburg & Peter, 2009). The capability of social media to enhance possibilities of relationship forming with strangers has also been studied (McKenna et al., 2002; Baym, 2010). Identity management on social networking sites is also being increasingly investigated (Dimicco & Millen, 2007). In nutshell, it can be said that researchers are investigating a wide range of phenomenon associated with the social media such as governance, democracy, creativity, productivity etc. (Anderson, 2007; Druin, 2009; Negroponte, 1995; Noveck, 2009; Shirky, 2008; Tapscott, 1998; Smith & Zook, 2011; Mangold & Fauds, 2009; Constantinides & Fountain, 2008).

From an extensive survey of empirical literature on the researches undertaken in the context of social media across many disciplines it can be concluded that social media connection has led to significant changes in the behavior of individuals and they are having a sense of plurality about their self identity. Having multiple self identities at the same time can be called as plurality of self.

Based on the above findings, this study has been guided throughout by the following research questions:

1. What is the role of social media in fulfilling the social as well as other needs of the individuals?
2. What is the influence of social media communication on the self-identity?
3. What are the implications of social media for businesses in the coming years?

The first research question has been mainly handled with the introspection technique. In order to seek answer to the second research question an extensive survey of secondary data and available literature was carried out. The literature that was consulted was both empirical as well as theoretical in orientation. It was mainly concerned with the impact of globalization on the self-identity, postmodernism school of identity, identity as an individualized project, communication in the technology savvy world and contemporary psychoanalytic approaches to self-identity. The third research question was addressed by the literature pertaining to instant gratification and social media, social comparison process in the contemporary scenario and online buying behavior of consumers.

SALUBRIOUSNESS OF SOCIAL MEDIA

Human being as social being is essentially showing-off, self-display, self presentation, including pretense (Eldred, 2008, p. 12). This is the reason why, in a given situation S_1 that provides more freedom to the individual to manipulate her identity in comparison to situation S_2, the identity will be more dynamic and fluid in situation S_1. Furthermore, self-identity is always a matter of how someone habitually lives, and is not a merely psychological self-image represented within consciousness, i.e. within a representational imagining of who one is. Such self-identity is always a reflection of oneself in the mirror of how I live in the world, understanding the practices I habitually practice as my own (Bandura, 1986).

Through identification with certain chosen states of existence in the real world, there evolves a self, contrast with the digital whoness - the digital counterpart of being is fundamentally nothing but strings of 0s and 1s. These strings of 0s and 1s are the basic units of any identity that circulates in the social media. But what the other ultimately views and perceives is the crucial point. The computer engineers might view the comment made by a close friend on the status update of his friend as a string of 0s and 1s (the privacy of which is a serious matter of concern), the digital whoness, but to the concerned individual it is a feedback to his projected self.

Self-identity is cast as a self-defining process that depends upon the monitoring of, and reflection upon psychological and social information about possible trajectories of life (Giddens, 1991). It is actually constitutive of what people do, who they think they are and how they live their identities. These three central acts of what, who and how in connection with identity have really taken an ironic turn with the arrival of social media. As for instance, "status updates" allows individuals to constantly examine and reform their perception of others as well as their self thereby altering their behavior. The social media have enabled this reflexivity.

The self-identity of individuals as soon as they join social networking sites becomes more and more open to choice, debate, scrutiny and revision. According to Beck, new demands, opportunities and controls are being placed on people today and that it is questionable whether collective or system units of meaning and action are socially significant (Beck, 2009). This is the living of lives in need of justification, re-elaboration, reworking, and above all reinvention. The examples of reinvention abound – rise of plastic surgery, instant identity makeovers of reality TV shows, making friends from far away land and so on.

Pressure to become what one is has paved the way to pressure to become what one desires of. This displacement has been coupled with another phenomenon of displaying one's whoness particularly digitally, which is referred to as Social media induced self (SMIS), to family, friends and colleagues, that one has truly made, it has been reinforced by the social media. With the passage of time, this SMIS becomes so much fluid and mobile that identity, if not lost, becomes confusing. In a nutshell, SMIS permits individuals to put round pegs in square holes.

Self-identity can be conceived to be composed of several sub identities as shown in the Figure 1.

Figure 1. The building blocks of identity
Source: Researchers' own creation

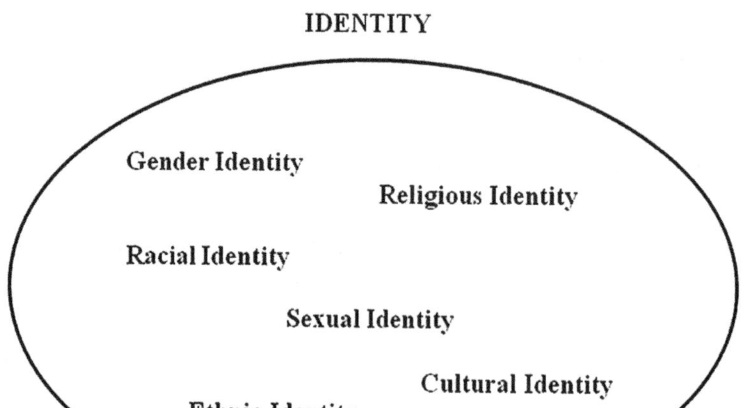

These sub identities act as the building blocks of the total identity. Hence, by manipulating these sub identities the individual is able to project the SMIS as she wishes. For example, suppose an individual joins a community composed of people belonging to her own religion. She will then first alter her religious sub identity whose effect will manifest itself in the identity later on. Thus, it is very important to think of identity in micro terms.

From the foregoing analysis, one might reasonably assume that the close connection of individuals with the social media has impacted on their psychological states, their sense of identity and selfhood; now perhaps more panicked, more fluid, more mobile, and more plural than before, but also more technologically mediated through the space provided by the social media. The multiplicity and networked connections with instant gratification as the dominating motive displace the initial self, introducing in its place a constant pressure to reinvent oneself resulting in a manipulated self called SMIS.

THE MODEL

Literally social media means the media, which is supposed to satisfy the social needs of individuals but to conclude this way will be a mistake. The researchers have presented a model of how social media, the needs and wants of the individual interact in Figure 2.

In the model, the social media does not simply act as a satisfier; instead, it has a dual role. It is both a satisfier to a need as well as modifier and generator of a need. The researchers have taken the Maslow's categorization of needs for the purpose of analysis. The social media acts as a satisfier to the upper level needs i.e. social needs, esteem needs, and self actualization needs both directly as well indirectly. The researchers rule out the possibility that it can satisfy the lower level needs, which are physiological needs, and security needs. At the best, sometimes it can act as an instrument to satisfy these lower level needs. But the second role of social media which is referred to as the (Modifier and Generator) MG role is now more significant than its role as a satisfier.

As mentioned in the preceding section, the pressure to constantly reinvent oneself and its augmentation by the autonomy provided by the social media motivate the individuals to redefine their needs,

Figure 2. Social media and need
Source: Researchers' own creation

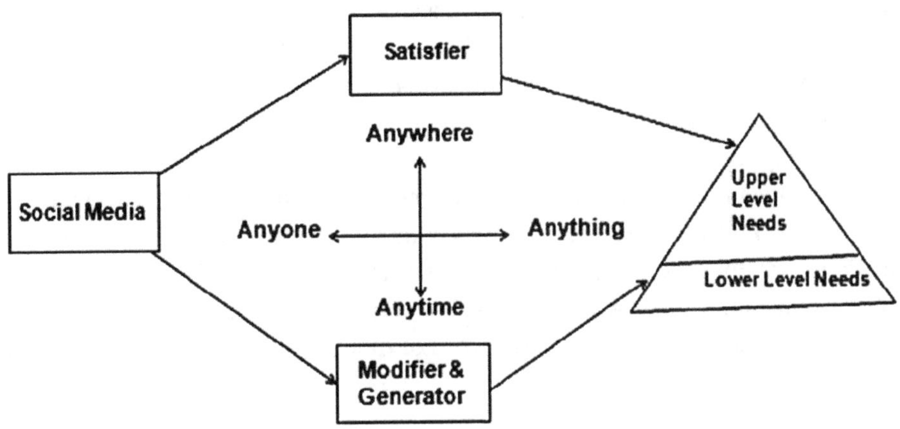

become aware to new needs, and in many cases even they expand the self actualization horizon. This however, is related to what one desires to be and not what he can be. Let us take an example. Consider an individual X who is acquainted with a stranger through social media and with whom he later forges a strong tie. He feels intimacy with her and wants to impress her. To accomplish it, he shall project a SMIS that will help him. Here, the social media has greatly modified the belongingness need, as now it will motivate the person to meet her. At the same time, it has allowed him to alter his identity according to the goal. Similarly, social media has enormous effect in case of esteem needs, given the fact that it is both intrinsic as well as extrinsic. It might happen that an individual who has failed to muster extrinsic esteem may replace it by intrinsic esteem need; clearly social media is a potent instrument in these situations. In contrast to higher level needs social media has generated serious concern about the security needs. It has made people more aware about safety and security needs.

The key elements that govern these two roles of social media can be expressed in 4A's:

- **Anyone**: Through social media, anyone can have access to the world, which was not possible earlier. It has diluted the boundary of income, race, religion, distance etc. As, for instance, income is a barrier which forbids individuals from becoming a member of clubs, associations etc. Social Media till date is virtually free. There are instances when individuals make fake profiles to have access to other individuals.
- **Anything**: At the click of a mouse, a colossal amount of information is available. Now individuals can even interact on a real time basis besides sharing feelings, exchanging photos etc.
- **Anytime**: The internet is 24×7. Therefore, there is no need to have a separate slot to enter the exciting world of social media.
- **Anywhere**: The arrival of smart phones has made it possible to remain connected to the family, friends and others from anywhere across the globe.

IMPLICATIONS FOR BUSINESSES

Ostensibly, the effects of social media on the evolution of self and hence behaviour has changed the entire way consumers recognize need, obtain information about the goods and services that can satisfy those need, evaluate those alternatives, decide upon a particular choice, use that product and finally dispose those products. What the researchers want to put forward is the fact that emergence of social media has exerted its influence on each stage of consumer decision-making process. This in turn, has several implications for the marketers for it could open a whole new world of opportunities for them, provided they are able to comprehend the consumer's changing psycho-social notions of products. Contemporaneously, it is a double edged sword for many sound businesses may decay if they fail to adapt themselves to the changing landscape.

Social media has direct influence on both the consumer behaviour as well as the conduct of businesses but it has more profound influence on the former as compared to the latter Mangold and Faulds (2009). The social media itself being a segment of businesses is also shaped by the factors that have a bearing on the consumer behaviour. This networking is likely to bring significant changes in the way businesses are conducted, for example, how to leverage the word of mouth communication, for brand building and positioning? How to communicate with the consumer especially the youth? What are its implications for the customer relationship management (CRM)? These all questions need to be answered within the above framework and adopting a holistic approach rather than a piecemeal approach.

How the intrusion of social media into the daily life of individuals is going to affect the future conduct of businesses can be well understood by looking at the Table 1.

Table 1 contains example of how different areas of business like sales and marketing, human resource management and production and operation management will have to factor in the growing influence of social media. The researchers would like to present here one fine example of how social media has influenced identity reinvention and in response to it, how companies have started to alter the way they communicate with the consumers. It is the classic Apple Computer's "Think Different" campaign launched in 1998:

Here's to the crazy ones. The misfits. The rebels. The troublemakers. The round pegs in the square holes. The ones who see things differently. They're not fond of rules. And they have no respect of the status quo. You can praise them, quote them, disbelieve them, glorify them or vilify them. Because they change things. They invent. They imagine. They heal. They explore. They create. They inspire. They push the human race forward. Maybe they have to be crazy... we make tools for these kinds of people. Because while some see them as the crazy ones, we genius. (Apple Computers, 1998).

This campaign is a departure from the traditional one in the sense that it allows the individual to appreciate their self (and thus be in the consonance with the product image!), but where does this self will find expression- nowhere but in the world of social media where the individual can add the hues of his choice to his identity at the click of a mouse.

Table 1. Social media and changing landscape of businesses

Management Arena	Social Media Influence	Implications for Businesses
Marketing Management	• Status update on first use of any product • Relying more on word of mouth • More involvement in comparing and contrasting • Consumer Awareness • Tweets by opinion leaders • Trending topics on social media; viral contents on social media	• Complex consumer psyche • More Attention on online Marketing research • Bigger role of data scientists • Product innovation • Quick decision making & more dynamic approach towards brand building • Customer relationship Management • Innovative Promotion strategies
Human Resource Management	• Liking or disliking the organization on social media • More information about Pay and social security benefits • Taking grievance to SNSs • Whistle blowing through Social Media	• Brand management/ Perception management • Appropriate Recruitment and Selection policies • Online Grievance redressal Procedure • Updated information on policies regarding pay and other benefits
Production and Operation Management	• Faster delivery • Good/ bad word of mouth about a product • Joining green Club on SNSs • Replacement/repair of faulty products based on customer reviews	• Supply chain Management • Quality control/ Honest introspection • Packaging • Environment friendly Products • Nimbler After sale service

Source: *Authors' own creation*

CONCLUSION

Social media is one of the most powerful forces today influencing almost every aspect of consumer behaviour and business operations. It influences consumer behaviour by allowing the individuals to change their identities as they want. Furthermore, it satisfies the social needs and higher level needs of individuals to a great extent, but at the same time it is a generator of some other needs. It is so because individuals become more aware about their needs and behaviour. Also social media provides an easy way of satisfying some needs as compared to real world scenario.

Furthermore, social media has made the self identity more fluid and plural. Individuals are free to project themselves as they want anytime. Also they project multiple self at the same time. It helps them to experiment with their identity but has some serious repercussions. For example, the mental agony the individual faces when the response is contrary to what he has expected. Hence, these influences of social media have far reaching consequences for the conduct of businesses. Businesses need to pay more attention to marketing research particularly, online. The consumer psychology will become increasingly complex and appropriate promotion strategy need to be designed. In fact, every aspect of business need to be revamped to deal with the changed situation.

The significance of the study lies in exposing the intricate interplay between the attributes of social media and the self. The study goes a long way in providing a deeper understanding of self concept in connection to social media which has immense importance not only for consumer behavior, but for businesses in general as it can aid and abet them to fine tune their strategies with the consumer psychology. The social media provides a platform for flexible, fervent and rapid response to the globalization process by the individuals. There is hardly any time to stand and stare, but incessant transformation and reinvention is required. As science and technologies offer alternative paradigm and possibilities of social life, the individual has come to occupy the centre stage and this has far-reaching consequences for the business. The businesses will have to respond in an appropriate way to the changing scenario in which the individuals want everything fast. But, what the researchers have not mentioned till now is a word of caution, since it was out of the ambit of the scope of study.

The study contributes to the existing scanty literature on how the social media affects and in turn is affected by the self and develops a conceptual model for understanding the mental states and the concept of self in relation to want satisfaction through social media. The researchers suggest that the spectacular rise of social media – self-discourse can tell us more about the present day state of instant gratification and its ramifications for the business and society. Further, its contribution lies in opening further research areas in this field.

REFERENCES

Anderson, C. (2007). *The long tail: how endless choice is creating unlimited demand.* Random House.

Anderson, K. J. (2001). Internet use among college students: An exploratory study. *Journal of American College Health, 50*(1), 21–26. doi:10.1080/07448480109595707 PMID:11534747

Bandura, A. (1986). *Social foundations of thought and action: A social cognitive theory.* Prentice-Hall, Inc.

Bargh, J. A., & McKenna, K. Y. (2004). The Internet and social life. *Annual Review of Psychology*, *55*(1), 573–590. doi:10.1146/annurev.psych.55.090902.141922 PMID:14744227

Baym, N. K., Zhang, Y. B., & Lin, M. C. (2004). Social interactions across media interpersonal communication on the internet, telephone and face-to-face. *New Media & Society*, *6*(3), 299–318. doi:10.1177/1461444804041438

Beck, U., & Beck-Gernsheim, E. (2009). Losing the Traditional: Individualization and Precarious Freedoms. In *Identity in question* (pp. 14-33).

Constantinides, E., & Fountain, S. J. (2008). Web 2.0: Conceptual foundations and marketing issues. *Journal of direct, data and digital marketing practice,9*(3), 231-244.

Cummings, J., Lee, J., & Kraut, R. (2006). Communication technology and friendship during the transition from high school to college. In *Computers, phones, and the Internet: Domesticating information technology* (pp. 265-278).

Druin, A. (2009). *Mobile technology for children: Designing for interaction and learning*. Morgan Kaufmann.

Eldred, M. (Ed.). (2008). *Social ontology: Recasting political philosophy through a phenomenology of whoness*. Walter de Gruyter. doi:10.1515/9783110333275

Flanagin, A. J. (2005). IM online: Instant messaging use among college students. *Communication Research Reports*, *22*(3), 175–187. doi:10.1080/00036810500206966

Giddens, A. (1991). *Modernity and self-identity: Self and society in the late modern age*. Stanford University Press.

Lenhart, A., Maddenn, M., & Hitlin, P. (2005). Teens and technology: Youth are leading the transition to a fully wired and mobile nation.

Mangold, W. G., & Faulds, D. J. (2009). Social media: The new hybrid element of the promotion mix. *Business Horizons*, *52*(4), 357–365. doi:10.1016/j.bushor.2009.03.002

Mangold, W. G., & Faulds, D. J. (2009). Social media: The new hybrid element of the promotion mix. *Business Horizons*, *52*(4), 357–365. doi:10.1016/j.bushor.2009.03.002

McKenna, K. Y., Green, A. S., & Gleason, M. E. (2002). Relationship formation on the Internet: What's the big attraction? *The Journal of Social Issues*, *58*(1), 9–31. doi:10.1111/1540-4560.00246

Negroponte, N. (1995). *Being Digital*. New York: Alfred A. Kopf.

Noveck, B. S. S. (2009). *Wiki government: how technology can make government better, democracy stronger, and citizens more powerful*. Brookings Institution Press.

Quan-Haase, A. (2008). Instant messaging on campus: Use and integration in university students' everyday communication. *The Information Society*, *24*(2), 105–115. doi:10.1080/01972240701883955

Shirky, C. (2008). *Here comes everybody: The power of organizing without organizations*. Penguin.

Smith, P. R., & Zook, Z. (2011). *Marketing communications: integrating offline and online with social media*. Kogan Page Ltd.

Tapscott, D. (1998). *Growing up digital* (Vol. 302). New York: McGraw-Hill.

Valkenburg, P. M., & Peter, J. (2009). The effects of instant messaging on the quality of adolescents' existing friendships: A longitudinal study. *Journal of Communication*, *59*(1), 79–97. doi:10.1111/j.1460-2466.2008.01405.x

KEY TERMS AND DEFINITIONS

Consumer Behavior: A field of study that deals with the various aspects of consumption behaviour of individuals, groups and organizations. Specifically, how consumers buy, use and dispose products.

Identity: All the characteristics that help in identifying individuals in social settings.

Need: A felt state of deprivation. It has been divided in five categories by Abraham Maslow.

Self-Concept: Generally means the conscious reflection of one's own being or identity as object separate from other or from the environment.

Social Comparison: Comparisons between the self and others.

Social Media Induce Self (SMIS): The self identity projected by individuals using social networking sites which may or may not be like their original self. Many individuals project multiple identities on social networking sites.

Social Media: Online technologies and practices that people use to share opinions, insights, experiences, and perspectives with each other.

Social Networking Sites (SNSs): A social networking website is an online platform, which individuals use to satisfy their social needs.

Section 5

Emerging Trends in Digital Marketing

Chapter 14
eWOM Marketing in Hospitality Industry

Saurabh Kumar Dixit
North Eastern Hill University, India

ABSTRACT

Due to its intangible nature, hospitality business finds it difficult to market its services. Past customer experiences are one of the best strategies that allow some quantification of the quality of the product. Word of mouth has been a key part of every effective marketing strategy for hospitality businesses. It is widely recognized that word of mouth, both positive and negative, has the potential to influence customer purchase decisions. With the technological advancement, the internet has been widely applied in various areas in the hospitality industry. Social media and the growth of web 2.0 have enabled word of mouth to be shared amongst millions of potential customers, one therefore can argue that electronic word of mouth (eWOM) has been the successor of the traditional word of mouth. Therefore, traditional Word-of-Mouth, which spread from person to person vocally has been replaced gradually by electronic Word-of-Mouth (eWOM). A growing trust on eWOM for making choices about hospitality products prompted the author to work on the present chapter.

INTRODUCTION

While planning to visit an unfamiliar place and need to avail hospitality services there, a tourist will definitely think about how to make a decision of an accommodation unit. He may seek help from his friends, check out a travel agency, or perhaps do an exploration on internet. All these strategies have in common is that people often seek the advice of others as part of their decision-making. Through recommendations or warnings obtained from friends or family members, Word-of-Mouth provides the opportunity for potential customers to learn about the positive and negative aspects of services offered by certain organizations before an actual purchase takes place.

Word of Mouth (WOM) has been described as person-to-person oral communication between a receiver and a communicator, whom the receiver perceives as non-commercial, regarding a brand, organization, product or service (Arndt, 1967). It represents the power of personal referral on consumer

DOI: 10.4018/978-1-5225-0332-3.ch014

decision-making. The advance into the internet age has brought some changes to this description. For instance, the presence of virtual WOM in bulletin boards is not face-to-face, oral and ephemeral. This form of WOM is usually referred as (Internet) iWOM or (electronic) eWOM in numerous studies.

The internet has transformed the way information flows across social circles and customers can use it to gather, distribute and publish information (Cakim, 2010). Virtual communities are becoming very influential in the hospitality business. The consumers trust their peers rather than marketing messages and therefore people exchange ideas/experiences through media channels. A virtual travel community makes it easier to obtain information and make decisions. By creating an understanding of these communities and their users, hospitality businesses can facilitate consumer centric marketing or relationships (Buhalis & Laws, 2008). Some types of e-Word of Mouth connect one consumer with another consumer, such as emails. Other marketing channels connect one consumer to wide range of consumers, such as web pages. E-mail and instant messaging is an asynchronous, one-to-one medium. The advantage of eWOM marketing is that it gives possibilities to create mailing lists and does not correlate with e - mailing costs. Once a list is obtained, it becomes a highly efficient means of communication between a hospitality provider and its past and potential guests.

However, recent increase of m - commerce and development of cheap and easy smart phone technology appears the next stage of electronic word of mouth (eWOM) to share hospitality experiences. With the rise of internet, visitors are using internet to talk about their brand experience on practically every available website. People do blog, write reviews on brands' or even independent websites; flushing their experiences they had with a certain product or service, a type of discussion also called as electronic word of mouth (eWOM). One form of Electronic Word-of-Mouth (eWOM) is online reviews generated by internet users regarding travel destinations, hotels, and tourism services, which has become an important source of information for decision making for other travelers (Pan, Mac Laurin, & Crotts, 2007).

Tourism industry is spending an increasing effort to monitor the eWOM in digital business environments, in order to respond to messages collected from customers shared on internet. These data are used to improve products and services, monitor brand image and competitors and adapting marketing strategies (Litvin et al., 2008). Some companies even have positions not only to monitor the shared content but also to manipulate eWOM to generate revenues, by creating and spreading positive WOM, and reinforcing existing desirable opinions.

Internet is both an opportunity and a challenge for hotel marketers. On one hand, it allows marketers to reach customers directly. On the other hand, it challenges them when trying to get their attention long enough to tell their stories (Mills & Law, 2004). To harness the power of Word of Mouth, organizations need to be prepared for the future where customers depend on online information sources (Cakim, 2010). Based on this, the study intends to study the influence and possibilities/challenges to create an understanding of electronic Word of Mouth, as a marketing channel for the hospitality industry.

The present research aims to look closer upon how hotels work with e-Word of Mouth marketing, with focus on online guest reviews. It aims to study how influential online reviews are for marketing in the hospitality industry and to suggest potential strategies for using online guest reviews when marketing. This will also investigate how online customer reviews, a particular form of electronic word of mouth (eWOM), affect consumer decision-making (willingness to purchase) during a first time purchase of services or products.

LITERATURE REVIEW

The advent of internet applications in tourism and hospitality industry has promoted new means of marketing and communications. One of these means is electronic word-of-mouth, which enjoys the advantage of being independent of any commercial influence. As large numbers of travellers are relying more and more on search engines to locate travel and accommodation information (Brey, So, Kim, & Morrison, 2007; Brown, Broderick, & Lee, 2007), electronic word-of-mouth will definitely change the structure of travel information, its accessibility, and subsequently travelers' knowledge and perception of various travel and accommodation products. The penetration of high-speed communications infrastructure into the homes of consumers gave birth to a new format of word-of-mouth advertising via computer-moderated channels (Golan & Zaidner, 2008).

The importance of recommendation is ever increasing with the development and diffusion of internet among personal users. As internet technology became more accessible, electronic interactions among customers increased (Goldsmith, 2006). The resulting term eWOM (electronic world of mouth) became large scale and very influential. Tourism is perceived as high-risk consumption and travellers appreciate almost any advice from former travellers before they make the final purchase decision (Litvin et al., 2008). Recommendation from others is ranked as the most important source of information when making high-risk purchase decisions such as tourism related services (Litvin, Goldsmith & Pan, 2008).

Academic researchers of marketing and consumer behavior have been investigating word-of-mouth technique as early as 1960s (Dichter, 1966; Arndt, 1967). Further, the investigation extended to explore the impact of word-of- mouth on the consumer's purchasing decisions (Godes & Mayzlin, 2004; Litvin et al. 2008; Wangenheim, 2005).

Litvin et al. (2008) defines eWOM as "all informal communications directed at consumers through internet-based technology related to the usage or characteristics of particular goods and services or their sellers." eWOM can also be described as sharing of information of products, services and brands through electronic communication mediums. Several mediums are available for consumers to create eWOM such as instant messaging, chat rooms, e-mail, blogs, newsgroups, review sites and other web pages. eWOM is low cost to access, broader in scope and harder to control (Dellarocas, 2003). Potential customers of most travel services are exposed to eWOM and the exposure rate is ever increasing. However, there is a danger in ease and anonymity of eWOM, the massages shared can be intentionally misleading.

Past studies in eWOM have explored the antecedents that affect the generation of WOM activities and the relationships of WOM characteristics such as valance (Celso and Carlos 2008); and the outcome variables that include customer equity and brand purchasing probability (Buttle 1998; East et al. 2008; Vermeulen and Seegers 2009). With the advent of the internet, eWOM has become the new focus of WOM research; however, there is a lack of studies that have focused on the causal relationships of the mechanisms that explain how eWOM leads to a customer's purchase action and hospitality marketing.

With recognition of the importance of eWOM, previous scholars in tourism and hospitality have mainly investigated the effect of online consumer reviews on two facets: predicting product sales (Ye, Law, Gu, & Chen, 2011) and the consumer decision making process (Vermeulen & Seegers, 2009). These studies consistently found that the characteristics of online reviews (i.e., star ratings, review richness, and valence of reviews) (Sparks & Browning, 2011) and of review providers (i.e., identity disclosure and level of expertise) (Vermeulen & Seegers, 2009) have positive influences on increasing revenues and assisting purchase decisions. However, research that attempts to identify what makes an online review helpful to consumers is limited (Mudambi & Schuff, 2010). Importantly, along with the increasing number of reviews available online, travellers can easily obtain information via internet (decreased search costs), whenever they find it difficult to choose specific information to help with the final decision (increased cognitive costs). Consumers, therefore, tend to seek heuristic information cues (i.e. star ratings in online reviews) to simplify the size of information involved due to their limited ability to arrive at the optimal solution, which is known as bounded rationality (Payne, Bettman, & Johnson, 1992)

METHODOLOGY

The current study is exploratory in nature. It attempts to assess the influence of eWOM on customers' purchasing decisions of hospitality products / services in India. It also evaluates the hotel management reactions in this aspect to find out the new methods of customers' retention and repeat business. The information about the customer's buying behaviour and their response towards eWOM is gathered through different secondary sources. In order to develop structural framework for the present paper, the previous similar research papers, websites, reputed books, journals and personal observation are referred. The main aim of the paper is to examine the customers' behavior towards eWOM and their buying decisions towards hospitality products/services besides the contribution of eWOM in marketing of hospitality products. The websites of the reputed hotel chains, consumer review websites and other similar web platforms are referred to highlight the outputs of the research paper. The eWOM strategies adopted in the premier hotel chains are also examined by visiting their official websites.

THE ROLE OF SOCIAL MEDIA IN MARKETING

Social media has become a preferred inexpensive marketing tool that encourages two-way communications between businesses and consumers, thus giving the latter a freedom like never before. With customers reacting and expressing their views on public domain, social media has become more than a mere marketing tool. It has become a channel that allows interaction and gives companies an opportunity to address the problems and concerns of their customers, which if done effectively, contributes in building the brand (Carraher, Buchanan, & Puia, 2010). In the present economic times where many businesses are cutting their marketing budgets, most successful hotels are also shifting from traditional marketing to social media as a means to communicate with consumers, build their brand and generate higher Return on Investment (ROI) for every marketing penny they spend. Unlike traditional channels of marketing, social media gives updated real time facts about a business such as the number of Facebook fans and likes, Twitter followers and Youtube views. Hotels can track the number of conversations taking place over a new product or service offered by them and can immediately respond to reviews, comments and feedback. Most successful hotels are finding innovative ways to integrate social media with traditional marketing methods to stay ahead in the race (Lanz, Fischhof, & Lee, 2010).

The importance of the internet for the tourism industry has been documented by various authors, e.g. Egger & Buhalis (2008), illustrating the need for developing and applying technological solutions for obtaining strategic benefits. Many scholars e.g. (Egger & Buhalis, 2008; McDonnell, 2006; Soteriades, & Avgeli, 2007) have examined marketing and management issues of electronic tourism; approaches, models and paradigms. A marketing approach that tourism destinations and business use in communicating and influencing connected/networked users and members is digital or viral marketing, essentially based on Social Media (Blery, 2010; Kabani, 2010; Kaplan & Haenlein, 2010). Tourism destinations and companies begin to understand that Information and Communications Technologies (ICT) and Social Media (SM) have forever changed the tourists' consumption behavior. Understanding the current tourists, but more importantly, predicting how to reach those tourists in coming years, will crucially impact how destinations and business develop, market and distribute their services and products (Moutinho, Ballantyne & Rate, 2011). Internet is used all over the world to interact, communicate, and share ideas, content, thoughts, experiences, perspectives, information, and relationships. Literature suggests various types of SM as are shown in Table 1.

Kabani (2010), suggests the following definitions: "Online marketing is the act of leveraging the internet in general to get your message across", "SM marketing is the act of leveraging specific social media platforms (places where people connect and communicate) to promote a product or a service to increase sales". Kirby & Marsden (2006, p. xviii) define viral marketing as "the promotion of a company or its products and services through a persuasive message designed to spread, typically online, from person to person", and connected marketing as "an umbrella term for viral, buzz and word of mouth marketing and any promotional activity that uses word-of-mouth connections between people, whether digital or traditional, as communications media to stimulate demand". McColl (2010, p. 17) defines viral marketing as "the marketing on the internet that spreads a message rapidly". Finally, Chan and Guillet (2011) define SM marketing as "a set of internet-based applications that enable interaction, communication, collaboration of user-generated content and hence, sharing of information such as ideas, thoughts, content, and relationships".

SM offers the opportunity for anyone to write or produce material and to publish this online. This material may then be communicated through their social network of 'friends' (Facebook), 'followers' (Twitter) or 'contacts' (LinkedIn). One of the key benefits of SM is that they are using one of the oldest forms of communication, WOM, and utilizing the power of the internet and the latest mobile technologies to provide the tools to connect people together quickly (Chan & Guillet, 2011).

Table 1. Social Media: Types and Content / Function

Type	Content/Function	Examples
Blogs and Micro - Blogs	Blogs are websites that allow blogger (s) to keep logs, share personal experiences and insights in a particular area, and interact with readers through the posting of comments. Micro-blogs: share the same function, except that the content of these blogs are mainly text-based and are limited to a certain number of characters.	Blogger (blogging) Twitter (microblogging) Travel Blog (travel blogging)
Social Networking Sites	Websites where people create personal profiles, virtually meet, connect, communicate, and develop relationships with other users.	Facebook (social networking) LinkedIn (professional networking)
Collaborative Projects	Aiming at aggregating the community intelligence, these sites highly depend on the users to work out the content. They are classified into two main types: wikis (sites with content open to users) and social bookmarking sites. In these sites, users interact with each other in the process of content collaboration.	Wikipedia (wiki)
Content Community Sites	Sites designed for sharing of materials (text, photos, videos, etc.) modified from pre-existing work or originated with people who upload the materials.	YouTube Flickr
Sites Dedicated for Feedback	Websites that allow users to post, read, review, discuss, and share experiences and opinions on a myriad of topics.	Typical forms: Online forums and sites dedicated for product reviews

Source: Retrieved from Kaplan & Haenlein (2010), O'Connor (2008), Solis (2010), and Wunsch-incent & Vickery (2007)

The one point that differentiates social media from traditional media is user participation. Like traditional media, social media serves as a vehicle to reach out to and inform consumers; however, it is only social media that allows consumers to participate and propagate their views. According to the Forrester Research on social media, approximately half of adults who go online take part in social networking. This number has a significant implication for businesses who want access to data rich information. Marketing companies use customized data mining software that enable them to keep a track of consumer behavior, spending pattern and satisfaction ratings. These findings are used to measure the effectiveness of marketing campaigns in terms of ROI and other performance indicators (Kasavana, 2008).

The parameters of social networking websites possess several unique implications for the hospitality industry including guests, staff, and management. These sites provide a platform for a rating system that can be used to generate, monitor, and evaluate reputation and image of the business. Online consumer-generated content is perceived as highly credible and in fact, more so than information attributed to the hospitality entity (Starkov & Mechoso, 2008). Hospitality company participation in online social networking has been shown to be a cost-effective means for interaction and engagement with potential clients. Participation in these websites provides businesses with direct access to active users without the need to adding any additional hardware, or software.

ONLINE CONSUMER REVIEWS FOR THE HOSPITALITY PRODUCTS

Current consumers largely consider online consumer reviews as a form of eWOM in a decision-making process to purchase products online and offline. Online reviews enable people to obtain detailed information with high trustworthiness and credibility compared to information provided by marketers. Based on the importance of online reviews, a number of researchers in marketing and information systems have concerned the characteristics of reviews and reviewers to estimate the effect of online reviews on three main aspects: product sales, consumer behaviours, and users' perceptions of information (Park & Nicolau, 2015).

The nature of tourism and hospitality products (inherently experiential, intangible, and heterogeneous) makes it hard for people to estimate the quality of products before actually purchasing them. Travellers actively seek detailed and reliable information to alleviate the level of uncertainty in the decision making process. Online reviews written by other consumers allow travellers to obtain sophisticated information as well as acquire indirect experience of tourism consumption (Litvin, Goldsmithb, & Pan, 2008).

With the recognition of these benefits of online reviews, different scholars have estimated the effect of consumer reviews on three areas: (1) product sales, (2) travel decisions, and (3) source evaluations. With regard to product sales in hospitality, several researchers estimated the changes of market share in hotels (Duverger, 2013; Xie, Chen, & Wu, 2012) and restaurants (Zhang, Ye, Law, & Li, 2010) by considering the characteristics of online reviews. Based on the assumption that the number of reviews per room for a hotel corresponds to sales per room, Ogut and Tas (2012) assessed the effect of review scores and star ratings on not only hotel room sales but also on price. The results of the study found that while hotel star ratings do not affect sales, improvement of customer rating increases the sales and price of hotel rooms. Ye et al. (2011) investigated a hotel consumer review website and found that a 10 percent increase in travel review ratings increases online hotel bookings by more than five percent. In the restaurant context, Zhang et al. (2010) showed that consumer-generated ratings representing the quality of food, environment and service of restaurants and volume of reviews have positive relationships with online restaurant popularity (i.e. number of page views). The study of Yacouel and Fleischer (2012) attempted to estimate the relationship between consumer review ratings and price premiums. The online reviews posted in online travel agencies reflecting service quality help prospective consumers trust their decisions; this increase in trustworthiness leads the travellers to pay higher price for hotel rooms.

In terms of travel decision-making, Leung, Law, van Hoof, and Buhalis (2013) suggested that online consumer-generated contents influence all the phases of the travel planning process, including pre-, during- and post-trips. For example, online reviews affect the formation of consideration sets (Vermeulen & Seegers, 2009) and purchasing intentions (Sparks & Browning, 2011) for travel products, whereby positive reviews with numerical ratings improve attitudes toward travel products and in turn, increase purchasing intentions. Filieri and McLeay (2014) used an elaboration likelihood model to identify the factors that lead to the adoption of consumer information, such as product ranking, information accuracy, value-added information, information relevance, and information timeliness. Several tourism and hospitality researchers explored travellers' responses to online reviews, which focuses on the trustiness, helpfulness, and usefulness of reviews (Racherla & Friske, 2012; Wei, Miao, & Huang, 2013). The study of Wei et al. (2013) revealed that positive consumer reviews enjoy more favourable evaluations than negative comments, and heuristic cues of online reviews lead readers to enlarge the perceived helpfulness of the reviews.

A research report from Cornell University's Center for Hospitality Research used data from three separate data sources to show the impact of online reputation upon hotel performance (Anderson, 2012). The report, using online reputation data from Review Pro and hotel performance data from Smith Travel Research, shows that a 1% improvement in review score translates into about a 1% gain in revenue per available room (RevPAR). Table 2 shows these gains with luxury hotels experiencing a 0.49% gain (percentage of gain in review score), increasing to 1.42% for mid-scale hotels. The results clearly demonstrate that online reputation, as measured by guest review score, has increasing impacts on hotel performance as the chains scale is decreased.

Similarly, using data from 13,341 reservations from 7 major US cities (The seven cities include Boston, Chicago, Dallas, Houston, Los Angeles, Miami, New York, Orlando, and Phoenix, with data consisting of hotel attributes like star level, price, guest review scores, number of reviews, etc. For each hotel booked, as well as all hotels displayed on the search results that were not booked) made through Travelocity during July 2012, the report indicates that the odds of a consumer booking a hotel increase

Table 2. Impact of Guest Reviews on Hotel Performance – Change in ADR, Occupancy and RevPAR (%) Given A Change in Review Score (%)

	Pricing Power (ADR)	Demand (Occupancy)	Performance (RevPAR)
All	0.80	0.20	0.96
Luxury	0.44	0.09	0.49
Upper upscale	0.57	0.30	0.74
Upscale	0.67	0.19	0.83
Upper midscale	0.74	0.42	1.13
Midscale	0.89	0.54	1.42

Source: Anderson, C. K. (2012)

by 1.142 if their Travelocity Review Score (five point scale) increases by one point, say from 3.1 to 4.1. As such, if the hotel chooses to increase price (versus market share), a 1-point gain translates into about an 11% gain in price while maintaining occupancy (WTO, 2014).

STRATEGIC ISSUES OF E - WOM IN HOSPITALITY MARKETING

- **Quality Assurance:** E-WOM seems particularly important to the marketing of hospitality products / services. Consumers need to rely on eWOM to reduce the level of perceived risk and uncertainty that are often associated with service purchase decisions (Murray, 1991). WOM have a greater influence on purchasers of services than on purchasers of products. The best eWOM of a hotel comes not from a sound sales budget or advertising, but from the high service quality itself and a good consumer experience, that is to say it is necessary to provide high-quality service and good experience before carrying out eWOM marketing. The quality of service is the most valuable things to sell to consumers for a long time, and a necessary condition to form a good eWOM. It is the presupposition for eWOM marketing to make consumers talk about companies' product or brand. Two major reasons could stimulate consumers to talk about companies' product or brand: one is that consumers gaining a good product experience during or after using it would like talk about with others; the other is that consumers express their dissatisfaction or complaint when they got bad experience. The attitude of eWOM marketing for a hotel is to achieve a positive information transmit effect, so it is necessary to provide consumers with high-quality service and good experience (Guo and Yang, 2006).
- **Choosing Well-Established Website:** The website reputation has a significant impact on the eWOM of a hotel. Due to low barriers of entry and lack of gatekeepers on the web, well-established and reputed websites have been more readily accepted by consumers than unknown sites (Shamdasani et al., 2001). A website's reputation could serve as extrinsic cues of eWOM information quality especially in the case of purchasing hotel's experience products. Consumer confidence brought about by a credible website might influence the eWOM posted on the website. Therefore, internet marketers may offset perceived risk by enhancing positive eWOM on well-established sites. This strategy could be more effective for hotel, which mainly provides service, the quality of which is inherently difficult for consumers to judge. This implies that a well-chosen website for eWOM placement can build and enhance eWOM effectiveness.
- **Avoiding Negative eWOM:** The importance of positive eWOM is generally recognized in the hotel industry, while the influence of the negative eWOM on a hotel has always been neglected. Evidence suggests that negative information is more attention grabbing in general and receives greater scrutiny than positive information (Homer and Yoon, 1992). Previous research suggests that the eWOM influence appears to be asymmetrical in that a negative eWOM has a stronger influence on customers' brand evaluations (Arndt, 1967; Mizerski, 1982) and on the purchase intentions of potential buyers than a positive eWOM. Hotel products may sustain great damage in the eWOM effect due to negative eWOM information. The reason is that the negative eWOM information magnifies consumers' prevailing uncertainty and fear initiated by their poor cognitive knowledge structure of a hotel. Therefore, the key point for company to carry out eWOM is to encourage and stimulate positive eWOM and avoid negative eWOM.

- **Open eWOM Environment:** Spreading true, clear, specific information to consumers is the guarantee to create a good brand image and successfully implement effective eWOM marketing. It is necessary for a hotel to spread true, clear, specific information to consumers from the beginning of eWOM marketing, for the reason that the dissemination speed of eWOM information is to be regulated to prevent the information from distortion. Clear and specific brand image more easily become the object of consumers' talking, while abstract and fuzzy image more easily leads to misunderstanding and is not conducive to eWOM communication.
- **Cultivate Opinion Leaders:** Although the eWOM marketing is long-term work, in most cases opinion leaders can help hotels in its effective application. Frequently, this information is transmitted by opinion leaders through eWOM communication. Opinion leaders are defined as individuals who transmit information about a topic to other people, in terms of the extent to which information is sought by those people (King and Summer, 1970). Therefore, it has become very important for a hotel to cultivate opinion leaders of online word-of-mouth marketing. Marketers of hotel could realize the initiative of eWOM marketing by cultivating opinion leaders to influence opinion seekers to carry out targeted eWOM marketing.

CONCLUSION

Since most goods and services offered by the hospitality business are experiential in nature, it is hard to predict their quality before the purchase. This makes the role of consumer review even more important for first timers or potential customers (Crotts, 1999). Companies that promote satisfied customers to share their experiences on web-based, company approved social networking platforms are more likely to draw new customers (Hardin & Kim, 2010). In addition, companies that address negative reviews retain dissatisfied customers; promote a positive impact on the word-of-mouth and improve their bottom line performance. According to Fornell and Wernfelt (1987), it is cheaper to retain existing satisfied customers than finding new ones. Since social media facilitates greater interaction between customers and company representatives, hospitality businesses today have more opportunities than ever before to respond promptly and effectively to customer complaints.

After a careful review of the literature on the use of social media among businesses, an argument was made about how customers of these businesses perceive this approach to marketing and brand formulation and management. According to Lanz, Fischhof, and Lee (2010) interactive marketing will comprise 21% of all marketing spending by 2014, and social media will represent 3% to 6% of the interactive marketing spend. If the above numbers are anything to go by, it is only logical to assume that social media will continue to grow as part of the hospitality industry landscape. According to Kasavana (2008) in order for better business outcomes companies need to continually use social media for monitoring, analyzing and evaluating customer reviews. In order to avoid inaccurate information and negative publicity businesses will have to come up with digital media policies to safeguard them. Just like any other technology social media should be embraced with proper planning and rigorous guidelines for maximum success.

Therefore, this research offers insights into the nature of the relationships that exist among marketing decisions (price and advertising expenditures), eWOM (customers' ratings and number of reviews), and the business performance of lodging establishments. In particular, both customer ratings and the number of reviews determine performance. The ratings measure refers to the overall evaluation of the establishment's offering by users. The conclusions being drawn with this study are that costumers tend to rely more on the virtual communities, their peers, online reviews and such stuff rather than traditional methods of marketing. Although, marketers tell that it is tough to determine the influence of e-Word of Mouth but they still believe that many people tend to read the e-reviews. It also enhances brand awareness along with influencing people.

In considering this finding, we note an argument in previous literature that the link between the number of reviews (i.e., the volume of the reviews) and sales represents an awareness effect. Overall then, negative feedback might enhance the credibility of reviews and websites, and more reviews can increase awareness. But, we caution against regarding negative feedback as harmless. If it grows overwhelming in reference to a particular establishment, it can have fatal effects (Vermeulen & Seegers, 2009). Therefore, lodging establishment must monitor the presence of low ratings and negative comments in online reviews, and then respond by resolving any problems that arose during the service delivery.

Online reviews give a company access to immediate assessments of its customers' evaluations, and offer strong predictors of tourists' adoption of information (Filieri & McLeay, 2014). Within the e- WOM strategy, review ratings represent an attempt to quantify service quality perceptions, which are determinant for customer satisfaction and behavioural intentions (Parasuraman, Zeithaml, & Malhotra, 2005).

Also, on account of the intangibility of tourism products, credibility is an essential point to be considered. According to the results obtained, this credibility can be achieved if reviewers' names are supported with their photographs. Note that this enhancement in credibility has to be considered in terms of both usefulness and enjoyment. In line with the uncertainty derived from intangibility, comments from ''expert'' and ''reputable'' reviewers seem to be perceived as more useful and more enjoyable, so emphasis should be placed on them when firms attempt to stress the content of specific reviews.

It is not just businesses that face challenges; even customers need to be aware of false reviews put up by companies. In many instances, businesses have used their own employees or promoters to write good reviews for themselves, and negative reviews for their competitors (Pogue, 2009). A full proof means of establishing authenticity of reviews on social media websites will therefore be very beneficial for customers. For instance, amazon.com requires users to have an account on Yahoo or Hotmail before they create a new Amazon.com account.

Therefore, eWOM marketing provides a cheap and effective marketing tool for hospitality enterprisers to stimulate a warm concern to consumers and helps to build company image, brand recognition and reputation; it has new characteristics that must be deeply understood. Otherwise, eWOM could not be exploited well. Therefore, hotels must be committed, before implementing the eWOM marketing, to provide consumers with high-quality product or service, combine with the characteristics of eWOM communication, boost positive eWOM, and avoid negative eWOM to enhance visibility, reputation, and promote sales as well.

REFERENCES

Anderson, C. K. (2012). The Impact of Social Media on Lodging Performance. *Center for Hospitality Research Report, 12*(15), 6–11.

Arndt, J. (1967). *Word of mouth advertising: A review of the literature*. New York: Advertising Research Foundation.

Arndt, J. (1967). Role of Product-Related Conversations in the Diffusion of a New Product. *JMR, Journal of Marketing Research*, *4*(3), 291–295. doi:10.2307/3149462

Blery, E. (2010). *Customer loyalty; marketing techniques to engender loyalty among customers*. Athens: Propompos Publications.

Brey, E. T., So, S., Kim, D., & Morrison, A. M. (2007). Web-based permission marketing: Segmentation for the lodging industry. *Tourism Management*, *28*(6), 1408–1416. doi:10.1016/j.tourman.2007.01.002

Brown, J., Broderick, A. J., & Lee, N. (2007). Word of mouth communication within online communities: Conceptualizing the online social network. *Journal of Interactive Marketing*, *21*(3), 2–20. doi:10.1002/dir.20082

Buhalis, D., & Law, R. (2008). Progress in information technology and tourism management: 20 years on and 10 years after the Internet – the state of Etourism research. *Tourism Management*, *29*(4), 609–623. doi:10.1016/j.tourman.2008.01.005

Buttle, F. A. (1998). Word of Mouth: Understanding and Managing Referral Marketing. *Journal of Strategic Marketing*, *6*(3), 241–254. doi:10.1080/096525498346658

Cakim, I. M. (2010). *Implementing Word of Mouth marketing: online strategies to identify influencers, craft stories, and draw customers. New Jersey*:John Wiley & Sons.

Carraher, S. M., Buchanan, J. K., & Puia, G. (2010). Entrepreneurial need for achievement in China, Latvia, and the USA. *Baltic Journal of Management*, *5*(3), 378–396. doi:10.1108/17465261011079767

Celso, A.M., & Carlos, A.V.R. (2008). Word-of-Mouth Communications in Marketing: A Meta-Analytic Review of the Antecedents and Moderators. *Journal of the Academy of Marketing Science*, 36(4), 578-96.

Chan, N. L., & Guillet, B. D. (2011). Investigation of social media marketing: How does the hotel industry in Hong Kong perform in marketing on social media websites? *Journal of Travel & Tourism Marketing*, *28*(4), 345–368. doi:10.1080/10548408.2011.571571

Crotts, J. (1999). Consumer decision making and prepurchase information search. In Y. Mansfield & A. Pizam (Eds.), *Consumer behavior in travel and tourism* (pp. 149–168). New York, NY: Haworth Press.

Dellarocas, C. (2003). The digitization of word of mouth: Promise and challenges on of online feedback mechanisms. *Management Science*, *49*(10), 1407–1424. doi:10.1287/mnsc.49.10.1407.17308

Dichter, E. (1966). How Word-of-Mouth Advertising Works. *Harvard Business Review*, *44*(6), 147–166.

Duverger, P. (2013). Curvilinear effects of user-generated content on hotels' market share: A dynamic panel-data analysis. *Journal of Travel Research*, *52*(4), 465–478. doi:10.1177/0047287513478498

East, R., Hammond, K., & Lomax, W. (2008). Measuring the Impact of Positive and Negative Word of Mouth on Brand Purchase Probability. *International Journal of Research in Marketing*, *25*(3), 215–224. doi:10.1016/j.ijresmar.2008.04.001

Egger, R., & Buhalis, D. (Eds.). (2008). *Etourism case studies: management and marketing issues in etourism*. Oxford: Elsevier.

Filieri, R., & McLeay, F. (2014). E-WOM and accommodation: An analysis of the factors that influence travelers' adoption of information from online reviews. *Journal of Travel Research*, *53*(1), 44–57. doi:10.1177/0047287513481274

Fornell, C., & Wernerfelt, B. (1987). Defensive marketing strategy by customer com- plaint management: A theoretical analysis. *JMR, Journal of Marketing Research*, *24*(4), 337–346. doi:10.2307/3151381

Godes, D., & Mayzlin, D. (2004). Using online conversations to study word-of-mouth communications. *Marketing Science*, *23*(4), 545–560. doi:10.1287/mksc.1040.0071

Golan, G. J., & Zaidner, L. (2008). Creative strategies in viral advertising: An application of Taylor's six segment message strategy wheel. *Journal of Computer-Mediated Communication*, *13*(4), 959–972. doi:10.1111/j.1083-6101.2008.00426.x

Goldsmith, R. E. (2006). Electronic word of mouth. In K. P. Mehdi (Ed.), *Encyclopedia of e-commerce, e-government and mobile commerce* (pp. 408–412). Hershey, PA: Idea Group. doi:10.4018/978-1-59140-799-7.ch067

Guoqing, G. U. O., & Xueeheng, Y. A. N. G. (2006). A Study of Word-of-Mouth Marketing and the Application Strategies in the Era of Internet. *Finance &Trade Economics*, *9*, 56–59.

Hardin, A., & Kim, J. (2010). The impact of virtual worlds on word-of-mouth: Improving social networking and servicescape in the hospitality industry. *Journal of Hospitality Marketing & Management*, *19*(7), 735–753. doi:10.1080/19368623.2010.508005

Homer, P. M., & Yoon, S. (1992). Message framing and the interrelationships among ad-based feelings, affect, and cognition. *Advert*, *21*(1), 19–33. doi:10.1080/00913367.1992.10673357

Kabani, S. (2010). *The Zen of social media marketing: an easier way to build credibility, generate buzz, and increase revenue*. Dallas: BenBella Books.

Kaplan, A. M., & Haenlein, M. (2010). Users of the world, unite! The challenges and opportunities of social media. *Business Horizons*, *53*(1), 59–68. doi:10.1016/j.bushor.2009.09.003

Kasavana, M. L. (2008). The unintended consequences of social media and the hospitality industry. *Hospitality Upgrade Fall 2008*. Retrieved from http://www.hospitalityupgrade.com/_files/File_Articles/HUFall08_Kasavana_SocialMediaandHospitality.pdf

King, C. W., & Summer, J. O. (1970). Overlap of opinion leadership across product categories. *JMR, Journal of Marketing Research*, *7*(1), 43–50. doi:10.2307/3149505

Kirby, J., & Marsden, P. (Eds.). (2006). *Connected marketing: the viral, buzz and word of mouth revolution*. Oxford: Butterworth/Heinemann, Elsevier.

Lanz, L., Fischhof, B., & Lee, R. (2010). *How are Hotels Embracing Social Media in 2010? Examples of How to Start Engaging*. New York: HVS Sales and Marketing Services.

Leung, D., Law, R., van Hoof, H., & Buhalis, D. (2013). Social media in tourism and hospitality: A literature review. *Journal of Travel & Tourism Marketing*, *30*(1-2), 3–22. doi:10.1080/10548408.2013.750919

Litvin, S. W., Goldsmith, R. E., & Pan, B. (2008). Electronic word-of-mouth in hospitality and tourism management. *Tourism Management*, *29*(3), 458–468. doi:10.1016/j.tourman.2007.05.011

McColl, P. (2010). *Viral explosions!: proven techniques to expand, explode, or ignite your business or brand online. Franklin Lakes*. Career Press.

McDonnell, I. (2006). *Etravel and tourism; marketing and management techniques*. Oxford: Elsevier.

Mills, E. J., & Law, R. (2004). *Handbook of consumer behavior, tourism and the Internet*. Binghamton, NY: Haworth Hospitality Press.

Mintel International Group. (2007). *Hotels and accommodations—US*. Chicago, IL: Author.

Mizerski, R. W. (1982). An attribution of the disproportionate influence of unfavorable information. *Consumer Research*, *9*(12), 301–310. doi:10.1086/208925

Moutinho, L., Ballantyne, R., & Rate, S. (2011). The new business environment and trends in tourism. In L. Moutinho (Ed.), *Strategic management in tourism* (2nd ed., pp. 1–19). Oxfordshire: CAB International. doi:10.1079/9781845935887.0001

Mudambi, S. M., & Schuff, D. (2010). What makes a helpful online review? A study of customer reviews on Amazon.com. *Management Information Systems Quarterly*, *34*(1), 185–200.

Murray, K. B. (1991). A test of services marketing theory: Consumer information acquisition activities. *Journal of Marketing*, *55*(1), 10–25. doi:10.2307/1252200

O'Connor, P. (2008). Online social media and travel international (Market research report). *Oxygen*. Retrieved from http://oxygen.mintel.com/sinatra/oxygen/display/id=387948

Ogut, H., & Tas, B. K. O. (2012). The influence of internet customer reviews on online sales and prices in hotel industry. *Service Industries Journal*, *32*(2), 197–214. doi:10.1080/02642069.2010.529436

Parasuraman, A., Zeithaml, V. A., & Malhotra, A. (2005). E-S-QUAL: A multiple-item scale for assessing electronic service quality. *Journal of Service Research*, *7*(3), 213–233. doi:10.1177/1094670504271156

Park, S., & Nicolau, J. L. (2015). Asymmetric Effects of Online Consumer Reviews. *Annals of Tourism Research*, *50*, 67–83.

Payne, J. W., Bettman, J. R., & Johnson, J. R. (1992). Behavioral decision research: A constructive processing perspective. *Annual Review of Psychology*, *43*(1), 87–131. doi:10.1146/annurev.ps.43.020192.000511

Racherla, P., & Friske, W. (2012). Perceived usefulness of online consumer reviews: An exploratory investigation across three services categories. *Electronic Commerce Research and Applications*, *11*(6), 548–559. doi:10.1016/j.elerap.2012.06.003

Shamdasani Prem, N., Stanaland Andrea, J. S., & Tan, J. (2001). Location, location, location: Insights for advertising placement on the Web. *Journal of Advertising Research*, *41*(4), 7–21. doi:10.2501/JAR-41-4-7-21

Solis, B. (2010). Defining social media 2006–2010. Retrieved from http://www.briansolis.com/2010/01/definingsocial-media-the-saga-continues

Soteriades, M., & Avgeli, V. (2007). Promoting tourism destinations: A strategic marketing approach. *Tourism: an International Interdisciplinary Journal*, *55*(3), 335–345.

Sotiriadis, M. D., & van Zyl, C. (2013). Electronic word-of-mouth and online reviews in tourism services: The use of twitter by tourists. *Electronic Commerce Research*, *13*(1), 103–124. doi:10.1007/s10660-013-9108-1

Sparks, B. A., & Browning, V. (2011). The impact of online reviews on hotel booking intentions and perception of trust. *Tourism Management*, *32*(6), 1310–1323. doi:10.1016/j.tourman.2010.12.011

Starkov, M. & Mechoso, M. (2008, August). Best Practices on Monitoring Hotel Review Sites. *Hospitality eBusiness Strategies*.

Vermeulen, I.E., & Daphne S. (2009). Tried and Tested: The Impact of Online Hotel Reviews on Consumer Consideration. *Tourism Management*, 30(1), 123-27.

Wangenheim, F. V. (2005). Post switching negative word of mouth. *Journal of Service Research*, *8*(1), 67–78. doi:10.1177/1094670505276684

Wei, W., Miao, L., & Huang, Z. J. (2013). Customer engagement behaviors and hotel responses. *International Journal of Hospitality Management*, *33*, 316–330. doi:10.1016/j.ijhm.2012.10.002

World Tourism Organization. (2014). *Online Guest Reviews and Hotel Classification Systems – An Integrated Approach Report, World Tourism Organization*. Madrid, Spain: UNWTO.

Wunsch-Vincent. S., & Vickery, G. (2007). Participative web and user-created content: Web 2.0, wikis and social networking. Paris: OECD.

Xie, K., Chen, C.-C., & Wu, S.-Y. (2012). Leveraging the ranking power of hotels by consumer reviews: Evidence from TripAdvisor.com. *Proceedings of the 18th annual graduate conference*, Washington State University.

Yacouel, N., & Fleischer, A. (2012). The role of cybermediaries in reputation building and price premiums in the online hotel market. *Journal of Travel Research*, *51*(2), 219–226. doi:10.1177/0047287511400611

Ye, Q., Law, R., Gu, B., & Chen, W. (2011). The influence of user-generated content on traveler behavior: An empirical investigation on the effects of e-word-of-mouth to hotel online bookings. *Computers in Human Behavior*, *27*(2), 634–639. doi:10.1016/j.chb.2010.04.014

Zhang, Z., Ye, Q., Law, R., & Li, Y. (2010). The impact of e-word-of-mouth on the online popularity of restaurants: A comparison of consumer reviews and editor reviews. *International Journal of Hospitality Management*, *29*(4), 694–700. doi:10.1016/j.ijhm.2010.02.002

KEY TERMS AND DEFINITIONS

eWOM: electronic Word-of-Mouth provides the opportunity for potential customers to learn about the positive and negative aspects of services offered by certain organizations through internet before an actual purchase.

Guest: The visitors availing the hospitality products / services.

Hospitality Business: the business covering hotels, restaurants, cafeterias, cruise liners and other similar catering establishments.

Marketing: Efforts to create awareness of the products/ services.

Online Review: Experience shared by the customers on different online portals.

Social Media: An important constituent affecting the eWOM behaviour.

Chapter 15
Interplay of Attitude, Satisfaction and Purchase Intentions:
A Study of Indian Youth in Online Shopping

Rajeev Kumar Malik
Banaras Hindu University, India

Priyanka
Banaras Hindu University, India

Sujit Kumar Dubey
Banaras Hindu University, India

ABSTRACT

On one hand entry of e-commerce is bringing a new dimension to competitive landscape, and on the other the customers are becoming more aware and are willing to exercise their choice more than ever before. Increased influence of social media among youth provide the opportunity for retailers to engage with customers in newer forms and to extend their relationship with the customers. All these things provided the motivation for researchers to undertake this endeavor to understand and examine the attitudes of youth towards Online Shopping. Efforts were made to understand the relationship between Attitudes towards Online Shopping, Satisfaction and Future Intentions to Shop Online. Satisfaction of online shoppers worked as a partial mediator between Attitude towards Online Shopping and purchase intentions.

INTRODUCTION

Indian Retailers are confronted with empowered customers; scattered markets and increased competition. The entry of e-commerce is bringing a new dimension to competitive landscape. The customers are becoming more aware and are willing to exercise their choice more than before. There is significant influence of social media among youth. This provides the retailers the opportunity to extend their relationship with the customers.

DOI: 10.4018/978-1-5225-0332-3.ch015

Online retailing has a growing prospect in the global marketplace. It provides location free, customer controlled, and information rich retail service. Internet has made a visible and authentic contribution towards the transformation in business nowadays. Internet has made E-commerce a possibility and it is inclusive of several pre purchase and post purchase activities. This, in turn, has led to purchase and sale of products, services and information over internet. Internet user of the twentieth century is young, professional, educated, and affluent with higher levels of income. They value time more than money, which automatically makes the working population and dual-income or single-parent households with time constraints a better candidate to be targeted by non-store retailers. E-commerce has stamped its authority over the market due to many impressive advantages – simpler, faster and efficient business transactions. It offers considerable opportunity for growth for a developing economy like India.

According to an American Express report, online shopping in India is expected to reach 38 million cyber shoppers in 2015. At present, there are 74 million internet users, which will continue to increase in coming years. India is third largest in terms of internet usage in world, with majority of internet users' age less than 35 years. The main factor for the growth of E-commerce is not only the growing internet usage, but also increase in the number of credit card users in India. As per the report, the number of Indians with credit cards increased by 4% in 2013. The e-commerce market in India was worth $16 billion in 2013 and is expected to touch $56 billion by 2023, according to the ASSOCHAM report. A huge number of choices, improved confidence and convenience drive the rapid growth of E-commerce in India. The e-commerce market in India will control 6.5% of total retail market by 2023.Without doubt; online retailing has most of its customers based in cities. Mumbai is the biggest contributor to the revenue of online retailers, followed by Delhi and Kolkata.

Youth's perception of shopping has changed dramatically. They now prefer to sit around, browse and shop from anywhere on their laptops or tabs or smartphones, then visiting the traditional markets. They do not want to invest time in travelling to different parts of the cities which costs money, roam around from shop to shop and buy something that was not their first choice but had to buy it because they had invested so much time into it. The reason why this significant change has taken place is the convenience of online retailing. This is mainly because online retailers have made available many features that are absolutely absent in the traditional markets like 'price comparisons'. Most of the students buy electronic items, books, etc. online and have the opportunity to compare prices of their choice, from hundreds of vendors who are selling that particular headphone, unlike in a traditional market where they would have to settle for the vendor's price. Many are still not confident enough to share credit/debit card information on online merchant websites. The online retailers have introduced the 'Cash on Delivery' option for such people and this has worked wonders. People, who used to be skeptical of the goods purchased online, now buy most of their necessities online including books, music and entertainment, kitchen and home décor, medicines etc. Online retailing has overcome the constraints through infinite choices, easy access to consumer reviews, no pressure sales and minimum time. Today's youth view this physical and online environment as a cohesive unit due to a combination of a fast paced lifestyle and increasing distances in which technology acts as a bridge. Fast evolution of mobility devices with decreased cost has enhanced this adoption. Focusing on same day delivery model, shipping within the minimum possible time, implementing a liberal return policy, and addressing trust and security concerns are some important ways retailers are working to ensure repeat purchases by existing customers.

Online shopping or "armchair shopping" as it is widely called, is expanding its horizons. It has definitely taken over a bunch of markets in India. Flipkart, eBay, Quickr and many more online retailers are enjoying positive response especially because of young and open minded citizens. Information technology has become a tool that has been used by retailers and it has created a dramatic shift in the purchasing process across the globe. The online channel is slowly making its presence felt in India. Indian companies are creating either their own web portal or are tying up with horizontal players like Rediff.com and Indiatimes.com to offer their products on the web.

The ICICI Bank supports the mobile cash venture in urban area, which enables the shoppers to purchase the consumer products through mobile phones. As the mobile network rollouts are growing with the increased pace in Tier-II cities and rural areas, it would be a matter of time before mobile phone penetration becomes significant in these areas. Mobile phones could eventually prove to be the medium that takes innovative retailers to places where computers and e- commerce are yet to arrive. Though this is in infant stage, it will serve as an important channel in coming future. Income generated from E-retailing is showing a growth of 50 per cent year on year with $10 billion in 2011. If it maintains the same growth rate, it is expected to be around $40billion in 2015. (Rebirth of e-Commerce in India, 2011 – E&Y)

REVIEW OF LITERATURE

With the advent of E-commerce, consumers can directly buy goods and/or services from a seller over the internet. This process is called business to consumer (B2C) commerce (Belanger et al., 2002). The use of E- commerce has created a new global market (Cohan, 2000). Nowadays, the business is no longer confined to physical boundaries or time constraint (Guo & Sun, 2004). Business is influenced in a dramatic manner through E-commerce, which in turn fuelling the growth of the retail sector (Nelson & Leon, 2012).

Demographic factors and personality traits are important factors in understanding why individuals shop online. Factors such as age, gender, education, and income, which form the demography, play an important moderating effect between the basic determinants and consumers' attitude toward online shopping (Burke, 2002). Dholakia and Rego (1999) studied the correlation between age and online shopping. The study revealed that younger consumers have more inclination towards online shopping. Younger consumers frequently visit the shopping sites for purchasing and they agree to the fact that online shopping is more convenient over traditional shopping which they felt is time consuming (Sorce et al., 2005; Wood, 2002; Ratchford et al., 2001). Coming to the next variable gender, men are more involved in online shopping, as compared to women who prefer shopping using catalogues at home. But the female shoppers who favours online shopping, has more frequency to shop online than their male counterparts (Burke, 2002; Li et al., 1999). Education also plays a significant role in shopping from web stores. Educated people are more comfortable to shop online as their level of internet literacy is high (Burke, 2002; Li et al., 1999). Income is an important determinant in online shopping. People in high-income bracket are more engaged in online shopping as compared to low income group, reasons may be various such as they have computers, internet access and higher education levels (Lohse et al., 2000).

ASSOCHAM report on E–commerce reveals the fact that in Indian E-retail market, the driving dynamism behind the growth of the online shopping is the younger age bracket. Nearly 90% of E-shoppers belong to the 18 – 35-year age group, while 8% shoppers are in the 36 – 45-year age group. Based upon shopper's gender, in India contribution of men is more than women in online shopping revenue. Approximately 65% of online shoppers are male as against 35%, who are female. Further, the survey revealed the reasons that restrict the people from online shopping. In reality, nearby 30% of people who purchase from retail outlets examine about the product online. 25% people are still not convinced about security in online shopping and hesitate to share their financial information online. 20% people consider high delivery costs as the main reason, while 15% are insecure about the handling of the product during shipment.

Indians prefer physical and tailored customer service, which is missing in E-commerce. Organisations need to use the internet along with their brick and mortar operations though some organisations have already initiated. Few issues like consistency in quality and in time shipment if considered by retailers will certainly lead to better performance in certain convenience categories (Vedamani, 2003).

In India, E-commerce is certainly becoming a hot opportunity. This growth can be attributed to demographics that are likely to be in favour of Indian retail sector. Currently India has the youngest population in the world. It is somewhat easier to alter the habits and conduct of young consumers as compared to elder one and this is equally true in case of online shopping. They will considerably have less free time, and so will possibly be willing to pay for the convenience that online channels aim to deliver (Srinivasan, 2012). Consumer's acceptance of online services can be attributed to a number of factors like trust, confidence, privacy and security (Hoffman et al., 1999; Yoon, 2002; Balasubramanian et al., 2003, Koufaris & Hampton-Sosa, 2004).

Several studies have focused on the consumers' attitudinal effect on online shopping (Cowles, Little & Kiecker, 2002; Harden, 1996; Kunz, 1997; Poel & Leunis, 1999). Poel and Leunis (1999) suggested that the internet as a medium for buying and selling of goods and services by the shoppers focused mainly on three elements, cash back assurances, price negotiation, and familiarity of brands.

During online transaction, a consumer has to provide personal and financial information for the right shipment of the product purchased. A number of risks are associated with online shopping, which may be apparent or real. The most often cited risks include financial risk, product risk, convenience risk, and non-delivery risk. Customers' insights in case of perceived risks to a great extent are influenced by the level of uncertainty surrounding the online shopping (Bhatnagar et al., 2000).

An examination of the social aspects of E-commerce, proposed that individuals behaviour regarding online shopping is reinforced by two major drives, functional and non-functional (Parsons, 2002; Sheth, 1983). The functional drives imply the shopping behaviour, the principal motive behind which is to gain the products, the need for which is actually felt by the individual (Westbrook & Black, 1985). In the non- functional drive, the principal motive behind shopping is distinct to the purchase of the product (Parsons, 2002). Parsons' study is mainly based on the two key categories of non-functional drives that are also acknowledged by Sheth (1983). One is personal drive that includes role playing, entertainment, pleasure-seeking activities, acknowledging new trends and styles, physical and mental exercises etc. Another is social drive which includes social involvements, communications with people having a similar interest, group interaction, position and power, bargaining and negotiation skills etc. The outcome of the examination is that out of the personal drives, non-functional drives for shopping, entertainment, pleasure seeking activities and acknowledging new trends and styles are the major motivators for online shopping. On the other side apart from bargaining and negotiation skills, all of the social drives were found to be significant for online shopping

Rice (1997) observed the factors that make the customers to visit a particular Web site again and again and found the design features such as content, layout, and ease of use and emotional experience i.e. entertaining features to be most important. Hoffman and Novak (1997) mentioned that personalization was the essence for online stores to materialize the internet as a unique consumer market. In E-commerce market, the success elements of web stores are categorised into four aspects *viz.* quality of information given, ease of use, system design, and playfulness (Liu & Arnett, 2000)

Basic elements of attitude towards online shopping and intention to shop online include ease of use, effectiveness and self-gratification. "Ease of use" refers to as the individual's awareness about the use of the new technology effortlessly (Davis, 1989). "Effectiveness" refers to as the individual's awareness that use of the new technology will improve the performance of individual (Davis, 1989) and "self-gratification" comes from the appreciation of an experience for its own sake, apart from any other consequence that may result (Holbrook, 1994).

Online shopping intention of consumers is also influenced by the frequency with which they use internet (Shim et al., 2001). Previous experiences of online shopping influence the shopping intentions of consumers. Helson (1964) advocates that person's reaction to a critical task is based on the individual's prior familiarities, the situation and the motivating factor. The individual's evaluation is based upon their past shopping experiences with the system. In case of E-shopping, consumers' evaluation of their shopping experiences depends on their awareness of the product/services, mode of payment, shipment policy, services rendered, risk association, confidentiality, security, personalization etc. (Burke, 2002; Parasuraman & Zinkhan, 2002). If the previous shopping experiences of consumer have yielded some satisfactory results, the tendency of consumer to shop online in near future is likely to increase (Shim et al., 2001). However, if the assessment of prior shopping experiences is disappointing, it will be more likely that he/she will be unwilling to shop online in future.

Using Fishbein and Ajzen's (1975) Theory of Reasoned Action that online buying behaviour is a function of attitude, Fishbein and Azjen (1980) defined, "attitude as a person's favourable or unfavourable feelings toward an object". Cognitive system forms the person's evaluations which are the results of cohesive awareness, beliefs etc. with respect to the concept. The relevance of the evaluation and whether it is favourable or not, is decided during the integration process (Peter et al., 1999). For that reason it is essential to envisage the behavioural intents besides their attitude as the consumers' intentions to participate in an actual behaviour proves to be a superior predictor of actual behaviour than their attitude towards a behaviour alone (Fishbein & Ajzen, 1975). However, they noticed that attitudes do impact a consumer's intention, which in turn influences their behaviour. There are different behavioural intentions of consumers' that could be measured. One such measured behavioural intention is to find out the possibility that the consumer is likely to purchase a particular product in near future. Other commonly measured behavioural intentions include the preparedness to pay a price superior and willingness to participate in word-of-mouth communication (Zeithaml, Berry & Parasuraman, 1996). In terms of online shopping it refers to a consumer's state of mind in terms of buying products or services on the internet (Yang et al., 2003).

Behaviour refers to the action and reaction of an individual in response to the changes in the environmental (social, economic, etc.) factors around him (Ajzen, 1985). In terms of online shopping it refers to ——the process of purchasing products or services via internet (Li & Zhang, 2002). Intention refers to an indication about the willingness of a person to perform a particular behaviour. Intention is governed by attitude, subjective norm and perceived behavioural control (Ajzen, 1985).

As per Magi (1999), loyalty means evaluating an object in a positive manner. Loyalty is a commitment that is deeply held by an individual to re- purchase a desired product/service again and again in the near future (Oliver, 1997). Loyalty induces an individual to purchase the products/services of same brand regularly although the situation and the marketing policies that keep on changing have the potential to switch the buyers' behaviour.

To understand the reason of shopping from the Web market, an important factor that should be considered is identifying the pre-purchase intentions of consumers. Research on behaviour of online consumers consists of studies that handle the variables influencing these intentions. Transaction security, dealer quality, price concerns, information and service quality, system quality, privacy and security risks, trust, shopping enjoyment and perceived product quality are the variables that affect the pre purchase intention (Varma, 2005).

Distrust among the customers is found to be one of the main factors for hesitating to shop online (Lee and Turban, 2001). Since online shopping is comparatively a new concept of shopping and only few people have some experience with it, most are reluctant to shop online. Rotter (1971) stated that in new situations, people rely on their general outlook to trust. Moreover, a certain level of risk is also associated with online shopping. Therefore, trust plays a vital role in between consumers' attitude towards online shopping and intention towards online shopping.

Attitude about online shopping differs among purchasers and non-purchasers (Lee & Johnson, 2002). Different levels of ease towards providing financial information over the internet are one of them. It is assumed that the online shoppers will have different attitudes as the attitudinal differences vary among the non-web purchasers, the web store visitor, and the web browser (Cowles, Kieker, & Little, 2002). Few researches suggested that the people who frequently use the internet are more likely to be future buyers because of their ease of use with the internet (Shim, et al., 2001). E-browsers are also more aware of the product, had a greater satisfaction for the product that they examined and bought and have a greater level of confidence in their online shopping ability (Fram & Grady, 1995; Lee & Johnson, 2002).

RESEARCH METHODOLOGY

Objectives of the Study

The study has following objectives.

1. To understand the relationship of Attitudes and Purchase Intentions in context of Online Shopping among Indian Youth.
2. To analyse the mediating role of Satisfaction between Attitudes and Purchase Intentions in context of Online Shopping among Indian Youth.

Hypotheses

In order to attain the objectives following hypotheses were made and tested through regression analysis.

H_{0a}: There is no relationship between attitude towards Online Shopping and Purchase Intentions to Online Shopping among Indian Youth.

H_{1a}: There is significant positive relationship between attitude towards Online Shopping and Purchase Intentions to Online Shopping among Indian Youth.

H_{0b}: Satisfaction does not mediate the relationship between attitude towards Online Shopping and Purchase Intentions to Online Shopping among Indian Youth.

H_{1b}: Satisfaction mediates the relationship between attitude towards Online Shopping and Purchase Intentions to Online Shopping among Indian Youth.

Design/Methodology/Approach

Research design chosen was exploratory cum descriptive. Data were collected through a structured, non-disguised questionnaire using non-probability convenience sampling. Both Online and Offline mode of survey were used. Instrument consisted of thirty items and responses were asked on Nominal as well as Interval and Ratio Scales. Participants were asked to respond to five-point, Likert Scale (1=strongly disagree, 5=strongly agree) by selecting the option that best represented how they felt about online shopping. An online questionnaire was also prepared using Google Doc and link was sent through personal email of the researchers. All questions were compulsory in the questionnaire and were regarding demographic profile and other predictor and criterion variables of the study.

Sample Size and Profile

Though researchers targeted to collect data from 500 youth from widespread geographical area in Northern India (300 online and 200 offline) but only 232 questionnaires were filled within given time despite several repeated attempts by researchers. Response rate in online survey was not very good since we got only 108 completed questionnaires via online mode out of 300-targeted respondents. 124 questionnaires were filled via offline mode. Out of 232 filled questionnaires, some were not fully responded to. Apart from that, some respondents reported that they have never done online shopping so their responses were not taken into account. Finally, we got 180 questionnaires that fulfilled the necessary criteria to be included in the further analysis. The demographic profile of the respondents is given in Table 1. This sample could be considered a good representative of Indian Youth.

Table 1. Demographic Profile of Respondents

Variables		Number	Percentage
Age (Mean=22.51, S.D.=4.49)	15-24 Years	141	78.33%
	25-34 Years	35	19.44%
	35 and above	04	2.22%
	Total	180	100
Gender	Male	75	41.7%
	Female	105	58.3%
	Total	180	100
Educational Qualification	Up to Graduation	105	58.3%
	Post Graduate	69	38.3%
	Above PG	06	3.3%
	Total	180	100
Monthly Income	Up to 25000	98	54.4%
	25001-50000	58	32.3%
	50001 & above	24	13.3%
	Total	180	100

Data Analysis

Primary data analysis through Pearson correlations coefficients revealed significant relationships between the independent and dependent variables. The results are shown in Table 2. Correlation coefficients are significant at the .01 level (1-tailed test).

Pearson correlations revealed significant, positive relationships between Purchase Intentions and attitude towards online shopping for Indian youth, r (180) = .527, p <0.01, supporting H_{1a}. There was also significant, positive relationship between satisfaction from online shopping and Purchase intensions, r (180) = .461, p <0.01. The above mentioned table 2 explains only the degree of association amongst the variables. So in order to find out the functional association and to examine the mediation researchers had to go for regression analysis.

Regression Analysis

The correlation coefficient describes only the degree of relationship existing between two variables but not the kind of relationship. Furthermore, correlation may researchers well occur coincidently. Therefore, to eliminate such sort of uncertainty and determine the type of relationship researchers went for regression analysis. The regression equation can be mathematically written as:

Purchase Intentions = $b_0 + b_1$*(Attitude towards Online Shopping)

Where $\mathbf{b_0}$ is the intercept and $\mathbf{b_1}$ is the gradient of the regression line fitted to data. Model summary and other statistical tables are mentioned in the discussion ut infra.

Model summary in table 3 represents the overall model fit. R, the correlation coefficient, is the linear correlation between the observed and model predicted values of the dependent variable; its large value indicates a strong relationship. $R^{2,}$ which is the main parameter in any regression model states that how much variance is explained by the model compared to how much variance is there to be explained in the first place. "It is the proportion of variance in the outcome variable that is shared by the predictor variables" (Field, 2009). The value of R^2 is .278, which explains that independent variable can account for 27.8% of the variation in dependent variable. It may be because that there are many factors explaining the variations in dependent variable, but our model, which includes only one independent variable, can explain approximately 28% of it. Around 72% of the variation in purchase intentions cannot be explained by the attitude towards online shopping alone which means there must be some other variables that have an influence on the purchase intention of the consumer.

Table 2. Correlations

		Attitude	Satisfaction
Purchase Intentions	Pearson Correlation	.527**	.461**
	Sig. (1-tailed)	.000	.000
	N	180	180
**Correlation is significant at the 0.01 level (1-tailed).			

Table 3. Model Summary

Model	R	R Square	Adjusted R Square	Std. Error of the Estimate
1	.527[a]	.278	.274	1.42249
a. Predictors: (Constant), Attitude towards online shopping				

Other parameters to look for in a regression model is F, which explains how much variability the model can explain relative to how much it can't explain i.e. it's the ratio of how good the model is compared to how bad it is (Field, 2009). If dependent and independent variables in a study come out to be unrelated then the slope of the regression line would be zero. When researchers run a regression analysis with sample data, they compute an estimated slope. It is critical to recognize that the estimated slope is a result of the particular sample at hand. Thus, it is subjected to sampling error, and is a matter for hypothesis testing. From the ANOVA table 4 given above, it is evident that F value is 68.507 and it is significant at $p< .001$ level (Sig .000). This means that there is less than 0.1% chance that an F ratio this large would happen if the null hypothesis (the slope is zero) were true. Therefore, researchers can conclude that our predicted slope of regression line is non-zero and the variance explained by model is not due to chance. Thus, researchers can say that regression model significantly predicts the purchase intentions for online shopping in Indian youth.

It is obvious from table 5 that intercept and gradients of the regression line are 2.03 and .081 respectively. The intercept signifies the value of dependent variable (Purchase intentions) when the independent variable is equal to zero. All values of unstandardized coefficients are significantly different from 0 as significance values for all 't' values are < .05. In other words, it simply means that probability of occurrence of these 't' values if the regression coefficients are zero in population is less than .05. The coefficients table also reports standardized coefficients, or beta value for independent variable. A standardized beta weight represents the number of standard deviations that dependent variable changes if the corresponding independent variable changes by one standard deviation. The significance level given in last column tells us that the independent variable has a statistically significant relationship to dependent variable. Therefore, the concluding remark is that in order to predict the purchase intentions of consumer, their attitude towards online shopping makes a noteworthy contribution. Finally, the regression equation of Purchase intentions on Attitude towards online shopping can be written as-

Purchase Intentions = 2.030 + .081*(Attitude towards Online Shopping)

Test of Mediation through Regression Analysis

Since our regression model between attitude towards online shopping and purchase intentions could explain around 28% of variance in purchase intentions, researchers must look for possible mediator variables. Researchers hypothesized satisfaction as a mediator variable between attitude towards online shopping and purchase intentions. Mediation is a hypothesized causal chain in which one variable affects a second variable that, in turn, affects a third variable. The intervening variable "mediates" the

Table 4. ANOVA^b

Model		Sum of Squares	Df	Mean Square	F	Sig.
1	Regression	138.622	1	138.622	68.507	.000^b
	Residual	360.178	178	2.023		
	Total	498.800	179			
a. Predictors: (Constant), Attitude towards online shopping						
b. Dependent Variable: Purchase intentions						

*Table 5. Coefficients**

Model		Unstandardized Coefficients		Standardized Coefficients	T	Sig.
		B	Std. Error	Beta		
	(Constant)	2.030	.634		3.205	.002
	Attitude	.081	.010	.527	8.277	.000
*Dependent Variable: Purchase intentions						

relationship between a predictor and an outcome variable. Baron and Kenny (1986) proposed a four step approach in which several regression analyses are conducted and significance of the coefficients is examined at each step. The purpose of first three steps is to establish the zero order correlations among the variables under study. If one or more of these relationships are non-significant, researchers usually conclude that mediation is not possible or likely (MacKinnon & Fairchild 2007). Since all correlational coefficients were found significant researchers could just examine the mediating role by looking the regression coefficients of mediator variable when controlling for the effect of independent variable. Proposed mediation analysis models are shown in Figure 1 and 2.

It is clearly inferred from the table 6 that since beta coefficients of both independent as well as mediator variable are significant in second model, our findings support partial mediation. Satisfaction partially mediates the relationship between attitude towards online shopping and purchase intentions. Hence, alternate hypothesis (H_{1b}) about mediation effect was supported. To calculate the regression coefficient of indirect effect i.e. the effect in criterion variable for every unit change in predictor variable that is mediated by mediator variable, researchers applied Judd and Kenny (1981) approach. This

Figure 1. Proposed mediation analysis model 1

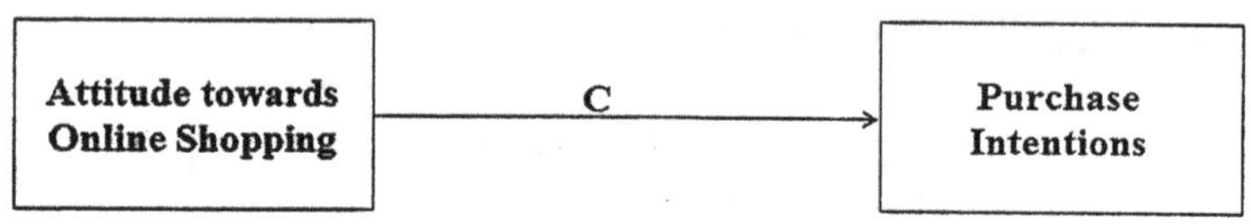

Figure 2. Proposed mediation analysis model 2

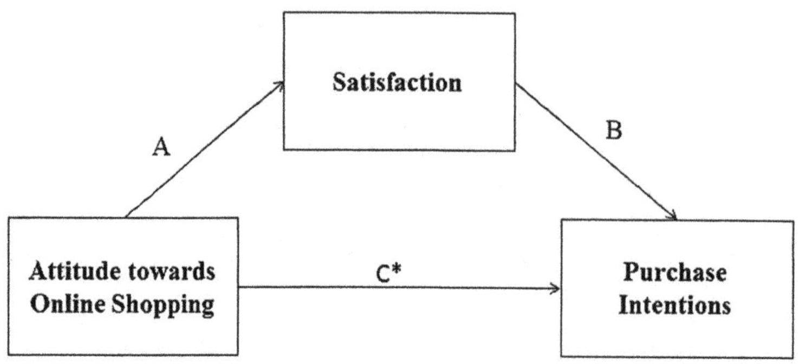

Table 6. Mediation Analysis through Regression

Model		Unstandardized Coefficients		Standardized Coefficients	T	Sig.
		B	Std. Error	Beta		
1	(Constant)	2.030	.634		3.205	.002
	Attitude towards online shopping	.081	.010	.527	8.277	.000
2	(Constant)	.191	.657		.291	.772
	Attitude towards online shopping	.068	.009	.443	7.387	.000
	Satisfaction	.690	.116	.357	5.947	.000

Dependent Variable in both models is Purchase Intention

approach involves subtracting the partial regression unstandardized coefficient obtained in Model 2 from the simple regression unstandardized coefficient obtained from Model 1. The indirect effect is the difference between these two coefficients.

Indirect Effect = C-C* =.081- .068 = .013

For checking the significance of indirect effect, Sobel (1982) test was also performed and found partial mediation in above regression model (Z=2.79, p = .005). Hence, researchers can conclude that satisfaction mediates the relationship between attitude towards online shopping and purchase Intentions to online shopping among Indian youth.

CONCLUSION

The growth of internet has altered the retail landscape and online shopping has become quite popular among the Indian consumers, particularly youth. This study was directed towards determining the determinants of online shopping behaviour among Indian youth and to investigate whether satisfaction has any mediating role in purchase intention in online shopping. Attitude towards online shopping emerged as a significant factor explaining 28% of the variance in purchase intention. The variable as well as the model both was found to be significant. As far as the role of satisfaction is concerned, it was clear that satisfaction mediates the relationship between attitude towards online shopping and purchase intentions to online shopping among Indian youth. In the light of these findings, it is clear that online shopping is going to grow at a rapid pace and retailers should focus on customer satisfaction. The website should be customer friendly and the shopping experience must be good enough to drive the customers again and again to the same website. To sum up just like in offline shopping, attitude and satisfaction play a crucial role in online shopping behaviour.

REFERENCES

Ajzen, I. (1985). *From intentions to actions: A theory of planned behavior* (pp. 11–39). Springer Berlin Heidelberg.

Ajzen, I., & Fishbein, M. (1980). Understanding attitudes and predicting social behaviour.

American Express Report. (2014, April 15). American Express. Retrieved from www.americanbaajaronline.com

ASSOCHAM Report on E-commerce market in India 2013-2023. (n. d.). Retrieved from http:www.assocham.org/

Balasubramanian, S., Konana, P., & Menon, N. M. (2003). Customer satisfaction in virtual environments: A study of online investing. *Management Science*, *49*(7), 871–889. doi:10.1287/mnsc.49.7.871.16385

Baron, R. M., & Kenny, D. A. (1986). The moderator–mediator variable distinction in social psychological research: Conceptual, strategic, and statistical considerations. *Journal of Personality and Social Psychology*, *51*(6), 1173–1182. doi:10.1037/0022-3514.51.6.1173 PMID:3806354

Belanger, F., Hiller, J. S., & Smith, W. J. (2002). Trustworthiness in electronic commerce: The role of privacy, security, and site attributes. *The Journal of Strategic Information Systems*, *11*(3), 245–270. doi:10.1016/S0963-8687(02)00018-5

Bhatnagar, A., Misra, S., & Rao, H. R. (2000). On risk, convenience, and Internet shopping behavior. *Communications of the ACM*, *43*(11), 98–105. doi:10.1145/353360.353371

Burke, R. R. (2002). Technology and the customer interface: What consumers want in the physical and virtual store. *Journal of the Academy of Marketing Science*, *30*(4), 411–432. doi:10.1177/009207002236914

Cohan, P. S. (2000). *E-profit: High-payoff Strategies for Capturing the E-commerce Edge*. American Management Assoc., Inc.

Cowles, D. L., Kiecker, P., & Little, M. W. (2002). Using key informant insights as a foundation for e-retailing theory development. *Journal of Business Research*, *55*(8), 629–636. doi:10.1016/S0148-2963(00)00203-4

Davis, F. D. (1989). Perceived usefulness, perceived ease of use, and user acceptance of information technology. *Management Information Systems Quarterly*, *13*(3), 319–340. doi:10.2307/249008

Dholakia, U. M., & Rego, L. L. (1999, January). What makes commercial web pages popular: An empirical study of online shopping.*Proceedings of 32nd Hawaii International Conference on System Sciences.*

DONNA. (1997). A new marketing paradigm for electronic commerce. *The Information Society*, *13*(1), 43–54. doi:10.1080/019722497129278

Field, A. (2009). *Discovering statistics using SPSS*. Sage publications.

Fishbein, M., & Ajzen, I. (1975). *Belief, attitude, intention and behavior: An introduction to theory and research.*

Fojt, M. (1996). Doing business on the information superhighway. *Internet Research*, *6*(2/3), 79–81.

Fram, E. H., & Grandy, D. B. (1995). Internet buyers: Will the surfers become buyers? *Direct Marketing*, *57*(10), 63–65.

Guo, J., & Sun, C. (2004). Global electronic markets and global traditional markets. *Electronic Markets*, *14*(1), 4–12. doi:10.1080/1019678042000175252

Harden, A. J. (1996). TV shopping: A summary of women's attitudes gained through focus group discussions. *Journal of Family and Consumer Sciences*, *88*(4), 58–62.

Helson, H. (1964). *Adaptation-level theory*. New York, NY: Harper & Row.

Hoffman, D. L., Novak, T. P., & Peralta, M. (1999). Building consumer trust online. *Communications of the ACM*, *42*(4), 80–85. doi:10.1145/299157.299175

Holbrook, M. B. (1994). The nature of customer value: an axiology of services in the consumption experience. *Service quality: New directions in theory and practice, 21*, 21-71.

Jahng, J., Hemant, J., & Ramamurthy, K. (2002). The impact of electronic commerce environment on user behaviour. *E-service Journal*, 1(1), 41-53.

Judd, C. M., & Kenny, D. A. (1981). Process analysis estimating mediation in treatment evaluations. *Evaluation Review*, *5*(5), 602–619. doi:10.1177/0193841X8100500502

Koufaris, M., & Hampton-Sosa, W. (2004). The development of initial trust in an online company by new customers. *Information & Management*, *41*(3), 377–397. doi:10.1016/j.im.2003.08.004

Kunz, M. B. (1997). *Online customers: Identifying store, product and consumer attributes which influence shopping on the Internet*. Knoxville: The University of Tennessee.

Lee, M., & Johnson, K. K. (2002). Exploring differences between Internet apparel purchasers, browsers and non-purchasers. *Journal of Fashion Marketing and Management: An International Journal*, *6*(2), 146–157. doi:10.1108/13612020210429485

Lee, M. K., & Turban, E. (2001). A trust model for consumer internet shopping. *International Journal of Electronic Commerce*, *6*(1), 75–91.

Li, H., Kuo, C., & Rusell, M. G. (1999). The impact of perceived channel utilities, shopping orientations, and demographics on the consumer's online buying behavior. *Journal of Computer-Mediated Communication, 5*(2).

Liu, C., & Arnett, K. P. (2000). Exploring the factors associated with Web site success in the context of electronic commerce. *Information & Management*, *38*(1), 23–33. doi:10.1016/S0378-7206(00)00049-5

Lohse, G. L., Bellman, S., & Johnson, E. J. (2000). Consumer buying behavior on the Internet: Findings from panel data. *Journal of Interactive Marketing*, *14*(1), 15–29. doi:10.1002/(SICI)1520-6653(200024)14:1<15::AID-DIR2>3.0.CO;2-C

MacKinnon, D. P., & Fairchild, A. J. (2009). Current directions in mediation analysis. *Current Directions in Psychological Science*, *18*(1), 16–20. doi:10.1111/j.1467-8721.2009.01598.x PMID:20157637

Mägi, A. (1999). *Store loyalty?: an empirical study of grocery shopping. Economic Research Institute Stockholm*. Stockholm: School of Economics.

Nelson, A. J., & Leon, A. (2012). Bricks and Clicks: Rethinking Retail Real Estate in the E– commerce Era (Research Report). *RREEF Real Estate.*

Oliver, R. L. (1997). *Satisfaction: A behavioral perspective on the customer.* New York.

Parasuraman, A., & Zinkhan, G. M. (2002). Marketing to and serving customers through the Internet: An overview and research agenda. *Journal of the Academy of Marketing Science, 30*(4), 286–295. doi:10.1177/009207002236906

Parsons, A. G. (2002). Non-functional motives for online shoppers: Why we click. *Journal of Consumer Marketing, 19*(5), 380–392. doi:10.1108/07363760210437614

Peter, J. P., Olson, J. C., & Grunert, K. G. (1999). *Consumer behavior and marketing strategy* (pp. 122–123). London: McGraw-Hill.

Ratchford, B. T., & Debabrata Talukdar, M. S. L. (2001). A model of consumer choice of the Internet as an information source. *International Journal of Electronic Commerce, 5*(3), 7–21.

Rice, M. (1997). What makes users revisit a Web site. *Marketing News, 31*(6), 12–13.

Rotter, J. B. (1971). Generalized expectancies for interpersonal trust. *The American Psychologist, 26*(5), 443–452. doi:10.1037/h0031464

Sheth, J. N. (1983). *An integrative theory of patronage preference and behavior.* College of Commerce and Business Patronage Behavior and Retail Management.

Shim, S., Eastlick, M. A., Lotz, S. L., & Warrington, P. (2001). An online prepurchase intentions model: The role of intention to search. *Journal of Retailing, 77*(3), 397–416. doi:10.1016/S0022-4359(01)00051-3

Sirni. R. Srinivasan (2012). *Strategic Retail Management.* Biztantra publications.

Sorce, P., Perotti, V., & Widrick, S. (2005). Attitude and age differences in online buying. *International Journal of Retail & Distribution Management, 33*(2), 122–132. doi:10.1108/09590550510581458

Van den Poel, D., & Leunis, J. (1999). Consumer acceptance of the Internet as a channel of distribution. *Journal of Business Research, 45*(3), 249–256. doi:10.1016/S0148-2963(97)00236-1

Varma, G. (2005). *On-line Marketing: Principles and Current Practices.* New Century Publications.

Vedamani, G. G. (2003). *Retail management.* Jaico Publishing House.

Westbrook, R. A., & Black, W. C. (1985). A motivation-based shopper typology. *Journal of Retailing, 61*, 78–103.

Wood, S. L. (2002). Future fantasies: A social change perspective of retailing in the 21 st century. *Journal of Retailing, 78*(1), 77–83. doi:10.1016/S0022-4359(01)00069-0

Yang, B., Lester, D., & James, S. (2006). Attitudes toward buying online as predictors of shopping online for British and American respondents. *Cyberpsychology & Behavior, 10*(2), 198–203. doi:10.1089/cpb.2006.9968 PMID:17474836

Yoon, S. J. (2002). The antecedents and consequences of trust in online-purchase decisions. *Journal of Interactive Marketing*, *16*(2), 47–63. doi:10.1002/dir.10008

Zeithaml, V. A., Berry, L. L., & Parasuraman, A. (1996). The behavioral consequences of service quality. *Journal of Marketing*, *60*(2), 31–46. doi:10.2307/1251929

KEY TERMS AND DEFINITIONS

Attitude: A predisposition or a tendency to respond positively or negatively towards a certain idea, object, person or situation.

Behaviour: The way in which one acts or conducts oneself especially towards others.

Belief: It is an idea one accepts as being true or real.

E-Commerce: Commercial transactions conducted electronically over the internet.

Intention: Intentions are the connecting chains between some desires and courses of action in order to fulfil those desires.

Mediation: It is a process through which one variable intervenes in the relationship between predictor and criterion variable.

Retailing: It is a process of selling consumer goods and/or services to customers through various channels of distribution to earn a profit.

Youth: The period between childhood and adulthood.

Compilation of References

5 steps to handling bad publicity. (2012). *TEC.com*. Retrieved from https://www.tec.com.au/resources/article-library/strategy/5-steps-to-handling-bad-publicity/

7 Step Action Plan to Deal with Negative Publicity on Social Media. (2012). *SmallBizViewpoints*. Retrieved from http://www.smallbizviewpoints.com/2012/03/06/7-step-action-plan-to-deal-with-negative-publicity-on-social-media/

Aaker, D. A. (1991). *Managing brand equity*. New York, NY: Free Press.

Aaker, D. A. (1996). *Building strong brands*. New York, NY: The Free Press.

Aasheim, H., & Stensønes, I. (2011). *Financial institutions in social media; Deliver traditional services in new channels*. Unpublished Master's thesis. Copenhagen Business School. CBS. Retrieved April 1, 2014 from http://hdl.handle.net/10417/2961 25

Aboim, S. (2005). A formação do casal: Formas de entrada e percursos conjugais. In K. Wall (Ed.), *Famílias em Portugal – percursos, interacções, relações sociais* (pp. 85–116). Lisbon: Imprensa de Ciências Sociais.

Acevedo, B. P., & Aron, A. (2009). Does a long-term relationship kill romantic love? *Review of General Psychology*, *13*(1), 59–65. doi:10.1037/a0014226

Agarwal, R., Ganco, M., & Ziedonis, R. H. (2009). Reputations for toughness in patent enforcement: Implications for knowledge spillovers via inventor mobility. *Strategic Management Journal*, *30*(13), 1349–1374. doi:10.1002/smj.792

Aggarwal, P., & Zhang, M. (2006). The moderating effect of relationship norm salience on consumers' loss aversion. *The Journal of Consumer Research*, *33*(3), 413–419. doi:10.1086/508524

Agrawal, J., & Kamakura, W. A. (1999). Country of origin: A competitive advantage? *International Journal of Research in Marketing*, *16*(4), 255–267. doi:10.1016/S0167-8116(99)00017-8

Ahmed, A. (2012). *Hypothesizing the aptness of social media and the information richness requirements of disaster management*. Proceedings of ECIS 2012. Retrieved from http://aisel.aisnet.org/ecis2012/157

Ahuja, V., & Medury, Y. (2010). Corporate blogs as e-CRM tools: Building consumer engagement through content management. *Journal of Database Marketing & Customer Strategy Management*, *17*(2), 91–105. doi:10.1057/dbm.2010.8

Ajzen, I., & Fishbein, M. (1980). Understanding attitudes and predicting social behaviour.

Ajzen, I. (1985). *From intentions to actions: A theory of planned behavior* (pp. 11–39). Springer Berlin Heidelberg.

Akar, E., & Topçu, B. (2011). An examination of the factors influencing consumers' attitudes toward social media marketing. *Journal of Internet Commerce*, *10*(1), 35–67. doi:10.1080/15332861.2011.558456

Alavi, M., & Leidner, D. E. (2001). Review: knowledge management and knowledge management systems: conceptual foundations and research issues. *Management Information Systems Quarterly*, *25*(1), 107–136. doi:10.2307/3250961

Alavi, S., Ahuja, V., & Medury, Y. (2011). Journal of Database Marketing & Customer Strategy Management. *Database Marketing & Customer Strategy Management*, *18*(2), 83–96.

Albert, P.C. & Muñoz, A.C. (1999). Signos distintivos en productos agroalimentarios. *Distribución y consumo*, *9*(45), 71-83.

Alcantara-Pilar, J. M., Del Barrio-García, S., & Porcu, L. (2013). A cross-cultural analysis of the effect of language on perceived risk online. *Computers in Human Behavior*, *29*(3), 596–603. doi:10.1016/j.chb.2012.10.021

Alfaro, M. (2004). *EDITAREDITARTemas clave de marketing relacional.*Madrid: McGraw-Hill.

Algesheimer, R., Dholakia, U. M., & Herrmann, A. (2005). The social influence of brand community: Evidence from European car clubs. *Journal of Marketing*, *69*(3), 19–34. doi:10.1509/jmkg.69.3.19.66363

Alsajjan, B., & Dennis, C. (2009). Internet banking acceptance model: Cross-market examination. *Journal of Business Research*, *63*(9-10), 957–963. doi:10.1016/j.jbusres.2008.12.014

American Express Report. (2014, April 15). American Express. Retrieved from www.americanbaajaronline.com

Amit, R., & Zott, C. (2001). Value creation in e-business. *Strategic Management Journal*, *22*(6-7), 49–520. doi:10.1002/smj.187

Anandarajan, M., Zaman, M., Dai, Q., & Arinze, B. (2010). Generation Y adoption of instant messaging: An examination of the impact of social usefulness and media richness of use richness. *IEEE Transactions on Professional Communication*, *53*(2), 132–143. doi:10.1109/TPC.2010.2046082

Andersen, P. H. (2005). Relationship marketing and brand involvement of professionals through web-enhanced brand communities: The case of Coloplast. *Industrial Marketing Management*, *34*(1), 39–51. doi:10.1016/j.indmarman.2004.07.002

Anderson, C. (2007). *The long tail: how endless choice is creating unlimited demand.* Random House.

Anderson, C. K. (2012). The Impact of Social Media on Lodging Performance. *Center for Hospitality Research Report*, *12*(15), 6–11.

Anderson, E., & Weitz, B. (1992). The use of pledges to build and sustain commitment in distribution channels. *JMR, Journal of Marketing Research*, *29*(1), 18–34. doi:10.2307/3172490

Anderson, K. J. (2001). Internet use among college students: An exploratory study. *Journal of American College Health*, *50*(1), 21–26. doi:10.1080/07448480109595707 PMID:11534747

Anderson, N. R., De Dreu, C., & Nijstad, B. A. (2004). The routinization of innovation research: A constructively critical review of the state-of-the-science. *Journal of Organizational Behavior*, *25*(2), 147–203. doi:10.1002/job.236

Anholt, S. (2006). *Competitive identity: The new brand management for nations, cities and regions.* Palgrave Macmillan. doi:10.1057/9780230627727

Argenti, P. A., & Druckenmiller, B. (2004). Reputation and the corporate brand. *Corporate Reputation Review*, *6*(4), 368–374. doi:10.1057/palgrave.crr.1540005

Arndt, J. (1967). Role of Product-Related Conversations in the Diffusion of a New Product. *JMR, Journal of Marketing Research*, *4*(3), 291–295. doi:10.2307/3149462

Arndt, J. (1967). *Word of mouth advertising: A review of the literature.* New York: Advertising Research Foundation.

Ashforth, B. E., & Mael, F. A. (1989). Social identity theory and the organization. *Academy of Management Review*, *14*(1), 20–35.

Ashtona, M. C., Paunonen, S. V., Helmes, E., & Jackson, D. N. (1998). Kin altruism, reciprocal altruism, and the big five personality factors. *Evolution and Human Behavior*, *19*(4), 243–255. doi:10.1016/S1090-5138(98)00009-9

ASSOCHAM Report on E-commerce market in India 2013-2023. (n. d.). Retrieved from http:www.assocham.org/

Aula, P. (2010). Social media, reputation risk and ambient publicity management. *Strategy and Leadership*, *38*(6), 43–49. doi:10.1108/10878571011088069

Aula, P. (2011). Meshworked reputation: Publicists' views on the reputational impacts of online communication. *Public Relations Review*, *37*(1), 28–36. doi:10.1016/j.pubrev.2010.09.008

Aula, P., & Mantere, S. (2008). *Strategic Reputation Management*. New York: Routledge.

Aviles, K. (2011, September). Mobile Convenience Stores Designed to Serve Japan's Earthquake Survivors. *Nasdaq*. Retrieved from http://community.nasdaq.com/News/2011-09/mobile-convenience-stores-designed-to-serve-japans-earthquake-survivors.aspx?storyid=94186

Bagozzi, R. P., & Dholakia, U. M. (2002). Intentional social action in virtual communities. *Journal of Interactive Marketing*, *16*(2), 2–21. doi:10.1002/dir.10006

Bagozzi, R. P., & Dholakia, U. M. (2006). Open source software user communities: A study of participation in Linux user groups. *Management Science*, *52*(7), 1099–1115. doi:10.1287/mnsc.1060.0545

Bagozzi, R. P., & Yi, Y. (1998). On evaluation of structural equations models. *Journal of the Academy of Marketing Science*, *16*(1), 74–94. doi:10.1007/BF02723327

Bajari, P., & Hortacsu, A. (2004). Economic Insights from Internet Auctions. *Journal of Economic Literature*, *42*(2), 457–486. doi:10.1257/0022051041409075

Baker, M. J., & Currie, C. A. (1993). Country of origin: the fifth element of the marketing mix? *Proceedings of theMarketing Education Group Conference* (pp. 149-167).

Baker, J. (1986). The role of the environment in marketing services: The consumer perspective. In A. John, J. A. Czepeil, C. A. Congrarn, & J. Shanahan (Eds.), *The service challenge: Integrating for competitive advantage* (pp. 79–84). Chicago, IL: American Marketing Association.

Baker, J., Grewal, D., & Parasuraman, A. (1994). The influence of store environment on quality inferences and store image. *Journal of the Academy of Marketing Science*, *22*(4), 328–339. doi:10.1177/0092070394224002

Bakos, Y. (1997). Reducing Buyer Search Costs: Implications for Electronic Marketplaces. *Management Science*, *43*(12), 1676–1692. doi:10.1287/mnsc.43.12.1676

Balakrishnan, B. K. P. D., Dahnil, M. I., & Yi, W. J. (2014). The impact of social media marketing medium toward purchase intention and brand loyalty among generation Y. *Procedia: Social and Behavioral Sciences*, *148*, 177–185. doi:10.1016/j.sbspro.2014.07.032

Balasubramanian, S., Konana, P., & Menon, N. M. (2003). Customer satisfaction in virtual environments: A study of online investing. *Management Science*, *49*(7), 871–889. doi:10.1287/mnsc.49.7.871.16385

Baldus, B. J., Voorhees, C., & Calantone, R. (2015). Online brand community engagement: Scale development and validation. *Journal of Business Research*, *68*(5), 978–985. doi:10.1016/j.jbusres.2014.09.035

Bandura, A. (1986). *Social foundations of thought and action: A social cognitive theory*. Prentice-Hall, Inc.

Banks. (n. d.) Jeff Bezos on customer service. Retrieved from http://blog.paylane.com/jeff-bezos-on-customer-service/

Bansal, A. (2013). Trends in Retail Banking Channels: Meeting Changing Client Preferences (Capgemini report). Retrieved from http://www.capgemini.com/resource-file-access/resource/pdf/trends_in_retail_banking_channels_meeting_changing_client_preferences.pdf

Bargh, J. A., & McKenna, K. Y. (2004). The Internet and social life. *Annual Review of Psychology*, *55*(1), 573–590. doi:10.1146/annurev.psych.55.090902.141922 PMID:14744227

Baron, R. M., & Kenny, D. A. (1986). The moderator–mediator variable distinction in social psychological research: Conceptual, strategic, and statistical considerations. *Journal of Personality and Social Psychology*, *51*(6), 1173–1182. doi:10.1037/0022-3514.51.6.1173 PMID:3806354

Barrow, S., & Mosley, R. (2005). *The employer brand: Bringing the best of brand management to people at work*. Chichester, UK: John Wiley & Sons.

Barwise, P., & Meehan, S. (2010). The one thing you must get right when building a brand. *Harvard Business Review*, *88*(12), 80–84.

Bateman, P. J., Gray, P. H., & Butler, B. (2010). The impact of community commitment on participation in online communities. *Information Systems Research*, *22*(4), 841–854. doi:10.1287/isre.1090.0265

Batra, R., Lehmann, D. R., & Singh, D. (1993). The brand personality component of brand goodwill: some antecedents and consequences. In D. A. Aaker & A. L. Biel (Eds.), *Brand equity and advertising* (pp. 83–96). Hillsdale, NY: Lawrence Erlbaum Associates Inc.

Baym, N. K., Zhang, Y. B., & Lin, M. C. (2004). Social interactions across media interpersonal communication on the internet, telephone and face-to-face. *New Media & Society*, *6*(3), 299–318. doi:10.1177/1461444804041438

Bearden, W. O., & Etzel, M. J. (1982). Reference group influence on product and brand purchase decisions. *The Journal of Consumer Research*, *9*(2), 183–194. doi:10.1086/208911

Beauchamp, M. (n. d.). *The Disadvantages of Bad Publicity.* Retrieved from http://yourbusiness.azcentral.com/disadvantages-bad-publicity-3495.html

Beck, T. (2013). Why the Japanese Love Twitter But Not Facebook. *Fast C@mpany*. Retrieved from http://www.fastcolabs.com/3016498/why-the-japanese-love-twitter-but-not-facebook

Beck, U., & Beck-Gernsheim, E. (2009). Losing the Traditional: Individualization and Precarious Freedoms. In *Identity in question* (pp. 14-33).

Belanger, F., Hiller, J. S., & Smith, W. J. (2002). Trustworthiness in electronic commerce: The role of privacy, security, and site attributes. *The Journal of Strategic Information Systems*, *11*(3), 245–270. doi:10.1016/S0963-8687(02)00018-5

Belson, K., & Bremner, B. (2003). *Hello Kitty: The Remarkable Story of Sanrio and the Billion Dollar Feline Phenomenon*. New York: John Wiley & Sons.

Bengtsson, A., & Servais, P. (2005). Co-branding on industrial markets. *Industrial Marketing Management*, *34*(7), 706–713. doi:10.1016/j.indmarman.2005.06.004

Bennett, R., & Rundle-Thiele, S. (2002). A comparison of attitudinal loyalty measurement approaches. *Journal of Brand Management*, *9*(3), 193–209. doi:10.1057/palgrave.bm.2540069

Berger, J., & Schwartz, E. M. (2011). What drives immediate and ongoing Word of mouth? *JMR, Journal of Marketing Research, 48*(5), 869–880. doi:10.1509/jmkr.48.5.869

Berger, J., Sorensen, A. T., & Scott, J. R. (2010). Positive Effects of Negative Publicity: When Negative Reviews Increase Sales. *Marketing Science, 29*(5), 815–827. doi:10.1287/mksc.1090.0557

Berkowitz, E. N. (2007). The evolution of public relations and the use of the internet: The implications for health care organizations. *Health Marketing Quarterly, 24*(3-4), 117–130. doi:10.1080/07359680802125154 PMID:19042531

Berman, C. (2015). *How Should Firms Respond to Negative Publicity?* Retrieved from http://smallbusiness.chron.com/should-firms-respond-negative-publicity-69199.html

Bernstein, D. (1984). *Company Image and Reality: A Critique of Corporate Communications. Holt, Rinehart and Winston.* Eastbourne: The Advertising Association.

Berry, L. L. (1983). *Relationship marketing.* American Marketing Association.

Berry, L. L. (1995). Relationship marketing of services—growing interest, emerging perspectives. *Journal of the Academy of Marketing Science, 23*(4), 236–245. doi:10.1177/009207039502300402

Berry, L. L., Bolton, R. N., Bridges, C. H., Meyer, J., Parasuraman, A., & Seiders, K. (2010). Opportunities for Innovation in the Delivery of Interactive Retail Services. *Journal of Interactive Marketing, 24*(2), 155–167. doi:10.1016/j.intmar.2010.02.001

Berry, L. L., Wall, E., & Carbone, L. (2006). Service clues and customer assessment of the service experience: Lessons from marketing. *The Academy of Management Perspectives, 20*(2), 43–57. doi:10.5465/AMP.2006.20591004

Berthon, P. R., Pitt, L. F., & Campbell, C. (2008). Ad lib: When consumers create the ad. *California Management Review, 50*(4), 6–30. doi:10.2307/41166454

Berthon, P. R., Pitt, L. F., McCarthy, I., & Kates, S. M. (2007). When customers get clever: Managerial approaches to dealing with creative consumers. *Business Horizons, 50*(1), 39–47. doi:10.1016/j.bushor.2006.05.005

Berthon, P. R., Pitt, L. F., Plangger, K., & Shapiro, D. (2012). Marketing meets Web 2.0, social media, and creative consumers: Implications for international marketing strategy. *Business Horizons, 55*(3), 261–271. doi:10.1016/j.bushor.2012.01.007

Bhagwat, R., & Sharma, M. K. (2007). Information system architecture: A framework for a cluster of small- and medium-sized enterprises (SMEs). *Production Planning and Control, 18*(4), 283–296. doi:10.1080/09537280701248578

Bharadwaj, A. S. (2000). A resource-based perspective on information technology capability and firm performance: An empirical investigation. *Management Information Systems Quarterly, 24*(1), 169–196. doi:10.2307/3250983

Bhatnagar, A., Misra, S., & Rao, H. R. (2000). On risk, convenience, and Internet shopping behavior. *Communications of the ACM, 43*(11), 98–105. doi:10.1145/353360.353371

Bhatt, G. D., & Grover, V. (2005). Types of information technology capabilities and their role in competitive advantage: An empirical study. *Journal of Management Information Systems, 22*(2), 253–277.

Bhatti, R. S. (1993). Changes in the institution of marriage and family structures: Problems and solutions. *Paper presented at the International Conference on Respect for Life: The Priority of the Nineties*, St. John's Medical College and Hospital, Bangalore, Karnataka.

Biel, A. L. (1992). How brand image drives brand equity. *Journal of Advertising Research, 32*(6), 6–12.

Bigne, J. E., Sanchez, M. I., & Sanchez, J. (2001). Tourism image, evaluation variables and after purchase behavior: Interrelationship. *Tourism Management*, *22*(6), 607–616. doi:10.1016/S0261-5177(01)00035-8

Birke, D. (2013). *Social Networks and their Economics: Influencing Consumer Choice*. Chichester: Wiley. doi:10.1002/9781118699638

Bitner, M. J. (1992). Servicescapes: The impact of physical surroundings on costumers employees. *Journal of Marketing*, *56*(2), 57–71. doi:10.2307/1252042

Blackshaw, P., & Nazzaro, M. (2004). *Consumer-generated media (CGM) 101: Word of mouth in the age of the web-fortified consumer*. Cincinnati, OH: Intelliseek.

Blackston, M. (1992). Observations: Building brand equity by managing the brand's relationships. *Journal of Advertising Research*, *32*(3), 79–83.

Blackston, M. (1995). The qualitative dimension of brand equity. *Journal of Advertising Research*, *35*(4), 2–7.

Blattberg, R. C., & Deighton, J. (1996). Manage marketing by the customer equity test. *Harvard Business Review*, *74*(4), 136–144. PMID:10158473

Blery, E. (2010). *Customer loyalty; marketing techniques to engender loyalty among customers*. Athens: Propompos Publications.

Bolton, R., & Saxena-Iyer, S. (2009). Interactive service: A framework, synthesis and research directions. *Journal of Interactive Marketing*, *23*(1), 91–104. doi:10.1016/j.intmar.2008.11.002

Bonabeau, E.M.D. (1999). Swarm Intelligence: From Natural to Artificial System. New York: Oxford University Press.

Bonsón, E., & Flores, F. (2011). Social media and corporate dialogue: The response of global financial institutions. *Online Information Review*, *35*(1), 34–49. doi:10.1108/14684521111113579

Bontis, N., Booker, L., & Serenko, A. (2007). The mediating effect of organizational reputation on customer loyalty and service recommendation in the banking industry. *Management Decision*, *45*(9), 1426–1445. doi:10.1108/00251740710828681

Booth, N., & Matic, J. A. (2011). Mapping and leveraging influencers in social media to shape corporate brand perceptions. *Corporate Communications: An International Journal*, *16*(3), 184–191. doi:10.1108/13563281111156853

Bordonaba-Juste, V., Lucia-Palacios, L., & Polo-Redondo, Y. (2012). Antecedents and consequences of e-business use for European retailers. *Internet Research*, *22*(5), 532–550. doi:10.1108/10662241211271536

Boush, D. M., Shipp, S., Loken, B., Gencturk, E., Crokett, S., Kennedy, E., & Strobel, J. et al. (1987). Affect generalization to similar and dissimilar brand extensions. *Psychology and Marketing*, *4*(3), 225–237. doi:10.1002/mar.4220040306

Bradley, A. J., & McDonald, M. P. (2011). *The social organization: How to use social media to tap the collective genius of your customers and employees*. Boston, MA: Harvard Business Review Press.

BRASS Programing Planning Committee. (2011). The business of social media: How to plunder the treasure trove. *Reference and User Services Quarterly*, *51*(2), 127–132. doi:10.5860/rusq.51n2.127

Brei, V. A. (2001). *Antecedentes e consequências da confiança do consumidor final em trocas relacionais com empresas de serviço: Um estudo com o usuário de internet banking no Brasil* [Unpublished master dissertation]. Universidade Federal do Rio Grande do Sul.

Bremner, B. (2002). In Japan, cute conquers all. *Businessweek*. Retrieved from http://www.businessweek.com/stories/2002-06-24/in-japan-cute-conquers-all

Brennan, B., & Schafer, L. (2010). *Branded! How Retailers Engage Consumers with Social Media and Mobility*. New Jersey: Wiley.

Brey, E. T., So, S., Kim, D., & Morrison, A. M. (2007). Web-based permission marketing: Segmentation for the lodging industry. *Tourism Management*, *28*(6), 1408–1416. doi:10.1016/j.tourman.2007.01.002

Bright, L. F., Kleiser, S. B., & Grau, S. L. (2015). Too much Facebook? An exploratory examination of social media fatigue. *Computers in Human Behavior*, *44*, 148–155. doi:10.1016/j.chb.2014.11.048

Brodie, R. J., Juric, B., Ilic, A., & Hollebeek, L. D. (2011, January). Consumer engagement in a virtual brand community: An exploratory analysis. *Journal of Business Research*, *66*(1), 105–114. doi:10.1016/j.jbusres.2011.07.029

Brown, J. B., Broderick, A. J., & Lee, N. (2007). Word of mouth communication within online communities: Conceptualizing the online social network. *Journal of Interactive Marketing*, *21*(3), 2–20. doi:10.1002/dir.20082

Brown, J. S., & Duguid, P. (2000). Balancing act: How to capture knowledge without killing it. *Harvard Business Review*, *78*(3), 73–80.

Brown, T. J., Barry, T. E., Dacin, P. A., & Gunst, R. F. (2005). Spreading the word: Investigating antecedents of consumers' positive word-of mouth intentions and behaviors in a retailing context. *Journal of the Academy of Marketing Science*, *33*(2), 123–138. doi:10.1177/0092070304268417

Bugshan, H. (2014). Co-innovation: The role of online communities. *Journal of Strategic Marketing*, *23*(2), 175–186. doi:10.1080/0965254X.2014.920905

Buhalis, D., & Law, R. (2008). Progress in information technology and tourism management: 20 years on and 10 years after the Internet – the state of Etourism research. *Tourism Management*, *29*(4), 609–623. doi:10.1016/j.tourman.2008.01.005

Buil, I., Martinez, E., & de Chernatony, L. (2013). The influence of brand equity on consumer responses. *Journal of Consumer Marketing*, *30*(1), 62–74. doi:10.1108/07363761311290849

Burke, F. (2010). Publicity and Social Media: A Match Made in Heaven. *Huffington Post*. Retrieved from http://www.huffingtonpost.com/fauzia-burke/publicity-and-social-medi_b_547672.html?ir=India

Burke, R. R. (2002). Technology and the customer interface: What consumers want in the physical and virtual store. *Journal of the Academy of Marketing Science*, *30*(4), 411–432. doi:10.1177/009207002236914

Burmann, C., Zeplin, S., & Riley, N. (2009). Key determinants of internal brand management success: An exploratory empirical analysis. *Journal of Brand Management*, *16*(4), 264–284. doi:10.1057/bm.2008.6

Businessess tap into growing power of social media. (2011, October 31). *The Asahi Shimbun*. Retrieved from http://ajw.asahi.com/article/behind_news/social_affairs/AJ2011103116169

Buttle, F. (2001). The CRM value chain. *Marketing Business*, February, 52–55. Retrieved from http://www.wtcbrescia.it/upload/0-FButtle_CRMvalchain.pdf

Buttle, F. A. (1998). Word of Mouth: Understanding and Managing Referral Marketing. *Journal of Strategic Marketing*, *6*(3), 241–254. doi:10.1080/096525498346658

Cakim, I. M. (2010). *Implementing Word of Mouth marketing: online strategies to identify influencers, craft stories, and draw customers. New Jersey*:John Wiley & Sons.

Callarisa, L., García, J. S., Cardiff, J., & Roshchina, A. (2012). Harnessing social media platforms to measure customer-based hotel brand equity. *Tourism Management Perspectives*, *4*, 73–79. doi:10.1016/j.tmp.2012.04.005

Campbell, R., Rogers, K., & Rezek, J. (2008). Efficient frontier estimation: A maximum entropy approach. *Journal of Productivity Analysis*, *30*(3), 213–221. doi:10.1007/s11123-008-0103-9

Capon, N., Farley, J. U., Hulbert, J., & Lehmann, D. R. (1992). Profiles of product innovators among large US manufacturers. *Management Science*, *38*(2), 157–169. doi:10.1287/mnsc.38.2.157

Cardwell, A. (2002, April 1). Viral marketing, subliminal advertising. *ZD Net Inter@ctive Week*. Retrieved from http://www.ennex.com/~Marshall/viral/ref/20020401-Cardwell.pdf

Carla, B. (2011). *Does Negative Publicity Help or Hurt your Business?* Retrieved from https://eotm.wordpress.com/category/publicity/

Carlson, B. D., Suter, T. A., & Brown, T. J. (2008). Social versus psychological brand community: The role of psychological sense of brand community. *Journal of Business Research*, *61*(4), 284–291. doi:10.1016/j.jbusres.2007.06.022

Carraher, S. M., Buchanan, J. K., & Puia, G. (2010). Entrepreneurial need for achievement in China, Latvia, and the USA. *Baltic Journal of Management*, *5*(3), 378–396. doi:10.1108/17465261011079767

Caruana, A., & Chircop, S. (2000). Measuring corporate reputation: A case example. *Corporate Reputation Review*, *3*(1), 43–57. doi:10.1057/palgrave.crr.1540098

Casaló, L. V., Flavián, C., & Guinalíu, M. (2010). Relationship quality, community promotion and brand loyalty in virtual communities: Evidence from free software communities. *International Journal of Information Management*, *30*(4), 357–367. doi:10.1016/j.ijinfomgt.2010.01.004

Celso, A.M., & Carlos, A.V.R. (2008). Word-of-Mouth Communications in Marketing: A Meta-Analytic Review of the Antecedents and Moderators. *Journal of the Academy of Marketing Science*, 36(4), 578-96.

Chan, F. T. S., & Chong, A. Y.-L. (2012). An empirical investigation of factors affecting e-collaboration diffusion in SMEs. *International Journal of Production Economics*, *138*(2), 329–344. doi:10.1016/j.ijpe.2012.04.004

Chan, K. W., & Li, S. Y. (2010). Understanding consumer-to-consumer interactions in virtual communities: The salience of reciprocity. *Journal of Business Research*, *63*(9-10), 1033–1040. doi:10.1016/j.jbusres.2008.08.009

Chan, N. L., & Guillet, B. D. (2011). Investigation of social media marketing: How does the hotel industry in Hong Kong perform in marketing on social media websites? *Journal of Travel & Tourism Marketing*, *28*(4), 345–368. doi:10.1080/10548408.2011.571571

Chaudhuri, A., & Holbrook, M. B. (2001). The chain of effects from brand trust and brand affect to brand performance: The role of brand loyalty. *Journal of Marketing*, *65*(2), 81–93. doi:10.1509/jmkg.65.2.81.18255

Chau, P. Y. K., & Tam, K. Y. (1997). Factors affecting the adoption of open systems: An exploratory study. *Management Information Systems Quarterly*, *21*(1), 1–25. doi:10.2307/249740

Cheng, S. S. (2011). A Corporate Hero with Scandal: Lessons Learned from Martha Stewart's Insider Trading Crisis. *International Journal of Humanities and Social Science*, *1*(15), 12–24.

Chen, Y.-H., & Barnes, S. (2007). Initial trust and online buyer behaviour. *Industrial Management & Data Systems*, *107*(1), 21–36. doi:10.1108/02635570710719034

Cherney, A. (2003). Reverse Pricing and Online Pricing Elicitation Strategies in Consumer Choice. *Journal of Consumer Psychology*, *13*(1), 51–62. doi:10.1207/153276603768344780

Chiao, Y. L., Lu, C. h., Chou, Y. Y., & Liu, P. l. (2011). Towards a human-centric and smarter convenience store service experience.*Proceedings of the International Conference of Social Science and Humanity* (pp. 84 – 88). Singapore: IACSIT Press.

Chong, A. Y. L., & Chan, F. T. S. (2012). Radio Frequency Identification (RFID) in the healthcare industry: A multi-stage diffusion analysis. *Expert Systems with Applications*, *39*(10), 8645–8654. doi:10.1016/j.eswa.2012.01.201

Choy, C. S., Yew, W. K., & Lin, B. (2006). Criteria for measuring KM performance outcomes in organisations. *Industrial Management & Data Systems*, *106*(7), 917–936. doi:10.1108/02635570610688850

Christodoulides, G., Jevons, C., & Blackshaw, P. (2011). The voice of the consumer speaks forcefully in brand identity: User-generated content forces smart marketers to listen. *Journal of Advertising Research*, *51*(1), 101–111. doi:10.2501/JAR-51-1-101-111

Christodoulides, G., Jevons, C., & Bonhomme, J. (2012). Memo to marketers: Quantitative evidence for change. How user-generated content really affects brands. *Journal of Advertising Research*, *52*(1), 53–64. doi:10.2501/JAR-52-1-053-064

Christopher, J. (n. d.). The 9 Golden Rules for Dealing With Bad Publicity. *Technori.com.* Retrieved from http://technori.com/2013/07/4516-the-9-golden-rules-for-dealing-with-bad-publicity/

Christou, E. (2015). Branding social media in the travel industry. *Procedia: Social and Behavioral Sciences*, *175*, 607–614. doi:10.1016/j.sbspro.2015.01.1244

Chua, A. Y. K., & Banerjee, S. (2013). Customer knowledge management via social media: The case of Starbucks. *Journal of Knowledge Management*, *17*(2), 237–249. doi:10.1108/13673271311315196

Churchill, G. A. (1979). A paradigm for developing better measures of marketing constructs. *JMR, Journal of Marketing Research*, *16*(1), 64–73. doi:10.2307/3150876

Chu, S., & Kim, Y. (2011). Determinants of consumer engagement in electronic word-of-mouth (eWOM) in social networking sites. *International Journal of Advertising*, *30*(1), 47–75. doi:10.2501/IJA-30-1-047-075

Clemons, E. K. (2009). The complex problem of monetizing virtual electronic social networks. *Decision Support Systems*, *48*(1), 46–56. doi:10.1016/j.dss.2009.05.003

Clifford, S. (2009). Video Prank at Domino's Taints Brand. Retrieved from http://www.nytimes.com/2009/04/16/business/media/16dominos.html?_r=0

Clifton, R. (2003). The future of brands. In R. Clifton (Ed.), *Brands and branding* (pp. 227–241). New York, NY: Bloomberg Press.

CNN. (2013, July 17). 2011 Japan Earthquake – Tsunami Fast Facts. *CNN Library*. Retrieved from http://www.cnn.com/2013/07/17/world/asia/japan-earthquake---tsunami-fast-facts/

Cohan, P. S. (2000). *E-profit: High-payoff Strategies for Capturing the E-commerce Edge*. American Management Assoc., Inc.

Coleman, J. S. (1988). Social capital in the creation of human capital. *American Journal of Sociology*, *94*, 95–120. doi:10.1086/228943

Colliander, J., & Dahlén, M. (2011). Following the fashionable friend: The power of social media. *Journal of Advertising Research*, *51*(1), 313–320. doi:10.2501/JAR-51-1-313-320

Collins, C. J., & Smith, K. G. (2006). Knowledge exchange and combination: The role of human resource practices in the performance of high-technology firms. *Academy of Management Journal*, *49*(3), 544–560. doi:10.5465/AMJ.2006.21794671

Comm, J., & Robbins, A. (2010). *Twitter Power 2.0: How to Dominate Your Market One Tweet at a Time*. New York: Wiley.

Constantinides, E., & Fountain, S. J. (2008). Web 2.0: Conceptual foundations and marketing issues. *Journal of direct, data and digital marketing practice,9*(3), 231-244.

Convenience stores turning to the elderly. (2014, January 16). *Japan Times*. Retrieved from http://www.japantimes.co.jp/life/2014/01/16/general/convenience-stores-turning-to-the-elderly/#.U9-5QpS1aCU

Cooley, S. C., & Cooley, A. B. (2011). An examination of the situational crisis communication theory through the general motors bankruptcy. *Journal of Media and Communication Studies*, *3*(6), 203–211.

Coombs, W. T. (2004). Impact of Past Crises on Current Crisis Communication: Insights from Situational Crisis Communication Theory. *Journal of Business Communication*, *41*(3), 265–289. doi:10.1177/0021943604265607

Copeland, J. (2007). The ethics of reputation management (or, "getting stuff deleted from Google"). *Moz.com*. Retrieved from http://moz.com/blog/reputation-management

Corbitt, B. J., Thanasankit, T., & Yi, H. (2003). Trust and e-commerce: A study of consumer perceptions. *Electronic Commerce Research and Applications*, *2*(3), 203–215. doi:10.1016/S1567-4223(03)00024-3

Cormode, G., & Krishnamurthy, B. (2008). Key differences between Web 1.0 and Web 2.0. *First Monday*, *13*(6), 2. doi:10.5210/fm.v13i6.2125

Corstjens, M., & Umblijs, A. (2012). The power of evil: The damage of negative social media strongly outweigh positive contributions. *Journal of Advertising Research*, *52*(4), 433–449. doi:10.2501/JAR-52-4-433-449

Cowles, D. L., Kiecker, P., & Little, M. W. (2002). Using key informant insights as a foundation for e-retailing theory development. *Journal of Business Research*, *55*(8), 629–636. doi:10.1016/S0148-2963(00)00203-4

Cox, J. L., Martinez, E. R., & Quinlan, K. B. (2008). Blogs and the corporation: Managing the risk, reaping the benefits. *The Journal of Business Strategy*, *29*(3), 4–12. doi:10.1108/02756660810873164

Craft, L. (2005, August 7). Japan As A World Leader In Pop Culture. *The Washington Times*. Retrieved from http://www.wpherald.com/storyview.php?StoryID=20050807-030608-2858r

Craig, T. (2000). *Japan Pop! Inside the World of Japanese Popular Culture*. New York: M.E. Sharpe, Inc.

Cretu, A. E., & Brodie, R. J. (2007). The influence of brand image and company reputation where manufacturers market to small firms: A customer value perspective. *Industrial Marketing Management*, *36*(2), 230–240. doi:10.1016/j.indmarman.2005.08.013

Crittenden, V. L., Hanna, R., & Rohm, A. (2011). We're all connected: The power of the social media ecosystem. *Business Horizons*, *54*(3), 265–273. doi:10.1016/j.bushor.2011.01.007

Crotts, J. (1999). Consumer decision making and prepurchase information search. In Y. Mansfield & A. Pizam (Eds.), *Consumer behavior in travel and tourism* (pp. 149–168). New York, NY: Haworth Press.

Culache, O., & Obadă, D. R. (2014). Multimodality as a premise for inducing online flow on a brand website: A social semiotic approach. *Procedia: Social and Behavioral Sciences*, *149*, 261–268. doi:10.1016/j.sbspro.2014.08.227

Culnan, M. J., McHugh, P. J., & Zubillaga, J. I. (2010). How large U.S. companies can use Twitter and other social media to gain business value. *MIS Quarterly Executive*, *9*(4), 243–260.

Cummings, J., Lee, J., & Kraut, R. (2006). Communication technology and friendship during the transition from high school to college. In *Computers, phones, and the Internet: Domesticating information technology* (pp. 265-278).

Curran, P. J., West, S. G., & Finch, J. F. (1996). The robustness of test statistics to nonnormality and specification error in confirmatory factor analysis. *Psychological Methods*, *1*(1), 16–29. doi:10.1037/1082-989X.1.1.16

Cutlip, S., Center, A., & Broom, G. (2000). *Effective Public Relations*. New Jersey: Prentice Hall.

Daft, R. L., & Lengel, R. H. (1984). Information richness: A new approach to manager information processing and organization design. In B. Staw & L. L. Cummings (Eds.), *Research in Organizational Behavior. Greenwhich, C.T.* JAJ Press.

Daft, R. L., & Lengel, R. H. (1986). Organizational information requirements, media richness and structural design. *Management Science*, *32*(5), 554–571. doi:10.1287/mnsc.32.5.554

Darnowski, C., & Wright, D. (2010). Tomorrow's professional: employer demand for public relations knowledge, skills and abilities. *Presented at Public Relations Society of America Leadership Assembly*. Retrieved from http://www.prsa.org/AboutPRSA/Documents/2010prsaemployerstudy.pdf

Darroch, J. (2003). Developing a measure of knowledge management behaviors and practices. *Journal of Knowledge Management*, *7*(5), 41–54. doi:10.1108/13673270310505377

Darroch, J. (2005). Knowledge management, innovation and firm performance. *Journal of Knowledge Management*, *9*(3), 101–115. doi:10.1108/13673270510602809

Davies, G., Chun, R., Da Silva, R. V., & Roper, S. (2003). *Corporate Reputation and Competitiveness*. UK: Routledge.

Davis, C. & Moy, C. (2007, October). Coming to Terms With Business Transparency. *Admap Magazine*, Issue 487, Oxon: WARC, pp. 19-22.

Davis, F. D. (1989). Perceived usufulness, perceived ease of use, and user acceptance of information technology. *Management Information Systems Quarterly*, *13*(3), 319–339. doi:10.2307/249008

Davis, R. A., & Sajtos, L. (2008). Measuring consumer interactivity in response to campaigns coupling mobile and television media. *Journal of Advertising Research*, *48*(3), 375–391. doi:10.2501/S0021849908080409

de Chernatony, L., & Segal-Horn, S. (2001). Building on services' characteristics to develop successful service brand. *Journal of Marketing Management*, *17*(7–8), 645–669. doi:10.1362/026725701323366773

De Valck, K., Van Bruggen, G., & Wierenga, B. (2009). Virtual communities: A marketing perspective. *Decision Support Systems*, *47*(3), 185–203. doi:10.1016/j.dss.2009.02.008

de Vries, L., Gensler, S., & Leeflang, P. S. H. (2012). Popularity of brand posts on brand fan pages: An investigation of the effects of social media marketing. *Journal of Interactive Marketing*, *26*(2), 83–91. doi:10.1016/j.intmar.2012.01.003

Dean, D. H., & Lang, J. M. (2008). Comparing three signals of service quality. *Journal of Services Marketing*, *22*(1), 48–58. doi:10.1108/08876040810851950

Decker, C. (1998). *P&G 99*. London: Harper Collins Business.

Deetz, S. (1986). Metaphors and the discursive production and reproduction of organization. In L. Thayer (Ed.), *Organization-Communication: Emerging Perspectives I* (pp. 168–182). Norwood, NJ: Ablex Publishing Co.

Deighton, J. (2008). Dove: Evolution of a brand. Harvard Business School (Case No. 9-508-047). Boston, MA: Harvard Business School Press.

Deighton, J., & Kornfeld, L. (2009). Interactivity's unanticipated consequences for marketers and marketing. *Journal of Interactive Marketing*, *23*(1), 2–12. doi:10.1016/j.intmar.2008.10.001

Del Aguila-Obra, A., & Padilla-Melendez, A. (2008). Organizational factors affecting Internet technology adoption. *Internet Research*, *16*(1), 94–110. doi:10.1108/10662240610642569

Delery, J. E., & Doty, D. H. (1996). Modes of theorizing in strategic human resource management: Test of universalistic contingency, and configurational performance predictions. *Academy of Management Journal*, *39*(4), 802–835. doi:10.2307/256713

Dellarocas, C. (2003). The Digitization of word-of-mouth: Promise and challenges of online reputation systems. *Management Science*, *49*(10), 1407–1424. doi:10.1287/mnsc.49.10.1407.17308

Dennis, C., Jayawardhena, C., & Papamatthaiou, E.-K. (2010). Antecedents of internet shopping intentions and the moderating effects of substitutability. *International Review of Retail, Distribution and Consumer Research*, *20*(4), 411–430. doi:10.1080/09593969.2010.504008

Dennis, C., Merrilees, B., Jayawardhena, C., & Wright, L. T. (2009). E-consumer behaviour. *European Journal of Marketing*, *43*(9/10), 1121–1139. doi:10.1108/03090560910976393

Devaraj, S., & Kholi, R. (2003). Performance impacts of information technology: Is actual usage the missing link? *Management Science*, *49*(3), 273–289. doi:10.1287/mnsc.49.3.273.12736

Dholakia, U. M., & Durham, E. (2010). One café chain's Facebook experiment. *Harvard Business Review*, *88*(3), 26.

Dholakia, U. M., & Rego, L. L. (1999, January). What makes commercial web pages popular: An empirical study of online shopping.*Proceedings of 32nd Hawaii International Conference on System Sciences.*

Dholokia, R. R., & Kshetri, N. (2004). Factors impacting the adoption of the internet among SMEs. *Small Business Economics*, *23*(4), 311–322. doi:10.1023/B:SBEJ.0000032036.90353.1f

Di Gangi, P., & Wasko, M. (2009). Steal My Idea! User Innovation Community Influence on Organizational Adoption of User Innovations: A Case Study of Dell Ideastorm. *Decision Support Systems*, *48*(1), 303–312. doi:10.1016/j.dss.2009.04.004

Dias, M. C., Zwicker, R., & Vicentin, I. C. (2003). Análise do modelo de aceitação de tecnologia de Davis. *Revista. SPEI*, *4*(2), 15–23.

Dichter, E. (1966). How Word-of-Mouth Advertising Works. *Harvard Business Review*, *44*(6), 147–166.

Dijkmans, C., Kerkhof, P., & Beukeboom, C. J. (2015). A stage to engage: Social media use and corporate reputation. *Tourism Management*, *47*, 58–67. doi:10.1016/j.tourman.2014.09.005

Dilworth, D. (2009, April 9). Ford debuts social media campaign for new Fiesta. *DM News*. Retrieved from www.dmnews.com/Ford-debuts-social-media-campaign-for-new-Fiesta/article/130445/

Dionísio, A., Reis, A. H., & Coelho, L. (2008). Utility function estimation: The entropy approach. *Physica A*, *387*(15), 3862–3867. doi:10.1016/j.physa.2008.02.072

Dobni, D., & Zinkhan, G. M. (1990). In Search of Brand Image: A Fundation Analysis. *Advances in Consumer Research. Association for Consumer Research (U. S.)*, *17*(1), 110–119.

Dong-Hun, L. (2010). Growing popularity of social media and business strategy. *SERI Quarterly*, *3*(4), 112–118.

DONNA. (1997). A new marketing paradigm for electronic commerce. *The Information Society*, *13*(1), 43–54. doi:10.1080/019722497129278

Donovan, R. J., & Rossiter, J. R. (1982). Store atmosphere: An environmental psychology approach. *Journal of Retailing, 58*(1), 34–57.

Dowling, G. (2001). *Creating Corporate Reputations: Identity, Image and Performance*. UK: Oxford University Press.

Dowling, G. R. (1993). Developing your corporate image into a corporate asset. *Long Range Planning, 26*(2), 101–109. doi:10.1016/0024-6301(93)90141-2

Drake, K. (2001, June 25). Kwest for kawaii. Time. Retrieved from http://content.time.com/time/arts/article/0,8599,131022,00.html

Druin, A. (2009). *Mobile technology for children: Designing for interaction and learning*. Morgan Kaufmann.

Duarte, C. (2011). Conflito e violência nas relações conjugais: Uma perspectiva sistémica. In P. M. Matos, C. Duarte, & M. E. Costa (Eds.), *Famílias: Questões de desenvolvimento e intervenção* (pp. 103–123). Oporto: LivPsic.

Dutton, J. E., Dukerich, J. M., & Harquail, C. V. (1994). Organisation images and member identification. *Administrative Science Quarterly, 39*(2), 239–263. doi:10.2307/2393235

Duverger, P. (2013). Curvilinear effects of user-generated content on hotels' market share: A dynamic panel-data analysis. *Journal of Travel Research, 52*(4), 465–478. doi:10.1177/0047287513478498

Eagleman, A. N. (2013). Acceptance, motivations, and usage of social media as a marketing communications tool amongst employees of sport national governing bodies. *Sport Management Review, 16*(4), 488–497. doi:10.1016/j.smr.2013.03.004

East, R., Hammond, K., & Lomax, W. (2008). Measuring the Impact of Positive and Negative Word of Mouth on Brand Purchase Probability. *International Journal of Research in Marketing, 25*(3), 215–224. doi:10.1016/j.ijresmar.2008.04.001

Edvardsson, B., Tronvoll, B., & Grubet, T. (2011). Expanding understanding of service exchange and value co-creation: A social construct approach. *Journal of the Academy of Marketing Science, 39*(2), 327–339. doi:10.1007/s11747-010-0200-y

Egger, R., & Buhalis, D. (Eds.). (2008). *Etourism case studies: management and marketing issues in etourism*. Oxford: Elsevier.

Eisenberger, R., Armeli, S., Rexwinkel, B., Lynch, P. D., & Roades, L. (2001). Reciprocation of perceived organizational support. *The Journal of Applied Psychology, 86*(1), 42–51. doi:10.1037/0021-9010.86.1.42

Eisingerich, A. B., Chun, H. H., Liu, Y., Jia, H., & Bell, S. J. (2015). Why recommend a brand face-to-face but not on Facebook? How word-of-mouth on online social sites differs from traditional word-of-mouth. *Journal of Consumer Psychology, 25*(1), 120–128. doi:10.1016/j.jcps.2014.05.004

Eldred, M. (Ed.). (2008). *Social ontology: Recasting political philosophy through a phenomenology of whoness*. Walter de Gruyter. doi:10.1515/9783110333275

Elliott, S. (2011, November 20). Redefining public relations in the age of social media. *New York Times,* Retrieved from http://www.nytimes.com/2011/2011/2021/business/media/redefining-public-relations-in-the-age-of-social-media.html

Enders, A., Hungenberg, H., Denker, H. P., & Mauch, S. (2008). The long tail of social networking: Revenue models of social networking sites. *European Management Journal, 26*(3), 199–211. doi:10.1016/j.emj.2008.02.002

Engel, J. E., Blackwell, R. D., & Kegerreis, R. J. (1969). How information is used to adopt an innovation. *Journal of Advertising Research, 9*(December), 3–8.

Enginkaya, E., & Yılmaz, H. (2014). What drives consumers to interact with brands through social media? A motivation scale development study. *Procedia: Social and Behavioral Sciences, 148*, 219–226. doi:10.1016/j.sbspro.2014.07.037

Erdem, M., & Cobanoglu, C. (2010). The impact of consumer-generated media and social networking in hospitality: The implications for consumers and hospitality managers. *Journal of Hospitality Marketing & Management, 19*(7), 697–699. doi:10.1080/19368623.2010.507990

Eroglu, S. A., Machleit, K. A., & Davis, L. M. (2001). Atmospheric qualities of online retailing: A conceptual model and implications. *Journal of Business Research, 54*(2), 177–184. doi:10.1016/S0148-2963(99)00087-9

Eroglu, S. A., Machleit, K. A., & Davis, L. M. (2003). Empirical testing of a model of online store atmospherics and shopper responses. *Psychology and Marketing, 20*(2), 139–150. doi:10.1002/mar.10064

Escalas, J. E. (2004). Narrative Processing: Building Consumer Connections to Brands. *Journal of Consumer Psychology, 14*(1–2), 168–180. doi:10.1207/s15327663jcp1401&2_19

Esch, F. R., Langner, T., Schmitt, B. H., & Geus, P. (2006). Are brands forever? How brand knowledge and relationships affect current and future purchases. *Journal of Product and Brand Management, 15*(2), 98–105. doi:10.1108/10610420610658938

Ewing, M. T., & Napoli, J. (2005). Developing and validating a multidimensional nonprofit brand orientation scale. *Journal of Business Research, 58*(6), 841–853. doi:10.1016/j.jbusres.2003.09.012

Eyrich, N., Padman, M., & Sweetser, K. (2008). PR practitioner's use of social media tools and communication technology. *Public Relations Review, 34*(4), 412–414. doi:10.1016/j.pubrev.2008.09.010

Faircloth, J. B. (2005). Factors influencing nonprofit resource provider support decisions: Applying the brand equity concept to nonprofits. *Journal of Marketing Theory and Practice, 13*(3), 1–15. doi:10.1080/10696679.2005.11658546

Fakharmanesh, S., & Miyandehi, R. (2013). The Purchase of Foreign Products: The Role of Brand Image, Ethnocentrism and Animosity: Iran Market Evidence. *Iranian Journal of Management Studies, 6*(1), 147–162.

Fang, Y., & Neufeld, D. (2009). Understanding sustained participation in open source software projects. *Journal of Management Information Systems, 25*(4), 9–50. doi:10.2753/MIS0742-1222250401

Ferguson, R. (2008). Word of mouth and viral marketing: Taking the temperature of the hottest trends in marketing. *Journal of Consumer Marketing, 25*(3), 179–182. doi:10.1108/07363760810870671

Fernando, I. (2010). Community creation by means of a social media paradigm. *The Learning Organization, 17*(6), 500–514. doi:10.1108/09696471011082367

Ferreira, P., Dionísio, A., & Pires, C. (2010). Adopt the euro? The GME approach. *Journal of Economic Interaction and Coordination, 5*(2), 231–247. doi:10.1007/s11403-010-0062-x

Ferris, G. R., Blass, R., Douglas, C., Kolodinsky, R. W., & Treadway, D. C. (2003). Personal reputation in organizations. In J. Greenberg (Ed.), *Organizational Behaviour: The State of the Science* (pp. 211–246). New Jersey: Lawrence Erlbaum Associates.

Fertik, M., & Thomson, D. (2010). *Wild West 2.0: How to Protect and Restore Your Online Reputation on the Untamed Social Frontier*. New York: AMA.

Fiegerman, S. (2012). 11 Biggest Social Media *Disasters*. Mashable.com. Retrieved from http://mashable.com/2012/11/25/social-media-business-disasters-2012/

Field, A. (2009). *Discovering statistics using SPSS*. Sage publications.

Filieri, R., & McLeay, F. (2014). E-WOM and accommodation: An analysis of the factors that influence travelers' adoption of information from online reviews. *Journal of Travel Research, 53*(1), 44–57. doi:10.1177/0047287513481274

Fill, C. (2005). *Marketing communications: engagements, strategies and practice*. Prentice Hall.

Firestein, P. J. (2006). Building and protecting corporate reputation. *Strategy and Leadership*, *34*(4), 25–31. doi:10.1108/10878570610676864

Fishbein, M., & Ajzen, I. (1975). *Belief, attitude, intention and behavior: An introduction to theory and research.*

Fishbein, M., & Ajzen, I. (1975). *Belief, attitude, intention and behavior: An introduction to theory and research*. Reading, Massachusetts: Addison-Wesley.

Flanagin, A. J. (2005). IM online: Instant messaging use among college students. *Communication Research Reports*, *22*(3), 175–187. doi:10.1080/00036810500206966

Fletcher, G. J. (2002). *The new science of intimate relationships*. New York: Blackwell. doi:10.1002/9780470773390

Flouri, E., & Buchanan, A. (2001). What predicts traditional attitudes to marriage? *Children & Society*, *15*(4), 263–271. doi:10.1002/chi.674

Fojt, M. (1996). Doing business on the information superhighway. *Internet Research*, *6*(2/3), 79–81.

Folgado, J. A., Oliveira, P. A., & Hernádez, J. M. (2011). Imagen del destino y marca turística: sinergias e implicaciones. *Proceedings of the International Conference on Tourism and management studies* (Book 1), Algarve Portugal (pp. 904-914).

Fombrun, C. J. (1996). *Reputation: Realizing Value from the Corporate Image*. Boston: Harvard Business School.

Fombrun, C. J., & Shanley, M. (1990). What's in a name? Reputation building and corporate strategy. *Academy of Management Journal*, *33*(2), 233–258. doi:10.2307/256324

Fombrun, C. J., & Van Riel, C. (1997). The reputational landscape. *Corporate Reputation Review*, *1*(1 & 2), 5–13. doi:10.1057/palgrave.crr.1540024

Fonseca, S., & Duarte, C. (2014). Do namoro ao casamento: Significados, expectativas, conflito e amor. *Psicologia: Teoria e Pesquisa (Brasília)*, *30*(2), 135–143. doi:10.1590/S0102-37722014000200002

Foo, M., Douglas, G., & Jack, M. A. (2008). Incentive schemes in the financial services sector: Moderating effects of relationship norms on customer-brand relationship. *International Journal of Bank Marketing*, *26*(2), 99–118. doi:10.1108/02652320810852772

Fornell, C., & Larcker, F. D. (1981). Evaluating structural equation models with unobservable variables and measurement error. *JMR, Journal of Marketing Research*, *18*(1), 39–50. doi:10.2307/3151312

Fornell, C., & Wernerfelt, B. (1987). Defensive marketing strategy by customer com- plaint management: A theoretical analysis. *JMR, Journal of Marketing Research*, *24*(4), 337–346. doi:10.2307/3151381

Fortin, D. R., Dholakia, R. R., & Dholakia, N. (2002). Emerging issues in electronic marketing: Thinking outside the square. *Journal of Business Research*, *55*(8), 623–627. doi:10.1016/S0148-2963(00)00202-2

Fournier, S., & Avery, J. (2011). The uninvited brand. *Business Horizons*, *54*(3), 193–207. doi:10.1016/j.bushor.2011.01.001

Fox, S. (2000). Communities of practice, foucault and actor network theory. *Journal of Management Studies*, *37*(6), 853–867. doi:10.1111/1467-6486.00207

Fram, E. H., & Grandy, D. B. (1995). Internet buyers: Will the surfers become buyers? *Direct Marketing*, *57*(10), 63–65.

Frías, D. M., Rodriguez, M. A., & Castañeda, J. A. (2008). Internet vs. travel agencies on pre-visit destination image formation: An information processing view. *Tourism Management*, *29*(1), 163–179. doi:10.1016/j.tourman.2007.02.020

Fuchs, G., & Reichel, A. (2006). Tourist destination risk perception: The case of Israel. *Journal of Hospitality & Leisure Marketing*, *14*(2), 83–108. doi:10.1300/J150v14n02_06

Gaines-Ross, L. (2008). *Corporate Reputation: 12 Steps to Safeguarding and Recovering Reputation*. Hoboken, NJ: John Wiley & Sons.

Gamboa, A. M., & Goncalves, H. M. (2014). Customer loyalty through social networks: Lessons from Zara on Facebook. *Business Horizons*, *57*(6), 709–717. doi:10.1016/j.bushor.2014.07.003

Gantz, J., & Reinsel, D. (2009). As the Economy Contracts, the Digital Universe Expands, IDC. Retrieved from http://idcdocserv.com/EMC_MMWP_Digital_Universe

Garbage News. (2014, October 9). Konbinishitennou no uriagedakanadowogurafukashitemiru. Retrieved from http://www.garbagenews.net/archives/1974644.html

Gardberg, N. A., & Fombrun, C. J. (2002). For better or worse – the most visible American corporate reputations. *Corporate Reputation Review*, *4*(4), 385–391. doi:10.1057/palgrave.crr.1540159

Gardner, H. K. (2012). Performance pressure as a double-edged sword: Enhancing team motivation but undermining the use of team knowledge. *Administrative Science Quarterly*, *57*(1), 1–46. doi:10.1177/0001839212446454

Gartner, W. C., & Ruzzier, M. K. (2011). Tourism destination brand equity dimensions: Renewal versus repeat market. *Journal of Travel Research*, *50*(5), 471–481. doi:10.1177/0047287510379157

Gefen, D. (2000). E-commerce: The role of familiarity and trust. *Omega*, *28*(6), 725–737. doi:10.1016/S0305-0483(00)00021-9

Gefen, D., Karahanna, E., & Straub, D. W. (2003). Trust and TAM in online shopping: An integrated model. *Management Information Systems Quarterly*, *27*(1), 51–90.

Gefen, D., & Straub, D. W. (2004). Consumer trust in B2C e-commerce and the importance of social presence: Experiments in e-products and e-services. *Omega*, *32*(6), 407–424. doi:10.1016/j.omega.2004.01.006

Gensler, S., Völckner, F., Liu-Thompkins, Y., & Wiertz, C. (2013). Managing brands in the social media environment. *Journal of Interactive Marketing*, *27*(4), 242–256. doi:10.1016/j.intmar.2013.09.004

Gibbs, J. L., & Kraemer, K. L. (2004). A cross-country investigation of the determinants of scope of e-commerce use: An institutional approach. *Electronic Markets*, *14*(2), 124–137. doi:10.1080/10196780410001675077

Gibson, D., Gonzales, J. L., & Castanon, J. (2006). The importance of reputation and the role of public relations. *Public Relations Quarterly*, *51*(3), 15–18.

Giddens, A. (1991). *Modernity and self-identity: Self and society in the late modern age*. Stanford University Press.

Giddens, A. D. M. (1999). *Introduction to Sociology, 5/e*. W. W. Norton & Company Inc.

Giglio, E. M. (2005). *O comportamento do consumidor*. São Paulo: Thomson.

Gillin, P., & Schwartzman, E. (2010). *Social marketing to the business customer: Listen to your B2B Market, generate major account leads, and build client relationships*. New York, NY: John Wiley & Sons, Inc.

Glazer, R. (2002). Measuring the value of information: The information-intensive organization. *IBM Systems Journal*, *32*(1), 99–110. doi:10.1147/sj.321.0099

Gobe, M. (2001). *Emotional Branding*. New York: Allworth Press.

Godes, D., & Mayzlin, D. (2004). Using online conversations to study word-of-mouth communications. *Marketing Science, 23*(4), 545–560. doi:10.1287/mksc.1040.0071

Godes, D., & Mayzlin, D. (2009). Firm-created word-of-mouth communication: Evidence from a field test. *Marketing Science, 28*(4), 721–739. doi:10.1287/mksc.1080.0444

Goh, K. Y., Heng, C. S., & Lin, Z. (2013). Social Media Brand Community and Consumer Behavior: Quantifying the Relative Impact of User- and Marketer-Generated Content. *Information Systems Research, 24*(1), 88–107. doi:10.1287/isre.1120.0469

Golan, A., & Dose, V. (2001). A generalized information theoretical approach to tomographic reconstruction. *Journal of Physics. A. Mathematical Nuclear and General, 34*(7), 1271–1283. doi:10.1088/0305-4470/34/7/304

Golan, A., Judge, G., & Miller, D. (1996). *Maximum Entropy Econometrics: Robust estimation with limited data.* Chichester: John Wiley & Sons.

Golan, G. J., & Zaidner, L. (2008). Creative strategies in viral advertising: An application of Taylor's six segment message strategy wheel. *Journal of Computer-Mediated Communication, 13*(4), 959–972. doi:10.1111/j.1083-6101.2008.00426.x

Goldsmith, R. E. (2006). Electronic word of mouth. In K. P. Mehdi (Ed.), *Encyclopedia of e-commerce, e-government and mobile commerce* (pp. 408–412). Hershey, PA: Idea Group. doi:10.4018/978-1-59140-799-7.ch067

González-Herrero, A., & Smith, S. (2008). Crisis communications management on the Web: How internet-based technologies are changing the way public relations professionals handle business crises. *Journal of Contingencies and Crisis Management, 16*(3), 143–153. doi:10.1111/j.1468-5973.2008.00543.x

Goode, M. M., & Harris, L. C. (2007). Online behavioural intentions: An empirical investigation of antecedents and moderators. *European Journal of Marketing, 41*(5/6), 512–536. doi:10.1108/03090560710737589

Gorry, G. A., & Westbrook, R. A. (2009). Winning the internet confidence game. *Corporate Reputation Review, 12*(3), 195–203. doi:10.1057/crr.2009.16

Greaves, M., & Mika, P. (2008). Semantic Web and Web 2.0. *Journal of Web Semantics, 6*(Jan), 1–3. doi:10.1016/j.websem.2007.12.002

Greenberg, P. (2009). CRM at the Speed of Light (4th ed.). New York, NY: McGraw-Hill.

Greenberg, J., & Elliott, C. (2009). A cold cut crisis: Listeriosis, Maple Leaf Foods and the politics of apology. *Canadian Journal of Communication, 34*(1), 189–204.

Grewal, D., & Gopalkrishnan, R. (2003). The Internet and The Price-Value-Loyalty Chain. *Journal of Business Research, 56*(5), 391–398. doi:10.1016/S0148-2963(01)00227-2

Grewal, D., Hardesty, D. M., & Iyer, G. R. (2004). The Effects of Buyer Identification and Purchase Timing on Consumers' Perceptions of Trust, Price Fairness and Repurchase Intentions. *Journal of Interactive Marketing, 18*(4), 87–100. doi:10.1002/dir.20024

Griffin, A., & Hauser, J. R. (1996). Integrating R&D and marketing: A review and analysis of the literature. *Journal of Product Innovation Management, 13*(3), 191–215. doi:10.1111/1540-5885.1330191

Gruen, T. W., Osmonbekov, T., & Czaplewski, A. J. (2006). eWOM: The impact of customer-to-customer online know-how exchange on customer value and loyalty. *Journal of Business Research, 59*(4), 449–456. doi:10.1016/j.jbusres.2005.10.004

Guo, J., & Sun, C. (2004). Global electronic markets and global traditional markets. *Electronic Markets, 14*(1), 4–12. doi:10.1080/1019678042000175252

Guoqing, G. U. O., & Xueeheng, Y. A. N. G. (2006). A Study of Word-of-Mouth Marketing and the Application Strategies in the Era of Internet. *Finance &Trade Economics*, *9*, 56–59.

Gu, V. C., Cao, Q., & Duan, W. (2012). Unified Modeling Language (UML) IT adoption— A holistic model of organizational capabilities perspective. *Decision Support Systems*, *54*(1), 257–269. doi:10.1016/j.dss.2012.05.034

Habibi, M. R., Laroche, M., & Richard, M. O. (2014). Brand communities based in social media: How unique are they? Evidence from two exemplary brand communities. *International Journal of Information Management*, *34*(2), 123–132. doi:10.1016/j.ijinfomgt.2013.11.010

Hagel, J. (1999). Net gain: Expanding markets through virtual communities. *Journal of Interactive Marketing*, *13*(1), 55–65. doi:10.1002/(SICI)1520-6653(199924)13:1<55::AID-DIR5>3.0.CO;2-C

Hagel, J. I., & Armstrong, A. G. (1997). *Net gain: Expanding markets through virtual communities*. Boston, MA: Harvard Business School Press.

Hall, J. (2012). *Accounting information systems*. Andover, Hampshire: Cengage Learning.

Hall, S. (2006). *Marital meaning: Exploring young adults' belief systems about handbook of couple therapy*. New York: Guilford Press.

Ham, C. D., Hong, H., & Cameron, G. T. (2012). Same Crisis, Different Responses: Case Studies of How Multiple Competing Corporations Responded to the Same Explosion-Related Crises. *International Journal of Business and Social Science*, *3*(20), 19–31.

Hankinson, P. (2002). The impact of brand orientation on managerial practice. *International Journal of Nonprofit and Voluntary Sector Marketing*, *7*(1), 30–44. doi:10.1002/nvsm.165

Hanlon, S. C., & Taylor, R. R. (1991). An examination of changes in work group communication behaviors following installation of a gain sharing plan. *Group and Organization Studies*, *16*(3), 238–267. doi:10.1177/105960119101600302

Harden, B. (2008, November 8). Japanese Stores Take Convenience To a New Level. *Washington Post Foreign Service*. Retrieved from http://www.washingtonpost.com/wp-dyn/content/article/2008/11/07/AR2008110703512.html

Harden, A. J. (1996). TV shopping: A summary of women's attitudes gained through focus group discussions. *Journal of Family and Consumer Sciences*, *88*(4), 58–62.

Harris, D. (2001). *Cute, Quaint, Hungry And Romantic: The Aesthetics of Consumerism*. New York: Da Capo Press.

Hassan, S., Nadzim, S. Z. A., & Shiratuddin, N. (2015). Strategic use of social media for small business based on the AIDA model. *Procedia: Social and Behavioral Sciences*, *172*, 262–269. doi:10.1016/j.sbspro.2015.01.363

Hausman, A. V., & Siekpe, J. S. (2009). The Effect of web interface features on consumer online purchase intentions. *Journal of Business Research*, *62*(1), 5–13. doi:10.1016/j.jbusres.2008.01.018

Havenstein, H. (2008, August 4). Exxon Mobil's brand 'hijacked' by impersonator on twitter. *Computer World*. Retrieved from www.computerworld.com/action/article.do?command1/4viewArticle Basic&articleId1/49111524

Haythornthwaite, C. (2005). Social networks and Internet connectivity effects. *Information, Communication, & Society. PubMed*, *8*(2), 125–147.

Heller Baird, C., & Parasnis, G. (2011). From social media to social customer relationship management. *Strategy and Leadership*, *39*(5), 30–37. doi:10.1108/10878571111161507

Helm, C., & Jones, R. (2010). Brand governance: The new agenda in brand management. *Journal of Brand Management, 17*(8), 545–547. doi:10.1057/bm.2010.20

Helson, H. (1964). *Adaptation-level theory*. New York, NY: Harper & Row.

Hemetsberger, A. (2002). Fostering cooperation on the internet: Social exchange processes in innovative virtual consumer communities. *Advances in Consumer Research. Association for Consumer Research (U. S.), 29*(1), 354–356.

Hendershot-Hurd, K. (2009). What to do when Social Media creates a Shit Storm. Retrieved from http://virtualimpax.com/2009/07/13/soial-media-shit-storm/

Henderson, A., & Bowley, T. (2010). Authentic dialogue? The role of "friendship" in a social media recruitment campaign. *Journal of Communication Management, 14*(3), 237–257. doi:10.1108/13632541011064517

Hendler, J., & Golbeck, J. (2008). Metcalfe's law, Web 2.0, and the Semantic Web. *Web Semantics: Science, Services, and Agents on the World Wide Web, 6*(1), 14–20. doi:10.1016/j.websem.2007.11.008

Hennig-Thurau, T., Gwinner, K., Walsh, G., & Gremler, D. (2004). Electronic word-of-mouth via consumer-opinion platforms: What motivates consumers to articulate themselves on the Internet? *Journal of Interactive Marketing, 18*(1), 38–52. doi:10.1002/dir.10073

Hobby, J. (1999). Looking after the one who matters. *Accountancy Age*, 28, 1741-2439.

Hoffman, D. L., & Fodor, M. (2010). Can you measure the ROI of your social media marketing? *MIT Sloan Management Review, 52*(1), 41–49.

Hoffman, D. L., & Novak, T. P. (1996). Marketing in hypermedia computer-mediated environments: Conceptual foundations. *Journal of Marketing, 60*(3), 50–68. doi:10.2307/1251841

Hoffman, D. L., Novak, T. P., & Peralta, M. (1999). Building consumer trust online. *Communications of the ACM, 42*(4), 80–85. doi:10.1145/299157.299175

Hofstede, G. (1980). *Culture's consequences: international differences in work-related values*. Beverly Hills: Sage.

Holbrook, M. B. (1994). The nature of customer value: an axiology of services in the consumption experience. *Service quality: New directions in theory and practice, 21*, 21-71.

Hollebeek, L. (2013). The customer engagement/value interface: An exploratory investigation. *Australasian Marketing Journal, 21*(1), 17–2. doi:10.1016/j.ausmj.2012.08.006

Homer, P. M., & Yoon, S. (1992). Message framing and the interrelationships among ad-based feelings, affect, and cognition. *Advert, 21*(1), 19–33. doi:10.1080/00913367.1992.10673357

Hong, W., & Zhu, K. (2006). Migrating to Internet-based e-commerce: Factors affecting e-commerce adoption and migration at the firm level. *Information & Management, 43*(2), 204–221. doi:10.1016/j.im.2005.06.003

Howell, D. C. (2012). *Statistical methods for psychology* (8th ed.). Independence, KY: Cengage Learning, Inc.

Hsieh, A. T., & Li, C. K. (2008). The moderating effect of brand image on public relations' perception and customer loyalty. *Marketing Intelligence & Planning, 26*(1), 26–42. doi:10.1108/02634500810847138

Huberman, B. A. (2008). Crowdsourcing and attention. *Computer, 41*(11), 103–105. doi:10.1109/MC.2008.450

Hudson, S., Roth, M. S., Madden, T. J., & Hudson, R. (2015). The effects of social media on emotions, brand relationship quality, and word of mouth: An empirical study of music festival attendees. *Tourism Management, 47*, 68–76. doi:10.1016/j.tourman.2014.09.001

Hughes, F. (2010, January 22). Naïve yurukyara win hearts across Japan. *The Japan Times*. Retrieved from http://blog.japantimes.co.jp/japan-pulse/naive-yuru-kyara-win-hearts-across-japan/

Humphreys, P., Samson, A., Roser, T., & Cruz Valdivieso, E. (2009). *Co creation: New pathways to value*. London: LSE Enterprise.

Hutton, J. G. (1997). A study of brand equity in an organizational-buying context. *Journal of Product and Brand Management*, *6*(6), 428–439. doi:10.1108/10610429710190478

Hutton, J. G., Goodman, M. B., Alexander, J. B., & Genest, C. M. (2001). Reputation management: The new face of corporate public relations? *Public Relations Review*, *27*(3), 247–261. doi:10.1016/S0363-8111(01)00085-6

Huy, L. V., Rowe, F., Truex, D., & Huynh, M. Q. (2012). An empirical study of determinants of e-commerce adoption in SMEs in Vietnam an economy in transition. *Journal of Global Information Management*, *20*(3), 23–54. doi:10.4018/jgim.2012070102

Hyde, K. F. (2008). Information processing and touring planning theory. *Annals of Tourism Research*, *35*(3), 712–731. doi:10.1016/j.annals.2008.05.001

Ibrahim, E., & Gill, J. (2005). A positioning strategy for a tourist destination, based on analysis of customers perceptions and satisfactions. *Marketing Intelligence & Planning*, *23*(2), 172–188. doi:10.1108/02634500510589921

Ind, N. (2003). *Beyond Branding: How the new values of transparency and integrity are changing the world of brands*. London: Kogan Page.

Ind, N., & Riondino, M. C. (2001). Branding on the Web: A real revolution? *The Journal of Brand Management*, *9*(1), 8–19. doi:10.1057/palgrave.bm.2540048

Iodhia, S. (2012). Web based social and environmental communication in the Australian minerals industry: An application of media richness framework. *Journal of Cleaner Production*, *25*, 73–85. doi:10.1016/j.jclepro.2011.11.040

Irwin, C., & Berge, Z. (2006). Socialization in the Online Classroom. E-Journal of Instructional Science and Technology, 9(1).

Iversen, N. M., & Hem, L. E. (2008). Provenance associations as core values of place umbrella brands: A framework of characteristics. *European Journal of Marketing*, *42*(5/6), 603–626. doi:10.1108/03090560810862534

Jahng, J., Hemant, J., & Ramamurthy, K. (2002). The impact of electronic commerce environment on user behaviour. *E-service Journal*, 1(1), 41-53.

Jang, H., Olfman, L., Ko, I., Koh, J., & Kim, K. (2008). The influence of on-line brand community characteristics on community commitment and brand loyalty. *International Journal of Electronic Commerce*, *12*(3), 57–80. doi:10.2753/JEC1086-4415120304

Janiszewski, C., & Van Osselaer, S. M. (2000). A connectionist model of brand-quality associations. *JMR, Journal of Marketing Research*, *37*(3), 331–350. doi:10.1509/jmkr.37.3.331.18780

Jansen, B. J., Zhang, M., Sobel, K., & Chowdury, A. (2009). Twitter power: Tweets as electronic word of mouth. *Journal of the American Society for Information Science and Technology*, *60*(11), 2169–2188. doi:10.1002/asi.21149

Japan Franchise Association. (2015, July). Retrieved from http://www.jfa-fc.or.jp/folder/1/img/20150820110725.pdf

Japan retail market. (2014, July). Retrieved from http://pdf.savills.asia/asia-pacific-research/japan-research/japan-retail/retail-spotlight-07-2014.pdf

Japan retails foods. (2013, December). Retrieved from http://gain.fas.usda.gov/Recent%20GAIN%20Publications/Retail%20Foods_Tokyo%20ATO_Japan_12-12-2013.pdf

Japanese convenient store operator orders 150 Mitsubishi electric cars. (2008, December 31). *EVWorld.* Retrieved from http://evworld.com/news.cfm?newsid=20038

Japanese culture is becoming a cult of cute. (2006, June 14). *NBC News*. Retrieved from http://www.nbcnews.com/id/13320352/ns/business-world_business/t/japanese-culture-becoming-cult-cute/#.VegFjiyqqko

Japanese department store rivals merge. (2007, March 14). *The New York Times*. Retrieved from http://www.nytimes.com/2007/03/14/business/worldbusiness/14iht-dai.4904532.html

Jap, S. (2003). An Exploratory Study of the Introduction of Online Reverse Auctions. *Journal of Marketing*, *67*(3), 96–107. doi:10.1509/jmkg.67.3.96.18651

Jayasingam, S., Ansari, M. A., Ramayah, T., & Jantan, M. (2013). Knowledge management practices and performance: Are they truly linked? *Knowledge Management Research & Practice*, *11*(3), 255–264. doi:10.1057/kmrp.2012.5

Jaynes, E. T. (1957a). Information theory and statistical mechanics. *Physical Review*, *106*(4), 620–630. doi:10.1103/PhysRev.106.620

Jaynes, E. T. (1957b). Information theory and statistical mechanics. II. *Physical Review*, *108*(2), 171–190. doi:10.1103/PhysRev.108.171

Jaynes, E. T. (2003). *Probability Theory – The Logic of Science*. Cambridge: Cambridge University Press. doi:10.1017/CBO9780511790423

Jin, S. A. A. (2012). The potential of social media for luxury brand management. *Marketing Intelligence & Planning*, *30*(7), 687–699. doi:10.1108/02634501211273805

Jitpleecheep, P. (2012, August 24). Saha Group in talks with Japan's Lawson. *The Bangkok Post.* Retrieved from http://www.bangkokpost.com/business/economics/309100/saha-group-in-talks-with-japan-lawson

Johnson, J. W., & Grimm, P. E. (2010). Communal and exchange relationship perceptions as separate constructs and their role in motivations to donate. *Journal of Consumer Psychology*, *20*(3), 282–294. doi:10.1016/j.jcps.2010.06.018

Johnson, R. D., & Keil, M. (2002). Media richness theory: Testing e-mail vs. v-mail for conveying student feedback. *Journal of Informatics Education*, *4*(2), 15–24.

Jolly, A. (2001). *Managing Corporate Reputations*. London: PRCA.

Jones, B., Bowd, R., & Tench, R. (2009). Corporate irresponsibility and corporate social responsibility: Competing realities. *Social Responsibility Journal*, *5*(3), 300–310. doi:10.1108/17471110910977249

Joo, J., & Normatov, I. (2013). Determinants of collective intelligence quality: Comparison between Wiki and Q&A services in English and Korean users. *Service Business*, *7*(4), 687–711. doi:10.1007/s11628-013-0183-0

Joseph, P. B., Peppers, D., & Rogers, M. (1995). Do you want to keep your customers forever. *Harvard Business Review*, *73*(2), 103–104.

Jothi, P. S. J., Neelamalar, M., & Prasad, R. S. (2011). Analysis of social networking sites: A study on effective communication strategy in developing brand communication. *Journal of Media and Communication Studies*, *3*(7), 234–242.

Judd, C. M., & Kenny, D. A. (1981). Process analysis estimating mediation in treatment evaluations. *Evaluation Review*, *5*(5), 602–619. doi:10.1177/0193841X8100500502

Juvva, S., & Bhatti, R. S. (2006). Epigenetic model of marital expectations. *Contemporary Family Therapy*, *28*(1), 61–72. doi:10.1007/s10591-006-9695-2

Kabani, S. (2010). *The Zen of social media marketing: an easier way to build credibility, generate buzz, and increase revenue*. Dallas: BenBella Books.

Kabani, S. (2012). *The Zen of Social Media Marketing: An Easier Way to Build Credibility, Generate Buzz, and Increase Revenue*. Dallas, Texas: Ben Bella Books.

Kacen, J. J., Hess, J. D., & Chiang, W. K. (2013). Bricks or Clicks? Consumer Attitudes Toward Traditional Stores and Online Stores. *Global Economics and Management Review*, *18*(1), 12–21. doi:10.1016/S2340-1540(13)70003-3

Kandampully, J., & Hu, H. H. (2007). Do hoteliers need to manage image to retain loyal customers? *International Journal of Contemporary Hospitality Management*, *19*(6), 435–443. doi:10.1108/09596110710775101

Kapferer, J. N. (1992). *Strategic Brand Management*. London: Kogan Page.

Kapferer, J. N. (1997). *Strategic brand management: Creating and sustaining brand equity long term*. London, UK: Kogan Page.

Kapferer, J. N. (2012). *The new strategic brand management: Advanced insights and strategic thinking*. Kogan Page.

Kaplan, A. M., & Haenlein, M. (2011). Two hearts in three-quarter time: How to waltz the social media/viral marketing dance. *Business Horizons*, *54*(3), 253–263. doi:10.1016/j.bushor.2011.01.006

Kaplan, A., & Haenlein, M. (2010). Users of the world, unite! The challenges and opportunities of social media. *Business Horizons*, *53*(1), 59–68. doi:10.1016/j.bushor.2009.09.003

Kasavana, M. L. (2008). The unintended consequences of social media and the hospitality industry. *Hospitality Upgrade Fall 2008*. Retrieved from http://www.hospitalityupgrade.com/_files/File_Articles/HUFall08_Kasavana_SocialMediaandHospitality.pdf

Kasavana, M. L., Nusair, K., & Teodosic, K. (2010). Online social networking: Redefining the human web. *Journal of Hospitality and Tourism Technology*, *1*(1), 68–82. doi:10.1108/17579881011023025

Kasemsap, K. (2015a). The role of social media in international advertising. In N. Taşkıran & R. Yılmaz (Eds.), Handbook of research on effective advertising strategies in the social media age (pp. 171–196). Hershey, PA: IGI Global. doi:10.4018/978-1-4666-8125-5.ch010

Kasemsap, K. (2014a). The role of social networking in global business environments. In P. Smith & T. Cockburn (Eds.), *Impact of emerging digital technologies on leadership in global business* (pp. 183–201). Hershey, PA: IGI Global. doi:10.4018/978-1-4666-6134-9.ch010

Kasemsap, K. (2014b). The role of social media in the knowledge-based organizations. In I. Lee (Ed.), *Integrating social media into business practice, applications, management, and models* (pp. 254–275). Hershey, PA: IGI Global. doi:10.4018/978-1-4666-6182-0.ch013

Kasemsap, K. (2014c). The role of brand management in emerging markets. In I. Samanta (Ed.), *Strategic marketing in fragile economic conditions* (pp. 167–184). Hershey, PA: IGI Global. doi:10.4018/978-1-4666-6232-2.ch009

Kasemsap, K. (2014d). The role of brand loyalty on CRM performance: An innovative framework for smart manufacturing. In Z. Luo (Ed.), *Smart manufacturing innovation and transformation: Interconnection and intelligence* (pp. 252–284). Hershey, PA: IGI Global. doi:10.4018/978-1-4666-5836-3.ch010

Kasemsap, K. (2015b). The roles of corporate marketing strategies and brand management in the global retail industry. In E. Pantano (Ed.), *Successful technological integration for competitive advantage in retail settings* (pp. 310–339). Hershey, PA: IGI Global. doi:10.4018/978-1-4666-8297-9.ch014

Kato, M. (2002). The Japanese obsession with adorable icons is rooted in cultural tradition. *Eye Magazine*. Retrieved from http://www.eyemagazine.com/feature/article/cute-culture

Katz, E., & Lazarsfeld, P. F. (1955). *Personal influence: The part played by people in the flow of mass communication*. New York: Free Press.

Kaynak, E., Kucukemiroglu, O., & Hyder, A. S. (2000). Consumers' country-of-origin (COO) perceptions of imported products in a homogenous less-developed country. *European Journal of Marketing*, *34*(9/10), 1221–1241. doi:10.1108/03090560010342610

Kelleher, T., & Miller, B. (2006). Organizational blogs and the human voice: Relational strategies and relational outcomes. *Journal of Computer-Mediated Communication*, *11*(2), 395–414. Retrieved from http://jcmc.indiana.edu/vol11/issue2/kelleher.html doi:10.1111/j.1083-6101.2006.00019.x

Keller, K. L. (1993). Conceptualizing, measuring, and managing customer-based brand equity. *Journal of Marketing*, *57*(1), 1–22. doi:10.2307/1252054

Keller, K. L. (1998). *Strategic brand management: Building, measuring, and managing brand equity*. Upper Saddle River, NJ: Prentice Hall.

Keller, K. L. (2008). *Strategic brand management: Building, measuring and managing brand equity*. Upper Saddle River, NJ: Prentice Hall.

Kent, M. L. (2010). Directions in social media for professionals and scholars. In R. Heath (Ed.), *Handbook of Public Relations* (2nd ed.). Thousand Oaks, CA: Sage.

Kerpen, D. (2011). *Likeable Social Media: How to Delight Your Customers, Create an Irresistible Brand, and Be Generally Amazing on Facebook (And Other Social Networks)*. New York: McGraw-Hill.

Kietzmann, J. H., Hermkens, K., McCarthy, I. P., & Silvestre, B. S. (2011). Social media? Get serious! Understanding the functional building blocks of social media. *Business Horizons*, *54*(3), 241–251. doi:10.1016/j.bushor.2011.01.005

Kim, A. J., & Ko, E. (2012). Do social media marketing activities enhance customer equity? An empirical study of luxury fashion brand. *Journal of Business Research*, *65*(10), 1480–1486. doi:10.1016/j.jbusres.2011.10.014

Kim, D. J., Ferrin, D. L., & Rao, H. R. (2008). A trust-based consumer decision-making model in electronic commerce: The role of trust, perceived risk, and their antecedents. *Decision Support Systems*, *44*(2), 544–564. doi:10.1016/j.dss.2007.07.001

Kim, E., Sung, Y., & Kang, H. (2014). Brand followers' retweeting behavior on Twitter: How brand relationships influence brand electronic word-of-mouth. *Computers in Human Behavior*, *37*, 18–25. doi:10.1016/j.chb.2014.04.020

Kim, H. B., & Kim, W. G. (2005). The relationship between brand equity and firms' performance in luxury hotels and chain restaurants. *Tourism Management*, *26*(4), 549–560. doi:10.1016/j.tourman.2004.03.010

Kim, H., Damhorst, M., & Lee, K. (2002). Apparel involvement and advertisement Processing. *Journal of Fashion Marketing and Management*, *6*(3), 277–302. doi:10.1108/13612020210441364

Kim, J., & Hardin, A. (2010). The impact of virtual worlds on word-of-mouth: Improving social networking and servicescape in the hospitality industry. *Journal of Hospitality Marketing & Management*, *19*(7), 735–753. doi:10.1080/19368623.2010.508005

Kim, J., Suh, E., & Hwang, H. (2003). A model for evaluating the effectiveness of CRM using the balanced scorecard. *Journal of Interactive Marketing*, *17*(2), 5–19. doi:10.1002/dir.10051

Kim, S., Haley, E., & Koo, G. Y. (2009). Comparison of the paths from consumer involvement types to ad responses between corporate advertising and product advertising. *Journal of Advertising*, *38*(3), 67–80. doi:10.2753/JOA0091-3367380305

King, C. W., & Summer, J. O. (1970). Overlap of opinion leadership across product categories. *JMR, Journal of Marketing Research*, *7*(1), 43–50. doi:10.2307/3149505

Kinsella, S. (1995). Cuties in Japan. In L. Skov & B. Moeran (Eds.), *Women, media, and consumption in Japan* (pp. 220–254). Honolulu: University of Hawaii Press.

Kirby, J., & Marsden, P. (Eds.). (2006). *Connected marketing: the viral, buzz and word of mouth revolution*. Oxford: Butterworth/Heinemann, Elsevier.

Kiss, C., & Bichler, M. (2005, October). Leveraging network effects for predictive modelling in customer relationship management. *Proceedings of the15th Annual Workshop on Information Technologies & Systems (WITS)*. doi:doi:10.2139/ssrn.883588 doi:10.2139/ssrn.883588

Klein, L. R. (1998). Evaluating the potential of interactive versus experience goods. *Journal of Business Research*, *41*(3), 195–203. doi:10.1016/S0148-2963(97)00062-3

Kohli, C., Suri, R., & Kapoor, A. (2015). Will social media kill branding? *Business Horizons*, *58*(1), 35–44. doi:10.1016/j.bushor.2014.08.004

Koo, C., Wati, Y., & Jung, J. J. (2011). Examination of how social aspect moderates the relationship between task characteristics and usage of social communication technologies in organizations. *International Journal of Information Management*, *31*(5), 445–459. doi:10.1016/j.ijinfomgt.2011.01.003

Koo, D.-M., & Ju, S.-H. (2010). The interactional effects of atmospherics and perceptual curiosity on emotions and online shopping intention. *Computers in Human Behavior*, *26*(3), 377–388. doi:10.1016/j.chb.2009.11.009

Kotler, P. (1998). *Administração de Marketing*. São Paulo: Atlas.

Kotler, P. H. (1991). *Marketing Management: Analysis, Planning, and Control* (8th ed.). Englewood Cliffs, NJ: Prentice-Hall, Inc.

Kotler, P., & Armstrong, G. (1996). *Principles of Marketing* (7th ed.). Englewood Cliffs, NJ: Prentice Hall, Inc.

Kotler, P., Kartajaya, H., & Setiawan, I. (2010). *Marketing 3.0: From products to customers to the human spirit*. New York: John Wiley & Sons Inc. doi:10.1002/9781118257883

Kotler, P., & Keller, K. L. (2007). *A framework for marketing management*. Upper Saddle River, NJ: Prentice Hall.

Koufaris, M., & Hampton-Sosa, W. (2004). The development of initial trust in an online company by new customers. *Information & Management*, *41*(3), 377–397. doi:10.1016/j.im.2003.08.004

Kozinets, R. (1999). E-tribalized marketing: The strategic implications of virtual communities of consumption. *European Management Journal*, *17*(3), 252–264. doi:10.1016/S0263-2373(99)00004-3

Kozinets, R. V. (2002). The field behind the screen: Using netnography for marketing research in online communities. *JMR, Journal of Marketing Research, 39*(1), 61–72. doi:10.1509/jmkr.39.1.61.18935

Krazit, T. (2011). A primer on online reputation management. *Cnet.com.* Retrieved from http://news.cnet.com/8301-30684_3-20028997-265.html

Kuan, K. Y., & Chau, Y. K. (2001). A perception model for EDI adoption in small businesses using a technology-organization-environment framework. *Information & Management, 38*(1), 507–521. doi:10.1016/S0378-7206(01)00073-8

Kucuk, S. U. (2008). Negative Double Jeopardy: The role of anti-brand sites on the internet. *Journal of Brand Management, 15*(3), 209–222. doi:10.1057/palgrave.bm.2550100

Kumamoto, Y. (2008, Sept. 26). Stores Defend 24-Hour Operations." The Japan Times Online. *The Japan Times.* Retrieved from http://www.japantimes.co.jp/text/nn20080926f2.html

Kumar, M., Townsend, J. D., & Vorhies, D. W. (2015). Enhancing consumers' affection for a brand using product design. *Journal of Product Innovation Management, 32*(5), 716–730. doi:10.1111/jpim.12245

Kunz, M. B. (1997). *Online customers: Identifying store, product and consumer attributes which influence shopping on the Internet.* Knoxville: The University of Tennessee.

Kunz, M. B., Hackworth, B., Osborne, P., & High, J. D. (2011). Fans, friends, and followers: Social media in the retailers' marketing mix. *Journal of Applied Business and Economics, 12*(3), 61–68.

Kupritz, V. W., & Cowel, E. (2011). Productive management communication: Online and face-to-face. *Journal of Business Communication, 48*(1), 54–82. doi:10.1177/0021943610385656

Kwon, E. S., & Sung, Y. (2011). Follow me! Global marketers' Twitter use. *Journal of Interactive Advertising, 12*(1), 4–16. doi:10.1080/15252019.2011.10722187

Kwon, O., & Wen, Y. (2010). An empirical study of the factors affecting social network service use. *Computers in Human Behavior, 26*(2), 254–263. doi:10.1016/j.chb.2009.04.011

Kyodo. (2012, July 26). Non-Japanese promoted to top posts to help in long-term bid to move into foreign markets. *The Japan Times.* Retrieved from http://www.japantimes.co.jp/text/nb20120726a7.html

Labrecque, L. I. (2014). Fostering consumer–brand relationships in social media environments: The role of parasocial interaction. *Journal of Interactive Marketing, 28*(2), 134–148. doi:10.1016/j.intmar.2013.12.003

Lampert, S. I., & Jaffe, E. D. (1998). A dynamic approach to country-of-origin effect. *European Journal of Marketing, 32*(1/2), 61–78. doi:10.1108/03090569810197471

Langerak, F., Verhorf, P. C., Verlegh, P. W., & de Valck, K. (2004). Satisfaction and participation in virtual communities. In B. E. Kahn & M. F. Luce (Eds.), *Advances in consumer research* (Vol. 31, pp. 56–57). Valdosta, GA: Association for Consumer Research.

Lanz, L., Fischhof, B., & Lee, R. (2010). *How are Hotels Embracing Social Media in 2010? Examples of How to Start Engaging*. New York: HVS Sales and Marketing Services.

Laroche, M., Habibi, M. R., & Richard, M. O. (2013). To be or not to be in social media: How brand loyalty is affected by social media? *International Journal of Information Management, 33*(1), 76–82. doi:10.1016/j.ijinfomgt.2012.07.003

Laroche, M., Habibi, M. R., Richard, M. O., & Sankaranarayanan, R. (2012). The effects of social media based brand communities on brand community markers, value creation practices, brand trust and brand loyalty. *Computers in Human Behavior, 28*(5), 1755–1767. doi:10.1016/j.chb.2012.04.016

Laroche, M., Papadopoulos, N., Heslop, L., & Mourali, M. (2005). The influence of country image structure on consumer evaluations of foreign products. *International Marketing Review*, *22*(1), 96–115. doi:10.1108/02651330510581190

Lawson, A. (2013, October 29). Akiko 4'koma' Lightning returns Final Fantasy XIII (Lawson HMV limited) release memorial collaboration. Plain clothes Light-chan is cute [Tweet]. Retrieved from https://twitter.com/akiko_lawson/status/395424838560403456/photo/1

Leal, G. P., Hor-Meyll, L. F., & Pessôa, L. A. (2013). Influence of virtual communities in purchasing decisions: The participants' perspective. *Journal of Business Research*, *67*(5), 882–890. doi:10.1016/j.jbusres.2013.07.007

LeBra, T. (1984). *Patterns of Japanese Behavior*. Honolulu: University of Hawaii Press.

Lee, D., Kim, H. S., & Kim, J. K. (2012). The role of self-construal in consumers' electronic word of mouth (eWOM) in social networking sites: A social cognitive approach. *Computers in Human Behavior*, *28*(3), 1054–1062. doi:10.1016/j.chb.2012.01.009

Lee, H., & Choi, B. (2003). Knowledge management enablers, processes, and organizational performance: An integrative view and empirical examination. *Journal of Management Information Systems*, *20*(1), 179–228.

Lee, M. K., & Turban, E. (2001). A trust model for consumer internet shopping. *International Journal of Electronic Commerce*, *6*(1), 75–91.

Lee, M.-C. (2008). Factors influencing the adoption of internet banking: An integration of TAM and TPB with perceived risk and perceived benefit. *Electronic Commerce Research and Applications*, *8*(3), 130–141. doi:10.1016/j.elerap.2008.11.006

Lee, M., & Johnson, K. K. (2002). Exploring differences between Internet apparel purchasers, browsers and non-purchasers. *Journal of Fashion Marketing and Management: An International Journal*, *6*(2), 146–157. doi:10.1108/13612020210429485

Lee, W., Xiong, L., & Hu, C. (2012). The effect of Facebook users' arousal and valence on intention to go to the festival: Applying an extension of the technology acceptance model. *International Journal of Hospitality Management*, *31*(3), 819–827. doi:10.1016/j.ijhm.2011.09.018

Leite, S. (2003). A união de facto em Portugal. *Revista de Estudos Demográficos*, *33*, 97–140.

Lenhart, A., Maddenn, M., & Hitlin, P. (2005). Teens and technology: Youth are leading the transition to a fully wired and mobile nation.

Letablier, M. T., & Nicolas, F. (1994). Genèse de la typicité. *Sciences des Aliments*, *14*(5), 541–556.

Leung, D., Law, R., van Hoof, H., & Buhalis, D. (2013). Social media in tourism and hospitality: A literature review. *Journal of Travel & Tourism Marketing*, *30*(1-2), 3–22. doi:10.1080/10548408.2013.750919

Levy, M. (2009). Web 2.0 implications on knowledge management. *Journal of Knowledge Management*, *13*(1), 120–134. doi:10.1108/13673270910931215

Lewis, S. (2001). Measuring corporate reputation. *Corporate Communications: An International Journal*, *6*(1), 31–35. doi:10.1108/13563280110381198

Li, H., Kuo, C., & Rusell, M. G. (1999). The impact of perceived channel utilities, shopping orientations, and demographics on the consumer's online buying behavior. *Journal of Computer-Mediated Communication*, *5*(2).

Liarte, S. (2013). Image de Marque et Internet. Comprendre, éviter et gérer l'effet «Streisand». Décisions marketing, (69, Janvier-Mars), pp.103-110

Li, C., & Bernoff, J. (2009). *Marketing in the groundswell*. Cambridge, MA: Harvard Business School Press.

Lica, L., & Tuta, M. (2011). Predicting product performance with social media. *Informatica Economica*, *15*(2), 46–56.

Li, L. H., Daugherty, T., & Biocca, F. (2002). Impact of 3-D advertising on product knowledge, brand attitude, and purchase intention: The mediating role of presence. *Journal of Advertising*, *31*(3), 43–59. doi:10.1080/00913367.2002.10673675

Lim, S., Trimi, S., & Lee, H. (2010). Web 2.0 service adoption and entrepreneurial orientation. *Service Business*, *4*(3-4), 197–207. doi:10.1007/s11628-010-0097-z

Lindquist, J. D., & Sirgy, J. M. (2009). *Shopper, Buyer and Consumer Behaviour theory, Marketing applications and Public Policy implications* (4th ed.). Ohio: Cengage Learning.

Lindstrom, M. (2005). *Brand Sense*. New York: Free Press.

Lin, J. S., & Pena, J. (2011). Are you following me? A content analysis of TV networks' brand communication on Twitter. *Journal of Interactive Advertising*, *12*(1), 17–29. doi:10.1080/15252019.2011.10722188

Lin, Z., Li, D., & Huang, W. (2003). Reputation, Reputation system and reputation distribution – An explanatory study in online consumer-to-consumer auctions. In R. Azari (Ed.), *Current security management & ethical issues of information technology* (pp. 249–266). USA: Idea Group Inc.

Litvin, S. W., Goldsmith, R. E., & Pan, B. (2008). Electronic word-of-mouth in hospitality and tourism management. *Tourism Management*, *29*(3), 458–468. doi:10.1016/j.tourman.2007.05.011

Liu, C., & Arnett, K. P. (2000). Exploring the factors associated with Web site success in the context of electronic commerce. *Information & Management*, *38*(1), 23–33. doi:10.1016/S0378-7206(00)00049-5

Li, Y. M., & Shiu, Y. L. (2012). A diffusion mechanism for social advertising over microblogs. *Decision Support Systems*, *54*(1), 9–22. doi:10.1016/j.dss.2012.02.012

Li, Z., & Li, C. (2014). Twitter as a social actor: How consumers evaluate brands differently on Twitter based on relationship norms. *Computers in Human Behavior*, *39*, 187–196. doi:10.1016/j.chb.2014.07.016

Lohse, G. L., Bellman, S., & Johnson, E. J. (2000). Consumer buying behavior on the Internet: Findings from panel data. *Journal of Interactive Marketing*, *14*(1), 15–29. doi:10.1002/(SICI)1520-6653(200024)14:1<15::AID-DIR2>3.0.CO;2-C

Loo, E. (2012, July 4). Dragon Quest's Slime is hired by convenience store. *Anime News Network*. Retrieved from http://www.animenewsnetwork.com/interest/2012-07-04/dragon-quest-slime-is-hired-by-convenience-store

Lopez-Cabrales, A., Pérez-Luño, A., & Cabrera, R. V. (2009). Knowledge as a mediator between HRM practices and innovative activity. *Human Resource Management*, *48*(4), 485–503. doi:10.1002/hrm.20295

López-Nicolás, C., & Meroño-Cerdán, A. L. (2011). Strategic knowledge management, innovation and performance. *International Journal of Information Management*, *31*(6), 502–509. doi:10.1016/j.ijinfomgt.2011.02.003

Lopez-Nicolas, C., & Soto-Acosta, P. (2010). Analyzing ICT adoption and use effects on knowledge creation: An empirical investigation in SMEs. *International Journal of Information Management*, *30*(6), 521–528. doi:10.1016/j.ijinfomgt.2010.03.004

Lorenzo-Romero, C., Constantinides, E., & Alarcon-Del-Amo, M. C. (2013). Social Media as Marketing Strategy: An Explorative Study on Adoption and Use by Retailers. In M.R. Olivas-Lujàn & Bondarouk (Eds.), Social Media in Strategic Management, (pp. 197–215). Bingley: Emerald Group Publishing Ltd.

Low, J., & Blois, K. (2002). The evolution of generic brands in industrial markets: The challenges to owners of brand equity. *Industrial Marketing Management*, *31*(5), 385–392. doi:10.1016/S0019-8501(00)00131-0

Luo, N., Zhang, M., & Liu, W. (2015). The effects of value co-creation practices on building harmonious brand community and achieving brand loyalty on social media in China. *Computers in Human Behavior*, *48*, 492–499. doi:10.1016/j.chb.2015.02.020

Luo, X., & Bhattacharya, C. B. (2006). Corporate social responsibility, customer satisfaction, and market value. *Journal of Marketing*, *70*(4), 1–18. doi:10.1509/jmkg.70.4.1

Macario, E., Ednacot, E., Ullberg, L., & Reichel, J. (2011). The changing face and rapid pace of public health communication. *Journal of Community Health*, *4*(2), 145–150. doi:10.1179/175380611X13022552566254

MacDonald, C. (2013) Ethics and online reputation management. *CSR news.net.* Retrieved from http://csr-news.net/main/2013/08/29/ethics-and-online-reputation-management/

Macedo, P., Silva, E., & Scotto, M. (2014). Technical efficiency with state-contingent production frontiers using maximum entropy estimators. *Journal of Productivity Analysis*, *41*(1), 131–140. doi:10.1007/s11123-012-0314-y

MacKinnon, D. P., & Fairchild, A. J. (2009). Current directions in mediation analysis. *Current Directions in Psychological Science*, *18*(1), 16–20. doi:10.1111/j.1467-8721.2009.01598.x PMID:20157637

Madden, M., Fox, S., Smith, A., & Vitak, J. (2007). Digital Footprints. *Pew Internet & American Life Project*. Retrieved from http://www.pewinternet.org/Reports/2007/Digital-Footprints/1-Summary-of-Findings.aspx?r=1

Mägi, A. (1999). *Store loyalty?: an empirical study of grocery shopping. Economic Research Institute Stockholm.* Stockholm: School of Economics.

Malthouse, E. C., Haenlein, M., Skiera, B., Wege, E., & Zhang, M. (2013). Managing customer relationships in the social media era: Introducing the social CRM house. *Journal of Interactive Marketing*, *27*(4), 270–280. doi:10.1016/j.intmar.2013.09.008

Mangold, W. G., & Faulds, D. J. (2009). Social media: The new hybrid element of the promotion mix. *Business Horizons*, *52*(4), 357–365. doi:10.1016/j.bushor.2009.03.002

Margalit, L. (2014, August 29). The psychology behind social media interactions. *Psychology Today*. Retrieved from https://www.psychologytoday.com/blog/behind-online-behavior/201408/the-psychology-behind-social-media-interactions

Mark, D. (2015). Apple is once again #1 most admired company in the world. *Loopinsight.com.* Retrieved from http://www.loopinsight.com/2015/02/20/apple-is-once-again-1-most-admired-company-in-the-world/

Marketo (2010). *The Definitive Guide to B2B Social Media: A Marketo Workbook.* San Mateo, CA Retrieved from http://docs.cdn.marketo.com/Guide-B2B-Social-Media-Part2.pdf

Martenson, R. (2007). Corporate brand image, satisfaction and store loyalty: A study of the store as a brand, store brands and manufacturer brands. *International Journal of Retail & Distribution Management*, *35*(7), 544–555. doi:10.1108/09590550710755921

Martin, P. D., Specter, G., Martin, D., & Martin, M. (2003). Expressed attitudes of adolescents toward marriage and family life. *Adolescence*, *38*(150), 359–367. PMID:14560887

Masabuchi, S. (1994). *Kawaiishokogun*. Tokyo: NHK Publishing.

McAlexander, J. H., Schouten, J. W., & Koenig, H. F. (2002). Building brand community. *Journal of Marketing*, *66*(1), 38–54. doi:10.1509/jmkg.66.1.38.18451

McCarthy, E. J. (1960). *Basic Marketing: A Managerial Approach*. Homewood, IL: Irwin.

McCarthy, I. P., Lawrence, T. B., Wixted, B., & Gordon, B. R. (2010). A multidimensional conceptualization of environmental velocity. *Academy of Management Review*, *35*(4), 604–626. doi:10.5465/AMR.2010.53503029

McColl, P. (2010). *Viral explosions!: proven techniques to expand, explode, or ignite your business or brand online. Franklin Lakes*. Career Press.

McCombs, M. E., & Shaw, D. L. (1993). The evolution of agenda-setting research: Twenty-five years in the marketplace of ideas. *Journal of Communication*, *43*(2), 58–67. doi:10.1111/j.1460-2466.1993.tb01262.x

McDonnell, I. (2006). *Etravel and tourism; marketing and management techniques*. Oxford: Elsevier.

McKee, S. (2010). *Creative B2B branding (no, really): Building a creative brand in a business world*. Oxford, UK: Goodfellow Publishers.

McKenna, R. (1991). Marketing is everything. *Harvard Business Review*, 69(1), 65-79.

McKenna, K. Y., Green, A. S., & Gleason, M. E. (2002). Relationship formation on the Internet: What's the big attraction? *The Journal of Social Issues*, *58*(1), 9–31. doi:10.1111/1540-4560.00246

McKenna, R. (1991). *Relationship Marketing: Successful Strategies for the Age of the Customer*. Perseus Book Group.

Mcknight, D. H., Choudhury, V., & Kacmar, C. (2002). The impact of initial consumer trust on intentions to transact with a web wite: A trust building model. *The Journal of Strategic Information Systems*, *11*(3/4), 297–323. doi:10.1016/S0963-8687(02)00020-3

McVeigh, B. (2000). How Hello Kitty commodities the cute, cool and camp: "Consumutopia" versus "control" in Japan. *Journal of Material Culture*, *5*(2), 225–245. doi:10.1177/135918350000500205

McWilliam, G. (2000). Building stronger brands through online communities. *Sloan Management Review*, *41*(3), 43–54.

McWilliam, G. (2012). Building stronger brands through online communities. *MIT Sloan Management Review*, *41*(3), 43–54.

Mead, R. (2002, March 18). Shopping Rebellion. What the kids wants. The New Yorker. Retrieved from http://www.newyorker.com/magazine/2002/03/18/shopping-rebellion

Mehrabian, A., & Russell, J. A. (1974). *An approach to environmental psychology*. Cambridge, MA: The MIT Press.

Melewar, T. C. (2008). *Facets of corporate identity, communication and reputation*. New York: Routledge. doi:10.4324/9780203931943

Merish, L. (1996). Cuteness and Commodity Aesthetics: Tom Thumb and Shirley Temple. In R.G. Thomson (Ed.), Freakery: Cultural spectacles of the extraordinary body (pp 185-203). New York: New York University Press.

Meroño-Cerdan, A., & Soto-Acosta, P. (2005). Examining e-Business impact on firm performance through website analysis. *International Journal of Electronic Business*, *3*(6), 583–598. doi:10.1504/IJEB.2005.008537

Meroño-Cerdan, A., Soto-Acosta, P., & Lopez-Nicolas, C. (2008). How do collaborative technologies affect innovation in SMEs? *International Journal of e-Collaboration*, *4*(4), 33–50. doi:10.4018/jec.2008100103

Merrit, J. (2015). The ultimate guide to ORM. *ReputationManagement.com.* Retrieved from https://www.reputationmanagement.com/

Merz, M. A., He, Y., & Vargo, S. L. (2009). The evolving brand logic: A service-dominant logic perspective. *Journal of the Academy of Marketing Science*, *37*(3), 328–344. doi:10.1007/s11747-009-0143-3

Meyou. (2015, September 3). Twitter nihonforowa ranking. Retrieved from http://meyou.jp/ranking/follower_allcat

Michaelidou, N., Siamagka, N. T., & Christodoulides, G. (2011). Usage, barriers and measurement of social media marketing: An exploratory investigation of small and medium B2B brands. *Industrial Marketing Management*, *40*(7), 1153–1159. doi:10.1016/j.indmarman.2011.09.009

Michaelson, D., & Stacks, D. W. (2011, Spring). Standardization in public relations measurement and evaluation. *The Public Relations Journal*, *5*(2), 1–22.

Michell, P., King, J., & Reast, J. (2001). Brand values related to industrial products. *Industrial Marketing Management*, *30*(5), 415–425. doi:10.1016/S0019-8501(99)00097-8

Miller, K. D., Fabian, F., & Lin, S. J. (2009). Strategies for online communities. *Strategic Management Journal*, *30*(3), 305–322. doi:10.1002/smj.735

Miller, R., & Lammas, N. (2010). Social media and its implications for viral marketing. *Asia Pacific Public Relations Journal*, *11*(1), 1–9.

Mills, E. J., & Law, R. (2004). *Handbook of consumer behavior, tourism and the Internet.* Binghamton, NY: Haworth Hospitality Press.

Mindruta, R. (2013). 5 Reasons Why Monitoring is Essential for PR. *BrandWatch*. Retrieved from http://www.brandwatch.com/2013/07/5-reasons-why-social-media-monitoring-is-essential-from-a-pr-perspective/

Mintel International Group. (2007). *Hotels and accommodations—US*. Chicago, IL: Author.

Mittelhammer, R., Cardell, N. C., & Marsh, T. L. (2013). The data-constrained generalized maximum entropy estimator of the GLM: Asymptotic theory and inference. *Entropy*, *15*(5), 1756–1775. doi:10.3390/e15051756

Mizerski, R. W. (1982). An attribution of the disproportionate influence of unfavorable information. *Consumer Research*, *9*(12), 301–310. doi:10.1086/208925

Moisescu, O. I. (2009). *Country branding: Conceptualization and review.* International Conference Marketing from Information to decision 2nd edition.

Mooradian, T., Renzl, B., & Matzler, K. (2006). Who trusts? Personality, trust and knowledge sharing. *Sage Journals Online Management Learning*, *37*(4), 523–540.

Moorman, C., Deshpandé, R., & Zaltman, G. (1993). Factors affecting trust in market research relationships. *Journal of Marketing*, *57*(1), 81–101. doi:10.2307/1252059

Moran, E., & Gossieaux, F. (2010). Marketing in a hyper-social world: The tribalization of business study and characteristics of successful online communities. *Journal of Advertising Research*, *50*(3), 232–239. doi:10.2501/S0021849910091397

Morgan, R. M., & Hunt, S. D. (1994). The commitment-trust theory of relationship marketing. *Journal of Marketing*, *58*(3), 20–38. doi:10.2307/1252308

Moutinho, K., & Roazzi, A. (2010). As teorias da ação planejada: Relações entre intenções e comportamentos. *Avalia-çãoPsicológica*, *9*(2), 279–287.

Moutinho, L., Ballantyne, R., & Rate, S. (2011). The new business environment and trends in tourism. In L. Moutinho (Ed.), *Strategic management in tourism* (2nd ed., pp. 1–19). Oxfordshire: CAB International. doi:10.1079/9781845935887.0001

Mou, Y., Atkin, D., Fu, H., Lin, C. A., & Lau, T. Y. (2013). The influence of online forum and SNS use on online political discussion in China: Assessing "Spirals of Trust.". *Telematics and Informatics*, *30*(4), 359–369. doi:10.1016/j.tele.2013.04.002

Mudambi, S. (2002). Branding importance in business-to-business markets three buyer clusters. *Industrial Marketing Management*, *31*(6), 525–533. doi:10.1016/S0019-8501(02)00184-0

Mudambi, S. M., & Schuff, D. (2010). What makes a helpful online review? A study of customer reviews on Amazon.com. *Management Information Systems Quarterly*, *34*(1), 185–200.

Mummalaneni, V. (2005). An empirical investigation of website characteristics, consumer emotional states and on-line shopping behaviors. *Journal of Business Research*, *58*(4), 526–532. doi:10.1016/S0148-2963(03)00143-7

Muniz, A. M. Jr, & O'guinn, T. C. (2001). Brand community. *The Journal of Consumer Research*, *27*(4), 412–432. doi:10.1086/319618

Muniz, A. M. Jr, & Schau, H. J. (2005). Religiosity in the abandoned Apple Newton brand community. *The Journal of Consumer Research*, *31*(4), 737–747. doi:10.1086/426607

Murray, K. B. (1991). A test of services marketing theory: Consumer information acquisition activities. *Journal of Marketing*, *55*(1), 10–25. doi:10.2307/1252200

Murray, K., & White, J. (2004). *CEO Views on reputation management*. London: Chimes Communications.

Murteira, B. J. F. (1993). *Análise exploratória de dados - Estatística descritiva*. Lisbon: McGraw-Hill.

Nahapiet, J., & Ghoshal, S. (1998). Social capital, intellectual capital, and the organizational advantage. *Academy of Management Review*, *23*(2), 242–266.

Nakata, H. (2011, October 25). Net super trend food for thought. Retrieved from http://www.japantimes.co.jp/news/2011/10/25/reference/net-super-trend-food-for-thought/#.VHxyLleUfpU

Nambisan, P., & Watt, J. H. (2011). Managing customer experiences in online product communities. *Journal of Business Research*, *64*(8), 889–895. doi:10.1016/j.jbusres.2010.09.006

Nambisan, S. (2002). Designing Virtual Customer Environments for New Product Development: Toward a Theory. *Academy of Management Review*, *27*(3), 392–413.

Nambisan, S., & Baron, R. A. (2007). Interactions in virtual customer environments: Implications for product support and customer relationship management. *Journal of Interactive Marketing*, *21*(2), 42–62. doi:10.1002/dir.20077

Nandan, S. (2005). An exploration of the brand identity-brand image linkage: A communications perspective. *The Journal of Brand Management*, *12*(4), 264–278. doi:10.1057/palgrave.bm.2540222

Naylor, R. W., Lamberton, C. P., & West, P. M. (2012). Beyond the like button: The impact of mere virtual presence on brand evaluations and purchase intentions in social media settings. *Journal of Marketing*, *76*(6), 105–120. doi:10.1509/jm.11.0105

Neff, J. (2010). How Pampers Battled Diaper Debacle. *Adage.com.* Retrieved from http://adage.com/article/news/pampers-battled-diaper-debacle/143777/

Negative Publicity Management. (2007). Vinove. Retrieved from http://www.vinove.com/mindscape/internet-marketing/negative-publicity-management/

Negroponte, N. (1995). *Being Digital*. New York: Alfred A. Kopf.

Nelson, A. J., & Leon, A. (2012). Bricks and Clicks: Rethinking Retail Real Estate in the E– commerce Era (Research Report). *RREEF Real Estate.*

Nemes, J. (2000) Domain names have brand impact. *B to B Chicago*, 85(12), 20.

Ngai, E. W. T., Tao, S. S. C., & Moon, K. K. L. (2015). Social media research: Theories, constructs, and conceptual frameworks. *International Journal of Information Management*, *35*(1), 33–44. doi:10.1016/j.ijinfomgt.2014.09.004

Ngwenyama, O. K., & Lee, A. S. (1997, June). Communication richness in electronic mail: Critical social theory and the contextuality of meaning. *Management Information Systems Quarterly*, *21*(2), 145–167. doi:10.2307/249417

Nifty Konbininitsuite no angketto ranking. (2013, May 24). Retrieved from http://chosa.nifty.com/life/chosa_report_A20130524/1/?theme=A20130524&report=1&theme=A20130524&report=1

Nonaka, I. (1994). A dynamic theory of organizational knowledge creation. *Organization Science*, *5*(1), 14–37. doi:10.1287/orsc.5.1.14

Nonaka, I., & Takeuchi, H. (1995). *The knowledge-creating company: how Japanese companies create the dynamics of innovation*. New York: Oxford University Press.

Noveck, B. S. S. (2009). *Wiki government: how technology can make government better, democracy stronger, and citizens more powerful*. Brookings Institution Press.

Nuttavuthisit, K. (2010). If you can't beat them, let them join: The development of strategies to foster consumers' co-creative practices. *Business Horizons*, *53*(3), 315–324. doi:10.1016/j.bushor.2010.01.005

Nye, J. (2006). Transformational Leadership and US grand strategy. *Foreign Affairs*, *85*(4), 139–148. doi:10.2307/20032047

O' Reilly, T. (2007). What is Web 2.0: Design patterns and business models for the next generation of software. *Communications & Stratégies*, *65*, 17–37.

O'Connor, P. (2008). Online social media and travel international (Market research report). *Oxygen.* Retrieved from http://oxygen.mintel.com/sinatra/oxygen/display/id=387948

O'Dell, J. (2009, January 5). Major Japanese retailer says Mitsubishi's I-MiEV battery electric car is way to go. Retrieved from www.edmunds.com/autoobserver-archive/2009/01/major-japanese-retailer-says-mitsubishis-i-miev-battery-electric-car-is-way-to-go.html

O'Connor, P. (2010). Managing a hotel's image on TripAdvisor. *Journal of Hospitality Marketing & Management*, *19*(7), 754–772. doi:10.1080/19368623.2010.508007

Ogut, H., & Tas, B. K. O. (2012). The influence of internet customer reviews on online sales and prices in hotel industry. *Service Industries Journal*, *32*(2), 197–214. doi:10.1080/02642069.2010.529436

Ohnemus, L. (2009). B2B branding: A financial burden for shareholders? *Business Horizons*, *52*(2), 159–166.

Oliver, R. L. (1997). *Satisfaction: A behavioral perspective on the customer*. New York.

O'Sullivan, D., & Dooley, L. (2010). Collaborative innovation for the management of information technology resources. *International Journal of Human Capital and Information Technology Professionals*, *1*(1), 16–30. doi:10.4018/jhcitp.2010091102

Otagaki, Y. (2013, November 13). Soft samurai wins hard battle of mascots. *The Wall Street Journal.* Retrieved from http://blogs.wsj.com/japanrealtime/2013/11/26/soft-samurai-wins-hard-battle-of-mascots/

Palacios-Marqués, D., Merigó, J. M., & Soto-Acosta, P. (2015a). Online social networks as an enabler of innovation in organizations. *Management Decision*, *53*(9), 1906–1920. doi:10.1108/MD-06-2014-0406

Palacios-Marqués, D., Soto-Acosta, P., & Merigó, J. M. (2015b). Analyzing the effects of technological, organizational and competition factors on web knowledge exchange in SMEs. *Telematics and Informatics*, *32*(1), 23–32. doi:10.1016/j.tele.2014.08.003

Palmer, A., & Koenig-Lewis, N. (2009). An experiential, social network-based approach to direct marketing. *Direct Marketing: An International Journal*, *3*(3), 162–176. doi:10.1108/17505930910985116

Pan & Lee. (2003). *Using E-CRM for a Unified View of the Customer*. New York, NY: ACM Press.

Pan, B., & Li, X. R. (2011). The long tail of destination image and online marketing. *Annals of Tourism Research*, *38*(1), 132–152. doi:10.1016/j.annals.2010.06.004

Panigrahy, R., Najork, M., & Xie, Y.-L. (2012, February 8-12). How user behavior is related to social affinity. *Proceedings of the Fifth ACM International Conference on Web Search and Data Mining WSDM '12,* Seattle, Washington (pp. 713-722).

Parasuraman, A., Zeithaml, V. A., & Malhotra, A. (2005). E-S-QUAL: A multiple-item scale for assessing electronic service quality. *Journal of Service Research*, *7*(3), 213–233. doi:10.1177/1094670504271156

Parasuraman, A., & Zinkhan, G. M. (2002). Marketing to and serving customers through the Internet: An overview and research agenda. *Journal of the Academy of Marketing Science*, *30*(4), 286–295. doi:10.1177/009207002236906

Parcell, L. M., Lame, M. O., & Cooley, S. C. (2011). Learning from the trades: Public relations, journalism and news release writing, 1945-2000. *American Journalism*, *28*(2), 81–111.

Park, H., & Kim, Y. K. (2014). The role of social network websites in the consumer–brand relationship. *Journal of Retailing and Consumer Services*, *21*(4), 460–467. doi:10.1016/j.jretconser.2014.03.011

Park, J., Cha, M., Kim, H., & Jeong, J. (2012). Managing Bad News in Social Media: A Case Study on Domino's Pizza Crisis. In J. G. Breslin, N. B. Ellison, J. G. Shanahan, & Z. Tufekci (Eds.), *ICWSM: The AAAI Press.*

Park, R., & Kim, J. (2013). Individual employees' responses to group incentives: The moderating role of innovation. *Journal of Business and Psychology*, *28*(2), 175–187. doi:10.1007/s10869-012-9270-9

Park, S. Y., & Bera, A. K. (2009). Maximum entropy autoregressive conditional heteroskedasticity model. *Journal of Econometrics*, *150*(2), 219–230. doi:10.1016/j.jeconom.2008.12.014

Park, S., & Nicolau, J. L. (2015). Asymmetric Effects of Online Consumer Reviews. *Annals of Tourism Research, 50,* 67–83.

Parsons, A. G. (2002). Non-functional motives for online shoppers: Why we click. *Journal of Consumer Marketing*, *19*(5), 380–392. doi:10.1108/07363760210437614

Parvatiyar, A., & Sheth, J. (Eds.). (2002). *Handbook of Relationship Marketing*. Thousand Oaks, CA: Sage.

Parveen, F., Jaafar, N. I., & Ainin, S. (2015). Social media usage and organizational performance: Reflections of Malaysian social media managers. *Telematics and Informatics*, *32*(1), 67–78. doi:10.1016/j.tele.2014.03.001

Payne, J. W., Bettman, J. R., & Johnson, J. R. (1992). Behavioral decision research: A constructive processing perspective. *Annual Review of Psychology*, *43*(1), 87–131. doi:10.1146/annurev.ps.43.020192.000511

Pentina, I., Zhang, L., & Basmanova, O. (2013). Antecedents and consequences of trust in a social media brand: A cross-cultural study of Twitter. *Computers in Human Behavior*, *29*(4), 1546–1555. doi:10.1016/j.chb.2013.01.045

Peppers, D., Rogers, M., & Dorf, B. (1999). 'Is your company ready for one-to-one marketing? *Harvard Business Review*, *77*(1), 151–160. PMID:10345390

Peppler, K. A., & Solomou, M. (2011). Building creativity: Collaborative learning and creativity in social media environments. *On the Horizon*, *19*(1), 13–23. doi:10.1108/10748121111107672

Pérez-López, S., & Alegre, J. (2012). Information technology competency, knowledge processes and firm performance. *Industrial Management & Data Systems*, *112*(4), 644–662. doi:10.1108/02635571211225521

Pestana, M. H., & Gageiro, J. N. (2003). *Análise de Dados para Ciências Sociais - A Complementaridade do SPSS*. Lisbon: Sílabo.

Peter, J. P., Olson, J. C., & Grunert, K. G. (1999). *Consumer behavior and marketing strategy* (pp. 122–123). London: McGraw-Hill.

Peters, P. (2011). *Reputations Management in Social Web*. Norderstedt: Social Media Verlag.

Peterson, S. J., & Luthans, F. (2006). The impact of financial and nonfinancial incentives on business-unit outcomes over time. *The Journal of Applied Psychology*, *91*(1), 156–165. doi:10.1037/0021-9010.91.1.156

Pew Research Centre social networking fact sheet. (n. d.). Pew Internet. Retrieved from http://www.pewinternet.org/fact-sheets/social-networking-fact-sheet/

Pinheiro, R. M., Castro, G. C., Silva, H. H., & Nunes, J. M. (2006). *Comportamento do consumidor e pesquisa de mercado*. São Paulo: FGV Management.

Ploof, R. (2009). Johnson & Johnson does new media. Retrieved from http://ronamok.com/ebooks/jnj_case_study.pdf

Plowman, K. D., Briggs, W. G., & Huang, Y. H. (2001). In R. L. Heath (Ed.), *Handbook of Public Relations* (pp. 301–310). California: Sage Publications. doi:10.4135/9781452220727.n23

Plummer, J. (1985). Brand personality: a strategic concept for multinational advertising. *Proceedings of theMarketing Educators Conference*. New York, NY: Young & Rubicam.

Podsakoff, P. M., Mackenzie, S. B., Lee, J., & Podsakoff, N. P. (2003). Common method biases in behavioral research: A critical review of the literature and recommended remedies. *The Journal of Applied Psychology*, *20*(5), 879–903. doi:10.1037/0021-9010.88.5.879

Pollitt, C. (2014). The Role of Social Media in Consumer Decision Making. *LinkedIn*. Retrieved from https://www.linkedin.com/pulse/20140331210413-36910198-the-role-of-social-media-in-consumer-decision-making

Popa, S., Soto-Acosta, P., & Loukis, E. (2016). Analyzing the complementarity of web infrastructure and eInnovation for business value generation. *Program*, *50*(1), 118–134. doi:10.1108/PROG-09-2015-0065

Porter, C. E., & Donthu, N. (2008). Cultivating trust and harvesting value in virtual communities. *Management Science*, *54*(1), 113–128. doi:10.1287/mnsc.1070.0765

Porter, M. E. (1985). *Competitive Advantage*. New York: Free Press.

Portmann, E., & Hutter, R. (2011). Blogosphäre –soziale Netzwerkeals Trendsetter. *HMD Praxis Der Wirtschaftsinformatik*, *48*(4), 37–48. doi:10.1007/BF03340604

Powers, T., Advincula, D., Austin, M. S., Graiko, S., & Snyder, J. (2012). Digital and social media in the purchase-decision process: A special report from the advertising research foundation. *Journal of Advertising Research*, *52*(4), 479–489. doi:10.2501/JAR-52-4-479-489

Prahalad, C. K., & Ramaswamy, V. (2003). The New Frontier of Experience Innovation. *Sloan Management Review*, *44*(4), 12–18. Retrieved from http://sloanreview.mit.edu/article/the-new-frontier-of-experience-innovation/

Prahalad, C. K., & Ramaswamy, V. (2004). Building New Strategic Capital for Co-Creation. Strategy. *Journal of Interactive Marketing*, *18*.

Prahalad, C. K., & Ramaswamy, V. (2004). Co-creation experiences: The next practice in value creation. *Journal of Interactive Marketing*, *18*(3), 5–14. doi:10.1002/dir.20015

Pratt, J. (2007). What is CRM. *Construction Business Development*, 71.

Preece, J., & Krichmar, D. M. (2003). Online communities: focusing on sociability and usability. In J. Jacko & A. Sears (Eds.), *Handbook of Human-Computer Interaction* (pp. 596–620). Mahwah, NJ: Lawrence Erlbaum Associates.

PRSA.org. (2012). What is Public Relations? PRSA's widely accepted definition. Retrieved from http://www.prsa.org/AboutPRSA/PublicRelationsDefined/#.U8wtf-NdXvE

Public Relations Office Government of Japan. (2011, Oct. 5). Retrieved from http://www.gov-online.go.jp/eng/publicity/book/hlj/html/201105/201105_03.html

Quan-Haase, A. (2008). Instant messaging on campus: Use and integration in university students' everyday communication. *The Information Society*, *24*(2), 105–115. doi:10.1080/01972240701883955

Qureshi, S., & Zigurs, I. (2001). Paradoxes and prerogatives in global virtual collaboration. *Communications of the ACM*, *44*(12), 85–88. doi:10.1145/501317.501354

Racherla, P., & Friske, W. (2012). Perceived usefulness of online consumer reviews: An exploratory investigation across three services categories. *Electronic Commerce Research and Applications*, *11*(6), 548–559. doi:10.1016/j.elerap.2012.06.003

Ratchford, B. T. (2009). Online Pricing: Review and Directions for Research. *Journal of Interactive Marketing*, *23*(1), 82–90. doi:10.1016/j.intmar.2008.11.001

Ratchford, B. T., & Debabrata Talukdar, M. S. L. (2001). A model of consumer choice of the Internet as an information source. *International Journal of Electronic Commerce*, *5*(3), 7–21.

Reilly, A. H., & Hynan, K. A. (2014). Corporate communication, sustainability, and social media: It's not easy (really) being green. *Business Horizons*, *57*(6), 747–758. doi:10.1016/j.bushor.2014.07.008

Report, L. I. (2014). Retrieved from http://lawson.jp/en/ir/library/annual_report.html

Reyneke, M., Pitt, L., & Berthon, P. R. (2011). Luxury wine brand visibility in social media: An exploratory study. *International Journal of Wine Business Research*, *23*(1), 21–35. doi:10.1108/17511061111121380

Reynolds, I. (2014, April 16). Japan's Population Shrinks For Third Year As Aging Increases. *Bloomberg News*. Retrieved from http://www.bloomberg.com/news/2014-04-15/japan-s-population-shrinks-for-third-year-as-ranks-of-aged-grow.html

Reynolds, G. (2006). *An army of Davids: How markets and technology empower ordinary people to beat big media, big government, and other Goliaths*. Nashville, TN: Thomas Nelson.

Ribeiro, T. (2002). Da diversidade do feminino e do masculino à singularidade do casal [Unpublished doctoral dissertation]. University of Lisbon.

Rice, M. (1997). What makes users revisit a Web site. *Marketing News*, *31*(6), 12–13.

Richins, M. L., & Root-Shaffer, T. (1988). The role of involvement and opinion leadership in consumer word-of-mouth: An implicit model made explicit. *Advances in Consumer Research. Association for Consumer Research (U. S.)*, *15*, 32–36.

Ridings, C., Gefen, D., & Arinze, B. (2006). Psychological barriers: Lurker and Poster motivation and behavior in online communities. *Communications of the Association for Information Systems*, *18*, 329–354.

Riedlinger, M. E., Gallois, C., Mckay, S., & Pittam, J. (2004). Impact of social group processes and functional diversity on communication in networked organizations. *Journal of Applied Communication Research*, *32*(1), 55–79. doi:10.1080/0090988042000178130

Rindova, V. P., Williamson, I. O., Petkova, A. P., & Sever, J. M. (2005). Being good or being known. *Academy of Management Journal*, *48*(6), 1033–1049. doi:10.5465/AMJ.2005.19573108

Roach, M. (1999, December 7). Cute Inc. *Wired*. Retrieved from http://archive.wired.com/wired/archive/7.12/cute.html

Robaina-Alves, M., Moutinho, V., & Macedo, P. (2015). A new frontier approach to model the eco-efficiency in European countries. *Journal of Cleaner Production*, *103*, 562–573. doi:10.1016/j.jclepro.2015.01.038

Robertson, J. (2012). Tell It All?: Challenging Crisis Communications' Rules. *The Public Relations Journal*, *6*(1), 1–19.

Rogers, E. M. (1962). *Diffusion of Innovations*. New York: Free Press.

Rogers, M., & Peppers, D. (1993). *The One to One Future*. New York, NY: Doubleday.

Romaniuk, J. (2011). Advertising is More Influential than Word-of-mouth? That would be Something to Talk About! *Proceedings of ANZMAC*. Retrieved from http://anzmac.info/conference/2011-proceedings

Roth, M. S., & Romeo, J. B. (1992). Matching Product Category and Country Image Perceptions: A Framework for Managing Country-Of-Origin Effects[corrected title: Matching Product Category and Country Image Perceptions: A Framework for Managing Country-Of-Origin Effects]. *Journal of International Business Studies*, *23*(3), 477–497. doi:10.1057/palgrave.jibs.8490276

Rotter, J. B. (1971). Generalized expectancies for interpersonal trust. *The American Psychologist*, *26*(5), 443–452. doi:10.1037/h0031464

Roy, D., & Banerjee, S. (2007). CARE-ing strategy for integration of brand identity with brand image. *International Journal of Commerce and Management*, *17*(1/2), 140–148. doi:10.1108/10569210710776512

Ryals, L., & Payne, A. F. T. (2001). Customer relationship management in financial services: Towards information-enabled relationship marketing. *Journal of Strategic Marketing*, *9*(1), 3–25. doi:10.1080/713775725

Sakaguchi, M. (2008). *Naruhodo Databook 1: Konbini No Shikake*. Tokyo: Otsuki Shoten.

Sakawee, S. (2014, March 27). Line now has 390 million users with Japan and Thailand as top countries. Retrieved from https://www.techinasia.com/line-390-million-users-japan-thailand-top-countries/

San Martín, S., López-Catalán, B., & Ramón-Jerónimo, M. A. (2012). Factors determining firms' perceived performance of mobile commerce. *Industrial Management & Data Systems*, *112*(6), 946–963. doi:10.1108/02635571211238536

Sánchez, M., Gil, I., & Mollá, A. (2000). Estatus del Marketing de Relaciones. *Revista Europea de Dirección y Economía de la Empresa*, *9*(3), 47–64.

Sands, S., Harper, E., & Ferraro, C. (2011). Customer-to-noncustomer interactions: Extending the "social" dimension of the store environment. *Journal of Retailing and Consumer Services*, *18*(5), 438–447. doi:10.1016/j.jretconser.2011.06.007

SAS. (2011). Improving Revenue and Customer Engagement with Social Media Analytics, *Retail Touchpoints White Paper*. Retrieved from http://www.sas.com/resources/whitepaper/wp_30521.pdf

Savilis World Research. (2014, July). Spotlight Japan retail market. Retrieved from http://pdf.savills.asia/asia-pacific-research/japan-research/japan-retail/retail-spotlight-07-2014.pdf

Sawhney, M., Verona, G., & Prandelli, E. (2005). Collaboration to Create: The Internet as a Platform for Customer Engagement in Product Innovation. *Journal of Interactive Marketing*, *19*(4), 4–17. doi:10.1002/dir.20046

Scarpi, D. (2010). Does size matter? An examination of small and large web-based brand communities. *Journal of Interactive Marketing*, *24*(1), 14–21. doi:10.1016/j.intmar.2009.10.002

Schau, H. J., Muñiz, A. M. Jr, & Arnould, E. J. (2009). How brand community practices create value. *Journal of Marketing*, *73*(5), 30–51. doi:10.1509/jmkg.73.5.30

Schiffman, L. G., & Kanuk, L. L. (2009). *Comportamento do consumidor*. São Paulo: LTC.

Schilling, M. (1997). *The encyclopedia of Japanese pop culture*. New York: Weatherhill.

Schmidt, H. J., & Baumgarth, C. (2015). Brand orientation: A case study approach within the context of social entrepreneurial businesses. *Procedia: Social and Behavioral Sciences*, *175*, 24–31. doi:10.1016/j.sbspro.2015.01.1170

Schmitt, B. H. (1999). *Experiential Marketing: How to Get Customers to Sense, Feel, Think, Act, Relate*. New York: Free Press.

Schoenbachler, D. D., Gordon, G. L., Foley, D., & Spellman, L. (1997). Understanding consumer database marketing. *Journal of Consumer Marketing*, *14*(1), 5–19. doi:10.1108/07363769710155820

Schouten, J. W., McAlexander, J. H., & Koenig, H. F. (2007). Transcendent customer experience and brand community. *Journal of the Academy of Marketing Science*, *35*(3), 357–368. doi:10.1007/s11747-007-0034-4

Schubert, P., & Ginsburg, M. (2000). Virtual communities of transaction: The role of personalization in electronic commerce. *Electronic Markets*, *10*(1), 45–55. doi:10.1080/10196780050033971

Schultz, M., Moritsen, J., & Gabrielsen, G. (2006). Sticky reputation: Analyzing a ranking system. *Corporate Reputation Review*, *4*(1), 24–41. doi:10.1057/palgrave.crr.1540130

Scott, D. M. (2011). *The New Rules of Marketing & PR: How to Use Social Media, Online Video, Mobile Applications, Blogs, News Releases, and Viral Marketing to Reach Buyers Directly*. New York: Wiley.

Sedley, R. (2006). cScape Customer Engagement Director. Retrieved from http://www.e-consultancy.com/publications/customer-engagement-report

Seebach, C., Beck, R., & Denisova, O. (2013). Analyzing social media for CR management: How firms can improve business agility. *International Journal of Business Intelligence Research*, *4*(3), 50–66. doi:10.4018/ijbir.2013070104

Seiryokuzu, K. (2014, March). Retrieved from http://todo-ran.com/t/kiji/10327

Sethi, V., & King, W. (1994). Development of Measures to Assess the Extent to Which an Information Technology Application provides Competitive Advantage. *Management Science*, *40*(12), 1601–1627. doi:10.1287/mnsc.40.12.1601

Shahkat, M. S. A. (2011). The use of Facebook to increase climate change awareness among employees. Proceedings of the International Conference on Social Science and Humanity (Vol. 5, pp. 266–270). Retrieved from http://www.ipedr.com/vol5/no2/59-H10164.pdf

Shainesh, G., & Sheth, J. (2006). *Conceptual Foundations of CRM, Customer Relationship Management, A Strategic Initiative*. Chennai, India: Macmillan.

Shamdasani Prem, N., Stanaland Andrea, J. S., & Tan, J. (2001). Location, location, location: Insights for advertising placement on the Web. *Journal of Advertising Research*, *41*(4), 7–21. doi:10.2501/JAR-41-4-7-21

Sheer, V. C., & Chen, L. (2004). Improving media richness theory: A study of interaction goals, message valence and task complexity in manager-subordinate communication. *Management Communication Quarterly*, *18*(1), 76–93. doi:10.1177/0893318904265803

Shen, Y.-C., Huang, C.-Y., Chu, C.-H., & Liao, H.-C. (2010). Virtual community loyalty: An interpersonal-interaction perspective. *International Journal of Electronic Commerce*, *15*(1), 49–74. doi:10.2753/JEC1086-4415150102

Sherman, E., Mathur, A., & Smith, R. B. (1997). Store environment and consumer purchase behavior: Mediating role of consumer emotions. *Psychology and Marketing*, *14*(4), 361–378. doi:10.1002/(SICI)1520-6793(199707)14:4<361::AID-MAR4>3.0.CO;2-7

Sheth, J. N. (1983). *An integrative theory of patronage preference and behavior*. College of Commerce and Business Patronage Behavior and Retail Management.

Sheth, J. N., & Parvatiyar, A. (2000). *'The evolution of relationship marketing', Handbook of Relationship Marketing* (pp. 119–148). India: Sage Publications Ltd. doi:10.4135/9781452231310.n5

Shevlin, R. (2006). Marketing Whims? Retrieved from http://marketingwhims.blogspot.com/2006/04/disengaging-from-arfs-definitionof05.html

Shih, C. C. (2009). *The Facebook era: Tapping online social networks to build better products, reach new audiences, and sell more stuff*. Boston, MA: Prentice Hall.

Shih, C. C., Lin, T. M. Y., & Luarn, P. (2014). Fan-centric social media: The Xiaomi phenomenon in China. *Business Horizons*, *57*(3), 349–358. doi:10.1016/j.bushor.2013.12.006

Shimp, T. A., Samiee, S., & Madden, T. J. (1993). Countries and their products: A cognitive structure perspective. *Journal of the Academy of Marketing Science*, *21*(4), 323–330. doi:10.1007/BF02894524

Shim, S., & Bickle, M. C. (1994). Benefit segments of the female apparel market: Psychographics, shopping orientations, and demographics. *Clothing & Textiles Research Journal*, *12*(2), 1–12. doi:10.1177/0887302X9401200201

Shim, S., & Chen, Y. Q.Yen Qiong Chen. (1996). Acculturation characteristics and apparel shopping orientations; Chinese students and spouses from the People's Republic of China residing in the Southwest. *Clothing & Textiles Research Journal*, *14*(3), 204–215. doi:10.1177/0887302X9601400306

Shim, S., & Drake, M. F. (1990). Consumer intention to utilize electronic shopping: The Fishbein behavioral intention model. *Journal of Direct Marketing*, *4*(3), 22–33. doi:10.1002/dir.4000040305

Shim, S., Eastlick, M. A., Lotz, S. L., & Warrington, P. (2001). An online prepurchase intentions model: The role of intention to search. *Journal of Retailing*, *77*(3), 397–416. doi:10.1016/S0022-4359(01)00051-3

Shirky, C. (2008). *Here comes everybody: The power of organizing without organizations*. Penguin books.

Shove, E. (2002). Converging Conventions of Comfort, Cleanliness and Convenience. Retrieved from http://www.lancaster.ac.uk/fass/resources/sociology-online-papers/papers/shove-converging-conventions.pdf

Sigala, M., & Chalkiti, K. (2013). Investigating the exploitation of web 2.0 for knowledge management in the Greek tourism industry: An utilisation–importance analysis. *Computers in Human Behavior*, *30*(1), 800–812.

Silva, P. M., & Dias, G. A. (2007). Teorias sobre aceitação de tecnologia: Por que os usuários aceitam ou rejeitam as tecnologias de informação? *Brazilian Journal of Information Science*, *1*(2), 69–91.

Silvestre, A. L. (2007). *Análise de dados e estatística descritiva*. Lisbon: Escolar Editora.

Simula, H., & Vuori, M. (2012). Benefits and barriers of crowdsourcing in B2B firms: Generating ideas with internal and external crowds. *International Journal of Innovation Management*, *16*(6), 1–19. doi:10.1142/S1363919612400117

Singh, R. (2015). 'Shake it off like the earthquake', says Lenskart ad after Nepal tragedy. *Zeenews*. Retrieved from zeenews.india.com/news/sci-tech/shake-it-off-like-the-earthquake-says-lenskart-ad-after-nepal-tragedy_1585108.html

Singh, D., & Agrawal, D. P. (2003). CRM practices in Indian industries. *International Journal of Customer Relationship Management*, *5*(3), 241–257.

Singh, S., & Sonnenburg, S. (2012). Brand performances in social media. *Journal of Interactive Marketing*, *26*(4), 189–197. doi:10.1016/j.intmar.2012.04.001

Sirni. R. Srinivasan (2012). *Strategic Retail Management*. Biztantra publications.

Smaiziene, I., & Jucevicius, R. (2009). Corporate Reputation: Multidisciplinary richness and search for a relevant definition. *Inzinerine Ekonomika-Engineering Economics*, *2*(62), 91–101.

Smith, A. D. (2009). The impact of e-procurement systems on customer relationship management: A multiple case study. *International Journal of Procurement Management*, *2*(3), 314–338. doi:10.1504/IJPM.2009.024814

Smith, A. N., Fischer, E., & Yongjian, C. (2012). How does brand-related user-generated content differ across YouTube, Facebook, and Twitter? *Journal of Interactive Marketing*, *26*(2), 102–113. doi:10.1016/j.intmar.2012.01.002

Smith, P. R., & Zook, Z. (2011). *Marketing communications: integrating offline and online with social media*. Kogan Page Ltd.

Smythe, J., Dorward, C., & Reback, J. (1992). *Corporate Reputation: Managing the New Strategic Asset*. London: Century Business.

Social Bakers. (n. d.) KLM: A Truly Socially devoted company. Retrieved from https://cdn.socialbakers.com/www/archive/storage/www/klm-sociallydevoted.pdf

Solis, B. (2010). Defining social media 2006–2010. Retrieved from http://www.briansolis.com/2010/01/definingsocial-media-the-saga-continues

Solomon, M. R. (2002). *O comportamento do consumidor: Comprando, possuindo e sendo*. São Paulo: Bookman.

Sorce, P., Perotti, V., & Widrick, S. (2005). Attitude and age differences in online buying. *International Journal of Retail & Distribution Management*, *33*(2), 122–132. doi:10.1108/09590550510581458

Soteriades, M., & Avgeli, V. (2007). Promoting tourism destinations: A strategic marketing approach. *Tourism: an International Interdisciplinary Journal*, *55*(3), 335–345.

Sotiriadis, M. D., & van Zyl, C. (2013). Electronic word-of-mouth and online reviews in tourism services: The use of twitter by tourists. *Electronic Commerce Research*, *13*(1), 103–124. doi:10.1007/s10660-013-9108-1

Soto-Acosta, P., Casado-Lumbreras, C., & Cabezas-Isla, F. (2010a). Shaping human capital in software development teams. The case of mentoring enabled by semantics. *IET Software*, *4*(6), 445–452. doi:10.1049/iet-sen.2010.0087

Soto-Acosta, P., Colomo-Palacios, R., & Popa, S. (2014). Web knowledge sharing and its effect on innovation: An empirical investigation in SMEs. *Knowledge Management Research & Practice*, *12*(1), 103–113. doi:10.1057/kmrp.2013.31

Soto-Acosta, P., Martinez-Conesa, I., & Colomo-Palacios, R. (2010b). An empirical analysis of the relationship between IT training sources and IT value. *Information Systems Management*, *27*(3), 274–283. doi:10.1080/10580530.2010.493847

Soto-Acosta, P., & Meroño-Cerdan, A. (2006). An analysis and comparison of web development between local governments and SMEs in Spain. *International Journal of Electronic Business*, *4*(2), 191–203. doi:10.1504/IJEB.2006.009790

Soto-Acosta, P., & Meroño-Cerdan, A. (2008). Analyzing e-Business value creation from a resource-based perspective. *International Journal of Information Management*, *28*(1), 49–60. doi:10.1016/j.ijinfomgt.2007.05.001

Soto-Acosta, P., Popa, S., & Palacios-Marqués, D. (2015). *E-business, organizational innovation and firm performance in manufacturing SMEs: An empirical study in Spain*. Technological and Economic Development of Economy;

Sparks, B. A., & Browning, V. (2011). The impact of online reviews on hotel booking intentions and perception of trust. *Tourism Management*, *32*(6), 1310–1323. doi:10.1016/j.tourman.2010.12.011

Sparks, L. (2000). Seven-Eleven Japan and The Southland Corporation: A marriage of convenience? *International Marketing Review*, *17*(4/5), 401–415. doi:10.1108/02651330010339923

Spies, K., Hesse, F., & Loesch, K. (1997). Store atmosphere, mood and purchasing behavior. *International Journal of Research in Marketing*, *14*(1), 1–17. doi:10.1016/S0167-8116(96)00015-8

Sprott, D., Czellar, S., & Spangenberg, E. (2009). Brand Engagement self concept. *JMR, Journal of Marketing Research*, Feb., 2009.

Srivastava, M. K., & Gnyawali, D. R. (2011). When do relational resources matter? Leveraging portfolio technological resources for breakthrough innovation. *Academy of Management Journal*, *54*(4), 797–810. doi:10.5465/AMJ.2011.64870140

Srivastava, R. K., Crosby, J. R., McInish, T. H., Wood, R. A., & Capraro, A. J. (1997). Part IV: How do reputations affect corporate performance: The value of corporate reputation: Evidence from the equity markets. *Corporate Reputation Review*, *1*(1), 62–68. doi:10.1057/palgrave.crr.1540018

Stahl, F., Heitmann, M., Lehmann, D. R., & Neslin, S. A. (2012). The impact of brand equity on customer acquisition, retention, and profit margin. *Journal of Marketing*, *76*(4), 44–63. doi:10.1509/jm.10.0522

Starkov, M. & Mechoso, M. (2008, August). Best Practices on Monitoring Hotel Review Sites. *Hospitality eBusiness Strategies*.

Statistic Brain. (2013). Twitter statistics. Retrieved on May 6, 2015 from http://www.statsticsbrain.com/twitterstatistics

Statistics Directory. (n. d.). Facebook. Retrieved from http://www.socialbakers.com/statistics/facebook/

Steenkamp, J. B. E. (1997). Dynamics in consumer behavior with respect to agricultural and food products. In Agricultural marketing and consumer behavior in a changing world (pp. 143-188). Springer US. doi:doi:10.1007/978-1-4615-6273-3_8 doi:10.1007/978-1-4615-6273-3_8

Steenkamp, J. B. E., & Dekimpe, M. G. (1997). The increasing power of store brands: Building loyalty and market share. *Long Range Planning*, *30*(6), 917–930. doi:10.1016/S0024-6301(97)00077-0

Steenkamp, M., & Hyde-Clarke, N. (2014). The use of Facebook for political commentary in South Africa. *Telematics and Informatics*, *31*(1), 91–97. doi:10.1016/j.tele.2012.10.002

Stegbauer, C. (2009). *Wikipedia: Das Ratsel der Kooperation*. Wiesbaden: VS. doi:10.1007/978-3-531-91691-0

Stephen, A. T., & Galak, J. (2009). The complementary roles of traditional and social media in driving marketing performance. Retrieved from http://www.insead.edu/facultyresearch/research/doc.cfm?did=46238

Stokburger-Sauer, N. (2010). Brand community: Drivers and outcomes. *Psychology and Marketing*, *27*(4), 347–368. doi:10.1002/mar.20335

Stuart, H., & Jones, C. (2004). Corporate branding in marketspace. *Corporate Reputation Review*, *7*(1), 84–93. doi:10.1057/palgrave.crr.1540213

Sugawa, K. (2000, April 25). Change in premiership and Japan's soft power. *The Asahi Shimbun.*

Sukoco, B. M., & Wu, W. Y. (2010). The personal and social motivation of customers' participation in brand community. *African Journal of Business Management*, *4*(5), 614–622.

Sun, T., Youn, S., Wu, G., & Kuntaraporn, M. (2006). Online word-of-mouth (or mouse): An exploration of its antecedents and consequences. *Journal of Computer-Mediated Communication*, *11*(4), 1104–1127. doi:10.1111/j.1083-6101.2006.00310.x

Suntornpithug, N., & Khamalah, J. (2010). Machine and person interactivity: The driving forces behind influences on consumers' willingness to purchase online. *Journal of Electronic Commerce Research*, *11*(4), 299–325.

Supa, D. W. (2014). A qualitative examination of the impact of social media on media relations practice. *The Public Relations Journal*, *8*(2). Retrieved from http://www.prsa.org/Intelligence/PRJournal/Vol8/No2/

Suresh, Shivaram, & Mohan (2004), Does Online Customer Experience Affect the Performance of E-commerce Firms. Journal of Business, 77(2 Part 2).

Suzuki, R. (2012, November 17). Nation in the grips of yurukyara fever. Yomiuri Online. Retrieved from http://www.yomiuri.co.jp/dy/photos/newjapan/newjapan121117.htm

Tang, Q., Gu, B., & Whinston, A. B. (2012). Content contribution for revenue sharing and reputation in social media: A dynamic structural model. *Journal of Management Information Systems*, *29*(2), 41–76. doi:10.2753/MIS0742-1222290203

Tapscott, D. (1998). *Growing up digital* (Vol. 302). New York: McGraw-Hill.

Taylor, M., & Kent, M. L. (2010). Anticipatory socialization in the use of social media in public relations: A content analysis of PRSA's public relations tactics. *Public Relations Review*, *36*(3), 207–214. doi:10.1016/j.pubrev.2010.04.012

Templeton, G. F., Lewis, B. R., & Snyder, C. A. (2002). Development of a measure for the organizational learning construct. *Journal of Management Information Systems*, *19*(2), 175–218.

Thackeray, R., Neiger, B. I., Hanson, C. L., & McKenzie, J. F. (2008). Enhancing promotional strategies within social marketing programs: Use of Web 2.0 social media. *Health Promotion Practice*, *9*(4), 338–343. doi:10.1177/1524839908325335 PMID:18936268

The Importance of Customer Satisfaction and Customer Engagement in Business Outcomes. (2010). *Peoplemetrics*, Retrieved from http://www.peoplemetrics.com/

The incredible shrinking country. (2014, March 25). *The Economist*. Retrieved from http://www.economist.com/blogs/banyan/2014/03/japans-demography

Thomas, J. B., Peters, C. O., Howell, E. G., & Robbins, K. (2012). Social Media and Negative Word of Mouth: Strategies for Handing Unexpecting Comments. *Atlantic Marketing Journal*, *1*(2), 87–108.

Thomas, J. B., Peters, C. O., Howell, E. G., & Robbins, K. (2012). Social media and negative wordof mouth: Strategies for handing unexpecting comments. *Atlantic Marketing Journal*, *1*(2), 7.

Thomke, S. (1998). Managing Experimentation in the Design of New Products. *Management Science*, *44*(6), 743–762. doi:10.1287/mnsc.44.6.743

Thomke, S., & Von Hippel, E. (2002). Customers as Innovators: A New Way to Create Value. *Harvard Business Review*, *80*(4), 74–81. PMID:12024760

Thompson, H. (2015). 6 Examples of Social Media Crises: What can we learn? *OurSocialTimes.com.* Retrieved from http://oursocialtimes.com/6-examples-of-social-media-crises-what-can-we-learn/

Thompson, C. J., & Troester, M. (2002). Consumer Value Systems in the Age of Postmodern Fragmentation: The Case of the Natural Health Microculture. *The Journal of Consumer Research*, *28*(4), 550–571. doi:10.1086/338213

Thompson, S. A., & Sinha, R. K. (2008). Brand communities and new product adoption: The influence and limits of oppositional loyalty. *Journal of Marketing*, *72*(6), 65–80. doi:10.1509/jmkg.72.6.65

Thomsen, S. R., Straubhaar, J. D., & Bolyard, D. M. (1998). *Ethnomethodology and the study of online communities: Exploring the cyberstreets.Proceedings of IRISS Conference*, Bristol.

Thong, J. Y. L. (1999). An integrated model of information systems adoption in small businesses. *Journal of Management Information Systems*, *15*(4), 187–214. doi:10.1080/07421222.1999.11518227

Tiwana, A. (2003). *The knowledge management toolkit: orchestrating it, strategy and knowledge platform.* Upper Saddle River, NJ: Prentice Hall.

Tokyo Drift: how Japan leads the way on m-payment. (2013, May 13). Vodafone Global Enterprise. Retrieved from http://enterprise.vodafone.com/insight_news/2013-08-13-tokyo-drift-how-japan-leads-the-way-on-m-payments.jsp

Toledano, M., & Riches, M. (2014). Brand alliance and event management for social causes: Evidence from New Zealand. *Public Relations Review*, *40*(5), 807–814. doi:10.1016/j.pubrev.2014.09.001

Tong, C. (2012, July 2). Japan-Based Convenience Store Chain. *Pacific Business News*. Retrieved from http://www.bizjournals.com/pacific/news/2012/07/02/japan-based-convenience-store-chain.html

Top 100 Twitterholics based on followers. (2015). *The Twitaholic.com.* Retrieved from http://twitaholic.com/top100/followers/

Tornatzky, L. G., & Fleischer, M. (1990). *The process of technological innovation. Lexington. MA.* Lexington: Lexington Books.

Torres, I. (2012, December 26). The battle for cute in Japan rages on in the 'yuru-kyara' mascot competition. Japan Daily Press. Retrieved from http://japandailypress.com/the-battle-for-cute-in-japan-rages-on-in-yuru-kyara-mascot-competition-2620436/

Tozzi, J. (2008). Do reputation management services work? *Businessweek.com.* Retrieved from http://www.businessweek.com/stories/2008-04-30/do-reputation-management-services-work-businessweek-business-news-stock-market-and-financial-advice

Trevino, L., Lengel, R., Bodensteiner, W., Gerloff, E., & Muir, N. K. (1990). The richness imperative and cognitive style: The role of individual differences in media choice behavior. *Management Communication Quarterly*, *4*(2), 176–197. doi:10.1177/0893318990004002003

Tsimonis, G., & Dimitriadis, S. (2014). Brand strategies in social media. *Marketing Intelligence & Planning*, *32*(3), 328–344. doi:10.1108/MIP-04-2013-0056

Tsui, A. S., Pearce, J. L., Porter, L. W., & Tripoli, A. M. (1997). Alternative approaches to the employee-organization relationship: Does investment in employees pay off? *Academy of Management Journal*, *40*(5), 1089–1121. doi:10.2307/256928

Tuominen, P. (2007). Emerging metaphors in brand in brand management: Towards a relational approach. *Journal of Communication Management*, *11*(2), 182–191. doi:10.1108/13632540710747398

Turner, J., & Qualman, E. (2013). The 83 Best Social Media and Mobile Marketing Tools for Small- to Mid-Sized Businesses. Retrieved from http://www.oahefcu.coop/elements/uploadFiles/83%20Best%20Tools.pdf

Turner, J. W., Grube, J. A., Tinsley, C. H., Lee, C., & O'Pell, C. (2006). Exploring the dominant media: How does media use reflect organizational norms and affect performance? *Journal of Business Communication*, *43*(3), 220–250. doi:10.1177/0021943606288772

Turning buzz into gold: How pioneers create value from social media. (2012). McKinsey & Company. Retrieved from https://www.mckinsey.com/~/media/.../Turning_buzz_into_gold.ashx

Urban, G. (2005). *Don't just relate-advocate: A blueprint for profit in the era of customer power*. Upper Saddle River, NJ: Wharton School Publishing.

Using Publicity and Social Media. (2011). IEEE. Retrieved from http://www.ieee.org/conferences_events/conferences/organizers/conference_publicity_social_media.html

Uyeno, K. (July 2005). Japanese convenience store debuts in Hawaii. Retrieved from http://www.khon2.com/mostpopular/story/Japanese-convenience-store-debuts-in-Hawaii/Dl5b-ZHMIEmDgcj_M-q44A.cspx

Valkenburg, P. M., & Peter, J. (2009). The effects of instant messaging on the quality of adolescents' existing friendships: A longitudinal study. *Journal of Communication*, *59*(1), 79–97. doi:10.1111/j.1460-2466.2008.01405.x

Valkokari, K., Paasi, J., & Rantala, T. (2012). Managing Knowledge within networked Innovation. *Knowledge Management Research & Practice*, *10*(1), 27–40. doi:10.1057/kmrp.2011.39

Vallaster, C., & von Wallpach, S. (2013). An online discursive inquiry into the social dynamics of multi-stakeholder brand meaning co-creation. *Journal of Business Research*, *66*(9), 1505–1515. doi: 10.1016/j.jbusres.2012.09.012

Van den Poel, D., & Leunis, J. (1999). Consumer acceptance of the Internet as a channel of distribution. *Journal of Business Research*, *45*(3), 249–256. doi:10.1016/S0148-2963(97)00236-1

van der Heijden, H., Verhagen, T., & Creemers, M. (2003). Understanding online purchase intentions: Contributions from technology and trust perspectives. *European Journal of Information Systems*, *12*(1), 41–48. doi:10.1057/palgrave.ejis.3000445

van Dijk, J., Antonides, G., & Schillewaert, N. (2014). Effects of co-creation claim on consumer brand perceptions and behavioural intentions. *International Journal of Consumer Studies*, *38*(1), 110–118. doi:10.1111/ijcs.12071

van Noort, G., & Willemsen, L. M. (2011). Online damage control: The effects of proactive versus reactive webcare interventions in consumer-generated and brand-generated platforms. *Journal of Interactive Marketing*, *26*(3), 131–140. doi:10.1016/j.intmar.2011.07.001

van Riel, C. B. M., & Balmer, J. M. T. (1997). Corporate identity: The concept, its measurement and management. *European Journal of Marketing*, *31*(5/6), 340–355. doi:10.1108/03090569710167574

Van Riel, C. B. M., & Berens, G. (2001). Balancing corporate branding policies in multi business companies. In P. J. Kitchen & D. E. Schultz (Eds.), *Raising the corporate umbrella: corporate communications in the 21st century*. Basingstoke: Palgrave.

Varadarajan, R., Srinivasan, R., Vadakkepatt, G. G., Yadav, M. S., Pavlou, P. A., Krishnamurthy, S., & Krause, T. (2010). Interactive technologies and retailing strategy: A review, conceptual framework and future research directions. *Journal of Interactive Marketing*, *24*(2), 96–110. doi:10.1016/j.intmar.2010.02.004

Vargo, S., & Lusch, R. (2004). Evolving to a new dominant logic for marketing. *Journal of Marketing*, *68*(1), 1–17. doi:10.1509/jmkg.68.1.1.24036

Varma, G. (2005). *On-line Marketing: Principles and Current Practices*. New Century Publications.

Vedamani, G. G. (2003). *Retail management*. Jaico Publishing House.

Venkatesh, V., & Davis, F. D. (2000). A theoretical extension of the technology acceptance model: Four longitudinal field studies. *Management Science*, *46*(2), 186–204. doi:10.1287/mnsc.46.2.186.11926

Venkatesh, V., & Morris, M. G. (2000). Why don't men even stop to ask for directions? Gender, social influence, and their role in technology acceptance and usage behavior. *Management Information Systems Quarterly*, *24*(1), 115–140. doi:10.2307/3250981

Vermeulen, I.E., & Daphne S. (2009). Tried and Tested: The Impact of Online Hotel Reviews on Consumer Consideration. *Tourism Management*, 30(1), 123-27.

Vickery, G., & Wunsch-Vincent, S. (2007). *Participative web and user-created content: Web 2.0 wikis and social networking*. Paris, France: Organization for Economic Cooperation and Development.

Vinod, H. D., & López-de-Lacalle, J. (2009). Maximum entropy bootstrap for time series: The meboot R package. *Journal of Statistical Software*, *29*(5), 1–19. doi:10.18637/jss.v029.i05

Visser, E. M., & Du Preez, R. (2001). Apparel shopping orientation: two decades of research. *Journal of Family Ecology and Consumer Sciences*, 29, 71-81. Retrieved from www.up.ac.za/academic/acadorgs/saafecs/vol29/visser.html

Vogt, P. (2009, April 24). Brands under attack: marketers can learn from domino's video disaster, *Forbes*. Retrieved from www.forbes.com/2009/04/24/dominos-youtube-twitter-leadership-cmonetwork- marketing.html

Vollenbroek, W., Vries, S., Constantinides, E., & Kommers, P. (2014). Identification of influence in social media communities. *International journal of web based communities*, 10(3), 280-297.

von Hippel, E. (2005). *Democratizing innovation*. Cambridge, MA: MIT Press.

Vorvoreanu, M. (2008). Society for new communication research study: ROI of online press releases. *Journal of New Communication Research*, *3*(1), 92–98.

Walker, E. (2008, May 21). Top car: how 'Hello Kitty' conquered the world. *The Independent*. Retrieved from http://www.independent.co.uk/news/world/asia/top-cat-how-hello-kitty-conquered-the-world-831522.html

Walker, K. (2010). A systematic review of the corporate reputation literature: Definition, measurement, and theory. *Corporate Reputation Review*, *12*(4), 357–387. doi:10.1057/crr.2009.26

Wangenheim, F. V. (2005). Post switching negative word of mouth. *Journal of Service Research*, *8*(1), 67–78. doi:10.1177/1094670505276684

Wang, S., & Hung, J. H. (2011). Voice of America in the post-Cold War era: Opportunities and challenges to external media services via new information and communication technology. *International Communication Gazette*, *73*(4), 343–358. doi:10.1177/1748048511398599

Wang, Y. M., Wang, Y. S., & Yang, Y. F. (2010). Understanding the determinants of RFID adoption in the manufacturing industry. *Technological Forecasting and Social Change*, *77*(5), 803–815. doi:10.1016/j.techfore.2010.03.006

Wang, Y., & Ahmed, P. (2009). The moderating effect of the business strategic orientation on e-commerce adoption: Evidence from UK family run SMEs. *The Journal of Strategic Information Systems*, *18*(1), 16–30. doi:10.1016/j.jsis.2008.11.001

Wang, Y., Hsu, K., Hsu, S., & Hsieh, P. (2011). Constructing an index for brand equity: A hospital example. *Service Industries Journal*, *31*(2), 311–322. doi:10.1080/02642060902759145

Warren Buffett: his best quotes. (2013). *The Telegraph*. Retrieved from http://www.telegraph.co.uk/finance/newsbysector/banksandfinance/8381363/Warren-Buffett-his-best-quotes.html

Wayne, S. J., Shore, L. M., & Liden, R. C. (1997). Perceived organizational support and leader-member exchange: A social exchange perspective. *Academy of Management Journal*, *40*(1), 82–111. doi:10.2307/257021

Weber, L. (2007). *Marketing on the Social Web: how digital customer communities build your business*. New Jersey: John Wiley and Sons.

Weick, K. E. (1995). *Sensemaking in organizations*. Thousand Oaks, CA: Sage Publications.

Weinberg, B. D., de Ruyter, K., Dellarocas, C., Buck, M., & Keeling, D. I. (2013). Destination social business: Exploring an organization's journey with social media, collaborative community and expressive individuality. *Journal of Interactive Marketing*, *27*(4), 299–310. doi:10.1016/j.intmar.2013.09.006

Weinberg, B. D., & Pehlivan, E. (2011). Social spending: Managing the social media mix. *Business Horizons*, *54*(3), 275–282. doi:10.1016/j.bushor.2011.01.008

Weinberg, T. (2009). *The new community rules: Marketing on the social web*. Sebastopol, CA: O'Reilly Media.

Weiner, B. (1986). *An Attributional Theory of Motivation and Emotion*. New York: Springer-Verlag. doi:10.1007/978-1-4612-4948-1

Weiss, A. M., Anderson, E., & Maclnniss, D. J. (1999). Reputation management as a motivation for sales structure decisions. *Journal of Marketing*, *63*(4), 74–89. doi:10.2307/1251975

Wei, W., Miao, L., & Huang, Z. J. (2013). Customer engagement behaviors and hotel responses. *International Journal of Hospitality Management*, *33*, 316–330. doi:10.1016/j.ijhm.2012.10.002

Westbrook, R. A., & Black, W. C. (1985). A motivation-based shopper typology. *Journal of Retailing*, *61*, 78–103.

West, M. I. (2008). *The Japanification of Children's Popular Culture: From Godzilla to Miyazaki*. Maryland: Scarecrow Press.

Wilcox, K., & Stephen, A. (2013). Are close friends the enemy? Online social networks, self-esteem, and self-control. *The Journal of Consumer Research*, *40*(1), 90–103. doi:10.1086/668794

Wilson, H. J., Gulnan, P. J., & Parise, S. (2011). What's your social media strategy? *Harvard Business Review*, (July - August), 23–25.

Wood, S. L. (2002). Future fantasies: A social change perspective of retailing in the 21 st century. *Journal of Retailing*, *78*(1), 77–83. doi:10.1016/S0022-4359(01)00069-0

World Association of Opinion and Marketing Research Professionals. (2011). *ESOMAR Guideline on Social Media Research*. Amsterdam, Netherlands: ESOMAR.

World Tourism Organization. (2014). *Online Guest Reviews and Hotel Classification Systems – An Integrated Approach Report, World Tourism Organization*. Madrid, Spain: UNWTO.

Wrench, J., Thomas-Madox, C., Peck Richmond, V., & McCroskey, J. (2008). *Quantitative research methods for communication: A hands on approach*. New York, NY: Oxford University Press.

Wright, J. (2006). The power of blogs for business. *Blog Marketing*. Retrieved from http://www.blogmarketingbook.com/

Wright, D. K., & Hinson, M. D. (2010, Summer). How new communication media are being used in public relations: A longitudinal analysis. *The Public Relations Journal*, *4*(3). Retrieved from http://www.prsa.org/Intelligence/PRJournal/Documents/2010tWrightHinson.pdf

Wright, D. K., & Hinson, M. D. (2014). An updated examination of social and emerging media use in public relations practice: A longitudinal analysis between 2006 and 2014. *The Public Relations Journal*, *8*(2), 1–35.

Wright, D. W., Simmons, L. A., & Campbell, K. (2007). Does a marriage ideal exist? Using Q-sort methodology to compare young adults and professional educators' views on healthy marriages. *Contemporary Family Therapy*, *29*(4), 223–236. doi:10.1007/s10591-007-9044-0

Wright, D., & Hinson, M. D. (2009). An updated look at the impact of social media on public relations practice. *The Public Relations Journal*, *3*(2), 2–23.

Wu, C.-S., Cheng, F.-F., & Yen, D. C. (2008). The atmospheric factors of online storefront environment design: An empirical experiment in Taiwan. *Information & Management*, *45*(7), 493–498. doi:10.1016/j.im.2008.07.004

Wu, J.-J., Chen, Y.-H., & Chung, Y.-S. (2010). Trust factors influencing virtual community members: A study of transaction communities. *Journal of Business Research*, *63*(9-10), 1025–1032. doi:10.1016/j.jbusres.2009.03.022

Wu, J.-J., & Tsang, A. S. (2008). Factors affecting members' trust belief and behaviour intention in virtual communities. *Behaviour & Information Technology*, *27*(2), 115–125. doi:10.1080/01449290600961910

Wunsch-Vincent. S., & Vickery, G. (2007). Participative web and user-created content: Web 2.0, wikis and social networking. Paris: OECD.

Wynne, R. (2014, April 28). Winning social media stratégies for public relations. *Forbes*. Retrieved from http://www.forbes.com/sites/robertwynne/2014/04/28/winning-social-media-strategies-for-public-relations/

Xiang, Z., & Gretzel, U. (2010). Role of social media in online travel information search. *Tourism Management*, *31*(2), 179–188. doi:10.1016/j.tourman.2009.02.016

Xie, K., Chen, C.-C., & Wu, S.-Y. (2012). Leveraging the ranking power of hotels by consumer reviews: Evidence from TripAdvisor.com. *Proceedings of the 18th annual graduate conference*, Washington State University.

Xie, J., & Shugan, S. M. (2001). Electronic Tickets, Smart Cards and Online Prepayments: When and How to Advance Sell. *Marketing Science*, *20*(3), 219–243. doi:10.1287/mksc.20.3.219.9765

Xin, J. Y., Ramayah, T., Soto-Acosta, P., Popa, S., & Ping, T. A. (2014). Analyzing the use of the Web 2.0 for brand awareness and competitive advantage: An empirical study in the Malaysian hospitability industry. *Information Systems Management*, *31*(2), 96–103. doi:10.1080/10580530.2014.890425

Xu, S., Zhu, K., & Gibbs, J. (2004). Global technology, local adoption: A cross-country investigation of Internet adoption by companies in the United States and China. *Electronic Markets*, *14*(1), 13–24. doi:10.1080/1019678042000175261

Yacouel, N., & Fleischer, A. (2012). The role of cybermediaries in reputation building and price premiums in the online hotel market. *Journal of Travel Research*, *51*(2), 219–226. doi:10.1177/0047287511400611

Yang, B., Lester, D., & James, S. (2006). Attitudes toward buying online as predictors of shopping online for British and American respondents. *Cyberpsychology & Behavior*, *10*(2), 198–203. doi:10.1089/cpb.2006.9968 PMID:17474836

Yan, J. (2011). Social media in branding: Fulfilling a need. *Journal of Brand Management*, *18*(9), 688–696. doi:10.1057/bm.2011.19

Yano, C.R. (2000). Dream girl: imagining the girl-next-door within the heart/ soul of Japan. *U.S-Japan Women's Journal* (English Supplement), 19, 122-141.

Yano, C. R. (2004). Kitty Litter: Japanese Cute At Home and Abroad. In J. Goldstein, D. Buckingham, & G. Brougere (Eds.), *Toys, Games, and Media* (pp. 57–58). New York: Routledge.

Yarow, J. (2012, January 6). There's one place in the world where Twitter is bigger than Facebook. Retrieved from http://www.businessinsider.com/theres-only-one-place-in-the-world-where-twitter-is-bigger-than-facebook-2012-1#ixzz3KYbyX0W0

Yates, D., & Paquette, S. (2011). Emergency knowledge management and social media technologies: A case study of the 2010 Haitian earthquake. *International Journal of Information Management*, *31*(1), 6–13. doi:10.1016/j.ijinfomgt.2010.10.001

Yeo, T.E.D. (2012). Social-media early adopters don't count: How to seed participation in interactive campaigns by psychological profiling of digital consumers. *Journal of Advertising Research*, *52*(3), 297–308. doi:10.2501/JAR-52-3-297-308

Ye, Q., Law, R., Gu, B., & Chen, W. (2011). The influence of user-generated content on traveler behavior: An empirical investigation on the effects of e-word-of-mouth to hotel online bookings. *Computers in Human Behavior*, *27*(2), 634–639. doi:10.1016/j.chb.2010.04.014

Yoo, B., Donthu, N., & Lee, S. (2000). An examination of selected marketing mix elements and brand equity. *Journal of the Academy of Marketing Science*, *28*(2), 195–211. doi:10.1177/0092070300282002

Yoon, S. J. (2002). The antecedents and consequences of trust in online-purchase decisions. *Journal of Interactive Marketing*, *16*(2), 47–63. doi:10.1002/dir.10008

Youndt, M. A., Snell, S. A., Dean, J. W. Jr, & Lepak, D. P. (1996). Human resource management, manufacturing strategy and firm performance. *Academy of Management Journal*, *39*(4), 836–866. doi:10.2307/256714

Yuanquan, L., Jiayin, Q., & Huaying, S. (2008). Review of relationships among variables in TAM. *Tsinghua Science and Technology*, *13*(3), 273–278. doi:10.1016/S1007-0214(08)70044-0

Zadeh, A. H., & Sharda, R. (2014). Modeling brand post popularity dynamics in online social networks. *Decision Support Systems*, *65*, 59–68. doi:10.1016/j.dss.2014.05.003

Zaglia, M. E. (2013). Brand communities embedded in social networks. *Journal of Business Research*, *66*(2), 216–223. doi:10.1016/j.jbusres.2012.07.015

Zarella, D. (2010). *The social media marketing book*. Sebastopol, CA: O'Reilly Media.

Zavattaro, S. M., Daspit, J. J., & Adams, F. G. (2015). Assessing managerial methods for evaluating place brand equity: A qualitative investigation. *Tourism Management*, *47*(1), 11–21. doi:10.1016/j.tourman.2014.08.018

Zeithaml, V. A. (1988). Consumer perceptions of price, quality, and value: A means-end model and synthesis of evidence. *Journal of Marketing*, *52*(3), 2–22. doi:10.2307/1251446

Zeithaml, V. A., Berry, L. L., & Parasuraman, A. (1996). The behavioral consequences of service quality. *Journal of Marketing*, *60*(2), 31–46. doi:10.2307/1251929

Zerfass, A., & Schramm, D. M. (2014). Social media newsrooms in public relations: A conceptual framework and corporate practices in three countries. *Public Relations Review*, *40*(1), 79–91. doi:10.1016/j.pubrev.2013.12.003

Zettelmeyer, F., Morton, S., & Silva-Risso, J. (2006). How the Internet Lowers Prices: Evidence from Matched Survey and Automobile Transaction Data. *JMR, Journal of Marketing Research*, *43*(2), 168–181. doi:10.1509/jmkr.43.2.168

Zhang, C., Hahn, J., & De, P. (2013). Continued participation in online innovation communities: Does community response matter equally for everyone? *Information Systems Research*, *24*(4), 1112–1130. doi:10.1287/isre.2013.0485

Zhang, K. Z. K., Benyoucef, M., & Zhao, S. J. (2015). Consumer participation and gender differences on companies' microblogs: A brand attachment process perspective. *Computers in Human Behavior*, *44*, 357–368. doi:10.1016/j.chb.2014.11.068

Zhang, K. Z. K., Zhao, S. J., Zhang, H., & Lee, M. K. O. (2014). An empirical research of the factors affecting users to follow companies' microblogs. *International Journal of Networking and Virtual Organisations*, *14*(1/2), 129–145. doi:10.1504/IJNVO.2014.065081

Zhang, Z., Ye, Q., Law, R., & Li, Y. (2010). The impact of e-word-of-mouth on the online popularity of restaurants: A comparison of consumer reviews and editor reviews. *International Journal of Hospitality Management*, *29*(4), 694–700. doi:10.1016/j.ijhm.2010.02.002

Zhou, Z., Zhang, Q., Su, C., & Zhou, N. (2012). How do brand communities generate brand relationships? Intermediate mechanisms. *Journal of Business Research*, *65*(7), 890–895. doi:10.1016/j.jbusres.2011.06.034

Zhu, K., & Kraemer, K. (2005). Post-adoption variations in usage and value of e-business by organizations: Cross-country evidence from the retail industry. *Information Systems Research*, *16*(1), 61–84. doi:10.1287/isre.1050.0045

Zhu, K., Kraemer, K. L., & Xu, S. (2006). The process of innovation assimilation by firms in different countries: A technology diffusion perspective on e-business. *Management Science*, *52*(10), 1557–1576. doi:10.1287/mnsc.1050.0487

Zhu, K., Kraemer, K. L., Xu, S., & Dedrick, J. (2004). Information technology payoff in e-business environments: An international perspective on value creation of e-business in the financial services industry. *Journal of Management Information Systems*, *21*(1), 17–54.

Zhu, K., Kraemer, K., & Xu, S. (2003). Electronic business adoption by European firms: A cross-country assessment of the facilitators and inhibitors. *European Journal of Information Systems*, *12*(4), 251–268. doi:10.1057/palgrave.ejis.3000475

Zhu, Y., Li, Y., Wang, W., & Chen, J. (2010). What leads to the post-implementation success of erp? An empirical study of the Chinese retail industry. *International Journal of Information Management*, *30*(3), 265–276. doi:10.1016/j.ijinfomgt.2009.09.007

Zins, A. (2001). Relative attitudes and commitment in customer loyalty models. International. *Journal of Service Industries management*, 12(3), 269-294.

About the Contributors

Anurag Singh has an affluent experience of more than sixteen years in teaching, research and training. He did his M.B.A., from Department of Business Administration, Bundelkhand University Jhansi and had the specialization in Marketing and Human Resource Management. He obtained his Ph. D. in Marketing area from FMS, Gurukul Kangri University, Haridwar, Uttarakhand. Dr. Singh has published more than 45 research papers in referred journals and edited volumes, which includes the prestigious International publishers like Palgrave, Springer, IGI global, IEEE, Bloomsbury etc. Dr. Singh has presented research papers in more than 45 National and International Seminars and Conferences on the contemporary issues in Management. Apart from organising Faculty Development Program on Time Series Analysis, Workshop on SEM and International Conference on Marketing, Dr. Singh has chaired a number of technical sessions in National and International Conferences and Seminar. Besides his active involvement as the trainer to various Government departments like MSME, and PVVNL, various Management Institutions are inviting him as a soft skill trainer. Dr. Singh has developed the curriculum for several management institutions in the Country. He has completed a minor research project funded by Banaras Hindu University and has edited a book titled "Integrated Marketing Communication: A Research Agenda", published by Global Publishing Ltd. Hyderabad. Dr. Singh is on the editorial board of five National journals of Management. Prior to taking his present assignment, Dr. Singh has worked with FMS, Gurukul Kangri University, Haridwar, Uttarakhand and Department of Business Administration, Assam University, Silchar, Assam. Presently, he is contributing as Assistant Professor in Faculty of Management Studies, Banaras Hindu University and is guiding doctoral research and master's dissertations students. He has special interests in contemporary issues like Behavioural Marketing, Digital Marketing and E-HRM.

Punita Duhan is a Doctoral Research Fellow in marketing area at Faculty of Management Studies, Banaras Hindu University, Varanasi and is pursuing research to study the influences of Social Media on consumer behaviour. She is faculty in Business Administration with Department of Training and Technical Education, Govt. of Delhi for the last 16 years. Prior to this, she has worked as Faculty of Management with University Business School, Panjab University, Chandigarh and IMT, Faridabad. She has attended 32 national as well as international seminars/conferences and has presented papers in 23 national and international seminars and conferences. She has published with prestigious national and international publishers such as Palgrave, Springer, IGI global, Bloomsbury etc. Besides, she has been actively involved in curriculum development of various universities and technical education departments of Delhi and Haryana State in management area.

***

Himadri Barman is an Assistant Professor at Centre for Management Studies, Dibrugarh University (CMSDU) since December 2003. He is an MSc (Mathematics) and MTech (IT), both from Tezpur University, Assam. He also has post graduate diplomas in Business Management and Operations Management from Gauhati University, Assam and IGNOU, New Delhi respectively. He underwent the Faculty Development Programme of Indian Institute of Management, Ahmedabad (IIMA). He has submitted his PhD thesis at Assam University, Silchar. He is a life member of Assam Academy of Mathematics, Aaranyak (North East India's largest wildlife conservation NGO) and the Tezpur University Alumni Association. He is the founder General Secretary of Samannay, the CMSDU Alumni Association and continues to be so. You may visit his website http://himadri.cmsdu.org or his blog http://himadri.rediffiland.com. His Twitter handle is http://twitter.com/zeroboyas and he may be reached on his Facebook page at http://facebook.com/BarmanHimadri.

Avani Desai is a Professor at GLS University, Ahmedabad and a Visiting Faculty at the Indian Institute of Management (IIM) Ahmedabad in the Communication Area. She holds an MBA in Finance and a PhD in the area of Investor Relations. She is the co-author of the book *Corporate Reputation Decoded* (2014), which is the first in this area in the Indian context. Her areas of interest are investor relations, corporate reputation, and corporate communication.

Saurabh K. Dixit, Ph. D., is an Associate Professor and Head, Department of Tourism and Hotel Management, North Eastern Hill University, Shillong, Meghalaya, India. He has graduated in Hotel Management and Catering Technology and possesses a Master's Degree in Tourism Management besides the Doctorate degree in Hotel Management. His areas of interest are Hospitality/Tourism Management and Guest Satisfaction. He has work experience from a number of Indian universities/educational institutes. He has successfully completed two research projects on Status of Hotel and Restaurant Industry in Bundelkhand Region with special reference to Jhansi, Gwalior and Khajuraho (India) and Guests' Satisfaction vis-à-vis Service Quality in the Luxury Hotels of Agra and Khajuraho (India) funded by University Grants Commission, New Delhi, India. He has six books to his credit besides the number of research papers in reputed peer reviewed journals and books. He is a member of the editorial board of number of scientific journals.

S. K. Dubey is B.Com (Hons), MBA, Ph.D. with a specialization in Marketing. Dr. Dubey, Professor in the Faculty of Management Studies, BHU has contributed several research papers/articles in national and international journals. He has organized several national conference/workshop/seminar/ Faculty Development Program/ Quality Improvement Program/Management Development Program. He has worked as Associate Professor, Pokhara University, Nepal. He has rich experience in academic administration. He is a member of AIMA, ISTE, IAMA and AIMS- International. Dr. Dubey is actively involved in training of corporate executives. His current areas of interest are Advertising, Retailing and Rural Marketing.

Mariana Mira Ferreira obtained her Bachelor's degree and her Master's degree in Management, both from the University of Aveiro. Her professional experience is related to marketing and market research activities.

Saurabh Gupta is a doctoral candidate in the Faculty of Management Studies, Banaras Hindu University. He is pursuing his doctoral degree in the field of strategic Management. He has been awarded Junior Research Fellowship in the discipline of Management as well as Human Resource Management by the UGC. He has edited one book in the area of Tourism Management. He has published more than 10 papers in national and international journals including book chapters. He has presented a number of papers in international and national conferences and seminars. He is an active researcher and his scholarly contributions are in the area of consumer behavior, services marketing and strategic management.

Manel Hamouda is an assistant professor at the Higher Institute of Management at the University of Gabès (Tunisia). She earned her Ph.D. degree in Marketing from the University of Tunis El Manar. Her research is focused mainly on consumer behavior, postmodern marketing, online marketing and international Marketing. She is the author of numerous research articles in peer reviewed journals, posters, conference proceedings and case studies. She was also a program committee member and co-chair of many international conferences. Her teaching experience includes teaching Bachelor and MBA degrees and she has taught different courses such as Business Administration, Marketing Management, International Marketing, Web Marketing, Retailing, Advertising strategy and Consumer Behavior. She also supervises undergraduate students in their major research projects."

Ana Isabel Jimenez-Zarco is an Associate Professor in the Innovation and Marketing Area of the Open University of Catalonia, and a Part-time professor at the Marketing Department of ICADE, Pontificia of Comillas University. PhD in Economics and Business Sciences from the University of Castilla-La Mancha, Spain. Postdegree in Bulding Models in Ecology and Natural Resources Management from the Polytechnic University of Catalonia. She is the author of several books and articles and serves as both a reviewer and as an associated editor of several international journals in the marketing area.

Kijpokin Kasemsap received his BEng degree in Mechanical Engineering from King Mongkut's University of Technology Thonburi, his MBA degree from Ramkhamhaeng University, and his DBA degree in Human Resource Management from Suan Sunandha Rajabhat University. He is a Special Lecturer in the Faculty of Management Sciences, Suan Sunandha Rajabhat University, Bangkok, Thailand. He is a Member of the International Association of Engineers (IAENG), the International Association of Engineers and Scientists (IAEST), the International Economics Development and Research Center (IEDRC), the International Association of Computer Science and Information Technology (IACSIT), the International Foundation for Research and Development (IFRD), and the International Innovative Scientific and Research Organization (IISRO). He also serves on the International Advisory Committee (IAC) for the International Association of Academicians and Researchers (INAAR). He has had numerous original research articles in top international journals, conference proceedings, and book chapters on business management, human resource management, and knowledge management published internationally.

Asha Kaul is a Professor in the Communication Area, Indian Institute of Management, Ahmedabad. She obtained her doctorate in stylistics from the Indian Institute of Technology, Kanpur in 1990. She is the author of *Effective Business Communication* (2000), *The Effective Presentation: Talk Your Way to Success* (2005), *Business Communication* (2nd edition, 2009), co-author of the book, *Corporate Reputation Decoded* (2014) and co-editor of two books: *Management Communication: Trends and Strategies* (2006) and *New Paradigms for Gender Inclusivity* (2013). Her current areas of interest include genderlect, politeness, managerial, corporate and digital communication. Currently, she is working on Indian cases to comprehend the intricacies involved in corporate decision making for enhancing reputation.

Pedro Macedo obtained a PhD in Mathematics (probability and statistics), a MSc in Economics, a postgraduate degree in Marketing and a licentiate degree in Applied Mathematics. He worked as a statistician in EDP Gas Distribution, a natural gas supply company from EDP Group, and is currently an Assistant Professor in the Department of Mathematics in the University of Aveiro and a member of CIDMA - Center for Research & Development in Mathematics and Applications.

R. K. Malik is Doctoral Research Fellow in Advertising area at FMS-BHU, Varanasi. He completed his Masters of Business Administration in Marketing & Finance from Madan Mohan Malviya Engineering College, Gorakhpur. Prior to joining the faculty as a full time research scholar, he worked around three years in CIPLA. He is currently pursuing his research in Advertising area.

Ana Isabel Gonzalez Michel received her M.A. from Department of Communication, The University of Texas at El Paso. Her research focuses on new media, public relations theory, and practices. She is currently working as a Community Education Liaison, in the Division of Professional and Graduate Studies, Albertus Magnus College in Connecticut.

António C. Moreira obtained a Bachelor's degree in Electrical Engineering and a Master's degree in Management, both from the University of Oporto, Portugal. He received his PhD in Management from UMIST-University of Manchester Institute of Science and Technology, England. He is an Assistant Professor in the Department of Economics Management and Industrial Engineering, University of Aveiro, Portugal, where he heads the Bachelor and Master's Degrees in Management for five years. He is also a member of GOVCOPP.

Simona Popa holds a PhD in MIS from the Department of Management and Finance at the University of Murcia, Spain. She received a BA in Accounting and data management from the University Alexandru Ioan Cuza (Iasi, Romania), a Master's in Business Research and a Master's in Sociology Applied to Research from University of Murcia (Spain). Her research interests are in the areas of eBusiness, Management Information Systems, Human-Computer Interaction and Business Information Management. Her work has been published in journals such as the International Journal of Information Management, Information Systems Management, Knowledge Management Research & Practice, and the Journal of Universal Computer Science and Service Business, among others.

Priyanka is a Doctoral Research Fellow in the retailing area at FMS-BHU, Varanasi. She did her Masters of Business Administration in Human Resource Management at Ranchi University, Ranchi. She is currently pursuing her research on Employee Attrition in the Indian Retail Industry. She has been awarded NET in the discipline on Human Resource Management and junior research fellowship in the discipline of management by the UGC. She has presented more than 20 research papers in several national and international conferences/seminars. Her area of interest is human resource management and Retail management.

Thomas E. Ruggiero is currently an Associate Professor and the designer and coordinator of the Multimedia Journalism Program at UTEP. He recently served as a Senior Lecturer in Journalism for one year in the Department of Culture, Media & Drama at the University of the West of England in Bristol, UK., where he established undergraduate and graduate courses in multimedia journalism. As a journalism professor for 12 years he teaches both practical and theoretical journalism courses including Public Affairs Reporting, Feature Writing, Journalism Ethics and Multimedia Journalism. He earned his Ph.D. from Bowling Green State University, his M.S. from Shippensburg University, and his B.A. from the University of Oregon School of Journalism. He has professional experience as a daily newspaper reporter with The San Jose Mercury News, The Herald Mail, Hagerstown, Md., The Record Herald, Waynesboro, Pa., The Press-Enterprise, Bloomsburg, Pa., and The Medford Mail Tribune, Medford, Or. As a researcher, his interests include: New Media Communication, Media Ethics, and Intercultural Media Effects. He has refereed articles published in many communication journals and books, including Communication Quarterly, Journal of Computer-Mediated Communication, Mass Communication & Society, and Journal of Mass Media Ethics; and regularly presents research papers at national and regional communication conferences. He co-created the borderzine.com e-magazine, serves as co-director of the Dow Jones Summer Minority High School Journalism Workshop, and is the official monitor for the Dow Jones Newspaper Fund Editing Intern Program.

Naman Sharma is currently working as an Assistant Professor with Amity School of Business, Amity University, Noida. He is UGC-NET qualified and has been awarded with the Centrally Administered Doctoral Fellowship 2015 by the Indian Council of Social Science Research (ICSSR). His area of research is Organizational Behavior and Human Resources specially the areas concerning Employees' Deviance and Ethics.

Rajshree Singh has over 7 years of experience in academia. She is the author of the book on Advertising Appeal - published by LAP Publications, Germany. She is currently working with Amity University as Assistant Professor. She has been actively researching the domain of Brand Management, with focus on its contributions to the fields of Marketing and CRM and has several years of research experience. She has published several manuscripts in International and National Journals. She also serves as reviewer of several International Journals and Books. At Amity School of Business, she teaches Sales and Distribution Management, International Marketing, Export Management and Strategy.

V. K. Singh is presently associated with FMS. He has served IAF for 7.5 years. He has authored 11 books. Under him, 14 research scholars have been awarded a Ph.D. He has 49 publications to his credit in international journals. He has traveled 14 countries on his academic & visiting professor clusters.

Neus Soler-Labajos is a Digital Marketing Consultant and a Part-time Professor of Marketing and Market Research at the Open University of Catalonia. Has a degree in Market Research and Techniques from the Open University of Catalonia as well as in Business Sciences. She holds a Master's in Business Administration and a Postdegree in Social Media and Community Management. She is also the author of several books and white papers on the area of Digital Marketing.

Pedro Soto-Acosta is an Associate Professor of Management at the University of Murcia (Spain). He attended Postgraduate Courses in Management at Harvard University (USA) and received his PhD in

MIS from University of Murcia. His work has been published in journals such as Behaviour & Information Technology, Computers in Human Behavior, Enterprise Information Systems, European Journal of Information Systems, European Management Journal, Information Research, International Journal of Information Management, Information Systems Management, Journal of Business Research, Management Decision and Online Information Review, among others. He is an Editorial Board Member and Associate Editor for several international journals and Chairman of various international conferences.

Caroline S. L. Tan is an Associate Professor of Marketing, Business Ethics and Corporate Social Responsibility at the University of Tsukuba. She is also a Visiting Associate Professor at Keio University and Rikkyo University. She received a Bac. of Soc. Sci. (Hons) from the University of Science, Malaysia, and an MBA from the University of Portsmouth. She holds a PhD in Marketing from Keio University. Prior to joining academia, she served as the Asia-Pacific Regional Supply Chain Manager at Teleplan NV and at Agilent Technologies (formerly Hewlett-Packard), as the Global Deployment Support Manager and Procurement Manager. Her research interests are consumer behavior, sustainable marketing, corporate social responsibility and marketing, cultural marketing and societal marketing. She has explored social media marketing, Yurukyara and place branding, metrosexuality and consumer behavior. She has examined the implications of trust and risk in influencing consumer decisions. She has also been involved in the planning and running of boutique training courses for companies such as Kirin, Mitsubishi, Sumitomo, Sony-Ericsson, KPMG and Mercedes-Benz.

Kenneth C.C. Yang (Ph.D.) is a Professor in the Department of Communication at the University of Texas at El Paso, USA. His research focuses on new media, consumer behavior, and international advertising. Some of his many works have been published in the International Journal of Consumer Marketing, the International Journal of Strategic Communication, the Journal of Intercultural Communication Studies, and Telematics and Informatics.

Index

N

O

P

R

S

T

U

V

W

Y

www.ingramcontent.com/pod-product-compliance
Lightning Source LLC
LaVergne TN
LVHW060412300926
849162LV00006B/1413
* 9 7 8 1 5 2 2 5 0 3 3 2 3 *